T0211778

Lecture Notes in Computer Science 11902

More information about this series at http://www.springer.com/series/7412

Yao Zhao · Nick Barnes ·
Baoquan Chen · Rüdiger Westermann ·
Xiangwei Kong · Chunyu Lin (Eds.)

Image
and Graphics

10th International Conference, ICIG 2019
Beijing, China, August 23–25, 2019
Proceedings, Part II

 Springer

Editors
Yao Zhao
Beijing Jiaotong University
Beijing, China

Nick Barnes
The Australian National University
Canberra, Australia

Baoquan Chen
Peking University
Beijing, China

Rüdiger Westermann
The Technical University of Munich
Munich, Bayern, Germany

Xiangwei Kong ⓘ
Zhejiang University
Hangzhou, China

Chunyu Lin ⓘ
Beijing Jiaotong University
Beijing, China

ISSN 0302-9743   ISSN 1611-3349   (electronic)
Lecture Notes in Computer Science
ISBN 978-3-030-34109-1   ISBN 978-3-030-34110-7   (eBook)
https://doi.org/10.1007/978-3-030-34110-7

LNCS Sublibrary: SL6 – Image Processing, Computer Vision, Pattern Recognition, and Graphics

This Springer imprint is published by the registered company Springer Nature Switzerland AG
The registered company address is: Gewerbestrasse 11, 6330 Cham, Switzerland

Preface

We would like to present the proceedings of the 10th International Conference on Image and Graphics (ICIG 2019), held in Beijing, China, during August 23–25, 2019.

The China Society of Image and Graphics (CSIG) has hosted this series of ICIG conferences since 2000. ICIG is a biennial conference organized by the CSIG, focusing on innovative technologies of image, video, and graphics in processing and fostering innovation, entrepreneurship, and networking. This time, the conference was organized by Tsinghua University, Peking University, and Institute of Automation, CAS. Details about the past nine conferences, as well as the current one, are as follows:

Conference	Place	Date	Submitted	Proceeding
First (ICIG 2000)	Tianjin, China	August 16–18	220	156
Second (ICIG 2002)	Hefei, China	August 15–18	280	166
Third (ICIG 2004)	Hong Kong, China	December 17–19	460	140
4th (ICIG 2007)	Chengdu, China	August 22–24	525	184
5th (ICIG 2009)	Xi'an, China	September 20–23	362	179
6th (ICIG 2011)	Hefei, China	August 12–15	329	183
7th (ICIG 2013)	Qingdao, China	July 26–28	346	181
8th (ICIG 2015)	Tianjin, China	August 13–16	345	170
9th (ICIG 2017)	Shanghai, China	September 13–15	370	172
10th (ICIG 2019)	Beijing, China	August 23–25	384	183

This time, the proceedings are published by Springer in the LNCS series. At ICIG 2019, 384 submissions were received, and 183 papers were accepted. To ease in the search of a required paper in these proceedings, the 161 regular papers have been arranged into different sections. Another 22 papers forming a special topic are included at the end.

Our sincere thanks to all the contributors, who came from around the world to present their advanced work at this event. Special thanks go to the members of the Technical Program Committee, who carefully reviewed every single submission and made their valuable comments for improving the accepted papers. The proceedings could not have been produced without the invaluable efforts of the publication chairs, the web chairs, and a number of active members of CSIG.

September 2019

Yao Zhao
Nick Barnes
Baoquan Chen
Rüdiger Westermann
Xiangwei Kong
Chunyu Lin

Organization

Organizing Committee

General Chairs

Tieniu Tan	Institute of Automation, CAS, China
Oliver Deussen	University of Konstanz, Germany
Rama Chellappa	University of Maryland, USA

Technical Program Chairs

Yao Zhao	Beijing Jiaotong University, China
Nick Barnes	ANU, Australia
Baoquan Chen	Peking University, China
Ruediger Westermann	TUM, Germany

Organizing Committee Chairs

Huimin Ma	Tsinghua University, China
Yuxin Peng	Peking University, China
Zhaoxiang Zhang	Institute of Automation, CAS, China
Ruigang Yang	Baidu, China

Sponsorship Chairs

Yue Liu	Beijing Institute of Technology, China
Qi Tian	University of Texas at San Antonio, USA

Finance Chairs

Zhenwei Shi	Beihang University, China
Jing Dong	Institute of Automation, CAS, China

Special Session Chairs

Jian Cheng	Institute of Automation, CAS, China
Gene Cheung	York University, Canada

Award Chairs

Yirong Wu	Institute of Electrics, CAS, China
Zixiang Xiong	Texas A&M University, USA
Yuxin Peng	Peking University, China

Publicity Chairs

Moncef Gabbouj	TUT, Finland
Mingming Cheng	Nankai University, China

Exhibits Chairs

Rui Li	Google, China
Jiang Liu	Meituan, China

Publication Chairs

Xiangwei Kong	Zhejiang University, China
Chunyu Lin	Beijing Jiaotong University, China

Oversea Liaison

Yo-Sung Ho	GIST, South Korea
Alan Hanjalic	Delft University of Technology, The Netherlands

Local Chairs

Xucheng Yin	USTB, China
Kun Xu	Tsinghua University, China

Tutorial Chairs

Weishi Zheng	Sun Yat-sen University, China
Chen Change Loy	NTU, Singapore

Workshop Chairs

Jiashi Feng	National University of Singapore, Singapore
Si Liu	Beihang University, China

Symposium Chair

Jinfeng Yang	Civil Aviation University of China, China

Website Chair

Bo Yan	Fudan University, China

Contents – Part II

Computer Vision and Pattern Recognition

Biological and Medical Image Processing

Artificial Intelligence

Computer Vision and Pattern Recognition

An Improved Image Positioning Method Based on Local Changed Plane Eliminated by Homography

Chunyang Wei[1,2,3], Hao Xia[2,3(✉)], and Yanyou Qiao[2,3]

[1] University of Chinese Academy of Sciences, Beijing, China
[2] Aerospace Information Research Institute, CAS, Beijing, China
xiahao@radi.ac.cn
[3] Institute of Remote Sensing and Digital Earth, CAS, Beijing, China

Abstract. Over the past two decades, advances in computer vision technology have allowed image-based positioning method to work in large scale with higher reliability and precision. However, this positioning technology has not been widely applied at present compare to GPS. One of the reasons is that large print advertisements on the surface of buildings which are common in cities are frequently updated. Positioning based on image may fail due to this scene changed relative to pre-build 3D model, which is still a challenge in the field of image-based location. To deal with positioning failure caused by changed plane, in this paper, we analyzed the effect of the changed plane size in query image on the positioning accuracy by systematic experiment with images collected regularly, and one improved 2D-to-3D positioning method based on local changed plane eliminated through homography transformation is proposed. Experiments show the method can raise the image-based localization success rate by 15%.

Keywords: Image positioning · 3D reconstruction · Local changed plane

1 Introduction

In the past two decades, image-based positioning has attracted many attentions from researchers as it does not rely on external hardware infrastructure compared to other methods such as Bluetooth or Wi-Fi positioning [1], and plenty of relative methods emerged recently [2]. Among them, the positioning method based on the SfM (Structure from Motion) [3, 4] has become an important research direction, due to more compact data structure and more stereoscopic positioning results it does [5]. The focus of image-based localization research during the first few years was to establish the correspondences between hundreds of query image features and millions of three-dimensional points with high efficiency [6]. With the advances in computer vision technology, real-time image positioning at city-scale has been achieved through years of efforts [7, 8]. However, image-based localization is still not widely applied currently, and the positioning failure result from changed scene due to frequent updating of urban appearance is one of the common reasons.

Y. Zhao et al. (Eds.): ICIG 2019, LNCS 11902, pp. 3–14, 2019.
https://doi.org/10.1007/978-3-030-34110-7_1

Since that image-based localization is based on Pre-built 3D model, there is an inevitable time lag between the model establishment and the positioning request. Once the building decorations changed, the relative features will change accordingly, and the query image may not be able to match with the pre-built 3D model. Therefore, there are still many challenges in image positioning under changing scenes [9–11], with no perfect solution to this question yet.

Large posters on the building is one of the common factors that change the appearance of the city. Aiming at positioning failure caused by local changed plane of query image, this paper tries to analyze the impact of various size of changed plane on positioning accuracy through systematic experiments, and one improved 2D-to-3D method based on changed plane eliminated through homography is proposed. Experiments show that this method can improve the success rate of image-based localization in changed condition to some extent. The remaining part of the essay proceeds as follows: Sect. 2 is a brief review of related work, and the improved method we proposed is described in Sect. 3, then in the following Sect. 4, we will validate our method by experiments, and draw a conclusion in Sect. 5 finally.

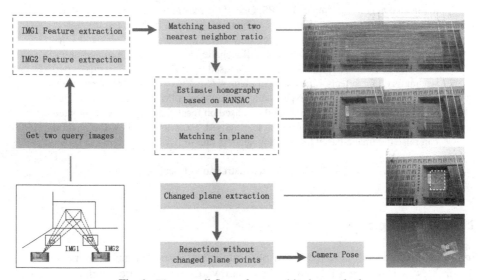

Fig. 1. The overall flow of our positioning method

2   Related Work

In the following, we will first briefly introduce the image localization process of the constant scene, and then the solutions for the image positioning in changed scene in recent years is reviewed.

Positioning based on the pre-built model procedures include three steps: feature extraction, correspondences establishment and pose solving. Image features are locally prominent structures such as corners, edges, and patches in image [12], which is the foundation of 3D reconstruction and image positioning. In terms of image scale, rotation transformation and illumination invariance, SIFT (Scale-invariant feature transform) [13] descriptor is robust for most of scenarios [14]. The typical image positioning based on 3D reconstruction model is 2D-to-3D [6, 15], which the core is to search for the nearest features in 3D model based on 2D query features. Once the correspondences established between the 2D features and 3D model, the combination of PnP [16] and RANSAC(Random Sample Consensus) algorithm [2, 7, 17] is used to solve the camera pose.

To address the problem of positioning failures in changed condition, focusing on approaches based on 3D model, the current methods to the best of our knowledge are mainly the following: Positioning based on several query images collected at same time, Positioning based on images set collected over multiple periods.

2.1 Positioning Based on Several Query Images Captured at Same Time

Notice the improvement of the place recognition through image sequences instead of single image in changing condition [18], many methods taking advantage of more images for positioning have proposed in recent years. Jonathan et al. proposed to combine the key frame based monocular SLAM and the global SfM model for image-based localization, which is robust even when partial occlusion occurring in query image [19]. Construction of local scenes is also helpful for positioning in changing condition, Deng et al. perform 3D-to-3D nonlinear optimization positioning based on multiple images to form a local 3D point cloud [20], more geometrically constrained features employed for camera pose solving.

2.2 Positioning Based on Images Set Collected Over Multiple Periods

Collecting image data over a long period of time is also aid in positioning performance improvement in changing condition. Mühlfellner et al. proposed to construct a vehicle summary map in changing scene by integrating image data from multiple seasons, weather and illumination to build 3D landmark [21], which enables the estimation of an vehicle pose by mixing landmarks from multiple sessions, this method requires manual selection of data in a wide range of seasons and lighting conditions in advance. For real-world vision-based vehicle positioning, Chen et al. deal with positioning failure through model update algorithm. Similar as Mühlfellner et al., they collected positioning data set in a range of month, but they propose a model verification process as unique active model to avoid data size increasing and matching ambiguities [22].

In summary, more images are employed in above studies to "suppress" local changed, which is essentially a "features increment" method. This paper attempts to propose one improved 2D-to-3D [15] positioning method based on local changed plane eliminated, which is essentially "features decrement" method though two images employed. The contributions of this paper are as follows: Firstly, the impact of various size of changed plane in query images on positioning accuracy is analyzed by systematic experiments. Secondly, for the problem of localization failure caused by local changed plane, one improved 2D-to-3D positioning method based on homography for changed plane elimi-nated is proposed. Experiment show this method improves the positioning performance for query image with local changed plane to a certain extent.

3 Proposed Method

In this section, we detail the procedure of our improved 2D-to-3D positioning approach. To eliminate changed plane in query image, we firstly estimate of the homography transformation matrix. For a pair of matching points p_1 and p_2 on same plane, there is,

$$p_1 = H \cdot p_2 \tag{1}$$

and H is the homography transformation matrix.

Firstly, different from the traditional one, we need to take two images with relative translation and same direction towards changed plane (as shown in Fig. 1), and then extract the features of two images. The rough matching of two images is calculated by Brute-Force matching with the first nearest to the second nearest distance threshold ratio which set as 0.8, then the homography transformation between the two images is estimated by RANSAC based on the correspondences with transfer error minimized [23] (Fig. 2).

Fig. 2. Homography transform to extract changed plane

Specifically, four pairs of correspondences are selected randomly, then the initial estimate of the homography transformation matrix is calculated with transfer error set as 1 pixel to extract the plane accurately. For initial matching of p_{1_i} and p_{2_i} ($i = 1, 2, 3, ..., N$), we consider the pair of points that satisfy the following formula (2) as inlier point.

$$\| p_{1_i} - H \cdot p_{2_i} \| < t \tag{2}$$

Following get inlier set which considered as good match in plane with the constrain by (2), we re-estimate H from inlier set with Levenberg-Marquardt algorithm [23].

After obtaining the homography matrix H, taking the left image as the query image, we approximate the changed plane by a rectangle formed by extremal points of homog-raphy features points in left, right, upper and lower of matching features coordinates. According to experiment, this approximation is reliable and can roughly represent the changed plane when the relative translation and rotation of the two cameras are relatively small.

Once the changed plane extracted through homography, the camera pose is estimated by the PnP + RANSAC algorithm. Assume that the camera intrinsic parameters are unknown, the six-point method is adopted to solve the camera pose. To verify the positioning accuracy and analyze the impact of the changed plane size in query image, images were captured towards newly poster on building in various distance and view angle regularly with constant camera high as 1.6 m on the square. The accuracy is judged by the Euclidean distance between the positioning calculated and the grids spatial points on the square where the query images captured is, then we represent the distance by D as following.

$$D = \sqrt[2]{(x_{ik} - \bar{x}_{ik})^2 + (y_{ik} - \bar{y}_{ik})^2 + (z_{ik} - \bar{z}_{ik})^2} \qquad (3)$$

In formula (3), $P(x_{ik}, y_{ik}, z_{ik})$ represents the query image location calculated by image-based positioning, and $\bar{P}(\bar{x}_{ik}, \bar{y}_{ik}, \bar{z}_{ik})$ represents grid coordinate position with constant $\bar{z}_{ik} = 1.6$ m. The smaller the distance D, the closer the positioning is to the true position, and vice versa.

The proposed method is summarized in Algorithm 1.

Algorithm 1 Local Changed Plane Eliminated by Homography

Input: img_1, img_2 /* two images with relative translation */
Output: $Pose_{img_1}$;
  1: Features extracted from img_1, img_2 ,get $feats_1$ and $feats_2$ respectively
  2: Establish matches C_p between $feats_1$ and $feats_2$ based nearest neighbors
  3: Estimate homography H by RANSAC based on C_p
  4: Select correspondences C_h meet homography H
  5: Get $x_{max}, x_{min}, y_{min}, y_{max}$ from $feats_1$ in C_h
  6: Appromixte changed plane by retangle $R(x_{min}, y_{min}, x_{max}, y_{max})$
  7: **for** $i = 1$ to N **do** /* N is number of features in img_1*/
  8:     **if** $feats_1[i]$ **not** in R **then**
  9:         search nearest 3D feature of $feats_1[i]$, save match in List M_{2d-3d}
 10:     **end if**
 11: **end for**
 12: Solve $Pose_{img_1}$ by $P6P + RANSAC$ algorithm based on M_{2d-3d}
 13: **return** $Pose_{img_1}$

Mismatches between the query features and the 3D points is one of the reasons for positioning failure. Therefore, eliminating of changed plane features in query image contribute to the improvement of the positioning success rate. In the next section, we will verify the effectiveness of this method through experiments.

4 Experiments

To facilitate the analysis and discussion, scene in small size was taken to explore the positioning accuracy with local changed plane. The images were collected in square of the Institute of Zoology of the Chinese Academy of Sciences, Beijing, China (shown in Fig. 3a, note that the time of satellite is inconsistent with the images collection, which the latter was in winter, and there were no green leaves on both sides of the square). In order to study the impact of the local changed scene on the positioning accuracy, the interval between two image collections we set is about 1 month.

      (a)   (b)

Fig. 3. Experimental field and 3D reconstruction point cloud

4.1   Image Acquisition and 3D Reconstruction

The first time of images acquisition for 3D reconstruction was 15:18 on December 4, 2018, and the images were captured by the common Smartisan U2 Pro mobile phone camera with resolution of 4160×3120 pixels. The images were taken by circular along the edge of the square with intervals of 0.5 m, and 454 images were collected totally. The 3D model (Fig. 3b) was built based on the openMVG library [24]. We set the upper left corner of the square lawn as the world coordinate origin, and the real scale of the model were established based on the field measurement. This 3D model (Fig. 3b) reconstruction was performed on the Alienware Aurora R6 desktop computer equipped with Ubuntu 16.04 operating system, Intel Core i7-7700K processor and 16 GB RAM; Finally, the model was established with 450 camera poses and 75,385 3D points.

The second time of images collection was in 15:40 on February 18, 2019 with same camera parameters as before, and those images were used for image-based localization experiments. As shown in Fig. 4, the scenes of the two shots have undergone local changing. Panels on both sides of square in first time of images collection were removed in the second shot, and a large poster was added on the front of the building. Next, we will analyze the impact of large poster newly added to the facade of the building after 3D model established, and compare the accuracy between direct 2D-to-3D positioning and the proposed improved one through changed plane eliminating.

Fig. 4. The scene in the experimental area changed

To analyze local plane change impact on positioning, we captured image set with equal rows and columns on experimental site. Since the equal space of square floor tiles (shown in Figs. 3a and 4), the natural coordinate formed by the floor tiles is served as the validation basis of positioning accuracy. Figure 5 shows the position of the images captured, where the triangle represents the direction of the cone and the larger yellow one represents the origin of the world coordinate of the 3D reconstruction model. The images are captured at uniform height of 1.6 m consist with the height of camera shooting held in hand, starting at the left of the southernmost of lawn and the left side of the square near trees. The sampling interval is 5.1 m in the north-south direction, and 2.55 m in the east-west, totally 6 rows and 9 columns (shown in Fig. 6).

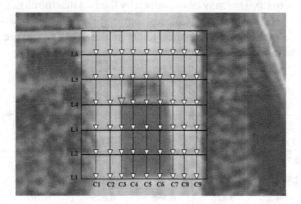

Fig. 5. Query images distribution

4.2 Positioning Experiment

Assume that the camera parameters of the query image unknown, the 6-point method is adopted to solve the camera pose. To validate the effect of proposed method, we compare the positioning accuracy based on the predefined coordinates between traditional direct 2D-to-3D positioning and the proposed improved one based on changed plane eliminated through homography.

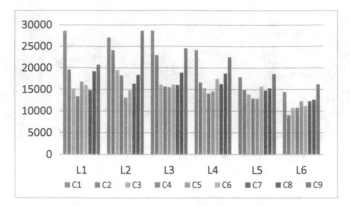

Fig. 6. Statistics of query image features

To study the effect of changed features on positioning, features extracted from images with different distances and angles on the front of the building are analyzed. The proportion of the features in changed plane of images taken from the view of square central is overall higher than two sides as the tree branches which contribute large number of features is outside of visual field. Figure 6 shows the number of features extracted from images captured with regular distribution on the square, what can be seen is features are less from the view of square central than two sides, and the features are generally decreasing from L1 to L6. This may be explained by the fact that the closer to the entrance of the building the less tree branches features captured is, and these features are mainly composed of corner points formed by brick joints on the walls, which are relatively rare compared to tree branches.

Table 1. Comparison results of two position methods I

| | L1 | | L2 | | L3 | |
	D_R	D_H	D_R	D_H	D_R	D_H
c01	0.729	0.735	1.439	1.451	1062.352	0.746
c02	2.892	2.519	0.25	0.318	0.167	0.136
c03	2.694	5.426	0.895	0.525	0.709	0.688
c04	3.627	6.224	0.377	0.253	0.264	0.211
c05	25.926	16.018	19.609	2.467	17.148	20.209
c06	19.766	0.378	20.301	5.579	90.78	7.814
c07	262.748	29.456	3.409	25.785	2.294	5.376
c08	41.842	39.328	10.741	31.802	19.256	29.571
c09	95.085	41.416	19.623	1.46	19.902	2.739

How the amount of image features affect positioning is the question we will explore following. Tables 1 and 2 provide the comparation of the positioning accuracy of two different positioning methods, in the two tables, L1–L9 represent sampling rows, C1–C9 represent sampling columns (as shown in Fig. 5), D_R represents the positioning error based on direct 2D-to-3D positioning method, and D_H represents the positioning error based on method proposed in this paper. The black bold font indicates effective positioning results, for the spatial error within 3 m is considered as acceptable positioning. As can be seen from the Table 1, the number of acceptable positioning by direct 2D-to-3D is 11 with success rate of 40%, and the other method proposed in this paper is 15 with success rate of 55%, one can see that our method improves the image-based localization to 15%. Figure 8 shows the success case of the positioning with changed plane eliminated while direct 2D-to-3D positioning failure, under the circumstances where large number of features generated by the branches which cannot be built in model, the exclusion of the features in changed plane helps to improve the positioning accuracy.

Table 2. Comparison results of two position methods II

	L4		L5		L6	
	D_R	D_H	D_R	D_{II}	D_R	D_H
c01	**0.648**	18.211	**0.596**	**0.613**	**0.375**	**2.022**
c02	**0.196**	**0.215**	**0.196**	**0.317**	**0.285**	**0.285**
c03	**0.442**	**0.643**	**0.477**	**0.569**	10.522	10.522
c04	**0.369**	**0.262**	**1.182**	**0.281**	10.827	10.827
c05	11.104	8.904	7.527	11.096	11.693	11.693
c06	166.778	19.97	9.808	9.07	13.009	13.009
c07	15.911	9.593	8.214	87.023	14.655	95.261
c08	3.831	5.349	13.773	54.813	**0.404**	**0.369**
c09	**0.648**	**2.467**	**0.268**	**0.171**	11.662	10.826

However, the proposed method may not always be as effective. From the Table 2 above we can see that the accuracy of the two positioning methods is relatively consistent. With the camera moves forward from L4 to L6, branches captured in image is getting less and less, and the features are more and more simple, mainly consisted of brick line crosses on wall and shadows in glass wall, eliminating of the changed plane in this circumstance make no difference on the positioning accuracy improvement.

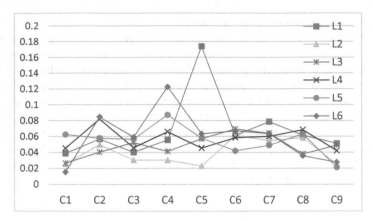

Fig. 7. The ratio of features in plane accounts for total query image

The positioning accuracy is related to the ration of changed features in query image. What stands out in Fig. 7 is the ratio of the homography features to the total features detected in query images captured in square regularly, where in the figure C1–C9 represent the images collected from left to right of the square, and the L1–L6 represent the imaged captured from north to south (as shown in Fig. 5). The numerical point indicates the ratio of the approximate changed plane image features to the total of the image. It can be seen from Fig. 7 that the proportion of the features in plane of L2, L3 and L3 is relatively low. Combining with Tables 1 and 2, a negative correlation between the ratio of changed points and the success rate of positioning can be found, that is, the higher the changed point ratio, the lower the success rate is. When the ratio of external points below 2%, the probability of successful positioning is greater.

Fig. 8. Positioning successful query image based on changed plane eliminated method

On the whole the eliminating of changed plane contributes to the improvement of image positioning accuracy to some extent. Figure 9 displays the acceptable positioning number of the direct 2D-to-3D and the our improved one. Overall, the positioning success rate of latter is higher than that of the former one, especially at row of L2. Where the features between L3 and L4 is relatively complicated, eliminating changed plane from resection is helpful to improve the positioning success rate.

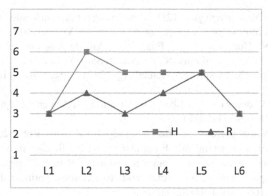

Fig. 9. Comparison of the successful positioning for direct 2D-to-3D positioning (R) and improved positioning through changed plane eliminated (H)

5 Conclusion

The aim of the present research is to address the image positioning failure caused by changed plane, and one improved method based on changed plane eliminated through homography transformation is proposed. Experiments show that this method can improve the success rate of image-based localization to 15% compared with the direct method under the circumstance of changed scenes.

However, there are still some shortcomings in this method. At present, only the scene where the change occurs in the whole plane can be positioned effectively. Once the change occurs only in a small part of the plane, many unchanged features may be excluded from the matching, leading to the positioning failure. Method proposed in this paper is not perfect yet, we hope provide a somewhat provocative idea for changing condition positioning based on 3D model.

Acknowledgements. This work is supported by the National Key R&D Plan (Grant No. 2017YFC0821902).

References

1. Davidson, P., Piché, R.: A survey of selected indoor positioning methods for smartphones. IEEE Commun. Surv. Tutor. **19**(2), 1347–1370 (2017)
2. Wu, Y., Tang, F., Li, H.: Image-based camera localization: an overview. Vis. Comput. Ind. Biomed. Art **1**(1), 8 (2018)
3. Agarwal, S., et al.: Building Rome in a day. In: 2009 IEEE 12th International Conference on Computer Vision (2009)
4. Özyeşil, O., et al.: A survey of structure from motion. Acta Numerica **26**, 305–364 (2017)
5. Cheng, L., et al.: Crowd-sourced pictures geo-localization method based on street view images and 3D reconstruction. ISPRS J. Photogram. Remote Sens. **141**, 72–85 (2018)
6. Sattler, T., Leibe, B., Kobbelt, L.: Efficient & effective prioritized matching for large-scale image-based localization. IEEE Trans. Pattern Anal. Mach. Intell. **PP**(99), 1 (2017)

7. Liu, L., Li, H., Dai, Y.: Efficient global 2D-3D matching for camera localization in a large-scale 3D map. In: IEEE International Conference on Computer Vision (2017)

8. Li, Y., Snavely, N., Huttenlocher, D., Fua, P.: Worldwide pose estimation using 3D point clouds. In: Fitzgibbon, A., Lazebnik, S., Perona, P., Sato, Y., Schmid, C. (eds.) ECCV 2012. LNCS, vol. 7572, pp. 15–29. Springer, Heidelberg (2012). https://doi.org/10.1007/978-3-642-33718-5_2

9. Piasco, N., et al.: A survey on visual-based localization: on the benefit of heterogeneous data. Pattern Recogn. **74**, 90–109 (2018)

10. Lowry, S., et al.: Visual place recognition: a survey. IEEE Trans. Rob. **32**(1), 1–19 (2016)

11. Sattler, T., et al.: Benchmarking 6DOF outdoor visual localization in changing conditions. In: 2018 IEEE/CVF Conference on Computer Vision and Pattern Recognition (2018)

12. Szeliski, R.: Computer Vision: Algorithms and Applications. Springer, Heidelberg (2010). https://doi.org/10.1007/978-1-84882-935-0. 812 p.

13. Lowe, D.G.: Distinctive image features from scale-invariant keypoints. Int. J. Comput. Vis. **60**(2), 91–110 (2004)

14. Karami, E., et al.: Image Matching Using SIFT, SURF, BRIEF and ORB: Performance Comparison for Distorted Images (2017)

15. Sattler, T., Leibe, B., Kobbelt, L.: Fast image-based localization using direct 2D-to-3D matching. In: IEEE International Conference on Computer Vision (2012)

16. Bujnak, M., Kukelova, Z., Pajdla, T.: A general solution to the P4P problem for camera with unknown focal length. In: IEEE Conference on Computer Vision & Pattern Recognition (2008)

17. Fischler, M.A., Bolles, R.C.: Random Sample Consensus: A Paradigm for Model Fitting with Applications to Image Analysis and Automated Cartography. Readings in Computer Vision, pp. 726–740 (1987)

18. Milford, M.: Vision-based place recognition: how low can you go? Int. J. Robot. Res. **32**(7), 766–789 (2013)

19. Jonathan, V., et al.: Global localization from monocular SLAM on a mobile phone. IEEE Trans. Vis. Comput. Graph. **20**(4), 531–539 (2014)

20. Deng, L., et al.: Image set querying based localization. In: 2015 Visual Communications and Image Processing (VCIP) (2015)

21. Mühlfellner, P., et al.: Summary maps for lifelong visual localization. J. Field Robot. **33**(5), 561–590 (2016)

22. Chen, K., et al.: Vision-based positioning for Internet-of-Vehicles. IEEE Trans. Intell. Transp. Syst. **18**(2), 364–376 (2017)

23. Hartley, R., Zisserman, A.: Multiple View Geometry in Computer Vision (2003)

24. Moulon, P., Monasse, P., Marlet, R.: Adaptive structure from motion with a Contrario model estimation. In: Lee, K.M., Matsushita, Y., Rehg, James M., Hu, Z. (eds.) ACCV 2012. LNCS, vol. 7727, pp. 257–270. Springer, Heidelberg (2013). https://doi.org/10.1007/978-3-642-37447-0_20

System Calibration for Panoramic 3D Measurement with Plane Mirrors

Wei Yin[1,2,3], Hao Xu[1], Shijie Feng[1,2,3], Tianyang Tao[1,2,3], Qian Chen[1,2], and Chao Zuo[1,2,3(✉)]

[1] School of Electronic and Optical Engineering,
Nanjing University of Science and Technology,
No. 200 Xiaolingwei Street, Nanjing 210094, Jiangsu, China
`zuochao@njust.edu.cn, surpasszuo@163.com`
[2] Jiangsu Key Laboratory of Spectral Imaging and Intelligent Sense,
Nanjing University of Science and Technology,
Nanjing 210094, Jiangsu, China
[3] Smart Computational Imaging (SCI) Laboratory,
Nanjing University of Science and Technology,
Nanjing 210094, Jiangsu, China

Abstract. In this paper, we propose a system calibration method for panoramic 3D shape measurement with plane mirrors. By introducing plane mirrors into the traditional fringe projection profilometry (FPP), our system can capture fringe images of the measured object from three different perspectives simultaneously including a real camera and two virtual cameras obtained by plane mirrors, realizing panoramic 3D shape reconstruction only by single-shot measurement. Furthermore, a flexible new technique is proposed to easily calibrate the mirror. In the proposed technique, the calibration of the mirror is discussed mathematically to ensure the effectiveness and rationality of the calibration process, it only requires the camera to observe a set of feature point pairs (including real points and virtual points) to achieve the solution of the reflection matrix for plane mirrors. The acquired calibration information is used to convert 3D point cloud data obtained from real and virtual perspectives into a common world coordinate system, making it possible to obtain full-surface 3D data of the object. Finally, benefited from the robust and high-performance calibration method, experimental results verify that our system can achieve high-accuracy and panoramic 3D shape measurement.

Keywords: Fringe projection profilometry · Plane mirrors · Calibration

1 Introduction

In recent years, Optical 3D shape measurement techniques are widely used in various fields such as biomechanics, intelligent monitoring, robot navigation,

© Springer Nature Switzerland AG 2019
Y. Zhao et al. (Eds.): ICIG 2019, LNCS 11902, pp. 15–26, 2019.
https://doi.org/10.1007/978-3-030-34110-7_2

industrial quality control, and human-computer interaction. Among plenty of state-of-the-art methods, fringe projection profilometry (FPP) [1–8], which is based on the principle of structured light and triangulation, has been proven to be one of the most promising techniques due to its inherent advantages of non-contactness, high accuracy, high efficiency, and low cost. In a conventional measurement system based on fringe projection profilometry (FPP) consisting of a camera and a projector, it cannot obtain the 360-degree overall 3D shape results of the object with complex surfaces due to the limited or occluded field of view, which leads to the limits on the application of FPP. Therefore, for such problems, it is necessary to carry out multiple measurements from different views to obtain the overall shape of the object.

In general, in order to achieve multiple measurements of the tested object from different views, it can be classified into three main categories: methods based on turn-table [9,10], methods based on movable robot arm [11,12], and measurement systems with plane mirrors [13–15]. In the first method, the tested object is placed on a turn-table, acquiring the whole 3D data by multiple rotations. Based on an idea contrary to the first method, the second method requires the measurement system to be mounted on a movable robot arm to perform multiple measurements around the tested object. Besides, the complicated post-processing operation for the scanned data must be performed using point cloud registration algorithms such as Iterated Closest Point (ICP). As a result, these fringe projection systems cannot be applied for the real-time overall acquisition of dynamic scenes, which requires multiple measurements and registration algorithms that are time-consuming and laborious. Different from the first two methods, measurement systems with plane mirrors can capture fringe images of the measured object from three different perspectives simultaneously including a real camera and two virtual cameras obtained by plane mirrors, making it possible to achieve panoramic 3D shape reconstruction only by single-shot measurement.

Several methods based on systems with plane mirrors has been presented in the survey articles and achieved remarkable success. Epstein et al. firstly introduced plane mirrors into FPP to create virtual cameras and projectors [13]. By tracking the relative positions of camera, projector, and mirrors, an interactive reconstruction system with structured light can provide 3D points to accurately estimate the pose of a mirror, while also reconstructing 3D points on the object. However, there are still some limitations in this system, which needs multiple measurements because the entire surface of the object cannot be illuminated at the same time. To solve this issue, Lanman et al. presented an orthographic projection system using a DLP projector and a Fresnel lens, which illuminated passive optical scatterers to create a volumetric display [14]. And then they designed an unambiguous Gray code sequence to facilitates the establishment of the correspondence of projectors and cameras, recovering a dense 3-D point cloud data of the entire object surface. In addition, some conventional calibration procedures are used to obtain accurate mirror calibration due to the lack of a suitable reflection model for the mirror, but it is complex and difficult to implement. Mariottini et al. systematically studied the catadioptric of the mirror to propose an ideal catadioptric model that helps convert the virtual surfaces reflected by the mirror into their true positions [16]. Following this idea, Chen et al. premade two speckle patterns on the mirrors to transform all surface portions into a common global coordinate thus allowing a straightforward full-surface 360-deg profile and deformation measurements [15]. However, this method requires the plane mirror with the front surface reflection, otherwise the thickness of the plane mirror should be considered [17]. In addition, it will inevitably introduce errors into the calibration of the mirror due to the nonuniform thickness of the print paper with speckles. On the other hand, since the paper is fixed on the plane mirror, it leads to limited 3D measurement volume for the system with plane mirrors.

In this work, a system calibration method for panoramic 3D shape measurement with plane mirrors is proposed. Firstly, the ideal reflection model for the plane mirror is review. Then, a flexible new calibration technique is proposed to easily calibrate the mirror. In the proposed technique, the calibration of the mirror is discussed mathematically to ensure the effectiveness and rationality of the calibration process, it only requires the camera to observe a set of feature point pairs (including real points and virtual points) to achieve the solution of the reflection matrix for plane mirrors. The entire calibration process is divided into two steps: the initial estimation of the reflection matrix and the precise calibration using the Levenberg-Marquardt algorithm with the bundle adjustment strategy. Finally, the estimated calibration information is used to convert 3D point cloud data obtained from real and virtual perspectives into a common world coordinate system, making it possible to obtain full-surface 3D data of the object. Benefitting from the robust and high-performance calibration method, experimental results verify that our method can achieve high-accuracy and panoramic 3D shape measurement.

2 Principle

2.1 The Reflection Model for the Plane Mirror

In this subsection, we will discuss in detail how to establish the ideal reflection model for the plane mirror. Firstly, let us consider the measurement system with a plane mirror as shown in Fig. 1, where an arbitrary 3D point of the tested object in the world coordinate system (X, Y, Z) is denoted by $X^o(x^o, y^o, z^o)$, O is the original point of the world coordinate system, d_w^r is the distance between O and the mirror, $X^r(x^r, y^r, z^r)$ represents the corresponding virtual point of X^o due to the reflection of the plane mirror, d_o^r is the distance between X^o and the mirror, and n^r is the normal vector of the mirror. From Fig. 1, we represent the reflection of plane mirror in the vector way:

$$\overrightarrow{OX^r} = \overrightarrow{OX^o} + \overrightarrow{X^oX^r}. \tag{1}$$

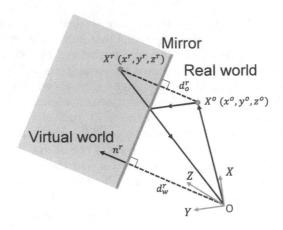

Fig. 1. The schematic diagram of the measurement system with a plane mirror.

Due to $\overrightarrow{X^o X^r} = 2d_o^r \overrightarrow{n^r}$, Eq. (1) can also be rewritten as:

$$\overrightarrow{OX^r} = \overrightarrow{OX^o} + 2d_o^r \overrightarrow{n^r}. \tag{2}$$

Besides, the relationship between d_o^r and $\overrightarrow{OX^o}$ can be calculated:

$$d_o^r = d_w^r - \overrightarrow{OX^o} \cdot \overrightarrow{n^r}, \tag{3}$$

where $\cdot$ is the dot product of vectors, $\overrightarrow{OX^o} \cdot \overrightarrow{n^r}$ is a value instead of a vector, so combining Eqs. (2) and (3) yields:

$$\overrightarrow{OX^r} = \overrightarrow{OX^o} + 2d_w^r \overrightarrow{n^r} - 2\overrightarrow{OX^o} \cdot \overrightarrow{n^r}\overrightarrow{n^r}. \tag{4}$$

In this subsection, X^o, X^r, and n^r are matrices with the size of 3×1. Due to $\overrightarrow{OX^o} \cdot \overrightarrow{n^r} = (X^o)^T n^r = (n^r)^T X^o$, Eq. (4) can also be rewritten in the matrix way:

$$X^r = (I - 2n^r(n^r)^T)X^o + 2d_w^r n^r, \tag{5}$$

where I is the 3×3 identity matrix. So we have:

$$\begin{bmatrix} X^r \\ 1 \end{bmatrix} = \begin{bmatrix} I - 2n^r(n^r)^T & 2d_w^r n^r \\ 0 & 1 \end{bmatrix} \begin{bmatrix} X^o \\ 1 \end{bmatrix}. \tag{6}$$

So the reflection matrix D^r for plane mirrors is defined as the following formula:

$$D^r = \begin{bmatrix} I - 2n^r(n^r)^T & 2d_w^r n^r \\ 0 & 1 \end{bmatrix}. \tag{7}$$

It is noted that D^r is involutory (e.g., $(D^r)^{-1} = D^r$) in [16]:

$$\begin{bmatrix} I - 2n^r(n^r)^T & 2d_w^r n^r \\ 0 & 1 \end{bmatrix} \begin{bmatrix} X^r \\ 1 \end{bmatrix} = \begin{bmatrix} X^o \\ 1 \end{bmatrix}. \tag{8}$$

It can be found according to Eq. (8) that the reflection matrix D^r for plane mirrors can be obtained immediately if n^r and d_w^r are known, and the 3D point cloud data obtained from virtual perspectives can be converted into the 3D point cloud data in the real world coordinate system. As a result, the core challenge for the panoramic 3D measurement is to calculate n^r and d_w^r quickly and accurately.

2.2   The Calibration Method for the Plane Mirror

At present, the conventional method requires artificially attaching a printing paper on the plane mirror to acquire the attitude information of the plane mirror for realizing the calibration of the plane mirror [15]. However, this method requires the plane mirror with the front surface reflection, otherwise, the thickness of the plane mirror should be considered [17]. In addition, it will inevitably introduce errors into the calibration of the mirror due to the nonuniform thickness of the print paper with speckles. On the other hand, since the paper is fixed on the plane mirror, it leads to limited 3D measurement volume for the system with plane mirrors.

In this subsection, the calibration of the mirror is discussed mathematically to ensure the effectiveness and rationality of the calibration process. The entire calibration process is divided into two steps: the initial estimation of the reflection matrix and the precise calibration using the Levenberg-Marquardt algorithm with the bundle adjustment strategy.

The Initial Estimation of the Reflection Matrix
Firstly, let n^r is (a^r, b^r, c^r), Eq. (8) can also be rewritten in detail:

$$\begin{bmatrix} 1 - 2(a^r)^2 & -2a^r b^r & -2a^r c^r & 2a^r d_w^r \\ -2a^r b^r & 1 - 2(b^r)^2 & -2b^r c^r & 2b^r d_w^r \\ -2a^r c^r & -2b^r c^r & 1 - 2(c^r)^2 & 2c^r d_w^r \\ 0 & 0 & 0 & 1 \end{bmatrix} \begin{bmatrix} x^r \\ y^r \\ z^r \\ 1 \end{bmatrix} = \begin{bmatrix} x^o \\ y^o \\ z^o \\ 1 \end{bmatrix}. \tag{9}$$

From Eq. (9), it requires the camera to observe N feature 3D point pairs (including real points X^o and virtual points X^r) to achieve the solution of the reflection matrix for plane mirrors. Minimizing Eq. (9) is a nonlinear minimization problem, which requires the accurate initial guesses of n^r and d_w^r obtained using the technique described in the following section. In addition, we have from Eq. (9):

$$[1 - 2(a^r)^2]x^r - 2a^r b^r y^r - 2a^r c^r z^r + 2a^r d_w^r = x^o, \tag{10}$$

$$- 2a^r b^r x^r + [1 - 2(b^r)^2]y^r - 2b^r c^r z^r + 2b^r d_w^r = y^o, \tag{11}$$

$$- 2a^r c^r x^r - 2b^r c^r y^r + [1 - 2(c^r)^2]z^r + 2c^r d_w^r = z^o. \tag{12}$$

Combining Eqs. (10) and (11) yields:

$$a^r(y^r - y^o) + b^r(x^o - x^r) = 0. \tag{13}$$

Likewise, the other two formulas can be derived from Eqs. (10), (11), and (12):

$$a^r(z^r - z^o) + c^r(x^o - x^r) = 0. \tag{14}$$

$$b^r(z^r - z^o) + c^r(y^o - y^r) = 0. \tag{15}$$

So combining Eqs. (13), (14), and (15) yields:

$$\begin{bmatrix} y^r - y^o & x^o - x^r & 0 \\ z^r - z^o & 0 & x^o - x^r \\ 0 & z^r - z^o & y^o - y^r \end{bmatrix} \begin{bmatrix} a^r \\ b^r \\ c^r \end{bmatrix} = 0. \tag{16}$$

Solving Eq. (16) is a least-squares minimization problem for obtaining an initial guess of $n^r(a^r, b^r, c^r)$. In our method, SVD can be implemented to yield the exact solution for the least-squares minimization problems, and the last column vector of V obtained using SVD is the initial guess $n_0^r(a_0^r, b_0^r, c_0^r)$. And Eqs. (10), (11), and (12) can also be rewritten for estimating the initial guess of d_w^r:

$$r_1(d_w^r) = 2a_0^r d_w^r + [1 - 2(a_0^r)^2]x^r - 2a_0^r b_0^r y^r - 2a_0^r c_0^r z^r - x^o = 2a_0^r d_w^r + c_1, \tag{17}$$

$$r_2(d_w^r) = 2b_0^r d_w^r - 2a_0^r b_0^r x^r + [1 - 2(b_0^r)^2]y^r - 2b_0^r c_0^r z^r - y^o = 2b_0^r d_w^r + c_2, \tag{18}$$

$$r_3(d_w^r) = 2c_0^r d_w^r - 2a_0^r c_0^r x^r - 2b_0^r c_0^r y^r + [1 - 2(c_0^r)^2]z^r - z^o = 2c_0^r d_w^r + c_3, \tag{19}$$

$$f(d_w^r) = \sum_{n=1}^{N} r_1^2(d_w^r) + r_2^2(d_w^r) + r_3^2(d_w^r), \tag{20}$$

where c_1, c_2, and c_3 are the constant values now. Since there is only one variable d_w^r in Eqs. (17), (18), and (19), minimizing Eq. (20) is a quadratic equation problem with one unknown, and the first-order derivative of $f(d_w^r)$:

$$f'(d_w^r) = \sum_{n=1}^{N} 8[(a_0^r)^2 + (b_0^r)^2 + (c_0^r)^2]d_w^r + 4(a_0^r c_1 + b_0^r c_2 + c_0^r c_3). \tag{21}$$

Due to the normal vector n_0^r (e.g., $(a_0^r)^2 + (b_0^r)^2 + (c_0^r)^2 = 1$), so we have:

$$f'(d_w^r) = \sum_{n=1}^{N} 8d_w^r + 4(a_0^r c_1 + b_0^r c_2 + c_0^r c_3). \tag{22}$$

Therefore, the initial guess of d_w^r is:

$$d_w^r = \frac{\sum_{n=1}^{N} -1/2(a_0^r c_1 + b_0^r c_2 + c_0^r c_3)}{N}. \tag{23}$$

There is the minimum value of $f(d_w^r)$ if Eq. (23) is established.

The Precise Calibration Using the Levenberg-Marquardt Algorithm with the Bundle Adjustment Strategy

Next, Eqs. (10), (11), and (12) can be rewritten again based on the Levenberg-Marquardt algorithm:

$$g_1(a^r, b^r, c^r, d_w^r) = [1 - 2(a^r)^2]x^r - 2a^r b^r y^r - 2a^r c^r z^r + 2a^r d_w^r - x^o, \quad (24)$$

$$g_2(a^r, b^r, c^r, d_w^r) = -2a^r b^r x^r + [1 - 2(b^r)^2]y^r - 2b^r c^r z^r + 2b^r d_w^r - y^o, \quad (25)$$

$$g_3(a^r, b^r, c^r, d_w^r) = -2a^r c^r x^r - 2b^r c^r y^r + [1 - 2(c^r)^2]z^r + 2c^r d_w^r - z^o, \quad (26)$$

$$\sum_{n=1}^{N} g_1^2(a^r, b^r, c^r, d_w^r) + g_2^2(a^r, b^r, c^r, d_w^r) + g_3^2(a^r, b^r, c^r, d_w^r), \quad (27)$$

where N is the total number of 3D point pairs. Minimizing Eq. (27) is a non-linear minimization problem, which is solved with the Levenberg-Marquardt algorithm. It is worth noting that there are two key factors (X^r and X^o) affecting the accuracy of the final optimization. It is well known that FPP is capable of acquiring high-precision 3D data of actual feature points. In our system, the precision of 3D measurement obtained using traditional multi-frequency phase-shifting profilometry is about 30 µm. Therefore, the influence of the second factor X^r should be considered primarily. In above calibration, X_n^r ($n = 1, 2, 3, \cdots, N$) were always taken as known input data. However, the low-precision 3D measurement for the virtual points (caused by the imperfect flatness of the mirror or the uneven reflectivity of the mirror) will introduce systematic errors into the final calibration results with low reliability. By further enhancing the manufacturing quality of the plane mirror, this disadvantage can be overcome to some extent to improve the performance of the calibration, but it is expensive and time-consuming. Therefore, the bundle adjustment strategy should be introduced to try to avoid problems caused by the mirror with low quality [18]. So Eq. (27) can be rewritten according to the bundle adjustment strategy:

$$\sum_{n=1}^{N} g_1^2(a^r, b^r, c^r, d_w^r, X_n^r) + g_2^2(a^r, b^r, c^r, d_w^r, X_n^r) + g_3^2(a^r, b^r, c^r, d_w^r, X_n^r). \quad (28)$$

Although the total number of variables has been increased from 4 to $4 + 3N$, minimizing Eq. (27) is still a nonlinear minimization problem that can be solved with the Levenberg-Marquardt method.

3   Experiments

In the experiment, a mirror-assisted FPP system is built to verify the actual performance of the proposed method as shown in Fig. 2. This system includes a monochrome camera (Basler acA2440-75 um with the resolution of 2448 × 2048), a DLP projector (LightCrafter 4500Pro with the resolution of 912 × 1140), two plane mirrors with the front surface reflection (the size of 30 cm × 30 cm). In

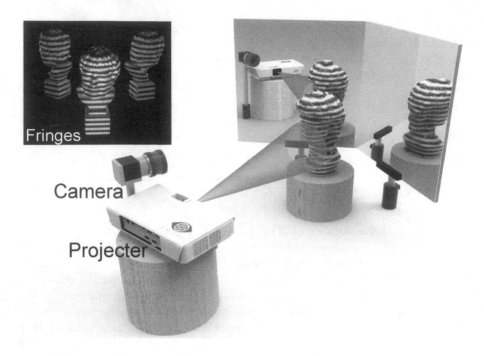

Fig. 2. The diagram of the mirror-assisted FPP system.

Fig. 2, since the camera is placed above the projector, a series of horizontal fringe patterns are projected by the projector and captured by the camera.

In the calibration process of the mirror, our calibration method needs to capture multiple pose data (6 postures are used in this experiment) of the circular calibration board with high precision, each of which can provide 15 feature point pairs as shown in Fig. 3. Then, these feature point pairs are used to perform in sequence the initial estimation of the reflection matrix and the precise calibration using the Levenberg-Marquardt algorithm with the bundle adjustment strategy. In order to quantitatively analyze the robustness of the proposed calibration method, the calibration residual errors at different steps are calculated as shown in Table 1. From the comparison results in Table 1, it can be found that our method can provide a relatively accurate initial guess of n^r and d_w^r with the RMS of 0.0704 mm or 0.0611 mm. Based on these estimations, the calibration residual errors can be further decreased to 0.0578 mm or 0.0534 mm using the Levenberg-Marquardt algorithm, which confirms its effectiveness. However, the low-precision 3D measurement for the virtual points will introduce systematic errors into the process of the calibration, which leads to the calibration results with low reliability. Therefore, the bundle adjustment strategy should be introduced into the calibration method to obtain results with high precision in Table 1.

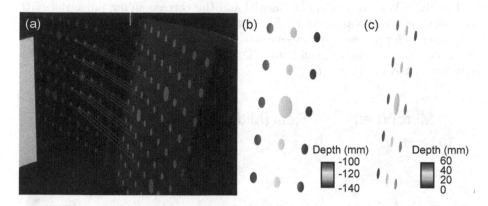

Fig. 3. The measurement result of the circular calibration board. (a) One pose data of the circular calibration board can provide 15 feature point pairs, (b) The 3D data of virtual points, (c) The 3D data of real points.

To further evaluate the accuracy of the proposed approach, a standard ceramic spheres with a diameter of 50.8 mm is measured using our system, and the single-view 3D measurement results and the full-surface 3D measurement results are presented in Figs. 4(a)–(c) and (g)–(i). Then, for the single-view 3D measurement results, we perform the sphere fitting to obtain separately the measured errors with the RMS of 27.577 μm, 47.531 μm, and 44.791 μm shown in Figs. 4(d)–(e), and the accuracy of full-surface measurement result is 65.122 μm shown in Figs. 4(j)–(l). This result verifies that the proposed method can realize high-accuracy and panoramic 3D shape measurement.

Table 1. Comparison of calibration residual errors.

RMS (mm)	IE[a]	L-M[b]	L-M with BA[c]
Mirror (left)	0.0704	0.0578	1.7911×10^{-5}
Mirror (right)	0.0611	0.0534	1.1588×10^{-5}

[a]IE = the initial estimation, [b]L-M = the Levenberg-Marquardt algorithm, [c]L-M with BA = the Levenberg-Marquardt algorithm with the bundle adjustment strategy.

Finally, a Voltaire model is measured and the corresponding full-surface 3D reconstruction results are shown in Fig. 5(a). And then, the corresponding results from three different views are presented to illustrate the reliability of our method which can achieve robust panoramic 3D shape measurement for objects with complex surfaces in Figs. 5(b)–(d).

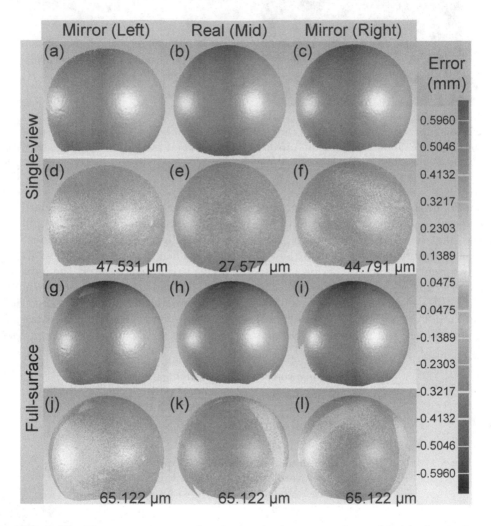

Fig. 4. The 3D measurement results of a standard ceramic spheres. (a)–(c) The single-view 3D measurement results. (d)–(f) The corresponding distribution of the errors of (a)–(c). (g)–(i) The full-surface 3D measurement results. (j)–(l) The corresponding distribution of the errors of (g)–(i).

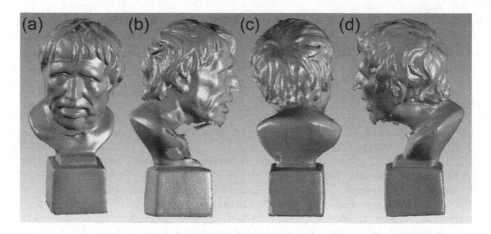

Fig. 5. The measurement results of a Voltaire model. (a) The full-surface 3D reconstruction results of a Voltaire model. (b)–(d) The corresponding results of (a) from three different views.

4   Conclusion

In conclusion, we proposed a system calibration method for panoramic 3D shape measurement with plane mirrors. By introducing plane mirrors into the traditional fringe projection profilometry (FPP), our system can capture fringe images of the measured object from three different perspectives simultaneously including a real camera and two virtual cameras obtained by plane mirrors, realizing panoramic 3D shape reconstruction only by single-shot measurement. Then, a flexible new calibration technique is proposed to easily calibrate the mirror. In this work, the calibration of the mirror is firstly discussed mathematically to ensure the effectiveness and rationality of the calibration process, it only requires the camera to observe a set of feature point pairs (including real points and virtual points) to achieve the solution of the reflection matrix for plane mirrors. By the initial estimation of the reflection matrix and the precise calibration using the Levenberg-Marquardt algorithm with the bundle adjustment strategy, the robust calibration information with high performance can be acquired to recovery full-surface 3D data of the object. Finally, experimental results verify that our method can achieve high-accuracy and panoramic 3D shape measurement with the precision of $65.122\,\mu m$.

Funding Information. This work was supported by National Natural Science Foundation of China (61722506, 61705105, 11574152), National Key R&D Program of China (2017YFF 0106403), Final Assembly "13th Five-Year Plan" Advanced Research Project of China (30102070102), Equipment Advanced Research Fund of China (614041502 02), The Key Research and Development Program of Jiangsu Province (BE20171 62), Outstanding Youth Foundation of Jiangsu Province (BK20170034), National Defense Science and Technology Foundation of China (0106173), "333 Engineering" Research Project of Jiangsu Province (BRA2016407), Fundamental Research Funds for the Central Universities (30917011204), China Postdoctoral Science Foundation (2017M621747), Jiangsu Planned Projects for Postdoctoral Research Funds (1701038A).

References

1. Gorthi, S.S., Rastogi, P.: Fringe projection techniques: whither we are? Opt. Laser Eng. **48**(2), 133–140 (2010)
2. Su, X., Zhang, Q.: Dynamic 3-D shape measurement method: a review. Opt. Laser Eng. **48**(2), 191–204 (2010)
3. Zhang, S.: High-speed 3-D shape measurement with structured light methods: a review. Opt. Laser Eng. **106**, 119–131 (2018)
4. Feng, S., Zhang, L., Zuo, C., Tao, T., Chen, Q., Gu, G.: High dynamic range 3-D measurements with fringe projection profilometry: a review. Meas. Sci. Technol. **29**(12), 122001 (2018)
5. Srinivasan, V., Liu, H.C., Halioua, M.: Automated phase-measuring profilometry of 3-D diffuse objects. Appl. Opt. **23**(18), 3105–3108 (1984)
6. Zuo, C., Feng, S., Huang, L., Tao, T., Yin, W., Chen, Q.: Phase shifting algorithms for fringe projection profilometry: a review. Opt. Laser Eng. **109**, 23–59 (2018)
7. Yin, W., et al.: High-speed 3D shape measurement using the optimized composite fringe patterns and stereo-assisted structured light system. Opt. Express **27**(3), 2411–2431 (2019)
8. Yin, W., et al.: High-speed three-dimensional shape measurement using geometry-constraint-based number-theoretical phase unwrapping. Opt. Laser Eng. **115**, 21–31 (2019)
9. Liu, X., Peng, X., Chen, H., He, D., Gao, B.Z.: Strategy for automatic and complete three-dimensional optical digitization. Opt. Lett. **37**, 3126–3128 (2012)
10. Song, L., Ru, Y., Yang, Y., Guo, Q., Zhu, X., Xi, J.: Full-view three-dimensional measurement of complex surfaces. Opt. Eng. **57**, 104106 (2018)
11. Rusinkiewicz, S., Hall-Holt, O., Levoy, M.: Real-time 3D model acquisition. ACM Trans. Graph. (TOG) **21**, 438–446 (2002)
12. Nießner, M., Zollhöfer, M., Izadi, S., Stamminger, M.: Real-time 3D reconstruction at scale using voxel hashing. ACM Trans. Graph. (TOG) **32**, 169 (2013)
13. Epstein, E., Granger, M., Potilin, P.: Exploiting mirrors in interactive reconstruction with structured light. In: Vision, Modeling, and Visualization, pp. 125–132 (2004)
14. Lanman, D., Crispell, D., Taubin, G.: Surround structured lighting: 3-D scanning with orthographic illumination. Comput. Vis. Image Underst. **113**(11), 1107 1117 (2009)
15. Chen, B., Pan, B.: Mirror-assisted panoramic-digital image correlation for full-surface 360-deg deformation measurement. Measurement **132**, 350–358 (2019)
16. Mariottini, G.L., Scheggi, S., Morbidi, F., Prattichizzo, D.: Planar mirrors for image-based robot localization and 3-D reconstruction. Mechatronics **22**, 398–409 (2012)
17. Wang, P., Wang, J., Xu, J., Guan, Y., Zhang, G., Chen, K.: Calibration method for a large-scale structured light measurement system. Appl. Opt. **56**(14), 3995–4002 (2017)
18. Liu, X., et al.: Calibration of fringe projection pro lometry using an inaccurate 2D reference target. Opt. Lasers Eng. **89**, 131–137 (2017)

Semantic SLAM Based on Joint Constraint in Dynamic Environment

Yuliang Tang[1,2], Yingchun Fan[1], Shaofeng Liu[1], Xin Jing[2], Jintao Yao[2], and Hong Han[1,2(✉)]

[1] School of Artificial Intelligence, Xidian University, Xi'an 710071, China
hanh@mail.xidian.edu.cn
[2] Shaanxi Key Laboratory of Integrated and Intelligent Navigation,
Xi'an 710071, China

Abstract. In most existing SLAM (Simultaneous localization and mapping) methods, it is always assumed that the scene is static. Lots of errors would occur when the camera enters a highly dynamic environment. In this paper, we present an efficient and robust visual SLAM system which associates dynamic feature points detection with semantic segmentation. We obtain the stable feature points by the proposed depth constraint. Combined with the semantic information provided by BlitzNet, every image in the sequence is divided into environment region and potential dynamic region. Then, using the fundamental matrix obtained from the environment region to construct epipolar line constraint, dynamic feature points in the potential dynamic region can be identified effectively. We estimate the motion of the camera using the stable static feature points obtained by the joint constraints. In the process of constructing environment map, moving objects are removed while static objects are retained in the map with their semantic information. The proposed system is evaluated both on TUM RGB-D dataset and in real scenes. The results demonstrate that the proposed system can obtain high-accuracy camera moving trajectory in dynamic environment, and eliminate the smear effects in the constructed semantic point cloud map effectively.

Keywords: SLAM · Semantic segmentation · Joint constraint · Dynamic objects

1 Introduction

SLAM plays an important role in the field of robot navigation and unmanned driving. Many excellent achievements have been produced in visual SLAM, which are mainly classified into direct method based on photometric error [1,2] and indirect method based on salient points matching [3]. The main purpose of both methods is to obtain environmental information through sensors to achieve camera pose estimation and map construction. It is a premise for most of the current

Supported by organization the open fund of Shaanxi Key Laboratory of Integrated and Intelligent Navigation (No. SKLIIN-20180102 and No. SKLIIN-20180107).

Y. Zhao et al. (Eds.): ICIG 2019, LNCS 11902, pp. 27–39, 2019.
https://doi.org/10.1007/978-3-030-34110-7_3

visual slam systems that the environment is static, which severely limits the application of visual SLAM due to lots of dynamic objects in the environment.

With the development of deep neural networks, target detection and semantic segmentation algorithms have achieved great progress, and many experts are committed to integrating visual SLAM with deep learning. Some studies specify dynamic targets by directly regarding people, cars or animals as dynamic objects, such as [4,22]. However, it may cause the loss of useful information in the constructed map.

In this work, a robust SLAM system to deal with dynamic objects on RGB-D data is proposed. The image is divided into environment region and potential dynamic region by the semantic information provided by the improved BlitzNet [17]. In order to eliminate the influence of missing values in the depth image and the sudden changes of the depth value in the edge of objects and environment, we proposed a depth constrain to obtain the stable feature points. And the dynamic feature points can be identified effectively by the epipolar line constraint constructed by the environment region. The static feature points are used to estimate the motion trajectory of the camera, while the dynamic feature points are used to determine the motion state of the potential dynamic objects. Finally, the point cloud map with semantic information is built.

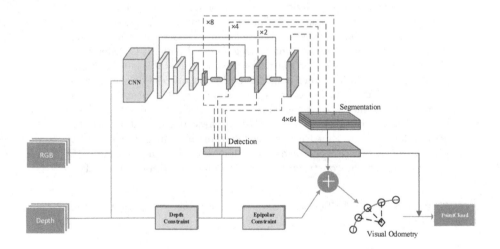

Fig. 1. Overview of the system.

2   Related Work

2.1   Dynamic SLAM

The presence of dynamic objects will seriously affect the mapping results and the estimation of the camera pose. Specified priori dynamic targets are utilized in [4,5] to handle dynamic environment. Burgard et al. [6] propose a data association technique to incorporate both dynamic and stationary objects directly into camera pose estimation. A different multi-camera combination strategy is introduced to deal with dynamic object effectively in [7]. Whats more, Henri Rebecq et al. [8] propose a method of using a special event camera which can achieve robust performances in highly dynamic environment, however, high cost limits the use of such methods.

2.2 Semantic Segmentation Based on Deep Learning

At present, most of the advanced semantic segmentation techniques based on deep learning are derived from full convolution network (FCN) [9], and different strategies are proposed to improve the segmentation effect. In terms of models, encoder-decoder architecture has been widely used, such as [10,11]. About convolution kernel, authors of [12,13] have done a lot of important work using dilated convolution to enhance receptive field to integrate context information. Starting from multi-scale feature fusion, Zhao et al. [14,15] use spatial pyramid pooling to integrate different scale features to obtain global information. As for instance segmentation, Mask R-CNN can detect objects in an image while simultaneously generating a segmentation mask for each instance, but it lacks real-time performance [16]. In this paper, a real-time semantic segmentation algorithm BlitzNet [17] is used to transform semantic segmentation into instance segmentation.

2.3 Semantic SLAM

Some approaches combine classic SLAM with semantic segmentation to build a more robust semantic map such as [18,19], but both of them do not focus on the localization of camera. Other approaches focus on locating and processing dynamic objects. For instance, Bowman et al. [20] propose probabilistic data association to improve the robustness of localization, and some algorithms [21,22] combine different deep network with moving consistency check to reduce the impact of dynamic objects. However, most of these methods roughly treat certain classes of objects as dynamic objects, even if these objects are static in the images, thus dynamic objects detection is not precise enough.

3 System Description

3.1 Framework of Our System

The overview of our system is presented in Fig. 1. Firstly, the RGB images pass through a CNN (Convolution Neural Network) that performs object detection and pixel-wise segmentation at the same time. The detected information includes some common objects such as people, screens, tables and chairs, etc. As for RGB-D data, we employ depth constraint and epipolar line constraint combined with object bounding box to determine potential dynamic points. After the instance segmentation result arrives, potential dynamic feature points will be added to the fusion module. Outliers located in the real moving objects can be removed effectively. More accurate camera trajectory can be obtained by the visual odometry. Finally, the constructed point cloud map and semantic information are integrated to obtain a semantic point cloud map.

3.2   Potential Dynamic Point Detection

Dynamic object detection algorithms are generally based on regional features of the image, such as texture, color, grayscale, and so on. In this paper, the potential dynamic points detection is realized by the proposed joint constraints. Finally, the dynamic objects can be detected by fusing the semantic segmentation algorithm.

For two adjacent frames of depth image, there are regions with incomplete depth (the depth value of these regions is 0), and there is a sudden change of depth value at the edge of the object [23]. The most stable feature points are on the surface of certain objects, such as the regions on the desk marked by the red dashed frame as shown in Fig. 2. Using image depth information to obtain stable feature points can effectively reduce the problem of high false alarm rate caused by strong parallax.

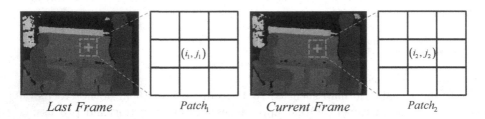

Last Frame   Patch₁   Current Frame   Patch₂

Fig. 2. Patches centered on the integer pixel coordinates of the feature points in two adjacent depth images. (Color figure online)

In order to find the stable feature points on the image, we consider a 3×3 image patch centered on the integer pixel coordinates of the feature points. As shown in Fig. 2, the red crosses represent the locations of the corresponding feature points on the two frames of depth image, where (i_1, j_1) and (i_2, j_2) are the integer pixel coordinates of the feature points on the previous and current frame, respectively. If any depth value on the image patch is 0, the depth value of the feature point is considered missing and the corresponding feature point pair is deleted. The depth value of the feature point is replaced by the average depth of the patch as shown in the following equation:

$$\hat{d} = \frac{1}{9} \sum_{x=1}^{3} \sum_{y=1}^{3} Patch(x, y) \tag{1}$$

where x, y are the coordinates of pixels in the patch. The Euclidean distance of the average depth of two feature points $\hat{d}_1$, $\hat{d}_2$ is used to exclude outliers with greater depth deviation to obtain stable feature points, as shown in Eq. 2.

$$D_d = \sqrt{(\hat{d}_1 - \hat{d}_2)^2} \tag{2}$$

By setting a threshold ξ, we can get the stable matching points P_{s1}, P_{s2} as shown in Eq. 3.

$$P_{s1}, P_{s2} = \{P_1, P_2 | D_d(\hat{d}_1, \hat{d}_2) < \xi\} \tag{3}$$

Using BlitzNet, the potential moving objects region can be obtained, such as the person region, and other region as the environment region. Therefore, the fundamental matrix F can be calculated by stable matching points in the environment region using RANSAC algorithm. Epipolar geometric describes the constraint relationship between the matching points in different angles of view. P_{m1}, P_{m2} denote feature points in the potential moving objects region of the previous frame and current frame, respectively.

$$P_{m1} = [u_1, v_1, 1]^T, P_{m2} = [u_2, v_2, 1]^T \tag{4}$$

We can distinguish the dynamic feature points in potential moving region by the epipolar line constraint as follows:

$$D_e = \frac{\left| P_{m2}{}^T F P_{m1} \right|}{\sqrt{l_x{}^2 + l_y{}^2}} \tag{5}$$

where l_x, l_y represent epipolar lines coordinate. D_e only depends on the epipolar geometry theory and the consistency relationship between the projection of the feature points. The specific algorithm process is described in Algorithm 1.

Algorithm 1. Joint Constraint Detection Algorithm

Input: Previous frame's feature points, P_1, Previous frame's depth, d_1; Current frame's depth, d_2;
Output: The set of potential dynamic points, S;
1: Calculate current frame's feature points P_2 by optical flow pyramid,
2: Obtain stable matching points P_{s1}, P_{s2} by depth constraint
3: Calculate fundamental matrix $F = findFundamentalMat(P_{s1}, P_{s2})$
4: for each matched point pair p_1, p_2 in P_1, P_2 do
5:       if p_1 is not in potential moving objects region then
6:             continue
7:       Calculate epipolar line $L = computeCorrespondEpilines(p_1, F)$
8:       Calculate distance from epipolar line constrain D_e by Eq. 5
9:       if $D_e > \xi$ then
10:             Append p_2 to$S$
11:       end if
12: end for

3.3　Sematic Segmentation

For scene analysis, BlitzNet, a deep neural network which can complete the object detection and semantic segmentation in one-time forward propagation, is used as the basic network in our experiment, whose backend is changed to meet the requirement of instance level segmentation tasks in our system.

BlitzNet only takes RGB image as input. In this experiment, VOC and COCO datasets are used for joint training and SSD300 is used as the backbone network, moreover, the object detection mAP on the VOC12 verification set can reach up to 83.6, while the semantic division mIOU reaches approximately 75.7. It has a good effect in the general scene, as shown in Fig. 3(a) and (b). The combination of the detection results and the segmentation results obtained by the network can get the desired instance segmentation image as shown in Fig. 3(c).

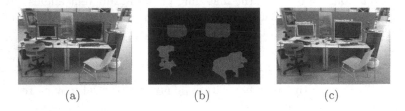

(a)　　　　　　　　(b)　　　　　　　　(c)

Fig. 3. Results of the improved BlitzNet. (a) Object detection. (b) Semantic segmentation. (c) Instance segmentation.

3.4　Dynamic Object Detection

In Sect. 3.2, the algorithm of detecting potential dynamic feature points is introduced, which can roughly find the dynamic feature points in the image. In this section, we will get more accurate dynamic points to detect dynamic objects in scene. Each segmented target in the image is enclosed by the detection box defined as the influence area. We divide feature points into four sets of points, as shown in Fig. 4: static points in potential moving region $U_s \in \mathbb{R}^{n \times 2}$, potential dynamic points $U_d \in \mathbb{R}^{m \times 2}$, outliers in environment $V_d \in \mathbb{R}^{M \times 2}$, and stable points in environment $V_s \in \mathbb{R}^{N \times 2}$. We propose two proportions, one is region dynamic point ratio τ_d, and the other is region points ratio τ_r, as shown in Eq. 6.

$$\tau_d = \frac{m}{m+n}, \tau_r = \frac{m+n}{m+n+N} \tag{6}$$

The value of threshold τ_d is 0.5 and τ_r is 0.15 in this experiment. Once the results of both equations are greater than their threshold, segmented targets within the detection box will be classified as dynamic targets, like the yellow part in the right figure in Fig. 4. The external parameter matrix to estimate trajectory of the camera can be obtained to estimate trajectory of the camera by solving the least squares problem shown below:

$$\min_{R,t} \sum_{i=1}^{N+n} \|P_{ai} - (RP_{bi} + t)\|^2 \tag{7}$$

where, $P_b \subseteq U_s \cup V_s$ and P_a is matching points in the previous frame.

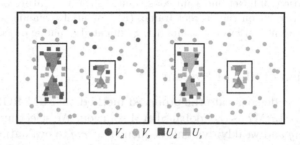

$\bullet\, V_d \quad \bullet\, V_s \quad \blacksquare\, U_d \quad \blacksquare\, U_s$

Fig. 4. Four types of points in dynamic objects detection. (Color figure online)

4 Experiments and Results

This section shows the experimental results of the proposed method. We have evaluated our system both on TUM RGB-D dataset [24] and in real-world environment.

4.1 Dynamic Points Detection

TUM datasets provide several image sequences in dynamic environment with accurate ground truth and camera parameters, and it is divided into categories of *walking, sitting,* and *desk.* We mainly test the dynamic feature points detection experiment in the *walking* sequence, and the motion amplitude of the dynamic object in this sequence is large.

The process of dynamic points detection and dynamic objects segmentation is shown in Fig. 5. The image can be divided into potential dynamic region and environment region by the semantic information provided by BlitzNet. The approximate distribution of the dynamic points in potential moving region can be obtained by the proposed joint constraint. According to the calculation results of τ_d and τ_r, we can judge that the two people in the bounding boxes are dynamic objects and feature points in the mask of people is regarded as dynamic points. It is obvious that the person is classified as dynamic object in this experiment automatically, and our algorithm retains a lot of static scenarios and removes dynamic part as much as possible.

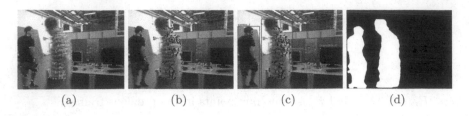

Fig. 5. Combination BlitzNet and joint constraint. (a) Stable feature points obtained by the depth constraint on the current frame. (b) Potential dynamic point detection by the joint constraint. (c) Fusion results. (d) Segmented dynamic objects.

4.2   Evaluation of SLAM System

In this section, we demonstrate the proposed method on TUM RGB-D datasets and adopt ORB-SLAM2 as the global SLAM solution. We select highly dynamic sequence *walking* and weakly dynamic sequence *sitting* to evaluation the SLAM system. Quantitative comparison results are shown in Tables 1, 2 and 3, where *static*, *rpy*, *xyz*, and *half* in the first column stand for four types of camera motions. The proposed dynamic detection thread combined with CNN is added to the system to accomplish the task of localization, thus metrics of absolute trajectory error (ATE) and relative pose error (RPE) are used for evaluation.

As we can see from Table 1, our method can make better performance in most high dynamic sequence such as *fr3/w/rpy*, *fr3/w/xyz* and *fr3/w/half*. Compared with ORB-SLAM2, our algorithm gets an order of magnitude improvement particularly in *walking* sequence, meanwhile, our positioning accuracy is better than DynaSLAM on *rpy*, *xyz*, and *half* camera motions in *walking* sequence.

What Table 2 gives is the relative attitude error under the same datasets, where RMSE (T) is the root mean square error of translation, and RMSE (R) the root mean square error of rotation. It can be seen from the data that our algorithm still has better robustness in relative posture than DynaSLAM and ORB-SLAM2.

Table 1. Results of absolute trajectory error

Sequence	ORB-SLAM2			DynaSLAM			Ours		
	RMSE	Mean	Median	RMSE	Mean	Median	RMSE	Mean	Median
fr3/w/static	0.3194	0.2626	0.3761	0.0068	0.0061	0.0056	0.0078	0.0068	0.0062
fr3/w/rpy	0.5391	0.4884	0.4419	0.0354	0.0302	0.0260	**0.0320**	**0.0260**	**0.0209**
fr3/w/xyz	0.5979	0.5421	0.4707	0.0164	0.0140	0.0121	**0.0153**	**0.0133**	**0.0118**
fr3/w/half	0.4543	0.3777	0.2740	0.0296	0.0251	0.0200	**0.0268**	**0.0228**	**0.0195**
fr3/s/half	0.0185	0.0145	0.0123	0.0229	0.0201	0.0179	0.0235	0.0204	0.0178

For ORB-SLAM2, camera trajectories are more complete because the dynamic targets are not eliminated. Although a large number of frames can

Table 2. Results of relative pose error

Sequence	ORB-SLAM2		DynaSLAM		Ours	
	RMSE (T)	RMSE (R)	RMSE (T)	RMSE (R)	RMSE (T)	RMSE (R)
fr3/w/static	0.1928	3.5992	0.0089	0.2612	0.0103	0.2714
fr3/w/rpy	0.3881	1.5906	0.0448	0.9894	**0.0426**	**0.9483**
fr3/w/xyz	0.4090	7.6553	0.0217	0.6284	**0.0199**	**0.6018**
fr3/w/half	0.3215	6.6515	0.0284	0.7842	**0.0261**	**0.7394**
fr3/s/half	0.0209	0.5614	0.0325	0.8822	0.0276	0.7475

Table 3. Results of successfully tracked trajectory

Sequence	Total	ORB-SLAM2		DynaSLAM		Ours	
		Tracked	Ratio (%)	Tracked	Ratio (%)	Tracked	Ratio (%)
fr3/w/static	717	714	99.6	375	52.3	692	96.5
fr3/w/rpy	866	825	99.8	546	63.0	806	93.1
fr3/w/xyz	827	795	91.8	757	91.5	**824**	**99.6**
fr3/w/half	1021	942	92.3	525	51.4	**1018**	**99.7**

be ensured to be tracked, the accumulation of errors can eventually lead to failure of the navigation. DynaSLAM achieves a more accurate camera trajectory than the ORB-SLAM2, however, the frames tracked ratio of DynaSLAM without inpainting is not as good as the ORB-SLAM2. As shown in Table 3, our algorithm can keep most of the frames tracked with high accuracy, which provides a guarantee for long-term navigation.

An example of the estimated trajectories of the three systems compared to the ground-truth in fr3/w/half are illustrated in Fig. 6. There is a large difference between the trajectory of ORB-SLAM2 and the real trajectory, while DynaSLAM and our system maintain a smaller difference but our trajectory is more complete than DynaSLAM. In addition, the translation error diagram shows that our algorithm has better stability and robustness.

Dynamic object removal can improve the mapping quality effectively. Because of the limitation of computing resources, we adopt the way of off-line mapping. As shown in Fig. 7 ORB-SLAM2 cannot handle the dynamic environment in fr3/w/xyz dataset, in which point cloud with smear will be built. DynaSLAM can get a point cloud without semantics because it only identifies people in TUM data, whereas our algorithm can deal with dynamic object effectively and eliminate the drag effect significantly. Furthermore, the semantic information is mapped to the point cloud. It is clear that the static objects such as screens are marked by blue and chairs are marked by red in our results.

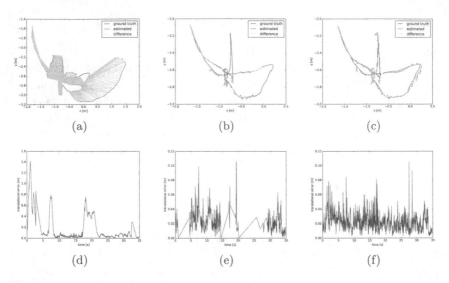

(a)   (b)   (c)

(d)   (e)   (f)

Fig. 6. Results of three algorithms in *fr3/w/half*. (a), (d) from ORB-SLAM2, (b), (e) from DynaSLAM, (c), (f) from our system.

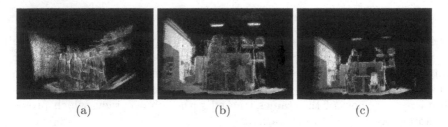

(a)   (b)   (c)

Fig. 7. Point cloud comparison of three algorithms in *fr3/w/xyz*. (a) ORB-SLAM2. (b) DynaSLAM. (c) Our system. (Color figure online)

4.3 Evaluation in Real-World Environment

In order to verify the robustness of moving object detection in dynamic environment, we use Xtion Pro camera to conduct extensive experiments in a laboratory environment. Xtion Pro camera can capture RGB images and depth images with 640×480 resolution. Before testing, we calibrate the camera in detail and use ROS to transmit the image data. The results obtained by the proposed method are shown in Fig. 8. In the experiment, the red points represent the dynamic feature points and the green points are the static feature points.

The first line shows a sequence of images taken in an office, there is a walker and a sitting person, and the sitting person can be regarded as a static target during this period of time. In the second line, most of the correct dynamic points can be constrained within the range of dynamic targets by the proposed joint constraints, but it is still a little insufficient, parts of the dynamic feature points on the walker are judged to be stationary. In the third line, combined with the

Fig. 8. Results in Lab environment. (Color figure online)

semantic information provided by the improved BlitzNet, the walker and the sitting person are distinguished effectively by the bounding boxes with region IDs. In the fourth line, we obtained a pixel-wise segmentation of the walker. In the real-world environment, the proposed algorithm is sample and feasible, and it can effectively identify the motion state of pedestrians.

5   Conclusion

In this paper, a semantic SLAM system based on joint constraint is proposed to detect the dynamic objects in the dynamic scene and accomplish the task of localization and mapping. The experiments on TUM dataset demonstrate the effectiveness and robustness of our system in localization. In addition, our system can obtain a more complete map with semantic information. Finally, we apply our algorithm to the real environment and it still has a notable performance. Future extensions of this work might include, among others, adaptive threshold method, on-line mapping and breaking the restrictions of application scope from semantic segmentation network.

References

1. Engel, J., Schöps, T., Cremers, D.: LSD-SLAM: large-scale direct monocular SLAM. In: European Conference on Computer Vision, pp. 834–849 (2014)
2. Engel, J., Koltun, V., Cremers, D.: Direct sparse odometry. IEEE Trans. Pattern Anal. Mach. Intell. 40(3), 611–625 (2018)

3. Mur-Artal, R., Tardós, J.D.: ORB-SLAM2: an open-source SLAM system for monocular, stereo, and RGB-D cameras. IEEE Trans. Robot. **33**(5), 1255–1262 (2016)
4. Wolf, D.F., Sukhatme, G.S.: Mobile robot simultaneous localization and mapping in dynamic environments. Auton. Robots. **19**(1), 53–65 (2005)
5. Wang, C.C., Thorpe, C., Thrun, S.: Online simultaneous localization and mapping with detection and tracking of moving objects: theory and results from a ground vehicle in crowded urban areas. In: IEEE International Conference on Robotics and Automation, pp. 842–849 (2003)
6. Bibby, C., Reid, I.: Simultaneous localisation and mapping in dynamic environments (SLAMIDE) with reversible data association. In: Proceedings of Robotics: Science and Systems, pp. 105–112 (2007)
7. Zou, D., Tan, P.: CoSLAM: collaborative visual SLAM in dynamic environments. IEEE Trans. Pattern Anal. Mach. Intell. **35**(2), 354–366 (2013)
8. Rebecq, H., Horstschaefer, T., Scaramuzza, D.: Real-time visual-inertial odometry for event cameras using keyframe-based nonlinear optimization. In: British Machine Vision Conference (2017)
9. Long, J., Shelhamer, E., Darrell, T.: Fully convolutional networks for semantic segmentation. In: Proceedings of the IEEE Conference on Computer Vision and Pattern Recognition, pp. 3431–3440 (2015)
10. Badrinarayanan, V., Kendall, A., Cipolla, R.: Segnet: a deep convolutional encoder-decoder architecture for image segmentation. IEEE Trans. Pattern Anal. Mach. Intell. **39**(12), 2481–2495 (2017)
11. Ronneberger, O., Fischer, P., Brox, T.: U-net: convolutional networks for biomedical image segmentation. In: International Conference on Medical Image Computing and Computer-Assisted Intervention, pp. 234–241 (2015)
12. Yu, F., Koltun, V.: Multi-scale context aggregation by dilated convolutions (2015). arXiv preprint arXiv:1511.07122
13. Chen, L.C., Papandreou, G., Kokkinos, I.: DeepLab: semantic image segmentation with deep convolutional nets, atrous convolution, and fully connected CRFs. IEEE Trans. Pattern Anal. Mach. Intell. **40**(4), 834–848 (2018)
14. Zhao, H., Shi, J., Qi, X.: Pyramid scene parsing network. In: Proceedings of the IEEE Conference on Computer Vision and Pattern Recognition, pp. 2881–2890 (2017)
15. Zhao, H., Qi, X., Shen, X., Shi, J., Jia, J.: ICNet for real-time semantic segmentation on high-resolution images. In: Ferrari, V., Hebert, M., Sminchisescu, C., Weiss, Y. (eds.) ECCV 2018. LNCS, vol. 11207, pp. 418–434. Springer, Cham (2018). https://doi.org/10.1007/978-3-030-01219-9_25
16. He, K., Gkioxari, G., Dollár, P.: Mask R-CNN. In: Proceedings of the IEEE International Conference on Computer Vision, pp. 2961–2969 (2017)
17. Dvornik, N., Shmelkov, K., Mairal, J.: BlitzNet: a real-time deep network for scene understanding. In: Proceedings of the IEEE International Conference on Computer Vision, pp. 4154–4162 (2017)
18. McCormac, J., Handa, A., Davison, A.: SemanticFusion: dense 3D semantic mapping with convolutional neural networks. In: IEEE International Conference on Robotics and Automation (ICRA), pp. 4628–4635 (2017)
19. Li, X., Belaroussi, R.: Semi-dense 3D semantic mapping from monocular SLAM (2016). arXiv preprint arXiv:1611.04144
20. Bowman, S.L., Atanasov, N., Daniilidis, K.: Probabilistic data association for semantic SLAM. In: IEEE International Conference on Robotics and Automation (ICRA), pp. 1722–1729 (2017)

21. Yu, C., Liu, Z., Liu, X.J.: DS-SLAM: a semantic visual SLAM towards dynamic environments. In: IEEE/RSJ International Conference on Intelligent Robots and Systems (IROS), pp. 1168–1174 (2018)
22. Bescos, B., Fácil, J.M., Civera, J.: DynaSLAM: tracking, mapping, and inpainting in dynamic scenes. IEEE Robot. Autom. Lett. **3**(4), 4076–4083 (2018)
23. Xiang, G., Tao, Z.: Robust RGB-D simultaneous localization and mapping using planar point features. Robot. Auton. Syst. **72**, 1–14 (2015)
24. Sturm, J., Engelhard, N., Endres, F.: A benchmark for the evaluation of RGB-D SLAM systems. In: IEEE/RSJ International Conference on Intelligent Robots and Systems, pp. 573–580 (2012)

A 3D Surface Reconstruction Method Based on Delaunay Triangulation

Wenjuan Miao, Yiguang Liu$^{(\boxtimes)}$, Xuelei Shi, Jingming Feng, and Kai Xue

Vision and Image Processing Lab (VIPL), College of Computer Science,
Sichuan University, Chengdu 610065, People's Republic of China
liuyg@scu.edu.cn

Abstract. Point cloud models acquired by passive three-dimensional reconstruction systems based on binocular or multi-view involve large amounts of noise and its distribution is uneven, which affects the accuracy of surface reconstruction. To tackle the problem, we proposed a three-dimensional surface reconstruction method based on Delaunay triangulation. First, use Delaunay triangulation to get a fully adaptive decomposition of point cloud, then the output triangular mesh was represented using dual graph, so by using graph cut optimization the initial surface model was obtained. Second, the deformation model was used to optimize the initial surface model, and then adopted photometric similarity function and Laplace operator to refine surface details. Finally, the refinement was transformed into an iterative procedure, by which the real surface of the object was accurately approximated. We experimented on four standard datasets of Castle-Entry, Castle, Fountain and Herzjesu. The result showed that compared with Poisson surface reconstruction and floating scale surface reconstruction algorithm, the proposed method was more adaptable and robust to noise and outliers, and the detailed information recovery of local surface reconstruction was better. It showed that the method proposed in this paper effectively improved the accuracy and completeness of surface reconstruction, which could reconstruct high quality three-dimensional surface models of object from the point cloud models with lots of noise and complex topological structures.

Keywords: Surface reconstruction · Deformation model · Photometric similarity function

1 Introduction

3D reconstruction technology is widely applied in many fields such as virtual simulation [1,23], non-contact measurement [21], virtual reality [7], battlefield environment perception [4,22], etc. Therefore, it is a significant problem to process 3D point cloud acquired by 3D digital scanning devices, and achieve 3D reconstruction effectively and accurately. In this paper, we focus on processing point cloud to restore the geometry and topology structure of objects. Considering that 3D cloud point acquired by passive 3D reconstruction systems

Supported by NSFC under Grant 61860206007 and 61571313.

based on binocular or multi-view involves large amounts of noise and outliers, which affects results of surface reconstruction, we proposed an approach based on Delaunay triangulation. First, Delaunay triangulation was constructed by incremental insertion, after that output triangular mesh was converted into the representation of dual graph, and then we transform the initial surface extraction problem into graph cut optimization. Then due to the loss of details and the roughness of initial surface model, we optimized the initial surface by minimizing the internal and external energy functions of deformation model globally. Finally, surface model was approximated to the real surface of the object through several iterations of all vertices on the surface.

2   Related Work

Surface reconstruction is a major field in computer vision at present. Many surface reconstruction methods is summarized in [2], in this section, we intend to introduce related approaches to our method, including implicit surface reconstruction approaches [5,9,10,20], and surface reconstruction approaches based on Delaunay triangulation [8,11–15].

Kazhdan et al. [9] formulates the surface reconstruction from oriented points as a spatial poisson problem, which suffers a tendency to oversmooth the data. Kazhdan et al. [10] modifies the poisson reconstruction algorithm to add incorporate positional constraints, which improves the geometric surface and detail characteristics of the surface. However, reconstruction results of the approach is easily affected by data redundancy. Fuhrmann et al. [5] achieves surface reconstruction by extracting the zero-level set of the implicit function. Their approach could be extended theoretically, but the interpolation ability of the approach is limited due to the small support area. Wang et al. [20] proposes a surface reconstruction approach based on implicit pht-splines. Their approach could reconstruct high-quality results, but which requires high demand of memory.

The visual hull introduced in [13] is unsuitable for outdoor scene reconstruction because of the dependence on separating object from background. Pan et al. [15] extracts surface by using probabilistic tetrahedron carving algorithm. But their approach is not resistant against outliers and inflexible for the batch processing of data. An approach of multi-view reconstruction is proposed in [12]. They define an energy equation based on visibility information and surface parameters, and minimize this energy by graph cuts [3]. Labatut et al. [11] improves the approach in [12], the photo-consistency is replaced by surface quality term in [11] and smoothing term is combined with a purely discrete visibility term. Their approach has good scalability, but it cannot construct weak-support surface well. Jancosek et al. [8] achieves multi-view reconstruction preserving weakly-supported surfaces which works on [11]. Mostegel et al. [14] proposes a scalable approach of surface reconstruction from 3D multi-scale multi-view stereo point clouds. Their approach extracts surface hypotheses from local Delaunay tetrahedralization and merges overlapping surface hypotheses by graph cuts [3],

finally a consistent mesh is generated. Their approach is resilient to outliers fragments and vast scale changes, but the results of reconstruction is limited by the
localized strategies taken in the original detection process.

3   Initial 3D Surface Reconstruction

In this paper, bundle system [16,17] is adopted to obtain camera parameters
and initial 3D point cloud. The point cloud is processed by PMVS [6], and then
we apply Delaunay triangulation to get a fully adaptive decomposition of point
cloud, which is constructed by incremental insertion. For the initial dense point
cloud, we find the nearest point of the point to be inserted in Delaunay triangulation based on the visibility information of the point, and then the maximum
reprojection error between two 3D points is computed. If the reprojection error
is above threshold e, the point would be inserted in Delaunay triangulation, or
the position of the nearest point would be recomputed. In addition, the visibility
information and confidence information of the nearest point would be updated.
This step outputs a Delaunay triangulation T through traversing all 3D points.

Next we convert the Delaunay tetrahedralization T into the representation of
a dual graph and set weight associated with it. Therefore, the surface is extracted
by performing graph cut optimization on this dual graph. The detailed procedure
is as follows: we assign weights to directed edges of dual graph based on visibility
information and smoothing terms. Accordingly, the minimum cut is extracted by
solving the energy equation as shown in formula (1). S is the initial reconstruction
surface, $E_{visibility}$ is the visibility term, E_{smooth} is the smoothing term and λ is
the weight coefficient. The energy equation is as follows:

$$E(S) = E_{visibility} + \lambda E_{smooth}(S) \tag{1}$$

According to the visibility constraints, all vertices v appearing on the final surface S should not be occluded from the viewpoints b they come from and therefore visibility item could be computed as the collision detection problem of the
line-face intersection conflict, as shown in Fig. 1. p_i is a 3D point, c_j is the center of camera j. We calculates the intersection of the ray $c_j p_i$ and Delaunay
tetrahedralization T. $\lambda_{visibility}$ is the size of visibility information set. $T_j(p_i)$ is

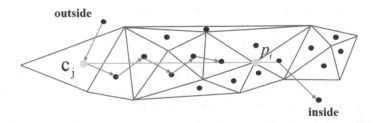

Fig. 1. The visibility conflict is the edge interested with ray $c_j p_i$, the arrowed edges
are parts of the representation of the dual graph, which weight the edge.

the credibility of the perspective, which represents the probability that vertex appears on the final surface model. Combining the Gaussian kernel function to reduce noise, the formula is as follows:

$$E_{visibility}(S) = \sum_{t \in T} \sum_{(p,c) \neq \varnothing} \lambda_{visibility}(1 - T_j(p_i)(1 - e^{\frac{-d^2}{2\sigma^2}})) \qquad (2)$$

In formula (2), t is the edge in the dual graph and the intersecting triangle of the adjacent tetrahedron in the Delaunay tetrahedralization, p is the vertex in the Delaunay, c is camera center, $(p,c) \cap t$ is the ray pc intersects t, d is the distance from the intersection with p_i, σ is the standard deviation of Gaussian function. Traversing all vertexes in the Delaunay tetrahedralization, we compute the visibility term by accumulating the directed edges weights as shown in formula (2).

The surface model will be uneven while the energy equation is only computed by $E_{visibility}$. In order to reduce the influence of outliers and noise points and restore the detailed information of the surface model. Triangle t is the intersecting of adjacent Delaunay tetrahedrons. The angle between the triangle plane and the external sphere of two tetrahedrons is α, β. The representation of the angle is shown in Fig. 2. While α, β is getting smaller, the possibility of cutting edge passing through triangle t is greater, which means the possibility of the cut edge appearing on the final surface is higher. α is calculated as.

$$\cos(\alpha) = \frac{\vec{pc} \cdot \boldsymbol{n}}{|\vec{pc}| \cdot |\boldsymbol{n}|} \qquad (3)$$

$\vec{pc}$ is the vector from vertex p to sphere centre c. $\boldsymbol{n}$ is the normal vector of triangle plane, E_{smooth} is computed as:

$$E_{smooth}(S) = \sum_{t \in T} 1 - min\{cos(\alpha), cos(\beta)\} \qquad (4)$$

The Smooth term is computed by traversing all the edges of dual graph. The Delaunay tetrahedron is labelled as inside/outside by graph cut optimization [3]. Triangles from label outside to inside are extracted as minimum cut edges and the initial reconstructed surface result S is obtained.

4   Surface Optimization Based on Deformation Model

Details are inevitably lost when smoothing the initial surface model. In this section, initial surface model is the input, which is optimized by deformation model to achieve surface optimization. In the deformation model, we adopted photometric similarity function as date term, and the internal energy function of the active contour model is calculated as regularization item by using Laplace operator. As the internal and external energy functions are minimized globally,

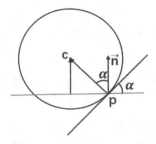

Fig. 2. It shows the 2D representation of the angle, α is the angle between triangle plane and external sphere of tetrahedrons, β is calculated the same way.

details of the surface model can be restored and a more refined surface reconstruction model can be obtained. The energy equation of the deformation model is as:

$$E(S) = E_{int}(S) + \lambda E_{ext}(S) \tag{5}$$

S is the initial surface model, λ is the weight of data item, $E_{int}(S)$ is the regularization item, which is responsible for constraining the topological structure of the surface model to prevent self-intersection and producing over smooth surface in the reconstruction process. $E_{int}(S)$ is computed by active contour model. $E_{ext}(S)$ is data item, which approximates the surface model to target model. $E_{ext}(S)$ is computed by photometric similarity function.

4.1   Data Term

The data term $E_{ext}(S)$ in the deformation model is computed by the photometric difference of images as:

$$\nabla E_{ext} = \sum_{I_i=0}^{n} \sum_{I_j=0 \cap I_i \neq I_j}^{n} \nabla M_{I_i,I_j}(S) \tag{6}$$

Matching function $M_{I_i,I_j}(S)$ is the difference between I_i and I_j, $\prod_j$ is the projection of the camera j, $\prod_{i,S}^{-1}$ is reprojecting I_i onto the surface, $I_j \circ \prod_j \circ \prod_{i,S}^{-1}$ is reprojecting the I_j onto I_i, $\Omega_{i,j}^{S}$ is the reprojection domain. $M_{I_i,I_j}(S)$ is as follows:

$$M_{I_i,I_j}(S) = M|_{\Omega_i \cap \Omega_{i,j}^{S}}(I_i, I_j \circ \prod_j \circ \prod_{i,S}^{-1}) \tag{7}$$

The data item gradient value of surface S is obtained by partial derivative of matching function with respect to variable x as:

$$\nabla M_{I_i,I_j}(S) = \int_{\Omega_i \cap \Omega_{i,j}^{S}} \partial M_{I_i,I_j}(x_i) DI_j(x_j) D \prod_j(x) \frac{n^T \delta S(x)}{n^T d_i} d_i dx_i \tag{8}$$

x is the reprojection 3D point of x_i, $DI_j(x_j)$ is the gradient of the image, $D\prod_j(x)$ is Jacobian matrix of $\prod_j$, d_i is the vector representing the camera i and the point x, n is the normal vector of 3D points.

4.2 Photometric Similarity Function

Matching function $M_{I,J}(S)$ is constructed by $L_{I,J}(x)$ on the basis of the local dependency between image I and image J.

$$M(I,J) = \int_{\Omega_i \cap \Omega^S_{i,j}} 1 - L_{I,J}(x_i)dx \tag{9}$$

$L_{I,J}(x)$ is photometric similarity function of image I and J at pixel x, $\Omega^S_{i,j}$ is the reprojection domain. In I_i, w_i is $n \times n$ pixel block centered on x_i, w_j is $n \times n$ pixel block centered on x_j. g_i is the grayscale value at pixel x_i, σ_g is the color standard deviation, σ_x is the distance standard deviation.

$$L_{I,J}(x_i) = \frac{cov(w_i, w_j)}{\sqrt{cov(w_i)cov(w_j, w_j)}} \tag{10}$$

$$E(x) = \frac{\sum_m^{n \times n} w_m x_m}{\sum_m^{n \times n} w_m} \tag{11}$$

$$w_m = e^{(-\frac{|g_m - g_i|^2}{2\sigma_g^2} + \frac{|x_m - x_i|^2}{2\sigma_x^2})} \tag{12}$$

4.3 Regularization Term

The regularization term is constructed by the internal function of the active contour models to prevent the self-intersection or producing over smooth of the surface model. We simplify the weight, λ_1 is the elasticity, λ_2 is the intensity coefficient to control the curves degree of surface, which ultimately makes the curvature of the surface tend to be stable. The minimum of energy function for equation is solved by Euler-Lagrange theorem as:

$$\nabla E_{int}(S) == \lambda_1 \triangle S - \lambda_2 \triangle^2 S \tag{13}$$

$\triangle$ is the laplace operator, $\triangle^2$ is the biharmonic Operator. For each vertex v in the surface S, the laplace operator is computed as formula (14), $N(v)$ is a set of 1-ring nearest vertices of v. n is the number of $N(v)$. The gradient of v is as:

$$\triangle v = (\sum_{i \in N(v)} (\frac{v_i}{n})) - v \tag{14}$$

$\triangle^2 v$ is calculated as:

$$\triangle^2 v = \sum_{i \in N(v)} (\frac{\triangle v_i}{n}) - \triangle v \tag{15}$$

For all vertices v of the surface, the $\nabla E_{int}(v)$ is accumulated by $\nabla E_{int}(S)$, as shown in formula (16):

$$\nabla E_{int}(S) = \sum_{v \in S} \nabla E_{int}(v) \tag{16}$$

4.4 Optimizing of the Final Surface

Finally, the surface is optimized by formula (5), and the discrete form of formula (5) is shown in formula (17). After several iterations of all vertices on the surface by gradient descent, surface model is approximated to the real surface of the object.

$$S^{k+1} = S^k + \triangle t(\nabla E_{int}(S) + \lambda \nabla E_{ext}(S)) \tag{17}$$

λ is the weight of data term, $\triangle t$ is the incremental step. All vertices v are iterated until the whole surface model converges. Finally, the reconstructed surface model is obtained.

5   Experiments

In this section, experiments are divided into two parts. To confirm the effectiveness of our method, we tested on four standard datasets [18]: Castle-Entry, Castle, Fountain and Herzjesu, and compared the experimental results with PSR [10] and FSSR [5]. Moreover, in order to verify the accuracy of our approach, we compared the reconstructed surface models with real three-dimensional models, and have experimented our method and GDMR on four datasets [18] to evaluate the similarity between the experiment results and ground truth of models.

In experiments, bundle system [16, 17] is adopted to obtain the initial 3D point cloud, and then we process the point cloud by PMVS [6], which is used as the input of the surface reconstruction. In the proposed approach, we get the initial reconstruction surface with parameter $\sigma = l/2$, where l represents the median of Delaunay side length, after that we optimize the surface by deformation model, and set threshold $n = 4$, we weight $\lambda_1 = 0.8$, $\lambda_2 = 0.2$ in optimation energy formulation, the weight factor λ of the iteration equation is set $\lambda = 0.5$, step $\triangle t$ at each iterations is set $\triangle t = 0.5$, which is reduced by 0.02 times after each iteration.

For the qualitative evaluation, we conducted on the four standard datasets [18] compared with PSR [10] and FSSR [5]. PSR is experimented at a depth of 11. Octree depth of FSSR is set to 10. As illustrated in Fig. 3, we can see that in the easily occluded areas such as pillars of the Herzjesu, our method reconstruct the surface with more details. In areas with uneven distribution of samples such as windows of the Herzjesu, our method reconstruct smoother wall than the others. In Fig. 4, surface details of spiral sculpture of the Fountain are more accurate and closer to the real model. In Fig. 5, the pillar and edge of Castle-entry are more detailed, while the reconstructed surfaces of PSR and FSSR are smoother and image details are lost. In Fig. 6, the reconstruction results of Castle show that the proposed algorithm is superior to PSR [10] and FSSR [5] in terms of detail recovery and reconstruction integrity.

Figures 3, 4, 5 and 6 demonstrate that our method increases the local details information of reconstructed surface, and it can be found that PSR [10] and FSSR [5] are vulnerable to a large number of noise points and outliers, resulting in poor reconstruction effect. Our method improves the precision of the surface reconstruction due to decomposing the surface model, and obtains accurate surface reconstruction by optimizing the surface details through the deformation model.

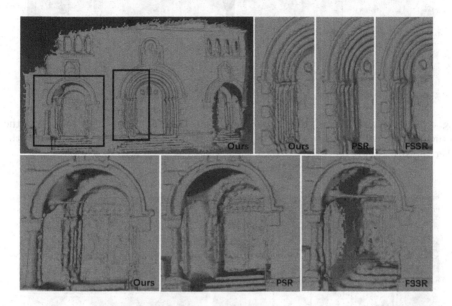

Fig. 3. The reconstruction result experimented on Herzjesu shows that the door and door frame reconstructed by the proposed method is more clearly than the other methods [5,10].

For the quantitative evaluation, we compared the reconstructed surface model and GDMR [19] with the real three-dimensional model respectively. We adopted the four standard datasets [18] as the assessment model. Table 1 and Table 2 show the error statistics of the surface model reconstructed by the algorithm and the ground truth on the Fountain and Herzjesu, and the error statistics of the GDMR and ground truth. In Table 1, the accuracy of the model after optimization of the deformation model in this paper is reduced when the error is 0.1. In Table 2, When the error is 0.045 and 0.06, the accuracy of the model is reduced, which is because the partial occlusion area increases the number of vertices and triangles of the occlusion area by triangulation during the deformation optimization process, resulting in an increase in the number of error points and optimization. In addition, from Table 1 and Table 2, it can be seen that the accuracy of the algorithm in this paper is better than that of GDMR. The initial

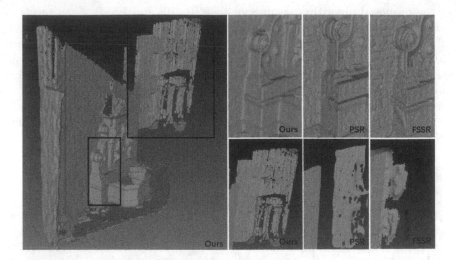

Fig. 4. The reconstruction result experimented on Fountain shows that outline of the statue and the wall reconstructed by the proposed method is more complete than the other methods [5,10].

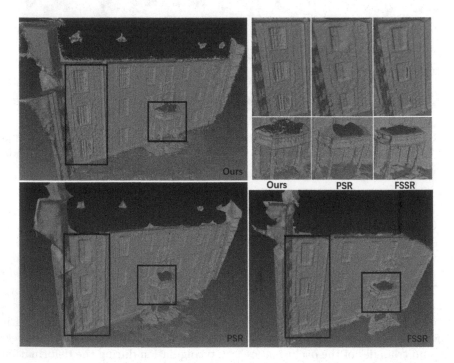

Fig. 5. The reconstruction result experimented on Castle-entry shows that the outline of the castle is clearer, and pillars is more complete than the other methods [5,10].

Fig. 6. The reconstruction result experimented on Castle shows that the completeness and detail of our approach is reconstructed better than the other methods [5,10].

Table 1. Relative errors between reconstructed results of our approach, GDMR [19] and the Fountain ground truth.

ratio(%) \ error(m) surface model	0.02	0.04	0.06	0.80	0.10
the initial surface	78.415	96.24	98.235	98.686	99.572
optimization surface	78.552	96.657	98.268	98.841	99.361
GDMR	76.436	95.985	98.379	98.794	99.358

Table 2. Relative errors between reconstructed results of our approach, GDMR [19] and the Herzjesu ground truth.

ratio(%) \ error(m) surface model	0.015	0.030	0.045	0.060	0.075
the initial surface	93.068	97.489	98.985	99.681	99.868
optimization surface	94.585	97.337	98.151	98.538	99.746
GDMR	94.385	97.364	98.086	98.479	99.685

model, deformation optimization model of our method and GDMR are quantitatively analyzed by experiments. The experiments show that our algorithm achieves higher accuracy than GDMR [19].

6   Conclusion

In this paper, we presented an approach of 3D surface reconstruction based on Delaunay triangulation. The initial surface model is derived by Delaunay triangulation and graph-cut optimization. Then we optimized the initial surface by deformation model and gradient descent to obtain the final surface. We experimented on four standard datasets of Castle-Entry, Castle, Fountain and Herzjesu. The proposed approach could reconstruct high quality three-dimensional surface models of object from the point cloud models with lots of noise and complex topological structures.

References

1. Bai, R., Qu, Y.: Study on three-dimensional visual simulation technology and its application in surface coal mine. In: 2012 Fourth International Conference on Computational and Information Sciences, pp. 14–16. IEEE (2012)
2. Berger, M., et al.: State of the art in surface reconstruction from point clouds. In: EUROGRAPHICS Star Reports, vol. 1, pp. 161–185 (2014)
3. Boykov, Y., Kolmogorov, V.: An experimental comparison of min-cut/max-flow algorithms for energy minimization in vision. IEEE Trans. Pattern Anal. Mach. Intell. **9**, 1124–1137 (2004)
4. Bruno, F., Bruno, S., De Sensi, G., Luchi, M.L., Mancuso, S., Muzzupappa, M.: From 3D reconstruction to virtual reality: a complete methodology for digital archaeological exhibition. J. Cult. Heritage **11**(1), 42–49 (2010)
5. Fuhrmann, S., Goesele, M.: Floating scale surface reconstruction. ACM Trans. Graph. (ToG) **33**(4), 46 (2014)
6. Furukawa, Y., Ponce, J.: Accurate, dense, and robust multiview stereopsis. IEEE Trans. Pattern Anal. Mach. Intell. **32**(8), 1362–1376 (2009)
7. Hafeez, J., Lee, S., Kwon, S., Hamacher, A.: Image based 3D reconstruction of texture-less objects for VR contents. Int. J. Adv. Smart Converg **6**(1), 9–17 (2017)
8. Jancosek, M., Pajdla, T.: Multi-view reconstruction preserving weakly-supported surfaces. In: CVPR 2011, pp. 3121–3128. IEEE (2011)
9. Kazhdan, M., Bolitho, M., Hoppe, H.: Poisson surface reconstruction. In: Proceedings of the Fourth Eurographics Symposium on Geometry Processing, vol. 7 (2006)
10. Kazhdan, M., Hoppe, H.: Screened poisson surface reconstruction. ACM Trans. Graph. (ToG) **32**(3), 29 (2013)
11. Labatut, P., Pons, J.P., Keriven, R.: Robust and efficient surface reconstruction from range data. In: Computer Graphics Forum, vol. 28, pp. 2275–2290. Wiley Online Library (2009)
12. Labatut, P., Pons, J.P., Keriven, R.: Efficient multi-view reconstruction of large-scale scenes using interest points, delaunay triangulation and graph cuts. In: 2007 IEEE 11th International Conference on Computer Vision, pp. 1–8. IEEE (2007)
13. Laurentini, A.: The visual hull concept for silhouette-based image understanding. IEEE Trans. Pattern Anal. Mach. Intell. **16**(2), 150–162 (1994)
14. Mostegel, C., Prettenthaler, R., Fraundorfer, F., Bischof, H.: Scalable surface reconstruction from point clouds with extreme scale and density diversity. In: Proceedings of the IEEE Conference on Computer Vision and Pattern Recognition, pp. 904–913 (2017)
15. Pan, Q., Reitmayr, G., Drummond, T.: Proforma: probabilistic feature-based online rapid model acquisition. In: BMVC, vol. 2, p. 6. Citeseer (2009)
16. Snavely, N., Seitz, S.M., Szeliski, R.: Photo tourism: exploring photo collections in 3D. In: ACM transactions on graphics (TOG), vol. 25, pp. 835–846. ACM (2006)

17. Snavely, N., Seitz, S.M., Szeliski, R.: Modeling the world from internet photo collections. Int. J. Comput. Vision **80**(2), 189–210 (2008)
18. Strecha, C., Von Hansen, W., Van Gool, L., Fua, P., Thoennessen, U.: On benchmarking camera calibration and multi-view stereo for high resolution imagery. In: 2008 IEEE Conference on Computer Vision and Pattern Recognition, pp. 1–8. IEEE (2008)
19. Ummenhofer, B., Brox, T.: Global, dense multiscale reconstruction for a billion points. In: Proceedings of the IEEE International Conference on Computer Vision, pp. 1341–1349 (2015)
20. Wang, J., Yang, Z., Jin, L., Deng, J., Chen, F.: Parallel and adaptive surface reconstruction based on implicit pht-splines. Comput. Aided Geom. Des. **28**(8), 463–474 (2011)
21. Wei, Z., Qi, G., Qiang, Z., Wang, Y., Jian, O.: A non-contact measurement method of cabin capacity based on structured light vision. In: IEEE International Conference on Mechatronics & Automation (2016)
22. Wu, H.N., Sun, X.R., Liu, W.J.: Research on 3D modeling technology of battlefield environment. Appl. Mech. Mater. **651–653**, 2020–2023 (2014)
23. Xie, A., Fang, C., Huang, Y., Fan, Y., Pan, J., Peng, F.: Application of three-dimensional reconstruction and visible simulation technique in reoperation of hepatolithiasis. J. Gastroenterol. Hepatol. **28**(2), 248–254 (2013)

A Visual Perspective for User Identification Based on Camera Fingerprint

Xiang Jiang[1,2], Shikui Wei[1,2(✉)], Ruizhen Zhao[1,2], Ruoyu Liu[1,2],
Yufeng Zhao[3], and Yao Zhao[1,2]

[1] Institute of Information Science, Beijing Jiaotong University, Beijing, China
{xiangj,shkwei,rzhzhao,12112062,yzhao}@bjtu.edu.cn
[2] Beijing Key Laboratory of Advanced Information Science and Network Technology,
Beijing 100044, China
[3] Institute of Clinic Basic Medicine, China Academy of Chinese Medical Sciences,
Beijing 100700, China
snowmanzhao@163.com

Abstract. User identification is to identify the online accounts' identity, which is a critical problem in many applications. The key problem in that is to find a typical pattern from the online accounts data. Different from the previous works, we identify users based on the camera fingerprint. The underlying idea is that the accounts belonging to the same individual contain the photos taken by the same cameras. Based on that, we propose a new framework to deal with the user identification problem. Specifically, the camera feature of each image is extracted by the PRNU (Photo Response Non-Uniformity) algorithm. With the proposed hierarchical clustering approach, the camera features of different camera source can be achieved. Extensive experiments on a collected photo dataset show that the proposed framework is effective for identifying users, especially in the scenarios that users have multiple cameras and photos forwarding behavior.

Keywords: User identification · Camera fingerprint · Multiple cameras · Reposted images

1 Introduction

Identifying the identity of online user accounts is an important problem for many practical applications. Such informative elements are referred to as user identification. With the rapid development of the Internet, the problem of user identifi-

This work was supported in part by National Key Research and Development of China (No. 2017YFC1703503), National Natural Science Foundation of China (No. 61532005, No. 61572065), Program of China Scholarships Council (No. 201807095006), Fundamental Research Funds for the Central Universities (No. 2018JBZ001).

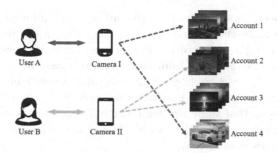

Fig. 1. The basic idea of our approach. Given four accounts, accounts 1 and 4 are asserted to belong to the same individual A, since all images in accounts 1 and 4 are captured by the same camera I.

cation can be the foundation of many practical applications, such as user migration [8], Enhancing Friend Recommendation [6], Information Diffusion [19], Multiple Network Group Interaction [5] and Analyzing Network Dynamics [1].

Identifying online accounts' identity is a challenging task. The core problem is how to find the person unique features from different accounts. Many efforts have been devoted to this problem, and many user features have been proposed. For example, the public personal informations such as real-name, e-mail, and IP address are employed in identifying the identity of online accounts. Linguistic stylistics [12], writing style [16] can also be viewed as an efficient pattern which indicates the real identity. Furthermore, other information which is summarized by the user behaviors, such as membership with other accounts and the points of interest, are also taken as the basis of user identification in many previous studies. Above works show the efficient performance in user identification. However, these studies show several limitations. For example, the personal information can be efficiently deliberate hidden with a different purpose, the linguistic stylistics shows much confusion with a few text data, and the user behaviors cannot precisely identify a specific users' identity.

In this paper, we attempt to identify users by matching their cameras. The underlying idea is that the accounts belong to the same person are usually post the same camera captured images, and the camera can be viewed as a person unique feature. As shown in Fig. 1, Account 1 and Account 4 are identified to User A since the images published in each account's album are all captured by Camera I. Therefore, we convert the user identification problem to camera identification problem. In previous studies of the forensic community, identifying the source of an image without extra information (*e.g.* EXIF file or JPEG Header) is an important problem. Just like the fingerprint, there exists the unique camera feature which is caused by the imperfection of the camera sensor, such as dust on the sensor, or sensor pattern noise (SPN). As the most popular camera fingerprints, the SPN extraction technique is applied in this paper to extract the person unique feature from the user account.

Extracting the camera features from the online users' albums is a challenging problem. According to the related technique, a fine camera fingerprint is the average of the residual noises of plenty same camera images. However, for a user album, the images may be taken from more than one camera device. Therefore, before we extract the camera fingerprint, we must know which images share with the same camera sources. Further, considering the user behavior of re-forwarding, the users that share the same camera fingerprints may not exist an excellent relationship in the offline world. Therefore, a mechanism that filters re-forwarding images is necessary.

In this paper, we propose a camera fingerprint-based user identification scheme to address user identification problem in image sharing platforms. To the best of our knowledge, it is the first work to tackle user identification from the forensic aspect. The main contributions can be summarized as follows:

- A new perspective is proposed to tackle the user identification problem in image sharing platforms.
- A camera feature extraction algorithm is proposed to extract the unique personal feature from the online account.
- A reposted images filter mechanism is proposed to restrain the confusion of photo forwarding behavior.

2   Related Work

User identification has been studied in different perspectives, such as a friend relationship. It is essential for user identification to find out whether online accounts could be associated with the same person or not in the real world. The core problem is how to seek a unique and reliable pattern among the accounts' public information.

One commonly adopted method is to extract personal information through users' public profiles, such as username and register address [13]. Based on these person-unique patterns, some simple but effective algorithms have been designed, and excellent performance on some datasets has been achieved. However, many users, especially malicious users, do not release any private information on social networks, which makes these methods fail.

Different from the methods mentioned above, [7] regards the social network as a large graph, where the nodes and edges represent the users and their link relationships, respectively. Therefore, the user identification problem can be converted into an approximate graph isomorphism problem. Similar works also reported in [9,17,18]. The essence of these kinds of methods is that the users' linking relationship is regarded as discrimination patterns. In recent years, plenty of similar works have been proposed and achieved good performance. However, such methods are not very suited to identify specific users, especially malicious users. Such methods may more suitable for identifying a user group.

To solve the above problem, many studies attempt to mine latent information from users' activities in accounts. An impressive work [12] shows that the users can be identified based on linguistic stylistics, which is trained through the person's text on the Internet. Furthermore, hobbies and interests patterns are also employed as user identification features. These methods can extract personal patterns through accounts' public information, and excellent performance has been achieved. However, the identification result obtained by such features is more like the inference instead of evidence, which makes such methods not reliable.

To address the above-mentioned problems, we extracting camera fingerprint as the person unique pattern. The camera fingerprint is a kind of invisible and camera-unique component in digital images, and the most widespread approach is PRNU (Photo Response Non-Uniformity) [10]. Recently, a plenty of works based on PRNU has been proposed and applied in many practical application. For example, citeValsesia2015 applied the PRNU to retrieval same camera source images on Internet, [9] attempt to tackle the problem of camera source cluster, [4] employed the PRNU to solve the problem of image forgery detection. Furthermore, [3] enhanced the detail of PRNU and further improved the performance. Due to the high reliability of camera fingerprint, it can be taken as the evidence in court. Therefore, it can make up the drawback of traditional user identification methods. Furthermore, similarity studies also mentioned in [11, 14, 15].

In the application of social network, [2] verified the feasibility of PRNU on social media images. Specifically, the images on social media are compressed and downsampling, however, the PRNU can still be detected. To the problem of user identification, to the best of our knowledge, [1] is the first work to tackle the user identification problem based on camera source. They proposed a novel algorithm, *i.e.* picture-to-identity linking, to identify the users via camera identification. However, this approach is based on the pairwise matching among all users' images, which means the time cost is very expensive, especially for the large scale dataset of online social network users.

3   Methodology

In this section, we propose a user feature extraction framework. The diagram is illustrated in Fig. 3. The details are given as follows.

3.1   Preliminaries

We first discuss how to extract camera fingerprint based on [10]. Given an image $\mathbf{I}$, its residual noise $\mathbf{R}$ can be extracted with

$$\mathbf{R} = \mathbf{I} - \mathcal{F}(\mathbf{I}), \tag{1}$$

where $\mathcal{F}(\cdot)$ is a denoising filter. Then for a set of same camera source images $\mathcal{I} = \{\mathbf{I}_i\}_{i=0}^{N}$, we can obtain the camera source $\mathbf{F}$ by

$$\mathbf{F} = \frac{\sum \mathbf{I}_i \cdot \mathbf{R}_i}{\sum \mathbf{I}_i^2} \tag{2}$$

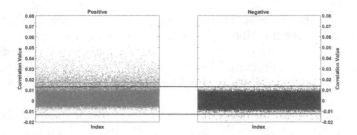

Fig. 2. The scatter plot to verify the proposed assumption. The spot in both diagrams is the correlation values among any pairs of images' residual noise. The orange spot means the two images have the same camera source (positive pair), and the blue spot in the right represents the images pair has different camera source. As we can see, high values (beyond the red line) are always achieved by the positive pairs and few negative pairs beyond it. (Color figure online)

The similarity $\mathbf{s}_{i,j}$ between two camera fingerprints $\mathbf{F}_i$ and $\mathbf{F}_j$ can be calculated by the normalized correlation as follow:

$$\mathbf{s}_{i,j} = \frac{(\mathbf{F}_i - \bar{\mathbf{F}}_i) \cdot (\mathbf{F}_j - \bar{\mathbf{F}}_j)}{||\mathbf{F}_i - \bar{\mathbf{F}}_i|| \cdot ||\mathbf{F}_j - \bar{\mathbf{F}}_j||} \tag{3}$$

where $\bar{\mathbf{F}}_i$ and $\mathbf{C\bar{F}}_j$ are the means of $\mathbf{F}_i$ and $\mathbf{F}_j$, respectively. If the score is greater than a predefined threshold, the two images set $\mathcal{I}_i$ and $\mathcal{I}_j$ are considered that they are captured by the same camera device.

3.2   User Feature Extraction Algorithm

Given a set of images $\mathcal{I} = \{\mathbf{I}_i\}_{i=0}^{N}$, the residual noise set $\mathcal{R} = \{\mathbf{R}_i\}_{i=0}^{N}$ can be obtained. Then, a pairwise similarity matrix $\mathbf{S}$ is calculated with Eq. 3, where $\mathbf{S}_{i,j}$ denotes the similarity between residual $\mathbf{R}_i$ and $\mathbf{R}_j$. The purpose algorithm is to segment the $\mathcal{I}$ based on their camera fingerprints $\mathcal{R}$ and pairwise similarities $\mathbf{S}$. The proposed algorithm is based on the hierarchical algorithm and contains three main steps, *i.e.* seeds selection, group merger, and residual assignment. The detail is introduced below.

Seeds Selection. The seeds selection step is to select initial segmentation of a user's album. As we mentioned before, the residual noise can be viewed as a noisy camera fingerprint, and the similarity between them is also noise so that the relationship of camera source cannot be surely determined. However, we observe an important phenomenon, which the large similarity can correctly predict the residuals with same camera source. In specific, *if the correlation of two images' residual noises is high enough; the two images have a high probability of being captured by the same camera.* To verify that, the pairwise similarities of 1,576 images of 11 cameras is calculated. For the same camera pair, we denote the similarity as the positive points, and others are negative points. They are drawn in Fig. 2. As we can see, the negative points show a more narrow range than positive scatters, and the points which are larger than 0.02 can be taken as positive points. Therefore, for the residual pairs whose similarities are larger than 0.02, we gather them into the same subset and take them as the initialized seed.

Group Merger. In the above step, plenty of seeds set can be obtained. However, the camera source of these subsets is not unique to each other. It is obvious that there are many positive pairs come from the same camera source. Therefore, merging these subsets can further restrain the noise of the camera fingerprint of each subset. Toward this end, a similar strategy to seed selection is employed here to merge consistent groups. In particular, given any two clusters $\mathbf{C}_j$, $\mathbf{C}_k$, we merge them into one cluster if the correlation value $\mathbf{S}_{ij}$ is greater than a 0.02. Formally, the updating procedure can be formulated as

$$\mathbf{C}_i = \mathbf{C}_j \bigcup \mathbf{C}_k, \; if \; \mathbf{S}_{i,j} > 0.02, \tag{4}$$

Residual Assignment. After the above two steps, we can obtain several small subsets. However, there are plenty of images not assigned. To assign these scatters into the correct subset, an iterative scheme is proposed. The residual noise of an image can be viewed as a camera fingerprint corrupted by the noise. To suppress the other noise and obtain a more reliable camera fingerprint, we need to collect more images with the same camera source. When more images are collected, a fine camera fingerprint can be obtained. For now, several subsets with multiple images are obtained, and we can get a relatively fine camera fingerprint for each of them. In this way, the similarities between residual images and the subsets' camera fingerprints may exceed the preset threshold. To avoid the extra error, we only add the residual image to a subset if they have the largest similarity than the similarities between other residual image and this subset. Therefore, for M camera fingerprints $\{\mathbf{F}_1, ..., \mathbf{F}_M\}$, a residual noise $\mathbf{R}_i$ should be assign to jth subset based on

$$j = \arg\max_{1 \leq j \leq M} \mathbf{S}_{i,j} \tag{5}$$

where $\mathbf{S}_{i,j}$ is the similarity value between $\mathbf{R}_i$ and $\mathbf{F}_j$.

Note that the camera fingerprint may be a strength after assigned new member, the similarity values between the current subsets may exceed than the preset threshold. It means that the subsets can be further merged since the strength of the camera fingerprints. Therefore, after adding a single residual image to each current subset, the group merger step will be processed. The iteration will not be terminated until there are no similarities between the residual images and subsets' camera fingerprints are larger than the preset threshold. After the terminated, we take all the camera fingerprints of every subset and the residual noises of every residual image as the user features. Algorithm 1 shows the detail of the proposed framework.

Algorithm 1. User Camera Fingerprint Extraction Algorithm

Input: An user's images set $\mathcal{I} = \{\mathbf{I}_i\}_{i=1}^{N}$;
 1: Get $\mathcal{R} = \{\mathbf{R}_i\}_{i=1}^{N}$ by Eq.1;
 2: Get pairwise similarities $\mathbf{S}$ by Eq.3;
 3: Get current subset $\mathcal{C} = \{\mathbf{C}_i\}_{i=1}^{N}$ and residual $\mathcal{I} = \{\mathbf{I}_i\}_{i=1}^{N^*}$ by **Seeds Selection**.
 4: Set $\Delta = 1$;
 5: **while** Δ **do**
 6:    Merge consistent groups $\mathcal{C}$ by Eq.4;
 7:    Merge residual images in $\mathcal{I}$ to each subset in $\mathcal{C}$ by Eq.5;
 8:    Update $\mathcal{I}$ to $\mathcal{I}^*$ and $\mathcal{C}$ to $\mathcal{C}^*$;
 9:    **if** $\mathcal{I} = \emptyset$ or $\mathcal{I}^* = \mathcal{I}$ **then**
10:       $\Delta = 0$
11:    **end if**
12:    $\mathcal{I}^* \leftarrow \mathcal{I}$, $\mathcal{C}^* \leftarrow \mathcal{C}$;
13: **end while**
Output: Camera fingerprints set $\mathcal{S}_i$

3.3   Feature Refinement

With the proposed feature extraction approach, several subsets and a plenty of images can be obtained, and their camera fingerprints and residual noise is taken as the users' feature. However, they may be confused by the re-posted images. The reposted images is the images which is captured by other person and posted by the current user. The shared camera fingerprint of reposted images cannot prove that the owner of these accounts have offline relationship. Therefore, eliminating the confusion of repost images is necessary to our purpose.

Distinguishing which images is the reposted image seems an impossible task. However, an important pattern of the reposted images is that they have been uploaded to the Internet many times. Considering the double compression processing provided by the service providers, the quality of an reposted image is very low. Fortunately, the camera fingerprint component exists in an image may be corrupted by the double compression, and the residual noises reposted images probably show weak response to the correlations. Therefore, for the image whose similarities with others is very low, it can be viewed as the *potential* reposted images.

In fact, small similarities with other data points indicate that they cannot be assigned to any exists subset. In other word, the reposted images probably exist in the residual images. Therefore, by discard all the residual images, we can restrain the confusion caused by the reposted images.

3.4   Similarity Estimation

Above algorithm can extract a fine user fingerprint under the challenges of multiple cameras and reposted images. How to measure the similarity between two users will be discussed in this part.

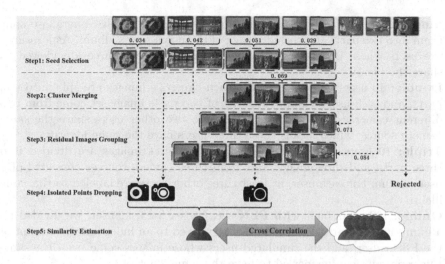

Fig. 3. The framework overview of proposed user feature extraction algorithm.

Given two accounts $\mathbf{A}_i$ and $\mathbf{A}_j$, $\mathcal{C}_i$ and $\mathcal{C}_j$ obtained by above algorithm are denoted to the features of $\mathbf{A}_i$ and $\mathbf{A}_j$, respectively. If $\mathbf{A}_i$ and $\mathbf{A}_j$ belong to the same person, their camera fingerprint sets may have an intersection. Therefore, the value of most similarity camera fingerprints from each feature is taken as the similarity between two users. Specifically, the mathematical expression is represented as follows:

$$\mathbf{d}(\mathbf{A}_i, \mathbf{A}_j) = \arg\max_{l,k} \frac{(\mathbf{C}_l^{(i)} - \mathbf{C}_l^{\overline{(i)}}) \cdot (\mathbf{C}_k^{(j)} - \mathbf{C}_k^{\overline{(j)}})}{||\mathbf{C}_l^{(i)} - \mathbf{C}_l^{\overline{(i)}}|| \cdot ||\mathbf{C}_k^{(j)} - \mathbf{C}_k^{\overline{(j)}}||} \tag{6}$$

where $\mathbf{d}(A_i, A_j)$ denotes the similarity between A_i, A_j; $\mathbf{C}_l^{(i)}$ and $\mathbf{C}_k^{(j)}$ denote the lth camera fingerprint of $\mathcal{C}_i$ and kth camera fingerprint of $\mathcal{C}_j$.

4 Experimental Evaluation

4.1 Settings

Before we present our experimental results, we will first introduce our settings, including dataset, metric, and baselines.

Dataset. The data set for user identification is difficult to obtain since these users are not fully labeled. Further, as our best knowledge, no public dataset has been released. Therefore, to verify the performance of user identification, we build several datasets based on a set of images. In specific, the base images comes from two sources, *i.e.* 1) 1,020 images with certain camera source (**ORI**) and 15,382 images crawled from 96 Flickr users' albums (**FLK**). We summarize our datasets as follow:

- **Single:** 20 users built with **ORI**. For the images of each camera, we split them into two parts and consider each of them is a user's album. As a results, the users whose images come from the same camera source are viewed to share the identity.
- **Double:** 10 users built with **ORI**. Each camera's images are split into two parts, and each user's album is consist of two parts image set come from two different cameras. For each user, there are two other users share the same camera source, which means these three users have the same identity.
- **Triple:** 10 users built with **ORI**. Each camera's images are divided into three parts, and three images sets from three camera sources consisted of a user' album. For each user, at least three other users are labeled to the same identity.
- **Online:** 192 users built with **FLK** set. For each Flickr user, we divided its album into two parts. Each part can be viewed to an independent account of the Filckr user, and the simulated users whose images come from the same Flickr account can be viewed to have the same identity.

Furthermore, to verify the influence of reposted images to the proposed scheme, we collect 102 images with the same camera source, and randomly assign them to all the simulated users in all above datasets. That means that all the users quote the collected camera' images.

Metrics. To verify the performance of the proposed algorithm, Purity, Precision, Recall, and F1-measure is employed. Further, we exploit the ROC curve to measure the distinct ability of extracted users' features. Finally, we treat the user identification as a retrieval problem, and the mAP (mean Average Precision) metric is exploited.

Baselines. To fully show the feasibility of the proposed framework, the above schemes are exploited as the baselines.

- **LtP:** The proposed algorithm (LinktoPicture) in [1]. Given two users, the camera fingerprints of each user's all images are extracted in the first. Then, the pairwise similarities between two users' images are calculated and take the maximum value as the users' similarity.
- **SCF:** Single Camera Fingerprints. In this scheme, the multi-camera issue is not taken into account, which means that they assume that a single camera captures all the images of an account. Therefore, a mixed camera fingerprint obtained by all the images is taken as the user' feature. The similarity between two camera fingerprints is considered as the similarity between two users.
- **MCF:** Multiple Camera Fingerprints. The scheme is similar to the proposed method, except the feature refinement step. The scattered images are taken as one of the user's camera fingerprint, and the reposted image issue is not taken into account.

4.2   Experimental Evaluation

Comparisons with the State-of-the-art Models. We treat the user identification to a retrieval problem, *i.e.* identify whether two users share the same cameras device. Therefore, the key to experiments is to evaluate the effectiveness of the proposed feature extraction algorithm. Toward this end, on all the built dataset, we compare our approach with the state-of-the-art schemes (*i.e.* **LtP**, **SCF**, and **MCF**). Table 1 shows experimental results, where the bold items denote the best performance and the runner-up are underlined.

Table 1. MAP of Users Identification

	LtP	SCF	MCF	Proposed
Single	0.4310	0.9660	_0.9870_	**0.9880**
Double	0.3300	0.4370	_0.8200_	**0.8340**
Triple	0.2910	0.3880	_0.6140_	**0.6200**
Online	0.4117	0.7790	_0.8736_	**0.9013**
Multi-Camera	-	-	✓	✓
Reposted-Image	-	-	-	✓

From Table 1, several conclusion can be obtained. First, the best performance is reported by the proposed scheme and **MCF** achieves the runner-up, which means that the multi-camera processing is an efficient step to user identification. Second, **LtP** achieves the worst performance and the reason mainly due to the confusion of reposted images. In our experiments, the highest similarity obtained by **LtP** always achieved by the reposted images, so that causes much false recognition. Therefore, restraining the reposted images is necessary for user identification problem. Furthermore, we find that **MCF** reports comparable results to the proposed method, and this indicates that the multi-camera processing step can restrain the confusion caused by reposted images. For example, some reposted images are mis-grouped to a group, and the confusion can be restraint by averaging the images in this group. Finally, we observe that the performance of the proposed algorithm shows a minor improvement to **MCF**, which means that the proposed refinement step is efficient.

Multi-camera Performance. Multi-camera processing is a necessary step in user identification, and its result may greatly influence the final performance of user identification. In this section, the purity, Precision, and Recall are exploited to evaluate the performance of the proposed scheme. Note that the images in **Online** don't have camera labels, we only conduct the experiments on **Single**, **Double** and **Triple** datasets. See the results on Table 2.

In Table 2, we observe that the proposed algorithm achieves high precision, that means most same camera source images are assigned to the same groups. It makes the result more robust, *i.e.* the outliers in groups may be restrained

Table 2. Multi-camera processing Performance

	Single	Double	Triple
Purity	0.76	0.54	0.45
Precision	0.91	0.90	0.85
Recall	0.72	0.50	0.42

by averaging the camera fingerprints of other images. We also observe that the increasing number of camera source makes the dataset more difficult, and the proposed algorithm shows a worse performance on the **Triple** dataset.

Evaluate Reposted Images Removing. Another import issue of user identification is to restrain the confusion of reposted images. In proposed algorithm, we discard the scatters to remove the reposted images. Let us denote the reposted images number is N_{rep}, and the removed images number is N_{rem}. Assume k reposted images are correctly removed, we can obtain the true removed ratio $\textbf{TR} = \frac{k}{N_{rep}}$, miss removed ratio $\textbf{MR} = \frac{N_{rem}-k}{N_{rem}}$ and false removed ratio $\textbf{FR} = \frac{N_{rep}-k}{N_{rep}}$. In this section, we exploit above metrics to evaluate the performance of reposted images removing. See detail in Table 3.

Table 3. Evaluation of Removing Reposted images

	Single	Double	Triple	Online
TR	0.497	0.590	0.578	0.578
MR	0.152	0.366	0.404	0.268
FR	0.503	0.410	0.422	0.422

In Table 3, we observe that more than half of the reposted images are correctly removed, which means that the proposed algorithm is efficient to restrain the reposted images. However, with the increasing of camera number, the missing discard images number is also increasing.

5   Conclusion

In this paper, we propose an algorithm to address the user identification problem. Different from previous work, we identify the users' identity based on the camera fingerprint. The underlying idea is that the accounts with the same cameras devices may share the same identity in the offline world. Toward this end, a novel algorithm is proposed to extract the user's feature, which can deal with the multi-camera and reposted images issue. The experimental results show that the proposed algorithm can deal with the multi-camera and reposted images issue, and efficiently tackle the user identification problem.

References

1. Bertini, F., Sharma, R., Iannì, A., Montesi, D.: Profile resolution across multilayer networks through smartphone camera fingerprint. In: Proceedings of the 19th International Database Engineering & Applications Symposium, pp. 23–32. ACM (2015)
2. Castiglione, A., Cattaneo, G., Cembalo, M., Petrillo, U.: Experimentations with source camera identification and Online Social Networks. J. Ambient Intell. Humaniz. Comput. **4**(2), 265–274 (2013)
3. Chang-tsun, L.: Source camera identification using enhanced sensor pattern noise. IEEE Trans. Inf. Forensics Secur. **5**(2), 280–287 (2010)
4. Chen, M., Fridrich, J., Goljan, M., Lukáš, J.: Determining image origin and integrity using sensor noise. IEEE Trans. Inf. Forensics Secur. **3**(1), 74–90 (2008)
5. Hao, H., Zhang, X., Yong, S.: Identifying evolving groups in dynamic multi-mode networks. Microcomput. Appl. **24**(1), 72–85 (2011)
6. Kimura, M., Saito, K., Nakano, R., Motoda, H.: Extracting influential nodes on a social network for information diffusion. Data Min. Knowl. Disc. **20**(1), 70 (2010)
7. Korula, N., Lattanzi, S.: An efficient reconciliation algorithm for social networks. Proc. VLDB Endowment **7**(5), 377–388 (2014)
8. Kumar, S., Zafarani, R., Liu, H.: Understanding user migration patterns in social media. In: AAAI Conference on Artificial Intelligence (2012)
9. Liu, S., Wang, S., Zhu, F.: Structured learning from heterogeneous behavior for social identity linkage. IEEE Trans. Knowl. Data Eng. **27**(7), 2005–2019 (2015)
10. Lukáš, J., Fridrich, J., Goljan, M.: Digital camera identification from sensor pattern noise. IEEE Trans. Inf. Forensics Secur. **1**(2), 205–214 (2006)
11. Marra, F., Poggi, G., Sansone, C., Verdoliva, L.: Blind prnu-based image clustering for source identification. IEEE Trans. Inf. Forensics Secur. **PP**(99), 1 (2017)
12. Narayanan, A., et al.: On the feasibility of internet-scale author identification. In: 2012 IEEE Symposium on Security and Privacy, pp. 300–314 (2012)
13. Perito, D., Castelluccia, C., Kaafar, M.A., Manils, P.: How unique and traceable are usernames? In: Fischer-Hübner, S., Hopper, N. (eds.) PETS 2011. LNCS, vol. 6794, pp. 1–17. Springer, Heidelberg (2011). https://doi.org/10.1007/978-3-642-22263-4_1
14. Phan, Q.T., Boato, G., Natale, F.G.B.D.: Accurate and scalable image clustering based on sparse representation of camera fingerprint. IEEE Trans. Inf. Forensics Secur. **PP**(99), 1
15. Phan, Q.T., Boato, G., Natale, F.G.B.D.: Image clustering by source camera via sparse representation. In: International Workshop on Multimedia Forensics and Security (2017)
16. Zafarani, R., Liu, H.: Connecting Users across Social Media Sites : A behavioral-modeling approach. In: Proceedings of the 19th ACM SIGKDD International Conference on Knowledge Discovery and Data Mining, pp. 41–49. ACM (2013)
17. Zafarani, R., Tang, L., Liu, H.: User identification across social media. ACM Trans. Knowl. Discov. Data **10**(2), 16 (2015)
18. Zhou, X., Liang, X., Zhang, H., Ma, Y.: Cross-platform identification of anonymous identical users in multiple social media networks. IEEE Trans. Knowl. Data Eng. **28**(2), 411–424 (2016)
19. Zhuang, J., Mei, T., Hoi, S.C.H., Hua, X.S., Zhang, Y.: Community discovery from social media by low-rank matrix recovery. ACM Trans. Intell. Syst. Technol. **5**(4), 1–19 (2015)

Feature Refine Network for Text-Based CAPTCHA Recognition

Chen Duan[1,2(✉)], Rong Zhang[1,2], and Ke Qing[1,2]

[1] Department of Electronic Engineering and Information Science, University of Science and Technology of China, Hefei 230027, China
duanch@mail.ustc.edu.cn
[2] Key Laboratory of Electromagnetic Space Information, Chinese Academy of Sciences, Hefei 230027, China

Abstract. Text-based CAPTCHA is a widely used security mechanism. Text-based CAPTCHA recognition aims to automatically detect characters in a text-based CAPTCHA. It reveals the weakness of current CAPTCHA and improves the security ability. In this paper, we propose a novel Feature Refine network (FRN) for text-based CAPTCHA with small-size characters. FRN consists of convolutional layers and deconvolution layers. The convolutional layers enhance the feature extraction capabilities of the network and expand the receptive field. The deconvolution layers increase the resolution of the feature map and restore the details of texts. In addition, our model uses skip ROI pooling to extract multi-scale features with multi levels of abstraction. We test our model on five popular text-based CAPTCHAs, namely eBay, Baidu, Hotmail, Sina and NetEase. The experimental compared with the state-of-the-art methods demonstrate the ability of FRN. The recognition rates are improved above 90%, and these results achieve the new state-of-the-art for real website CAPTCHAs.

Keywords: Text-based CAPTCHA · Internet security · Feature refine network · Feature fusion

1 Introduction

CAPTCHA (Completely Automatic Public Turing tests to tell Computers and Humans Apart) is a program that most humans can pass but the machine can hardly pass. As a kind of Turing test [1], the CAPTCHA has important significance in website security. CAPTCHAs are widely used to prevent malicious batch operations, dictionary attacks, ensure the authenticity of online voting and other aspects. Since it was proposed by Louis Von Ahn et al. in 2003 [2], CAPTCHAs have been widely used in Google, Microsoft, eBay, and other websites. The most popular CAPTCHA is text-based scheme in which distorted and overlapped characters are contained in a single image. In order to study the security and reliability of the text-based CAPTCHAs, the breaking technique is proposed. The research of text-based CAPTCHAs recognition technology can

© Springer Nature Switzerland AG 2019
Y. Zhao et al. (Eds.): ICIG 2019, LNCS 11902, pp. 64–73, 2019.
https://doi.org/10.1007/978-3-030-34110-7_6

reveal the weakness of current text-based CAPTCHAs and lead to the design of a more secure CAPTCHA. Since that, the research of text-based CAPTCHAs recognition technology contributes to the security of websites on network.

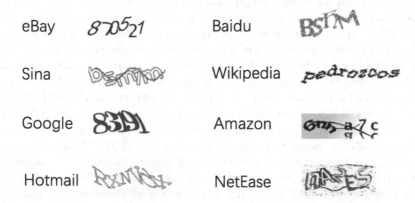

Fig. 1. Different types of text-based CAPTCHAs. Wikipedia and Hotmail use the waving method to prevent recognition. Amazon and NetEase use the complex background methods. Sina prevents recognition by adding lines. Google, Baidu and eBay use the Collapsing to prevent recognition.

With the development of text-based CAPTCHA technology, the most widely used text-based CAPTCHA schemes use combinations of distorted characters and obfuscation techniques that humans can recognize but difficult for automated scripts [3]. In order to recognize these complex text-based CAPTCHAs, various recognition methods have been proposed. According to whether segmentation involved in the recognition algorithm or not. These methods can be divided into segmentation based algorithm and non-segmentation based algorithm. segmentation based algorithm splits text-based CAPTCHA into individual characters firstly, then recognizes each character individually. Jeff Yan and El Ahmad [4] use projection and color filling algorithms to segment Microsoft's CAPTCHA. Their simple attack has achieved a segmentation success rate of higher than 90%, and overall (segmentation and recognition) success rate is more than 60%. However, the segmentation method is valid for simple text-based CAPTCHAs, which have no complicated background and the Collapsing. In addition, The method of segmentation needs to preprocess the text-based CAPTCHA image first. These preprocessing methods are not universal, and each type of text-based CAPTCHA needs to design a corresponding preprocessing algorithm. Once the website updates the text style of text-based CAPTCHA, a new preprocessing algorithm needs to be designed. Methods that based on non-segmentation directly recognize characters in a text-based CAPTCHA image without segmentation, such as shape context matching [5], multi-label convolutional neural network [6,7] and hidden Markov models (HMMs) [15].

The great challenge of non-segmentation is that characters in the text-based CAPTCHA image are Collapsed and distorted, which leads to low recognition rate.

In this paper, we use detection method to recognize text-based CAPTCHA. In recent years, the detection method based on deep learning has made sufficient progress, and yields better detection performance than the traditional method. Faster R-CNN [8] is a representative network in object detection which improves the precision of object detection. Compared with other detection networks [9,10]. Faster R-CNN has been proved to have good detection performance for deformed and rotating objects. The rotation and deformation of characters in the image are a bottleneck for improving the recognition rate of text-based CAPTCHA. So we adopt Faster R-CNN in our framework to recognize text-based CAPTCHA. Due to the problem of large differences in the scale of the characters. If we use the Faster R-CNN network to recognize text-based CAPTCHA directly, it will struggles in small-size character detection and precise localization, mainly due to the coarseness of its feature maps [11]. To solve such problem, we propose Feature Refine Network (FRN). FRN is composed of convolutional layer and deconvolution layer. The convolutional layer in FRN can deepen the network, making the extracted features have larger receptive field and more informative. The deconvolution layer in FRN can increase the resolution of the feature map and restore the object details by upsampling. In addition, our model uses skip ROI pooling to extract features at multiple scales to increase small object detection capabilities.

We test our model on text-based CAPTCHAs of eBay, Baidu, Hotmail, Sina and Netease. For each type of text-based CAPTCHA, we train our model with 1400, 3862, 3000, 2357, 3700 images respectively and test each type of text-based CAPTCHA with 1000 images. The recognition rates are all above 90%. Compared with other researchers' models [6, 7, 12–14, 16], our model is universal and achieves better performance.

2   Approach

In this section, we propose an effective and fast text-based CAPTCHA recognition method. Our framework is based on object detection. We use Faster R-CNN as the basis network for detection and recognition. The characters in the text-based CAPTCHA are not the same size, in which some are too tiny to be detected by Faster R-CNN effectively. Therefore, We propose Feature Refine Network (FRN) to extract more informative features. Then, we use ROI pooling to extract features at multiple scales and levels of abstraction. The framework of our model is shown in Fig. 2.

2.1   Feature Refine Network

Faster R-CNN uses VGG-16 as the basic feature extraction layers, which is pre-trained with ImageNet dataset [17]. VGG-16 has 4 pooling layers, and the

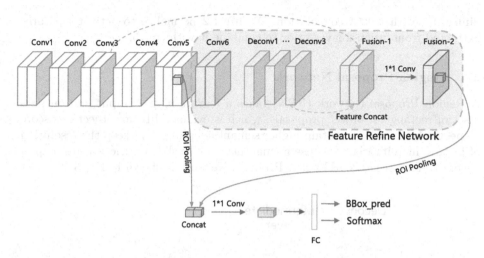

Fig. 2. Framework of our model. Convolutional layers are used to extract feature map from input image, and then the resolution of the feature map is expanded by deconvolution. According to the propsals of Region Proposal Network (RPN), features will be concatenated which are extracted on conv5 and fusion-2 respectively by ROI pooling. After reducing the dimension of these concatenate features by 1 * 1 convolution, the last step is classification and bounding boxes regression.

output feature map is 16 times smaller than the input image. Therefore, the output feature map of VGG-16 is coarse. To solve the problem, We propose Feature Refine Network (FRN). The FRN consists of convolutional layers and deconvolution layers. FRN uses 2 convolutional layers and 1 pooling layer to deepen the network and make the abstracted features more informative. Then 3 deconvolution layers in FRN is designed follow the convolutional layers to increase the resolution of the feature map. The dimension of the feature map output by the deconvolution layer is consistent with conv3. The output feature map of deconv3 has high-level semantic information [18]. The lower layer has more finer information, combination of conv3 layer and deconv3 layer makes our model finer detail, while retaining high-level semantic information.

2.2 Multi-scale Feature Fusion

Previous work has shown that multi-scale representation will significantly improve object detection capabilities at various scales [19]. Our model uses skip ROI pooling to extract features at multiple scales to increase small object detection capabilities. The ROI pooling layer uses max pooling to convert the features inside any valid region of interest to a small feature map. In our model, ROI is a rectangular window with a fixed spatial extent of 7 * 7. Skip layer connection is to route lower layers directly to higher layers while by-passing the middle layers. We concatenate each ROI pooling feature along the channel axis and reduce the dimension with a $1*1$ convolution. We use L2 normalize to activate features extracted from fusion-2 layer prior to combine it with conv5.

2.3 Region Proposal Network

A Region Proposal Network (RPN) takes a feature map as input and outputs a set of rectangular object proposals, which is evaluated by an objectness score respectively. In order to obtain higher semantic features and keep the resolution of feature map invariant, we use a small network to slide on the feature map of deconv1. The structure of Region Proposal Network is shown in Fig. 3.

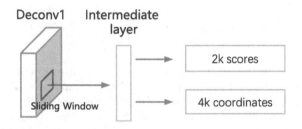

Fig. 3. The construction of Region Proposal Network.

2.4 Loss Function

We use a multi-task loss $\mathcal{L}$ to jointly train the network end-to-end for object classification and bounding-box regression. The loss of our model is given below:

$$\mathcal{L} = L_{RPN} + L_{obj} + \alpha L_{Fusion-2} \tag{1}$$

L_{RPN} is used to train Region Proposal Network (RPN) which consists of classification loss $L_{RPN-cls}$ and regression loss $L_{RPN-reg}$. The classification loss $L_{RPN-cls}$ is log loss over two classes (object/not object). The regression loss $L_{RPN-reg}$ targets at minimizing the smoothed L1 loss between the predict location offsets $t = (t_x, t_y, t_w, t_h)$ and the object offsets $t^* = (t_x^*, t_y^*, t_w^*, t_h^*)$. We denote the object detection loss with L_{obj}. L_{obj} includes object classification loss $L_{obj-cls}$ and regression loss $L_{obj-reg}$. The classification loss $L_{obj-cls}$ determines which class the object belongs to and is computed by softmax. The definition of the regression loss $L_{obj-reg}$ is the same as $L_{RPN-reg}$. The loss function of $L_{Fusion-2}$ is used to supervise the training of the FRN. $L_{Fusion-2}$ consists of classification loss $L_{Fusion-2-cls}$ and regression loss $L_{Fusion-2-reg}$. And their definition are the same as $L_{obj-cls}$ and $L_{obj-reg}$. The parameter α controls the balance between the object loss and FRN loss. In our experiment, $\alpha = 0.5$.

3   Experiment and Analysis

3.1   Dataset

We create a dataset of real-world text-based CAPTCHAs to evaluate the effectiveness of our model. This dataset contains the text-based CAPTCHAs for five websites, including eBay, Baidu, Hotmail, Sina, and NetEase. These popular websites use complex text-based CAPTCHAs to improve security. All types of text-based CAPTCHAs are rotated, distorted, and some text-based CAPTCHAs have complex backgrounds to resist recognition. In particular, Hotmail's CAPTCHA is hollow, which makes it harder for recognition. The dataset is shown in the Table 1. At the same time, we list the size of training data and testing data for each website.

Table 1. Dataset for experiments

Scheme	Sample image	Training images	Testing images
NetEase		3700	1000
Sina		2357	1000
Hotmail		3000	1000
Baidu		3862	1000
eBay		1400	1000

3.2   Implementation Details

Text-based CAPTCHAs on five websites are tested on a computer with a 3.40-GHz Intel Core i5-7500 central processing unit (CPU) and 8 GB of random-access memory (RAM), Linux 16.04 x64, and the graphics card NVIDIA GTX1060. We use Tensorflow as experiment software environment.

We make the length and width of the image identical by padding. Then we re-scale the image such that their width is $s = 448$. We fix the IoU threshold for NMS at 0.7 in the RPN. And the IoU threshold for NMS at 0.3 in the classification. The classification confidence for each output box is set to 0.7. The learning rate adaptively changes with the number of iterations. The basic learning rate is $lr = 0.001$. When the number of iterations exceeds 50,000, the learning rate is $lr = 0.0001$. Our model has been iterated 70,000 times and saved every 5,000 times. We use the model with the highest recognition rate as the final result.

3.3   Experimental Results

We propose Feature Refine Network, a very effective text-based CAPTCHAs recognition model. We will make comparisons to evaluate the effectiveness of our approach. Faster R-CNN takes the feature map of conv5 for detection and recognition. We use the Faster R-CNN recognition results as a baseline. To increase small-size character detection capabilities, we extract features at multiple scales, there are conv5 layer and conv3 layer. Table 2 shows the recognition results of multi-scale (conv5+conv3) feature fusion, which proves that multi-scale is effective for text-based CAPTCHAs recognition. In order to solve the problem that conv3 layer does not contain high-level semantic information. We extract features at fusion-2 layer. As can be seen from Table 2, the features of the fusion-2 layer are very informative. The performance of the CAPTCHA recognition of Sina is even better than that of the multi-scale feature fusion method. To demonstrate the effectiveness of our model, we compare the experimental results with other methods. Table 2 shows the performance of different methods for text-based CAPTCHAs recognition. The results indicate that our model significantly outperform previous works.

Table 2. Recognition rates for real-world schemes

Method	NetEase	Sina	Hotmail	Baidu	eBay
Tang et al. [12]	-	75%	50.9%	-	-
Bursztein et al. [13]	-	-	-	-	51.39%
Gao et al. [14]	-	-	-	-	58.8%
Qing and Zhang [6]	-	-	-	43.05%	-
Hu et al. [7]	-	4%	-	-	68.7%
Hussain et al. [16]	-	-	27.01%	-	53.2%
Baseline	87.2%	92.6%	93%	95.3%	96.9%
Multi-scale fusion	87.4%	95.9%	94%	95.7%	97.4%
Fusion-2	82.3%	96.2%	82.5%	94.6%	95.6%
Our model	**90%**	**96.8%**	**94.2%**	**96.8%**	**97.3%**

Figure 4 gives some example of our recognition results, we can see that our model is effective for complex text-based CAPTCHAs. In addition to character recognition, our model can detect the location of characters in an image.

(a) Input image   (b) Baseline   (c) Our results

Fig. 4. Comparison between the baseline and proposed framework. In the first row, the character "z" is not detected at the baseline. In the second row, the character "l" is not detected at the baseline. In the third row, the character "1" is not detected at the baseline. In our model, these characters can be detected.

The average attack speed of text-based CAPTCHAs for the mentioned is evaluated for ranges from 0.087 to 0.09 s. And the results are shown in Table 3. This shows that our breaking method is a real-time attack. Compared to the model in [12] which recognizes Sina and Hotmail text-based CAPTCHAs at a rate of 0.14 and 0.44 s. Our model recognition speed is significantly faster than [12].

Table 3. Average attack speed of different websites

Website	Average attack speed (s)
Sina	0.087
Netease	0.090
Hotmail	0.088
eBay	0.089
Baidu	0.088

4 Conclusion

In this paper, we propose Feature Refine Network (FRN) for text-based CAPTCHA recognition in real websites. FRN is a architecture that leverages convolutional layers and deconvolution layers to obtain more informative features. The convolutional layer in FRN can deepen the network, making the extracted features have larger receptive field and more informative. The deconvolution layer in FRN can increase the resolution of the feature map and restore the object details by upsampling. In addition, we uses skip ROI pooling to extract features at multiple scales to increase small object detection capabilities. We achieve state-of-the-art performance on five text-based CAPTHA websites, and our model is effective in improving recognition rate of text-based CAPTCHAs. The text-based CAPTCHAs may not be suitable for Turing test to identify whether the other person is a human or a machine.

References

1. Turing, A.M.: Computing machinery and intelligence. In: Epstein, R., Roberts, G., Beber, G. (eds.) Parsing the Turing Test, pp. 23–65. Springer, Dordrecht (2009)
2. Von Ahn, L., Blum, M., Langford, J.: Telling humans and computers apart automatically. Commun. ACM **47**(2), 56–60 (2004)
3. Bursztein, E., Martin, M., Mitchell, J.: Text-based CAPTCHA strengths and weaknesses. In: Proceedings of the 18th ACM Conference on Computer and Communications Security, pp. 125–138 (2011)
4. Yan, J., El Ahmad, A.S.: A Low-cost attack on a microsoft CAPTCHA. In: Proceedings of the 15th ACM Conference on Computer and Communications Security, pp. 543–554 (2008)
5. Mori, G., Malik, J.: Recognizing objects in adversarial clutter: breaking a visual CAPTCHA. In: Computer Vision and Pattern Recognition (2003)
6. Qing, K., Zhang, R.: A multi-label neural network approach to solving connected CAPTCHAs. In: 14th IAPR International Conference on Document Analysis and Recognition, pp. 1313–1317 (2017)
7. Hu, Y., Chen, L., Cheng, J.: A CAPTCHA recognition technology based on deep learning. In: 13th IEEE Conference on Industrial Electronics and Applications, pp. 617–620 (2018)
8. Ren, S., He, K., Girshick, R., Sun, J.: Faster R-CNN: towards real-time object detection with region proposal networks. In: Advances in Neural Information Processing Systems, pp. 91–99 (2015)
9. Girshick, R., Donahue, J., Darrell, T., Malik, J.: Rich feature hierarchies for accurate object detection and semantic segmentation. In: Proceedings of the IEEE Conference on Computer Vision and Pattern Recognition, pp. 580–587 (2014)
10. Girshick, R.: Fast R-CNN. In: Proceedings of the IEEE Conference on Computer Vision and Pattern Recognition, pp. 1440–1448 (2015)
11. Kong, T., Yao, A., Chen, Y., et al.: Hypernet: towards accurate region proposal generation and joint object detection. In: Proceedings of the IEEE Conference on Computer Vision and Pattern Recognition, pp. 845–853 (2016)
12. Tang, M., Gao, H., Zhang, Y., et al.: Research on deep learning techniques in breaking text-based captchas and designing image-based captcha. IEEE Trans. Inf. Forensics Secur. **13**(10), 2522–2537 (2018)
13. Bursztein, E., Aigrain, J., Moscicki, A.: The end is nigh: Generic solving of text-based captchas. In: Workshop on Offensive Technologies (2014)
14. Gao, H., Yan, J., Cao, F., et al.: A simple generic attack on text captchas. In: The Network and Distributed System Security Symposium (2016)

15. Sano, S., Otsuka, T., Itoyama, K., Okuno, H.G.: HMM-based attacks on Google's ReCAPTCHA with continuous visual and audio symbols. J. Inf. Process. **23**(6), 814–826 (2015)
16. Hussain, R., Gao, H., Shaikh, R.A.: Segmentation of connected characters in text-based CAPTCHAs for intelligent character recognition. Multimedia Tools Appl. **76**(24), 25547–25561 (2017)
17. Simonyan, K., Zisserman, A.: Very deep convolutional networks for large-scale image recognition. arXiv preprint (2014)
18. Long, J., Shelhamer, E., Darrell, T.: Fully convolutional networks for semantic segmentation. In: Proceedings of the IEEE Conference on Computer Vision and Pattern Recognition, pp. 3431–3440 (2015)
19. Bell, S., Zitnick, C.L., Bala, K., Girshick, R.: Inside-outside net: detecting objects in context with skip pooling and recurrent neural networks. In: Proceedings of the IEEE Conference on Computer Vision and Pattern Recognition, pp. 2874–2883 (2016)

Concept Factorization with Optimal Graph Learning for Data Representation

Zhenqiu Shu[1,2], Xiao-jun Wu[2(✉)], Honghui Fan[1], Congzhe You[1], Zhen Liu[2], and Jie Zhang[1]

[1] School of Computer Engineering, Jiangsu University of Technology, Changzhou 231001, China
shuzhenqiu@163.com
[2] Jiangsu Provincial Engineering Laboratory of Pattern Recognition and Computational Intelligence, Jiangnan University, Wuxi 214122, China
wu_xiaojun@jiangnan.edu.cn

Abstract. In recent years, concept factorization methods become a popular data representation technique in many real applications. However, conventional concept factorization methods cannot capture the intrinsic geometric structure embedded in data using the fixed nearest neighbor graph. To overcome this problem, we propose a novel method, called Concept Factorization with Optimal Graph Learning (CF_OGL), for data representation. In CF_OGL, a novel rank constraint is imposed on the Laplacian matrix of the initial graph model, which encourages the learned graph with exactly c connected components for the data with c clusters. Then the learned optimal graph regularizer is integrated into the model of concept factorization. Therefore, this learned structure is benefit to the clustering analysis. In addition, we develop an efficient and effective iterative optimization algorithm to solve our proposed model. Extensive experimental results on three benchmark datasets have demonstrated that our proposed method can effectively improve the performance of clustering.

Keywords: Concept factorization · Data representation · Geometric structure · Rank constraint · Laplacian matrix · Regularizer

1 Introduction

Data representation methods have been widely applied to various fields in pattern recognition and machine learning [1–3]. Over the past few decades, matrix factorization methods have become one of the most popular data representation

This work was supported by the National Natural Science Foundation of China [Grant No. 61603159, 61672265, U1836218], Natural Science Foundation of Jiangsu Province [Grant No. BK20160293], China Postdoctoral Science Foundation [Grant No. 2017M611695] and Jiangsu Province Postdoctoral Science Foundation [Grant No. 1701094B] and Excellent Key Teachers of QingLan Project in Jiangsu Province.

Y. Zhao et al. (Eds.): ICIG 2019, LNCS 11902, pp. 74–84, 2019.
https://doi.org/10.1007/978-3-030-34110-7_7

techniques due to its efficiency and effectiveness. Many classical matrix factorization techniques, such as Singular Value Decomposition (SVD) [4], Principal Component Analysis (PCA) [5], Nonnegative Matrix Factorization (NMF) [6] and Concept Factorization (CF) [7], have shown the encouraging performances in image classification, object tracking, document clustering, etc. [8,9].

NMF has aroused increasing interests due to its physical and theoretical interpretations. NMF naturally leads to a part-based representation of data by imposing the nonnegative constraint on both coefficient and basis matrices. The basic idea behind NMF is to seek two nonnegative matrices to approximate the original data matrix. However, NMF cannot deal with the data matrix containing with some negative elements due to the noise or outlier. Therefore, Xu et al. [7] proposed a variation of NMF, called Concept Factorization (CF), for document clustering. Different from the NMF methods, CF can deal with the data matrix mixed with nonnegative elements. In order to discover the local geometric structure of data, Cai et al. [10] proposed a Locally Consistent Concept Factorization (LCCF) method for data representation. It models the manifold structure of data using the graph regularizer. Shu et al. [11] proposed a Local Learning Concept Factorization (LLCF) method to learn the discriminant structure and the local geometric structure, simultaneously, by adding the local learning regularization term into the model of CF. Motivated by the deep learning, Li et al. [12] proposed a multilayer concept factorization method to discover the structure information hidden in data using the multilayer framework. Pei et al. [13] developed a CF with adaptive neighbors method for clustering. The idea of this proposed method is to integrate an ANs regularizer into the CF decomposition. However, the aforementioned methods cannot update dynamically the optimal graph model, which is used to explore the intrinsic geometric manifold structure of data in matrix decomposition.

To solve this issue, we propose a novel method named as Concept Factorization with Optimal Graph Learning (CF_OGL) in this paper. Specifically, we impose a rank constraint on the Laplacian matrix of the initially given graph, and then iteratively update it. Therefore, the learned graph has exactly c connected components, whose structure is beneficial to the clustering applications. Then the learned graph regularizer is used to constrain the model of the concept factorization method, and thus the geometric structure of data can be better preserved in low dimensional feature space. Extensive experimental results on three datasets demonstrate that our proposed CF_OGL method outperforms other state-of-the-art methods in clustering.

This paper is organized as follows: We briefly describe both CF and LCCF algorithms in Sect. 2. In Sect. 3, we introduce our proposed CF_OGL algorithm and then derive its updating rules. In Sect. 4, we carry out some experiments to investigate the proposed CF_OGL algorithm. Finally, conclusions are drawn in Sect. 5.

2 The Relative Work

In this section, the models of both CF and LCCF are briefly presented.

2.1 CF

Concept factorization is a popular matrix factorization technique to deal with high dimensional data. Given a data matrix $X = [x_1, x_2, ..., x_n] \in R^{m \times n}$, x_i denotes a m-dimensional vector. In CF, the entire data points are used to lineally represent each underlying concept, and all the concepts seek to lineally approximate to each data point, simultaneously. Therefore, we can give the objective function of CF as

$$X = XUV^T \tag{1}$$

where $U \in R^{n \times k}$ and $V \in R^{n \times k}$. Using the Euclidean distance metric to measure the reconstruction error, its minimization problem can be given as follows:

$$\min_{U,V} \left\| X - XUV^T \right\|_F^2 \tag{2}$$
$$s.t. U \geq 0, V \geq 0$$

where $\|\cdot\|_F$ denotes the matrix *Frobenius norm*. Using the multiplicative updating algorithm, we derive the updating rules of Eq. (2) as follows:

$$u_{ij}^{t+1} \leftarrow u_{ij}^t \frac{(KV)_{ij}}{(KUV^TV)_{ij}}$$
$$v_{ij}^{t+1} \leftarrow v_{ij}^t \frac{(KW)_{ij}}{(VW^TKW)_{ij}} \tag{3}$$

where $K = X^TX$. To deal with the nonlinear data, CF is easily kernelized using kernel trick.

2.2 LCCF

Traditional CF method fails to consider the manifold structure information of data. To solve this issue, Cai et al. [10] proposed the LCCF method, which models the manifold structure embedded in data using the fixed graph model. Therefore, the objective function of LCCF can be given as follow:

$$\min_{U,V} \left\| X - XUV^T \right\|_F^2 + \lambda tr(V^TLV) \tag{4}$$
$$s.t. U \geq 0, V \geq 0$$

where λ stands for a balance parameter, and $tr(.)$ denotes the trace of a matrix. D is a diagonal matrix, $D_{ii} = \sum_S W_{ij}$, $L = D - W$. Similarly, we derive the updating rules of Eq. (4) as follows:

$$u_{ij}^{t+1} \leftarrow u_{ij}^t \frac{(KV)_{ij}}{(KUV^TV)_{ij}}$$
$$v_{ij}^{t+1} \leftarrow v_{ij}^t \frac{(KW+\lambda WV)_{ij}}{(VW^TKW+\lambda DV)_{ij}} \tag{5}$$

According to the rules (5), we can achieve a local minimum of Eq. (4).

3   The Proposed Method

3.1   Motivation

Traditional CF methods cannot effectively explore the intrinsic geometric manifold structure embedded in high dimensional data using the fixed graph model. By addint the rank constraint into the Laplacian matrix of the initially given graph, we learn an optimal graph model with exactly c connected components. In CF_AGL, the learned graph regularizer is further constructed, and then imposed on the model of CF. Therefore, our proposed method explores the semantic information hidden in high dimensional data effectively.

3.2   Constrained Laplacian Rank (CLR)

A graph learning method, called Constrained Laplacian Rank (CLR), was proposed to explore the intrinsic geometric structure of data, whose goal is to learn an optimal graph model [14]. Therefore, the CLR method is formulated by the following optimization problem:

$$J_{CLR} = \min_{\sum_j a_{ij}=1, a_{ij} \geq 0, rank(L_Q)=n-k} \|Q - W\|_F^2 \tag{6}$$

where L_Q stands for the Laplacian matrix of the matrix Q. Denote $\sigma_i(L_Q)$ as the i-th smallest eigenvalue of L_A. It is worth noting that $\sigma_i(L_Q) > 0$ because of its positive semidefinition. Therefore, Eq. (6) can be reformulated as the following problem for a large enough value of σ_i:

$$J_{CLR} = \min_{\sum_j q_{ij}=1, q_{ij} \geq 0} \|Q - W\|_F^2 + 2\lambda \sum_{i=1}^{k} \sigma_i(L_Q) \tag{7}$$

According to the Ky Fans Theorem, we have the following equivalent definition as

$$\sum_{i=1}^{k} \sigma_i(L_Q) = \min_{F \in n \times k, F^T F=I} Tr(F^T L_Q F) \tag{8}$$

Therefore, we can further rewrite the problem (7) as follows:

$$\min_{Q} \|Q - W\|_F^2 + \lambda Tr(F L_Q F^T) \\ s.t. \, FF^T = I, Q1 = 1, Q \geq 0, Q \in R^{n \times n} \tag{9}$$

3.3   Our Proposed Method

By integrating the learned graph regularization term into the model of CF, the objective function of our proposed CF_OGL method can given as follows:

$$\min_{Q,U,V} (\|Q - W\|_F^2 + \beta Tr(F L_Q F^T) + \lambda Tr(V L_Q V^T) \\ + \mu \|X - XUV^T\|) \\ s.t. FF^T = I, V \geq 0, U \geq 0, Q1 = 1, Q \geq 0, Q \in R^{n \times n} \tag{10}$$

It is impractical to find the global optimal solution of problem (10) because it is not a convex problem in U, V and A together. Fortunately, we can achieve a local solution by optimizing the variables alternatively. Therefore, the optimization scheme of our proposed CF_OGL method mainly consists of two parts:

Fixing Q and F, Update U and V. By fixing the variables A and F, the Eq. (10) can be rewritten as the following problem:

$$\min_{U,V}(\lambda Tr(VL_QV^T) + \mu\|X - XUV^T\|)$$
$$s.t.VV^T = I, Q \geq 0, U \geq 0 \tag{11}$$

Similarly, it is easy to derive the updating rules of problem (10) as follows:

$$u_{ij}^{t+1} \leftarrow u_{ij}^t \frac{(KV)_{ij}}{(KUV^TV)_{ij}} \tag{12}$$

$$v_{ij}^{t+1} \leftarrow v_{ij}^t \frac{(KW+\lambda WV)_{ij}}{(VW^TKW+\lambda DV)_{ij}} \tag{13}$$

Fixing U and V, Update Q and F. By fixing U and V, we can rewrite the Eq. (10) as the following optimization problem:

$$\min_{Q,U,V}(\|Q - W\|_F^2 + \beta Tr(FL_QF^T))$$
$$s.t.FF^T = I, Q1 = 1, Q \geq 0, Q \in R^{n\times n} \tag{14}$$

(A) When Q is fixed, the Eq. (14) becomes

$$\min_{FF^T=I}(\beta Tr(FL_QF^T)) \tag{15}$$

It is easy to know that the solution scheme of F can be converted into solving the k smallest eigenvalues problem of L_Q.

(B) When F is fixed, the problem (14) becomes the following optimization problem:

$$\min \sum_{i,j=1} (q_{i,j} - w_{i,j})^2 + \frac{\beta}{2}\sum_{i,j=1}\|f_i - f_j\|_2^2 q_{i,j}$$
$$s.t.\sum_j q_{ij} = 1, q_{ij} \geq 0 \tag{16}$$

For each row w_i, we have the vector form as

$$\min_{q_i \geq 0, q_i 1=1}\left\|q_i - (w_i - \frac{\beta}{2}d_i^T)\right\|_2^2 \tag{17}$$

where $d_{ij} = \|f_i - f_j\|_2^2$. The problem (17) can be solved by the optimization algorithm proposed in [14].

4   Experimental Results

In this section, we carry out some experiments to investigate the proposed CF_OGL method on the Yale, ORL and FERET datasets. To demonstrate its effectiveness, the proposed CF_OGL method is compared with several state-of-the-art methods, such as K-means, PCA, NMF, CF and LCCF. Two well accepted measurements, such as accuracy (AC) and normalized mutual information (NMI), are used as metrics to quantify the performance of data representation in clustering.

Algorithm 1. Summary of the proposed CF_OGL method

Input: Initial graph W, parameter β, λ, μ, Data matrix X.
Output: The coefficient matrix V;
Initialization: $W \leftarrow W_0$, $Q \leftarrow Q_0$, $L_Q = Laplace(Q)$
Repeat
Fixing Q and F:
  Update U by Eq.(12);
  Update V by Eq.(13);
Fixing U and V:
  Update F by Eq.(15);
  Update Q by Eq.(17);
  Compute L_Q by $L_Q = D_Q - \frac{Q+Q^T}{2}$;
Until convergence

4.1 Yale Face Dataset

The Yale face dataset includes a total of 165 face images from 15 individuals. In each experiment, the P categories images were randomly sampled from the Yale dataset to evaluate the performances of all methods. We run all methods ten times for each value of P, and recorded their average results. The results of all methods on the Yale dataset are shown in Table 1. We can clearly see that our proposed CF_OGL method outperforms other state-of-the-art methods regardless of the choices of P. Specifically, the average AC and NMI of the proposed CF_OGL method are 3.7% and 5.1% higher than those of LCCF, respectively. The main reason is that our propose CF_OGL method can learn an optimal graph structure, which can significantly improve the clustering performance than LCCF.

4.2 ORL Face Dataset

The ORL face dataset contrains 400 face images from 40 distinct subjects. For some subjects, the face images were taken at different times, varying the lighting and facial expressions. In this experiment, we adopted the above similar experimental scheme to investigate the effectiveness of our proposed CF_OGL method. Table 2 provides the clustering results of six methods on the ORL face dataset. It can be observed that CF_OGL can achieve the best performance among all the compared methods. The main reason is that our proposed CF_OGL method can learn the optimal graph and thus effectively preserve the intrinsic geometric structure of data. Therefore, it outperforms other state-of-the-art methods on this dataset (Figs. 1 and 2).

Fig. 1. Some samples from the Yale dataset

Table 1. The clustering performances on the Yale face dataset

P	AC						NMI					
	K-means	PCA	NMF	CF	LCCF	CF_OGL	K-means	PCA	NMF	CF	LCCF	CF_OGL
8	0.536	0.520	0.511	0.545	0.556	**0.575**	0.602	0.590	0.589	0.561	0.592	**0.628**
9	0.480	0.458	0.477	0.438	0.454	**0.505**	0.560	0.540	0.558	0.516	0.542	**0.575**
10	0.489	0.469	0.465	0.490	0.460	**0.514**	0.589	0.575	0.577	0.551	0.533	**0.604**
11	0.462	0.480	0.461	0.480	0.480	**0.497**	0.587	0.596	0.577	0.559	0.569	**0.604**
12	0.440	0.451	0.431	0.437	0.428	**0.456**	0.564	0.566	0.564	0.530	0.536	**0.575**
13	0.439	0.427	0.423	0.400	0.422	**0.449**	0.573	0.566	0.564	0.513	0.534	**0.585**
14	0.448	0.454	0.422	0.432	0.431	**0.474**	0.589	0.602	0.581	0.542	0.546	**0.610**
15	0.427	0.423	0.408	0.396	0.386	**0.429**	0.583	0.582	0.568	0.519	0.518	**0.596**
AVG	0.468	0.461	0.451	0.456	0.453	**0.490**	0.581	0.577	0.572	0.536	0.546	**0.597**

Fig. 2. Some samples from the ORL dataset

Table 2. The clustering performances on the ORL face dataset

P	AC						NMI					
	K-means	PCA	NMF	CF	LCCF	CF_OGL	K-means	PCA	NMF	CF	LCCF	CF_OGL
20	0.386	0.384	0.373	0.244	0.377	**0.394**	0.582	0.578	0.573	0.367	0.571	**0.584**
22	0.375	0.382	0.364	0.230	0.370	**0.391**	0.596	0.592	0.575	0.371	0.591	**0.596**
24	0.368	0.374	0.357	0.239	0.373	**0.406**	0.592	0.598	0.579	0.388	0.585	**0.613**
26	0.356	0.364	0.342	0.228	0.344	**0.374**	0.585	0.595	0.569	0.384	0.577	**0.596**
28	0.341	0.350	0.328	0.209	0.339	**0.360**	0.586	0.588	0.568	0.376	0.575	**0.591**
30	0.334	0.324	0.332	0.206	0.328	**0.355**	0.587	0.582	0.580	0.382	0.578	**0.589**
32	0.326	0.339	0.330	0.200	0.338	**0.361**	0.587	0.582	0.580	0.382	0.578	**0.589**
34	0.332	0.332	0.334	0.206	0.330	**0.345**	0.588	0.597	0.578	0.385	0.589	**0.607**
36	0.328	0.324	0.312	0.204	0.336	**0.345**	**0.600**	0.595	0.585	0.392	0.584	0.597
38	0.320	0.315	0.315	0.185	0.320	**0.322**	0.596	0.600	0.583	0.383	0.587	**0.604**
40	0.3075	0.315	0.302	0.192	0.315	**0.318**	0.589	0.597	0.581	0.400	0.5953	**0.598**
AVG	0.343	0.346	0.335	0.213	0.343	**0.361**	0.591	0.593	0.577	0.385	0.585	**0.598**

4.3   FERET Face Dataset

The FERET face database contains 200 different individuals with about 7 face samples for each individual. Here, we randomly chose P categories samples from the FERET dataset, and mixed them as the experimental subset for clustering. All methods were run ten times, and then their average performances were recorded as the final results. The clustering performances for each method on the FERET dataset are summarized in Table 3. It is easy to find that the average performance of our proposed CF_OGL method has certain advantage compared with other methods in clustering (Fig. 3).

Fig. 3. Some samples from the FERET dataset

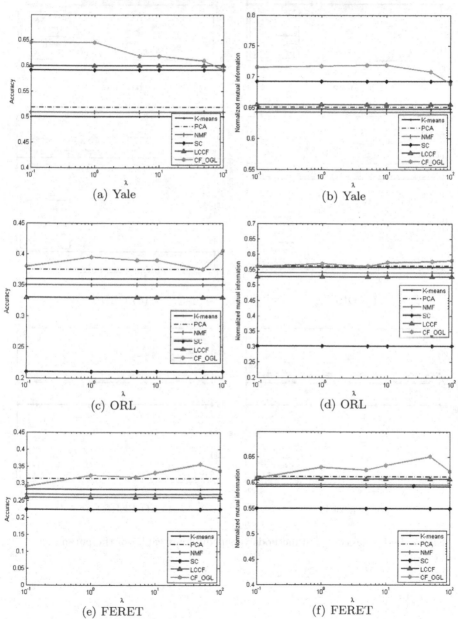

Fig. 4. Performances of all methods versus different vaules of the parameter λ

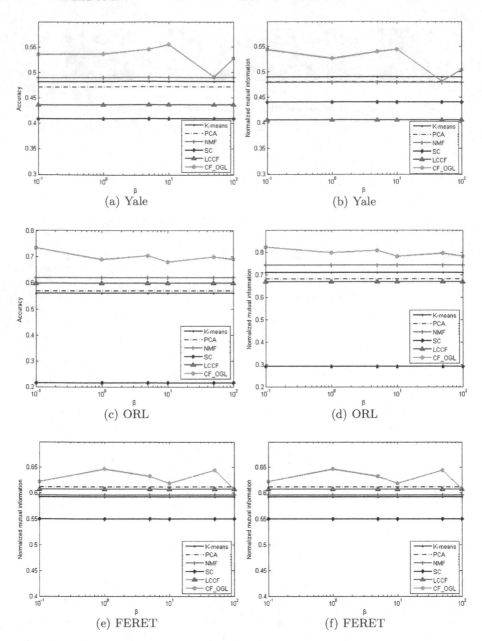

Fig. 5. Performances of all methods versus different vaules of the parameter β

Table 3. The clustering performances on the FERET face dataset

P	AC						NMI					
	K-means	PCA	NMF	CF	LCCF	CF_OGL	K-means	PCA	NMF	CF	LCCF	CF_OGL
80	0.283	0.283	0.270	0.205	0.256	**0.315**	0.596	0.600	0.594	0.527	0.601	**0.617**
100	0.273	0.274	0.255	0.200	0.248	**0.298**	0.606	0.611	0.596	0.546	0.613	**0.622**
120	0.271	0.274	0.253	0.187	0.239	**0.283**	0.617	0.619	0.604	0.543	0.618	**0.629**
140	0.260	0.269	0.243	0.184	0.232	**0.276**	0.619	0.633	0.611	0.545	0.631	**0.642**
160	0.258	0.262	0.233	0.175	0.228	**0.272**	0.627	0.638	0.613	0.537	0.632	**0.643**
180	0.249	0.253	0.231	0.173	0.223	**0.254**	0.632	**0.642**	0.622	0.546	0.639	0.641
200	0.246	**0.257**	0.228	0.171	0.220	0.251	0.634	**0.649**	0.622	0.549	0.645	0.644
AVG	0.263	0.267	0.245	0.185	0.235	**0.278**	0.619	0.627	0.609	0.542	0.626	**0.632**

4.4 The Analysis of the Parameters

In our proposed CF_OGL, the parameters β, λ and μ have an effect on the clustering performance. Specifically, we randomly chose 10, 20, 80 categories samples as the dataset to carry out the experiments. However, the parameter selection of the proposed CF_OGL method is still an open problem. Therefore, we determine the parameters by grid search at first and then change them within certain ranges. Here, we only investigate the parameters β and λ. The Figs. 4 and 5 show the performances of all methods varied with different values of β and λ on three datasets, respectively. It is clear to see that our proposed method can achieve a relative stable performance in a large range.

5 Conclusion

In this paper, a novel matrix factorization technique, called Concept Factorization with adaptive graph learning (CF_OGL), is proposed for data representation. In order to learn an optimal graph, we impose a rank constraint on the Laplacian matrix of the initially given graph. Then the learned graph regularizer is integrated into the model of CF. Therefore, our proposed CF_OGL method effectively exploits the geometric manifold structure embedded in high dimensional data. Experimental results have shown that the proposed CF_OGL algorithm achieves better performance in comparison with other state-of-the-art algorithms.

References

1. Wu, X., Josef, K., Yang, J., et al.: A new direct LDA (D-LDA) algorithm for feature extraction in face recognition. In: International Conference on Pattern Recognition, vol. 4, pp. 545–548. IEEE Xplore (2004)
2. Shu, Z., Wu, X., Huang, P., et al.: Multiple graph regularized concept factorization with adaptive weights. IEEE Access **6**, 64938–64945 (2018)
3. Zheng, Y., Yang, J., Yang, J., et al.: Nearest neighbour line nonparametric discriminant analysis for feature extraction. Electron. Lett. **42**(12), 679–680 (2006)

4. Zhou, B., Chen, J.: A geometric distortion resilient image watermarking algorithm based on SVD. Chin. J. Image Graph. **9**, 506–512 (2004)
5. Turk, M., Pentland, A.: Eigenfaces for recognition. J. Cogn. Neurosci. **3**(1), 71–86 (1991)
6. Lee, D., Seung, H.: Learning the parts of objects by non-negative matrix factorization. Nature **401**, 788–791 (1999)
7. Xu, W., Gong, Y.: Document clustering by concept factorization. In: Proceedings of ACM SIGIR, pp. 202–209 (2004)
8. Shu, Z., Wu, X.J., Hu, C., et al.: Structured discriminative concept factorization for data representation. In: The Third IEEE International Smart Cities Conference (ISC2), pp. 1–4 (2017)
9. Shu, Z., Wu, X., Hu, C.: Structure preserving sparse coding for data representation. Neural Process. Lett. **48**, 1–15 (2018)
10. Cai, D., He, X., Han, J.: Locally consistent concept factorization for document clustering. IEEE Trans. Knowl. Data Eng. **23**(6), 902–913 (2011)
11. Shu, Z., Zhou, J., Huang, P., et al.: Local and global regularized sparse coding for data representation. Neurocomputing **198**(29), 188–197 (2016)
12. Li, X., Shen, X., Shu, Z., Ye, Q., Zhao, C.: Graph regularized multilayer concept factorization for data representation. Neurocomputing **238**, 139–151 (2017)
13. Pei, X., Chen, C., Gong, W.: Concept factorization with adaptive neighbors for document clustering. IEEE Trans. Neural Netw. Learn. Syst. **29**(2), 343–352 (2018)
14. Nie, F., Wang, X., Jordan, M.I., et al.: The constrained Laplacian rank algorithm for graph-based clustering. In: Thirtieth AAAI Conference on Artificial Intelligence. AAAI Press (2016)

An End-to-End Practical System for Road Marking Detection

Chaonan Gu, Xiaoyu Wu$^{(\boxtimes)}$, He Ma, and Lei Yang

Communication University of China, Beijing, China
wuxiaoyu_hai@163.com, {gcn,mahe,yanglei}@cuc.edu.cn

Abstract. Road marking is a special kind of symbol on the road surface, used to regulate the behavior of traffic participants. According to our survey, it seems that no papers has yet proposed a mature, highly practical method to detect and classify these important fine-grained markings. Deep learning techniques, especially deep neural networks, have proven to be effective in coping with a variety of computer vision tasks. Using deep neural networks to construct road marking detection systems is a practical solution.

In this paper, we present an accurate and effective road marking detection system to handle seven common road markings. Our model is based on the R-FCN network framework, with the ResNet-18 model as backbone. SE blocks and data balancing strategies are also used to further improve the accuracy of the detection model. Our model has made a good trade-off between accuracy and speed, and achieved quite good results in our self-built road marking dataset.

Keywords: Road marking · Detection · R-FCN · SE block · Median frequency balancing

1 Introduction

Road markings refer to the special symbols that are drawn on the surface of the road, usually including arrows, characters, etc., which play an important role in guiding, restricting, and warning to the traffic participants. Although the problem of road marking recognition is solved in [1], there seems to be no mature, highly practical method to detect road markings currently, which not only requires to classify but also to locate the markings. The detection of road markings has great practical value, that could be used in many fields such as GPS positioning, the decision making and path planning of automatic driving systems. It is of great practical significance to construct an accurate and efficient detection system.

It is very difficult for computers to locate and identify the road markings from the images. As shown in Fig. 1, the road scene is changeable. Affected by weather, illumination, angle of view and other factors, outdoor road images will change to a lot of different forms. Furthermore, the worn-out road markings, the complex urban road environment, and the markings occlusion, also increase the difficulty of road marking detection. According to our survey, there seems to be no published paper presenting a

© Springer Nature Switzerland AG 2019
Y. Zhao et al. (Eds.): ICIG 2019, LNCS 11902, pp. 85–93, 2019.
https://doi.org/10.1007/978-3-030-34110-7_8

Fig. 1. Various types of road markings: under different lighting condition; worn out marking; marking occlusion.

practical classification and detection method, to deal with these important and variable fine-grained markings.

We plan to use deep learning algorithms to build our detection system, in which data plays a critical role. Currently, there are very few road marking datasets proposed. Existing datasets, such as Caltech, KITTI [2], Berkeley datasets, etc., contain only a small amount of image data, far from meeting the needs of deep learning. However, in a large dataset: Apollo [3], since the images are mainly extracted from the video, the changes between them are relatively small and cannot meet the requirements of diversity. In another large dataset, the Tsinghua-Tencent-100k dataset, some pictures are distorted, and only a few pictures contain road markings, which means it will take a lot of time to filter. All of these datasets have certain drawbacks. The lack of road marking data is a huge challenge for building our systems. In addition, there is another big problem in the data, that is, the numbers of various road markings are not balanced. The number of straight arrows is much larger than that of other classes, such as U-turns, which is very disadvantageous for deep learning.

At present, there are two main ideas for road marking detection algorithms using deep learning: based on object segmentation and based on object detection. The segmentation-based road marking detection algorithm (VPG [4], TT100k [5], Mask R-CNN [6]) spends a lot of computing resources on pixel-by-pixel segmentation, which results in long test times. However, the segmentation result is superfluous for road marking detection. Therefore, it is not suitable to construct a road marking detection system based on segmentation.

Currently, road marking detection algorithms based on object detection are more common. There are two main ideas in the field of object detection: one-stage networks, two-stage networks based on region proposal and classification [7–9]. Through our experiments, it is found that typical single-stage network structures, such as YOLO [10], SSD [11] and its improved method DSSD [12], although with high detection speed, are not accurate enough for detecting relatively small objects in images. It still has a certain gap from our requirements.

A two-stage detection network based on region proposal has higher accuracy than single-stage networks, but its detection speed is usually slow (e.g., Faster R-CNN [9]). Another two-stage network, the R-FCN model with two-stage network structure can achieve similar detection accuracy compared with Faster R-CNN while maintaining relatively fast speed. The R-FCN [13] model adopts fully convolutional network [14]. Through the design of the position-sensitive score map, all convolution calculations are shared by all candidate regions, thus getting a good trade-off between speed and accuracy. The R-FCN network is a relatively suitable basic model for road marking detection.

For the significant problems of detecting road marking: the insufficient and imbalance data, the lack of mature road marking detection model, we propose our own road marking detection system drawing on the SE (squeeze and excitation) blocks [15]: (i) we build our own dataset, which contains 40k images for seven common road markings; (ii) the basic model is R-FCN with ResNet-18 [16] as backbone; (iii) median frequency balancing is used to compensate for the adverse effects of imbalance data; (iv) SE blocks are adopted to further improve the accuracy of the model. Our model has a good balance between speed and accuracy, and achieves good results in self-built dataset.

2 Our Approach

The structure of our model is shown in Fig. 2. We use the R-FCN as basic model, with ResNet-18 as the backbone network. Two SE blocks are added to stage 4 and stage 5 of ResNet-18 to further enhance model performance with negligible effect on speed.

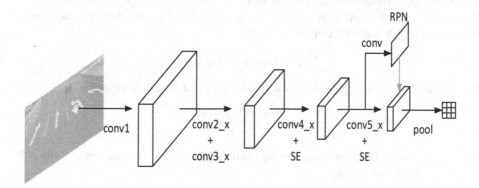

Fig. 2. Road marking detection model

2.1 Basic Model

We selected 3269 original images containing seven common road markings from the public dataset, and finally obtained our own dataset containing 40k images through data augmentation. The dataset is described in more detail in Sect. 3.1.

We build our road marking detection system based on the R-FCN network. Compared to other detection models, the R-FCN model is relatively fast, while still maintaining high accuracy. We use the residual network as the backbone network of the model. The detection model is fine-tuned using ResNet model pre-trained on ImageNet. Images were preprocessed before sent to the network. Since the road markings usually appear in the lower half of the image, the top pixels in the image do not contain the required information, so we cropped 1/3 of the image from the top. In order to achieve good trade-off between speed and accuracy, each cropped image is resized to 900 * 600.

We tested two residual network models, ResNet-50 and ResNet-18, and the experimental results are shown in Sect. 3.2. Compared to ResNet-50, the accuracy of ResNet-18 has dropped by 0.6%, but the time is shortened by half to 56 ms. The ResNet-18 network gets a better balance between speed and accuracy, making it more suitable for road marking detection.

2.2 Median Frequency Balancing

The dataset we get is not balanced. The number of straight arrows is much larger than the number of other classes of road markings, while, on the opposite, the number of U-turn arrows is much smaller than others. Since the goal of the neural network algorithm is to minimize the overall error rate, which may result in poor performance of classes with less instances. On the one hand, we try to ensure a balance of different road markings in the data augmentation process. On the other hand, we adopted median frequency balancing referring [17].

In RFCN [13], the loss of each RoI is defined as the summation of the cross-entropy loss and the box regression loss: $L(s, t_{x,y,w,h}) = L_{cls}(s_{c*}) + \lambda[c^* > 0]L_{reg}(t, t^*)$. Here c^* means the ground-truth label of the RoI, s_{c*} is the predicted probability of the RoI belonging to c^*. We keep the bounding box regression loss L_{reg} not changed, and change the cross-entropy loss of the classification to:

$$L_{cls}(s_{c*}) = w_{c*}[-log(s_{c*})] \tag{1}$$

w_{c*} is the weight the original loss of the RoI multiplied. It is defined as:

$$w_c = \frac{median(\{f_c | c \in C\})}{f_c} \tag{2}$$

Here, we have C classes of road markings to be detected, f_c is the frequency of the c-th category. We define f_c as:

$$f_c = \frac{Number\ of\ c\text{-}th\ instances\ in\ dataset}{Number\ of\ instances\ in\ dataset} \tag{3}$$

w_c varies from class to class to compensate for the adverse effects of the unbalanced data. The class with the most instances has the least weight, and the class with the fewest instances has the largest weight. By using the median frequency balancing strategy, the contribution of each class to overall loss will be more balanced. According to experimental, the accuracy of the model using the strategy is about 0.4% higher than the original model.

2.3 SE Blocks

Since the accuracy dropped with resnet18 as the backbone network, the SE module [15] is used to compensate. The literature [15] studies the relationship of channels and explicitly models the relationship between convolutional feature maps by using SE blocks. Through two operations, the model can use the global information to strengthen the beneficial channels and suppress the useless channels, thus achieving the characteristic response re-correction between the channels and improving the accuracy of our model.

The first operation of SE block is squeeze. Each feature map is compressed using global average pooling. The convolutional layer outputs a feature map of H*W*C, which will be compressed into a real sequence of 1*1*C through squeeze, so that the global information of the network can be utilized by all layers. The second operation of the SE block is called excitation. Using the gate mechanism, the output of the squeeze is transformed into a series of weights to measure the importance of each channel.

The SE block is easy to port and can be inserted into the non-linear operation after convolution of all standard models. Therefore, SE blocks can also be easily applied to ResNet-18. We place the SE blocks after the non-linear operation of the residual block, before the identity branch summation. In Sect. 3.4, we will examine in detail the impact of the position of SE blocks and the number of SE blocks.

Although each SE block introduces extra parameters, it does not significantly affect the detection speed while improving the accuracy of the model, which is very suitable for application to our model. The experimental results show that adding SE blocks to res4b and res5b respectively, the model achieves the best results. The accuracy was improved by 0.6% while maintaining almost the same detection speed.

3 Experiments

3.1 Dataset

Since existing datasets do not meet our research needs, due to their limitations, we have built our own road marking dataset shown in Table 1. We choose seven types of most common road markings as a study aims: right turn arrow, left turn arrow, straight arrow, straight or right turn arrow, straight or left turn arrow, U-turn arrow, and crosswalk.

Table 1. Weights for all classes

	Right turn arrow	Left turn arrow	Straight or right turn arrow	Straight or left turn arrow	Straight arrow	U-turn arrow	Crosswalk
Number of instances	10656	13171	10263	8550	23619	5994	15067
Weight	1.0	0.8204	1.0404	1.2511	0.4831	2.2189	0.7067

Then we picked out 3269 original images containing these road markings from public datasets such as KITTI, RoadMarking, Baidu Apollo and TT100k. Among these images, there are video frames extracted from the video sequence, and pictures taken in various different scenes to meet the requirements of different application scenarios. The pictures contain simple scenes such as highways, and also contains complex scenes such as urban areas. All original images are manually labeled.

We random selected 1k origin images as test set, others as training set. We adopted a series of data augmentation methods to improve the diversity and quantity of the training set. We adjust the brightness and contrast of the image to simulate the effects of different shooting times. We also rotated the original image by 5° to simulate the change in perspective. Other methods such as cropping and mirroring are also used. Images that do not match the actual situation have been deleted. Finally, we got a training of 40k images.

3.2   Basic Model

In general, deeper networks have abilities to learn more high-level abstract features. However, for road marking detection tasks, deeper network like the Resnet-50 network takes up a lot of computation time, reducing the practicability of the model. And because road markings are relatively simple, the features extracted by very deep network model are quite redundant. Network models with less layers like ResNet-18 may have better results.

Based on a single computer with a Nvidia 1080ti GPU, we studied the effects of different residual network models. The experimental results are shown in Table 2.

Table 2.   Performance with different residual networks

	mAP (%)	Test time (ms)
ResNet-50	88.9	105
ResNet-18	88.3	56

According to the experiments results, the ResNet-18 model is sufficient enough for road marking feature extraction and does not lead to a sharp drop in accuracy. With the ResNet-18 network, the accuracy is dropped by about 0.6% to 88.3% compared to the model with ResNet50, and the time is shortened by half to 56 ms. This means that ResNet-18 is more suitable for road marking detection systems than ResNet-50.

3.3   Median Frequency Balancing

We explored the effect of median frequency balancing. The weights are calculated on the training set. The distribution of various class instances in the dataset as well as the calculation results of weights are shown in Table 1.

The effects of the median frequency balancing strategy are shown in Table 3. We can see that, whether with or without SE blocks, the accuracy of the model with median frequency balancing is improved compared to the model without it, which proves the validity and applicability of this data balancing strategy.

Table 3. The mAP of models with and without median frequency balancing

	Without (%)	With (%)
R-FCN + ResNet-18	88.3	88.8
R-FCN + ResNet-18 + SE	89.2	89.5

3.4 SE Blocks

We explore the impact of SE blocks in terms of both quantity and location. The reduction factor for all SE blocks is set to 16, which is consistent with [15]. The experimental results are shown in Tables 4 and 5.

Table 4. The impact of different SE block position

Position	mAP (%)
No SE block	88.3
Res2b	88.3
Res3b	88.5
Res4b	88.9
Rcs5b	88.6

Table 5. The impact of different number of SE blocks

Position	mAP (%)
No SE block	88.3
Res4b	88.8
Res4b+5b	89.2
Res3b+4b+5b	88.9

When using a single SE block, it works best on the second residual block of stage 4 called res4b which is the last residual block shared by the RPN subnetwork and the classification subnetwork. When two SE blocks placed in res4b and res5b respectively, the model achieves the highest accuracy, which is 0.6% higher than the model without any SE block. More than two SE blocks seem to have contributed nothing to improving accuracy.

Through calculation, two SE blocks in res4b and res5b add a total of 40k parameters. The model size increased by only 0.1M, and the test time on each image barely increases. Adding two SE blocks to the original model, combined with median frequency balancing in training process, we get the final model with an accuracy of 89,5% and 56 ms of test time for a single image, which means our model achieves a good balance between speed and accuracy.

In summary, ResNet-18, combined with median frequency balancing and SE module, ensures that our model has a relatively fast speed and a high accuracy. Results on different models are shown in Table 6, where MFB means median frequency balancing. The visualization of test result is shown in Fig. 3. Our model can deal with illumination changing, worn-out marking and marking occlusion relatively well.

Table 6. Results on different model

	mAP (%)
Basic model: R-FCN + ResNet-18	88.3
Basic model + MFB	88.8
Basic model + SE	88.9
Basic model + MFB + SE	89.5

Fig. 3. Visualization of test results of our model

4   Conclusion

In this paper, in order to the deal with the problem of insufficient and imbalance data, we first built a dataset containing seven common classes of road markings. Secondly, we constructed a road marking model based on R-FCN structure with ResNet-18. We further improved the accuracy of the model through median frequency balancing and SE blocks. The experimental results show that our model has a good result on our self-built dataset, and achieves a good balance between testing speed and accuracy.

Acknowledgement. This work was supported by National Natural Science Foundation of China (61801441) and the Fundamental Research Funds for the Central Universities.

References

1. Touqeer, A., David, I., Ebrahim, E., George, B.: Symbolic road marking recognition using convolutional neural networks. In: Intelligent Vehicles Symposium (IV), pp. 1428–1433. IEEE, Los Angeles (2017)
2. Geiger, A., Lenz, P., Stiller, C., Urtasun, R.: Vision meets robotics: the KITTI dataset. Int. J. Robot. Res. **32**(11), 1231–1237 (2013)
3. Xinyu, H., et al.: The ApolloScape dataset for autonomous driving. In: Computer Vision and Pattern Recognition (CVPR) Workshops, pp. 954–960. IEEE, Salt Lake City (2018)
4. Seokju, L., et al.: VPGNet: vanishing point guided network for lane and road marking detection and recognition. In: International Conference on Computer Vision (ICCV), pp. 1947–1955. IEEE, Venice (2017)
5. Zhe, Z., Dun, L., Songhai, Z., Xiaolei, H., Baoli, L., Shimin, H.: Traffic-sign detection and classification in the wild. In: Conference on Computer Vision and Pattern Recognition (CVPR), pp. 2110–2118. IEEE, Las Vegas (2016)
6. Kaiming, H., Georgia, G., Piotr, D., Ross, G.: Mask R-CNN. In: The IEEE International Conference on Computer Vision (CVPR), pp. 2961–2969. IEEE, Hawaii (2017)
7. Ross, G., Donahue, J., Darrell, T., Malik, J.: Rich feature hierarchies for accurate object detection and semantic segmentation. In: Conference on Computer Vision and Pattern Recognition (CVPR), pp. 580–587. IEEE, Columbus (2014)
8. Ross, G.: Fast RCNN. In: The IEEE International Conference on Computer Vision (ICCV), pp. 1440–1448. IEEE, Santiago Chile (2015)
9. Shaoqing, R., Kaiming, H., Ross, G., Jian, S.: Faster RCNN: towards real-time object detection with region proposal networks. In: Advances in Neural Information Processing Systems(NIPS), Curran Associates, Montreal (2015)
10. Joseph, R., Santosh, D., Ross, G., Ali, F.: You only look once: unified, real-time object detection. In: The IEEE International Conference on Computer Vision (ICCV), pp. 779–788. IEEE, Las Vegas (2016)
11. Liu, W., et al.: SSD: single shot multibox detector. In: Leibe, B., Matas, J., Sebe, N., Welling, M. (eds.) ECCV 2016. LNCS, vol. 9905, pp. 21–37. Springer, Cham (2016). https://doi.org/10.1007/978-3-319-46448-0_2
12. Cheng-Yang, F., Wei, L., Ananth, R., Ambrish, T., Alexander, C.B.: DSSD: deconvolutional single shot detector. In: The IEEE International Conference on Computer Vision (ICCV), arXiv preprint arXiv:1701.06659 (2017)
13. Jifeng, D., Yi, L., Kaiming, H., Jian, S.: R-FCN: object detection via region-based fully convolutional networks. In: Advances in Neural Information Processing Systems (NIPS), pp. 379–387. Curran Associates, Barcelona (2016)
14. Jonathan, L., Evan, S., Trevor, D.: Fully convolutional networks for semantic segmentation. In: The IEEE International Conference on Computer Vision (ICCV), pp. 3431–3440. IEEE, Boston (2015)
15. Hu, J., Shen, L., Sun, G.: Squeeze-and-excitation networks. In: Conference on Computer Vision and Pattern Recognition (CVPR), pp. 7132–7141. IEEE, Hawaii (2018)
16. Kaiming, H., Xiangyu, Z., Shaoqing, R., Sun, J.: Deep residual learning for image recognition. In: Conference on Computer Vision and Pattern Recognition (CVPR), pp. 770–778. IEEE, Las Vegas (2016)
17. Vijay, B., Alex, K., Roberto, C.: SegNet: a deep convolutional encoder-decoder architecture for image segmentation. arXiv preprint arXiv:1511.00561 (2015)

Face Verification Between ID Document Photos and Partial Occluded Spot Photos

Yunfei Zhao, Shikui Wei$^{(\boxtimes)}$, Xiang Jiang, Tao Ruan, and Yao Zhao

School of Computer and Information Technology, Beijing Jiaotong University, Beijing, China
{17120335,shkwei,14112058,16112024,yzhao}@bjtu.edu.cn

Abstract. ID-spot face verification is an important problem in face verification area, which aims to identify whether the spotted face is the same to the ID photo. Although some face verification systems have been deployed in many application scenarios, most of them are used in a constrained environment and many key problems need to be addressed furthermore. In this paper, we focus on a challenging ID-spot face verification task, in which the spot photo is partially occluded. Toward this end, a two-stream network is employed to learn more discriminative feature for distinguishing different ID-Spot face pairs. In addition, to suppress the negative effect of background and occlusion, a global weight pooling method is proposed, which makes the available face area more significant than the background and occlusion. The experimental results show that the proposed method obtains 10% improvements on FAR@0.01 compared with previous schemes.

Keywords: Face verification · Occluded face · ID document photo versus spot photo

1 Introduction

As one of the most important biometrics, face recognition plays an important role in many application scenarios, such as device unlocking, application login and mobile payment. In the past decades, lots of face recognition algorithms are reported and great progress has been made. In recent years, the advances in deep learning techniques have greatly boosted the performance of face recognition. In fact, one of most important research topics lies in the extraction of more discriminative facial features by employing convolutional neural networks, which can be discussed from three aspects. Firstly, more powerful network architectures are adapted by introducing deeper or wider networks from VGG [1] to ResNet [2]. Secondly, large and refined face datasets are constructed to simulate real-world scenarios. For example, more wild MS1M [4] dataset is constructed to replace CASIA-WebFace [3]. Finally, more rigorous loss functions are designed to enable the network to learn more discriminative face features. In fact, most of commercial face recognition systems required the users to actively cooperate with the cameras so as to acquire clear face images. That is, most of them only work well in certain constrained environment. However, in some more tough application scenarios, it is almost impossible to meet the conditions. For example, the face recognition systems in public safety can

© Springer Nature Switzerland AG 2019
Y. Zhao et al. (Eds.): ICIG 2019, LNCS 11902, pp. 94–105, 2019.
https://doi.org/10.1007/978-3-030-34110-7_9

even acquire a clear and complete face image. In this application scenario, the law enforcement agency has frequent requirements to compare ID document photos with spotted face images. What the face verification system needs to do is to help the police find out the faces of the criminals from these spotted images based on the ID document photos. In fact, this kind of face verification systems is quite different from existing commercial face recognition systems. First, the images are generally acquired in more natural environment, in which some factors like the capturing views and light conditions are uncontrolled. Second, criminals always have a psychological tendency to hide their faces, which further increases the difficulties of verification. Finally, the ID document photos are generally normative but low-quality, while the images from surveillance cameras or spot cameras are generally high-quality but arbitrary. That is, two types of faces are heterogeneous, which makes the matching of faces more difficult. Figure 1 illustrates the difference between ID faces and Spot faces. In this paper, we focus mainly on the ID-Spot face verification problem.

Fig. 1. The sample photo shows the three situations. Each column is a matching pair of images, from left to right, representing normal, sunglasses, and mask. It should be noted that the black rectangular block is for privacy protection, not the information that the image carries.

In the ID-Spot face verification scenario, the ID document photo is unified and clear, while may be covered by some stuffs like sunglasses and masks. Due to this special nature, when we follow the standard face feature extraction method, we can't get a very effective and discriminative face representation. Therefore, we employ a pseudo-siamese network to solve the heterogeneous problem. In the network architecture, the network for processing ID document photos is different from the one for handling spot photos. That is, the two networks don't share parameters, while they have the same architecture and trained jointly. In this manner, we can effectively enhance the discriminative ability of heterogeneous faces. In addition, a global weight pooling method is proposed to suppress the negative effect of background and occlusion. Using the global weight method, the available face area are assigned more significant weight than the background and occlusion, which makes face representation more discriminative.

In brief, we aim to create a fast and effective face verification system for face verification in wild conditions. In order to achieve this goal, we have proposed a face representation method and achieved good performance. The main contributions of this article are as follows:

1. We explored the face verification problem with partial occlusion and quantitatively analyzed the impact of occlusion on face verification.
2. We adjusted the global average pooling in CNN and achieved performance improvement. At FAR = 0.01%, we increased the TAR from 47.58% to 57.63%.
3. Our model achieved the best results on a Chinese ID-Spot dataset.

2   Related Works

2.1   Face Recognition Based on Deep Learning

Due to the emergence of massive data and the tremendous increase in computing power, deep learning has shown great vitality in the field of computer vision. Face recognition is a special type of task in image classification.

The use of softmax to classify faces is the most basic method for studying face recognition. Since softmax is only used for classification, it has a weak ability to increase the distance between classes and reduce the distance within the class. Therefore, a series of methods such as center loss [5], SphereFace [6], CosineFace [7], and arcface [8] have appeared. Center loss [9] adds an additional supervisory signal for compressing the intraclass distance. In order to enhance the softmax loss ability, the multiplicative margin and the additive margin are introduced into the angle space by ArcFace [8] and SphereFace [6] respectively. CosineFace [7], AMSoftmax [9] adds additive margins to the cosine space to increase the penalty power for more discerning facial representations. The Softmax series method classifies the face of the training set globally. Its advantage is that it can converge quickly. The disadvantage is that when the class of the training set is large, more memory space is needed.

The DeepID [10, 11] combines softmax and validation signals to train the network. Facenet [12] uses the triple loss function to learn facial representations in large-scale databases. Contrastive loss and triplet loss are both data-using strategies. So, we need to build data pairs before training, and the method of building the data pairs will have a big impact on the result. Hard samples are often used as a choice for triples. Such methods search for optimal solutions in local space, and often require longer training time on large-scale training data.

2.2   ID Versus Spot

ID-Spot verification can be considered as a special case of heterogeneous face verification. Although the image structures of the two are the same, the data distribution of the two has a huge gap that is hard to cross. There are usually two types of methods for solving heterogeneous problems. One is to first convert the image so that the two types of data are similarly distributed, and the other is to map the two types of images into the same shared feature space. There are many researchers [13–16] who have conducted a lot of experiments and explorations on this issue.

Large-scale [17] and DocFace [18, 19] explored ID-Scene validation issues. The two adopted a similar strategy in the general direction. Pre-training on open large-scale datasets to obtain a pretrained model that is sensitive to human faces is the first step. Then, what needs to be done is to fine-tune the model on the ID-Spot dataset, also known as transfer learning, so that the model has a stronger ability to process heterogeneous ID photos and spot photos. More specifically, Large-scale adopted a classification-verification-classification strategy to gradually improve the performance of the model. DocFace designed an optimization method called DWI to update the weights.

2.3 Face Verification with Partial Occlusion

In the development of face recognition, many researchers have conducted great explorations and experiments on occlusion problems. Subspace regression transforms the occlusion face recognition problem into an unoccluded face image and occlusion respectively return to their respective subspaces; robust error coding attempts to separate the occlusion image into occluded and unoccluded regions; Robust feature extraction method decomposes the image features, reduces the mutual interference between the features, and provides sufficient fine features for subsequent recognition.

In recent years, there have been many works on partially occluded faces. Robust LSTM [20] proposes a robust long- and short-term memory network-automatic coding model to restore occluded faces. DFI [21] recognizes a human face by forming a facial star network map by connecting key points of the face area. Enhancing [22] improves the recognition rate by finding areas that have a significant impact on recognition.

3 Approach

In this section, we will describe our approach in detail. This method improves the face verification performance in the case of partial occlusion.

3.1 The Impact of Occlusion on Face Verification

It is well known that partial occlusion like sunglasses can cause trouble for face verification. We conduct a quantitative analysis of the effects of sunglasses on face verification, and give the effect of sunglasses on face verification from numerical values. We first compare the matching similarities between images, and obtain the cosine similarity of scene-scene, glass-glass, and scene-glass. The three groups are all compared by different people. Second, we use the same model to verify the dataset with occlusion and the dataset without occlusion, and get the verification result. In the process, we use the mobilefacenet [23] model trained by ArcFace [8].

3.2 Network Architecture

Global Weight Pooling (GWP). In practice, face verification should achieve an ideal balance between speed and accuracy. Mobilefacenet [23] is a lightweight network designed for face recognition that can be deployed on mobile devices. Mobilefacenet draws on mobilenetv1 [24], mobilenetv2 [25], and shufflenet [26] networks, which use many separable convolutions to reduce the amount of computation and parameters. Mobilefacenet uses the global separable convolution instead of the global average pooling for down sampling at the end of the convolution.

We use the backbone network of mobilefacenet, so the size of the final feature map is 7*7, and the channel is 512. In the global average pooling layer, we use a global pooling operation with weights. The weights on each channel are not shared, and the weight parameter size is 512*7*7. After each iteration in the training, the 49 weights on each channel are processed to ensure that the result of each inference is a weighted average. Please see Fig. 2.

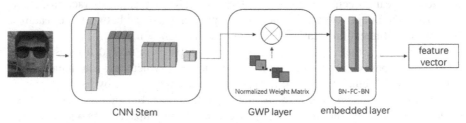

CNN Stem   GWP layer   embedded layer

Fig. 2. A 512*7*7 feature map will be obtained after the image has passed the CNN stem. CNN stem consists of four parts. there are two convolution modules in the first part. Then, 4 residual blocks and 6 residual blocks and 2 residual blocks, which contain many separable convolution operations, are executed sequentially. Usually, there is a global average pooling operation after convolution layer. We use GWC, which constrains the sum of the weights of each channel to 1, instead of GAP(Global Average Pooling). The physical meaning of GWC is to perform a weighted average operation, like its name. An embedded layer consisting of BN-FC-BN is executed at the end.

The global average pooling layer is calculated as:

$$Output_{GAP-c} = \sum_{i,j} \frac{1}{W*H} \cdot F_{i,j,c} \tag{1}$$

The global separable convolution is calculated as:

$$Output_{GSC-c} = \sum_{i,j} W_{i,j,c} \cdot F_{i,j,c} \tag{2}$$

The global weighted average pooling layer is calculated as:

$$Output_{GWP-c} = \sum_{i,j} W_{i,j,c} \cdot F_{i,j,c}$$

$$\sum_{i,j} W_{i,j,c} = 1 \tag{3}$$

Where F is the input feature map of size $W \times H \times C$. W is the weight matrix of size $W \times H \times C$. The (i, j) denotes the spatial position in W and F, and c denotes the channel index.

We use three methods for weight processing to ensure that it is a weighted average. They are:

- Option-A: Use Softmax function
- Option-B: Use Softmax function after relu
- Option-C: Use Rescale process after relu

The GWP structure can increase the effective area weight of the face in the image to obtain more discriminative facial features, and process the parameter matrix into weights, which can highlight the importance of each region of the face.

Pseudo-siamese Network. Most of the existing face verification networks are based on the siamese network, and the siamese network is used to handle similar input situations. In the ID-Spot verification, although the input is a human face, our task is to verify the face, that is, to find a larger dissimilarity in similarity. Especially in the case of the difference in the distribution of data between the ID photo and the Spot photo, and the existence of obvious heterogeneous characteristics, the pseudo-siamese network will be able to solve the problem better.

We use a pseudo-siamese network to solve the heterogeneity of ID photo and Spot photo. Two networks of the same structure process the ID photo and the spot photo separately, and the two networks do not share parameters. In addition, we do a comparative experiment, the performance of the shared embedded layer will be lower than that of a single network. The embedded layer is shown in Fig. 2 and the structure is BN-FC-BN. Therefore, we used two networks with completely independent parameters. Figure 3 shows the pipeline.

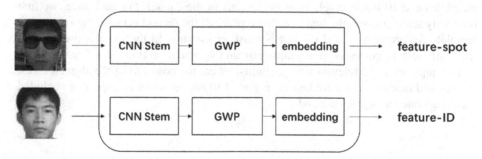

Fig. 3. This is the pipeline for extracting facial features.

4 Experiments

Our code is based on the MXNet framework. All experiments run on 2 NVIDIA 1080Ti (12G). The specific settings for the experiment will be described in detail below.

4.1 Dataset

MS1M. MS1M [4] is currently the largest open source face dataset, which contains approximately 100k identities and 10Million images. However, the original MS1M had a lot of noise, and ArcFace [8] cleaned it up and got the cleaned dataset. The cleaned dataset contains approximately 85K identities and 5.8 Million images. We used a refined dataset [27] for training.

LFW, AgeDB, CFP-FP. lfw [28] is a well-known face test dataset in the field of face recognition, which contains 13,233 images from 5,749 IDs collected from online. The agedb [29] is a test data set for age. The image in cfp-fp [30] emphasizes the side face. 6000 pairs, 6000 pairs, and 7000 pairs of images were obtained from lfw, agedb, and cfp_fp, respectively. We use these three datasets as validation sets to select the optimal model.

IDSpot. The IDSpot dataset is a private dataset that includes 19,500 pairs of matched images and 100k pairs of unmatched images. Each pair of images is a ID photo and a spot photo. The matching image pairs are from the same ID and do not match from different IDs. The types of ID photos are uniform, with the same size, degree of blur, image type; the style of spot photos is very different, there is a big difference.

We adjust the size of the ID photos to 112*112 by image processing functions such as crop and resize. Then we use MTCNN [31] to preprocess the spot photos, make face alignment on the face images according to the 5 landmarks, and finally adjust the size of the spot photos to 112*112.

Because it is difficult to collect enough occlusion images with labels, we obtain a synthetic occlusion dataset IDSpot-paste by image processing. We chose 100 sunglasses templates and 10 mask templates as occlusions in the dataset. For each face, we first randomly select 3 cases, the first is to do no process, the second is to use the sunglasses template for processing, and the last is mask processing. In the latter two cases, we randomly select a corresponding template again to generate an occlusion face. We paste these templates to the relevant face positions, where the positions of the aligned faces, glasses and mouth corners are known. Figure 4 illustrates some examples of occluded faces generated using this method.

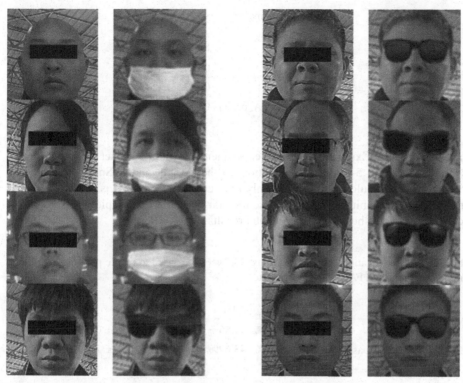

Fig. 4. Here are some spot photos and generated occlusion photos. It should be noted that the black rectangular block is for privacy protection, not the information that the image carries.

We selected 15600 pairs of matching images for training, using the remaining 3900 pairs of matching images and 100K pairs of unmatched images for verification, and repeating the above process 5 times for 5-fold cross-validation. It should be noted that the IDs appearing in the matching image pair do not appear in the unmatched image pair. This will ensure that the same ID does not appear in the training set and verification set.

4.2 Occlusion Impact Analysis

Random Matching Experiment. We randomly select 10,000 images from the spot photos, and divide them into 2 groups, named A and B respectively. According to the occlusion generation method, A and B are processed to obtain A_paste and B_paste, respectively. We use the mobilefacenet pretrained model to extract the features of the above four datasets. Finally, we compare three groups according to the four groups of features: first, A and B calculate the cosine similarity, get 5000 cosine similarity, calculate the mean and variance; the second group is to calculate the cosine similarity of A_paste and B_paste, then get the mean and variance. the last group is to calculate the cosine similarity between A and B_paste, B and A_paste and to obtain 10000 cosine similarities, and calculate mean and variance. Table 1 shows the experimental results.

Table 1. Random matching experiment results

Type	Similarity
A-B	0.5473 ± 0.0622
A_paste – B_paste	0.6135 ± 0.0664
(A, B) – (B_paste, A_paste)	0.5034 ± 0.0438

Face Verification Experiment. In this experiment, the mobilefacenet pretrained model is used to perform 5-fold cross-validation on the IDSpot and IDSpot-paste datasets respectively. It should be noted that only the verification process is performed here, and there is no training process. We use tar@far as a metric to explore the effects of occlusion. Table 2 shows the experimental results.

Table 2. Face verification experiment results: TAR@FAR is used to metric performance. TAR: True Accept rate, and FAR: False Accept rate

Dataset	FAR = 0.01%	0.1%	1%
IDSpot	67.45% ± 1.00%	90.56% ± 0.41%	98.63% ± 0.18%
IDSpot-paste	31.30% ± 0.81%	43.69% ± 0.94%	65.11% ± 1.39%

We explore partial occlusion through the above two experiments. We can see that occlusion has a huge impact on face verification from Tables 1 and 2. The experimental results show that face verification with local occlusion is a much more difficult task than conventional face verification.

4.3 Metrics

We use two evaluation metrics in all the experiments in this paper. We evaluate the models trained on MS1M on the lfw, agedb, and cfp-fp datasets, and use Accuracy as the evaluation metric. According to Accuracy, the optimal model is selected as the pretrained model. Accuracy is the ratio of the model's correct number of samples to the total number of samples, which reflects the overall predictive power of the model.

In addition, we also use tar@far as the evaluation metric. Different far values correspond to different tar values. This metric can reflect the prediction ability of the model at a certain extreme, and can pay more attention to a certain aspect of performance.

4.4 Training on MS1M [4]

According to ArcFace [8], we train the mobilefacenet [23] network on the refined MS1M dataset [27]. We take ArcFace with a margin of 0.5 as the loss function. We set the batchsize to 128, the learning rate is divisible from 10 at 50K, 80K, 100K iterations, and the total number of iterations is 140K. We set the momentum to 0.9, and the weight decay to 5e-4.

Finally, we get the pretrained model. The pretrained model achieves the results of 99.47%, 95.67%, and 93.45% on lfw [28], agedb [29], and cfp_fp [30].

4.5 Transfer Learning

In this part of the experiment, we take a triplet loss. We use hard samples to design triples, each time looking for the hardest sample from a batch of samples as a negative sample. We set up a 5-fold cross-validation experiment. With 50 epochs per experiment, the learning rate starts at 0.1 and droppes to 0.01 and 0.001 at the beginning of the 11th epoch and 26 epochs, respectively. We set the batchsize to 32.

In GWP, we use several different ways to process weights. The first is to process by using the softmax function; the second is relu processing before softmax; the third is relu processing and process by using rescaling (Table 3).

Table 3. GAP, GSC, GWC experiments results, TAR@FAR is used to metric performance. TAR: True Accept rate, and FAR: False Accept rate. A, B, C denote option-A, option-B, option-C. S denotes pseudo-siamese network. GAP-S(EMB) denotes pseudo-siamese network sharing embedding layer parameters.

Model	FAR = 0.01%	FAR = 0.1%	FAR = 1%
GAP	47.58% ± 2.00%	77.68% ± 0.59%	94.65% ± 0.61%
GSC	46.41% ± 3.41%	79.43% ± 0.71%	94.76% ± 0.50%
GWP-A	48.63% ± 2.83%	78.72% ± 0.21%	94.80% ± 0.37%
GAP-S(EMB)	46.57% ± 4.14%	70.23% ± 2.55%	90.32% ± 0.89%
GAP-S	56.66% ± 2.40%	81.73% ± 0.91%	95.73% ± 0.28%
GSC-S	55.33% ± 2.18%	**82.87% ± 0.33%**	**95.95% ± 0.41%**
GWP-AS	57.01% ± 3.07%	81.94% ± 0.59%	95.79% ± 0.38%
GWP-BS	56.97% ± 0.95%	81.76% ± 0.64%	95.87% ± 0.36%
GWP-CS	**57.63% ± 2.55%**	82.29% ± 0.76%	95.91% ± 0.31%

From the experimental results, we can analyze that the pseudo-siamese network can effectively improve the representation of heterogeneous human faces, which also proves that the data distribution of ID photos and Spot photos is very different. The sharing of the embedded layer leads to a significant drop in performance, indicating that different distributed data should be subjected to different linear transformations. Both GSC and GWP can achieve performance improvements over GAP. At far = 0.01%, GWP performed best, indicating that GWP performs better under low false accepted rate.

5 Conclusion

In this paper, we explore face verification with partial occlusion and quantitatively analyze the impact of occlusion on face verification. We improve the representation of the face by adjusting the GAP part of the CNN. In addition, pseudo-siamese network is used to explore and analyze the heterogeneity of ID photos and spot photos.

Acknowledgement. This work was supported in part by National Key Research and Development of China (No. 2017YFC1703503), National Natural Science Foundation of China (No. 61532005, No. 61572065), Program of China Scholarships Council (No. 201807095006), Fundamental Research Funds for the Central Universities (No. 2018JBZ001).

References

1. Simonyan, K., Zisserman, A.: Very deep convolutional networks for large-scale image recognition. In: ICLR (2015)
2. He, K., Zhang, X., Ren, S., Sun, J.: Deep residual learning for image recognition. In: Proceedings of the IEEE Conference on Computer Vision and Pattern Recognition, pp. 770–778 (2016)
3. Yi, D., Lei, Z., Liao, S., Li, S.Z.: Learning face representation from scratch. Technical report arXiv:1411.7923 (2014)
4. Guo, Y., Zhang, L., Hu, Y., He, X., Gao, J.: MS-Celeb-1M: a dataset and benchmark for large-scale face recognition. In: Leibe, B., Matas, J., Sebe, N., Welling, M. (eds.) ECCV 2016. LNCS, vol. 9907, pp. 87–102. Springer, Cham (2016). https://doi.org/10.1007/978-3-319-46487-9_6
5. Wen, Y., Zhang, K., Li, Z., Qiao, Y.: A discriminative feature learning approach for deep face recognition. In: Leibe, B., Matas, J., Sebe, N., Welling, M. (eds.) ECCV 2016. LNCS, vol. 9911, pp. 499–515. Springer, Cham (2016). https://doi.org/10.1007/978-3-319-46478-7_31
6. Liu, W., Wen, Y., Yu, Z., Li, M., Raj, B., Song, L.: Sphereface: deep hypersphere embedding for face recognition. In: CVPR (2017)
7. Wang, H., Wang, Y., Zhou, Z., Ji, X., Gong, D., Zhou, J., et al.: CosFace: large margin cosine loss for deep face recognition. arXiv:1801.0941 (2018)
8. Deng, J., Guo, J., Zafeiriou, S.: ArcFace: additive angular margin loss for deep face recognition. arXiv:1801.07698 (2018)
9. Wang, F., Liu, W., Liu, H., Cheng, J.: Additive margin softmax for face verification. arXiv: 1801.05599 (2018)
10. Sun, Y., Chen, Y., Wang, X., Tang, X.: Deep learning face representation by joint identification-verification. In: NIPS (2014)
11. Sun, Y., Wang, X., Tang, X.: Deeply learned face representations are sparse, selective, and robust. In: Computer Vision and Pattern Recognition, pp. 2892–2900 (2015)
12. Schroff, F., Kalenichenko, D., Philbin, J.: FaceNet: a unified embedding for face recognition and clustering. In: CVPR (2015)
13. Tang, X., Wang, X.: Face photo recognition using sketch. In: ICIP (2002)
14. Liu, Q., Tang, X., Jin, H., Lu, H., Ma, S.: A nonlinear approach for face sketch synthesis and recognition. In: CVPR (2005)
15. Liao, S., Yi, D., Lei, Z., Qin, R., Li, S.Z.: Heterogeneous face recognition from local structures of normalized appearance. In: Tistarelli, M., Nixon, M.S. (eds.) ICB 2009. LNCS, vol. 5558, pp. 209–218. Springer, Heidelberg (2009). https://doi.org/10.1007/978-3-642-01793-3_22

16. Klare, B.F., Jain, A.K.: Heterogeneous face recognition using kernel prototype similarities. IEEE Trans. PAMI 35(6), 1410–1422 (2013)
17. Zhu, X., et al.: Large-scale bisample learning on id vs. spot face recognition. arXiv:1806.03018 (2018)
18. Shi, Y., Jain, A.K.: DocFace: matching ID document photos to selfies. arXiv:1805.02283 (2018)
19. Shi, Y., Jain, A.K.: DocFace+: ID document to selfie matching. arXiv:1809.05620 (2018)
20. Zhao, F., Feng, J., Zhao, J., Yang, W., Yan, S.: Robust LSTM-autoencoders for face de-occlusion in the wild. arXiv:1612.08534 (2016)
21. Singh, A., Patil, D., Reddy, M., Omkar, S.: Disguised face identification (DFI) with facial keypoints using spatial fusion convolutional network. In: The IEEE International Conference on Computer Vision (ICCV), pp. 1648–1655 (2017)
22. Trigueros, D.S., Meng, L., Hartnett, M.: Enhancing convolutional neural networks for face recognition with occlusion maps and batch triplet loss. In: Image and Vision Computing (2018)
23. Chen, S., Liu, Y., Gao, X., Han, Z.: MobileFaceNets: efficient CNNs for accurate real-time face verification on mobile devices. arXiv:1804.05737 (2018)
24. Howard, A.G., et al.: MobileNets: efficient convolutional neural networks for mobile vision applications. CoRR, abs/1704.04861 (2017)
25. Sandler, M., Howard, A., Zhu, M., Zhmoginov, A., Chen, L.C.: MobileNetV2: inverted residuals and linear bottlenecks. CoRR, abs/1801.04381 (2018)
26. Zhang, X., Zhou, X., Lin, M., Sun, J.: ShuffleNet: an extremely efficient convolutional neural network for mobile devices. CoRR, abs/1707.01083 (2017)
27. InsightFace github. https://github.com/deepinsight/insightface
28. Huang, G.B., Ramesh, M., Berg, T., et al.: Labeled faces in the wild: a database for studying face recognition in unconstrained environments (2007)
29. Moschoglou, S., Papaioannou, A., Sagonas, C., Deng, J., Kotsia, I., Zafeiriou, S.: AgeDB: the first manually collected in-the-wild age database. In: CVPRW (2017)
30. Sengupta, S., Chen, J.-C., Castillo, C., Patel, V.M., Chellappa, R., Jacobs, D.W.: Frontal to profile face verification in the wild. In: WACV, pp. 1–9 (2016)
31. Zhang, K., Zhang, Z., Li, Z., Qiao, Y.: Joint face detection and alignment using multi-task cascaded convolutional networks. IEEE Signal Proc. Lett. 23(10), 1499–1503 (2016)

Road Detection of Remote Sensing Image Based on Convolutional Neural Network

Yuting Zhu$^{(\boxtimes)}$ ⓘ, Jingwen Yan ⓘ, Cong Wang ⓘ, and Yiqing Zhou ⓘ

Department of Electronic Engineering, Shantou University, Shantou, Guangdong, China
18ytzhu@stu.edu.cn

Abstract. We propose an end-to-end framework for the road detection in satellite imagery with convolutional neural networks (CNNs). Firstly, we analyze the limitations of patch-based network and full convolution neural network and propose a new method. In our approach, CNNs are directly trained to produce classification maps out of the input images without losing much edge information. The method, called M-FCN, extends FCN by using a new activation function instead of the traditional activation function. We then address the issue of imperfect training data through a traditional approach: labeled images manually to form a new dataset. Finally, we show that such a network can be trained on remote sensing images with a composite loss function. At the same time, we validate the effect of label accuracy in dataset on the model. To ensure the accuracy of our method, we apply different methods to train in the same dataset. A series of experiments show that our networks consider a large amount of context to provide fine-grained classification maps, M-FCN outperforms SVM, patch-based network and full convolution network.

Keywords: Road detection · Convolutional neural networks (CNNs) · Deep learning · Satellite images

1 Introduction

The analysis of remote-sensing images is very important in many practical applications, such as meteorological monitoring, city planning [1]. Recent technological developments have significantly increased the amount of available satellite imagery. Road, as an important support and guarantee of the national economic lifeline, plays an indispensable role in the process of urbanization in China. In this paper, A new pixel-based classification method for remote sensing images is proposed.

There is a vast literature on road-detection approaches that can be divided into two parts: automatic road feature acquisition and semi-automatic road feature acquisition. The first method [2] mainly includes the automatic recognition and location technology of the main road information. The second method [3] combines the human vision system with the computer system organically. It relies on the high resolution of the road in the

Supported by the NSF of China (No. 61672335 and 61601276), and by Department of Education of Guangdong Province (No. 2016KZDXM012 and 2017KCXTD015).

© Springer Nature Switzerland AG 2019
Y. Zhao et al. (Eds.): ICIG 2019, LNCS 11902, pp. 106–118, 2019.
https://doi.org/10.1007/978-3-030-34110-7_10

remote sensing image and the powerful computing ability of the computer system. In a large-scale setting, however, these approaches are not effective. On the one hand, current large-scale satellite imagery doesn't use high spectral resolution sensors, making it difficult to distinguish object classes solely by their spectrum. On the other hand, due to the large spatial extent covered by the data sets, classes have a considerable internal variability, which further challenges the class separability when simply observing the spectral signatures of a restricted neighborhood. We argue that a more thorough understanding of the context, such as the shape of objects, is required to aid the classification process.

Recently, convolution neural networks (CNNs) have attracted great attention due to their excellent capability in spectral image classification, target detection and image categorization problems [4]. CNNs consist of a stack of learned convolution filters that extract hierarchical contextual image features, and are a popular form of deep learning networks. They are already outperforming other approaches in various domains [5].

In this paper, we show that an algorithmic change-use maximum feature mapping (MFM) instead of traditional activation function-leads to an elegant and effective solution which could prevent the loss of edge information. At the same time, we show that such a network can be trained on remote sensing images with a composite loss function. To this end, We manually made labels to create a new dataset.

Our method, called M-FCN, extends FCN [12] by using MFM instead of Relu on each activation function. We comprehensively evaluate our method on the different datasets with several methods. The experimental results show that the performance of the proposed method, such as IoU and ACC, is better than that of traditional machine learning SVM algorithm, patch-based neural network and traditional full convolution neural network algorithm. At the same time, the obtained road detection is more accurate, the road is clearer and more continuous, and the location is more accurate.

2 Related Work

We now review road detection methods in remote sensing. They can be roughly divided into two parts: traditional methods and the use of CNNs.

Machine learning based on probability and statistics provides many feasible methods for remote sensing image detection. Typical machine learning methods include support vector machines (SVM), decision trees, principal component analysis (PCA) and K-means. Maulik et al. [6] constructed a set of semi-supervised SVM classifiers to solve the problem of remote sensing image classification. SVM has the characteristics of stability and ease of use, but its performance in solving multi-class target classification problem is not very well, and there is no relevant theoretical basis for how to correctly select the kernel function. In recent years, stochastic forest model based on decision tree algorithm and CART decision tree have been used in remote sensing image classification. Decision tree algorithm is easy to understand, highly operable, and can deal with multi-output problems. The disadvantage is that the generalization ability is too poor and the performance is not good when dealing with high-dimensional data. However, remote sensing image information shows a trend of massive growth. The above classification methods belong to shallow learning network. It is difficult to establish complex function representation, and can't adapt to the classification of complex samples of remote sensing images.

In remote sensing, CNNs can improve the accuracy of detection through massive training data and model learning with many hidden layers. Manih [8] uses semantic tags to label aerial image pixels and uses CNNs to train these aerial images. He proposed a special architecture for feature learning of annotated aerial images. It is derived from common image categorization networks by increasing the output size of the final layer. Instead of outputting a single value to indicate the category, the final layer produces an entire dense classification. This network successfully learns contextual spatial features to better distinguish the object classes. However, this patch-wise procedure has the disadvantage of introducing artifacts on the border of the classified patches.

In the methods mentioned above, traditional road detection methods mainly extract shallow features, such as SVM and other algorithms. They have a common disadvantage that they can't separate the target from the background well, which makes the target detection deviate. CNNs can better learn the features of remote sensing images with rich road information, so that the trained model can be used to accurately detect and locate the road.

3 Proposed CNN Architecture

In this paper, we address the problem of dense classification, i.e., not just the categorization of an entire image, but a full pixelwise labeling into the different categories. Firstly, we introduce an existing approach, the patch-based network, point out its limitations. Then we transform the traditional Full Convolution Neural Network (FCN) and use the Maximum Feature Mapping (MFM) instead of the Rectified Linear Unit (ReLU) as the activation function to form a new architecture of convolution Neural Network, which is named M-FCN.

3.1 Patch-Based Network

Patch-based approaches infer the label of each pixel independently based on its small surrounding region. In these approaches, a classifier is designed and trained to predict a single label from a small image patch. In the inference phase, a sliding window is used to extract patches around all pixels in the input image, which are subsequently forwarded through the classifier to get the target labels. The way to create dense predictions is to increase the number of outputs of the last fully connected classification layer, in order to match the size of the target patch.

Although the patch-based convolution neural network can complete the classification of remote-sensing images, it still has some shortcomings. The resolution of these filters is 1/4 of the input resolution, because the stride of the first convolution layer is 4. This means that the fully connected layer does not only compute the classification scores, but also learns how to upsample them. Outputting a full-resolution patch is then the result of upsampling and not of an intrinsic high-resolution processing. We also observe that the fully connected layer allows outputs at different locations to have different weights with respect to the previous layer. Nevertheless, pixel-based approaches are often outperformed by patch-based methods in remote sensing semantic segmentation tasks [7, 8]. As a result, in this work, we put more emphasis on the pixel-based approach and follow such a paradigm in our design.

3.2 Pixel-Based Network

Unlike patch-based approaches, pixel-wise methods infer the labels for all of the pixels in the input image at the same time. One of the first CNN architectures for pixel-wise semantic segmentation is the fully-convolutional network (FCN) method introduced by Long et al. in [12]. In this method, a transposed convolutional layer is employed to perform up-sampling. This operation is essential in order to produce outputs of the same spatial dimensions as the inputs.

The FCN architecture was recently employed for semantic segmentation of remote sensing images in [10]. Every layer in the fully convolutional network is a three-dimensional array of $h \times w \times d$, which h and w are spatial dimensions and d is feature or channel dimension. Firstly, the layer is an image with h $\times$ w pixel size and d color channels. In the network, the area size of the output layer corresponding to an element in the output result of a certain layer is called the receptive field. Convolution is based on translation invariance. Their basic components (convolution, merge and activation functions) run on the local input area and depend only on relative spatial coordinates. Write x for data vectors in the location of a particular layer at (i, j). Calculate y in the next layer by the following function:

$$y_{ij} = f_{ks}\left(\{x_{si+\Delta i, sj+\Delta j}\}_{0 \le \Delta i, \Delta j \le k}\right) \tag{1}$$

K is called kernel size and S is stride or sub-sampling factor. F determines the type of layer: convolution or average pooling, a maximum spatial pooling, or a non-linear activation function of an element and other types of layer. This form of functionality is maintained under composition, and the stride and pace of the kernel follow the following transformation:

$$f_{ks} \circ g_{k's'} = (f \circ g)_{k'+(k-1)s', ss'} \tag{2}$$

The input of the FCN can be of any size and produce the corresponding output (possibly resampling) spatial dimension. The decoder uses pooling indices computed in the max-pooling step of the corresponding encoder to perform non-linear up-sampling, followed by mirror-structured convolution layers to produce the pixel-wise full size label map.

Full Convolutional Neural Network (FCN), as an improved framework of convolutional neural network, can be effectively applied to semantic segmentation and target detection [9].

3.3 Maximum Feature Mapping (MFM)

Firstly, the structure we proposed no longer uses the traditional sigmoid activation function or Relu activation function. The reason is that sigmoid function has many shortcomings, it is easy to saturate. When the initial value is very large, most of the neurons will be saturated, which will affect the gradient curve, and ultimately make the neural network difficult to train. In order to overcome the problem of gradient vanish, people begin to use Rectified Linear Unit (ReLU) as activation function, which is a sparse representation. The characteristics of ReLU learning are usually high-dimensional, and one drawback it may have in the process of optimization is that if its value is not positive, it will be assigned a value of 0. In this case, it is possible to lose some important information, especially in the previous convolution layers, the impact of this phenomenon may be more obvious. In order to address the above shortcomings, three extended activation functions, Leaky-ReLu, Parametric relu (P-ReLu) and Randomized relu (R-ReLu), appear. But they still have the defect of losing information, this is disadvantageous to the result of semantic segmentation.

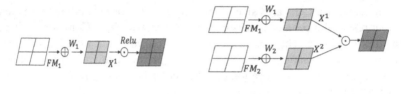

(a) Relu:$h(x) = \max(0, C^1)$ (b) MFM:$f(x) = \max(C^1, C^2)$

Fig. 1. A comparison between Relu and MFM, (a) Relu suppresses a neuron by thresholding magnitude response. (b) MFM suppresses a neuron by a competitive relationship. It is the simplest case of maxout activations.

FCN is an end-to-end, pixels-to-pixels network. If we use Relu activation functions, the details will be lost in the previous layers, which will lead to lack of spatial consistency. In remote sensing image road detection, we need neural network to extract road edge details. Considering the above problems, we use maximum feature mapping (MFM) [11] to replace ReLUs as activation function in CNNs. MFM is an alternative of ReLU to suppress low-activation neurons in each layer, so that it can be considered as a special implementation of maxout activation to separate noisy signals and informative signals.

In the Maximum Feature Mapping (MFM), if the input convolution layer is assumed, the specific operation can be calculated using the flow shown in Fig. 1.

Figure 1(b) can be written as:

$$f_{ij}^k = \max_{1 \leq k \leq n}(C_{ij}^k, C_{ij}^{k+n}) \tag{3}$$

where the channel of input convolution layer is $2n$, $1 \leq i \leq h$, $1 \leq j \leq w$. As shown in Eq. (1), the output C via MFM operation is in $R^{H \times W \times N}$.

The gradient of Eq. (1) takes the following form,

$$\frac{\partial f}{\partial C^{k'}} = \begin{cases} 1, & if\ C_{ij}^k \geq C_{ij}^{k+n} \\ 0, & otherwise \end{cases} \tag{4}$$

$1 \leq k' \leq 2n$, and:

$$k = \begin{cases} k' & 1 \leq k' \leq n \\ k' - n & n + 1 \leq k' \leq 2n \end{cases} \tag{5}$$

As we can see above, the 50% gradient of this activation layer is 0. Therefore, the maximum feature mapping activation function can obtain sparse gradient, which can reflect the data variance under the condition of phase strain. Furthermore, the maximum feature mapping (MFM) activation function can be regarded as a sparse connection between two convolution layers, thus encoding spatial information into the feature space.

In this paper, maximum feature mapping (MFM) is introduced into full convolution neural network (FCN) to form a new architecture of neural network: M-FCN.

4 Implement Details

We set hyper-parameters following existing FCN work. Although these decisions were made for semantic segmentation in original papers [12], we found our road detection system is robust to them.

Fine-tuning is a very common procedure in the neural network literature. The idea is to adapt an existing pretrained model to a different domain by executing a few training iterations on a new data set. The notion of fine-tuning is based on the intuition that low-level information/features can be reused in different applications, without training from scratch. Even when the final classification objective is different, it is also a relevant approach for initializing the learnable parameters close to good local minima, instead of initializing with random weights. After proper fine-tuning, low-level features tend to be quite preserved from one data set to another, while the higher layers' parameters are updated to adapt the network to the new problem.

We now incorporate the idea of neural network fine-tuning, in order to perform training on our data. We train on a GPU (mini-batch size is 16) for 240k iteration, with a learning rate which is decreased by 0.1 every 50k iteration. We use a weight decay of 0.0001 and a momentum of 0.9.

4.1 M-FCN

Similar to FCN, our M-FCN architecture follows the generic encoder-decoder paradigm, as illustrated in Fig. 2. In the figure, the encoder and decoder parts are delimited by continuous and dashed rectangular boxes, respectively. Novel components are brought in the network design. Inspired by the face recognition technology, we propose a network that features (i) using MFM instead of ReLU as activation function and (ii) forwarding information from the encoding layers directly to decoding ones by skip connections.

We implemented the CNNs using the Caffe deep learning framework [13]. The network starts with the input layer, which is responsible for reading the three-channel remote sensing images of the training set and cutting the input remote sensing images randomly into 256×256 sizes for training. After dimension reduction by downsampling, the hidden layer of the neural network is entered, which is shown as UnitModule layer,

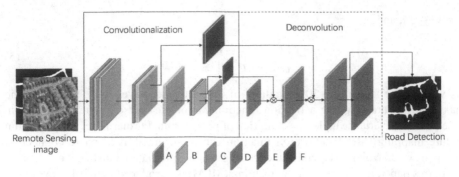

Fig. 2. The proposed Maximum-feature-mapping fully convolution network (M-FCN) architecture. A is convolutional layer; B is the MFM layer; C is the max pooling layer; D is the Deconvolution layer, E is the loss layer. F is the residuals modules.

which includes convolution layer, pooling layer and MFM layer. Among them, 64 kernels are set in the convolution layer, the size is 5×5, the stride is 2, and the zero-filling expansion is adopted in 2. The maximum pooling method is adopted in the pooling layer, the kernel size is set to 2×2, and the stride is 2. The input layer corresponding to the MFM layer is the output of the convolution layer, and the characteristics processed by the MFM layer are used as the input of the pooling layer. After several hidden layers, the training features are input into the deconvolution layer, and then the deconvolution layer is processed into the final input layer, loss layer, which is used to classify the target and background in a two-class way, thus forming the final training model.

In the decoding part, the layer serve as the transposed convolutional layer, with the same up-sampling factor of two. After the first and second up-sampling, data directly forwarded from the encoding part are concatenated with the outputs of the transposed convolutional layers. Finally, loss layer, which is a weighted softmax layer, is used in the training phase of the network. M-FCN has the following advantages:

1. The size of the input image of the full convolution network is not limited;
2. After one convolution, the features of multiple regions can be obtained, which can avoid the problem of repeatedly calculating convolution by introducing convolution neural network into the sub-region, and make the training network more efficient.
3. The deconvolution layer used in full convolution network eliminates the discontinuity caused by block boundary when full connection layer was used before.
4. Compared to the Patch-based network, our network uses fewer parameters to make the model more efficient.

4.2 Composite Loss Function

As the loss function we used a weighted sum of the binary cross-entropy BCE combined with the Lovasz-Softmax loss (also known as over union). By observing our predicted results and labels, this loss was inspired by [14] which proposed an special loss for IoU. It can be defined as following:

$$J(A, B) = \frac{|A \cap B|}{|A \cup B|} = \frac{|A \cap B|}{|A| + |B| - A \cap B} \tag{6}$$

$$J = \frac{1}{n} \sum_{c=1}^{2} w_c \sum_{i=1}^{n} \left(\frac{y_i^c \widehat{y_i^c}}{y_i^c + \widehat{y_i^c} - y_i^c \widehat{y_i^c}} \right) \tag{7}$$

Where y_i^c is the binary values (label) and corresponding predicted probability for the pixel I of the class c.

The final loss function contains H (the binary cross-entropy) and J (Lovasz-Softmax) as following:

$$L = \alpha H + (1 - \alpha)(1 - J) \tag{8}$$

Based on validation, we chose the optimal values of loss parameters: $\alpha = 0.7$. By minimizing this loss function, we found that the accuracy of IoU has increased.

5 Experimental Results

We carried out extensive experiments to assess the effectiveness of our proposed M-FCN architecture. We employed three Remote Sensing Image datasets. The three datasets are CasNet, Massachusetts Roads Dataset and Aerial Image Dataset, which are published by Cheng et al. [15], Mnih [8] and Maggiori [16]. In this section, we describe our experimental settings and report quantitative and qualitative results. We evaluate the benefits of each of the components in our proposed method and compare our results to those of the SVM, Patch-based and FCN networks.

5.1 Datasets

Training CNNs requires lots of data. Manih's dataset (MRD) uses computer technology to form corresponding road labels, but there are some deviations in the accuracy of these road labels, because the labels formed by computer technology can't guarantee the complete road identification and label. Arial Image Dataset corresponds to labels about houses, but in order to have more data for training, in this paper, the road in the data set is labeled in the form of manual labels. It takes about a month to label the Aerial Image Dataset manually. The road and background are successfully divided into corresponding road labels (Fig. 3).

One of the characteristics of CasNet data set is that the size of images in the data set is inconsistent, and the size is about 1000×1000, consisting of 224 images, but the input of M-FCN does not need a fixed size. All the images in Massachusetts Roads Dataset (MRD) are fixed at 1500×1500 in size, consisting of 2342 images, belongs to the large-scale remote sensing input image. In Manual Aerial Image Dataset (MAID), the size of the image is fixed at 5000×5000, consisting of 360 images, which belongs to the super large-scale remote sensing image.

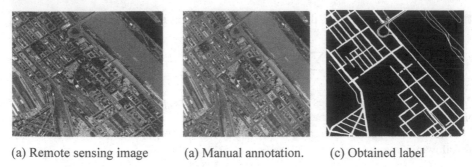

(a) Remote sensing image   (a) Manual annotation.   (c) Obtained label

Fig. 3. We label roads in remote sensing images by a drawing tool. Then we use Matlab to generate corresponding road labels.

5.2 Result Contrast

The reason for comparing the experimental results of three datasets is that we want to verify that the accuracy of labeling data sets will have an impact on the results of road detection. We used 80% of the images in three datasets for training, 10% for validation, and 10% for testing. We trained M-FCN for about 6 days, got three different caffe models, and tested them in the corresponding testset.

The experimental results show that in CasNet and MAID, for different width roads, the corresponding label positions will show different width sizes. Different road data labels reflect the width and narrowness, which enables the convolutional network framework to better learn road features without losing some important features. Because there are many road edge features in learning, their test samples can predict most of the roads. Because the resolution of CasNet is relatively small, all of them are within 1000×1000, so using computer to generate corresponding labels and then adjust them manually can restore the image labels fairly well. In MAID, the resolution of each remote sensing image is 5000×5000. For large remote sensing images, the labels generated by machine will have large deviation. Therefore, in order to get more accurate labels, the paper labels the road manually. The marked roads include highways, viaducts, country roads and other roads that may be seen. In MRD, the resolution of each remote sensing image is 5000×5000. The road of each remote sensing image has been marked, but for the dataset, no matter how wide the road is, it is marked with the same width in the corresponding label. Therefore, when learning the corresponding road features, convolution network will lose a large part of the edge information, making the results unsatisfactory.

In order to display this error more intuitively, we use three colors to mark the results, as shown in Fig. 4. Through comparison, we can find that most data of CasNet and MAID in the comparison result images show the red part, while the green part (road but not predicted) and the blue part (not road but misidentified road) account for a relatively small proportion. For MRD, the most frequently displayed color is green, because the accuracy of labels is not high enough, which leads to that the model trained by the dataset can't predict the continuous path well and the location is biased.

That's why we label manually to improve accuracy. Finally, we use CasNet and MAID as the training datasets of M-FCN.

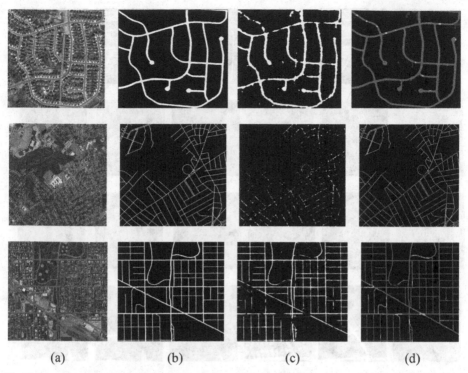

(a)   (b)   (c)   (d)

Fig. 4. Red means that the label matches the predicted results. Green means unpredictable roads. Blue indicates that the prediction is wrong. (a) Input images. (b) Label. (c) Output results. (d) Comparison results (Color figure online)

5.3 Comparing Algorithms

To verify the performance, the proposed M-FCN is compared with other methods in two aspects: IoU and ACC.

(1) *SVM:* Shi et al. [17] use Support Vector Machine to fuse the spectral-spatial features and homogenous properties to obtain the road detection result.
(2) *Patch-based Network:* To perform road detection of aerial imagery, Mnih [8] proposed a patch-based CNN. We used his method as our comparative experiment.
(3) *FCN:* Long et al. [12] proposed FCN for the semantic segmentation. In our experiments, we modified the architecture of FCN with much feature maps and much convolution layers.
(4) *M-FCN:* Based on the FCN, extends FCN by using a new activation function instead of the traditional activation function. At the same time, we provide a new composite loss function to train the network.

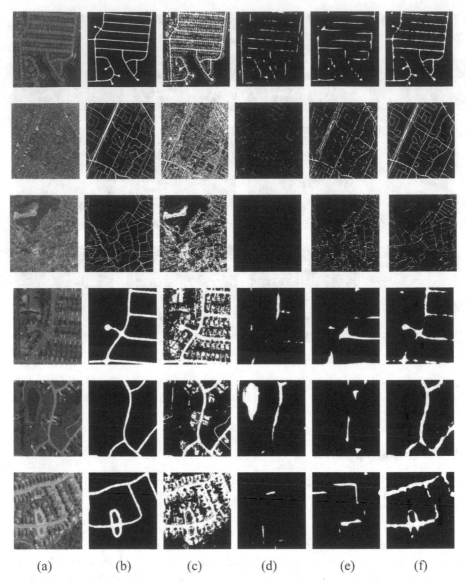

(a)   (b)   (c)   (d)   (e)   (f)

Fig. 5. Classified fragments of the predicted test images. (a) Color image. (b) Label (c) SVM. (d) Patch-based network. (e) FCN. (f) M-FCN

5.4 Main Results

We compare M-FCN with several methods described in detail above. Full tile prediction results from different networks are depicted in Fig. 5. The test pictures displayed are of different sizes.

From the experimental results we can see that SVM can't separate the house from the road, and the prediction results will show the house and the road together. This is because the color of roads and houses in remote sensing images is very similar. SVM can't be used to train and predict them well, so the road and houses can be predicted together. We now point out some limitations of the patch-based approach. In the process of training, the patch is sampled from the training set. The size of each patch is 64×64, and the corresponding label size is 16×16. The center pixel is used to predict the surrounding area. Through comparative analysis, whether the block belongs to road or background is obtained. This means that the fully connected layer doesn't only compute the classification scores, but also learns how to upsample them. Outputting a full-resolution patch is then the result of upsampling and not of an intrinsic high-resolution processing. For example, as shown in Fig. 5, a large white area is likely to appear, which is not the right road area. Compared with the patch-based convolution neural network, the prediction results of the traditional full convolution neural network (FCN) are better. For small-scale remote sensing images, the location of roads can be better predicted, and not too many parts that are not roads can be predicted. For large-scale remote sensing images, FCN can also predict the roads very well, but there may be a lot of road make-and-break, which is not well coherent. Without bells and whistles, M-FCN shows the best results.

Whether for small-scale remote sensing images or large-scale remote sensing images, compared with other algorithms, our method can better predict the location of roads by the naked eye, and the predicted road coherence is better among the other algorithms (Tables 1 and 2).

Table 1. IoU and ACC of Prediction Results of different Algorithms on CasNet.

	SVM	Patch-based	FCN	FCN+MF	FCN+MF+CLoss
IoU	0.210521	0.378275	0.464929	0.552423	0.600996
ACC	0.5992	0.9214	0.9242	0.9322	0.9381

Table 2. IoU and ACC of Prediction Results of different Algorithms on MAID.

	SVM	Patch-based	FCN	FCN+MF	FCN+MF+CLoss
IoU	0.175852	0.036527	0.363183	0.454234	0.507785
ACC	0.6298	0.8784	0.9162	0.9323	0.9418

6 Conclusion

We introduce M-FCN, a unified model for road detection in remote sensing images. Our model is simple to construct and can be trained directly on full images. Unlike patch-based approaches and fully convolution network (FCN), M-FCN can extract image features better without losing most edge information. At the same time, we propose a new composite loss function to improve IoU. We also use manual label to form our own new remote sensing road image dataset-MAID, to solve the problem of insufficient remote sensing road label dataset.

References

1. Bonnefon, R., Dhérété, P., Desachy, J.: Geographic information system updating using remote sensing images. Pattern Recogn. Lett. **23**(9), 1073–1083 (2002)
2. Sun, W., Yang, G., Wu, K., et al.: Pure endmember extraction using robust kernel archetypoid analysis for hyperspectral imagery. ISPRS J. Photogramm. Remote Sens. **131**, 147–159 (2017)
3. Du, B., Zhang, M., Zhang, L., et al.: Patch-based low-rank tensor decomposition for hyperspectral images. IEEE Trans. Multimed. **19**(1), 67–79 (2017)
4. Li, X., Chen, G., Liu, X., et al.: A new global land-use and land-cover change product at a 1-km resolution for 2010 to 2100 based on human-environment interactions. Ann. Am. Assoc. Geogr. **107**, 1040–1059 (2017)
5. Tupin, F., Houshmand, B., Datcu, M.: Road detection in dense urban areas using SAR imagery and the usefulness of multiple views. IEEE Trans. Geosci. Remote Sens. **40**(11), 2405–2414 (2002)
6. Udomhunsakul, S.: Semi-automatic road detection from satellite imagery. In: International Conference on Image Processing, pp. 1723–1726. IEEE (2004)
7. Dahl, J.V., Koch, K.C., Kleinhans, E., et al.: Convolutional networks and applications in vision. In: IEEE International Symposium on Circuits and Systems, pp. 253–256. IEEE (2010)
8. Mnih, V.: Machine learning for aerial image labeling. Ph.D. dissertation, University of Toronto (2013)
9. Sermanet, P., Eigen, D., Zhang, X., Mathieu, M., Fergus, R., LeCun, Y.: Overfeat: integrated recognition, localization and detection using convolutional networks. In: Proceedings of the International Conference on Learning Representations (ICLR), Banff, AB, Canada, pp. 14–16 (2014)
10. Kampffmeyer, M., Salberg, A.B., Jenssen, R.: Semantic segmentation of small objects and modeling of uncertainty in urban remote sensing images using deep convolutional neural networks. In: Proceedings of the IEEE Conference on Computer Vision and Pattern Recognition Workshops (CVPRW), Las Vegas, NV, USA, pp. 1–9 (2016)
11. Huang, L., Yang, Y., Deng, Y., et al.: DenseBox: unifying landmark localization with end to end object detection. Computer Science (2015)
12. Long, J., Shelhamer, E., Darrell, T.: Fully convolutional networks for semantic segmentation. IEEE Trans. Pattern Anal. Mach. Intell. **39**(4), 640–651 (2014)
13. Jia, Y., Shelhamer, E., et al.: Caffe: convolutional architecture for fast feature embedding (2014)
14. Iglovikov, V., Mushinskiy, S., Osin, V.: Satellite imagery feature detection using deep convolutional neural network: a Kaggle competition (2017)
15. Cheng, G., Wang, Y., Xu, S., et al.: Automatic road detection and centerline extraction via cascaded end-to-end convolutional neural network. IEEE Trans. Geosci. Remote Sens. **55**(6), 3322–3337 (2017)
16. Maggiori, E., Tarabalka, Y., Charpiat, G., et al.: Can semantic labeling methods generalize to any city? The Inria aerial image labeling benchmark. In: IEEE International Geoscience and Remote Sensing Symposium (IGARSS) (2017)
17. Shi, W., Miao, Z., Debayle, J.: An integrated method for urban main-road centerline extraction from optical remotely sensed imagery. IEEE Trans. Geosci. Remote Sens. **52**(6), 3359–3372 (2014)

Real-Time 3D Object Detection and Tracking in Monocular Images of Cluttered Environment

Guoguang Du$^{(\boxtimes)}$ ⓘ, Kai Wang ⓘ, Yibing Nan ⓘ, and Shiguo Lian ⓘ

CloudMinds Technologies, Beijing, China
`george.du@cloudminds.com`

Abstract. This paper presents a novel method for real-time 3D object detection and tracking in monocular images. The method build maps of a user-specified object from a video sequence, and stores the data for 3D object detection and tracking. The main advantage of the method lies in that it does not need existing 3D models of the objects. Instead, it first detects the target object using the state-of-the-art deep learning-based object detection method, and constructs its map using visual Simultaneous Localization and Mapping (vSLAM). The maps only need to be built once and multiple maps of different objects can be stored. A fast method is proposed to recognize the object in the map with the aid of deep learning-based detection. The method needs only one camera and is robust in cluttered environment. The mode of multiple maps allows the reuse of pre-reconstructed maps. Experimental results show that accurate, fast and robust detection and tracking are achieved.

Keywords: 3D object detection · 3D object tracking · Deep learning · SLAM

1 Introduction

3D object detection and tracking plays a pivotal role in many areas such as augmented reality, robotic manipulation, and autonomous driving, et al. Most of the current 3D object detection and tracking methods depend on the existence of 3D digital models [1]. Detection and tracking are implemented by matching local features such as feature points, contours, or normals between the current 2D image and the projected images of the 3D model. However, it is difficult to obtain the accurate textured 3D model or the CAD model of a 3D object with a monocular camera merely. Besides, traditional methods show limited capabilities in cluttered scenes especially. Therefore, it is essential to propose convenient and effective 3D object detection and tracking strategies.

This paper presents a novel method for 3D object detection and tracking in monocular images, which combines visual Simultaneous Localization and Mapping (vSLAM) and deep learning-based object detection. The method contains the 3D object reconstruction stage, the recognition and tracking stage. During

© Springer Nature Switzerland AG 2019
Y. Zhao et al. (Eds.): ICIG 2019, LNCS 11902, pp. 119–130, 2019.
https://doi.org/10.1007/978-3-030-34110-7_11

the first stage, only 3D feature points that are reconstructed from the target object areas are reserved with the help of deep learning-based object detection. The 3D object map does not contain the points of the environment, and will not bring interference to the tracking. During the second stage, candidate objects are first detected in the observed image to assist the recognition. The ambition of this paper is to put forward a method to interact with the 3D object effectively and quickly, which eliminates the need for an existing 3D model and improves the capabilities in cluttered environment. The deep learning-based detection is utilized to recognize and detect the object, which improves the robustness in cluttered environment. Besides, an effective and efficient outliers removal algorithm is proposed particularly for the maps reconstructed from vSLAM.

2   Related Work

Methods of 3D object detection and tracking can be roughly divided into two kinds according to whether needing existing 3D models or not.

Most of the current methods are conducted with the assist of existing 3D models. Multiple images are generated by projecting the existing 3D models in various angles, and these images are regarded as the templates. The problem is then transformed into comparing the current image and the templates. Lepetit et al. [1] presented a survey about monocular model-based 3D tracking methods of rigid objects. Prisacariu et al. [2] proposed a probabilistic framework for simultaneous region-based 2D segmentation and 2D to 3D pose tracking using a known 3D model. Hinterstoisser et al. [3] proposed a novel image representation based on spread image gradient orientations for template matching and represented a 3D object with a limited set of templates. Their method can be extended by taking 3D surface normal orientations into account if a dense depth sensor is available. With the development of deep learning, convolutional neural network-based methods are proposed. Crivellaro et al. [4] predicted the 3D pose of each part of the object in the form of the 2D projections of a few control points with the assist of a Convolutional Neural Network(CNN). The 6D pose can be calculated with an efficient PnP algorithm [5]. However, these algorithms need large amounts of data for training and are difficult to be extended.

Some works are conducted without the need of 3D models, whereas, they utilized the SLAM methods. Feng et al. [6] proposed an on-line object reconstruction and tracking system, which segments the object from the background, reconstructs and tracks the object using the visual simultaneous localization and mapping (SLAM) techniques. However, their method shows weak resistance to cluttered environments and the reconstruction error accumulates when dealing with the full object. Besides, Jason et al. [7] proposed a system that first scans the object and then start tracking. Whereas, their 3D scanning is based on the structured light principle. Compared with these methods, we propose to reconstruct the sparse points of the object ahead of detection and tracking, by utilizing the real-time SLAM system. Besides, in order to increase the resistance to cluttered environment, we utilize the deep learning-based object detection.

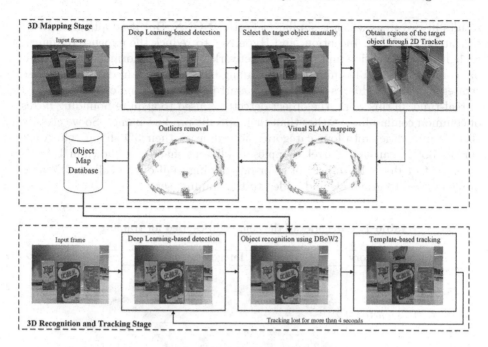

Fig. 1. Architecture of the proposed method.

3 Method

Overview of our method is illustrated in Fig. 1 and detailed processing steps are elaborated in two subsections, namely 3D object mapping, 3D object recognition and tracking.

3.1 3D Object Mapping

The object mapping stage consists three steps: 3D object detection, 3D object mapping and outliers removal. In the first step, the 2D bounding box of the target object is detected firstly in the observed frame. In the second step, the target object is mapped using vSLAM. In the third step, a novel filtering step is conducted to remove noisy points.

3D Object Detection. The 2D bounding box of the target object in the observed frame should be detected firstly, since we need to reconstruct the 3D map of the target object without the points of the environment.

A deep learning-based 3D object detection method is used to accomplish this task. The current deep learning-based detection network, such as Faster R-CNN [8], PVANET [9], show satisfactory results in object detection tasks. We select PVANET [9] as the algorithm to obtain the 2D bounding box of the object considering the tradeoff between speed and accuracy. PVANET predict results in two steps which is similar to Faster R-CNN. But it adopts modules of concatenated ReLU, Inception, and HyperNet to reduce the expense on multi-scale feature extraction and trains the network with batch normalization, residual connections, and learning rate scheduling based on plateau detection. These strategies make it achieves the state-of-the-art performance and can be processed in real-time. In this work, the object detector is used to acquire bounding boxes of common commodities rather than their specific product names. So we classify these commodities into four categories according to their 3D shape, which are carton, bottle, cans and barrel. Samples of different shapes are shown in Table 1. In order to reduce the impact of color on training, half of the collected images are converted to grayscale and added to the training set.

Table 1. Categories of the commodities used for training.

Since all regions of the potential objects are detected in the observed frame, the target object is manually selected. During the following frames, 2D tracking algorithms will be conducted to obtain regions of the target object consistently. Among the most 2D trackers, TLD [10] is selected for its high accuracy. Note that we enlarged each tracking results to 10%, which ensures that the target object lies in the detected region and improves the stability.

Visual SLAM-Based 3D Object Mapping. In order to conduct the object reconstruction in real-time, we utilize visual SLAM algorithms. Among the algorithms, we select ORB-SLAM [11] since it achieves more stable and accurate results. The input of ORB-SLAM is a video stream. During mapping, the object is kept stable on a desk. ORB-SLAM finds two frames to initialize and computes the initial map through the matched ORB features automatically. During mapping, the poses of the camera with respect to the object are estimated, new keyframes are added, and new 3D points are added into the map. Meanwhile, the object region is tracked through the 2D tracker, and the bounding boxes are stored for each keyframe of ORB-SLAM. After scanning the object for a round, the 3D points of the map that are mapped from the bounding boxes region of the object will be segmented from the original map, as shown in Fig. 2(b).

Outliers Removal. Since we use detection rather than segmentation, noisy points are be brought in. The use of detection is quite fast than segmentation. Besides, the background improves the accuracy and robustness of pose estimation by providing more feature points. The bounding box region in Fig. 2(a) contains areas that belong to the background, and these areas are reconstructed into those green points in Fig. 2(b). Aiming at these noisy points, an outlier removal algorithm is proposed particularly for the map built by visual SLAM.

The algorithm of outliers removal is illustrated in Algorithm 1. The initial map is reconstructed by the first two keyframes, and the $z - axis$ is pointing to the center of the object. This information is utilized for the removal of outliers. Since there exist many outliers that are far away from the object, the resolution is computed in a subset of the map. Otherwise, the resolution will be too large for filtering. Since the object region could be quite sparse in some area, it is not suitable to remove outliers according to the point cloud density as well. S_I in Algorithm 1 is regarded as the final map of the target object, and stored into the object map database. Results of outliers removal are shown in Fig. 2(c).

Algorithm 1. Outliers removal for VSLAM maps

Input: The set of point cloud S with N_S points built by visual SLAM;
Output: The set of inliers S_I;
  1: Extract the start point p_s from S, with $p_s = \arg\min_{p_s} d(p_s, p_o) \& \theta(\overrightarrow{p_o p_s}, Z) < 5°$,
    where p_o represents the origin point and Z represents $z - axis$;
  2: Compute the subset S_p which is the nearest M points form p_s in S, where $M = 0.6 * N_S$;
  3: Compute the resolution r_p of S_p, which is the average point-to-point distance;
  4: Set $S_I = \{p_s\}$, set threshold as $T = 4 * r_p$, compute $p_i = \arg\min_{p_i} d(p_i, S_I)$, with
    $p_i \in S$, if $d(p_i, S_I) < T$, $S_I = S_I \cup \{p_i\}$. Compute p_i iteratively until $d(p_i, S_I) \geq T$;
  5: **return** S_I;

3.2   3D Object Recognition and Tracking

The 3D object recognition and tracking stage consists two steps: 3D object recognition and 3D object tracking. In the first step, the target object is recognized

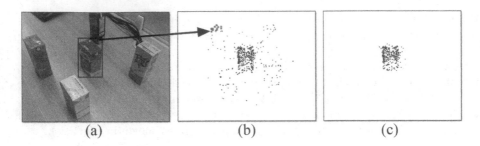

(a)   (b)   (c)

Fig. 2. The reconstructed maps. (a) One of the keyframes. (b) The segmented object points. Since the object area contains the background region, outliers are imported. (c) The results of outliers removal.

and the corresponding map is loaded for relocalization. In the second step, the target object is tracked using template-based methods.

3D Object Recognition. Meanwhile, we've already stored many maps about the commodities in the object map database. The object in the current frame should be recognized firstly, and the corresponding map is then loaded for relocalization and tracking.

In order to improve the recognition robustness in cluttered environment, candidate objects will be detected firstly using deep learning-based detection algorithm in Sect. 3.1, since background may bring extreme interference. Aiming at the candidate object regions, the target object will be recognized by comparing the current image and keyframes of the object maps in the object map database, as shown in Fig. 3.

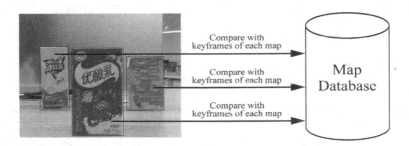

Fig. 3. Each candidate object region will compared with keyframes of each map.

We propose a fast method for comparing the current frame and keyframs which utilizes DBoW2 [12]. During the reconstruction of the object map, the DBoW2 features are extracted for all keyframes of each map. Firstly, the reverse order files, which contain the relationships between each word and the related keyframes, are extracted for each object map. Secondly, the DBoW2 words are extracted for the input frame. Thirdly, for keyframes of one object map, find the keyframe that has the largest number of similar words according to the reverse order files. Fourthly, traverse all maps and record the number of the similar words of the most similar keyframe. Finally, select the keyframe that have the most words, load the corresponding map and conduct relocalization. A successful relocalization illustrates a correct recognition. When the relocalization fails, another frame will be imported and conducted another recognition step.

3D Object Tracking. After a successful recognition, the map is loaded and an initial pose is achieved by relocalization. Template matching-based tracking method is adopted to conduct tracking.

The tracking follows the thread of the ORB-SLAM. Firstly, a new frame is acquired from the camera, and a prior pose is estimated according to a constant velocity motion model. Secondly, the reconstructed object map points are projected into the image according to the frame's prior pose estimation. Correspondences between the 2d feature points in the current frame and the projected 2D points are obtained by comparing ORB features. A local bundle adjustment is performed to optimize the camera pose. This motion-only BA optimizes the camera orientation $R \in SO(3)$ and position $t \in R^3$, minimizing the reprojection error between matched 3D points $X^i \in R^3$ in world coordinates and keypoints $x^i \in R^2$, with $i \in \chi$ the set of all matches, as is shown in Eq. 1.

$$\{R, t\} = \arg \min_{R,t} \sum_{i \in \chi} \rho(\left\|x^i - \pi(RX^i + t)\right\|^2) \tag{1}$$

where ρ is the robust Huber cost function and $\pi()$ is the projection function.

The poses of the camera w.r.t the target object are achieved since no environmental points exist in the 3D object map. In case the tracking is lost, and the relocalization fails for many times, the deep learning-based object detector is conduct to detect candidate objects. Then, the reverse order files are used to recognize the object in the input frame and conduct relocalization again. In our method, when the tracking is lost for four seconds, the object recognition will be conducted until the success of relocalization.

4   Experiments

In this section, we evaluated the accuracy and robustness of the proposed method, and made comparisons and discussions. The experiments are conducted on a PC with an Inter(R) Core(TM) i5-4460 processor (3.2 GHz), a NVIDIA GeForce GTX 1080 graphics card and a calibrated Logitech Pro C920 (640×480) webcam. The proposed method achieves real-time performance.

4.1   Accuracy

3D Object Detection. In this section, we evaluate the accuracy of the detection for commodities in daily environment.

We captured and labeled more than 2.1 million bounding boxes for 75 kinds of commodities. These categories cover different colors, shapes, and textures of commodities that are common in daily life. One tenth of the dataset is regarded as the test set. We classified these goods into 4 categories described in Sect. 3.1 during the training process. The detection accuracy is evaluated by Intersection over Union (IoU) score. Average Precision (AP) in each single category and mean Average Precision (mAP) across all the 4 categories are exhibited in Table 2 and some detection results of different kinds of commodities are shown in Fig. 4.

Table 2. Accuracies of the 4 categories.

	carton	bottle	cans	barrel	average
mAP	93.6	81.93	93.59	93.83	90.74

Fig. 4. The detected commodities in the images. Each commodity is detected with a high confidence.

3D Object Mapping. In this section, we evaluated the accuracy of the mapping on four commodities, which have different textures and different geometries. Two factors are evaluated which are the accuracy of the 2D tracking during reconstruction and the accuracy of the reconstructed 3D object map.

For the accuracy of 2D tracking, we calculate the average IoU score on keyframes of the map. During the reconstruction, we stored the images of keyframes, and recorded 2D tracking results for the target object. We manually selected bounding boxes of the target object to obtain the Ground Truth.

The average IoU score for each kind of commodity is shown in Table 3. And we can see that accurate tracking results are achieved.

For the accuracy of the reconstructed 3D object map, two metrics are adopted which are the repetition ratio L_r and the reference error ratio δ_r. Let the reconstructed 3D object map be M_R. We manually segment the object of the keyframes, and extract the 3D points that are reconstructed from these object regions. These 3D points are regarded as the Ground Truth 3D object map M_G. Let N_L represents the repetitive number of points between M_R and M_G, the repetition ratio L_r is measured as the ratio between N_L and N_R, where N_R represents the number of points in the reconstructed map. The reference error ε_r represents the average Euclidean distance between each point on M_R and its nearest point on M_G, as is shown in Eq. 2. The reference error ratio δ_r is measured as a percentage of the diameter of M_G. The distances between the reconstructed map and the Ground Truth map of two commodities is shown in Fig. 5, from which we can see that most points in the reconstructed map belong to the Ground Truth map. The results of L_r and δ_r for four commodities are illustrated in Table 3. From the table, we can see that accurate results are achieved.

$$\varepsilon_r = \sum_{p_r \in M_R} \arg\min_{p_r} d(p_r, M_G)/N_R \qquad (2)$$

Fig. 5. The distances between the reconstructed map and the Ground Truth map.

Table 3. Accuracies of the tracking results and the reconstructed map.

Category	IoU	L_r	δ_r
o1	0.79	94.2%	1.2%
o2	0.82	90.6%	2.1%
o3	0.85	95.7%	1.4%
o4	0.87	92.3%	2.3%

3D Object Tracking. In this section, we evaluate the accuracy of our tracking system by conducting experiments similar to the one in Ref. [13]. A drink box, whose map has been reconstructed, is moved on a planar desk, and the trajectory

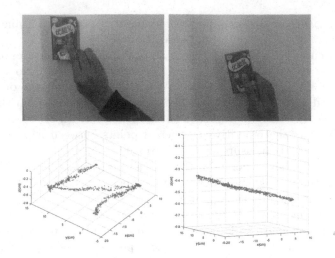

Fig. 6. Estimated trajectories of the centroid of the target box.

of the box is estimated by our system. The estimated trajectory of the centroid of the target box is shown in Fig. 6. We can see that our system does retrieve a trajectory approximately lying on a plane.

4.2 Robustness

In this section, we evaluated the robustness of our tracking system. The tracking is stable when at least 15 pairs of matched feature points are detected in the current frame. In order to shown the tracking results vividly, we designed an augmented reality system, in which a virtual toy is attached with the target object according to the poses achieved from our system. The criteria we use contain robust to scale change, small visible regions, different angles, dynamic background, fast motion and partial occlusion. From the Fig. 7, we conclude that our tracking system have a strong capabilities in resistance to these situations.

4.3 Comparisons and Discussions

In this section, we compared our algorithm with existing methods. The largest advantage of our system lies in that we do not need the 3D model of the target object, which extends the range of objects that can be augmented. Whereas, most of current methods [2,3] need existing 3D models. The work that is most similar with us is Feng et al. [6]. Compared with them, our method is more versatile and allows the reuse of 3D maps. Besides, the reconstruction of the target object utilized the ORB-SLAM, which involves the loop closure detection, and the maps built are more precise. What's more, our method supports multiple objects, as long as the 3D maps are reconstructed.

Fig. 7. Robustness on different situations: scale, dynamic environment, different angles and small visible regions.

There exist situations when our reconstruction fails. Since ORB-SLAM relies on the feature points for finding correspondences, our algorithms can not handle commodities without texture or with high reflection. This is the case where current feature point-based methods all face difficulties.

5   Conclusions

Most of the current 3d object detection and tracking methods require existing 3D models as a prior condition. However, this limits the creativity of individuals. In this paper, we present a method for 3D object detection and tracking without the need for existing 3D models. Instead, we reconstruct the coarse models in advance and then conduct the recognition and tracking. Our method combines deep learning-based 2D object detection, visual SLAM and template-based object tracking together. Users can "scan" the object firstly and then track it. The deep learning-based detection framework can handle objects in cluttered environment and can handle multiple objects. Our method has been verified on commodities and illustrated satisfactory results.

References

1. Lepetit, V., Fua, P., et al.: Monocular modelbased 3D tracking of rigid objects: a survey. Found. Trends Comput. Graph. Vis. **1**(1), 1–89 (2005)
2. Prisacariu, V.A., Reid, I.D.: PWP3D: real-time segmentation and tracking of 3D objects. IJCV **98**(3), 335–354 (2012)
3. Hinterstoisser, S., et al.: Gradient response maps for real-time detection of textureless objects. TPAMI **34**(5), 876–888 (2012)
4. Crivellaro, A., Rad, M., Verdie, Y., Yi, K.M., Fua, P., Lepetit, V.: Robust 3D object tracking from monocular images using stable parts. TPAMI **40**, 1465–1479 (2018)

5. Lepetit, V., Moreno-Noguer, F., Fua, P.: EPnP: an accurate O(n) solution to the PnP problem. IJCV **81**(2), 155–166 (2009)
6. Feng, Y., Wu, Y., Fan, L.: On-line object reconstruction and tracking for 3D interaction. In: International Proceedings on International Conference on Multimedia and Expo, pp. 711–716. IEEE, Melbourne (2012)
7. Rambach, J., Pagani, A., Schneider, M., Artemenko, O., Stricker, D.: 6DoF object tracking based on 3D scans for augmented reality remote live support. Computers **7**(1), 6 (2018)
8. Ren, S., He, K., Girshick, R., Sun, J.: Faster R-CNN: towards real-time object detection with region proposal networks. TPAMI **6**, 1137–1149 (2017)
9. Kim, K.-H., Hong, S., Roh, B., Cheon, Y., Park, M.: PVANET: deep but lightweight neural networks for real-time object detection. arXiv preprint arXiv:1608.08021 (2016)
10. Kalal, Z., Mikolajczyk, K., Matas, J., et al.: Tracking-learning-detection. TPAMI **34**(7), 1409–1422 (2012)
11. Mur-Artal, R., Montiel, J.M.M., Tardos, J.D.: ORB-SLAM: a versatile and accurate monocular SLAM system. Trans. Rob. **31**(5), 1147–1163 (2015)
12. Gálvez-López, D., Tardos, J.D.: Bags of binary words for fast place recognition in image sequences. Trans. Rob. **28**(5), 1188–1197 (2012)
13. Park, Y., Lepetit, V., Woo, W.: Multiple 3D object tracking for augmented reality. In: 7th International Proceedings on IEEE and ACM International Symposium on Mixed and Augmented Reality in ISMAR, pp. 117–120. IEEE Computer Society, Cambridge (2008)

Embedding Rotate-and-Scale Net for Learning Invariant Features of Simple Images

Zihang He[2(✉)], Xiang Ye[1]⑩, Zuguo He[2], and Yong Li[1]⑩

[1] School of Electronic Engineering, Beijing University of Posts and Telecommunications, Beijing, People's Republic of China
[2] School of Science, Beijing University of Posts and Telecommunications, Beijing, People's Republic of China
zhe@bupt.edu.cn

Abstract. Learning invariant features is important to computer vision tasks such as image classification or object detection. Rotation and scaling may dampen the classification/detection performance regardless of how deep nets are because most objects in image datasets are upright and have a suitable size. Existing methods often implicitly employ the data augmentation strategy to accomplish a better recognition performance. The problem with the data augmentation strategy is that it significantly increases the computational complexity and the training time. To address this problem, we propose Rotate-and-Scale Net (RSN) to be easily embedded in convolutional neural networks, making them invariant to rotation and scaling. The key insight of RSN is to mimic the recognition mechanism of human beings through parallel Siamese networks. It does not require data augmentation strategy hence have the advantages of having fewer parameters and needing fewer samples. We have validated the proposed method on three datasets including MNIST, MNIST-12k, MNIST-scaled and MNIST-rand datasets. Experiment results show that RSN compares favourably to the state-of-the-art in classifying/recognising rotated and scaled images in some way.

Keywords: Convolutional neural network · Deep learning · Invariant features

1 Introduction

Though convolutional neural networks have evolved many times, invariance is still an existing subject in computer vision tasks that have been studied for years. Classical hand-crafted features including Weber's Law descriptor [4], Gabor features [7,9], HOG [6], SIFT [17], and LBP [1,19] are designed for different tasks to encode orientation and size information. Although they all have invariance,

Thanks to the Fund for Beijing University of Posts and Telecommunications (Grants No. 2013XD-04, 2015XD-02), Fund for the Beijing Municipal Natural Science Foundation (No. 4172024), and Fund for Beijing Key Laboratory of Work Safety and Intelligent Monitoring.

© Springer Nature Switzerland AG 2019
Y. Zhao et al. (Eds.): ICIG 2019, LNCS 11902, pp. 131–142, 2019.
https://doi.org/10.1007/978-3-030-34110-7_12

classical hand-crafted ways usually can not extract enough features from images for recognition. Recently, the success of AlexNet [12] proved the effectiveness of CNN which can extract countless features that are more abstract for many fields and have good properties such as translation invariance. However, the lack of rotation and scale invariant features still limit its applications.

In order to recognize rotated and scaled simples, data augmentation, e.g., rotating each training sample into multi-oriented versions, is often implemented into CNN. The CNN trained by learning-by-rote strategy just learns the appearance of the augmented data. Although it improves the performance by extending the training set, data augmentation has the disadvantages of increasing computational complexity, lengthening training time, and introducing image noise. The increase of samples leads to the difficulty of training while the decrease of samples leads to the fall of accuracy, in other words, leads to a larger chance of underfitting or overfitting [13].

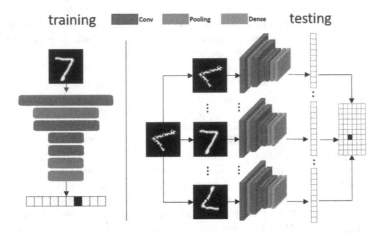

Fig. 1. The comparison of RSN and data augmentation. In the method of Data augmentation, CNN is trained by lots of augmented data and can recognize the test sample if a similar augmented sample is trained. RSN can recognize images rotated by different angles without augmenting the train dataset. The forth part is the structure of RSN, the fed image is rotated by different angles to ensure that at least one rotated version is close to a certain training sample.

Unlike data augmentation, other methods are proposed to gain networks the ability to learn rotation and scale invariant features. Jaderberg *et al.* [11] proposed STN (Spatial transformer networks) to use a learnable matrix to make the image upright before extracting features. Although it owns a complete theory, our experiment found out that it is only suitable for small angle rotation, e.g., less than 45°. Laptev *et al.* [13] employed parallel siamese networks and input different transformations to train a TI-Pooling (Transformation-invariant) layer to tackle vary images. But it needed augmented training datasets and would even cause side-effect if only given original datasets. Zhou *et al.* [24] proposed a new method named ORN (Oriented Response Networks) that can work entirely without data augmentation and learn rotation invariant features. So the same with [22] proposed by Su *et al.* It gains the deep neural networks the ability to identify images rotated by any degree once it is well trained to correctly recognize the samples without rotation. This is realized by rotating convolutional kernels at different angles evenly arrange 360°. Plural refitted kernels filter out the right orientation by enhancement and suppression. Other methods such as SWN [3] and H-Net [23] will not be introduced here.

ORN [24] realized this rotation invariance, but human beings seem to recognize rotated objects differently. People typically rotate a not upright image to canonical pose instead of rotating our heads. The way that ORN takes is to rotate its head to a particular angle so that rightly correspond to the given image.

In this work, we designed a method, dubbed RSN, by mimicking human beings when they look at and understand image content. It utilizes geometric knowledge to reasonably designing the transformation by siamese networks [2] in the testing phase as shown in Fig. 1,

The three main contributions of this work are summarized as follows:

– The proposed RSN can effectively empower CNNs to learn invariant feature representations to both rotation and scale without the need of data augmentation.
– RSN can be readily embedded into existing models with CNNs as backbone networks with a negligible increase of parameter.
– RSN yields a stronger ability to represent invariant features and hence outperforms other transformation invariant methods when embedded in existing models for the classification task on randomly rotated and scaled images.

When models are trained on MNIST training dataset [16] and tested on three datasets including MNIST-rot dataset [14], MNIST-scale dataset and MNIST-rand dataset, RSN outperformed STN [17], MobileNetV2 [20] and VGG-16 [21], had advantages over each other when compared with ORN.

2   The Proposed Approach

The insufficient ability to learn rotation and scaling invariant features limits the performance of deep neural networks in the task of recognizing/classifying objects. To enhance the ability of deep neural networks dealing with transformed images, we proposed RSN. Invariances of RSN originate from the architecture of parallel siamese networks [2] that are shown in Fig. 1. It successfully enhances the recognition ability of CNNs based on the observation that the more similar the fed image samples appear to the training samples, the higher confidence the trained deep neural networks will output. Therefore, rotating (scaling) a test image by different angles (scales) can ensure that at least one rotated version appears close to a certain training sample. Theoretical validity on RSN and the steps of embedding it into existing architectures of CNNs will be discussed in Sect. 2.2.

2.1   Architecture

This section firstly analyzes the reason of performance decrease on rotated images for CNNs and the relationship between the confidence score of a test image and its visual affinity to training image samples. Then based upon the analysis RSN is proposed to alleviate the performance decrease of classifying rotated images with CNNs.

One reason that features extracted by CNNs are not invariant to rotations is that the learned kernel weights through training process explicitly or implicitly encodes the orientations of image samples and hence they will provide a better classification/detection performance on test images that have a similar orientation to the training samples, as shown in Fig. 2. This makes it difficult for CNNs to tackle many computer vision tasks including object boundary detection [8,18], multi-oriented object detection [5], and image classification [11,13].

To make CNNs more capable of addressing images subject to rotation and scaling, this work aims to look for an architecture that can well classify/recognize on rotated and scaled images while does not dramatically increase the computational complexity.

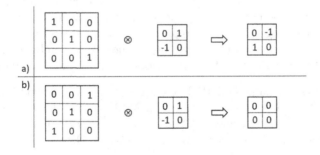

Fig. 2. What a fixed kernel extract from un-rotated and rotated images respectively. It extracts no information when the image is rotated by 90°.

We observed that the more similar the fed image samples appear to the training samples, the higher confidence the trained deep neural networks will output. This indicates that well-trained CNNs only make mistakes when the test image appears to be very close to another class. And therefore, the visual appearance similarity between a test image and its correct class of training images will have a significant effect on its classification accuracy. Based on this observation, a natural conclusion is that an unrotated image can be more likely classified correctly than the rotated image by a CNN model that is trained solely on unrotated samples. So transforming an image to a canonical pose or appearance will potentially boost the recognition accuracy. This work aims to extract the canonical features from any input image as if its canonical image were available. To this end, we proposed RSN to transform an image to cover all its possible poses and then reserve the canonical pose by the siamese structure.

To introduce the structure of RSN, we will firstly explain the difference between data augmentation and RSN. For data augmentation, CNN is trained by lots of augmented data which requires larger model size and more training time. As a comparison, RSN can recognize images rotated by different angles without the need for augmenting the training dataset as shown in Fig. 1. The architecture of RSN is composed of M siamese networks with inputs transformed by different rotations and/or scales. These transformations ought to cover a sufficiently wide range of rotation degrees and scaling factors such that these samples contain at least one canonical pose. Siamese networks output a $M \times N$ matrix, denoted by A and the i_{th} row of A is of dimension $1 \times N$ that stores the classification probability for every class by the i_{th} network. Then the $M \times N$ matrix A is max-pooled along the first dimension, i.e., finding the highest output score of all branches for each class, ending with a $1 \times N$ array $B = [b_j], 0 \leq j \leq n - 1$, where $b_j = \max_i a_{ij}$. Finally, the produced $1 \times N$ matrix will be used to identify by a softmax layer. The whole way is as follows:

$$A = [a_{ij}], \quad 0 \leq i \leq m - 1, 0 \leq j \leq n - 1$$
$$b_j = \max_i a_{ij}$$
$$B = [b_j], \quad 0 \leq j \leq n - 1 \tag{1}$$
$$C = \max_j b_j$$
$$def: \quad C = RMax(A)$$

At last, we defined the final output confidence to be $C = RMax(A)$.

2.2   Implementation Details

This section discusses the means of embedding the RSN module in CNNs to introduce rotation and scale invariant feature representation.

Designing the RSN structure follows two basic principles. The first is that RSN should be easily incorporated in any existing CNN architectures such as LeNet [15], MobileNetV2 [20], VGGNet [21], and ResNet [10]. The second is that RSN should gain them the ability to classify rotated and/or scaled images. According to the discussion in Sect. 2.1, one can opt for transforming images instead of kernels for the CNNs to robustly learn the rotation and scaling invariant features. The steps of empowering rotation invariance by the RSN are stated in what follows.

We first discuss the rotation invariance and then extend to both rotation and scaling invariance. Given a well trained deep model for the classification task, a test input image I is firstly rotated by N angles distributed uniformly in $[0, 2\pi]$ denoted by ω_i:

$$\omega_i = \frac{2\pi}{N} \cdot i \quad i \in \{0, \dots, N-1\} \tag{2}$$

and let I_i denote the image transformed by ω_i. Next, we duplicate the model N copies (here copied models mean siamese networks [2]), the ith branch is fed with I_i, shown as input rotated images in Fig. 3. For the Siamese architecture, every branch shares the same parameters with other branches and yields a list of M similarity scores, encoding the probability of a test input image belongs to different classes. Then the $M \times N$ matrix is max-pooled along the first dimension, i.e., finding the highest output score of all branches for each class, ending with a $1 \times N$ array. Finally, the produced $1 \times N$ matrix will be used to identify by a softmax layer.

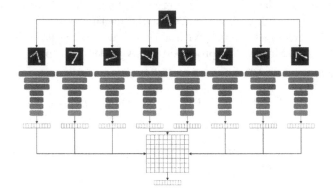

Fig. 3. The way of empowering RSN rotation invariance, whatever angle the start of first image be rotated at, there will always be one rotated to $0°$.

The whole architecture is shown in Fig. 3. Our experiment found that CNN trained by original MNIST training set can achieve 95% and 85% accuracy on the same dataset rotated by degrees fall in $[-\frac{\pi}{6}, \frac{\pi}{6}]$ and $[-\frac{\pi}{4}, \frac{\pi}{4}]$ respectively. Therefore to prove that the capability of being invariant to rotation can be introduced by RSN module, we only need to verify that at least one transformed version of an input image will fall in $[-\frac{\pi}{6}, \frac{\pi}{6}]$, i.e., appearing to be close to the canonical pose. Assume an input test image I needs to be rotated by α degrees to come to the canonical pose, for any arbitrary $\alpha \in [0, 2\pi]$, there always exists an integer $i \in [0, N-1]$ such that makes it as close as $[-\frac{\pi}{N}, \frac{\pi}{N}]$ to canonical pose's degree as follows:

$$|\alpha - \omega_i| \leq \frac{\pi}{N} \tag{3}$$

Since $\omega_i = \frac{2\pi}{N} \cdot i$, (3) holds if only there exists an integer $i \in [0, N-1]$ such that:

$$\frac{\pi}{N}(2i-1) \leq \alpha \leq \frac{\pi}{N}(2i+1) \tag{4}$$

But (4) is evident as $[\frac{\pi}{N}(2i-1), \frac{\pi}{N}(2i+1)] = [0, 2\pi]$.

Simply setting N to 6, we can obtain poses of some I_i lying in $[-\frac{\pi}{6}, \frac{\pi}{6}]$, so the recognition accuracy will be expected to 95%.

The scaling invariant feature representation is accomplished by a similar process to rotation invariance that is discussed in former paragraphs, but is fine tuned to: Given a well trained deep model for the classification task and a test image, the ratio of the area occupied by the symbol over that of the entire image S is firstly scaled by N distributed uniformly in $[\theta_1, \theta_2]$ denoted by ω_i:

$$\omega_i = \theta_1 + \frac{\theta_2 - \theta_1}{N} \cdot i \quad i \in \{0, \dots, N\} \tag{5}$$

and let S_i denote the transformed image by ω_i. The theory of rotation invariance can also be explained for scale invariance. How to resize test images is shown in Fig. 4.

$$\exists i \in \{0, \dots, N\} \quad s.t.$$

$$(\theta_1 + \omega_i)S - S_{ori} \leq \left| \frac{\theta_2 - \theta_1}{2 \times N} \right| \cdot S \tag{6}$$

Here S_{ori} represents the original ratio of the area occupied by the symbol over that of the entire image.

Fig. 4. The way of empowering RSN scale invariance, however the start of first image be scaled, there will always be one scaled to original size.

Relating these two invariances is also not difficult by increasing the number of siamese networks [2]. Every degree we designed can be companied with different sizes flexibly as shown in Fig. 5.

Fig. 5. The way of empowering RSN rotation and scale invariances, however the start of first image be scaled or rotated, there will always be one scaled and rotated to original size and degree. Rotated by 4° and scaled each degree to two sizes.

2.3   Computational Complexity

RSN increase the testing time roughly proportional to the number of siamese networks. However, RSN decrease the training time compared with data augmentation strategy for fewer training samples and fewer times of back propagation. Also, the parameters of models do not increase because of the parameters of Siamese networks are shared. Moreover, RSN can work with data augmentation to achieve better results which will be mentioned in the next section.

3   Experiment

This section evaluates RSN on three datasets, MNIST-rot [14], MNIST-scale, and MNIST-rand. MNIST-rot is generated by randomly rotating each sample in the MNIST dataset in $[0, 2\pi]$. We generated MNIST-scale by randomly scaling the ratio of the area occupied by the symbol over that of the entire image by a factor in $[0.5, 1]$, and generated MNIST-rand by scaling and rotating images in MNIST [16] simultaneously.

3.1   Rotation Invariance

RSN was embedded to a trained Baseline CNN to build a parallel siamese structure, and then compared the recognition performance with the baseline CNN, MobileNetV2 [20], VGG-16 [21], STN [11] and ORN [24]. Some performance of STN and ORN is from [24]. Specific configure of STN [11] and ORN [24] can also be found in their papers. TI-Pooling [13] is excluded from the comparison since it requires augmented data to well train its Ti-pooling layer.

To explain the constructed siamese structure, the first branch of it is discussed. Similar to the baseline 5-layer CNN network in STN [11], the branch starts with two convolutional layers that have channels of 40 and 80, and kernel size of 9×9 and 7×7 pixels, respectively. The next two layers are the 3×3 convolutional ones with 80 and 160 channels respectively. All the convolutional layers have 1-pixel stride, 1-pixel padding, and the rectified linearities (ReLU) following. The next one is a global average pooling layer which is followed by 10-D fully-collected layer and a softmax classifiers successively. Two 2×2 max-pooling operators with stride 2 follow the first and fourth layers respectively. Other branches have the same layers and share the weights with the first branch.

The experiment results are shown in Table 1. For original MNIST dataset, RSN performed worse than baseline CNN for introducing noises from multiple siamese networks. This truth revealed the trade-off between the stronger rotation invariance and extra noises brought by the numbers of siamese networks. For MNIST-rot dataset (training without augmentation), the baseline CNN achieves 44.1% accuracy with $0.33M$ parameters, MobileNetV2 achieves 43.4% accuracy with $43.4M$ parameters, and VGG-16 achieves 45.8% accuracy with $17.25M$ parameters. Since VGG-16 has $16.92M$ parameters more than the baseline CNN and its classification accuracy dose not outperform the baseline

Table 1. The second column describes the parameters of each model. Following columns describe the accuracy rates achieved on the original and rotated testing set (training without rotation). The last column describes the accuracy rates achieved on rotation testing set when trained by augmented training set.

Method	Params	Original%	O→rot%	A→rot%
Baseline CNN	0.33M	99.27	44.13	97.18
MobileNetV2	0.43M	99.04	43.48	97.45
VGG-16	17.25M	99.40	45.85	97.61
STN (affine)	13.35M	99.39	43.67	97.48
STN (rotation)	13.35M	99.34	44.41	97.12
ORN-4	2.12M	**99.43**	72.08	98.31
ORN-8	4.18M	99.34	**83.79**	**98.58**
RSN-3	0.33M	99.25	66.3	97.20
RSN-4	0.33M	99.21	74.3	97.54
RSN-5	0.33M	99.19	76.8	97.69
RSN-6	0.33M	99.23	78.3	97.83
RSN-8	0.33M	99.24	77.5	97.71

CNN, increasing CNN's parameters solely dose not enhance the invariance of networks to rotation. On the contrary, the baseline CNN embedded with RSN-4 (Input test images are rotated to 4 orientations) achieves 74.3% with $0.33M$ parameters, has advantages on both model size and performance compared with ORN-4 (ORAlign), 16.0% parameters and 1.7% accuracy increase. The baseline CNN embedded with RSN-6 (Input test images are rotated to 6 orientations), achieves 78.3% with $0.33M$ parameters, performed a little weaker than OSN-8, but only has 7.9% parameters. They both improve more than 30% accuracy with only 2.5% parameters over STN [11]. Since the baseline CNN embedded with RSN-8 (Input test images are rotated to 8 orientations) achieves 77.5% accuracy, continually increasing the number of orientations does not boost performance. For MNIST-rot dataset (training with augmentation), RSN-6 yielded 97.83% accuracy with $0.33M$ parameters, improved 0.65% and 0.35% accuracy over the baseline CNN and STN, respectively. Although RSN still performed worse than ORN, this results showed RSN can work with data augmentation together to get higher accuracy.

3.2 Scaling

On MNIST-scale, RSN-4 in Table 2 denotes we expanded the size of the input image by factors including 1, 1.3, 1.6, and 1.9 and then centre-cropped patches which have the same size as the input image from them to feed into siamese networks. Since VGG-16 achieves 93.2% accuracy, outperforming MobileNetV2 and the baseline CNN which give 91.0% accuracy and 89.0% accuracy respectively with the largest number of parameters, the invariance of networks to scaling increases with the increase of parameters. While RSN-4 achieves 97.4% accuracy, improving 4.2% accuracy over VGG-16 with only 1.9% parameters of the later. This indicates the strong invariance of RSN to scaling.

Table 2. Results on the MNIST-scale and MNIST-rand datasets. The second column describes the parameters of each model. The third column describes the accuracy rates achieved on the scale testing set (with random scaling) by models trained on the original training set (without scaling). The last column describes the accuracy rates achieved on the random testing set (with random scaling and rotation) by models trained on the original training set (without scaling).

Method	Params	O→scale(%)	O→rand(%)
Baseline CNN	0.33M	89.0	36.8
MobileNetV2	0.43M	91.0	33.0
VGG-16	17.25M	93.2	38.4
RSN-4	0.33M	**97.4**	**69.6**

On MNIST-rand, RSN-4 × 2 includes 4 orientations, 0, 90, 180, and 270°, each associated with two scaling factors, 1 and 1.3. It achieved 69.6% accuracy, outperforming the baseline CNN, MobileNetV2, and VGG-16 that gives 36.8%, 33.0%, and 38.4% accuracy, respectively.

4   Conclusion

In this paper, we proposed a simple and effective strategy which mimics human beings named Rotate-and-Scale Net (RSN). It can be embedded to any CNN model to make it invariant to rotation and/or scaling by way of rotating and/or scaling images to all poses first, then reserving the canonical pose for final classifying. On the one hand, CNNs embedded with RSN can recognize rotated and/or scaled images while only trained with canonical poses. On the other hand, RSN improves the performance of CNNs while trained with augmented data. RSN has advantages of negligible parameters increase, short training time, and flexible handling of transformation compared with STN and ORN. It performs considerably to state-of-the-art when tested on MNIST, MNIST-rot, MNIST-scale and MNIST-rand datasets.

References

1. Ahonen, T., Hadid, A., Pietikainen, M.: Face description with local binary patterns: application to face recognition. IEEE Trans. Pattern Anal. Mach. Intell. **28**(12), 2037–2041 (2006)

2. Bertinetto, L., Valmadre, J., Henriques, J.F., Vedaldi, A., Torr, P.H.S.: Fully-convolutional siamese networks for object tracking. In: Hua, G., Jégou, H. (eds.) ECCV 2016. LNCS, vol. 9914, pp. 850–865. Springer, Cham (2016). https://doi.org/10.1007/978-3-319-48881-3_56

3. Bruna, J., Mallat, S.: Invariant scattering convolution networks. IEEE Trans. Pattern Anal. Mach. Intell. **35**(8), 1872–1886 (2013)

4. Chen, J., et al.: WLD: a robust local image descriptor. IEEE Trans. Pattern Anal. Mach. Intell. **32**(9), 1705–1720 (2010)

5. Cheng, G., Zhou, P., Han, J.: RIFD-CNN: rotation-invariant and fisher discriminative convolutional neural networks for object detection. In: Computer Vision and Pattern Recognition, pp. 2884–2893 (2016)

6. Dalal, N., Triggs, B.: Histograms of oriented gradients for human detection. In: IEEE Computer Society Conference on Computer Vision and Pattern Recognition, pp. 886–893 (2005)

7. Haley, G.M., Manjunath, B.S.: Rotation-invariant texture classification using modified Gabor filters. In: Proceedings of International Conference on Image Processing, 1995, vol. 1, pp. 262–265 (1995)

8. Hallman, S., Fowlkes, C.C.: Oriented edge forests for boundary detection. In: Computer Vision and Pattern Recognition, pp. 1732–1740 (2015)

9. Han, J., Ma, K.K.: Rotation-invariant and scale-invariant Gabor features for texture image retrieval. Image Vis. Comput. **25**(9), 1474–1481 (2007)

10. He, K., Zhang, X., Ren, S., Sun, J.: Deep residual learning for image recognition, pp. 770–778 (2015)

11. Jaderberg, M., Simonyan, K., Zisserman, A., Kavukcuoglu, K.: Spatial transformer networks. In: IEEE Conference on Computer Vision and Pattern Recognition, pp. 2017–2025 (2015)

12. Krizhevsky, A., Sutskever, I., Hinton, G.E.: Imagenet classification with deep convolutional neural networks. In: International Conference on Neural Information Processing Systems, pp. 1097–1105 (2012)

13. Laptev, D., Savinov, N., Buhmann, J.M., Pollefeys, M.: TI-Pooling: transformation-invariant pooling for feature learning in convolutional neural networks. In: IEEE Conference on Computer Vision and Pattern Recognition, pp. 289–297 (2016)

14. Larochelle, H., Erhan, D., Courville, A., Bergstra, J., Bengio, Y.: An empirical evaluation of deep architectures on problems with many factors of variation. In: International Conference on Machine Learning, pp. 473–480 (2007)

15. Lecun, Y., Bottou, L., Bengio, Y., Haffner, P.: Gradient-based learning applied to document recognition. Proc. IEEE **86**(11), 2278–2324 (1998)

16. Liu, C.L., Nakashima, K., Sako, H., Fujisawa, H.: Handwritten digit recognition: benchmarking of state-of-the-art techniques. Pattern Recogn. **36**(10), 2271–2285 (2003)

17. Lowe, D.G.: Object recognition from local scale-invariant features. In: ICCV, p. 1150 (1999)

18. Maninis, K.-K., Pont-Tuset, J., Arbeláez, P., Van Gool, L.: Convolutional oriented boundaries. In: Leibe, B., Matas, J., Sebe, N., Welling, M. (eds.) ECCV 2016. LNCS, vol. 9905, pp. 580–596. Springer, Cham (2016). https://doi.org/10.1007/978-3-319-46448-0_35

19. Ojala, T., Pietikäinen, M., Mäenpää, T.: Multiresolution gray-scale and rotation invariant texture classification with local binary patterns. IEEE Trans. Pattern Anal. Mach. Intell. **24**(7), 971–987 (2002)

20. Sandler, M., Howard, A., Zhu, M., Zhmoginov, A., Chen, L.C.: MobileNetv2: inverted residuals and linear bottlenecks (2018)
21. Simonyan, K., Zisserman, A.: Very deep convolutional networks for large-scale image recognition. Comput. Sci. (2014)
22. Su, H., Maji, S., Kalogerakis, E.: Multi-view convolutional neural networks for 3D shape recognition (2015)
23. Worrall, D.E., Garbin, S.J., Turmukhambetov, D., Brostow, G.J.: Harmonic networks: deep translation and rotation equivariance. In: IEEE Conference on Computer Vision and Pattern Recognition, pp. 7168–7177 (2017)
24. Zhou, Y., Ye, Q., Qiu, Q., Jiao, J.: Oriented response networks. In: IEEE Conference on Computer Vision and Pattern Recognition, pp. 4961–4970 (2017)

Person Re-identification with Patch-Based Local Sparse Matching and Metric Learning

Bo Jiang[✉], Yibing Lv, Aihua Zheng, and Bin Luo

School of Computer Science and Technology, Anhui University, Hefei, China
{jiangbo,ahzheng214,luobin}@ahu.edu.cn, yibing95@foxmail.com

Abstract. Recently, patch based matching has been demonstrated effectively to address the spatial misalignment issue caused by camera-view changes or human pose variations in person re-identification (Re-ID) problem. In this paper, we propose a novel local sparse matching model to obtain a reliable patch-wise matching for Re-ID problem. In particular, in the training phase, we develop a robust Local Sparse Matching model to learn more precise corresponding relationship between patches of positive sample image pairs. In the testing phase, we adopt a local-global distance metric learning for Re-ID task by considering global and local information simultaneously. Extensive experiments on four benchmarks demonstrate the effectiveness of our approach.

Keywords: Person re-identification · Graph matching · Metric learning

1 Introduction

Person re-identification (Re-ID) is an active research problem in computer vision and visual surveillance. The aim of Re-ID is to identify a specific probe person image from a set of gallery images captured from cross-view cameras. Many existing methods [12, 15, 28, 30] generally first extract a kind of global feature representation for person images and then utilize some metric learning methods to conduct a holistic comparison between test images for Re-ID.

One main challenge for Re-ID is to deal with the misalignment issue between image pair caused by large variations in camera views or human poses. Obviously, traditional global-based methods generally ignore spatial misalignment. To alleviate this issue, one kind of popular ways is to use part (or patch) based metric learning methods [16, 20, 23, 29, 33, 36]. These methods generally first partition each person image into a set of local patches. Then, they aim to conduct online patch-wise matching to obtain the spatial correspondences between patches of different images. Finally, the computed patch-wise matching is combined with local patch features to generate a robust metric learning for person Re-ID. However, one main issue for this online patch-wise matching is that it may lead to some mismatching among patches due to (1) lacking spatial and visual context information among local patches and (2) existing similar patch appearances or occlusions.

To overcome this issue, recent works [16, 23, 36] propose to develop some matching learning strategies for Re-ID. These methods generally first obtain a kind of reliable patch-wise matchings between training images in the training phase. Then, these

© Springer Nature Switzerland AG 2019
Y. Zhao et al. (Eds.): ICIG 2019, LNCS 11902, pp. 143–154, 2019.
https://doi.org/10.1007/978-3-030-34110-7_13

learned matchings are utilized or transferred to guide the robust patch-wise matching between test images in the testing phase.

However, the graph matching methods they used generally do not explicitly consider the one-to-one matching constraint and the impact of outlier patches which may lead to inaccurate correspondence relationships. In this paper, we propose a novel patch graph matching model for Re-ID problem. The aim of the proposed matching model is that it can obtain a robust one-to-one matching solution for the patches of two images. In particular, in the training phase, we first use the proposed matching model to learn an optimal correspondence relationship between positive sample pairs. In the testing phase, we then select the former R pairs references by pose pairs similarity, and use their correspondence relationship for the new testing image pair. Finally, we adopt the local-global distance metric for Re-ID problem. Overall, this paper makes the following contributions.

- In order to reduce the impact of outliers and obtain robust patch-wise correspondence relationships, we propose a novel graph matching model to make the spatial misalignment problem better solved.
- We propose a novel person Re-ID approach by employing both visual context information and spatial correspondence relationship learning simultaneously to avoid the limitations caused by local information and misalignment issues.
- Experimental results demonstrate that the proposed Re-ID method outperforms the other state-of-the-art approaches, validating the effectiveness of the method.

2 Related Work

Here, we briefly review some related works that are devoted to spatial misalignment for person Re-ID. Oreifej et al. [20] propose to utilize Earth Movers Distance (EMD) to obtain the whole similarity based on similarities between extracted patches. However, it ignores the spatial context of patches which may lead to mismatching for the patches with similar appearance or occlusions. Cheng et al. [9] propose to alleviate the influence of misalignment based on body part detection. The effectiveness of this approach generally relies on the detection result of the body part, which may be less effective in presence of occlusion. Some recent works [2,17,33] also propose to explore saliency or body prior to guiding the patch-wise matching between image pair.

One main limitation for the above online matching is that it may lead to some mismatching among patches due to (1) lacking using spatial context information among patches and (2) similar patch appearances or occlusions. To alleviate this limitation, Zhou et al. [36] recently propose to use a graph matching technique to obtain the optimal correspondence between each image pair during the training phase. Then, it transfers the learned patch-wise correspondence directly to the test image pair based on pose-pair configuration. This approach generally relies on image-level matching results obtained in the training phase. Lin et al. [16,23] propose to learn a correspondence structure via a boosting based approach for each camera (pose) pair in the training phase. The learned correspondence structure is then utilized to guide the robust patch matching between test images. However, this method lacks considering spatial context information of patches in the matching process, which may be less effective in the presence of similar patch appearances.

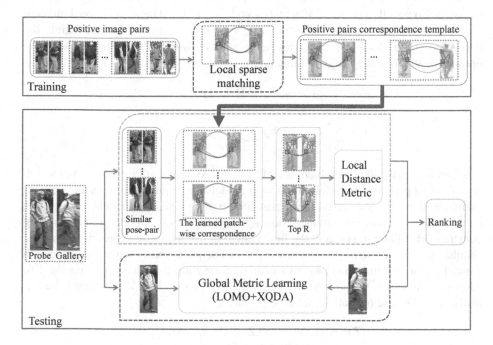

Fig. 1. Framework of the proposed approach

3   The Proposed Model

In this section, we propose our patch matching model, followed by an effective update algorithm to compute it. We present our complete Re-ID approach in Sect. 4.

3.1   Model Formulation

Given a positive image pair I and I', we first divide them into several overlapping patches $P = (p_1, p_2 \cdots p_n)$ and $P' = (p'_1, p'_2 \cdots p'_m)$, respectively. Then, we extract feature descriptor for each patch of the image. Our aim is to find the correspondence relationship between patches of two images. In order to do so, we construct an attributed relation graph $G = (V, E, A, R)$ for image I, where nodes V represent patches P and edges E denote the relationship among patches. Each node $v_i \in V$ has an associated attribute vector $\mathbf{a}_i \in A$ and each edge $e_{ih} \in E$ has a weight value $\mathbf{r}_{ih} \in R$. Similarly, we can construct a graph $G' = (V', E', A', R')$ for I'. Based on this graph representation, the above patch matching problem can be reformulated as finding the correspondences between nodes of two graphs. Let $\mathbf{Z} \in \{0, 1\}^{n \times m}$ denote the correspondence solution between two graphs, in which $\mathbf{Z}_{ij} = 1$ implies that node $v_i \in G$ corresponds to node $v_j' \in G'$, and $\mathbf{Z}_{ij} = 0$ otherwise. To obtain the optimal $\mathbf{Z}$, we define an affinity matrix $\mathbf{K}$. The diagonal term $\mathbf{K}_{ij,ij}$ of $\mathbf{K}$ represents the unary affinity $f_a(\mathbf{a}_i, \mathbf{a}_j)$ that measures how well node $v_i \in V$ matches node $v_j' \in V'$. The non-diagonal element $\mathbf{K}_{ij,hk}$ contains the pair-wise affinity $f_r(\mathbf{r}_{ih}, \mathbf{r}_{jk})$ that measures how compatible the nodes (v_i, v_h) in G are with the nodes (v_j', v_k') in G'. We can obtain the optimal $\mathbf{Z}$ by optimizing the following objective function,

$$\max_{\mathbf{Z}} \quad \mathcal{Q}_{IQP} = \text{vec}(\mathbf{Z})^T \mathbf{K} \, \text{vec}(\mathbf{Z}),$$

$$s.t. \forall i \sum_{j=1}^{n} \mathbf{Z}_{ij} = 1, \forall j \sum_{i=1}^{m} \mathbf{Z}_{ij} \leq 1, \mathbf{z}_{ij} \in \{0, 1\} \tag{1}$$

It is known that the above problem is an Quadratic Assignment Problem (QAP) which is a NP-hard problem. Therefore, relaxation models are required to find some approximate solutions. For the person image matching problem, an ideal matching relaxation model should be satisfied with the following two aspects. (1) An one-to-one matching constraint should be imposed in the final matching results, i.e., each patch in image I should correspond to at most one patch in I'. (2) There may exist outlier patches in both I and I'. Thus, the matching process should perform robustly to the outlier patches. To address these issues, we propose to obtain the optimal matching $\mathbf{Z}$ by solving the following novel sparse relaxation matching problem,

$$\max_{\mathbf{Z}} \quad \text{vec}(\mathbf{Z})^T \mathbf{K} \, \text{vec}(\mathbf{Z}) - \beta \|\mathbf{Z}\|_2^2 \quad s.t. \quad \|\mathbf{Z}\|_{1,2} = 1, \mathbf{Z} \geq 0 \tag{2}$$

where $\|\mathbf{Z}\|_{1,2} = (\sum_i (\sum_j |\mathbf{Z}_{ij}|)^2)^{1/2}$ is used to encourage local sparse and thus one-to-one matching constraint [3]. The ℓ_2-norm regularization term is used to control the compactness of all inlier, which make the model perform robustly to the outlier patches, as discussed in work [26].

3.2 Computational Algorithm

The proposed patch matching model can be solved effectively via a simple multiplicative update algorithm. Starting from $\mathbf{Z}^{(0)}$, the proposed algorithm conducts the following update until convergence.

$$\mathbf{Z}_{ij}^{(t+1)} = \mathbf{Z}_{ij}^{(t)} \sqrt{\frac{\mathbf{M}_{ij}^{(t)}}{\lambda \sum_j \mathbf{Z}_{ij}^{(t)}} + \beta \mathbf{Z}_{ij}^{(t)}} \tag{3}$$

where matrix $\mathbf{M}^{(t)} \in \mathbb{R}^{m \times n}$ is the matrix form of the vector $[\mathbf{K}^{(t)} \text{vec}(\mathbf{Z}^{(t)})]$, and λ is computed as,

$$\lambda = \text{vec}(\mathbf{Z}^{(t)})^T \mathbf{K} \text{vec}(\mathbf{Z}^{(t)}) - \beta \text{vec}(\mathbf{Z}^{(t)}) \tag{4}$$

Theoretical Analysis. The optimality and convergence of the algorithm are guaranteed by Theorems 1 and 2, respectively.

Theorem 1. *Update rule of Eq. (3) satisfies the first-order Karush-Kuhn-Tucker (KKT) optimality condition.*

Theorem 2. *Under the update rule Eq. (3), the Lagrangian function $\mathcal{L}(X)$ Eq. (5) is monotonically increasing.*

$$\mathcal{L}(\mathbf{Z}) = vec(\mathbf{Z})^{\mathrm{T}} \mathbf{K} \, vec(\mathbf{Z}) - \beta \|\mathbf{Z}\|_2^2 - \lambda (\sum_i (\sum_j \mathbf{Z}_{ij})^2 - 1) \tag{5}$$

The proof of them can be similarly derived from work [3] which is omitted here due to limited space.

4 Person Re-ID

In this section, we describe our Re-ID approach based on the proposed patch matching model. The complete process is shown in Fig. 1.

4.1 Training Stage

Given a positive image pair I_p and I_g, we decompose them into many overlapping patches at the start. Then, we construct a graph for these patch features and learn the patch-wise correspondence $\mathbf{Z}$ of them via the proposed matching model. Of course, the part of graph matching can also be replaced by some classic graph matching methods such as [4, 11].

In Re-ID, $\mathbf{Z}_{ij} = 1$ means the ith patch in I_p semantically corresponds to the jth patch in I_g. And the graph matching model was detailed in the previous section. In this stage, we can obtain satisfactory patch-wise matching results for Re-ID, and these correspondence relationships will be used to distance measure.

4.2 Testing Stage

We use the local-global pattern for the final distance metric learning due to local information is one-sided and global information is easily lead to misalignment. We compute the final distance D as follows,

$$D(I_p', I_g') = \alpha D_l + (1 - \alpha) D_g \tag{6}$$

where D_g and D_l represent global and local distance between test images I_g' and I_p' respectively, and α is a balance parameter.

Local Distance Metric. When we have learned the patch-wise correspondence relationships of all trained positive sample pairs from the training stage, we can get the most similar R pairs of positive references to test pair by comparing the pose similarity. The local distance compute is as follows,

$$D_l(I_p', I_g') = \sum_{i=1}^{R} w_i \sum_{j=1}^{S_i} \zeta(f_p', f_g') \tag{7}$$

where f'_p and f'_g represent features of patches in probe image I'_p and gallery image I'_g, and $\zeta(.)$ denotes the KISSME metric [12]. We use $\Phi = \{\phi_i\}_{i=1}^R$ to represent the R templates selected, where each template $\phi_i = \{z_{ij}\}_{j=1}^{S_i}$ contains a total of S_i patch-wise correspondences, and each correspondence z_{ij} denotes the positions of matched patches calculated by $\mathbf{Z}_{ij}$, which is consistent with the original method [36]. The difference with the method lies in that we normalized weighted and summed the selected R pairs of references, so that the more similar the pose is, the higher the weight is, where the weight is represented by w_i.

Global Distance Metric. For the test pair I'_p and I'_g, we adopt the LOMO+XQDA [15] to supplement the global distance compute. We combine global information into patch-wise feature distances between each correspondence of selected references, so we can calculate the local and global distances between the test image pairs. In all our experiments, we use Local Maximal Occurrence features [15] for the patch features representation, whether local or global.

5 Experiments

5.1 Datasets

VIPeR Dataset: The VIPeR dataset [10] includes 1264 images of 632 pedestrians, and each pedestrian has two images collected from cameras A and B. Each image is adjusted to the size of 128×48. The dataset is characterized by a diversity of perspectives and lighting.

Road Dataset: This dataset [23] is captured from a crowd road scene by two cameras and consists of 416 image pairs. It is very challenging due to the large variation of human pose and camera view.

PRID450S Dataset: This dataset [22] consists of 450 image pairs from two camera views. The low image qualities and camera viewpoint changes make it very challenging for person re-identification.

CUHK01 Dataset: This dataset [13] consists of 971 individuals captured from two disjoint camera views. The images on this dataset are of higher resolutions. We also adopt the commonly utilized 485/486 setting for person re-identification evaluation.

5.2 Evaluation Settings

Parameter Setup. We follow previous methods and perform experiments under the half-training and half-testing setting. All images are scaled to 128×48. The patch size is set to 32×24. The stride size between neighboring patches is 6 horizontally and 8 vertically for probe images and gallery images. More specifically, for each stripe in the probe image, patch-wise correspondences are established between the corresponding gallery stripe within the search range in the gallery image.

Evaluation. On all datasets, both the training/testing set partition and probe/gallery set partition are performed 10 times and average performance is reported. The performance is evaluated by using the Cumulative Matching Characteristic (CMC) curve, which represents the expected probability of finding the correct match for a probe image in the top r matches in the gallery list [36]. Tables 1, 2, 3 and 4 show the CMC results of different methods on four datasets and Fig. 2 shows the CMC curves on three datasets.

Table 1. Comparisons of top r matching rate using CMC on VIPeR dataset. The best results are marked in bold.

Methods	Rank = 1	Rank = 5	Rank = 10	Rank = 20	Reference
KISSME	27.3%	55.3%	69.0%	82.7%	CVPR2012
SVMML	30.0%	64.7%	79.0%	91.3%	CVPR2013
SalMatch	30.2%	52.3%	65.5%	79.2%	T-PAMI2017
ELS	31.3%	62.1%	75.3%	86.7%	TIP2015
KLFDA	32.4%	65.9%	79.8%	90.8%	ECCV2014
CSL	34.8%	68.7%	82.3%	91.8%	ICCV2015
IDLA	34.8%	64.5%	-	-	CVPR2015
JLR	35.8%	68.0%	-	-	CVPR2016
LOMO + XQDA	40.0%	68.1%	80.5%	91.1%	CVPR2015
Semantic	41.6%	71.9%	86.2%	95.1%	CVPR2015
Single-KMFA	43.3%	77.4%	88.2%	92.7%	TIP2017
LMF + LADF	43.4%	73.0%	84.9%	93.7%	CVPR2014
DCSL	44.6%	73.4%	82.6%	-	IJCAI2016
TCP	47.8%	74.7%	84.8%	91.1%	CVPR2016
TMA	48.2%	-	87.7%	95.5%	ECCV2016
GCT	49.4%	77.6%	87.2%	94.0%	AAAI2018
LOMO-fusing	51.2%	82.1%	90.5%	95.9%	CVPR2016
Multi-mamu-KMFA	51.4%	82.5%	91.2%	**96.0%**	TIP2017
Our	**59.7%**	**83.2%**	**91.4%**	**96.0%**	

Table 2. Comparisons of top r matching rate using CMC on Road dataset. The best results are marked in bold.

Methods	Rank = 1	Rank = 5	Rank = 10	Rank = 20	Reference
eSDC-knn	52.4%	74.5%	83.7%	89.9%	CVPR2013
SVMML	57.2%	85.2%	92.1%	96.1%	CVPR2013
MFA	58.3%	85.5%	92.4%	96.2%	ECCV2014
kLFDA	59.1%	86.5%	91.8%	95.8%	ECCV2014
CSL	61.5%	91.8%	95.2%	98.6%	ICCV2015
Single-KMFA	71.4%	92.5%	95.6%	97.1%	TIP2017
Multi-manu-KMFA	73.1%	92.8%	96.4%	97.8%	TIP2017
GCT	88.8%	**96.7%**	98.4%	99.6%	AAAI2018
Our	**88.9%**	96.6%	**99.0%**	**100%**	

5.3   Results

To evaluate the effectiveness of the proposed method, we evaluate the proposed Re-ID method by comparing it with some other methods including KISSME [12], SVMML [14], SalMatch [35], ELS [6], MFA [28], kLFDA [28], IDLA [1], JLR [27], LOMO + XQDA [15], Semantic [25], LMF + LADF [34], DCSL [32], deCPPs + MER [24], TCP [9], TMA [18], LOMO-fusing [31], SCNCD [30], Mirror-KMFA [8], eSDC-knn [33], CSL [23], single-KMFA [16], multi-manu-KMFA [16], DeepRanking [7], ME [21], GOG [19], SalMatch [35], CSBT [5], and GCT [36].

Table 3. Comparisons of top r matching rate using CMC on PRID450S dataset. The best results are marked in bold.

Methods	Rank = 1	Rank = 5	Rank = 10	Rank = 20	Reference
KISSME	33.0%	-	71.0%	79.0%	CVPR2012
SVMML	42.8%	69.7%	79.2%	86.6%	CVPR2013
CSL	44.4%	71.6%	82.2%	89.8%	ICCV2015
MFA	44.7%	71.9%	80.2%	86.9%	ECCV2014
Semantic	44.9%	71.7%	77.5%	86.7%	CVPR2015
kLFDA	46.9%	73.1%	81.7%	87.2%	ECCV2014
TMA	54.2%	73.8%	83.1%	90.2%	ECCV2016
Mirror-KMFA	55.4%	79.3%	87.8%	93.9%	IJCAI2015
GCT	58.4%	77.6%	84.3%	89.8%	AAAI2018
Single-KMFA	63.2%	82.7%	90.5%	94.8%	TIP2017
Multi-manu-KMFA	65.1%	84.9%	91.2%	95.4%	TIP2017
Our	**75.6%**	**91.2%**	**95.1%**	**97.5%**	

Table 4. Comparisons of top r matching rate using CMC on CUHK01 dataset. The best results are marked in bold.

Methods	Rank = 1	Rank = 5	Rank = 10	Rank = 20	Reference
Semantic	32.7%	51.2%	-	76.3%	CVPR2015
kLFDA	32.8%	59.0%	69.6%	-	ECCV2014
IDLA	47.5%	71.5%	80.0%	-	CVPR2015
DeepRanking	50.4%	75.9%	84.1%	-	TIP2016
ME	53.4%	76.3%	84.4%	-	CVPR2015
GOG	57.8%	79.1%	86.2%	-	CVPR2016
SalMatch	28.5%	46.0%	-	67.3%	T-PAMI2017
CSBT	51.2%	76.3%	-	91.8%	CVPR2017
TCP	53.7%	84.3%	91.0%	96.3%	CVPR2016
GCT	61.9%	81.9%	87.6%	92.8%	AAAI2018
Our	**82.7%**	**93.6%**	**96.9%**	**98.6%**	

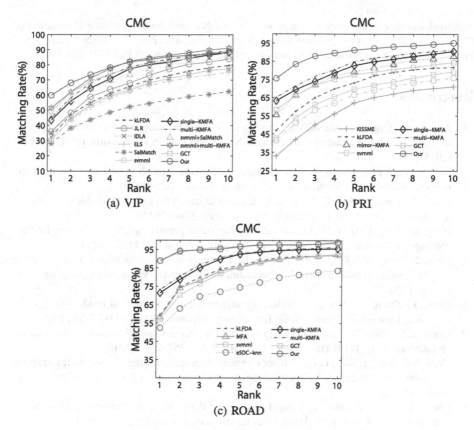

Fig. 2. CMC scores comparison on different datasets.

Tables 1, 2, 3 and 4 summarize the comparison results. Here, we can note: (1) Our approach performs better than graph correspondence transfer (GCT) [36], which demonstrates the effectiveness and robustness of the proposed patch matching model by reducing the impact of outliers. (2) Our method also outperforms many other Re-ID methods and obtains the best performance on all datasets, which indicates the effectiveness of the proposed Re-ID approach.

6 Conclusion

In this paper, we propose a new model to solve the problem of cross-view spatial mis-alignment of person Re-id. We first propose a novel local sparse matching model to learn the corresponding relationship between patches of image pair in the training stage. Then, in the testing phase, we adopt local-global distance measure method to make the learning result of person images more accurate. Extensive experimental results on several benchmarks demonstrate the effectiveness of the proposed Re-ID method.

Acknowledgment. This work was supported by the National Natural Science Foundation of China (61602001), Natural Science Foundation of Anhui Province (1708085QF139), Open Project Program of the National Laboratory of Pattern Recognition (NLPR) (201900046).

References

1. Ahmed, E., Jones, M., Marks, T.K.: An improved deep learning architecture for person re-identification. In: Proceedings of Computer Vision and Pattern Recognition, pp. 3908–3916 (2015)
2. Bak, S., Carr, P.: Person re-identification using deformable patch metric learning. In: International Workshop on Applications of Computer Vision, pp. 1–9 (2016)
3. Jiang, B., Tang, J., Ding, C., Luo, B.: A local sparse model for matching problem. In: American Association for Artificial Intelligence, pp. 3790–3796 (2015)
4. Jiang, B., Tang, J., Ding, C., Luo, B.: Binary constraint preserving graph matching. In: Proceedings of Computer Vision and Pattern Recognition, pp. 4402–4409 (2017)
5. Chen, J., Wang, Y., Qin, J., Liu, L., Shao, L.: Fast person re-identification via cross-camera semantic binary transformation. In: Proceedings of Computer Vision and Pattern Recognition, p. 1 (2017)
6. Chen, J., Zhang, Z., Wang, Y.: Relevance metric learning for person re-identification by exploiting listwise similarities. IEEE Trans. Image Process. **24**(12), 4741–4755 (2015)
7. Chen, S.Z., Guo, C.C., Lai, J.H.: Deep ranking for person re-identification via joint representation learning. IEEE Trans. Image Process. **25**(5), 2353–2367 (2016)
8. Chen, Y.C., Zheng, W.S., Lai, J.: Mirror representation for modeling view-specific transform in person re-identification. In: International Joint Conference on Artificial Intelligence, pp. 3402–3408 (2015)
9. Cheng, D., Gong, Y., Zhou, S., Wang, J., Zheng, N.: Person re-identification by multi-channel parts-based cnn with improved triplet loss function. In: Proceedings of Computer Vision and Pattern Recognition, pp. 1335–1344 (2016)
10. Gray, D., Brennan, S., Tao, H.: Evaluating appearance models for recognition, reacquisition, and tracking. In: Proceedings of International Workshop on Performance Evaluation for Tracking and Surveillance, pp. 1–7 (2007)
11. Jiang, B., Tang, J., Ding, C., Gong, Y., Luo, B.: Graph matching via multiplicative update algorithm. In: Proceedings of Neural Information Processing Systems, pp. 3187–3195 (2017)
12. Koestinger, M., Hirzer, M., Wohlhart, P., Roth, P.M., Bischof, H.: Large scale metric learning from equivalence constraints. In: Computer Vision and Pattern Recognition, pp. 2288–2295 (2012)
13. Li, W., Zhao, R., Wang, X.: Human reidentification with transferred metric learning. In: Lee, K.M., Matsushita, Y., Rehg, J.M., Hu, Z. (eds.) ACCV 2012. LNCS, vol. 7724, pp. 31–44. Springer, Heidelberg (2013). https://doi.org/10.1007/978-3-642-37331-2_3
14. Li, Z., Chang, S., Liang, F., Huang, T.S., Cao, L., Smith, J.R.: Learning locally-adaptive decision functions for person verification. In: Proceedings of Computer Vision and Pattern Recognition, pp. 3610–3617 (2013)
15. Liao, S., Hu, Y., Zhu, X., Li, S.Z.: Person re-identification by local maximal occurrence representation and metric learning. In: Proceedings of Computer Vision and Pattern Recognition, pp. 2197–2206 (2015)
16. Lin, W., et al.: Learning correspondence structures for person re-identification. IEEE Trans. Image Process. **26**(5), 2438–2453 (2017)
17. Ma, L., Yang, X., Xu, Y., Zhu, J.: A generalized emd with body prior for pedestrian identification. J. Vis. Commun. Image Represent. **24**(6), 708–716 (2013)

18. Martinel, N., Das, A., Micheloni, C., Roy-Chowdhury, A.K.: Temporal model adaptation for person re-identification. In: Leibe, B., Matas, J., Sebe, N., Welling, M. (eds.) ECCV 2016. LNCS, vol. 9908, pp. 858–877. Springer, Cham (2016). https://doi.org/10.1007/978-3-319-46493-0_52

19. Matsukawa, T., Okabe, T., Suzuki, E., Sato, Y.: Hierarchical gaussian descriptor for person re-identification. In: Proceedings of Computer Vision and Pattern Recognition, pp. 1363–1372 (2016)

20. Oreifej, O., Mehran, R., Shah, M.: Human identity recognition in aerial images. In: Computer Vision and Pattern Recognition, pp. 709–716 (2010)

21. Paisitkriangkrai, S., Shen, C., Van Den Hengel, A.: Learning to rank in person re-identification with metric ensembles. In: Proceedings of Computer Vision and Pattern Recognition, pp. 1846–1855 (2015)

22. Roth, P.M., Hirzer, M., Köstinger, M., Beleznai, C., Bischof, H.: Mahalanobis distance learning for person re-identification. In: Gong, S., Cristani, M., Yan, S., Loy, C. (eds.) Person Re-Identification. ACVPR, pp. 247–267. Springer, London (2014). https://doi.org/10.1007/978-1-4471-6296-4_12

23. Shen, Y., Lin, W., Yan, J., Xu, M., Wu, J., Wang, J.: Person re-identification with correspondence structure learning. In: Proceedings of International Conference on Computer Vision, pp. 3200–3208 (2015)

24. Sheng, H., Huang, Y., Zheng, Y., Chen, J., Xiong, Z.: Person re-identification via learning visual similarity on corresponding patch pairs. In: Zhang, S., Wirsing, M., Zhang, Z. (eds.) KSEM 2015. LNCS (LNAI), vol. 9403, pp. 787–798. Springer, Cham (2015). https://doi.org/10.1007/978-3-319-25159-2_73

25. Shi, Z., Hospedales, T.M., Xiang, T.: Transferring a semantic representation for person re-identification and search. In: Proceedings of Computer Vision and Pattern Recognition, pp. 4184–4193 (2015)

26. Suh, Y., Adamczewski, K., Lee, K.M.: Subgraph matching using compactness prior for robust feature correspondence. In: Proceedings of Computer Vision and Pattern Recognition, p. 1 (2015)

27. Wang, F., Zuo, W., Lin, L., Zhang, D., Zhang, L.: Joint learning of single-image and cross-image representations for person re-identification. In: Proceedings of Computer Vision and Pattern Recognition, pp. 1288–1296 (2016)

28. Xiong, F., Gou, M., Camps, O., Sznaier, M.: Person re-identification using kernel-based metric learning methods. In: Fleet, D., Pajdla, T., Schiele, B., Tuytelaars, T. (eds.) ECCV 2014. LNCS, vol. 8695, pp. 1–16. Springer, Cham (2014). https://doi.org/10.1007/978-3-319-10584-0_1

29. Yang, Y., Wen, L., Lyu, S., Li, S.Z.: Unsupervised learning of multi-level descriptors for person re-identification. In: American Association for Artificial Intelligence, p. 1 (2017)

30. Yang, Y., Yang, J., Yan, J., Liao, S., Yi, D., Li, S.Z.: Salient color names for person re-identification. In: Fleet, D., Pajdla, T., Schiele, B., Tuytelaars, T. (eds.) ECCV 2014. LNCS, vol. 8689, pp. 536–551. Springer, Cham (2014). https://doi.org/10.1007/978-3-319-10590-1_35

31. Zhang, L., Xiang, T., Gong, S.: Learning a discriminative null space for person re-identification. In: Proceedings of Computer Vision and Pattern Recognition, pp. 1239–1248 (2016)

32. Zhang, Y., Li, X., Zhao, L., Zhang, Z.: Semantics-aware deep correspondence structure learning for robust person re-identification. In: International Joint Conference on Artificial Intelligence, pp. 3545–3551 (2016)

33. Zhao, R., Ouyang, W., Wang, X.: Unsupervised salience learning for person re-identification. In: Proceedings of Computer Vision and Pattern Recognition, pp. 3586–3593 (2013)

34. Zhao, R., Ouyang, W., Wang, X.: Learning mid-level filters for person re-identification. In: Proceedings of Computer Vision and Pattern Recognition, pp. 144–151 (2014)
35. Zhao, R., Oyang, W., Wang, X.: Person re-identification by saliency learning. IEEE Trans. Pattern Anal. Mach. Intell. **39**(2), 356–370 (2017)
36. Zhou, Q., et al.: Graph correspondence transfer for person re-identification, p. 1. arXiv preprint. arXiv:1804.00242 (2018)

Shot Segmentation Based on Feature Fusion and Bayesian Online Changepoint Detection

Qiannan Bai and Fang Dai[✉]

School of Sciences, Xi'an University of Technology, Xi'an 710054, Shaanxi, China
daifang@xaut.edu.cn

Abstract. Shot segmentation is an important technology in video analysis. Traditional shot segmentation methods usually need to set thresholds in advance. Due to the diversity of shot types, it is usually difficult to set appropriate thresholds for these segmentation. In this paper, a new shot segmentation method is proposed, which combines feature fusion with Bayesian online changepoint detection. Firstly, the HSV quantitative color features of video frames are extracted and a new feature MEP is constructed. The comprehensive similarity of MEP features of two adjacent frames is calculated. Then, Bayesian online changepoint detection algorithm is applied to detect the comprehensive similarity. The location of the changepoint detected is the position of shot segmentation in the video. The experimental results show that Bayesian online changepoint detection has the ability to distinguish different shots. The average Recall and Precision of our method are over 0.90, which is more accurate than the results of the methods which used to compare with our method.

Keywords: Shot segmentation · Bayesian online changepoint detection · Feature fusion · Color features

1 Introduction

Video, as a carrier of information, is becoming more and more popular and widely used in various fields. In the face of massive video data, how to quickly and accurately find the required video resources is the current research hotspot. Shot segmentation is a key step in the process of video analysis. The subsequent keyframe extraction and video summary generation are mainly depended on the accuracy of shot segmentation.

In recent years, researchers have proposed many shot segmentation methods, most of which work on the principle of using frame difference as a measure of shot segmentation. The method of shot segmentation based on pixel difference in literature [1] is easy to understand and implement, but sensitive to camera motion, intensity change and noise. For this reason, the adaptive shot segmentation methods with robustness to camera motion and illumination intensity are proposed in literature [2] and literature [3], respectively. The disadvantage is that the computational cost is expensive. In order to reduce the computational cost, a shot segmentation method based on visual word bag is proposed in literature [4]. However, this method can not detect gradual shot very well.

© Springer Nature Switzerland AG 2019
Y. Zhao et al. (Eds.): ICIG 2019, LNCS 11902, pp. 155–166, 2019.
https://doi.org/10.1007/978-3-030-34110-7_14

Literature [5] sets two thresholds, one for detecting gradual transformation and the other for detecting abrupt transformation. It can detect gradual shots very well, but there are still some shortcomings for detecting dissolved shots. In order to solve this problem, a method of detecting fade-in, fade-out and dissolve-in based on the combination of double contrast and black-and-white frame detection is proposed in [6]. This method can effectively segment the gradual shots, but it is very sensitive to change of illumination and fast motion of objects.

In addition, the above methods need to determine the threshold ahead of time in shot segmentation. However, due to the diversity of shot types, it is difficult to set the appropriate threshold for shot switching. If the shot switching in video data is regarded as a state transition with statistical significance, we can apply changepoint detection to shot segmentation. Bayesian online changepoint detection [7] describes data conversion [8] by estimating the probability that the incoming data points belong to the distribution related to the run length of the previous changepoint. Although previous studies have applied the changepoint method to human-computer interaction system [9], joint motion model [10], and physiological changes in medicine [11], the changepoint detection has not yet been involved in the field of shots segmentation. Therefore, on the basis of multi-feature fusion, Bayesian online changepoint detection is applied to shot segmentation of video data, and a new shot segmentation method is proposed in this paper.

2   Multi-feature Fusion

2.1   HSV Quantitative Color Feature

HSV color space histogram is selected as the description feature of frame to participate in shot segmentation. HSV is a color model that conforms to human visual characteristics. For the sake of storage efficiency, it is necessary to quantize the feature at unequal intervals. Firstly, the H, S, V components are divided into 8, 3, 3 levels respectively. Then, the three color components are converted into a quantity L according to the formula (1). Thus, the image color is divided into 72 levels [12].

$$L = 9H + 3S + V \tag{1}$$

The value of L is taken as $0, 1, \cdots, 71$, and the one-dimensional histogram of the image can be obtained by calculating the L value of the image. Record the histogram feature vectors of the ith frame as $f_i = (a_{i1}, a_{i2}, \cdots, a_{il})$, where $a_{ij} \in [0, 1]$ is a normalized proportional value, $i = 1, 2, \cdots, n$, $j = 1, 2, \cdots, l$, n is the total number of frames of the video, $l = 72$ is the dimension of the one-dimensional histogram vector. The normalization formula is as follows:

$$a_{ij} = A_{ij} / \sum_{j=1}^{l} A_{ij} \tag{2}$$

Among them, A_{ij} is the number of pixels whose L value is $j - 1$ of the ith frame.

2.2 The MEP Feature

In order to segment shots more accurately, the color mean (M), image information entropy (E) and the number of eigenvalues larger than 1 (P) in the image correlation coefficient matrix of Principal Component Analysis (PCA) are further extracted. These three features are combined linearly to obtain the final MEP comprehensive features.

Assuming that the resolution of the frame is $N_w \times N_h$ and any pixel in the ith frame is (x_p, y_q), the mean value of the pixel in the ith frame [13] is:

$$m_i = \frac{1}{N_w \times N_h} \sum_{p=1}^{N_w} \sum_{q=1}^{N_h} f_i'(x_p, y_q) \tag{3}$$

where $f_i'(x_p, y_q)$ represents the pixel value at the pixel coordinate point (x_p, y_q) in the ith frame.

Image information entropy [14] is a description of the average amount of information in an image. In this paper, when calculating the image information entropy, the first step is to convert the color image to the gray image. Secondly, the information entropy of the gray image is calculated by formula (4). Then the information entropy of the ith frame is:

$$e_i = -\sum_{j=1}^{N} p_{ij} \log p_{ij} \tag{4}$$

Among them, p_{ij} is the proportion of the pixels whose gray value is $j - 1$ in the gray image in all the pixels of the ith frame, $j = 1, 2, \cdots 256$. The e_i is the information entropy of the ith frame.

PCA [15] refers to the transformation of a set of variables that may have correlation into a set of linear independent variables by orthogonal transformation. In this paper, image information is depicted by the number of eigenvalues greater than 1 in the correlation coefficient matrix of principal component analysis. Firstly, the gray image matrix is standardized, that is to subtract the mean value of each element in the gray image matrix to get x_{jk}, $j = 1, 2, \cdots N_w$, $k = 1, 2, \cdots N_h$. Secondly, the correlation coefficient matrix of standardized data $X = (x_{jk})_{N_w \times N_h}$ is calculated. Then, the eigenvalues of the correlation coefficient matrix are calculated by Jacobian method; Finally, counting the number of eigenvalues greater than 1, the number of eigenvalues greater than 1 in the ith frame is counted as p_i.

After calculating the pixel mean m_i, information entropy e_i and the number of eigenvalues greater than 1 in the correlation coefficient matrix p_i of the ith frame, these three quantities are normalized. The normalized three features are recorded as M_i, E_i, P_i, and the integrated features of MEP in the ith frame is $F_i = (M_i, E_i, P_i)$.

2.3 Similarity Measure

The Euclidean distance is used to calculate the similarity between two image feature vectors. Taking the HSV quantitative color feature of video frames as an example, two image feature vectors are given as f_i, f_{i+1}. The similarity between video frames is calculated using the following formula:

$$s_i^{HSV}(f_i, f_{i+1}) = \sqrt{\sum_{j=1}^{l} (a_{ij} - a_{(i+1)j})^2} \tag{5}$$

So, the HSV color similarity matrix of adjacent frames is $S_{HSV} = [s_1^{HSV}, s_2^{HSV}, \cdots s_{n-1}^{HSV}]$. For the same reason, the similarity matrix of MEP features of adjacent frames is $S_{MEP} = [s_1^{MEP}, s_2^{MEP}, \cdots s_{n-1}^{MEP}]$, then the comprehensive similarity between frames is constructed as following:

$$S = S_{HSV} + S_{MEP} \tag{6}$$

The plus sign represents the sum of the corresponding elements of two vectors,

$$S = [s_1, s_2, \cdots s_{n-1}], \ s_i = s_i^{HSV} + s_i^{MEP}, \ i = 1, 2, \cdots n - 1$$

3 Bayesian Online Changepoint Detection for Shots Segmentation

3.1 Bayesian Online Changepoint Detection

The objective of this paper is to separate different shots from feature $s_1, s_2, \cdots s_{n-1}$ (denoted as $s_{1:n-1}$), and the boundary between each shots can be called a changepoint. In order to determine these shot boundaries, the run length method [8] is used, which is based on Bayesian theorem and assumes that the changepoints are generated by random processes, and that the data between the changepoints are independent and identically distributed. If run length r_t falls to zero, the changepoint occurs; otherwise, run length increases by 1. Firstly, assuming that the predicted distribution $P(s_{t+1}|r_t, s_t^{(r)})$ can be calculated under the condition of given run length r_t, then the posterior distribution $P(r_t|s_{1:t})$ can be integrated on the current run length to find the marginal predicted distribution $P(s_{t+1}|s_{1:t})$, as shown in formula (7):

$$P(s_{t+1}|s_{1:t}) = \sum_{r_t} P(s_{t+1}|r_t, s_t^{(r)}) P(r_t|s_{1:t}) \tag{7}$$

And, the posterior distribution is:

$$P(r_t|s_{1:t}) = \frac{P(r_t, s_{1:t})}{P(s_{1:t})} \tag{8}$$

$s_t^{(r)}$ represents the data set s associated with run length r_t. Furthermore, in order to find $P(r_t, s_{1:t})$, the run length distribution $P(r_{ti}, s_{1:t})$ is estimated using an iterative approach, $r_{ti} \in r_t$, $i = 1, 2, \cdots t$, $\sum_{i=1}^{t} r_{ti} = 1$.

By maximizing each run length distribution, it can be determined that when the probability of $i = t$ element of the run length distribution is the highest, if $r_t = 0$, the changepoint has occurred (i.e., the shot boundary is detected); otherwise, there is no changepoint (i.e., the shot boundary is not detected), and the run length is increased to $r_t = r_{t-1} + 1$. Run length distribution can be expressed as:

$$P(r_{ti}|s_{1:t}) = \frac{P(r_{ti}, s_{1:t})}{\sum\limits_{r_{ti}} P(r_{ti}, s_{1:t})} \tag{9}$$

The joint distribution $P(r_{ti}, s_{1:t})$ of run length r_t at time t and observation data $s_{1:t}$ can be updated recursively online according to formula (10):

$$\begin{aligned} P(r_{ti}, s_{1:t}) &= \sum_{r_{(t-1)i}} P(r_{ti}, r_{(t-1)i}, s_{1:t}) \\ &= \sum_{r_{(t-1)i}} P(r_{ti}, s_t | r_{(t-1)i}, s_{1:t-1}) P(r_{(t-1)i}, s_{1:t-1}) \\ &= \sum_{r_{(t-1)i}} P(r_{ti} | r_{(t-1)i}) P(s_t | r_{(t-1)i}, s_{t-1}^{(r)}) P(r_{(t-1)i}, s_{1:t-1}) \end{aligned} \tag{10}$$

where

$$P(r_{ti}|r_{(t-1)i}) = \begin{cases} H(r_{(t-1)i} + 1), & r_{ti} = 0 \\ 1 - H(r_{(t-1)i} + 1), & r_{ti} = r_{(t-1)i} + 1 \\ 0, & others \end{cases} \tag{11}$$

$H(\cdot)$ is usually a constant. The predicted distribution $P(s_t | r_{(t-1)i}, s_{1:t-1})$ depends only on the latest data $s_{t-1}^{(r)}$, which can be obtained by marginalizing the parameters in the conjugate exponential model [16].

3.2 Shot Segmentation

For the comprehensive similarity sequence $s_1, s_2, \cdots s_{n-1}$ of two adjacent frames, Bayesian online changepoint detection algorithm is employed to detect the existence of shot boundary. We use t-distribution to calculate the prediction function. The specific algorithm is as follows.

Step 1. Initialization parameter $\alpha_1^{(0)}, \beta_1^{(0)}, \kappa_1^{(0)}, u_1^{(0)}$, corresponding initialization mean μ, variance σ^2 and degree of freedom υ are as follows:

$$\sigma_1^{2(0)} = \frac{\beta_1^{(0)}(\kappa_1^{(0)} + 1)}{\alpha_1^{(0)} \kappa_1^{(0)}}, \upsilon_1^{(0)} = 2\alpha_1^{(0)} \tag{12}$$

run length distribution $P(r_{0i}) = 1$;

Step 2. Read in data s_t and use t distribution to calculate the prediction function:

$$\xi_t^{(r)} = P\left(s_t | \mu_t^{(r)}, \sigma_t^{2(r)}, \upsilon_t^{(r)}\right)$$

$$= \frac{\Gamma(\frac{v_t^{(r)}+1}{2})}{\sqrt{v_t^{(r)}\pi\sigma_t^{2(r)}}\Gamma(\frac{v_t^{(r)}}{2})} \left(1 + \frac{\left(s_t - v_t^{(r)}\right)^2}{v_t^{(r)}\sigma_t^{2(r)}}\right)^{(-\frac{v_t^{(r)}+1}{2})} \tag{13}$$

Γ is a Gamma function.

Step 3. Loop $i = 1$ to $t - 1$, calculate growth probability:

$$P(r_{ti}, s_{1:t}) = P(r_{(t-1)i}, s_{1:t-1})\xi_t^{(r)}(1 - H) \tag{14}$$

Assume that the hazard function $H = \lambda^{-1}$, λ is a time scale parameter, usually take $\lambda = 250$.

Step 4. Calculate the changepoint probability (i.e. shot boundary probability):

$$P(r_{tt}, s_{1:t}) = \sum_{r_{(t-1)i}} P(r_{(t-1)i}, s_{1:t-1})\xi_t^{(r)} H \tag{15}$$

Step 5. Calculate run length distribution:

$$P(r_{ti}|s_{1:t}) = \frac{P(r_{ti}, s_{1:t})}{\sum\limits_{r_{ti}} P(r_{ti}, s_{1:t})} \tag{16}$$

Step 6. Update the parameters α, β, κ, u and mean μ, variance σ^2 and degree of freedom v as follows:

$$
\begin{aligned}
\alpha_{t+1}^{(r+1)} &= \alpha_t^{(r)} + 0.5 \\
\beta_{t+1}^{(r+1)} &= \beta_t^{(r)} + \frac{\kappa_t^{(r)}\left(s_t^{(r)} - \mu_t^{(r)}\right)^2}{2\left(\kappa_t^{(r)}+1\right)} \\
\kappa_{t+1}^{(r+1)} &= \kappa_t^{(r)} + 1 \\
u_{t+1}^{(r+1)} &= \mu_{t+1}^{(r+1)} = \frac{\kappa_t^{(r)}\mu_t^{(r)} + s_t}{\kappa_t^{(r)}+1} \\
\sigma_{t+1}^{2(r+1)} &= \frac{\beta_{t+1}^{(r+1)}\left(\kappa_{t+1}^{(r+1)}+1\right)}{\alpha_{t+1}^{(r+1)}\kappa_{t+1}^{(r+1)}} \\
v_{t+1}^{(r+1)} &= 2\alpha_{t+1}^{(r+1)}
\end{aligned}
\tag{17}
$$

Step 7. If $t = \arg\max\limits_{i} P(r_{ti}|s_{1:t})$, A changepoint occurs and the run length is reset to 0. If not, run length $r_t = r_{t-1} + 1$;

Step 8. Iterate until there is no data input and the algorithm ends. Finally, the position of the changepoint returned is the location where shot segmentation occurs in the video.

4   Experimental Results and Analysis

In order to verify the effectiveness of the proposed shot segmentation method, 50 videos are selected as experimental material. The types of videos include movies, news, advertisements, sports, historical films, animation, documentaries, man-made videos, animal videos and educational films. All videos are downloaded in different formats on the network, and they are converted to AVI format with resolution 320×240, 30 frames per second by using MATLAB software. The Recall (R), Precision (P) and F_1 measurement (F_1) [17] are used as the criteria to test the effectiveness of the algorithm to measure the advantages and disadvantages of our method in shot detection. The definitions of Recall rate, Precision rate and F_1 measurement are as follows.

$$R = \frac{N_c}{N_c + N_m} \times 100\% \tag{18}$$

$$P = \frac{N_c}{N_c + N_f} \times 100\% \tag{19}$$

$$F_1 = \frac{2 \times R \times P}{R + P} \times 100\% \tag{20}$$

Referring to the artificial recognition statistics of shot boundary, N_c is the correct number of shot boundary detected by this method, N_m is the number of missed shot boundary detected by this method, and N_f is the number of false shot boundary detected by this method.

When using Bayesian online changepoint detection method to segment shots of video, the method of selecting initialization parameters is as follows. Take 02 video with both abrupt and gradual shots for example. In order to avoid the denominator equal to zero in the variance update formula (12), let's take $\alpha_1^{(0)} = \kappa_1^{(0)} = 0.1$, $u_1^{(0)} = 0$, Fig. 1 shows the F_1 value of $\beta_1^{(0)} = [0.002, 0.01, 0.02, 0.04, 0.07, 0.1, 0.14, 0.17]$ when $\alpha_1^{(0)}, \kappa_1^{(0)}, u_1^{(0)}$ is fixed.

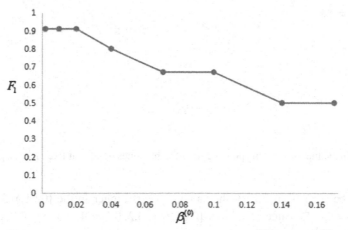

Fig. 1. The value of F_1 corresponding to different values of $\beta_1^{(0)}$ at fixed $\alpha_1^{(0)}, \kappa_1^{(0)}, u_1^{(0)}$

Figure 1 shows the value of F_1 is higher in the $(0, 0.02]$ interval. Fig. 2 shows the F_1 value of $u_1^{(0)} = [0, 0.1, 0.2, 0.3, 0.4, 0.5, 0.6, 0.7]$ when $\alpha_1^{(0)} = \kappa_1^{(0)} = 0.1$, $\beta_1^{(0)} = 0.01$.

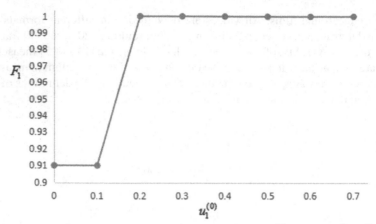

Fig. 2. The value of F_1 corresponding to different values of $\mu_1^{(0)}$ at fixed $\alpha_1^{(0)}, \kappa_1^{(0)}, \beta_1^{(0)}$

As can be seen from Fig. 2, the value of F_1 is higher in the $[0.2, 0.7]$ interval. Fig. 3 shows the F_1 value of $\alpha_1^{(0)} = [0.01, 0.1, 0.2, 0.3, 0.4, 0.5, 0.6, 0.7]$ when $\beta_1^{(0)} = 0.01$, $\kappa_1^{(0)} = 0.1$, $u_1^{(0)} = 0.5$.

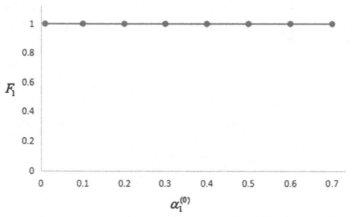

Fig. 3. The value of F_1 corresponding to different values of $\alpha_1^{(0)}$ at fixed $\mu_1^{(0)}, \kappa_1^{(0)}, \beta_1^{(0)}$

As can be seen from Fig. 3, the value of F_1 is higher in the $[0.01, 0.7]$ interval. Fig. 4 shows the F_1 value of $\kappa_1^{(0)} = [0.01, 0.1, 0.2, 0.3, 0.4, 0.5, 0.6, 0.7, 0.8]$ when $\alpha_1^{(0)} = 0.01$, $\beta_1^{(0)} = 0.1$, $u_1^{(0)} = 0.5$. As can be seen from Fig. 4, the value of F_1 is higher in the $[0.01, 0.4]$ interval.

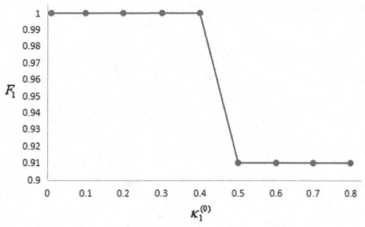

Fig. 4. The value of F_1 corresponding to different values of $\kappa_1^{(0)}$ at fixed $\mu_1^{(0)}, \alpha_1^{(0)}, \beta_1^{(0)}$

When using Bayesian online changepoint detection algorithm for shot segmentation, the initial parameters adopted in this paper are $\alpha_1^{(0)} = 0.1, \beta_1^{(0)} = 0.01$ $\kappa_1^{(0)} = 0.1, u_1^{(0)} = 0.5$ in turn. Firstly, the previous six videos are taken as examples. Table 1 gives the basic information of the previous six videos.

Table 1. The basic information of the previous six videos.

Video sequence	Video type	Total frames	Abrupt shot	Gradual shot	Total shots
01	Movie	510	6	0	6
02	Movie	585	2	5	7
03	News	1445	11	0	11
04	News	1785	13	0	13
05	Advertisement	750	26	1	27
06	Advertisement	450	12	2	14

To illustrate the effectiveness of proposed method in this paper, Fig. 5 shows the run length of the video segment with serial number 01 obtained by Bayesian online changepoint detection algorithm, in which the position with zero run length corresponds to the position where shot segmentation occurs in the video. From Fig. 5, we can see that Bayesian online changepoint detection has the ability to distinguish different shots.

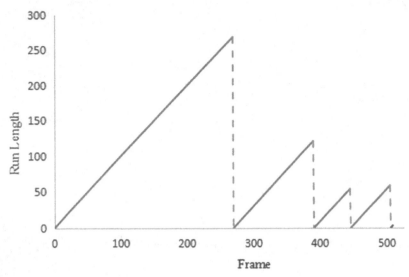

Fig. 5. Run length of sequence 01 video segment

Take the previous six videos for example, Our method is compared with the classical Otsu algorithm [17] and the method in literature [3]. The experimental results are shown in Table 2.

Table 2. Comparison of the results of our method with those of other literature methods

Video sequence	Otsu algorithm [17]			Literature [3] method		
	R	P	F_1	R	P	F_1
01	1.00	0.71	0.83	1.00	1.00	1.00
02	1.00	0.60	0.75	1.00	0.67	0.80
03	1.00	1.00	1.00	1.00	1.00	1.00
04	0.75	1.00	0.86	1.00	0.92	0.96
05	0.96	0.77	0.85	0.96	0.85	0.90
06	1.00	0.67	0.80	1.00	0.67	0.80
Video sequence	HSV+Bayesian			Our method		
	R	P	F_1	R	P	F_1
01	1.00	0.83	0.91	0.80	1.00	0.89
02	0.83	1.00	0.91	1.00	1.00	1.00
03	1.00	1.00	1.00	1.00	0.91	0.95
04	1.00	1.00	1.00	1.00	1.00	1.00
05	0.96	0.85	0.90	0.96	0.92	0.94
06	0.67	0.80	0.73	0.75	0.82	0.78

In 01, 03 and 04 video segments, all of them are abrupt shots, and the accuracy of the four methods is relatively high, the average F_1 of Otsu algorithm is 0.90, the average F_1 of literature [3] method is 0.98, the average F_1 of HSV and Bayesian method is 0.97, and the average F_1 of our method is 0.95. It can be seen that our method is superior to Otsu algorithm only for video with abrupt shots, but slightly inferior to the combination of HSV and Bayesian method in literature [3].

In 02, 05 and 06 video segments, there are more gradual shots, and the picture changes between shots are more intense, so the recall, precision and value of F_1 have decreased. The average F_1 of Otsu algorithm is 0.80, the average F_1 of literature [3] method is 0.83, the average F_1 of HSV and Bayesian method is 0.85, and the average F_1 of our method is 0.92. It can be seen that our method is superior to the other three algorithms in terms of video with a large number of gradual shots. Especially in shot gradual detection, the false detection rate is obviously less than the other three algorithms.

Table 3. Average Recall rate, average Precision rate and average F_1 of different methods

	Average Recall rate	Average Precision rate	Average F_1
Otsu algorithm [17]	0.88	0.61	0.72
Literature [3] method	0.77	0.71	0.74
HSV+Bayesian	0.77	0.87	0.82
Our method	0.83	0.87	0.85

Table 3 gives the average Recall, average Precision and average F_1 of the 01–50 six-segment videos. As can be seen from Table 3, the average F_1 value of Otsu algorithm is 0.72, the average F_1 value of literature [3] method is 0.74, the average F_1 value of HSV and Bayesian method is 0.82, and the average F_1 value of our method is 0.85. The average F_1 value of our method is 0.13 higher than that of Otsu algorithm, 0.11 higher than that of literature [3] method, and 0.03 higher than that of the combination of HSV and Bayesian method.

5 Conclusion

In this paper, a new shot segmentation method is proposed. Bayesian online change point detection is applied to shot segmentation, which realizes online shot segmentation and avoids the determination of traditional shot boundary threshold. In order to improve the accuracy of shot segmentation, a new MEP feature is proposed and fused with HSV quantitative color feature. Three different types of video sequences are used to evaluate the proposed method. The experimental results show that the proposed method is superior to the classical Otsu-based adaptive threshold method, the literature [3] method and the combination of HSV and Bayesian method. The next step is to apply the shot segmentation method to video summary generation, so as to achieve online video summary generation.

Acknowledgement. This research was financially supported by the Xi'an Science and Technology Innovation Guidance Project (No. 201805037YD15CG21(7)).

References

1. Boreczky, J.S., Rowe, L.A.: Comparison of video shot boundary detection techniques. J. Electron. Imaging **5**(2), 8–32 (1996)
2. Don, A., Uma, K.: Adaptive edge-oriented shot boundary detection. EURASIP J. Image Video Process. **2009**(1), 1–13 (2009)
3. Hannane, R., Elboushaki, A., Afdel, K.: Efficient video summarization based on motion SIFT-distribution histogram. In: 13th International Conference on Computer Graphics, Imaging and Visualization, Beni Mellal, Morocco, pp. 312–317. IEEE (2016)
4. Lankinen, J., Kämäräinen, J.K.: Video shot boundary detection using visual bag-of-words. In: International Conference on Computer Vision Theory and Application (2013)
5. Hanjalic, A.: Shot-boundary detection: unraveled and resolved. IEEE Trans. Circuits Syst. Video Technol. **12**(2), 90–105 (2002)
6. Chavan, S., Akojwar, S.: An efficient method for fade and dissolve detection in presence of camera motion & illumination. In: International Conference on Electrical, Electronics, and Optimization Techniques, pp. 3002–3007. IEEE (2016)
7. Aminikhanghahi, S., Cook, D.J.: A survey of methods for time series change point detection. Knowl. Inf. Syst. **51**(2), 339–367 (2017)
8. Adams, R.P., Mackay, D.J.C.: Bayesian online changepoint detection. Statistics (2007)
9. Lau, H.F., Yamamoto, S.: Bayesian online changepoint detection to improve transparency in human-machine interaction systems. In: 49th IEEE Conference on Decision and Control. IEEE (2010)
10. Niekum, S., Osentoski, S., Atkeson, C.G., et al.: Online Bayesian changepoint detection for articulated motion models. In: International Conference on Robotics & Automation. IEEE (2015)
11. Gee, A.H., Chang, J., Ghosh, J., et al.: Bayesian online changepoint detection of physiological transitions. In: Annual International Conference of the IEEE Engineering in Medicine and Biology Society (EMBC). IEEE (2018)
12. Su, C.: Research and system implementation of video abstraction technology. Central South University, Hunan (2009)
13. Sun, Y., Jiang, Z., Shan, G., et al.: Key frame extraction based on optimal distance clustering and feature fusion expression. J. Nanjing Univ. Sci. Technol. **42**(4), 416–423 (2018)
14. Zheng, J.: Research on no-reference image quality assessment based on image information entropy. Beijing Jiaotong University, Beijing (2015)
15. Jiang, X., Xue, H., Zhang, C., et al.: Study on influencing factors of air quality in Hohhot city based on principal component analysis. Saf. Environ. Eng. **23**(01), 75–79 (2016)
16. Snelson, E., Ghahramani, Z.: Compact approximations to Bayesian predictive distributions. In: International Conference on Machine Learning, pp. 840–847. ACM (2005)
17. Otsu, N.: A threshold selection method from gray-level histograms. IEEE Trans. Syst. Man Cybern. **9**(1), 62–66 (1979)

MMA: Motion Memory Attention Network for Video Object Detection

Huai Hu, Wenzhong Wang, Aihua Zheng, and Bin Luo$^{(\boxtimes)}$

Anhui University, Hefei, China
huaihu5831@foxmail.com, {wenzhong,luobin}@ahu.edu.cn,
ahzheng214@foxmail.com

Abstract. Modern object detection frameworks such as Faster R-CNN achieve good performance on static images, benefiting from the powerful feature representations. However, it is still challenging to detect tiny, vague and deformable objects in videos. In this paper, we propose a Motion Memory Attention (MMA) network to tackle this issue by considering the motion and temporal information. Specifically, our network contains two main parts: the dual stream and the memory attention module. The dual stream is designed to improve the detection of tiny object, which is composed of an appearance stream and a motion stream. Our motion stream can be embedded into any video object detection framework. In addition, we also introduce the memory attention module to handle the issue of vague and deformable objects by utilizing the temporal information and distinguishing features. Our experiments demonstrate that the detection performance can be significantly improved when integrating the proposed algorithm with Faster R-CNN and YOLO$_{v2}$.

Keywords: Video object detection · Dual stream · Memory attention module

1 Introduction

Object detection is a fundamental task in computer vision. It has been widely used in many applications, such as monitoring system and autonomous driving, etc. In recent years, a lot of detectors based on ConvNets have been proposed to improve the accuracy and speed in object detection task [3,13,16]. Although they have achieved great success of object detection in image, the performance in the video object detection is still not satisfying for tiny, vague and deformable objects. Furthermore, distant objects on RGB frames are usually mixed with the background. The response of these objects on the feature map is not distinguishable enough, which significantly limits the performance of conventional detectors.

The temporal information in video plays an import role in video object detection [21,22]. They usually estimate the optical flow information between consecutive frames to improve the final detection results. However, the estimation of optical flow is time consuming for practical scenarios.

© Springer Nature Switzerland AG 2019
Y. Zhao et al. (Eds.): ICIG 2019, LNCS 11902, pp. 167–178, 2019.
https://doi.org/10.1007/978-3-030-34110-7_15

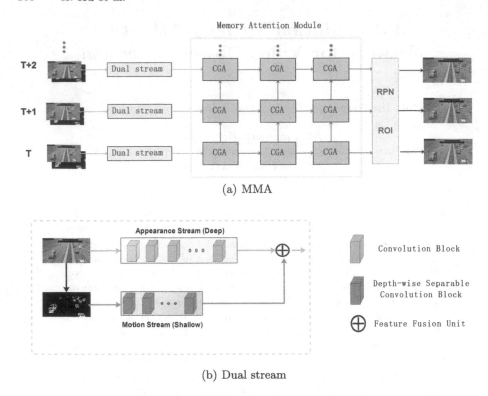

(a) MMA

(b) Dual stream

Fig. 1. (a) **Motion Memory Attention Network (MMA).** Our approach is comprised by dual stream and memory attention module. The memory attention module is shown in Fig. 3; (b) **Dual stream.** The appearance stream is the Faster R-CNN network pre-trained on the COCO dataset. The motion stream is composed of a number of column Depth-wise separable convolution blocks and takes temporal difference frames as input.

To handle aforementioned issues, in this paper, we propose a dual stream video object detection framework which composed of appearance and motion stream, to encode generic appearance and motion cues respectively. The appearance stream is the Faster R-CNN network pre-trained on the COCO dataset. The motion stream is used to mine the motion information. Our motion stream is composed of a number of column depth-wise separable convolution blocks and takes temporal difference frames as input, which greatly reduces computation cost compared to the optical flow based methods. For the tiny and blurry object in the temporal difference frames, the position response of the moving object on the feature map is obvious when the object moves, so our motion streams can capture these objects. Since the temporal difference frames is not valid for stationary objects, the appearance stream can provide complementary cues for object detection.

Furthermore, some detected objects maybe lost in subsequent frames due to occlusion or motion blur. To tackle this issue, we propose to introduce a memory attention module to exploit the temporal correlation in adjacent video frames. Given object states in one frame, we can reliably predict their states in the neighbouring frames using these inter-frame correlations. We use states vectors to describe each video frame and infer the states of any frame from a sequence of the states of its adjacent frames. Specially, the attention model is introduced into the recurrent memory network to refine the states vectors of the video frames. Therefore, the memory attention module can effectively capture the inter-frame correlations. By utilizing the states of adjacent frames, we can improve the detection results of occluded and blurred objects significantly.

The contributions of this paper can be summarized in the following three aspects:

- We propose a dual stream to capture motion information in consecutive video frames, in addition, to the appearance information, the motion information can enhance the response of the moving object in the feature map.
- A memory attention module is proposed to exploit the temporal correlation in adjacent video frames, and refine the states vector of each frame, which can recover the lost object encountering deformation and blurring.
- Our method leads to competitive performance on benchmark video object detection dataset DETRAC [20] across different detectors and backbone networks.

2   Related Work

2.1   Object Detection

Benefiting from the power of Deep ConvNes, object detectors such as Faster R-CNN [16] has shown dramatic improvements in accuracy. Two-stage detectors like R-CNN [4] directly combine the steps of cropping box proposals like Selective Search and classifies them through the CNN model. Compared with the traditional method, it obtains significant precision improvement and opens the deep learning era in object detection. Its descendants like Fast R-CNN [19] performs end-to-end classification and position regression loss training on convolutional neural networks. The Faster R-CNN suggests replacing the selective search with a Regional Recommendation Network (RPN), to generate candidate bounding boxes (anchor boxes) while filtering out background areas. Then it uses another tiny network based on these proposals for classification and bounding box location regression. In recent years, one-stage detectors like SSD [13] and YOLO [15] have been proposed for real-time detection with satisfactory accuracy. However, in contrast to these methods of still-image object detection, our method focuses on object detection in videos.

2.2 Object Detection in Video

Many researchers have focused on more generic categories and realistic videos, but their methods focus on post-processing class scores by static-image detectors to enforce temporal consistency of the scores. MCMOT [12] regards post-processing as a multi-object tracking problem, then uses the tracking target confidence to re-evaluate the confidence of detection. T-CNN [11] propagates the predicted boundary box to adjacent frames according to the pre-computed optical flow, and then uses the tracking algorithm of high confidence boundary box to select multiple candidate frames around the last frame and select the candidate box with the highest score. Han et al. [5] correlated the initial test results into the sequence. The weaker class scores in the same video sequence are improved, and the initial frame-by-frame detection results are improved. In contrast, our approach considers temporal information at the feature layer rather than post-processing the detected object frames. The entire framework completes video object detection via an end-to-end training.

2.3 Long Short Term Memory

LSTM [8] is a structure of Rnn cell that has been proven to be stable and powerful for modeling long-term dependencies, uses three gates (input, output, and forgetting gates) to control the transfer of information between units, and each gate has its own set of weights. The long-term short-term memory (LSTM) and the gated recursive unit (GRU) [2] as the advanced versions of RNN, can alleviate the problem of gradient disappearance to some extent [7,14]. GRU is simpler than LSTM since the output gate is removed from the unit and the output stream is indirectly controlled by the other two gates. Cell memory is also updated in different ways in the GRU. But the traditional GRU are designed to process text data rather than images. Using them on images may causes some problems, such as excessive training parameters to converge. Therefore, we need to convert a gated architecture to a convolutional architecture, replace dot product with convolutions, which effectively utilizes spatial information.

2.4 Attention Modules

Attention module can model long-term dependencies and has been widely used in the Natural Language Processing (NLP) field in recent years. Squeeze-and-Excitation Networks [10] enhance the representational power of the network by modeling channel-wise relationships in an attention mechanism. Chen et al. [1] makes use of several attention masks to fuse feature maps or predictions from different branches. Vaswani et al. [18] applies a self-attention model on machine translation. The attention modules are also increasingly applied in the image vision flied. For example, the work [9] proposes an object relation module to model the relationships among a set of objects, which improves object recognition. Our approach is motivated by the success of attention modules in the above works.

3   The Proposed Approach

Our approach is to detect generic objects in video, calibrate object locations and classify them without any manual intervention. Our method is composed of two modules: the dual stream and the memory attention module, as shown, in Fig. 1. Firstly, we pre-train the appearance and motion stream separately to get better feature representation. Then, the output of these two streams are summed together as the encoding results. After that, we utilize the memory attention module to capture temporal information. The augmented features are then fed into the RPN module and the bounding box regression and classification are conducted for object detection.

3.1   Dual Stream Architecture

Appearance Stream. Our appearance stream is used to extract the object appearance features, based on Faster R-CNN, which is an advanced method for detection. In order to get a general appearance stream, we use an advanced CNN structure for this stream, such as ResNet50 [6]. It takes RGB frames as input and outputs $H/4 \times W/4$ feature map. It is pre-trained on an object detection dataset, $i.e.$, the COCO dataset, to locate object position.

Motion Stream. It is difficult for our appearance stream to separate tiny objects that are blended with the background. Then our proposed temporal difference frames, as shown in Fig. 2(a), can not only eliminate the background interference, but also enhance the expression of the object in the feature map. After adding the motion stream, the response of object motion feature is significantly enhanced, and the tiny object undetected in original red bounding box can be recovered accurately.

However, our motion stream is invalid for static objects. When an object moves through the scene, motion stream enhances the response of the object position on the feature map. But once it becomes stationary as shown in Fig. 2(b), the motion network can not estimate the object like the appearance stream. Therefore, we leverage this complementary nature to fuse the appearance and motion streams in our pipeline.

For the motion stream, we use Depth-wise separable convolution (DWConv) to reduce computational complexity. Since temporal difference frames is not as complex as RGB frames, shallow Depth-wise separable convolution layers fits them well. This stream decomposes standard convolution into DWConv which can also be called spatial or channel-wise convolution, followed by a 1×1 point-wise convolution layer. Therefore, cross-channel and spatial correlation can be calculated independently, which greatly reduce the number of parameters, and make the structure of the motion network simpler and faster to execute. This method is trained to estimate the location of independently moving objects, based on temporal difference frames calculations from consecutive three frames as input. For the temporal difference method, we set the threshold to 25 and set

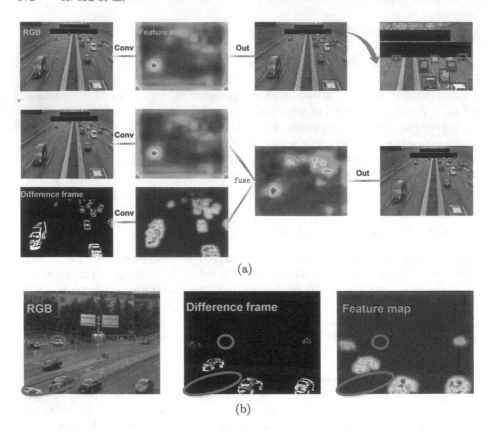

(a)

(b)

Fig. 2. (a) Appearance and motion stream feature visualization. It can be clearly seen that, for the feature response of the object position, the effect of the temporal difference frames are much higher than that of the RGB frame. But when we added them together, the objects missed in the red box is restored. (b) Visualization of motion stream features, including stationary objects in red circle. (Color figure online)

the brightness value between 30 and 100 as the background. Then we use some morphology processing (such as corrosion, expansion) to reduce the interference of the motion background. The time cost of obtaining these temporal difference frames is much less than the optical flow picture. We train the motion stream to estimate independently moving objects that produce a H/4 × W/4 prediction output, where each value represents the status of the corresponding pixel motion.

3.2   Memory Attention Module

To capture temporal information in the video sequence, we propose a memory attention module which comprised two key components: ConvGRU module and attention module. The ConvGRU module is designed to exploit the temporal correlation in adjacent video frames, and the attention module is to refine the status feature matrix h_t in ConvGRU, as shown in the Fig. 3. Our memory

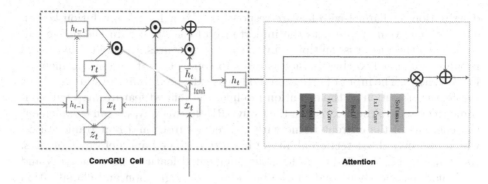

Fig. 3. Memory attention module. Our memory attention module is composed two key components: ConvGRU module and an Attention module.

attention module is computed with convolutional operators and non-linearities as follows.

$$z_t = \sigma(W_{hz} * h_{t-1} + W_{xz} * x_t + b_z) \tag{1}$$

$$r_t = \sigma(W_{hr} * h_{t-1} + W_{xr} * x_t + b_r) \tag{2}$$

$$\overline{h}_t = tanh(W_h * (r_t \odot h_{t-1}) + W_{xr} * x_t + b_r) \tag{3}$$

$$h_t = (1 - z_t) \odot h_{t-1} + z \odot \overline{h} \tag{4}$$

$$c_t = Softmax(W_{1*1}(ReLU(W_{1*1} * GAP(h_t)))) \tag{5}$$

$$h'_t = (c_t * h_t + h_t) \tag{6}$$

Firstly, ConvGRU obtains the states of the two control gates (reset gate and update gate) by the last transmitted state h_{t-1} and the input x_t of the current node. As shown in Eq. (1). The state and gate are 3D tensors that characterize the spatiotemporal pattern in the video, effectively remember each object trajectory and their direction. σ stands for the activation function, acting as a gating signal. After getting the gating signal, we use the reset gate to handle the state of the previous frame h_t, and then splice it with the input x_t, and get the implicit state of the current frame through a *tanh* activation function. $\odot$ denotes the multiplication of the corresponding element. The last and most critical step, as we call it the memory update phase, is used to simultaneously forget and remember. According to Eq. (4), we can see that z_t and $1 - z_t$ are interlocked, selectively forgetting or retaining the previous state and the hidden state. Module learning combines the characteristics of the current frame with the video representation of the memory to improve motion predictions, or to fully recover them from previous observations even if the moving objects become stationary.

Our attention module is to refine the state feature h_t in ConvGRU, and to improve the representation of specific context by mining the interrelationships between channels. As shown in Fig. 3, the module is built upon deep CNN features to achieve the feature selection. Detailed steps are shown in Eq. (5). The *GAP* represents the global average pooling. This descriptor embeds the global distribution of channel-wise feature responses. W is a 1×1 convolution kernel. The *Softmax* value represents the importance of each region in the image feature. Then the output is multiplied by the original features. Finally the extracted features are added to the original features to complete feature enhancement as Eq. (6) shows. The input of attention module is extracted from the state h_t. After the feature selection of the attention module, the refined feature map will continue to be sent to the next cell in the ConvGRU. In this way, we can complement the contents of the current frame with the refined front and rear frame states, which improves the detection ability of blurred, occluded and deformed objects. As shown in Fig. 4. Finally, we feed the augmented features into the RPN and ROI module, and then conduct the bounding box regression and classification for object detection. The details of RPN and ROI module can be referred in [16].

Faster R-cnn   no Memory Attention   with Memory Attention

Fig. 4. Our memory attention module recovers the object in the current frame that was lost due to occlusion and blurring based on the state vector of the previous frame.

4   Experiments

We evaluate our approach on a public dataset DETRAC [20]. We first introduce the dataset and implementation details, followed by a series of ablation experiments. Finally, we present the comparison results with other state-of-the-art methods.

DETRAC: The DETRAC [20] is a large object detection dataset of urban street scene, with 10 h at 24 different locations in Beijing and Tianjin. The frame rate is 25 frames per second with a resolution of 960×540. The entire dataset contains 100 videos with 140,000 frames manually labeled with 8,250 vehicles for a total of 1.21 million labeled objects. The training set contains 60 videos, and the rest 40 videos for the test set.

4.1   Implementation Details

In this subsection, we will decompose our approach to verify the contribution of each component. We implement our method based on Pytorch. Our proposed network is based on the ResNet-50 and ResNet-101 pre-trained on ImageNet [17].

Training: We respectively use the Faster R-CNN and YOLO$_{v2}$ as our basic object detection frameworks, most of the parameters are set according to the original publication. SGD training is performed, with 6 image at each mini-batch. 120 K iterations are performed on 4 GPUs, each of which holding two mini-batch. All our experiments are performed on a workstation with Nvidia 1080ti, CUDA 9.0 and cuDNN V7.5.

Table 1. The performance on DETRAC [20] dataset. APP represents appearance stream, MOT represents motion stream, and MA represent memory attention. The Faster R-CNN is based on ResNet-50. The YOLO$_{v2}$ is based on darknet19.

Method	APP	MOT	MA	mAP(%)
Faster R-CNN	✓			71.71
		✓		61.00
	✓	✓		72.83
	✓		✓	72.92
	✓	✓	✓	**73.96**
YOLO$_{v2}$	✓			71.23
		✓		60.16
	✓	✓		72.47
	✓		✓	72.24
	✓	✓	✓	**73.39**

Table 2. Per-class results on DETRAC [20] testing set. MMA net outperforms existing approaches and achieves 74.88% in mAP.

Method	Backbone	mAP (%)	Car	Van	Bus	Others
R-FCN	Res50	71.73	88.42	74.04	90.49	33.97
R-FCN	Res101	73.27	88.63	73.73	90.61	40.11
SSD	Vgg16	70.16	87.29	72.13	87.21	34.02
FSSD	Vgg16	71.75	89.16	73.25	88.46	36.12
YOLO$_{v2}$	darknet19	71.23	89.93	65.84	87.83	41.31
Faster R-CNN	Res50	71.71	88.95	73.08	90.55	34.27
Faster R-CNN	Res101	73.11	88.91	73.23	90.63	39.66
MMA + YOLO$_{v2}$	darknet19	**73.39**	90.41	69.53	91.23	**42.37**
MMA + FasterR − CNN	Res50	**73.96**	90.25	74.78	93.32	37.48
MMA + FasterR − CNN	Res101	**74.88**	**90.87**	**75.06**	**93.33**	40.26

YOLOv2   MMA + YOLOv2   Faster R-cnn   MMA + Faster R-cnn

Fig. 5. Detection results of YOLO$_{v2}$, Fater R-cnn and our algorithm. The car in the red box is missed by YOLO$_{v2}$ and FastrRcnn, but detected by our algorithm. (Color figure online)

4.2   Ablation Study

For better understanding MMA net, we investigate the impact of each component in its design. The results are summarized in Table 1.

As show in Table 1, our MMA net improves the performance. Compared with the baseline Faster R-CNN (ResNet-50), our MMA yields to a result of 73.96% in mAP, which brings 2.25% improvement. (1) APP: The appearance stream is the backbone of base detectors like Faster R-CNN. As we can see, our baseline accuracy is 71.71%. (2) MOT: When we add motion steam separately, the accuracy is reduced by a few points compared to the baseline. The reason is that there are many static objects in the dataset. For example, cars stopping at traffic lights are almost equivalent to stationary targets in consecutive frames, which leads to inaccurate temporal difference frame and low precision. Therefore, adding appearance stream can facilitate compensating the ineffective prediction of motion stream, which improves the mAP to 72.83%. (3) MA: Employing memory attention module individually outperforms the baseline by 1.21%. When we integrate these modules together, the performance further achieves to 73.96%. In addition, when we apply a deeper pre-trained network (ResNet-101), our module detection performance is improved to 74.88%. After integrating our components to YOLO$_{v2}$, the performance consistently improves.

4.3   Comparison to the State-of-the-art

Table 2 compares our approach to the state-of-the-art methods on DETRAC [20]. In order to verify the superiority of our approach, we use different backbone networks for verification. The results show that we perform much well than above of method. Figure 5 visualizes some representative results of the Faster R-CNN, YOLO$_{v2}$ baseline and our proposed framework. It is clear that the visualization quality of our method is much better than the baselines.

5   Conclusion

In this paper, we propose a novel module for object detection in video with competitive performance, which introduces a dual stream network with memory attention module. In our network, we make full use of the object motion information and send it into a memory attention module, followed by the refined consecutive frames states for improving detection accuracy. Specifically, the motion stream improves the detection accuracy of the tiny objects, but it can not detect the stationary object, so we merge it with the appearance stream to form a complementary module and memory attention module to recover the lost object due to deformation and blur. Our ablation study shows that our proposed module can achieve competitive results and outperforms other advanced methods. More importantly, our modules can be easily embedded in other object frameworks such as Faster R-CNN and YOLO$_{v2}$, which demonstrates the generality of our method.

Acknowledgements. This work was supported by the Open Project Program of the National Laboratory of Pattern Recognition (NLPR) (201900046) and the National Natural Science Foundation of China (61472002).

References

1. Chen, L.C., Yang, Y., Wang, J., Xu, W., Yuille, A.L.: Attention to scale: scale-aware semantic image segmentation. In: Proceedings of the IEEE Conference on Computer Vision and Pattern Recognition (2016)
2. Cho, K., et al.: Learning phrase representations using RNN encoder-decoder for statistical machine translation. arXiv preprint. arXiv:1406.1078 (2014)
3. Dai, J., Li, Y., He, K., Sun, J.: R-FCN: object detection via region-based fully convolutional networks. In: Advances in Neural Information Processing Systems (2016)
4. Girshick, R., Donahue, J., Darrell, T., Malik, J.: Rich feature hierarchies for accurate object detection and semantic segmentation. In: Proceedings of the IEEE Conference on Computer Vision and Pattern Recognition (2014)

5. Han, W., et al.: Seq-NMS for video object detection. arXiv preprint. arXiv:1602.08465 (2016)
6. He, K., Zhang, X., Ren, S., Sun, J.: Deep residual learning for image recognition. In: Proceedings of the IEEE Conference on Computer Vision and Pattern Recognition (2016)
7. Hochreiter, S.: The vanishing gradient problem during learning recurrent neural nets and problem solutions. Int. J. Uncertainty Fuzziness Knowl. Based Syst. 6(02), 107–116 (1998)
8. Hochreiter, S., Schmidhuber, J.: Long short-term memory. Neural Comput. 9(8), 1735–1780 (1997)
9. Hu, H., Gu, J., Zhang, Z., Dai, J., Wei, Y.: Relation networks for object detection. In: Proceedings of the IEEE Conference on Computer Vision and Pattern Recognition (2018)
10. Hu, J., Shen, L., Sun, G.: Squeeze-and-excitation networks. In: Proceedings of the IEEE Conference on Computer Vision and Pattern Recognition (2018)
11. Kang, K., et al.: T-CNN: tubelets with convolutional neural networks for object detection from videos. IEEE Trans. Circuits Syst. Video Technol. 28(10), 2896–2907 (2018)
12. Lee, B., Erdenee, E., Jin, S., Nam, M.Y., Jung, Y.G., Rhee, P.K.: Multi-class multi-object tracking using changing point detection. In: Hua, G., Jégou, H. (eds.) ECCV 2016. LNCS, vol. 9914, pp. 68–83. Springer, Cham (2016). https://doi.org/10.1007/978-3-319-48881-3_6
13. Liu, W., et al.: SSD: single shot multibox detector. In: Leibe, B., Matas, J., Sebe, N., Welling, M. (eds.) ECCV 2016. LNCS, vol. 9905, pp. 21–37. Springer, Cham (2016). https://doi.org/10.1007/978-3-319-46448-0_2
14. Pascanu, R., Mikolov, T., Bengio, Y.: On the difficulty of training recurrent neural networks. In: International Conference on Machine Learning (2013)
15. Redmon, J., Divvala, S., Girshick, R., Farhadi, A.: You only look once: unified, real-time object detection. In: Proceedings of the IEEE Conference on Computer Vision and Pattern Recognition (2016)
16. Ren, S., He, K., Girshick, R., Sun, J.: Faster R-CNN: towards real-time object detection with region proposal networks. In: Advances in Neural Information Processing Systems (2015)
17. Russakovsky, O., et al.: Imagenet large scale visual recognition challenge. Int. J. Comput. Vis. 115(3), 211–252 (2015)
18. Vaswani, A., et al.: Attention is all you need. In: Advances in Neural Information Processing Systems (2017)
19. Wang, L., Ouyang, W., Wang, X.: Visual tracking with fully convolutional networks. In: Proceedings of the IEEE International Conference on Computer Vision (2015)
20. Wen, L., et al.: UA-DETRAC: a new benchmark and protocol for multi-object detection and tracking. arXiv preprint. arXiv:1511.04136 (2015)
21. Zhu, X., Dai, J., Yuan, L., Wei, Y.: Towards high performance video object detection. In: Proceedings of the IEEE Conference on Computer Vision and Pattern Recognition (2018)
22. Zhu, X., Wang, Y., Dai, J., Yuan, L., Wei, Y.: Flow-guided feature aggregation for video object detection. In: Proceedings of the IEEE International Conference on Computer Vision (2017)

Fitting Cuboids from the Unstructured 3D Point Cloud

Chengkun Cao[1,2] and Guoping Wang[1,2(✉)]

[1] School of Electronics Engineering and Computer Science,
Peking University, Beijing, China
{cck,wgp}@pku.edu.cn
[2] Beijing Engineering Research Center for Virtual Simulation and Visualization,
Beijing, China

Abstract. The structural of 3D point cloud data is very important. This paper proposes an algorithm for fitting the cuboid from the unstructured point cloud data directly. In this paper, a 3D point cloud is fitted into a combination of multiple cuboids. Initializing several seeds randomly, and then segment the point cloud and fitting cuboids from the segmented point cloud through iteration. The method in this paper has obvious advantages than traditional methods, with better robustness and more accurate fitting results.

Keywords: Point cloud · Fitting cuboids · Graph cut · Levenberg-Marquardt algorithm

1 Introduction

As we all know, getting data of the three-dimensional models from the real world is an accurate and efficient method. With the rapid development of related equipment and algorithms, the application of this method is becoming more and more extensive. In this circumstance, the gotten data is always unstructured point cloud data which has some unavoidable problems such as noise, incomplete quantity, uneven density, etc. So we can use structured fitting on these data to solve the mentioned problems effactually. The method used in [14] is a classical fitting method, which can fitting the point cloud data of the familiar plane, cylinder, cone and sphere partly and respectively. We can use this method to fitting the point cloud data on the surface of cylinder or cone in one time; But for the point cloud data on the surface of the cuboid, we need to fitting six surfaces respectively in this method. However, in real life, there are so many cuboids in man-made objects. The fitting result via the above method can not guarantee the parallel or vertical of the correlative surfaces, and especially in the case that the point cloud data has a lot of noise or missing data we can not fitting the

Supported by The National Key Technology Research and Development Program of China (No. 2017YFB1002705, 2017YFB1002601); and the National Natural Science Foundation of China (NSFC) (61632003,61661146002).

© Springer Nature Switzerland AG 2019
Y. Zhao et al. (Eds.): ICIG 2019, LNCS 11902, pp. 179–190, 2019.
https://doi.org/10.1007/978-3-030-34110-7_16

integrated six surfaces. In conclusion, we need a method that can fitting the cuboid directly and improve the fitting-quality of this point cloud data.

The surface of sphere can be expressed by a continuous equation. Theoretically, we can use 4 points on different sphere surfaces to fitting the only sphere accurately. But the fitting of the cuboid is differ from sphere, we need to get a point on every surface in order to fitting the only cuboid accurately. For the point cloud data on surface, using this method has computing complexity. In the circumstance where a surface has incomplete data, we can not confirm the only result.

This paper puts forward an iteration-fitting method that can proceed the affine transformation on an infinitesimal unit cuboid. On this basis, it applies the strategies including random seeds, dynamic segmentation of the point cloud and combination of fitting cuboid to fitting multi-cuboid in the complex scene simultaneously. This method has good-robustness, and in the complex multi-cuboid scene it can also fitting every cuboid. Even in the data-losing or noise condition, it will get a good fitting result.

The main contributions of this paper are as follows:

1. We propose an algorithm for directly fitting multiple cuboids from a 3D point cloud data by iterative segmentation and fitting;
2. We propose a formula for calculating the exact result of the shortest distance from any point in the space to the surface of the cuboid.

2   Related Works

2.1   Surface Reconstruction

Surface reconstruction on point cloud data is the most direct method. [4] proposed a general algorithm of surface reconstruction, which can construct a smooth and watertight surface mesh model with certain anti-noise ability, but it can not maintain the sharp features of the model. For the area with data sparse or missing, the area is difficult to maintain the flatness of the surface. [1] using a noisy point cloud as input, quickly sketch out each plane through interaction, thus constructing a complex model. [13] For the reconstruction of LiDAR data, an algorithm with an interaction-based, using common features between floors is proposed, it can solve a large amount of data loss. [12] using interactive means to outline the general appearance of the building, and then the detailed building elements such as windows are constructed by interaction to reconstruct the complex architectural model. The above works are general algorithm that are from the point cloud to mesh reconstruction, and some of them are optimized for urban scenes, some combined interactions to enhance the express ability of details.

2.2   Parameterization of the Point Cloud

[9] abstracts a complex model using several ellipsoids of varying sizes. [15] proposes a way to represent Mesh with spheres, using a series of spheres of varying

sizes and theirs joints between the spheres to abstract a complex Mesh. [7,8] proposes a way to represent a Manhattan urban scene with cuboids, which are constituted by cutting space by planes that is parallel and vertical, so we get a number of cuboids with axis in the same representing a building in a Manhattan scene. The above method proposes a parametric representation of the point cloud for different data and different application fields.

2.3 Plane Extraction and Processing of the Point Cloud

Many scenes are made up of many planes. To combat the effects of data noise and other factors, [14] is widely used to fit planes. Due to the single type of the fitted features, the accuracy of the fitting is improved, and the low-quality point cloud data can still fit the original plane. Most of these works are deal with urban scene data. [6] establishes a regular surface mesh model by extracting the plane features of the point cloud and solving its intersection. [10] is designed for urban scenes with many plane structures and errors. It correct the errors by organizing the plane of the scene, grouping the parallel and vertical relationships of the planes in the scene. The main idea of the above method is to fit the plane in the point cloud, and then use the relationship between the planes to process the point cloud data to reduce the impact of data noise and other issues.

This paper fitting the cuboids from the point cloud directly. On the one hand, it proposes an abstract representation of the scene represented by cuboids. On the other hand, it has better fitting ability to the plane works in many cases.

3   Algorithm

The algorithm of this paper includes 4 parts: Setting the seeds The distance of a point to cuboid & Point cloud segmentation Cuboid fitting and The deleting & adding of cuboids. The input of algorithm is an unstructured point cloud data $C = \{P_i\}_{i \in \mathbb{I}} \subset \mathbb{R}^3 (0 < i < N)$ which include N points. The algorithm initialize some seeds randomly, then make segmentation and fitting on the segmented point cloud by iteration. The point cloud C is segmented by the distance from the point cloud to seeds, which is solved by the algorithm Graph Cut [2,3,5]. The fitted cuboids are affine transformed from the seeds. In the iteration progress, it will segment the point cloud again after every iteration in order to avoid local result. In the segment progress, it may combine the 2 neighboring seeds and delete the seeds that can not be fitting. In order to guarantee the variety of the algorithm, in the fitting progress, it will increase some points as new seeds randomly. When all the fitting cuboid is stable or the fitting time is achieved, it will stop fitting. The flow chart of algorithm is as Fig. 1.

3.1   Pretreatment

Creating a KD-tree for the input point cloud C, and for each point P in the point cloud, finding all points less than the radius r as the neighbor point $Nb(P)$ for that point.

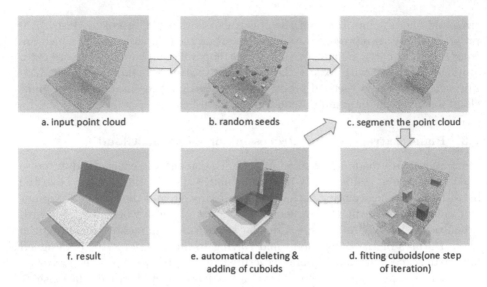

a. input point cloud   b. random seeds   c. segment the point cloud

f. result   e. automatical deleting & adding of cuboids   d. fitting cuboids(one step of iteration)

Fig. 1. Flow chart of the algorithm. (a) is a input point cloud. Then generate the seeds(b) randomly. In the iteration progress, we segment the point cloud(c) (note: not all seeds are assigned to the point), and then fitting cuboids of the segmented point cloud(d). In every iteration progress, there are automatically deleting & adding of cuboids(e). If every cuboids' fitting energy is small enough or reach to the max iteration, stop the iteration and get the result(f), or continue the iteration to(c).

3.2 Setting the Seeds

This paper put forward an infinitesimal cuboid concept. Due to the computer can not represent an infinitesimal value really, we will use a minimum that can be expressed to instead. Because a minimum will increase the number of iterations, we use the $\frac{1}{10000}$ of the point cloud AABB bounding box diagonal length to represent, marked as L. The cuboid in this paper is expressed by a center c and 3 vectors that are mutually perpendicular. The length of vectors is half of the 3 edges respectively. And the length of 3 vectors on infinitesimal fundamental cuboid is L, the center c is a random point from the input point cloud. In this paper, the infinitesimal fundamental cuboid with the length of vector is L and the center is c seed. Theoretically, the initial number of seed K can be a random integer, but the initial number K shouldn't be too small in order to cover all the situations and boost the calculation. So we choose about 10 times of the real cuboids numbers of the scene as K.

3.3 The Distance of a Point to Cuboid and Point Cloud Segmentation

The Distance of a Point to Cuboid. The distance of a point to cuboid is the shortest distance of a point to a cuboid surface. If we use the infinite surface of the 6 cuboid surface, we can divide the 3d space into 27 parts which 26 parts are in the external and 1 part is in the interior. For the distance of a random point on the cuboid surface to cuboid is 0. For the distance of a point in the interior, we use the minimum value of the point to cuboid surface's vertical distance. For the external points, there are 3 cases: (1) the point is above cuboid surface, the vertical distance of the point to surface is the shortest distance of the point to cuboid surface, this case is 6 among 26; (2) the point is in the angle place of 2 neighboring cuboid surfaces, the vertical distance of the point to edge which the 2 surface intersections pass, this case is 12 among 26; (3) the point is in the angle place of 3 neighboring cuboid surfaces, the shortest distance of the point to cuboid surface is the distance of the point to the intersection (the corresponding cuboid vertex) of 3 surfaces, this case is 8 among 26. No matter what above case it is, we need to calculate the distance of the point to a cuboid surface to get the shortest distance of the point to cuboid surface. We define the direction of the center to outward on the cuboid surface as this surface vector. Due to the surface expressing equation is $ax + by + cz + d = 0$, and $a^2 + b^2 + c^2 = 1$. From the solid geometry science, the distance $D_0 = ax_0 + by_0 + cz_0 + d$ of a random point in the space $P(x_0, y_0, z_0)$ to the surface. Because we define the outward normal, there are 3 cases: (1) when the point is above surface, $D_0 > 0$; (2) the point is on the surface, $D_0 > 0$; (3) the point is below the surface, $D_0 < 0$. We define $D_1, D_2, D_3, D_4, D_5, D_6$ as the distance of a random point $P(x_0, y_0, z_0)$ in the space to the planes of the 6 faces of the cuboid. If we calculate the 27 cases respectively, it will be very inconvenient. So we combine the 27 cases including the point is in external and interior to calculate together. From the solid geometry science, when $D_1, D_2, D_3, D_4, D_5, D_6$ are less than 0, the point P is in the interior, the distance of it to cuboid B is:

$$D(B, P) = \min\{D_1, D_2, D_3, D_4, D_5, D_6\} \tag{1}$$

When D_x (among $D_1, D_2, D_3, D_4, D_5, D_6$) is 0 and the others are all less than 0, it means the point P is on the x cuboid surface. The distance of the point to cuboid is 0, which is a special case in the interior. The 26 cases where the point P is in the external, from the solid geometry science,

$$D(B, P) = \sqrt{\sum_{i=1}^{6} \lambda \cdot D_i^2}, \quad \begin{cases} \lambda = 1 \; D_i > 0 \\ \lambda = 0 \; D_i \leq 0 \end{cases} \tag{2}$$

is the distance of the point P to cuboid.

The Point Cloud Segmentation. When the seed is selected, it will segment the point cloud according to the distance of a point to seed. Every point only can belong to one seed, so it belong to the seed which is nearest. Just considering the distance segmentation can not guarantee the smoothness of the segmentation boundary, so consider the neighbor of each point as a smoothing term, and optimize the following energy:

$$E(l) = \sum_{i \in C} D_i(l_i) + \gamma \sum_{\{i,j\} \in Edge} V_{i,j}(l_i, l_j) \tag{3}$$

Among them, l means every point's ID of all seed; $D_i(l_i)$ means the distance of every point P_i to the seed l; γ is a constant on the interval $[0,1]$, and it is the balance weight of the two items, in results section we will express the effect in the value of the *gamma*; *Edge* is the set of all pairs of P_i in C with its neighbors $NB(P_i)$. The smoothing term $V_{i,j}$ aims to make the closing points belong to the same seed as much as possible. Therefore, we define as follows:

$$V_{i,j} = \frac{L}{\lambda \cdot (\epsilon + DP(i,j))}$$

L is the length of the point cloud C bounding box diagonal; λ is constant term, its value and the smooth capability have a proportional relationship. We adopt 10^3. $DP(i,j)$ is the Euclidean distance of point P_i and point P_j. The energy formula E is solved by the Graph Cut algorithm. The speed of the solution is related to the number of points in the point cloud and the number of neighbors. In order to speed up the calculation, the number of neighbors at each point in this paper is limited to 16. Fitting each cuboid using the method Sect. 3.4 for each segment result, then recalculate the distance from each point to the fitted cuboid using the formula (3) to solve the new segmentation.

3.4   Cuboid Fitting

We define a subset CS segmented from the point cloud C to fitting a cuboid. Given an initial result, a final result can be obtained by optimizing the distance from all points in the CS to the cuboid. We solve the 3 transformed parameter including rotate $R(r_x, r_y, r_z)$, pan $T(t_x, t_y, t_z)$ and zoom S by applying affine transformation on the seeds, then make the distance from the point cloud to cuboid after transformation. We define the distance from point cloud subset CS to the cuboid B is as follows:

$$D_{cuboid}(B) = D_{points\_to\_cuboid}(B) + D_{cuboid\_to\_points}(B) \tag{4}$$

Among them, $D_{points\_to\_cuboid}(B)$ is the distance from all points in the point cloud belonging to the seeds to the point, using the formulas (1) and (2). $D_{cuboid\_to\_points}(B)$ can avoid points where some of the six planes of the cuboid are unconstrained, which is defined as:

$$D_{cuboid\_to\_points}(B) = \frac{\sum_{m=1}^{6} \min_{i=1}^{|CS|} (is\_empty_m \cdot DF(m,i))}{\sum_{m=1}^{6} is\_empty_m}$$

$|CS|$ indicates the number of points in the subset CS; is_empty_m indicates whether there is a point on the m plane of the cuboid. If there is not, it is 1, if there is, it is 0; $DF(m,i)$ indicates the distance from the i point to the m plane. Thus, for a plane without a point constraint, we use the distance from the nearest point in all points as the constraint for that plane. The scaling in the affine transformation is scaled separately along the three axes of the cuboid, so we need to solve three scaling parameters S_1, S_2, S_3. According to the transformation rules, the final result is obtained by solving the following formula:

$$B_{new} = R \cdot S \cdot B_{old} + T \tag{5}$$

B_{old} is the cuboid before the transformation, and B_{new} is the transformed cuboid. $S = \begin{bmatrix} s_1 & & \\ & s_2 & \\ & & s_3 \end{bmatrix}$ compared to the standard affine transformation, the scaling parameters have changed from one to three. From the formula (4) and (5), we can solve these 9 parameters by optimizing energy:

$$E = \min(D_{cuboid}(B_{new}))$$
$$= \min(D_{cuboid}(R \cdot S \cdot B_{old} + T))$$

Since the function $D(B, p_i)$ is a piecewise function, it is not conducive to directly finding its derivative. Therefore, for this optimization problem, we use the numerical derivative to calculate the function, using Levenberg – Marquardt, LM algorithm [11] solves. The LM algorithm is an iteration optimized algorithm that requires us to provide an initial result. We use the value of the seed as the initial result.

The input data cannot be modified in each iteration step using the standard LM algorithm, that is, the point cloud data cannot be dynamically segmented at each step. Therefore, we redesigned the iterative step to re-segment the point cloud data before recalculating the input data before using each step of the LM algorithm. Since we have to perform the point cloud segmentation and cuboid fitting in every iteration step, the points where each iteration step participates in the fitting are likely to change, so the algorithm does not converge quickly. In the experiment of this paper, the final result is generally approached after 20 50 iterations. The energy E will not change significantly after 100 iterations, so the maximum number of iterations of the algorithm in this paper is set to 200.

3.5   The Deleting and Adding of Cuboids

Since not all point clouds is guaranteed to fit a cuboid, such as when there is no result when all points are in one or two planes, or if the count of the points is too small, the only result cannot be determined. In this case, the fitting algorithm will make the volume of cuboid is very large or the LM algorithm exits abnormally. Such seed need to be deleted.

In addition, when using the Graph cut algorithm in the point cloud segmentation, some seeds will not be assigned points in the point cloud C, and the seed that are not assigned to the point will be deleted. This is the seed deleted most in this paper.

In order to fitting all the cuboids as much as possible, the distance from each point to the cuboid is calculated after each segmentation, and the distance value is used as the probability density, and a point is randomly selected as a new seed.

This algorithm is very insensitive to the setting of the number K of the initial seeds.

Figure 2d is the fitting result in the case where the initial value of K is 1, and Fig. 2b and c is the result of step (3,4), which automatically increases the seeds.

Figure 2h is the result of the fitting in the case where the initial value of K is 30, and Fig. 2f and g is the result of step (2, 4). The algorithm automatically merges the majority of the seeds belonging to the same cuboid.

a. step = 1, seeds = 1   b. step = 3, seeds = 3   c. step = 4, seeds = 4   d. step = 28, seeds = 3

e. step = 1, seeds = 30   f. step = 2, seeds = 5   g. step = 4, seeds = 4   h. step = 23, seeds = 4

Fig. 2. Auto adding & deleting of the seeds. The above line are showing the step of adding seeds, and the underside line are showing the steps of deleting of the seeds.

4   Results and Discussion

The experimental environment of this paper is a normal desktop computer, configured as i5-7500CPU and 8 GB DDR4 memory, and the program is single-threaded. We tested different types of data in different situations.

4.1   Noisy Data

Figure 3a is a surface point cloud data with 5% noise. Figure 3b is the fitting result of the noisy point cloud. Figure 2 is the fitting result of the raw data without noise.

4.2   The Effect of the Smooth Parameter γ

The value of the smoothing parameter γ effects the accuracy of the final result. The smaller the value of γ, the more the cuboids in the final result; the larger the value of γ, the fewer cuboids in the final result, as shown in Fig. 4.

Fig. 3. Noisy data. (a) is the input point cloud with 5% noisy. (b) is the result cuboids and the input point cloud. (c) is the distance of each point to the cuboids using the jet colormap. (d) is the result cuboids only.

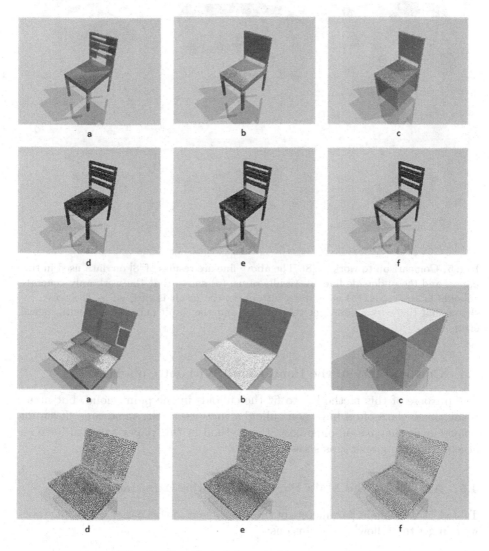

Fig. 4. The effect of the smooth parameter γ.

4.3   Compare to Work in [8]

Figure 5 is a comparison of the method in this paper and the method in [8]. Since [8] can only process Manhattan scenes, and the algorithm relies on the method of [14] as the pretreatment. It can be seen that it cannot process multiple cuboids in any orientation at one time, and if the fitting plane is missing, the correct result is generally not obtained.

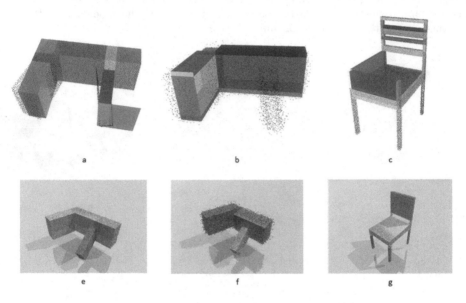

Fig. 5. Comparison to work in [8]. The above line are results of [8] on data used in this paper, and the underside line are results of us. (a) shows that the work only generate cuboids in same axis. (b) is on data with noise, the result is effected by the noise. (c) shows that the work cannot get thin planes, and the result cuboids may with logical errors.

4.4   Compatibility of the Point Cloud Without Cuboids

The purpose of this method is to fit the cuboids in the point cloud, but many point clouds data often have non-cuboid structures at the same time. Even for point clouds that no cuboids exist, the method in this paper can still have an acceptable fitting result, as shown in Fig. 6.

4.5   Analysis of the Main Parameters of the Experiment

Table 1 lists the main parameters of the experiment in this paper. From the table we can get the following conclusions:

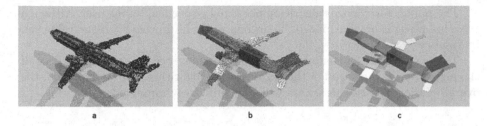

a   b   c

Fig. 6. Compatibility of point clouds without cuboids.

1. Here is basically no correlation between the initial seeds K and the final cuboid number, but it affects the calculation speed.
2. The smoothing parameter γ of the segmentation algorithm is an important parameter affecting the final number of cuboids.
3. The small Root Mean Square Error (RMSE) of the final experimental results does not necessarily mean that the results of the fitting are good.

Table 1. The main parameters of the experiment in this paper.

Name	Points no	Final cuboids no	initial K	γ	time(s)	RMSE	Figure no
laptop_0141	4236	1	20	1E-2	21	0.7666	Fig. 4
laptop_0141	4236	2	20	2E-3	59	0.0424	Figs. 1 and 4
laptop_0141	4236	10	20	5E-4	157	0.0434	Fig. 4
chair_0007	5841	2	40	3E-3	57	0.0156	Fig. 4
chair_0007	5841	6	60	5E-4	266	0.0135	Figs. 4 and 5
chair_0007	5841	22	150	9E-5	788	0.0236	Fig. 4
brick	7298	3	1	8E-4	80	0.0384	Fig. 2
brick	7298	4	30	8E-4	99	0.0246	Figs. 2 and 5
brick.noisy	7298	3	50	8E-4	50	0.0348	Figs. 3 and 5
airplane_0002	3464	20	150	2E-5	375	0.0275	Fig. 6

5 Conclusion and Future Work

This paper proposes a method for directly fitting multiple cuboids from the unstructured 3D point cloud data, which has obvious advantage compared with the traditional methods. The fitting results can be well applied in the structured processing of point cloud data and the presentation of the model.

This algorithm is well robust, but the fitting efficiency of the flat cuboid is less, and the fitting ability to the detail part needs to be improved.

The parameter γ in this algorithm needs to be specified by the user. Although its value range is obvious, it will be an important improvement if the value can be calculated automatically.

The point cloud segmentation part of this paper occupies the main time of the algorithm. If the speed of the segmentation algorithm can be improved, the overall efficiency of the algorithm will be significantly improved.

References

1. Arikan, M., Schwärzler, M., Flöry, S., Wimmer, M., Maierhofer, S.: O-snap: optimization-based snapping for modeling architecture. ACM Trans. Graph. (TOG) **32**(1), 6 (2013)
2. Boykov, Y., Kolmogorov, V.: An experimental comparison of min-cut/max-flow algorithms for energy minimization in vision. IEEE Trans. Pattern Anal. Mach. Intell. **9**, 1124–1137 (2004)
3. Boykov, Y., Veksler, O., Zabih, R.: Fast approximate energy minimization via graph cuts. In: Proceedings of the Seventh IEEE International Conference on Computer Vision, vol. 1, pp. 377–384. IEEE (1999)
4. Kazhdan, M., Bolitho, M., Hoppe, H.: Poisson surface reconstruction. In: Proceedings of the fourth Eurographics Symposium on Geometry Processing, vol. 7 (2006)
5. Kolmogorov, V., Zabih, R.: What energy functions can be minimizedvia graph cuts? IEEE Trans. Pattern Anal. Mach. Intell. **2**, 147–159 (2004)
6. Lafarge, F., Alliez, P.: Surface reconstruction through point set structuring. In: Computer Graphics Forum, vol. 32, pp. 225–234. Wiley Online Library (2013)
7. Li, M., Nan, L., Liu, S.: Fitting boxes to manhattan scenes using linear integer programming. Int. J. Digital Earth **9**(8), 806–817 (2016)
8. Li, M., Wonka, P., Nan, L.: Manhattan-world urban reconstruction from point clouds. In: Leibe, B., Matas, J., Sebe, N., Welling, M. (eds.) ECCV 2016. LNCS, vol. 9908, pp. 54–69. Springer, Cham (2016). https://doi.org/10.1007/978-3-319-46493-0_4
9. Lu, L., Choi, Y.K., Wang, W., Kim, M.S.: Variational 3d shape segmentation for bounding volume computation. In: Computer Graphics Forum, vol. 26, pp. 329–338. Wiley Online Library (2007)
10. Monszpart, A., Mellado, N., Brostow, G.J., Mitra, N.J.: Rapter: rebuilding man-made scenes with regular arrangements of planes. ACM Trans. Graph. **34**(4), 103:1–103:12 (2015)
11. Moré, J.J.: The Levenberg-Marquardt algorithm: implementation and theory. In: Watson, G.A. (ed.) Numerical Analysis. LNM, vol. 630, pp. 105–116. Springer, Heidelberg (1978). https://doi.org/10.1007/BFb0067700
12. Nan, L., Jiang, C., Ghanem, B., Wonka, P.: Template assembly for detailed urban reconstruction. In: Computer Graphics Forum, vol. 34, pp. 217–228. Wiley Online Library (2015)
13. Nan, L., Sharf, A., Zhang, H., Cohen-Or, D., Chen, B.: Smartboxes for interactive urban reconstruction. In: ACM Transactions on Graphics (TOG), vol. 29, p. 93. ACM (2010)
14. Schnabel, R., Wahl, R., Klein, R.: Efficient ransac for point-cloud shape detection. In: Computer Graphics Forum, vol. 26, pp. 214–226. Wiley Online Library (2007)
15. Thiery, J.M., Guy, É., Boubekeur, T.: Sphere-meshes: shape approximation using spherical quadric error metrics. ACM Trans. Graph. (TOG) **32**(6), 178 (2013)

Computer Graphics and Visualization

Blending Polyhedral Edge Clusters

Pei Zhou[1]([✉]) and Wen-Han Qian[2]

[1] Beijing Institute of Astronautical Systems Engineering, Beijing 100076, China
zhoup2@126.com
[2] Robotics Institute, School of Mechanical Engineering,
Shanghai Jiao Tong University, Shanghai 200240, China

Abstract. This paper presents an efficient method for blending edge clusters on polyhedra, where an edge cluster means a set of polyhedral edges connected together by polyhedral vertices. It extends the vertex-first algorithm in (P. Zhou, W.H. Qian, A vertex-first parametric algorithm for polyhedron blending, Computer-Aided Design 41 812–824(2009)) from a single vertex to several vertices with relevant edges together, so that a tensor product or multisided Bézier surface can blend an edge cluster of diverse configurations. This is achieved simply by placing the control points of the Bézier surface on the vertices and edges properly. If the clusters can not cover the whole polyhedron, the left C^0 corner points can be handled by Hartmann method. Thus the complete G^g (geometrically continuous up to order g) blending surfaces can be produced faster. Their shapes can be adjusted by utilizing certain freedoms of placing the control points. The implementation of this method is demonstrated with various practical examples.

Keywords: Multivariate bernstein polynomials · Multisided bézier surfaces · S-patches · Vertex blending · Geometric continuity

1 Introduction

Blending is a basic technique in computer aided geometric design (CAGD) for aesthetic, strength, safety, manufacturing and functional purposes. Polyhedra are commonly selected as the initial models to blend. According to the analytical forms of resulting blending surfaces, the relevant methods can be classified into implicit and parametric. In implicit forms, algebraic surfaces [1–3] and functional splines [4] are often used. In general, however, the parametric forms are more popular with engineers. For example, it is easy to determine points, curves and trimmed patches on a parametric surface.

The traditional parametric methods always blended the edges first by use of the rolling ball technique [5]. Many researchers focused on the vertex blending, which was transformed into hole-filling problems after edge blending. Some of them used a whole multisided patch [6, 7]. Loop and DeRose [8] developed a kind of multisided Bézier surfaces, called S-patches. Later, they made use of S-patches to blend the vertices [9]. Zhou and Qian [10] applied the rational S-patches to setback vertex blending. The others paid attention to stitching several rectangular topology patches [11–14]. Piegl and Tiller [15] filled n-sided holes with B-spline boundaries in user-specified tolerance. Moreover, Yang et al. [16] extended their method to rational form.

© Springer Nature Switzerland AG 2019
Y. Zhao et al. (Eds.): ICIG 2019, LNCS 11902, pp. 193–207, 2019.
https://doi.org/10.1007/978-3-030-34110-7_17

The blending processes of the above edge-first parametric methods often become complicated because of continuity conditions with edge blending surfaces and twist compatibility problems, especially when the vertex gathers more edges. Moreover, achieving higher continuity is difficult, because the vertex blending surface is required to contact continuously with the constructed edge blending surfaces, rather than the primary planar faces. In [17], a vertex-first blending strategy is proposed, simplifying the blending process. In addition, this vertex-first parametric algorithm could get the higher order blending surfaces. Figure 1 shows the processes of two different blending strategies for a tetrahedron. Nevertheless, as a polyhedron ordinarily involves many vertices, handling them one by one [17] is time consuming. Fortunately we found a ubiquitous phenomenon that there are miscellaneous edge clusters on the polyhedron, which can be blended as a whole. An edge cluster means a series of polyhedral edges connected together by polyhedral vertices. Sometimes an edge is so short that the two vertices linked by it can not be blended separately. Figure 2 shows some edge clusters lying on polyhedra, where the number of edges of an edge cluster refers to the open edges. For example, the open edges in Fig. 2(b) are $\overline{v_1a_1}$, $\overline{v_2a_2}$, $\overline{v_2a_3}$, $\overline{v_2a_4}$, $\overline{v_1a_5}$, while the open edges in Fig. 2(d) are $\overline{v_1a_1}$, $\overline{v_5a_2}$, $\overline{v_5a_3}$, $\overline{v_4a_4}$, $\overline{v_3a_5}$, $\overline{v_2a_6}$, $\overline{v_1a_7}$. Note that, developed by Krasauskas [18], toric surface patches are another important multisided Bézier surfaces which contain triangular Bézier (briefly TB) and tensor product Bézier (briefly TPB) surfaces. However, for the sake of multivariate de Casteljau algorithm, we prefer to blend the edge clusters using the S-patches.

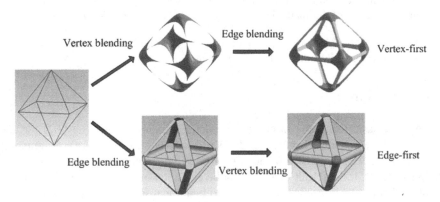

Fig. 1. The blending processes of edge-first and vertex-first methods.

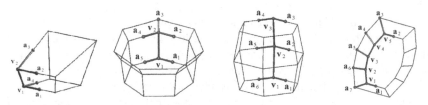

(a) A 4-edge cluster (b) A 5-edge cluster (c) A 6-edge cluster (d) A 7-edge cluster

Fig. 2. Edge clusters on polyhedra.

This paper deals with the edge cluster blending, aiming to find a blending surface smoothing the vertices and edges of an m-edge cluster on a polyhedron and having G^g-contact with m surrounding planar faces. Especially, we apply a single TPB surface for 4-edge clusters and an m-sided Bézier surface for m-edge clusters ($m > 4$). Compared with the vertex-first method, the main advantage of edge cluster blending lies in: repeated vertex and edge blending operations for an m-edge cluster can be replaced by only one edge cluster blending. Figure 3 illustrates a 7-edge cluster blending (Fig. 3(b)) instead of five vertex blending and four edge blending operations (Fig. 3(a)). Moreover, the varieties of edge clusters increase with the number of edges steeply.

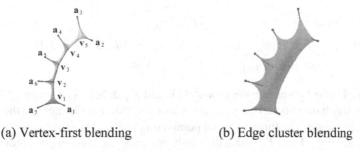

(a) Vertex-first blending   (b) Edge cluster blending

Fig. 3. Blending a 7-edge cluster.

In what follows, Sect. 2 recalls some basic properties of TPB surfaces and multisided Bézier surfaces. The 4-edge cluster blending is discussed in Sect. 3. Section 4 gives different configurations in 5-edge and 6-edge clusters, and deduces the G^g edge cluster blending condition of m-sided Bézier surfaces of degree n. Section 5 analyzes how to select edge clusters on a polyhedron and how to settle the free control points for adjusting the blend shape. These two problems are explained in detail through a practical examples — a blood pressure meter. Finally, a flower pot and a door knob are blended by the proposed method.

2 Preliminaries

From now on, if an index ranges from 1 to m, then $m + 1$ should be replaced by 1 and 0 by m.

2.1 TPB Surfaces

A TPB surface of degree (n_1, n_2) can be expressed by

$$\mathbf{b}(u, v) = \sum_{i=0}^{n_1} \sum_{j=0}^{n_2} \mathbf{b}_{i,j} B_i^{n_1}(u) B_j^{n_2}(v), \ u, v \in [0, 1] \tag{1}$$

where $B_i^{n_1}(u)$ and $B_j^{n_2}(v)$ are the univariate Bernstein polynomials, and $\mathbf{b}_{i,j}$ are the Bézier control points. Without loss of generality, we assume $n_1 \geq n_2$. The control point sets F_k, $k = 1, 2, 3, 4$ shown in Fig. 4 are defined as

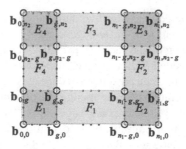

Fig. 4. Schematic control points for TPB surfaces.

$$F_1 = \{\mathbf{b}_{i,j} | 0 \le i \le n_1, 0 \le j \le g\}, \quad F_2 = \{\mathbf{b}_{i,j} | n_1 - g \le i \le n_1, 0 \le j \le n_2\},$$
$$F_3 = \{\mathbf{b}_{i,j} | 0 \le i \le n_1, n_2 - g \le j \le n_2\}, \quad F_4 = \{\mathbf{b}_{i,j} | 0 \le i \le g, 0 \le j \le n_2\},$$
$$\text{and } E_k = F_{k-1} \cap F_k, \ k = 1, 2, 3, 4.$$

Remark 1. Control points are the root of TPB and S-patches. As a matter of fact, their illustration may have two versions: one is irrelevant to their coordinates and the other has real geometric sense. The former control points compose a schema like knots in a regular polygonal net (Figs. 4 and 7), so that their indices can be specified in good order to guide the generation of a patch mentioned above. Determined by the boundary number and surface degree, the schema has nothing to do with the shape of the edge cluster. The latter control points show their positions in a 3-D space, maybe accompanying the generated patch (Figs. 5 and 8). For distinguishing we call them *schematic* and *positional* control points respectively.

Lemma 1. *If the positional control points corresponding to F_1 (resp. F_2, F_3, F_4) fall on a plane, then $\mathbf{b}(u, v)$ will have G^g-contact with the plane along $v = 0$ (resp. $u = 1$, $v = 1$, $u = 0$) (see Theorem 2 in [17]).*

Figure 5 shows a TPB surface of degree $(3, 3)$ having G^2-contact with a plane $\mathbf{n}$ along $v = 0$ when its control points corresponding to $F_1 = \{\mathbf{b}_{i,j} | 0 \le i \le 3, 0 \le j \le 2\}$ fall on the plane $\mathbf{n}$.

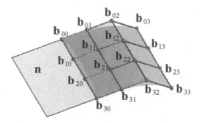

Fig. 5. A TPB surface of degree $(3, 3)$ contacts with a plane G^2-continuously.

2.2 Multisided Bézier Surfaces

The regular S-patch, often called multisided Bézier surfaces, was first defined by Loop and DeRose [8] on the affine image of a regular polygon.

Figure 6 shows an m-sided Bézier surface of degree n defined on P, and the symbol $\mathbf{e}_k$ denotes a multi-index whose components are all zero except for the kth component which is one. A regular S-patch can be formulated as [8]:

$$S(p) = \mathbf{B} \circ L(p) = \sum_{|\mathbf{i}|=n} \mathbf{b_i} B_{\mathbf{i}}^n(l_1(p), \dots, l_m(p)), \; p \in P \tag{2}$$

which is the composition of an embedding L and a Bézier simplex $\mathbf{B}$, where $L : P \to \Omega$, and $\Omega = \{v_1, \dots, v_m\}$ is a simplex of dimension $m - 1$. $\mathbf{B} : \Omega \to \mathbb{R}^3$ is given by

$$\mathbf{B}(\mathbf{u}) = \sum_{|\mathbf{i}|=n} \mathbf{b_i} B_{\mathbf{i}}^n(\mathbf{u}) = \sum_{|\mathbf{i}|=n} \mathbf{b_i} B_{\mathbf{i}}^n(u_1, \dots, u_m), \; \mathbf{u} \in \Omega \tag{3}$$

where $\mathbf{u} = (u_1, \dots, u_m)$ and $\sum_{k=1}^m u_k = 1$. Besides, $u_1, \dots, u_m$ are the barycentric coordinates of $\mathbf{u}$ with respect to Ω. $\mathbf{i} = (i_1, \dots, i_m) = \sum_{k=1}^m i_k \mathbf{e}_k$, and its components are nonnegative integers. $|\mathbf{i}| = n$ denotes $\sum_{k=1}^m i_k = n$. $\mathbf{b_i} \in \mathbb{R}^3$ are the control points.

$$B_{\mathbf{i}}^n(\mathbf{u}) = B_{\mathbf{i}}^n(u_1, \dots, u_m) = \binom{n}{\mathbf{i}} u_1^{i_1} \cdots u_m^{i_m} \tag{4}$$

are the $(m - 1)$-variate Bernstein polynomials of degree n, where $\binom{n}{\mathbf{i}} = \frac{n!}{i_1! \cdots i_m!}$.

Thus,

$$B_{\mathbf{i}}^n(l_1(p), \dots, l_m(p)) = \binom{n}{\mathbf{i}} l_1(p)^{i_1} \cdots l_m(p)^{i_m}, \tag{5}$$

where $l_k(p), k = 1, \dots, m$ are rational functions that partition unity. They mean

$$l_k(p) = \frac{\pi_k(p)}{\pi_1(p) + \cdots + \pi_m(p)}, \; k = 1, \dots, m, \; \sum_{k=1}^m l_k(p) = 1, \tag{6}$$

where $\pi_k(p) = \sigma_1(p) \cdots \sigma_{k-2}(p)\sigma_{k+1}(p) \cdots \sigma_m(p)$. As shown in Fig. 6, $\sigma_k(p)$ denotes the signed area of the triangle $pp_k p_{k+1}$, which is positive when p is inside P.

Figure 7 illustrates the schematic control point sets $F_k, k = 1, \dots, m$ of the m-sided Bézier surface $\mathbf{S}(p)$. They are defined as

$$F_k = \{\mathbf{b_i} | \mathbf{i} = \mathbf{i}_0 + \mathbf{e}_{k_1} + \cdots + \mathbf{e}_{k_g}, \mathbf{i}_0 = (0, \dots, 0, i_k, i_{k+1}, 0, \dots, 0),$$
$$|\mathbf{i}_0| = n - g, \text{ and } k_1, \dots, k_g = 1, \dots, m\}$$
$$\text{and } E_k = F_{k-1} \cap F_k, \; k = 1, \dots, m. \tag{7}$$

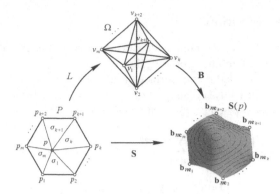

Fig. 6. An m-sided Bézier surfaces of degree n defined on a regular polygon P.

Lemma 2. *If the positional control points corresponding to F_k fall on a plane, then $\mathbf{S}(p)$ will have G^g-contact with the plane along $l_k(p) + l_{k+1}(p) = 1$ (see Theorem 3 in [17]).*

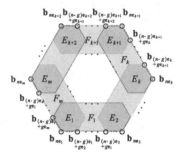

Fig. 7. Schematic control points for m-sided Bézier surfaces.

When $m = 5$, $n = 2$, and $g = 1$, for example, from Eq. (7), we have

$$F_1 = \{\mathbf{b_i} | \mathbf{i} = \mathbf{i}_0 + \mathbf{e}_{k_1}, \ \mathbf{i}_0 = (i_1, i_2, 0, 0, 0), |\mathbf{i}_0| = i_1 + i_2 = 1 \text{ and } k_1 = 1, \ldots, 5\}$$
$$= \{\mathbf{b}_{20000}, \mathbf{b}_{11000}, \mathbf{b}_{10100}, \mathbf{b}_{10010}, \mathbf{b}_{10001}, \mathbf{b}_{02000}, \mathbf{b}_{01100}, \mathbf{b}_{01010}, \mathbf{b}_{01001}\}.$$

When all the members of F_1 fall on a plane, the 5-sided Bézier surface of degree 2 has tangent-plane continuity with the plane along $l_1(p) + l_2(p) = 1$. Figure 8 depicts the result. For more properties about multisided Bézier surfaces, please refer to [8, 19].

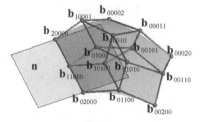

Fig. 8. A 5-sided Bézier surface of degree 2 contacts with a plane G^1-continuously.

3   Starting from a 4-Edge Cluster Blending

For brevity, we define a notation "→" in the formula

$$S \rightarrow \mathbf{g}, \tag{8}$$

where S denotes a set of schematic control points (e.g., the foregoing F_k or E_k in Sect. 2) and $\mathbf{g}$ is a geometric entity in the 3-D space (e.g., vertex, edge or face). This formula means that the positional control points corresponding to S fall on $\mathbf{g}$.

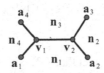

Fig. 9. A 4-edge cluster.

Figure 9 shows a typical and the simplest 4-edge cluster with two vertices $\mathbf{v}_1$ and $\mathbf{v}_2$, four open edges $\overline{\mathbf{v}_1\mathbf{a}_1}$, $\overline{\mathbf{v}_2\mathbf{a}_2}$, $\overline{\mathbf{v}_2\mathbf{a}_3}$, $\overline{\mathbf{v}_1\mathbf{a}_4}$, and four faces $\mathbf{n}_k$, $k = 1, 2, 3, 4$. Note that $\mathbf{n}_1$ and $\mathbf{n}_3$ intersect at the edge $\overline{\mathbf{v}_1\mathbf{v}_2}$. To achieve G^g-blending of this 4-edge cluster using a TPB surface, F_k, $k = 1, 2, 3, 4$ defined in Subsect. 2.1 need to fall on the faces $\mathbf{n}_k$, $k = 1, 2, 3, 4$ respectively based on Lemma 1. Besides, the points in E_1 falling on $\mathbf{n}_1$ and $\mathbf{n}_4$ simultaneously only lie on the intersection $\overline{\mathbf{v}_1\mathbf{a}_1}$, and likewise for E_k, $k = 2, 3, 4$. Symbolically, $E_1 \rightarrow \overline{\mathbf{v}_1\mathbf{a}_1}$, $E_2 \rightarrow \overline{\mathbf{v}_2\mathbf{a}_2}$, $E_3 \rightarrow \overline{\mathbf{v}_2\mathbf{a}_3}$, $E_4 \rightarrow \overline{\mathbf{v}_1\mathbf{a}_4}$ respectively and $F_k \backslash (E_k \cup E_{k+1}) \rightarrow \mathbf{n}_k, k = 1, 2, 3, 4$ respectively. However, since $\overline{\mathbf{v}_1\mathbf{a}_1} \cap \overline{\mathbf{v}_2\mathbf{a}_3} - \emptyset$, so $E_1 \cap E_3 = \emptyset$. Referring to Fig. 4,

$$E_1 = \Gamma_4 \cap F_1 = \{\mathbf{b}_{i,j} | 0 \le i \le g, 0 \le j \le g\},$$

$$E_3 = F_2 \cap F_3 = \{\mathbf{b}_{i,j} | n_1 - g \le i \le n_1, n_2 - g \le j \le n_2\},$$

In addition,

$$E_1 \cap E_3 = \{\mathbf{b}_{i,j} | n_1 - g \le i \le g, n_2 - g \le j \le g\} = \emptyset. \tag{9}$$

It follows from the above three equations that $n_1 > 2 g$. Otherwise, G^g blending of this kind of edge clusters is impossible. Thus,

Theorem 1. (a) *If $n_1 \ge n_2 > 2 g$, then $\mathbf{b}(u, v)$ is a G^g-blending surface for the 4-edge cluster when $E_1 \rightarrow \overline{\mathbf{v}_1\mathbf{a}_1}$, $E_2 \rightarrow \overline{\mathbf{v}_2\mathbf{a}_2}$, $E_3 \rightarrow \overline{\mathbf{v}_2\mathbf{a}_3}$ and $E_4 \rightarrow \overline{\mathbf{v}_1\mathbf{a}_4}$ respectively and $F_k \backslash (E_k \cup E_{k+1}) \rightarrow \mathbf{n}_k, k = 1, 2, 3, 4$ respectively.*

(b) *If $n_1 > 2 g \ge n_2$, then $\mathbf{b}(u, v)$ is a G^g-blending surface for the 4-edge cluster when $V_1 \rightarrow \mathbf{v}_1$, $V_2 \rightarrow \mathbf{v}_2$, $E_1 \backslash V_1 \rightarrow \overline{\mathbf{v}_1\mathbf{a}_1}$, $E_2 \backslash V_2 \rightarrow \overline{\mathbf{v}_2\mathbf{a}_2}$, $E_3 \backslash V_2 \rightarrow \overline{\mathbf{v}_2\mathbf{a}_3}$ and $E_4 \backslash V_1 \rightarrow \overline{\mathbf{v}_1\mathbf{a}_4}$, $\overline{E} \rightarrow \overline{\mathbf{v}_1\mathbf{v}_2}$, $F_1 \backslash (E_1 \cup E_2 \cup \overline{E}) \rightarrow \mathbf{n}_1$, and $F_3 \backslash (E_3 \cup E_4 \cup \overline{E}) \rightarrow \mathbf{n}_3$, where $V_1 = E_1 \cap E_4$, $V_2 = E_2 \cap E_3$, $\overline{E} = (F_1 \cap F_3) \backslash (V_1 \cup V_2)$.*

Proof. (a) It is apparent. (b) When $n_1 > 2\,g \geq n_2$, since $V_1 \subset E_1$ and $V_1 \subset E_4$, so $V_1 \rightarrow \overline{v_1 a_1}$ and $V_1 \rightarrow \overline{v_1 a_4}$ simultaneously. Thus $V_1 \rightarrow v_1$, $E_1 \backslash V_1 \rightarrow \overline{v_1 a_1}$, $E_4 \backslash V_1 \rightarrow \overline{v_1 a_4}$. In words, the positional control points corresponding to V_1 falling on $\overline{v_1 a_1}$ and $\overline{v_1 a_4}$ simultaneously is equivalent to falling on their intersection v_1, but the positional images of other members of E_1 except V_1 are still free on $\overline{v_1 a_1}$, and likewise for E_4. A similar result holds for V_2. Moreover, $(V_1 \cup V_2) \subseteq (E_1 \cup E_2) \cap (E_3 \cup E_4) \subset (F_1 \cap F_3)$, $F_1 \cap F_3 \rightarrow n_1 \cap n_3 = \overline{v_1 v_2}$, hence $\overline{E} \rightarrow \overline{v_1 v_2}$. Furthermore,

$$E_1 \cup E_4 = \{\mathbf{b}_{i,j} | 0 \leq i \leq g, 0 \leq j \leq n_2\} = F_4,$$

$$E_2 \cup E_3 = \{\mathbf{b}_{i,j} | n_1 - g \leq i \leq n_1, 0 \leq j \leq n_2\} = F_2.$$

Therefore the theorem is valid. $\square$

Example 1. Figure 10(a) and (b) depict that TPB surfaces of degree $(4, 2)$ are adopted to blend a hexahedron with four 4-edge clusters G^1-continuously as a blood pressure meter. The related sets are as follows:

$$F_1 = \{\mathbf{b}_{i,j} | 0 \leq i \leq 4, 0 \leq j \leq 1\}, \ F_2 = \{\mathbf{b}_{i,j} | 3 \leq i \leq 4, 0 \leq j \leq 2\},$$
$$F_3 = \{\mathbf{b}_{i,j} | 0 \leq i \leq 4, 1 \leq j \leq 2\}, \ F_4 = \{\mathbf{b}_{i,j} | 0 \leq i \leq 1, 0 \leq j \leq 2\},$$
$$E_1 = \{\mathbf{b}_{i,j} | 0 \leq i \leq 1, 0 \leq j \leq 1\}, \ E_2 = \{\mathbf{b}_{i,j} | 3 \leq i \leq 4, 0 \leq j \leq 1\},$$
$$E_3 = \{\mathbf{b}_{i,j} | 3 \leq i \leq 4, 1 \leq j \leq 2\}, \ E_4 = \{\mathbf{b}_{i,j} | 0 \leq i \leq 1, 1 \leq j \leq 2\},$$
$$V_1 = \{\mathbf{b}_{0,1}, \mathbf{b}_{1,1}\}, \ V_2 = \{\mathbf{b}_{3,1}, \mathbf{b}_{4,1}\}, \ \overline{E} = \{\mathbf{b}_{2,1}\}.$$

From Theorem 1(b), referring to Figs. 9 and 2(a),

$$V_1 \rightarrow v_1; \ V_2 \rightarrow v_2;$$

$$E_1 \backslash V_1 = \{\mathbf{b}_{0,0}, \mathbf{b}_{1,0}\} \rightarrow \overline{v_1 a_1}; \ E_2 \backslash V_2 = \{\mathbf{b}_{3,0}, \mathbf{b}_{4,0}\} \rightarrow \overline{v_2 a_2};$$

$$E_3 \backslash V_2 = \{\mathbf{b}_{3,2}, \mathbf{b}_{4,2}\} \rightarrow \overline{v_2 a_3}; \ E_4 \backslash V_1 = \{\mathbf{b}_{0,2}, \mathbf{b}_{1,2}\} \rightarrow \overline{v_1 a_4};$$

$$\overline{E} \rightarrow \overline{v_1 v_2};$$

$$F_1 \backslash (E_1 \cup E_2 \cup \overline{E}) = \{\mathbf{b}_{2,0}\} \rightarrow n_1; \ F_3 \backslash (E_3 \cup E_4 \cup \overline{E}) = \{\mathbf{b}_{2,2}\} \rightarrow n_3.$$

The sets V_1, V_2, and $\overline{E}$ are indicated in Fig. 10(a).

Example 2. Figure 10(c) shows the schematic control points of a TPB surface of degree $(5, 5)$. The associated sets E_k, $k = 1, 2, 3, 4$ are also indicated. Figure 10(d) depicts the G^2-blending operations based on Theorem 1(a).

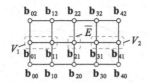

(a) Schematic control points of a TPB surface of degree $(4, 2)$ (b) G^1 blending

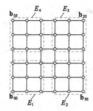

(c) Schematic control points of a TPB surface of degree $(5, 5)$ (d) G^2 blending

Fig. 10. 4-edge cluster blending using TPB surfaces.

4 Multi-edge Cluster Blending Using Multisided Bézier Surfaces

4.1 Edge Cluster Configurations

The edge cluster configurations will become more and more complicated and diversified with the increase of edge number. In the sequel, we denote an m-edge cluster with n non-terminal vertices by $\{n + m\}$. For instance, we denote the 4-edge cluster with 2 vertices (i.e., v_1 and v_2) in Fig. 9 by $\{2 + 4\}$.

Figure 11 shows two 5-edge clusters. Compared with Figs. 9, 11(a) has an additional branch at the vertex v_2, while Fig. 11(b) has a bifurcation at an original open end. Figure 12 shows eight 6-edge clusters.

(a) $\{2+5\}$ (b) $\{3+5\}$

Fig. 11. 5-edge clusters.

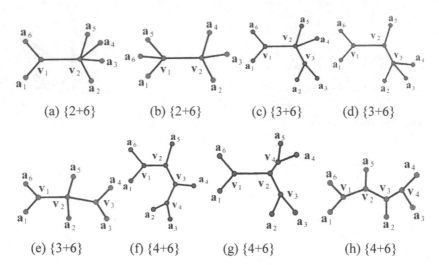

(a) {2+6}   (b) {2+6}   (c) {3+6}   (d) {3+6}

(e) {3+6}   (f) {4+6}   (g) {4+6}   (h) {4+6}

Fig. 12. 6-edge clusters.

4.2 Blending Condition

According to Lemma 2, F_k, $k = 1, \ldots, m$ are required to fall on $\mathbf{n}_k$, $k = 1, \ldots, m$ simultaneously to realize G^g-blending. Obviously, a sufficient condition for blending all edge clusters is $E_k \cap E_l = \emptyset$, $l \neq k$, $k, l = 1, \ldots, m$. In terms of the central symmetry of the schematic control points of m-sided Bézier surfaces (see Fig. 7), $E_1 \cap E_2 = \emptyset$ is sufficient. Therefore, from Eq. (7), we have

$$F_1 = \{\mathbf{b_i} | \mathbf{i} = \mathbf{i}_0 + \mathbf{e}_{k_1} + \cdots + \mathbf{e}_{k_g}, \mathbf{i}_0 = (i_1, i_2, 0, \ldots, 0),$$
$$|\mathbf{i}_0| = n - g, \text{ and } k_1, \ldots, k_g = 1, \ldots, m\},$$

$$F_2 = \{\mathbf{b_i} | \mathbf{i} = \mathbf{i}_0 + \mathbf{e}_{k_1} + \cdots + \mathbf{e}_{k_g}, \mathbf{i}_0 = (0, i_2, i_3, 0, \ldots, 0),$$
$$|\mathbf{i}_0| = n - g, \text{ and } k_1, \ldots, k_g = 1, \ldots, m\},$$

$$F_m = \{\mathbf{b_i} | \mathbf{i} = \mathbf{i}_0 + \mathbf{e}_{k_1} + \cdots + \mathbf{e}_{k_g}, \mathbf{i}_0 = (i_1, 0, \ldots, 0, i_m),$$
$$|\mathbf{i}_0| = n - g, \text{ and } k_1, \ldots, k_g = 1, \ldots, m\}.$$

Hence,

$$E_1 = F_m \cap F_1 = \{\mathbf{b_i} | \mathbf{i} = \mathbf{i}_0 + \mathbf{e}_{k_1} + \cdots + \mathbf{e}_{k_g}, \mathbf{i}_0 = (n - g, 0, \ldots, 0)$$
$$\text{or } \mathbf{i} = \mathbf{i}_0 + \mathbf{e}_{k_1} + \cdots + \mathbf{e}_{k_{g-1}}, \mathbf{i}_0 = (n - g - 1, 1, 0, \ldots, 0, 1)$$
$$\text{or } \mathbf{i} = \mathbf{i}_0 + \mathbf{e}_{k_1} + \cdots + \mathbf{e}_{k_{g-2}}, \mathbf{i}_0 = (n - g - 2, 2, 0, \ldots, 0, 2)$$
$$\cdots$$
$$\text{or } \mathbf{i} = \mathbf{i}_0, \mathbf{i}_0 = (n - 2g, g, 0, \ldots, 0, g), k_1, \ldots, k_g = 1, \ldots, m\}.$$

Equivalently,

$$E_1 = \{\mathbf{b_i} | \mathbf{i} = \mathbf{i}_0^x + \sum_{j=1}^{g-x} \mathbf{e}_{k_j}, \mathbf{i}_0^x = (n - g - x, x, 0, \ldots, 0, x), 0 \leq x \leq g,$$

$$|\mathbf{i}_0^x| = n - g + x, \text{ and } k_1, \ldots, k_g = 1, \ldots, m\}. \tag{10}$$

Similarly, we derive

$$E_2 = \{\mathbf{b_i}|\mathbf{i} = \mathbf{i}_0^y + \sum_{j=1}^{g-y} \mathbf{e}_{k_j}, \mathbf{i}_0^y = (y, n-g-y, y, 0, \ldots, 0), 0 \le y \le g,$$
$$|\mathbf{i}_0^y| = n - g + y, \text{ and } k_1, \ldots, k_g = 1, \ldots, m\}. \tag{11}$$

Since $\mathbf{e}_{k_j}, j = 1, \ldots, g - x$ (resp. $j = 1, \ldots, g - y$) can be freely added to $\mathbf{i}_0^x$ (resp. $\mathbf{i}_0^y$) in E_1 (resp. E_2) to produce $\mathbf{i}$, they can be regarded as freedoms to equalize the $\mathbf{i}$ in E_1 and the $\mathbf{i}$ in E_2. Thus, the freedoms are $g - x + g - y = 2g - x - y$. On the other hand, the constraints between $\mathbf{i}_0^x$ and $\mathbf{i}_0^y$ are the sum of the differences between corresponding components, i.e. $(n - g - x - y) + (n - g - y - x) + (y - 0) + (x - 0) = 2n - 2g - x - y$. Therefore, to ensure $E_1 \cap E_2 = \emptyset$, the constraints should be more than the freedoms, namely $2n - 2g - x - y > 2g - x - y$, that is $n > 2g$. Note that it unifies the 4-edge case when $n_1 = n_2$ in Theorem 1. Hence, we have

Corollary 1. *If $n > 2g$, then $\mathbf{S}(p)$ is a G^g-blending surface for an m-edge cluster when E_k falls on the open edge ending at $\mathbf{a}_k, k = 1, \ldots, m$ respectively and $F_k \backslash (E_k \cup E_{k+1}) \rightarrow \mathbf{n}_k, k = 1, \ldots, m$ respectively.*

Example 3. Figure 13(a) and (b) show that 5-sided Bézier surfaces of degree 3 are used to blend seven $\{2 + 5\}$ like Fig. 11(a) G^1-continuously. Therefore,

$$F_k = \{\mathbf{b_i}|\mathbf{i} = \mathbf{i}_0 + \mathbf{e}_{k_1}, \mathbf{i}_0 = (0, \ldots, 0, i_k, i_{k+1}, 0, \ldots, 0), |\mathbf{i}_0| = 2, \text{ and } k_1 = 1, \ldots, 5\},$$

$$E_k = F_{k-1} \cap F_k, k = 1, \ldots, 5$$

From Corollary 1, referring to Figs. 11(a) and 2(b), we have

$$E_1 \rightarrow \overline{\mathbf{v_1 a_1}}; \; E_2 \rightarrow \overline{\mathbf{v_2 a_2}}; \; E_3 \rightarrow \overline{\mathbf{v_2 a_3}}; \; E_4 \rightarrow \overline{\mathbf{v_2 a_4}}; \; E_5 \rightarrow \overline{\mathbf{v_1 a_5}};$$

$$F_1 \backslash (E_1 \cup E_2) = \{\mathbf{b}_{11010}\} \rightarrow \mathbf{n}_1; \; F_2 \backslash (E_2 \cup E_3) = \{\mathbf{b}_{01101}\} \rightarrow \mathbf{n}_2;$$

$$F_3 \backslash (E_3 \cup E_4) = \{\mathbf{b}_{10110}\} \rightarrow \mathbf{n}_3; \; F_4 \backslash (E_4 \cup E_5) = \{\mathbf{b}_{01011}\} \rightarrow \mathbf{n}_4;$$

$$F_5 \backslash (E_5 \cup E_1) = \{\mathbf{b}_{10101}\} \rightarrow \mathbf{n}_5.$$

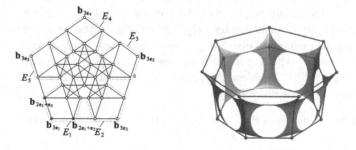

(a) The control net for $m = 5, n = 3, g = 1$ (b) 5-edge clusters like Fig. 11(a)

Fig. 13. Edge cluster blending using 5-sided Bézier surfaces.

5 How to Select the Edge Clusters and Settle the Free Positional Control Points

In general, there often exist multiple choices of edge clusters on a given polyhedron. Different edge cluster blending strategies lead to different blending results. Hence, the intention of designers determines how to choose the edge clusters. However, because the blending surfaces are shaped depending on the edge cluster configurations, distorted edge clusters sometimes uglify the blending shape. From our experience, the smaller an edge cluster backbone (connecting the open edges together) *distorts*, the fairer the blending surfaces are. Besides, the edge cluster revealing main features of the polyhedron or symmetrical edge clusters should be given priority.

The following will illustrate the influence of the control points on the edge cluster blending shape with a typical practical example. In Example 1, a blood pressure meter has been smoothed by four edge cluster blending. Referring to the analysis in Example 1, we have that the control points with freedoms are: $\mathbf{b}_{0,0}$ and $\mathbf{b}_{1,0}$ can move along the edge $\overline{v_1 a_1}$; $\mathbf{b}_{3,0}$ and $\mathbf{b}_{4,0}$ can move along $\overline{v_2 a_2}$; $\mathbf{b}_{3,2}$ and $\mathbf{b}_{4,2}$ can move along the edge $\overline{v_2 a_3}$; $\mathbf{b}_{0,2}$ and $\mathbf{b}_{1,2}$ can move along the edge $\overline{v_1 a_4}$; $\mathbf{b}_{2,1}$ can move along the edge $\overline{v_1 v_2}$; $\mathbf{b}_{2,0}$ can move in the face $\mathbf{n}_1$; $\mathbf{b}_{2,2}$ can move in the face $\mathbf{n}_3$. As shown in Fig. 14, the smooth region of edge cluster blending can be enlarged by adjusting $\mathbf{b}_{2,0}$ and $\mathbf{b}_{2,2}$, meanwhile the aesthetic is also improved. Moreover, the bottom supporting region the blood pressure meter can be extended by adjusting $\mathbf{b}_{0,0}$ and $\mathbf{b}_{0,2}$.

adjust $\mathbf{b}_{20}, \mathbf{b}_{22}$ adjust $\mathbf{b}_{00}, \mathbf{b}_{02}$

Fig. 14. Influence of the control points' position on the blending shape.

6 Practical Examples

Example 4. To model a flower pot, involving two regular pentagons and one decagon horizontally at increasing height from the bottom. The decagon comes out if sharp corners are cut away from an auxiliary regular pentagon, whose orientation is the same as the real regular pentagons. Five 5-edge convex-concave vertices around the waist and five 3-edge convex vertices at the bottom together construct five 6-edge clusters like Fig. 12(a) in Fig. 15(d). We blend the $\{2 + 6\}$ using 6-sided Bézier surfaces of degree 3. The associated sets are as follows:

$$F_k = \{\mathbf{b_i} | \mathbf{i} = \mathbf{i}_0 + \mathbf{e}_{k_1}, \mathbf{i}_0 = (0, \ldots, 0, i_k, i_{k+1}, 0, \ldots, 0), |\mathbf{i}_0| = 2, \text{ and } k_1 = 1, \ldots, 6\},$$

$$E_k = F_{k-1} \cap F_k, \ k = 1, \ldots, 6$$

From Corollary 1 and Fig. 15(a), we have

$$E_1 \to \overline{v_1 a_1};\ E_2 \to \overline{v_2 a_2};\ E_3 \to \overline{v_2 a_3};\ E_4 \to \overline{v_2 a_4};\ E_5 \to \overline{v_2 a_5};\ E_6 \to \overline{v_1 a_6};$$

$$F_1 \backslash (E_1 \cup E_2) = \{ \mathbf{b}_{110100}, \mathbf{b}_{110010} \} \to \mathbf{n}_1;$$

$$F_2 \backslash (E_2 \cup E_3) = \{ \mathbf{b}_{011010}, \mathbf{b}_{011001} \} \to \mathbf{n}_2;$$

$$F_3 \backslash (E_3 \cup E_4) = \{ \mathbf{b}_{001101}, \mathbf{b}_{101100} \} \to \mathbf{n}_3;$$

$$F_4 \backslash (E_4 \cup E_5) = \{ \mathbf{b}_{100110}, \mathbf{b}_{010110} \} \to \mathbf{n}_4;$$

$$F_5 \backslash (E_5 \cup E_6) = \{ \mathbf{b}_{010011}, \mathbf{b}_{001011} \} \to \mathbf{n}_5;$$

$$F_6 \backslash (E_6 \cup E_1) = \{ \mathbf{b}_{101001}, \mathbf{b}_{100101} \} \to \mathbf{n}_6.$$

Note that the face $\mathbf{n}_6$ is spanned by $\mathbf{v}_1$, $\mathbf{a}_1$ and $\mathbf{a}_6$.

As shown in Fig. 15(a), Γ_1 (resp. Γ_2) is a cubic Bézier curve determined by $\mathbf{b}_{300000}$, $\mathbf{b}_{210000}$, $\mathbf{b}_{120000}$, $\mathbf{b}_{030000}$ (resp. $\mathbf{b}_{030000}$, $\mathbf{b}_{021000}$, $\mathbf{b}_{012000}$, $\mathbf{b}_{003000}$). Since $\mathbf{b}_{030000}$, $\mathbf{b}_{120000}$, and $\mathbf{b}_{021000}$ all lie on $\overline{v_2 a_2}$, so $\mathbf{b}_{030000}$ (coinciding with $\mathbf{a}_2$) is a degenerate point at $S(p)$, whose normal vector at $\mathbf{b}_{030000}$ is undefined. So are $\mathbf{b}_{300000}$, $\mathbf{b}_{003000}$, $\mathbf{b}_{000300}$, $\mathbf{b}_{000030}$ and $\mathbf{b}_{000003}$. To avoid these C^0 points appearing around the waist and bottom of the flower pot, we use Hartmann method [20, 21] to smooth them.

A G^h-blending surface generated by Hartmann method is defined as

$$\mathbf{x}(s, t) = f(t) \mathbf{x}_1(s, t) + (1 - f(t)) \mathbf{x}_2(s, t),\ s, t \in [0, 1], \tag{12}$$

where $\mathbf{x}_1(s, t)$, $\mathbf{x}_2(s, t)$ are reparameterized local base patches, and $\mathbf{x}(s, t)$ has C^h-contact with $\mathbf{x}_1(s, t)$ and $\mathbf{x}_2(s, t)$ along the contact curves $\mathbf{x}_1(s, 0)$ and $\mathbf{x}_2(s, 1)$, $s \in [0, 1]$ respectively. Besides,

$$f(t) = \frac{\mu(1 - t)^{h+1}}{\mu(1 - t)^{h+1} + (1 - \mu)t^{h+1}},\ t \in [0, 1], \tag{13}$$

where $\mu \in (0, 1)$ is the design parameter. As illustrated by Fig. 15(c), $x_1(s, t)$ and $x_2(s, t)$ are bilinear reparameterized domains in respective regular hexagon domains. Then maps $\mathbf{S}_1$ and $\mathbf{S}_2$ give rise to the reparameterized local base patches $\mathbf{x}_1(s, t) = \mathbf{S}_1(x_1(s, t))$ and $\mathbf{x}_2(s, t) = \mathbf{S}_2(x_2(s, t))$. Based on Eqs. (12) and (13) with $h = 1$ and $\mu = 0.5$, the edge blending surface $\mathbf{x}(s, t)$ is generated and shown in Fig. 15(b). Here $\mathbf{x}(s, t)$ not only contacts with $\mathbf{S}_1(P)$ and $\mathbf{S}_2(P)$ G^1-continuously, but also with the primary faces in tangent-plane continuity [17]. Naturally, graceful setbacks are created and degenerated points are trimmed off. The final blending of a flower pot is shown in Fig. 15(e).

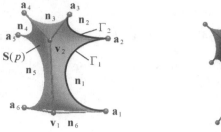

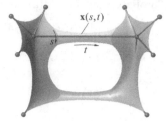

(a) A 6-edge cluster like Fig. 12(a)   (b) Edge blending using Hartmann method

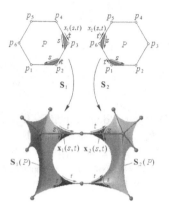

(c) Reparameterized local base patches (d) Edge cluster blending   (e)   Edge blending

Fig. 15. Blending a flower pot.

Example 5. To construct a door knob, the initial polyhedron is shown in Fig. 16(a). Four 6-edge clusters like Fig. 12(b) are located in this polyhedron. Figure 16(b) shows the resulting edge cluster blending. Figure 16(c) depicts the final blending.

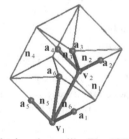

(a) A 6-edge cluster like Fig. 12(b) (b) Edge cluster blending   (c) Edge blending

Fig. 16. Blending a door knob.

References

1. Braid, I.C.: Non-local blending of boundary models. Comput. Aided Des. **29**, 89–100 (1997)
2. Kosters, M.: Quadratic blending surfaces for complex corners. Vis. Comput. **5**, 134–146 (1989)
3. Mou, H.N., Zhao, G.H., Wang, Z.R., Su, Z.X.: Simultaneous blending of convex polyhedra by algebraic splines. Comput. Aided Des. **39**, 1003–1011 (2007)
4. Hartmann, E.: Implicit Gn-blending of vertices. Comput. Aided Geom. Des. **18**, 267–285 (2001)
5. Choi, B.K., Ju, S.Y.: Constant-radius blending in surface modeling. Comput. Aided Des. **21**, 213–220 (1989)
6. Varady, T.: Overlap patches: a new scheme for interpolating curve networks with n-sided regions. Comput. Aided Geom. Des. **8**, 7–27 (1991)
7. Warren, J.: Creating multisided rational bézier surfaces using base points. ACM Trans. Graph. **11**, 127–139 (1992)
8. Loop, C., DeRose, T.: A multisided generalization of Bézier surfaces. ACM Trans. Graph. **8**, 204–234 (1989)
9. Loop, C., DeRose, T.: Generalized B-spline surfaces of arbitrary topology. Comput. Graph. (ACM) **24**, 347–356 (1990)
10. Zhou, P., Qian, W.H.: Polyhedral vertex blending with setbacks using rational S-patches. Comput. Aided Geom. Des. **27**, 233–244 (2010)
11. Szilvasi-Nagy, M.: Flexible rounding operation for polyhedra. Comput. Aided Des. **23**, 629–633 (1991)
12. Gregory, J.A., Zhou, J.W.: Filling polygonal holes with bicubic patches. Comput. Aided Geom. Des. **11**, 391–410 (1994)
13. Varady, T., Rockwood, A.: Geometric construction for setback vertex blending. Comput. Aided Des. **29**, 413–425 (1997)
14. Hsu, K.L., Tsay, D.M.: Corner blending of free form n-sided holes. IEEE Comput. Graph. Appl. 72–78 (1998)
15. Piegl, L.A., Tiller, W.: Filling n-sided regions with NURBS patches. Vis. Comput. **15**, 77–89 (1999)
16. Yang, Y.J., Yong, J.H., Zhang, H., Paul, J.C., Sun, J.G.: A rational extension of Piegl's method for filling n-sided holes. Comput. Aided Des. **38**, 1166–1178 (2006)
17. Zhou, P., Qian, W.H.: A vertex-first parametric algorithm for polyhedron blending. Comput. Aided Des. **41**, 812–824 (2009)
18. Krasauskas, R.: Toric surface patches. Adv. Comput. Math. **17**, 89–113 (2002)
19. Goldman, R.: Multisided arrays of control points for multisided Bézier patches. Comput. Aided Geom. Des. **21**, 243–261 (2004)
20. Hartmann, E.: Parametric G^n blending of curves and surfaces. Vis. Comput. **17**, 1–13 (2001)
21. Song, Q.Z., Wang, J.Z.: Generating G^n parametric blending surfaces based on partial reparameterization of base surfaces. Comput. Aided Des. **39**, 953–963 (2007)

A New Coefficient for a Two-Scale Microfacet Reflectance Model

Hongbin Yang[1,2][✉], Mingxue Liao[1], Changwen Zheng[1], and Pin Lv[1]

[1] Science and Technology on Integrated Infomation System Laboratory,
Institute of Software, Chinese Academy of Sciences, Beijing, China
{hongbin2017,mingxue,changwen,lvpin}@iscas.ac.cn
[2] University of Chinese Academy of Sciences, Beijing, China

Abstract. Reflectance properties express how objects in a virtual scene interact with light; they control the appearance of the object: whether it looks shiny or not, whether it has a metallic or plastic appearance. Having a good reflectance model is essential for the production of photo-realistic pictures. A considerate reflectance model needs to consider both specular peak and wavelength dependency. So a model combining reflection and diffraction is a reasonable idea. Holzschuch and Pacanowski proposed a two-scale microfacet model combining reflection and diffraction. However, the coefficient that connects the two parts of this model is not very physically-based since reflection part gets close to zero for a wide angle range while the surface roughness is excessive. In this paper, we design a new coefficient which controls the two parts of this model in a more reasonable range. As a result, the improved model produces a good approximation to measured reflectance. Moreover, we compute the integral of the diffraction part with higher efficiency by using Monte Carlo integration. Finally we use piecewise sampling to fit the parameters, and we can get model parameters faster.

Keywords: Microfacet model · Diffraction model · Monte Carlo integration

1 Introduction

In computer graphics, reflection microfacet reflectance model has been extensive used to express reflectance properties. Based on a surface geometric model at the microscopic level, they predict the overall materials appearance at the macroscopic level.

Microfacet reflectance model are simply divided into parametric reflectance models and data-driven models. Parametric reflectance models give exact analytical forms with a few parameters to fit different materials. The most commonly used microfacet model is the Cook-Torrance model [1], based on earlier work from optic [2], to model light reflection from rough surface. It assumes that light follows the principle of optical geometry: it is reflected by the surface micro-geometry but also potentially occluded. The main contributing parameter is

© Springer Nature Switzerland AG 2019
Y. Zhao et al. (Eds.): ICIG 2019, LNCS 11902, pp. 208–219, 2019.
https://doi.org/10.1007/978-3-030-34110-7_18

the *normal distribution function* (NDF) of the microfacet. Another reflectance model assumes that the micro-geometry diffracts the incoming light. This model computes diffraction effects caused by differences in height in the surface micro-geometry, and predicts visual appearance from the frequency content of the height distribution. This reflectance model has an intrinsic wavelength dependency.

Both models provide relatively good fits with measured reflectance properties for some aspects. However, any of the two models can not express specular peak and wide-angle scattering well simultaneously. Previous experiments has shown that fitting measured materials to parametric models is hard. Ngan et al. [3] proved that diffuse and glossy materials are well approximated using the Cook-Torrance. The models are less accurate for specular materials such as metals, metallic paints and shiny plastic with lobe width varies at different wavelengths.

It is interesting to compare measured reflectance with what the models predict. Bagher et al. [4] introduced a new microfacet distribution for the Cook-Torrance model. It provides a very good fit with measured data, if you use different parameters for each color channel, implying that the geometry of microfacet is different for each channel. Löw et al. [5] showed that the diffraction model provides a good fit for measured data, but they removed the wavelength dependency from the model.

HOLZSCHUCH et al. [6] presented a surface reflectance model. It assumes that surface geometry details are present at all scales, from the size of the wavelength of incoming light to much large. It express the overall material properties as a sum of a standard Cook-Torrance lobe and a Cook-Torrance-Diffraction lobe. This model provides a good fit with measured reflectance. But the reflection part is close to zero in a wide range because the coefficient that connects the two parts of the model is not well.

In this paper, we provide a new coefficient to combine reflection and diffraction. We express this coefficient with a piecewise function. As a result, this coefficient makes reflection part vary in a more proper range.

In the next section, we review previous work on material reflectance, both in the microfacet models and diffraction models. We then describe in Sect. 3 the background of the microfacet reflectance model and the Generalized Harvey-Shack diffraction theory and describe reflectance model, combining reflection and diffraction in Sect. 4, and explain the computation of diffraction part. In Sect. 5, we fit with all measured materials, and discuss the results. In Sect. 6, we conclude and present field for future work.

2 Previous Work

2.1 Microfacet Model

Several physically-based BRDF models connect the surface micro-geometry with the way the surface interacts with light. The microfacet model [2] assumes that surface micro-geometry is made of specular microfacet. It predicts the overall surface appearance from the probability distribution of these microfacet normal.

Existing models include Gaussian [1], rational fraction [7], fraction to the power p [8], Shifted-Gamma Distribution [4], exponential of a power function [9].

The shadowing and masking term is essential for energy conservation in the microfacet model. Assuming that microfacet position and orientation are independent, Smith [10] computes the shadowing/masking term from two successive integration of the slope distribution. Heitz [11] shows that this is the most physically consistent method to compute the shadowing and masking term, and provides an improved shadowing term taking into account correlation between input and output directions.

Ward [12] introduced a simplified version of the Cook-Torrance model and extended it to reflections from anisotropic materials. He also provided a method for sampling his model, and Beckmann distributions in general, but see [13] for the correct sampling weights. An alternative sampling method using fitted separable approximations was proposed by Lawrence et al. [14]. Schlick [15] used rational approximation to create a cheaper approximation to the Cook-Torrance model including a widely adopted approximation to the Fresnel formula.

2.2 Diffraction Model

The diffraction model is widely used in Optical Engineering community. It assumes that surface micro-geometry is roughly the same size as the wavelength of the incoming light, as a function of the Power Spectral Distribution (PSD) of surface height. Löw et al. [5] showed that this model is consistent with the lobe shape in measured BRDFs. They also showed that the diffraction model provides a good fit with measured reflectance. To conduct the fitting, they removed the wavelength dependency from the diffraction model. Their model also does not account for energy conservation.

Holzschuch and Pacanowski [6] show that measured reflectances appear to be a combination of the two phenomena: diffraction for wide-angle scattering, microfacet reflection close to the specular direction. They also show that summing the two components provides a good approximation to all measured reflectance. But the coefficient that combines reflection part and diffraction part is not very suitable. Compared to their work, we provide a more physically-based coefficient for the connection between the two lobes, as well as present the computation of diffraction part. We also provide a good fit with measured materials while reducing the scale of fitting process.

3   Background

3.1   Microfacet Model

The microfacet model [1] is widely used in computer graphics. It assumes that the surface of the object is made of specular microfacet, large enough that we can assume the rules of geometrical optics. The resulting BRDFs model then depends mainly on the probability distribution of the microfacet normal $D(\theta_h)$ Summing the contributions of all microfacet results in the Cook-Torrance reflectance model:

$$\rho_{CT}(\boldsymbol{i},\boldsymbol{o}) = \frac{F(\eta,\theta_d)D(\theta_h)G(\boldsymbol{i},\boldsymbol{o})}{4\cos\theta_i\cos\theta_o}. \tag{1}$$

The Fresnel term F is responsible for the color of the microfacet. The shadowing-masking term G expresses the probability for light to be blocked before or after the specular reflection on the microfacet. It is usually computed using Smith's method through a double integration of D. The only wavelength dependency comes from the Fresnel term F.

3.2 Diffraction: Modified Harvey-Shack Theory

For the diffraction reflectance model [5], the dimensions of the surface micro-geometry are close the incoming light wavelength. Diffraction effects are dominant. We focus on the Harvey-Shack theory [16], as it is suitable for wide-angle scattering and has been found to provide a good approximation to measured reflectance.

According to the Harvey-Shack theory, reflectance is separated in two different lobes: a peak in the direction of specular reflection, connecting to a Dirac delta function, surrounded by a halo of scattered [17]. The relative intensity of those two components depend on the surface roughness σ_s^2, defined as the variance of height distribution h:

$$\rho_{diff.}(\boldsymbol{i},\boldsymbol{o}) = AF(\boldsymbol{i},\boldsymbol{o})\frac{\delta(refl(\boldsymbol{i}),\boldsymbol{o})}{\cos\theta_o} + (1-A)Q(\boldsymbol{i},\boldsymbol{o})S_{HS}(\boldsymbol{f}) \tag{2}$$

$$\text{with } A = e^{-\left(2\pi\frac{\sigma_s}{\lambda}(\cos\theta_i+\cos\theta_o)\right)^2} \tag{3}$$

where S_{HS} is a scattering function, F is the Fresnel term for reflectance, and Q is the color term for diffraction.

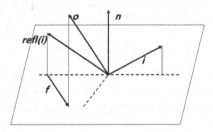

Fig. 1. Diffraction effects depend on f, projected vector between reflected incoming direction and outgoing direction.

The main parameter controlling the diffraction lobe is the 2D vector f, defined as the projection on the tangent plane of the difference between the reflected incoming direction and the outgoing direction, divided by the wavelength (see Fig. 1).

$$f = \frac{1}{\lambda}(o - refl(i)).\tag{4}$$

$$f = \|f\| = \frac{2}{\lambda}\sin\theta_h\cos\theta_d.\tag{5}$$

The scattering function can be expressed as [6]:

$$S_{HS}(f) = \frac{c-1}{2\pi}\frac{\sigma_s^2 b^2}{(1+b^2 f^2)^{\frac{c+1}{2}}}.\tag{6}$$

Where $1/b$ specifies the width parameter of the diffraction lobe, c ($c > 1$) is the exponent parameter of the diffraction lobe.

4   Two-Scale BRDF Model and New Coefficient

4.1   Two-Scale BRDF Model

The two-scale reflectance model [6] is based on the fact: reflectance and diffraction effects are not mutually exclusive. The Generalized Harvey-Shack theory [17] explicitly allocates energy to the reflection and diffraction lobes, combining a specular reflection with a diffraction lobe. It compute the surface reflectance at the macroscopic level by integrating the contributions over all visible microfacet which is the original microfacet framework to work with any kind of reflectance on the microfacet:

$$\rho(i, o) = \int_\Omega \left|\frac{i \cdot m}{i \cdot n}\right| f_s(i, o, m) \left|\frac{o \cdot m}{o \cdot n}\right| G(i, o)D(m)d\omega_m.\tag{7}$$

where f_s is assumed that comes from diffraction effects, due to slight imperfections on each microfacet:

$$f_s(i, o, m) = AF(i, o)\frac{\delta(refl(i), o)}{\cos\theta_o} + (1 - A)Q(i, o)S_{HS}(f)\tag{8}$$

$$\text{with } A = e^{-\left(2\pi\frac{\sigma_s}{\lambda}(i\cdot m + o\cdot m)\right)^2}.\tag{9}$$

The first term is the standard Cook-Torrance lobe, multiplied by A evaluated where $refl(i) = o$, or $m = h$. The combined two-scale reflectance is the sum of a Cook-Torrance lobe multiplied by $A_{spec}(\theta_d)$, and of a combined Cook-Torrance diffraction lobe, ρ_{CTD}:

$$\rho(i, o) = A_{spec}(\theta_d)\rho_{CT}(i, o) + \rho_{CTD}(i, o)\tag{10}$$

$$\text{with } A_{spec}(\theta_d) = e^{-\left(2\pi\frac{\sigma_s}{\lambda}(2\cos\theta_d)\right)^2}\tag{11}$$

$$\rho_{CT}(i, o) = \frac{F(\eta, \theta_d)D(\theta_h)G(i, o)}{4\cos\theta_i\cos\theta_o}\tag{12}$$

$$\text{with } D(\theta_h) = \frac{\chi_{[0,\pi/2]}(\theta_h)}{\cos^4 \theta_h} \frac{p}{\pi \beta^2 \Gamma(1/p)} e^{-\left(\frac{\tan^2 \theta_h}{\beta^2}\right)^p} \tag{13}$$

$$\rho_{CTD}(i,o) = \int_\Omega \left|\frac{i \cdot m}{i \cdot n}\right| (1 - A) Q(i,o) S_{HS}(f) \left|\frac{o \cdot m}{o \cdot n}\right| G(i,o) D(m) d\omega_m. \tag{14}$$

Where β controls the width of the peak, while p controls its kurtosis, that is whether is drops sharply at origin or not.

4.2 New Coefficient and the Computation of Diffraction Part

It is obvious that the coefficient A (Eq. 1) correspond to adjust the relationship between Cook-Torrance lobe and Cook-Torrance diffraction lobe. So a good fitting result depends largely on whether A is suitable. The coefficient A expresses the energy repartition between the reflection and diffraction lobes. It depends on the incoming and outgoing directions and on the σ_s/λ ratio (see Fig. 2(a)). For $\sigma_s/\lambda > 0.3$, it is close to 0 on most parameters range.

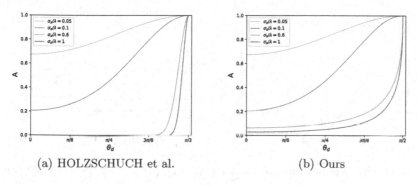

(a) HOLZSCHUCH et al.   (b) Ours

Fig. 2. Coefficient A for θ_d. (a) is HOLZSCHUCH et al. (b) is Ours

An interesting effect appears for rough surfaces (where $\sigma_s > 0.5\lambda$). For these materials, A is negligible for almost all direction (see Fig. 2(a)). The impact of the microfacet lobe is only felt at grazing angles. As a result, it can not get any input on the microfacet distribution from the fitting. It is self-evident that this result is not very reasonable. Based on this effect, we propose a new coefficient to connect those two parts of the two-scale BRDF model. The new coefficient is express as:

$$A = \begin{cases} e^{-\left(2\pi\frac{\sigma_s}{\lambda}(\cos\theta_i + \cos\theta_o)\right)^{1/2}} & \text{if } \sigma_s/\lambda > 0.5, \\ e^{-\left(2\pi\frac{\sigma_s}{\lambda}(\cos\theta_i + \cos\theta_o)\right)^2} & \text{otherwise.} \end{cases} \tag{15}$$

Now, we can see the effect of the new coefficient (see Fig. 2(b)). The variety of the two parts of the model is expressed more physically-based by our new coefficient. Not only can microfacet lobe change in a wider angle range, but also it can faster growth at grazing angles which is more physically-based. There is no closed-form version for the diffraction part. It can be approximated by a product integral by neglecting the variations of some terms in the integral.

We then need to convert these local properties into global properties. Based on this, we use the fact that $(\boldsymbol{i}, \boldsymbol{o}) = 2 \cos \theta_d \boldsymbol{h}$, where $\boldsymbol{h}$ is the normalized half-vector.

$$\boldsymbol{i} \cdot \boldsymbol{m} + \boldsymbol{o} \cdot \boldsymbol{m} = 2 \cos \theta_d (\boldsymbol{h} \cdot \boldsymbol{m}) \tag{16}$$

$$A_{spec}(\theta_d) = e^{-\left(2\pi \frac{\sigma_s}{\lambda}(2\cos\theta_d)\right)^t} \tag{17}$$

$$A = e^{-\left(2\pi \frac{\sigma_s}{\lambda}(\boldsymbol{i}\cdot\boldsymbol{m}+\boldsymbol{o}\cdot\boldsymbol{m})\right)^t} \tag{18}$$

$$1 - A \approx (1 - A_{spec}(\theta_d))(\boldsymbol{h} \cdot \boldsymbol{m})^t \tag{19}$$

$$\text{where } t = 1/2 \text{ or } t = 2. \tag{20}$$

This approximation is exact for extreme values $(\boldsymbol{h} \cdot \boldsymbol{m}) = 0$ and $(\boldsymbol{h} \cdot \boldsymbol{m}) = 1$. It is also a good approximation for other range (see Fig. 3).

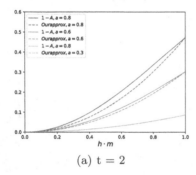
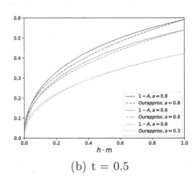

(a) $t = 2$ (b) $t = 0.5$

Fig. 3. Quality of approximation $1 - A$ for $(\boldsymbol{h} \cdot \boldsymbol{m})$. (a) is $t = 2$. (b) is Ours $t = 0.5$

Two functions in the integration, $S_H S$ and D, vary quickly and are almost null over a large part of the interval. We approximate the other functions, which very more slowly, by their values when $S_H S$ and D are maximal:

$$\rho_{CTD}(\boldsymbol{i}, \boldsymbol{o}) \approx Q(\boldsymbol{i}, \boldsymbol{o})G(\boldsymbol{i}, \boldsymbol{o}) \int_{\Omega} (1 - A)S_{HS}(\boldsymbol{f})D(\boldsymbol{m})d\omega_m \tag{21}$$

$$\approx Q(\boldsymbol{i}, \boldsymbol{o})G(\boldsymbol{i}, \boldsymbol{o})(1 - A_{spec}(\theta_d)) \int_{\Omega} (\boldsymbol{h} \cdot \boldsymbol{m})^t S_{HS}(\boldsymbol{f})D(\boldsymbol{m})d\omega_m. \tag{22}$$

The last integral is between two functions defined on the sphere. To evaluate this integral, we compute the Spherical Harmonics coefficients of each function. This integral is equal to the dot product of the two coefficients vectors (see Appendix A). Both functions have rotational symmetry: their Spherical Harmonics decomposition is Zonal Harmonics(coefficients with $m \neq 0$ are null), and we can exploit Monte Carlo integration to compute the Spherical Harmonics coefficients of each function as there are enough samples, speeding up computations.

5   Validation with Measured Materials

5.1   Fitting Process

Considering that when θ_i is small, the BRDF energy change is relatively gentle, and when θ_i is relatively large, especially when approaching the glancing angle, the BRDF energy changes drastically, so we can sample θ_o at different frequencies. Specifically, we sample the θ_o at a higher frequency when approaching the glancing angle. As a result, although some parameters' accuracy may be slightly lost, the parameters fitting calculation scale are greatly reduced. Specifically, it is about one tenth of the computational cost of the original, and greatly accelerates the fitting speed.

5.2   Result and Comparision

To test the validity of our model, we have use it to fit all 100 materials in the MERL database [18], which are then used to render imagines with 4096 samples per pixel. We use two metrics (average image difference using sMAPE, BRDF energy difference using RMSE, see Table 1) to compare with two-scale model [6].

Table 1. Metrics used for comparison

sMAPE: Symmetric Mean Absolute Percentage Error

$$E_{sMAPE} = \frac{\left| V_{measured} - V_{predicted} \right|}{V_{measured} + V_{predicted}}$$

RMSE: Root Mean Square Error

$$E_{RMSE}(\theta_i) = \left(\int \left(\rho(\boldsymbol{i},\boldsymbol{o}) - f(\boldsymbol{i},\boldsymbol{o}) \right)^2 \cos^2 \theta_i d\omega_o \right)^{1/2}$$

Both our model and HOLZSCHUCH et al. [6] model provide a good approximation of measured data, with a few spectacular exceptions. Look at both qualitative (imagine comparison) and quantitative metrics (sMAPE, RMSE), our model gives a good representation for most materials. We show one of the best rendering result which is almost no difference left between the measured data and what our model predicts, and one of the worst rendering result.(see Fig. 4). We also show the quantitative metrics (sMAPE, RMSE) for those two materials(see Tables 2 and 3).

Specifically, our model has a smaller RMSE than HOLZSCHUCH et al. [1] model for 57 materials, corresponding to some glossy to specular materials, from $color - changing - paint3$ to $violet - acrylic$ (see Fig. 5). Since we model reduced the scale of the parameter fitting calculation, the RMSE value was slightly larger

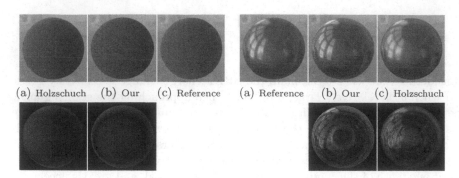

Fig. 4. Qualitative metric (image comparison) for the MERL isotropic materials. The left part (light-brown-fabric) is one of the best rendering result of our model and HOLZSCHUCH et al compared with reference. The right part (grease-covered-steel) is one of the worst rendering result of our model and HOLZSCHUCH et al compared with reference. The second line are the difference from the reference. (Color figure online)

Table 2. Quantitative metrics (sMAPE, RMSE) for light-brown-fabric material

	BRDF metric	Image metric		
	RMSE	Mean sMAPE	(r,g,b) sMAPE	
Our model	0.0066622	**0.0726365**	**0.0727764**	0.07113	0.0740031
HOLZSCHUCH et al.	**0.00339263**	0.0915575	0.0765452	0.0976629	0.100464

Table 3. Quantitative metrics (sMAPE, RMSE) for grease-covered-steel material

	BRDF metric	Image metric		
	RMSE	Mean sMAPE	(r,g,b) sMAPE	
Our model	**0.00708712**	0.0923099	0.0933661	0.0902866	0.0932769
HOLZSCHUCH et al.	0.101091	**0.0887874**	**0.0887973**	0.0826365	0.0949283

than HOLZSCHUCH et al. model for some materials, but at the same time we also greatly accelerated the parameter fitting speed.

The material roughness is critical to the relative intensities of diffraction effects and Cook-Torrance effects. Diffraction effects are visually more important for smooth surfaces. Our model does not perform so well for very rough and diffuse surfaces, including diffuse paint and fabrics. This may be due to different cause: other effects are present including back-scattering and multiple scattering inside the micro-geometry, and the fitting process has difficulties separating between the different phenomena.

6   Conclusion and Future Work

We have presented a exploration of material reflectance model, based on two-scale micro-facet reflectance model. Considering the physically-based allocation

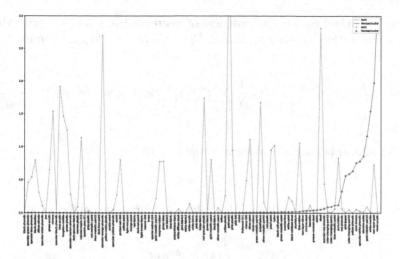

Fig. 5. Root Mean Square Error (RMSE) for all materials in the MERL database, computed on the whole BRDF, sorted according to the RMSE for the HOLZSCHUCH et al. (Color figure online)

of BRDF energy between diffraction and Cook-Torrance reflection, we provide a new coefficient to control the partition of BRDF energy. As a result, our model gives a good representation for measured materials. In order to speed up the calculation, we also provide a new way to compute diffraction part by using Monte Carlo integration.

In future work, we will focus on making a simplified model by applying a new NDF and reducing the number of paramerters. For a more compact representation, it is possible to remove the imaginary part k of the index of refraction, as its influence over material behaviour is relatively small. This would bring the total number of parameters to 8 for the single layer model, at the expense of physical consistency.

A   The Integral Between D and S_{SH}

We compute the integral between D and S_{SH} of diffraction part in two steps.

- compute the Spherical Harmonics coefficients vectors of each function.

$$Y_l^0(\theta, \varphi) = \sqrt{\frac{2l+1}{4\pi}} P_l(\cos\theta) \tag{23}$$

$$S_l = \int_\Omega S(\theta) Y_l^0(\theta) d\omega \tag{24}$$

$$D_l = \int_\Omega D(\theta) Y_l^0(\theta) d\omega \tag{25}$$

where P_l is the Legendre polynomical of degree l. Here, we can apply Monte Carlo integration to compute S_l and D_l as there are adequate samples.

$$S_l = \int_\Omega S(\theta)Y_l^0(\theta)d\omega \quad \approx \frac{1}{N}\sum_{i=1}^N S(\theta)Y_l^0(\theta)\omega(\theta_i), \text{weight } \omega(\theta_i) = \frac{1}{p(\theta_i)}.$$ (26)

For a uniform hemispherical surface, the weights are:

$$\omega(\theta_i) = 2\pi$$ (27)

So the numerical estimation of the Spherical Harmonic coefficient is:

$$S_l = \int_\Omega S(\theta)Y_l^0(\theta)d\omega$$ (28)

$$\approx \frac{2\pi}{N}\sum_{i=1}^N S(\theta)Y_l^0(\theta).$$

$$D_l = \int_\Omega D(\theta)Y_l^0(\theta)d\omega$$ (29)

$$\approx \frac{2\pi}{N}\sum_{i=1}^N D(\theta)Y_l^0(\theta).$$

- multiply them to obtain the Spherical Harmonics coefficients of the integral:

$$\int_\Omega S_{HS}Dd\omega = \sum_l S_lD_lP_l(\cos\theta).$$ (30)

References

1. Cook, R.L., Torrance, K.E.: A reflectance model for computer graphics. ACM Trans. Graph. **1**(1), 7–24 (1982)
2. Torrance, K.E., Sparrow, E.M.: Theory for off-specular reflection from roughened surface. J. Opt. Soc. Am. **57**(9), 1105–1114 (1967)
3. Ngan, A., Durand, F., Matusik, W.: Experimental analysis of BRDF models. In: Eurographics Symposium on Rendering, pp. 117–226 (2005)
4. Bagher, M.M., Soler, C., Holzschuch, N.: Accurate fitting of measured reflectances using a shifted gamma micro-facet distribution. Comput. Graph. Forum **31**(4), 1509–1518 (2012)
5. Löw, J., Kronander, J., Ynnerman, A., Unger, J.: BRDF models for accurate and efficient rendering of glossy surfaces. ACM Trans. Graph **31**(1), 9:1–9:14 (2012)
6. Holzschuch, N., Pacanowski, R.: A two-scale microfacet reflectance model combining reflection and diffraction. ACM Trans. Graph **36**(4), 66:1–66:12 (2017)

7. Walter, B., Marschner, S., Li, H., Torrance, K.E.: Microfacet models for refraction through rough surfaces. In: Eurographics Symposium on Rendering, pp. 195–206 (2007)
8. Burley, B.: Physically-based shading at Disney. In: Hill, S., McAuley, S. (eds.) Siggraph Course: Practical Physically Based Shading in Film and Game Production. ACM (2012)
9. Brady, A., Lawrence, J., Peers, P., Weimer, W.: genBRDF: discovering new analytic BRDFs with genetic programming. ACM Trans. Graph **33**(4), 114:1–114:11 (2014)
10. Smith, B.: Geometrical shadowing of a random rough surface. IEEE Trans. Antennas Propag. **15**(5), 668–671 (1967)
11. Heitz, E.: Understanding the masking-shadowing function in microfacet-based BRDFs. J. Comput. Graph. Tech. **3**(2), 32–91 (2014)
12. Larson, G.J.W.: Measuring and modeling anisotropic reflection. In: Computer Graphics (Proceedings of SIGGRAPH 1992), pp. 265–272 (1992)
13. Walter, B.: Notes on the ward BRDF. Technical report PCG-05-06, Cornell Program of Computer Graphics (2005)
14. Lawrence, J., Rusinkiewicz, S., Ramamoorthi, R.: Efficient BRDF importance sampling using a factored representation. ACM Trans. Graph. **23**(3), 496–505 (2004)
15. Schlick, C.: An inexpensive BRDF model for physically-based rendering. Comput. Graph. Forum **13**(3), 233–246 (1994)
16. Harvey, J.E.: Light-scattering characteristics of optical surface. Ph.D. thesis, University of Arizona. Adviser: R.V. Shack (1975)
17. Krywonos, A.: Predicting surface scatter using a linear systems formulation of non-paraxial scalar diffraction. Ph.D. thesis, University of Central Florida. Adviser: J.E. Harvey (2006)
18. Matusik, W., Pfister, H., Brand, M., McMillan, L.: A data-driven reflectance model. ACM Trans. Graph. **22**(3), 759–769 (2003)

An Automatic Base Expression Selection Algorithm Based on Local Blendshape Model

Ziqi Tu[1], Dongdong Weng[1,2(✉)], Dewen Cheng[1], Yihua Bao[2],
Bin Liang[1], and Le Luo[1]

[1] Beijing Engineering Research Center of Mixed Reality and Advanced Display,
School of Optics and Photonics, Beijing Institute of Technology, Beijing, China
crgj@bit.edu.cn
[2] AICFVE of Beijing Film Academy, Beijing, China

Abstract. In order to give a virtual human rich and realistic facial expression in the film production process, a good blendshape model is needed. But selecting and capturing base expressions for blendshape model requires a lot of manual work, time and effort, and the model also lacks expressiveness. A method for automatically selecting a set of base expressions from a sequence of facial motions is proposed in this paper. In this method, the Procrustes analysis is used to estimate the difference between face meshes and determine the composition of the base expressions. And the base expressions are used to build a local blendshape model which can enhance expressiveness. The results of reconstructing facial expressions by the local blendshape model are shown in this paper. By this method, the base expressions can be automatically selected from the expression sequence, reducing the manual operation.

Keywords: Base expression selection · Local blendshape model · Facial expression reconstruction

1 Introduction

In the process of making movies, lifelike facial expressions of virtual human play an important role in expressing the character's emotions and language. The commonly used method of facial expression acquisition is through facial motion capture devices and blendshape models. In order to achieve a good effect of blending, it is necessary to capture as many expressions as possible. In the process of facial expression scanning, Facial Action Coding System (FACS) [7] is commonly used to guide the selection of expressions to be captured. FACS is based on the anatomical structure of the face and the laws of facial movement.

This project was funded by the National Key Research and Development Program of China (No. 2017YFB1002805), the National Natural Science Foundation of China (No. U1605254) and Microsoft Research Asia.

It contains more than 100 expressions. During the scanning of the models, some other expressions will also be added empirically based on FACS. For example, in the movie "The Curious Case of Benjamin Button", 170 blendshapes based on FACS principles were used [6]. However, choosing the expressions that need to be scanned mostly depend on the experience of artists. During the scanning, actors may make different expressions each time, and the description of the expressions is often confusing, so the same expressions need to be scanned many times. These reasons lead to a cost of time and manual operation in the process of constructing a blendshape model, and the actors also need to make a lot of effort. How to select the base expressions automatically for a blendshape model is worth studying.

Disney Research proposed a local blendshape model based on facial anatomical constraints [15]. They selected 10 from a subset of FACS containing 26 expressions as the base expressions for their blendshape model. Thus realizing monocular facial expression capture. Their way of choosing base expressions is inspiring.

For the local blendshape model, the entire face is divided into several local regions, each region can perform an independent blendshape. The local blendshape model is more flexible because it provides more degrees of freedom and has the advantage of exploiting hidden data [19]. Features that each face region is independent of each other can help fuse multiple locally deformations of the face together, which can further reduce the number of base expressions for blendshape model.

In this paper, a method for automatically selecting base expressions for blendshape model from a set of random expressions is proposed. The method is based on the local blendshape model. In a set of facial expression models with randomness, a subset is selected iteratively as the base expressions, and the unselected expressions are reconstructed by the facial expression reconstruction algorithm with the selected subset. The one with the greatest reconstruction error in the model to be selected as the next base expression. Finally, a set of base expressions that are most suitable are obtained. This paper shows the set of basic expressions that are automatically selected and the results of facial expression reconstructions.

2 Related Work

For building a blendshape model, most of the base expression selection are based on FACS. Ichim [9] proposed a physical based facial animation method. They used 48 blendshapes inspired by FACS as templates, sculptured by the artists, for facial animation. In the movie "King Kong", the expression space used in the reconstruction of facial animation was a superset of FACS [12]. Cao created a 3D facial expression database [4], which contains 150 individual's expression data, and created blendshape contains 46 expression units for each person. These 46 expression units are from FACS. Weise proposed a performance-driven real-time facial expression system [14], in which 39 facial expressions based on FACS were used to construct the blendshape model. FACS plays an important role in guiding the process of blendshape. However, in the current method, the number of base expressions that need to be scanned is too large, and the actor may need to make an expression many times because each time may have a different expression, which is challenging for the actor, and the scans also need to be selected later.

The local blendshape model is to divide the face into different regions and construct blendshape for each part so that every face region can deform independently. The local blendshape model is more flexible and can express the shape of the face that is not in the base expression. As early as 1995, Black [1] has studied the local parametric model for the recovery and recognition of non-rigid facial motion. Decarlo [5] manually created a parameterized 3D face model for tracking faces in the video; the shape of the model is controlled by parameterized deformation, which is used for a specific region of the face, from a single region to the entire face. Blanz [2] manually divided the face into 5 parts, creating a deformation model for each part. JOSHI [10] used a region-based blendshape model for keyframe facial animation and automatically determines the best segmentation through the physical model. Zhang [17] proposed a system for synthesizing facial expressions for 2D images and 3D face models. They empirically divided the face into several regions in order to synthesize asymmetric expressions. Tena [13] built a region-based PCA model based on motion capture data, allowing manual manipulation of face models. Brunton [3] used many local multi-linear models to reconstruct faces from noisy point cloud model. Neumann et al. [11] proposed a method for extracting sparse spatial local deformation patterns from animated mesh sequences. The local blendshape model has more parameters than the global blendshape model and provides more degrees of freedom, so it is more flexible, and can still perform well with a small number of base expressions.

Based on the local blendshape model, this paper automatically selects the base expressions in a set of random face models iteratively, and reconstruct the unselected expressions, realizing covering the whole with a small number of expressions.

3   Overview

The overall process of automatically selecting the base expression is shown in the Fig. 1. First, obtaining a series of random facial expression models is required. Starting with the neutral expression, select the base expressions from the set of models, and the unselected expressions for reconstruction. Then use the base expressions to construct a local blendshape model. Next, treat each unselected expression as the target model, perform monocular facial expression reconstruction with the constructed local blendshape model to obtain the corresponding reconstructed expression models. Then reconstructed expression meshes are compared with the target models, and the difference d_i between the reconstructed expression and the target expression is calculated as the error using the Procrustes analysis [8]. After that, the expression model with the largest error is

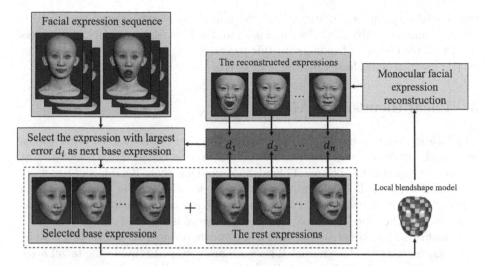

Fig. 1. The whole process for auto-selecting base expressions. The facial expression sequence is divided into selected base expressions and the rest expressions. d_i Represent the distances between the reconstructed meshes and the rest expressions calculated by Procrustes analysis.

selected as the new base expression, and the next iteration is performed. When the change rate of the error becomes relatively small, a set of suitable base expressions can be obtained. Each part will be introduced as follows.

4   Facial Expression Sequence

Before performing 3D face modeling, it is necessary to determine all the expressions to be scanned, to inform the actor of the expressions in advance, and tell the actor the essentials of facial expressions, and let the actors practice. In the process of scanning, in order to prevent the movement from being insufficient, a plurality of scans are generally performed for each expression. The goal of this paper is to simplify this process.

This paper refers to the requirements of the facial animation capture device Dynamixyz, select 56 extreme expressions as a sequence of expressions. These expressions are also based on FACS. This set of 56 expressions can be used as the base expression for the global blendshape model, for reconstructing most facial expressions. If a subset can be chosen to cover this set of expressions, then the subset can also be used to construct most facial expressions. Additional 10 expressions are added to the subset, supplementing some Chinese pronunciations and random expressions.

There are many ways to obtain 3D facial expression models. This paper uses a multi-view face reconstruction method similar to [18]. The images of different angles of the face are acquired by the multi-view camera array, and then the facial feature points are matched and the point cloud is calculated, and finally, the face model is obtained. In order to build a blendshape model, all models need to have the same topology. In this paper, a face model template is used to fit the reconstructed face with the help of ZBrush and R3DS warp3 software.

5   Local Blendshape Model

The base expressions need to include the deformation form of all the face regions, and on the basis of the global blendshape model, it is necessary to select a large number of expressions. The local blendshape model is more flexible and has more degrees of freedom. The deformation state of each region can be determined with a small number of base expressions, thus realizing the reconstruction of facial expressions. Therefore, the local blendshape model is necessary for this paper.

The first step in constructing the local blendshape model is to divide the facial area and segment the face model. There are many ways to divide the facial area, such as along the lines of the skin's surface, or according to the distribution of muscles. In a word, face segmentation is a very challenging task. Wu [15] used an UV-based partitioning method to segment the face model with 700k points into 1000 patches. This paper uses a similar approach. The facial area is selected in the UV map and is divided in the horizontal and vertical directions, and the corresponding portion of the face model is segmented. In order to ensure that each patch contains the appropriate number of points, the face model used in this paper has about 50k points and is divided into 100 patches. In order to ensure the integrity of the face model, there are overlap areas between the patches, which is convenient for fusing the patches into a whole. Each patch has approximately 20% overlapping vertices with neighboring patches by adjusting the patch size.

After segmenting the face model, all the blendshape models are segmented in the same way. Assuming that N is the number of expressions other than neutral expressions, then each patch has $N + 1$ shapes and can blend separately. Let X_i be the shape of the i-th patch, it can be obtained by the following formula

$$X_i = \left(U_i + \sum_{n=1}^{N} \alpha_i^n D_i^n \right) \tag{1}$$

Where U_i represents the shape of the i-th patch in the neutral expression, α_i^n is the weight of the blendshape in the patch and D_i^n refers to the deformation of the i-th patch with the n-th blendshape. Let S_i^n be the n-th shape of the i-th patch, then $D_i^n = S_i^n - U_i$.

6   Select the Base Expression

This paper will select a subset of N expressions as the base expression from 66 random face models. In order to ensure the efficiency of facial expression reconstruction, and considering the accuracy, it is important to select an appropriate number of basic expressions. This paper uses an iterative approach. The facial expression reconstruction method based on local blendshape is used to reconstruct the unselected expressions. The Procrustes analysis is used to estimate the errors of the reconstructed models. And the expression with the largest error is added to the set base expression. Then proceed to the next iteration. Finally, a set of appropriate base expressions is acquired.

6.1 Facial Expression Reconstruction

In order to reconstruct facial expressions, it is necessary to get the blendshape parameters of each patch, as well as the position and pose of the patch in three-dimensional space. Given that the current trend of facial expression reconstruction algorithms is for a monocular RGB camera, the method used in this paper is also for the same situation. In the energy function built in this paper, the blendshape parameters and pose of each patch are taken as the unknown quantity, and the selected two-dimensional feature points in the face image and the corresponding three-dimensional points in the model are taken as inputs. The formula is as follows:

$$E = E_M + E_O \qquad (2)$$

Wherein, the energy E is composed of E_M and E_O. E_M is the constraint on the patch shape and the pose, and it is used for determining the blendshape parameters of each patch in the face model and the position of the patch in the space; E_O is the constraint on the overlap of the patch and the neighboring patch.

In the local blendshape model, each patch can be independently deformed. The shape X_i of each patch can be obtained by Eq. 1, assuming that x_i is the three-dimensional coordinate of the feature point selected in the i-th patch, $P_i = K \cdot [R_i|T_i]$ is the projection matrix of the i-th patch. K is the camera intrinsic matrix obtained by the calibration. R_i and T_i are the rotation matrix and the translation matrix of the i-th patch. p_i is the corresponding 2D feature point coordinate in the i-th patch. E_M is computed as:

$$E_M = \lambda_M \sum_{i=1}^{V} \|P_i \cdot x_i - p_i\| \qquad (3)$$

Where V represents the number of patches for local blendshape model, $V = 100$. λ_M is the weight of the shape constraint. $\lambda_M = 1$ in this paper.

The overlap constraint of the patch is used to limit the position and shape of the neighboring patches to ensure the integrity of the facial expression.

$$E_O = \lambda_O \sum_{i=1,j=1}^{V} \|x_i - x_j\|^2 \qquad (4)$$

Where x_j represents the three-dimensional coordinates of the vertices in the j-th patch neighboring to the i-th patch. λ_O is the weight of the overlap constraint. Through adjustment, it is found that $\lambda_O = 7$ is suitable for this paper.

By minimizing the energy function $E = E_M + E_O$, we can get the blendshape weight α_i^n and the poses R_i and T_i of each patch. Through these parameters, the face model can be reconstructed. But there still have seams between the patches, so we need to fuse all the patches into a full face model. According to the distances between the vertexes in the patch and the center of the patch, the fusion weight of each point is calculated, and the coordinates of the patch vertexes of the overlapping portion are adjusted according to the weight to obtain a whole face model.

6.2   Select Base Expression Iteratively

Selecting the base expression begins with the neutral expression. By comparing the neutral expression with all the rest expressions, using the Procrustes analysis to calculate the difference between the neutral expression and the rest expressions, selecting the expression with the largest difference as the new base expression. Construct the first local blendshape model with the selected base expressions. Then use the local blendshape model to reconstruct all the unselected expressions, the reconstructed models of all expressions are obtained as results. And then use the Procrustes analysis again, compare the reconstructed models with the corresponding expression models, select the expression model with the largest error, and add to the base expression. Then proceed to the next iteration. When all the errors are small enough and the rate of error changing is small, the current set of expressions is the selected base expressions.

7   Result

For each iteration, the currently selected base expression and the reconstruction error are recorded. Figure 2 shows the line chart of the number of base expressions and the maximum error in each iteration.

In Fig. 2, the abscissa represents the number of base expressions, and the ordinate represents the maximum value of the Procrustes distance between the

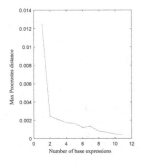

Fig. 2. The error of reconstruction is reduced very quickly when there are 2 base expressions. As the number of the base expressions increases, the error decreases and the rate of change becomes slows.

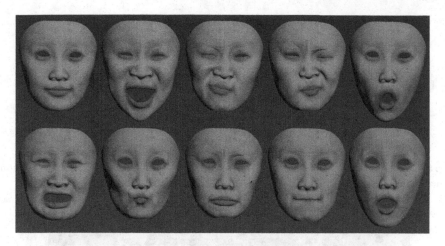

Fig. 3. The selected 10 base expressions including mouth wide open, frown, amazing, kiss and so on. Each represents the extreme expression of a certain area of the face.

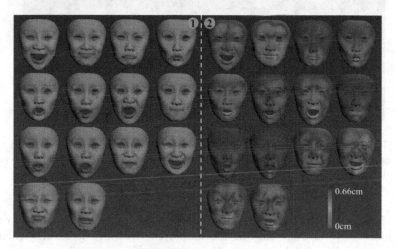

Fig. 4. Different facial expressions are reconstructed. (1) Some of the unselected expressions and (2) the corresponding reconstructed models. The color indicates the error of reconstructed models. (Color figure online)

reconstructed model and the corresponding unselected model, and also represents the reconstruction error of the blendshape model. As can be seen from the figure, when the number of base expression reaches 10 (including the neutral expression), the error has been significantly reduced, and the rate of change of the error is 0.0878, indicating that the error changes slowly. The 10 facial expressions are chosen as the set of base expressions and are shown in Fig. 3.

Using the local blendshape model constructed by this set of basic expressions, the remaining expressions are reconstructed, and some of the result is shown in Fig. 4. The color of the reconstructed mesh represents the reconstruction error,

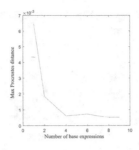

Fig. 5. The max Procrustes distance is decreasing when the number of base expression is increasing.

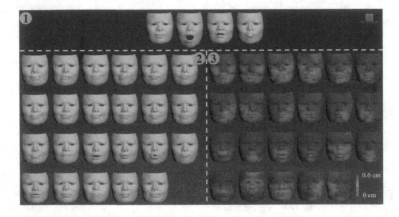

Fig. 6. (1) The selected 4 base expressions, (2) the face models for reconstruction, (3) the reconstructed face expressions, the color represents the reconstruction error. (Color figure online)

red is 0.5 and blue is 0. Assuming that the distance between the inner corners of the human eye is 3 cm, and in the model the distance is 2.2572, then the error represented by 0.5 is 0.66 cm. As can be seen from the figure, the overall error is relatively small. In some expressions, there is little error in the corners of the mouth and the chin, which may be due to the small number of overall expressions, it is not enough to cover the rich mouth deformations.

Besides using this set of scanned face models. Two additional public face datasets are also used in this paper. A set of facial blendshape models contains 47 facial expressions (with neutral face) are selected from Facewarehouse [4]. Face retopology is applied to all the models to facilitate the segmentation process. With the same procedure of Fig. 1, the base expressions are selected iteratively. The Procrustes distance is shown in the line chart of Fig. 5.

Four base expressions are selected according to Fig. 5. The rest expressions are reconstructed with the selected base expressions. The result is shown in Fig. 6.

The other dataset to be used is provided by the University of Washington Graphics and Imaging Laboratory [16], it contains 384 frames of facial meshes with different facial expression. In order to reduce computing time, this paper select one mesh from every 4 frames, and 96 face models are selected as random expressions. The result of base expression selection and reconstruction is shown in Figs. 7 and 8.

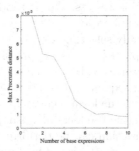

Fig. 7. When the number of base expression reaches 7, the max Procrustes distance changes slow.

Fig. 8. (1) The set of base expression selected, (2) the face models to be reconstructed, (3) the reconstructed expressions and the error.

These results show that the number and the composition of base expressions are different due to the random expression sequence used, but the errors of facial expression reconstruction are all relatively small.

8 Conclusion

This paper attempts to automatically select the base expressions. In a set of 66 random facial expression scans, a set of 10 base expressions is selected by an iterative method, and a local blendshape model is constructed using the set of base expressions to reconstruct the unselected expressions. This paper also tests the method of base expression selection on two public face model datasets. The result of the test is similar to the result of the expression sequence acquired in this paper. Which indicates that the method has the ability to choose a set of base expressions from a sequence of facial expressions. The constructed local blendshape model with the base expressions can cover all facial expressions. According to the reconstruction results, the method proposed in this paper is practical for facial expression animation.

The method of automatically selecting a set of base expressions proposed in this paper can be used in the process of facial expression tracking and reconstruction. Without requiring an actor to make a specific set of facial expressions many times, only need to capture a sequence of facial expressions, and then the base expressions needed to construct the local blendshape model is selected automatically. The process of constructing the local blendshape model can be simplified, and facial expression reconstruction can be performed more conveniently.

This paper attempts to auto select a set of base expressions and builds a local blendshape model. But in the reconstruction process, the scanned expression model instead of the real face image is used as input. In the future, feature points extracted from the real face image will be used for reconstructing facial expressions.

The local blendshape model used in this paper also can be improved. The current method to segment face is by UV mapping, but the deformation of different parts of the face is different. In the future, the method of face segmentation can be further studied.

References

1. Black, M.J., Yacoob, Y.: Tracking and recognizing rigid and non-rigid facial motions using local parametric models of image motion. In: Proceedings of IEEE International Conference on Computer Vision, pp. 374–381. IEEE (1995)
2. Blanz, V., Vetter, T., et al.: A morphable model for the synthesis of 3D faces. In: Siggraph 1999, pp. 187–194 (1999)
3. Brunton, A., Bolkart, T., Wuhrer, S.: Multilinear wavelets: a statistical shape space for human faces. In: Fleet, D., Pajdla, T., Schiele, B., Tuytelaars, T. (eds.) ECCV 2014. LNCS, vol. 8689, pp. 297–312. Springer, Cham (2014). https://doi.org/10.1007/978-3-319-10590-1_20
4. Cao, C., Weng, Y., Zhou, S., Tong, Y., Zhou, K.: Facewarehouse: a 3D facial expression database for visual computing. IEEE Trans. Visual Comput. Graph. 20(3), 413–425 (2014)
5. Decarlo, D., Metaxas, D.: Optical flow constraints on deformable models with applications to face tracking. Int. J. Comput. Vision 38(2), 99–127 (2000)
6. Flueckiger, B.: Computer-generated characters in avatar and Benjamin button. Digitalitat und Kino 1 (2011). Translation from German by B. Letzler
7. Friesen, E., Ekman, P.: Facial action coding system: a technique for the measurement of facial movement. Palo Alto 3 (1978)
8. Gower, J.C.: Generalized procrustes analysis. Psychometrika 40(1), 33–51 (1975)

9. Ichim, A.E., Kadleček, P., Kavan, L., Pauly, M.: Phace: physics-based face modeling and animation. ACM Trans. Graph. (TOG) **36**(4), 153 (2017)

10. Joshi, P., Tien, W.C., Desbrun, M., Pighin, F.: Learning controls for blend shape based realistic facial animation. In: ACM Siggraph 2006 Courses, p. 17. ACM (2006)

11. Neumann, T., Varanasi, K., Wenger, S., Wacker, M., Magnor, M., Theobalt, C.: Sparse localized deformation components. ACM Trans. Graph. (TOG) **32**(6), 179 (2013)

12. Sagar, M.: Facial performance capture and expressive translation for King Kong. In: ACM SIGGRAPH 2006 Courses, p. 7. ACM (2006)

13. Tena, J.R., De la Torre, F., Matthews, I.: Interactive region-based linear 3D face models. ACM Trans. Graph. (TOG) **30**, 76 (2011)

14. Weise, T., Bouaziz, S., Li, H., Pauly, M.: Realtime performance-based facial animation. ACM Trans. Graph. (TOG) **30**, 77 (2011)

15. Wu, C., Bradley, D., Gross, M., Beeler, T.: An anatomically-constrained local deformation model for monocular face capture. ACM Trans. Graph. (TOG) **35**(4), 115 (2016)

16. Zhang, L., Snavely, N., Curless, B., Seitz, S.M.: Spacetime faces: high-resolution capture for modeling and animation. In: ACM Annual Conference on Computer Graphics, pp. 548–558, August 2004

17. Zhang, Q., Liu, Z., Quo, G., Terzopoulos, D., Shum, H.Y.: Geometry-driven photorealistic facial expression synthesis. IEEE Trans. Visual Comput. Graph. **12**(1), 48–60 (2006)

18. Zhang, Y., Ji, Q., Zhu, Z., Yi, B.: Dynamic facial expression analysis and synthesis with MPEG-4 facial animation parameters. IEEE Trans. Circuits Syst. Video Technol. **18**(10), 1383–1396 (2008)

19. Zollhöfer, M., et al.: State of the art on monocular 3D face reconstruction, tracking, and applications. In: Computer Graphics Forum, vol. 37, pp. 523–550. Wiley Online Library (2018)

OpenFACS: An Open Source FACS-Based 3D Face Animation System

Vittorio Cuculo$^{(\boxtimes)}$ (iD) and Alessandro D'Amelio (iD)

PHuSe Lab - Dipartimento di Informatica, University of Milan, Milan, Italy
{vittorio.cuculo,alessandro.damelio}@unimi.it

Abstract. We present OpenFACS, an open source FACS-based 3D face animation system. OpenFACS is a software that allows the simulation of realistic facial expressions through the manipulation of specific action units as defined in the Facial Action Coding System. OpenFACS has been developed together with an API which is suitable to generate real-time dynamic facial expressions for a three-dimensional character. It can be easily embedded in existing systems without any prior experience in computer graphics. In this note, we discuss the adopted face model, the implemented architecture and provide additional details of model dynamics. Finally, a validation experiment is proposed to assess the effectiveness of the model.

Keywords: Facial expression · FACS · Emotion · 3D facial animation · HCI

1 Introduction

The chief purpose of systems that realise natural interactions is to remove the mediation between human and machine typical of classic interfaces. Among the main modalities of interaction there are speech, gestures, gaze and facial expressions (see [24] for a thorough review). The latter is particularly relevant because it plays a fundamental role in non-verbal communication between human beings. In particular, as to the human-computer interaction (HCI) aspects, the ability to recognize and synthesize facial expressions allows the machines to gain significant communication skills, on the one hand by interpreting emotions relying on the face of a subject; on the other hand by translating their communicative intent through an output, such as movement, sound response or colour change [7]. The latter skill is the one specifically addressed by the system presented here (Fig. 1), which aims at providing the scientific community with a tool that can be easily used and integrated into other systems.

2 Related Works

A significant body of work concerning facial animation has been reported since its early stages [19]. In recent years, thanks also to the entertainment industry, this

Y. Zhao et al. (Eds.): ICIG 2019, LNCS 11902, pp. 232–242, 2019.
https://doi.org/10.1007/978-3-030-34110-7_20

Fig. 1. Visualization of the OpenFACS 3D face animation system with the actor showing a neutral facial expression.

field of research has undergone a boost in the technologies developed, reaching high levels of realism [14]. However, the demand for specific skills in the computer graphics field or, alternatively, the high cost of third-party software, creates a barrier to the effective usability of an animated 3D model by researchers not directly involved in the computer graphics field but who still require a precise and realistic visible facial response for emotion research [4,5,8,20].

In terms of facial movements coding systems two are the prominent approaches: MPEG-4 and the Facial Action Coding System (FACS). The former [18] identifies a set of Face Animation Parameters (FAP), each corresponding to the displacement of a subset of 84 Feature Points (FP) of the face. These displacements are measured in FAP Units, defined as the distance between the fiducial points of the face. A similar approach, but with different motivation, has been realized by Paul Ekman [10] in the Facial Action Coding System (FACS). As the name suggests, the work presented here is based on the FACS, and related works that share the same system will be taken in consideration below. In 2009 a 3D facial animation system named FACe! [23] has been presented. This system was able to reproduce 66 action units from FACS as single activations or combined together. In the same year, Alfred [3] provided a virtual face with 23 facial controls (AUs) connected with a slider-based GUI, a gamepad, and a data glove. They concluded that the use of a gamepad for facial expression generation can be promising, reducing the production time without causing a loss of quality. A few years later, FACSGen 2.0 [15] provides a new animation software for creating facial expressions adopting 35 single AUs. The software has been evaluated by four FACS-certified coders resulting in good to excellent classification levels for all AUs. HapFACS 3.0 [1] was one of the few free software, providing an API based on the Haptek 3D-character platform. It has been developed to address the needs of researchers working on 3D speaking characters and facial expression generation. Among the most recent software based on FACS, FACSHuman [12] represents a suite of plugins for MakeHuman 3D tool. These should permit the creation of complex facial expressions manipulating the intensity of all known action units.

All the above tools, when still available, are not free to use, nor cross-platform or easily integrable within a pre-existing system. The only exception could be represented by FACSHuman but, at the time of writing, no technical details or software are still provided.

3   Theoretical Background

As mentioned in the introduction, facial expressions play a very important role in social interaction and their analysis has always represented a complex challenge [6,24]. They have been under study since 1872 when Charles Darwin published "The Expression of the Emotions in Man and Animals" [9], positing his thesis on the universality of emotions as a result of the evolutionary process, and considering facial expressions as a residue of behaviour, according to the principle of the "serviceable habits". From Darwin's work also stems the view addressing the communicative function of emotions (*emotions as expressions*). Researchers have expanded on Darwin's evolutionary framework toward other forms of emotional expression. The most notable ones are from Tomkins [22], proposing that there is a limited number of pan-cultural basic emotions, such as surprise, interest, joy, rage, fear, disgust, shame, and anguish, and by Ekman and Friesen [11]. In particular, Ekman's facial action coding system (FACS, [10]) influenced considerable research that tackles the affect detection problem developing systems that identify the basic emotions through facial expressions (and in particular extracting facial action units). According to the FACS, the emotional manifestations occur through the activation of a series of facial muscles which are described by 66 action units (AU). This encoding system allows the realisation of about 7000 expressions that can be found on a human face by the combination of such atoms. Each AU is identified by a number (AU1, AU2, AU4 ...) and correspond to the activation of a single facial muscle (e.g. *Zygomatic Major* for AU12). Intensities of FACS are expressed by letters from A (minimal intensity) to E (maximal intensity) postponed to the action unit number (e.g. AU1A is the lowest representation of the Inner Brow Raiser action unit).

4   OpenFACS System

The system presented here is an open-source, cross-platform, stand alone software. It relies on a 3D face model where FACS AUs are employed as a reference for creating specific muscle activations, that can be manipulated through a specialized API. OpenFACS software, including examples of usage and Python interface with the API are freely available at https://github.com/phuselab/openFACS.

4.1   Model

The 3D model adopted in OpenFACS is instantiated by exploiting the free software Daz3D[1]. It consists of approximately 10000 vertices and 17000 triangles (ref. Fig. 2). The handling of its parts relies on the so-called morph targets (also known as blend shapes), that describe the translation of a set of vertices in the 3D space to a new target position. In the proposed system, each of the 18 considered action units is implemented by the contribution of one or more morph targets. Table 1 summarizes the correspondence between the considered action units and the respective morph targets.

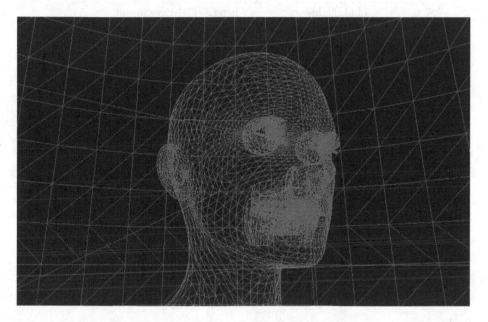

Fig. 2. Wireframe visualisation of the adopted 3D face model consisting of ∼10000 vertices and 17000 triangles.

To reproduce the FACS standard, the intensities for each of the action units are expressed with a value in the range [0, 5], where 0 corresponds to the absence of activation and 1 to 5 follows the A to E encoding. The value of muscle activation speed ranges from 0 to 1 and directly affects the linear interpolation speed from the current to the target configuration (e.g.: speed equal to 0.25 means that every tick it goes 25% of the way to the target). In Fig. 3 are shown the prototypical facial expressions of six basic emotions: anger, disgust, fear, happiness, sadness and surprise. These were obtained following the FACS [10], for instance, the surprise is made up by the combination of AU1, AU2, AU5 and AU26 (all with intensities equal to C).

---

[1] https://www.daz3d.com/.

Table 1. List of considered FACS action units and corresponding model morph targets.

Action unit	Description	Morph target
1	Inner Brow Raiser	head_CTRLBrowInnerUp
2	Outer Brow Raiser	head_CTRLBrowOuterUp
4	Brow Lowerer	head_PHMBrowSqueeze
5	Upper Lid Raiser	head_CTRLEyeLidsTopUp
6	Cheek Raiser	head_PHMSSmileFullFace
		head_PHMMouthSmile
		head_CTRLEyesSquint
7	Lid Tightener	head_CTRLEyesSquint
9	Nose Wrinkler	head_PHMNoseWrinkle
10	Upper Lip Raiser	head_CTRLLipTopUp
12	Lip Corner Puller	head_PHMMouthSmile
14	Dimpler	head_PHMCheeksBaloonPucker
15	Lip Corner Depressor	head_PHMMouthFrown
17	Chin Raiser	head_CTRLLipBottomOut
		head_PHMMouthOpen
20	Lip Stretcher	head_PHMLipsPucker
23	Lip Tightener	head_CTRLMouthNarrow
25	Lips parter	head_PHMLipsPart
26	Jaw Drop	head_PHMMouthOpenWide
28	Lip Suck	head_CTRLLipTopDown
		head_CTRLLipBottomIn
45	Blink	head_CTRLEyeLidsTopDown
		head_CTRLEyeLidsBottomUp

4.2 Architecture

The 3D model presented above is imported and managed by the source-available game engine Unreal Engine[2]. In such environment, an UDP based API server has been developed. Such API permits to an external software, even remotely, to communicate action units intensity values as well as the speed of muscle activation. This information must be serialized following the JSON data-interchange format and exchanged via classical client-server pattern. This implementation choice paves the way to a cross-platform and language-independent embedding into external systems. The engine, in real-time, takes care to realise the desired facial movement.

A sequence diagram of the implemented architecture can be found in Fig. 4, it includes the *ServerListener* that implements the UDP server, the *JSONParser*

---

[2] http://www.unrealengine.com/.

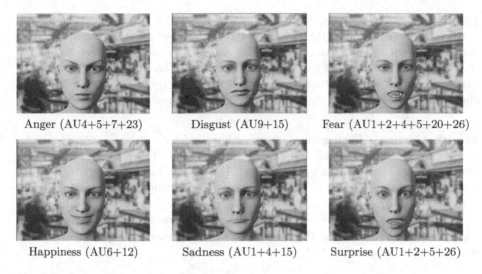

Anger (AU4+5+7+23)   Disgust (AU9+15)   Fear (AU1+2+4+5+20+26)

Happiness (AU6+12)   Sadness (AU1+4+15)   Surprise (AU1+2+5+26)

Fig. 3. Examples of six different facial expressions resulting from the combination of a specific set of action units, reported in brackets.

receives and interprets the JSON messages, the *AUInfos* keeps the information about action unit intensities and speed, while the *HumanMesh* is the only who can operate on the 3D model.

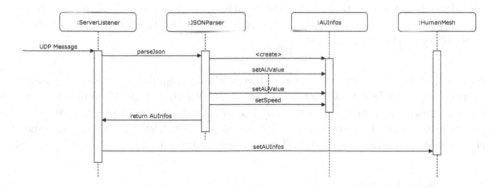

Fig. 4. Sequence diagram of the system to set a new facial expression.

4.3   Additional Details

In order to increase the realism of the simulation, in addition to a natural background and a clearer and realistic lighting, some basic automatic movements were added, unrelated to the action units. Bearing in mind that movements could amplify the effect of the so called *uncanny valley* [16,17], we modelled very slight movements of mouth corners, eyelids, neck and eye blink as described below.

Eye Blink. It has been shown that the average blink rate varies between 12 and 19 blinks per minute [13]. Here it is determined by sampling from a Normal distribution with $\mu = 6.0$ and $\sigma = 2.0$. The sampled value represents the waiting time (in seconds) between two consecutive blinks. The blink duration, in this case, is constant and set to 360 ms following the findings of Schifmann [21] who claims that blink duration lies between 100 and 400 ms.

Mouth Corners. Each mouth corner is handled by a specific morph target, namely *PHMMouthNarrowR* and *PHMMouthNarrowL*. The position (m) of such morph targets assume values in range $[-1, 1]$. At each tick, the probability that a corner is moved is equal to 0.8. In this case, when the morph target position is $m = 0$, it assumes probability 0.5 to be increased or decreased. The step done at each tick (t) is equal to $\Delta_m = 0.02$. A movement in any direction makes that direction less likely in the next step, in other words the probability that $m_{t+1} = m_t + \Delta_m$ is equal to

$$p = 1 - (0.5 + 0.5 * m) \tag{1}$$

This choice allows to keep constrained mouth corner movements reducing the possibility of abrupt changes.

Eyelids. Eyelids movement results in a constant and slight vibration of the interested vertices. The algorithm behind this movement is the same as the one described for mouth corners. Differently from Eq. 1, the probability that $m_{t+1} = m_t + \Delta_m$ is equal to $p = 1 - (0.8 + 0.2 * m)$, thus obtaining a lower probability of these movements.

Neck. Neck movement is realised through the manipulation of two different morph targets: *CTRLNeckHeadTwist* and *CTRLNeckHeadSide*. Even in this case the two morph targets are governed by the approach described for the previous movements, where Eq. 1 becomes $p = 1 - (0.6 + 0.4 * m)$, and $\Delta_m = 0.001$, since the neck movements require to be much more contained.

5   Validation

To characterise the behaviour of proposed simulation model, in terms of its expressive abilities, we conceived an experimental setup where an "expert" evaluates the unfolding of the facial dynamics of human $\mathcal{H}$ and artificial $\mathcal{A}$ expressers. In this perspective, a human expert (e.g., a FACS certified psychologist) would compare AUs' behaviour of $\mathcal{H}$ and $\mathcal{A}$ while expressing the same emotion.

We use in the role of a "synthetic expert" a freely available AU detector [2]. The inputs to the detector are the original frame sequence of $\mathcal{H}$'s facial actions and $\mathcal{A}$'s output. The AU detector provides, at each frame, the activation level of the following AUs ($N_{AU} = 12$): $AU k, k = 1, 2, 5, 9, 12, 14, 15, 17, 20, 23, 25, 26$.

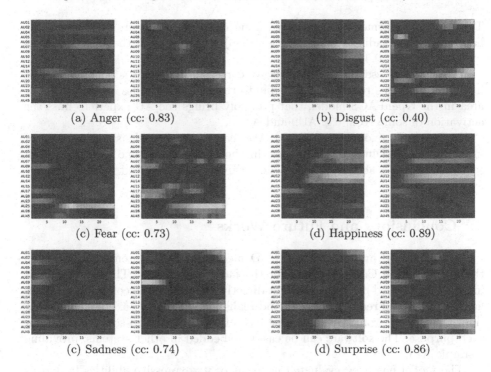

(a) Anger (cc: 0.83) (b) Disgust (cc: 0.40)

(c) Fear (cc: 0.73) (d) Happiness (cc: 0.89)

(c) Sadness (cc: 0.74) (d) Surprise (cc: 0.86)

Fig. 5. AU activation maps for the expression associated with each of the six basic emotions performed by the human actor (left) and OpenFACS model (right). Each row represents the activation over time of a single AU (brighter colours for higher activations). In brackets the 2D correlation coefficient between human and simulated AU activation maps. (Color figure online)

For each of the six basic emotions (anger, disgust, fear, happiness, sadness and surprise), we run the AU detector over either an original $\mathcal{H}$'s sequence, excerpted from the classic Cohn-Kanade dataset, and its synthetic reproduction, i.e., $\mathcal{A}$'s actual expression sequence resulting from the prototypical activation of facial action units as conceived in [10]. It is worth mentioning that no explicit expression design has been carried out, conversely the generated facial expression is the result of simultaneous activation of those AUs that, according to [10], are responsible for displaying the emotion at hand.

To quantify the expressive abilities of OpenFACS we compared the AU activations of $\mathcal{H}$ and $\mathcal{A}$ in terms of their two dimensional correlation coefficient. This was done for each of the six emotion categories. No specific tuning was adopted for optimizing detector performance, namely, it was used as black box AU expert.

Figure 5 illustrates the results achieved in terms of time-varying AU activation maps (each row denoting a single AU activation in time, brighter colour corresponding to higher activation). It can be noted at a glance that human's patterns of activation, for each expression, are similar to artificial's patterns.

This is also confirmed by the fairly strong correlation (anger: 0.83, fear: 0.73, happiness: 0.89, sadness: 0.74, surprise: 0.86) achieved in all the basic emotions but one (disgust: 0.40).

In the latter case, although a positive correlation exists it is not as strong as in the others. This result is mostly due to the lack of wrinkles around the nose area in the OpenFACS model, that probably brings the AU expert to miss the activation of some AUs, e.g. AU9 and AU10.

Interestingly enough, associated AUs can be activated as surrogates, for instance AU14 (Dimpler, that forms in the cheeks when one smiles) as consequence of AU12 activation. This effect can be easily noticed for the "happy" expression.

6   Conclusions and Future Works

In this paper we presented a novel 3D face animation system that relies on the Facial Action Coding System for the facial movements. This framework is intended to be used by researchers not directly involved in the computer graphics field but who still require a precise and realistic visible facial expression simulation. OpenFACS would overcome the lack of a free and open-source system for such purpose. The software can be easily embedded in other systems, providing a simple API.

The model has been evaluated in terms of its expressive abilities by means of quantitative comparison with the unfolding of humans' facial dynamics, for each of the six basic emotions. Obtained results proved the effectiveness of the proposed model.

In a future work, in addition to the objective evaluation already done, OpenFACS could be validated by a set of FACS-certified coders, in order to consolidate the operational definitions of the implemented AUs. Moreover, OpenFACS could benefit from the implementation of phonemes actions that that may be used to simulate speech, increasing its communication skills.

Acknowledgements. We gratefully acknowledge the support of NVIDIA Corporation with the donation of the Quadro P6000 GPU used for this research.

References

1. Amini, R., Lisetti, C., Ruiz, G.: HapFACS 3.0: facs-based facial expression generator for 3D speaking virtual characters. IEEE Trans. Affect. Comput. **6**(4), 348–360 (2015). https://doi.org/10.1109/TAFFC.2015.2432794
2. Baltrušaitis, T., Mahmoud, M., Robinson, P.: Cross-dataset learning and person-specific normalisation for automatic action unit detection. In: 11th IEEE International Conference and Workshops on Automatic Face and Gesture Recognition, vol. 6, pp. 1–6. IEEE (2015)
3. Bee, N., Falk, B., André, E.: Simplified facial animation control utilizing novel input devices: a comparative study. In: Proceedings of the 14th International Conference on Intelligent User Interfaces, pp. 197–206. ACM (2009)

4. Boccignone, G., Bodini, M., Cuculo, V., Grossi, G.: Predictive sampling of facial expression dynamics driven by a latent action space. In: Proceedings of the 14th International Conference on Signal-Image Technology Internet-Based Systems (SITIS), Las Palmas de Gran Canaria, Spain, pp. 26–29 (2018)
5. Boccignone, G., Conte, D., Cuculo, V., D'Amelio, A., Grossi, G., Lanzarotti, R.: Deep construction of an affective latent space via multimodal enactment. IEEE Trans. Cogn. Dev. Syst. **10**(4), 865–880 (2018). https://doi.org/10.1109/TCDS.2017.2788820
6. Ceruti, C., Cuculo, V., D'Amelio, A., Grossi, G., Lanzarotti, R.: Taking the hidden route: deep mapping of affect via 3D neural networks. In: Battiato, S., Farinella, G.M., Leo, M., Gallo, G. (eds.) ICIAP 2017. LNCS, vol. 10590, pp. 189–196. Springer, Cham (2017). https://doi.org/10.1007/978-3-319-70742-6_18
7. Cuculo, V., Lanzarotti, R., Boccignone, G.: The color of smiling: computational synaesthesia of facial expressions. In: Murino, V., Puppo, E. (eds.) ICIAP 2015. LNCS, vol. 9279, pp. 203–214. Springer, Cham (2015). https://doi.org/10.1007/978-3-319-23231-7_19
8. D'Amelio, A., Cuculo, V., Grossi, G., Lanzarotti, R., Lin, J.: A note on modelling a somatic motor space for affective facial expressions. In: Battiato, S., Farinella, G.M., Leo, M., Gallo, G. (eds.) ICIAP 2017. LNCS, vol. 10590, pp. 181–188. Springer, Cham (2017). https://doi.org/10.1007/978-3-319-70742-6_17
9. Darwin, C.: The Expression of the Emotions in Man and Animals. John Murray (1872)
10. Ekman, P.: Facial action coding system (FACS). A human face (2002)
11. Ekman, P., Friesen, W.V.: Constants across cultures in the face and emotion. J. Pers. Soc. Psychol. **17**(2), 124 (1971)
12. Gilbert, M., Demarchi, S., Urdapilleta, I.: FACSHuman a software to create experimental material by modeling 3D facial expression. In: Proceedings of the 18th International Conference on Intelligent Virtual Agents - IVA 2018, pp. 333–334. ACM Press, New York (2018)
13. Karson, C.N., Berman, K.F., Donnelly, E.F., Mendelson, W.B., Kleinman, J.E., Wyatt, R.J.: Speaking, thinking, and blinking. Psychiatry Res. **5**(3), 243–246 (1981)
14. Klehm, O., et al.: Recent advances in facial appearance capture. In: Computer Graphics Forum, pp. 709–733. Wiley Online Library (2015)
15. Krumhuber, E.G., Tamarit, L., Roesch, E.B., Scherer, K.R.: FACSGen 2.0 animation software: generating three-dimensional FACS-valid facial expressions for emotion research. Emotion **12**(2), 351 (2012)
16. MacDorman, K.F., Ishiguro, H.: The uncanny advantage of using androids in cognitive and social science research. Interact. Stud. **7**(3), 297–337 (2006)
17. Mori, M.: The uncanny valley. Energy **7**(4), 33–35 (1970)
18. Pandzic, I.S., Forchheimer, R.: MPEG-4 Facial Animation: The Standard, Implementation and Applications. Wiley, Hoboken (2003)
19. Parke, F.I., Waters, K.: Computer Facial Animation. AK Peters/CRC Press (2008)
20. Roesch, E.B., Sander, D., Mumenthaler, C., Kerzel, D., Scherer, K.R.: Psychophysics of emotion: the quest for emotional attention. J. Vision **10**(3), 4–4 (2010)
21. Schiffman, H.R.: Sensation and Perception: An Integrated Approach. Wiley, Hoboken (1990)
22. Tomkins, S.: Affect, Imagery, Consciousness, vol. 1. Springer, New York (1962)

23. Villagrasa, S., Sánchez, S., et al.: FACe! 3D facial animation system based on FACS. In: IV Iberoamerican Symposium in Computer Graphics, pp. 203–209 (2009). https://doi.org/10.1002/9780470682531.pat0170
24. Vinciarelli, A., et al.: Bridging the gap between social animal and unsocial machine: a survey of social signal processing. IEEE Trans. Affect. Comput. **3**(1), 69–87 (2012)

Overview on Vision-Based 3D Object Recognition Methods

Tianzhen Dong[1], Xiao Qi[1], Qing Zhang[1], Wenju Li[1], and Liang Xiong[2(✉)]

[1] School of Computer Science and Information Engineering, Shanghai Institute of Technology,
Shanghai 201418, China
[2] School of Humanities, Shanghai University of Finance and Economics, Shanghai 200433,
China
dongtianzhen@126.com

Abstract. In the fields of computer vision and pattern recognition, 3D object recognition has always been one of the most challenging problems, and has become an important direction of current image recognition research. This paper introduces the main methods of 3D object recognition and its key technologies comprehensively. It compares the advantages and disadvantages of various methods, and hopes to have a more comprehensive learning and grasp of 3D object recognition, and further clarify the future research direction.

Keywords: Computer vision · 3D object recognition · Overview

1 Introduction

Object recognition refers to obtaining environmental information by a set of sensors, and identifying specific objects in the scene through computer analysis. Its task is to realize the recognition of specific objects in the scene and give the position and posture of the object. The general process includes object detection, feature extraction, and recognition. About 80% come from vision when humans perceive external information. Therefore, vision-based object recognition has become a popular research in recent years, and is widely used in many fields such as robot navigation, industrial inspection, aerospace, military reconnaissance and so on.

As the complexity of the object to be identified increases, the object recognition of the traditional 2D image cannot meet the practical application, while the 3D object recognition can objectively describe the shape and structure and improve the recognition rate. According to the research status at home and abroad, the existing 3D object recognition methods are roughly divided into five categories: geometric or model-based method, appearance or view-based method, feature matching-based method, depth image-based method and intelligent algorithm-based method. The methods are introduced and compared, respectively.

© Springer Nature Switzerland AG 2019
Y. Zhao et al. (Eds.): ICIG 2019, LNCS 11902, pp. 243–254, 2019.
https://doi.org/10.1007/978-3-030-34110-7_21

2   Geometric or Model-Based Method

In the process of object recognition, the prior knowledge of the shape and structure of the object is generally called geometric or model-based 3D object recognition [1]. The method obtains a 3D geometric feature description from the input graphic data, and matches it with the model description to achieve recognition and positioning of the object.

Qian [2] proposed a new 3D object recognition method. The method segments a 3D point set into a number of planar patches and extracts the Inter-Plane Relationships (IPRs) for all patches. Based on the IPRs, the High Level Feature (HLF) for each patch is determined. A Gaussian-Mixture-Model-based plane classifier is then employed to classify each patch into one belonging to a certain model object. Finally, a recursive plane clustering procedure is performed to cluster the classified planes into the model objects.

Lin et al. [3] described the geometric component model in a combined way to describe the contour of the object, and established an ordered chain structure to show the degree of matching. The method can solve the matching problem of complex object contours, and the detection time is reduced by 60%–90% compared with previous methods. For a rigid object with a clear outline, the effect is better. Ding [4] used the forward method to establish a 3D scattering center model from the object CAD model offline. This model can effectively predict the object in arbitrary posture.

This method is generally applicable to the object with a regular shape, and the shape comparison is relatively intuitive and easy to understand. However, the algorithm has a large amount of computation, and a geometric model needs to be established, which is not suitable for environments with complex backgrounds and noise interference. When there is occlusion between objects, it will also produce poor recognition results.

3   Appearance or View-Based Method

3.1   Single-View Feature-Based Method

This method is to analyze the observed image of the object by a certain viewpoint, and to identify the object by feature extraction and feature matching. It requires that the object posture is relatively stable and the structure is relatively simple.

Eigen et al. [5] used multi-scale DNN to obtain depth information from single-view images. This method has only been improved in scale and has limitations for other 3D geometric information. Lee et al. [6] proposed an automatic pose estimation method to obtain depth information values from a given single image, suitable for various image sequences containing objects with different appearances and poses. Yan et al. [7] used the point, line and surface information in the image as the correction of the input image to eliminate the distortion problem. However, most are used in symmetrical building scenarios, and the robustness of the algorithm needs to be further improved.

In this recognition system, the identification feature of the higher dimension is generally required to represent the object, and the feature vector is compared with the template feature vector to complete the recognition. Single-view acquisition is susceptible to factors such as viewing angles, lighting and the complex background.

3.2 Multi-view Feature-Based Method

Based on the single-view object recognition, the multi-view compensate for the misidentification under similar 2D images formed by different objects and background occlusion. Feature matching is performed on images from two different viewing angles, which can realize camera calibration and restore the 3D coordinates of spatial points, thereby gradually developing SFM [8], three views [9] and multiple views [10] were following developed.

Chen [11] extracted features and reduced dimensions, then input these features into the SVM [12] for classification and identification, which solved the problems of classification complexity and low recognition efficiency caused by the increase of feature dimension. Zhan [13] extracted multiple features and then used PCA to eliminate the redundant information between the features. Finally, the genetic algorithm-optimized SVM is used for classification and recognition, which improves the accuracy and speed of 3D object recognition.

In order to objectively and accurately identify the object, a larger number of views are usually required, so that the complexity of the classification is significantly improved. If a smaller number of views are used, the recognition accuracy is reduced.

3.3 Optical Operation-Based Method

The basic principle is to obtain 2D graphics or images by optical imaging method, and to identify the object according to the optical characteristic parameters [14]. In the process of recognition, the object to be identified and the template are measured for similarity, and a set of related features are used to determine the category, position and posture of the object.

The classical optical operation, such as the optical flow method, changes the intensity of the light, and the motion is projected onto the image plane after being irradiated, and the change of the optical flow is formed by the pixel variation of the discrete sampling of the sensor. This method has high accuracy and can adapt to the motion situation, but due to the large amount of calculation and the sensitivity to environment, so the application is relatively small.

Zhang [15] encoded the depth information of the 3D object into the 2D image, and used optical 2D image recognition technology to identify the object. However, this method is limited to simple spherical objects, and the impact in practical applications has not been estimated. Vallmitjana [16] designed different filters according to different views of the object, integrated all the data into the object-centered coordinate system. However, excessive use of filters is likely to cause noise limitations in practical applications.

The optical operation recognition speed is fast, and the information can be processed in parallel, but the calculation amount is large and the time is long. Therefore, it is necessary to extract the 2D information based on the 3D object, and finally realize the optical 3D object recognition.

4 Feature Matching-Based Method

4.1 Global Feature-Based Method

The traditional image description method is to select features from a large number of images containing the object that can represent the whole, such as color, texture, etc., and use statistical classification technology to classify the object to achieve the purpose of recognition. The color histogram [17] describes the proportion of each color in the entire image, but it does not clearly describe the specific distribution and spatial position of the color. Texture features [18] describe a surface property that ignores other properties of the object and is highly flawed in the acquisition of high-level images.

The features selected are comprehensively representative, small in computation and easy to implement, but weak in detail resolution, sensitive to occlusion and background, and the object to be recognized is independent and the data is complete, so the application range is limited [19], and may have the following three shortcomings:

(1) Under the complex image structure, image segmentation technology affects the object recognition;
(2) The amount of learning data is large and the training time is long;
(3) When the object undergoes a large deformation, it will cause a sudden change in the global feature.

The model-based and view-based methods mentioned above show disadvantages in this respect.

4.2 Local Feature-Based Method

The local feature refers to the set of attributes that can objectively and stably describe the object, and combines the local features to form the feature vector, thereby realizing the effective representation of the object. The algorithm based on local feature matching has achieved good results in the field of object recognition [20–22].

The selected feature points must satisfy the following conditions [23]: (1) Repeatable extraction; (2) It can define a unique 3D coordinate system; (3) Its neighborhood contains valid description information. Subsequent feature point matching can be performed after feature point selection is completed [24]. The most widely used descriptors are the SIFT [25], the SURF [26], the Harris detector [27], the Hessian detector [28], HOG [29] and LBP [30].

Wei et al. [31] extracted the feature description of the invariant angle contour, obtained the feature vector of the object by invariant moment transformation, and compared the cosine of the angle to achieve feature matching. This method can be used for object recognition in complex scenes.

Although existing local feature-based techniques have high accuracy and can handle occlusion and chaos, these methods still have high computational complexity. In order to solve these problems, the literature [32] proposed keypoints-based surface representation (KSR), which does not need to calculate local features, using the geometric relationship between the detected 3D key points to local surface representation, to some extent, it suppresses the noise level.

Local features have good stability and are not easily affected by environmental factors. Even though the amount of data is too large, fast registration can be achieved, but at the cost of algorithm complexity and computational addition. The global feature is invariant, small calculation amount and convenient to understand. Therefore, they can be combined to improve the recognition rate and reduce the calculation amount.

5 Depth Image-Based Method

A narrow depth image [33] is defined as acquiring depth information of an object using a depth sensor such as a microwave or a laser. At present, the methods frequently used for obtaining depth images are stereoscopic vision technology [34], microwave ranging principle and lidar imaging [35].

The more commonly used depth image types are grid representation [36] and point cloud representation [37].

5.1 Grid Representation

The grid consists of points, edges and planes. It is an irregular data structure and has a rich description of the shape and other details.

Fang et al. [38] introduced the grid structure into the multi-view image, so that the grid point position corresponds to the viewpoint image feature vector, and then the model is built according to the local invariant feature statistics of the object. Wang et al. [39] proposed an end-to-end depth learning framework that can generate 3D mesh directly from a single color picture. The CNN is used to represent the 3D mesh, and features are extracted from the input image to produce the correct geometry shape.

Grid data is informative and has a topology. However, when drawing a large scene, performing grid reconstruction will bring about problems such as long calculation time and large amount of information storage.

5.2 Point Cloud Representation

The point cloud is a set of 3D point coordinates of a scene or an object. Due to the huge amount of point cloud scene data, each object contains a large number of features, and each feature corresponds to a high-dimensional description vector, resulting in large computational complexity and low computational efficiency [40].

The PointNet network [41] can process the unordered point cloud and the rotated point cloud data. On this basis, PointNet++ [42] adds a hierarchical structure to the network structure to process local features. The SO-Net [43] network structure simulate the spatial distribution of the point cloud in a self-organizing map (SOM) manner. In Model-Net40 classification, PointNet achieved 86.2%, PointNet++ is remarkably stronger than PointNet, and SO-Net was up to 90.8%.

The graph-based method is a novel method for 3D point cloud object recognition. Wang et al. [44] proposed an EdgeConv module in DGCNN. By stacking or reusing the

EdgeConv module, global shape information can be extracted. DGCNN has improved performance by 0.5% over PointNet++. The key to RS-CNN [45] is learning from relation, i.e., the geometric topology constraint among points. RS-CNN reduces the error rate of PointNet++ by 31.2% and with a stronger robustness than PointNet, PointNet++ and DGCNN.

6 Intelligent Algorithm-Based Method

Intelligent algorithm is a kind of engineering practice algorithm realized by computer. It reflects the simulation and reproduction of biological system, human intelligence and physical chemistry. It is widely used in object recognition and image matching. The following is an introduction to several major intelligent algorithms:

6.1 Ant Colony Algorithm

According to the characteristics of ant colonies' foraging behavior, a population-based simulated evolutionary algorithm was proposed, called Ant Colony Optimization [46].

The idea is that during the foraging process of the ant, information exchanged and transmission will be carried out, and the next walking path will be selected according to the length of the path taken, showing a positive feedback phenomenon [47]. When the ant is unable to move in the next step, the path taken at this time corresponds to a feasible solution in the optimization problem. Zhang et al. [48] combined the relative difference of gradient and statistical mean with image edge detection. The relative difference between the gradient value and the statistical mean is extracted as an ant search for image edge detection. In the future, parallel ACO algorithms can be used to further reduce the computational complexity of the algorithm.

6.2 Particle Swarm Optimization

According to the birds' foraging behavior, Kennedy and Eberhart proposed Particle Swarm Optimization [49]. Considering the flock of birds as a group of random particles, with the two attributes of direction and distance, with the nearest solution from the food and the optimal solution currently found by the whole population as a reference, the area closest to the food can be regarded as the best solution to the problem.

Due to the rapid loss of diversity, PSO suffers from premature convergence. In order to improve the performance, Wang et al. [50] proposed a hybrid PSO algorithm (DNSPSO), which uses diversity enhancement mechanism and domain search strategies. By combining these two strategies, DNSPSO achieves a trade-off between exploration and development capabilities. Compared to standard PSO, DNSPSO does not increase computation time and has better results on low-dimensional issues.

6.3 Artificial Fish-Swarm Algorithm

The Artificial Fish-Swarm Algorithm [51] was derived from the characteristics of fish movement. Supposing that in a water area, the fish population will gather together according to the behavior of foraging, so the place where the fish population gathers the most is the best nutritional water quality, which is the best solution to the problem.

Due to the computational complexity of the artificial fish algorithm and the slow convergence rate at the later stage, Ma et al. [52] proposed an adaptive vision-based fish swarm algorithm (AVAFSA), which changed the field of view of the fish foraging, and gradually reduced when the algorithm iterated. The small field of view value stops the iteration until the field of view value is less than half of the initial value. The improved algorithm has fast convergence speed and small calculation amount, and is more accurate and stable than the basic AFSF algorithm.

6.4 Genetic Algorithm

The Genetic Algorithm (GA) [53] is an evolutionary algorithm that utilizes the natural laws of the biological world. The parameters in the optimization problem are regarded as chromosomes, and the chromosomes in the population are optimized by iterative methods such as selection, crossover and mutation, and the chromosomes that meet the optimization object are feasible solutions.

Aiming at the defects of GA, the immune genetic algorithm is used to combine the immune algorithm [54] with the GA to solve the problem of premature convergence of GA, to ensure the diversity of the group [55]. Tao et al. [56] combined GA with SVM to classify data classes, and the classification accuracy were greatly improved.

6.5 Simulated Annealing Optimization

Simulated Annealing Optimization [57] simulates the process of heating and cooling solid matter in physics, referring to the solution process of general optimization problems. Shieh et al. [58] proposed a hybrid algorithm combining particle swarm optimization with simulated annealing behavior (SA-PSO), which has good solution quality advantages in simulated annealing and has fast search capability in particle swarms, which can increase efficiency and speed up convergence.

It can be improved by combining with other algorithms, such as the combination with PSO [59], GA [60] and ant colony algorithm [61].

6.6 Neural Networks

The neural network [62] is a mathematical model that simulates the laws of human beings in various things in nature, solves some problems with its working principle, and adjusts the connection relationship between internal nodes to adapt to the processing of different information.

The advantage of the neural network is that it can be self-learning, and the learning rules are simple, easy to implement by computer, and has broad application prospects. The disadvantage is that it is impossible to explain its own reasoning process and reasoning basis. Once the data is insufficient, it will lose the ability to work normally.

Intelligent algorithms are an emerging research direction, and Table 1 lists the comparison of these six algorithms.

Table 1. Comparison of intelligent algorithms

Name	Advantage	Disadvantage	Application
Ant Colony Algorithm	Strong robustness and strong parallel computing power	Easy to fall into the local optimal solution	Discrete optimization problem
Particle Swarm Optimization	Strong versatility, few parameters, fast convergence	Easy to fall into the local optimal solution	Real number optimization problem
Artificial Fish-Swarm Algorithm	The local optimum value is easy to determine and the convergence speed is fast	Multi-extreme function is inefficient and easy to fall into local optimal solution	Various continuous function solution
Genetic Algorithm	Global optimization algorithm, fast solution	The algorithm is complex, the search speed is slow, and the choice of the population is large	Multiple optimization problems
Simulated Annealing Optimization	Robust and versatile, global optimization	Longer optimization process	Global optimization problems
Neural Networks	Strong nonlinear mapping ability, high learning and self-adaptive ability, generalization ability	Easy to fall into local extreme value, slow convergence, different structural choices, sample dependence	Multiple optimization problems

7   Conclusion

Vision-based 3D object recognition has always been a research hotspot in the field of computer vision. According to the foregoing, both method (1) and method (2) can compare shapes intuitively. In the absence of the shape description of the object, method (2) can be used. However, they all require that the object is independent and the data is complete, sensitive to occlusion and background, so the scope of application is limited. In contrast, Method (3) has better robustness in the presence of overlapping and complex backgrounds and has become the most common method. Method (4) embodies the shape contour of the object space, which has the advantages that the ordinary CCD camera does not have and change the idea of 2D image recognition. The difference is that Method (5) uses an optimized strategy combined with the first four methods to improve.

At present, the most widely used recognition methods are object recognition for uniform point cloud distribution or scenes with less objects. The 3D point cloud scene data is sensitive to noise and there is a case where the density distribution is uneven. How to reduce point cloud noise, reduce the impact of uneven density distribution, and how to apply the mature technology in 2D object recognition to 3D point cloud data will be an important research direction. Table 2 lists the comparison of various recognition algorithms.

Table 2. Comparison of various recognition algorithms

Algorithm	Introduction	Advantage	Disadvantage
Geometric or model-based method	Get a description of the object from the input images or data	It is relatively straightforward to compare shapes and is easy to understand	Computationally and not suitable for environments with noise interference or complex backgrounds
Appearance or view-based method	The object recognition is realized by view similarity	The image is easy to obtain and relatively simple	Susceptible to viewing angles and illumination, and sensitive to occlusion and noise environments
Feature matching-based method	Area with high discriminability as a feature	Good robustness to complex backgrounds, noise, local occlusion and changes in pose	The selection of features determines the complexity and the accuracy
Depth image-based method	Get geometric information from the depth data	Unaffected by illumination and surface texture	Affected by sensor performance
Intelligent algorithm-based method	Come form natural phenomena	Novel and widely used	Has limitations and still needs to be verified

References

1. Ying, C., Ji, Z., Hua, C.: 3-D model matching based on distributed estimation algorithm. In: 2009 Chinese Control and Decision Conference, CCDC 2009, pp. 5063–5067. IEEE (2009)
2. Qian, X., Ye, C.: 3D object recognition by geometric context and Gaussian-mixture-model-based plane classification. In: IEEE International Conference on Robotics and Automation. IEEE (2014)
3. Lin, Y.D., He, H.J., Chen, F., et al.: A rigid object detection model based on geometric sparse representation of profile and its hierarchical detection algorithm. Acta Automatica Sinica **41**(4), 843–853 (2015)
4. Ding, B., Wen, G.: Target reconstruction based on 3-D scattering center model for robust SAR ATR. IEEE Trans. Geosci. Remote Sens. **56**, 3772–3785 (2018)
5. Eigen, D., Puhrsch, C., Fergus, R.: Depth map prediction from a single image using a multi-scale deep network. In: International Conference on Neural Information Processing Systems, pp. 2366–2374. MIT Press (2014)

6. Lee, J., Kim, Y., Lee, S., et al.: High-quality depth estimation using an exemplar 3D model for stereo conversion. IEEE Trans. Visual Comput. Graph. **21**(7), 835–847 (2015)
7. Miao, Y.W., Feng, X.H., Yu, L.J., et al.: 3D building interactive progressive modeling based on single image. J. Comput. Aided Des. Comput. Graph. **28**(09), 1410–1419 (2016)
8. Widya, A.R., Torii, A., Okutomi, M.: Structure from motion using dense CNN features with keypoint relocalization. IPSJ Trans. Comput. Vis. Appl. **10**(1), 6 (2018)
9. Wu, C.: Towards linear-time incremental structure from motion. In: International Conference on 3D Vision, pp. 127–134. IEEE Computer Society (2013)
10. Zou, G.F., Fu, G.X., Li, H.T.: A survey of multi-pose face recognition. Pattern Recogn. Artif. Intell. **28**(7), 613–625 (2015)
11. Chen, G., Deng, C.W.: Research on 3D object recognition based on KPCA-SVM. Comput. CD Softw. Appl. **07**, 77–78 (2012)
12. Gedam, A.G., Shikalpure, S.G.: Direct kernel method for machine learning with support vector machine. In: International Conference on Intelligent Computing. IEEE (2018)
13. Zhan, N.: Three-dimensional object recognition method based on multiple features and support vector machine. Comput. Simul. **30**(3), 375–380 (2013)
14. Xu, S.: Research on three dimensional object recognition. University of Electronic Science and Technology of China (2010)
15. Zhang, H.H.: Study on three-dimensional recognition of the spatial object based on optical correlation pattern recognition. Hubei University of Technology (2009)
16. Vallmitjana, S., Juvells, I.P., Carnicer, A., et al.: Optical correlation from projections of 3D objects. In: Proceedings of SPIE - The International Society for Optical Engineering, vol. 81, pp. 148–169 (2017)
17. Aloraiqat, A.M., Kostyukova, N.S.: A modified image comparison algorithm using histogram features (2018)
18. Tyagi, V.: Texture feature. Content-Based Image Retrieval (2017)
19. Guo, Y.L., Lu, M., Tan, Z.G., Wan, J.W.: Survey of local feature extraction on range image. Pattern Recogn. Artif. Intell. **25**(05), 783–791 (2012)
20. Xiao, Q., Luo, Y., Hu, X.: Object detection based on local feature matching and segmentation. In: IEEE International Conference on Signal Processing. IEEE (2012)
21. Zhou, D.B., Huo, L.J., Gang, L.I., et al.: Automatic object recognition based on local invariant features. Acta Photonica Sinica **44**(2) (2015)
22. Kechagias-Stamatis, O., Aouf, N., Gray, G., et al.: Local feature based automatic object recognition for future 3D active homing seeker missiles. Aerosp. Sci. Technol. **73**, 309–317 (2018)
23. Mian, A., Bennamoun, M., Owens, R.: On the repeatability and quality of keypoints for local feature-based 3D object retrieval from cluttered scenes. Int. J. Comput. Vis. **89**(2–3), 348–361 (2010)
24. Wei, X.: The research of image matching method and application based on local feature detection. Anhui University (2015)
25. Xie, J., Xu, Z., Liu, Y., et al.: A remote sensing image object recognition method based on SIFT algorithm. In: International Conference on Mechatronics, Robotics and Automation (2015)
26. Guan, F., Liu, X., Feng, W., et al.: Multi object recognition based on SURF algorithm. In: International Congress on Image and Signal Processing, pp. 448–453. IEEE (2013)
27. Karthik, O.S., Varun, D., Ramasangu, H.: Localized Harris-FAST interest point detector. In: India Conference, pp. 1–6. IEEE (2017)
28. Tahery, S., Drew, M.S.: A novel colour Hessian and its applications. Electron. Imaging (2017)
29. Jebril, N.A., Al-Zoubi, H.R., Al-Haija, Q.A.: Recognition of handwritten arabic characters using histograms of oriented gradient (HOG). Pattern Recogn. Image Anal. **28**(2), 321–345 (2018)

30. Fan, H., Cosman, P.C., Hou, Y., et al.: High speed railway fastener detection based on line local binary pattern. IEEE Signal Process. Lett. **25**, 788–792 (2018)
31. Yong-Chao, W., Feng, C., Xia, Z., et al.: 3D target recognition based on invariant angle contour. J. Sichuan Univ. (Nat. Sci. Edn.) (2017)
32. Shah, S.A.A., Bennamoun, M., Boussaid, F.: Keypoints-based surface representation for 3D modeling and 3D object recognition. Pattern Recogn. **64**, 29–38 (2017)
33. Fisher, R.B., Breckon, T.P., Dawson-Howe, K., et al.: Dictionary of Computer Vision and Image Processing. Wiley, New York (2014)
34. Kaehler, A., Bradski, G.: Learning OpenCV 3: Computer Vision in C++ with the OpenCV Library. O'Reilly Media Inc., Sebastopol (2016)
35. Wang, Y., Huang, J., Liu, Y., et al.: Simulation of lidar imaging for space object. Infrared Laser Eng. **45**(9) (2016)
36. Li, Y.: Research on key techniques of 3D surface reconstruction based on depth camera. Zhejiang University (2015)
37. Zhuang, Z.Y., Zhang, J., Sun, G.F.: Extended point feature histograms for 3D point cloud representation. J. Natl. Univ. Defense Technol. **38**(6), 124–129 (2016)
38. Fang, X., Yu, R.X.: Grid-based statistical model for 3D object recognition. Comput. Mod. **2014**(4), 24–28 (2014)
39. Wang, N., Zhang, Y., Li, Z., Fu, Y., Liu, W., Jiang, Y.-G.: Pixel2Mesh: generating 3D mesh models from single RGB images. In: Ferrari, V., Hebert, M., Sminchisescu, C., Weiss, Y. (eds.) ECCV 2018. LNCS, vol. 11215, pp. 55–71. Springer, Cham (2018). https://doi.org/10.1007/978-3-030-01252-6_4
40. Hao, W., Wang, Y.H., Ning, X.J., et al.: Survey of 3D object recognition for point clouds. Comput. Sci. **44**(09), 11–16 (2017)
41. Qi, C.R., Su, H., Mo, K., et al.: PointNet: deep learning on point sets for 3D classification and segmentation (2016)
42. Qi, C.R., Yi, L., Su, H., et al.: PointNet++: deep hierarchical feature learning on point sets in a metric space (2017)
43. Li, J., Chen, B.M., Lee, G.H.: SO-Net: self-organizing network for point cloud analysis (2018)
44. Wang, Y., Sun, Y., Liu, Z., et al.: Dynamic graph CNN for learning on point clouds. ACM Trans. Graph. (TOG) **38**(5), 146 (2018)
45. Liu, Y., Fan, B., Xiang, S., et al.: Relation-shape convolutional neural network for point cloud analysis (2019)
46. Bisht, A., Kumar, R.: An efficient multi-level clustering approach using improved ant colony optimization. In: International Conference on Advances in Computing, Communication and Automation, pp. 1–5. IEEE (2018)
47. Xia, X.Y., Zhou, Y.R.: Advances in theoretical research of ant colony optimization. CAAI Trans. Intell. Syst. **11**(01), 27–36 (2016)
48. Zhang, J., He, K., Zheng, X., et al.: An ant colony optimization algorithm for image edge detection. In: International Conference on Artificial Intelligence and Computational Intelligence, pp. 215–219. IEEE (2010)
49. Jain, N.K., Nangia, U., Jain, J.: A review of particle swarm optimization. J. Inst. Eng. **99**, 407–411 (2018)
50. Wang, H., Sun, H., Li, C., et al.: Diversity enhanced particle swarm optimization with neighborhood search. Inf. Sci. **223**, 119–135 (2013)
51. Zhang, L.H., Dou, Z.Q., Sun, G.L.: An improved artificial fish-swarm algorithm using cluster analysis. In: Qiao, F., Patnaik, S., Wang, J. (eds.) ICMIR 2017. AISC, vol. 690, pp. 49–54. Springer, Cham (2018). https://doi.org/10.1007/978-3-319-65978-7_8
52. Ma, X.-M., Liu, N.: Improved artificial fish-swarm algorithm based on adaptive vision for solving the shortest path problem. J. Commun. (2014)

53. Roberge, V., Tarbouchi, M., Labonte, G.: Comparison of parallel genetic algorithm and par-
    ticle swarm optimization for real-time UAV path planning. IEEE Trans. Ind. Inform. **9**(1),
    132–141 (2013)
54. Jia, C., Fan, Y.: Application of immune genetic algorithm in image segmentation. Beijing
    Surv. Mapp. (2018)
55. Shi, J., Su, Y.D., Xie, M.: Research on application of IGA (immune genetic algorithm) to the
    solution of Course-Timetabling Problem. In: International Conference on Computer Science
    and Education, pp. 1105–1109. IEEE (2009)
56. Tao, Y., Zhou, J.: Automatic apple recognition based on the fusion of color and 3D feature
    for robotic fruit picking. Comput. Electron. Agric. **142**, 388–396 (2017)
57. Awange, J.L., Paláncz, B., Lewis, R.H., et al.: Simulated annealing (2018)
58. Shieh, H.L., Kuo, C.C., Chiang, C.M.: Modified particle swarm optimization algorithm with
    simulated annealing behavior and its numerical verification. Appl. Math. Comput. **218**(8),
    4365–4383 (2011)
59. Chen, S., Ren, L., Xin, F.: Reactive power optimization based on Particle Swarm Optimization
    and Simulated Annealing cooperative algorithm. In: Control Conference, pp. 7210–7215.
    IEEE (2012)
60. Mann, M., Sangwan, O.P., Tomar, P., et al.: Automatic goal-oriented test data generation using
    a genetic algorithm and simulated annealing. In: International Conference - Cloud System
    and Big Data Engineering, pp. 83–87. IEEE (2016)
61. Rong, X.J.: Research on hybrid task scheduling algorithm simulation of ant colony algorithm
    and simulated annealing algorithm in virtual environment. In: International Conference on
    Computer Science and Education, pp. 562–565. IEEE (2015)
62. Schmidhuber, J.: Deep learning in neural networks. Neural Netw. **61**, 85–117 (2015)

An Improved Indoor Image Registration Algorithm Based on Shallow Convolutional Neural Network Descriptor

Yun Gong and Mengjia Yang[✉]

Xi'an University of Science and Technology, Xi'an 710054, China
2504853112@qq.com

Abstract. At present, the application demand of indoor simultaneous localization and mapping (SLAM) technology increases greatly, among which, image matching is the most basic and critical content. Compared with traditional image registration, indoor image registration has higher requirements on the real-time and robustness of the algorithm. The shallow convolutional neural network is a deep machine learning model based on supervised learning with the characteristics of centralized and automatic learning from data. Aiming at the problems of slow processing and strong rotation failure of feature descriptors in traditional registration algorithms, this paper proposed an improved algorithm of local feature descriptor of triple-sample shallow convolutional neural network, which has strong feature expression ability. In addition, the performance of our improved algorithm was compared with that of three traditional algorithms (SIFT, ORB and SURF) in rotation change of indoor image matching. The results show that the improved algorithm performs better than the other three traditional methods and has a certain antagonistic effect on image rotation.

Keywords: Feature detection · Feature matching · Neural network · Descriptor

1 Introduction

Feature matching refers to a process of seeking common connection points between two images with overlapping areas, which provides a basic support for subsequent data applications. Feature matching is a crucial step in computer vision visualization. Feature matching solves the problem of data association [1] in computer vision, which determine the correspondence between the features seen currently and those seen previously. By accurately matching the descriptors between images or between images and maps, a large burden can be reduced for subsequent posture estimation, optimization, and the like. However, due to the local characteristics of image features, mismatches widely exist and have not been effectively solved for a long time, which has become a major bottleneck restricting performance improvement in computer vision [2].

After feature points are detected in the process of image matching, feature descriptors are used to express the detected feature points in a certain mathematical way so that the machine can recognize them. Meanwhile, the uniqueness of the expression of feature

© Springer Nature Switzerland AG 2019
Y. Zhao et al. (Eds.): ICIG 2019, LNCS 11902, pp. 255–265, 2019.
https://doi.org/10.1007/978-3-030-34110-7_22

points is taken into consideration, so that mismatching will not occur. The ideal feature descriptor needs to satisfy the invariance of scale, rotation, and even affine transformation, and is not sensitive to noise. Only when the feature descriptors corresponding to different feature points have little correlation can different feature points be well distinguished. Therefore, improving the recognition and expression ability of feature descriptors is conducive to improving the overall matching quality. For image matching, local feature space distribution descriptor [3] is most widely used. One of the most representative studies is the SIFT descriptor. In 2004, KeY et al. developed the PCA-SIFT [4] descriptor by removing some insignificant direction gradient values through Principal Component Analysis (PCA), which significantly improved the speed. Mikolajczyk obtained the GLOH (Gradient Location and Orientation Histogram) descriptor [5] by using the expression of polar coordinate system instead of the expression expansion of European coordinate system. In 2008, Bay et al. proposed a 64-dimensional SURF descriptor to speed up the calculation. In 2010, Enign et al. proposed the DAISY [6] descriptor, which replaced the weighted calculation of some previous operators by means of convolution kernel, and it has a good application in the region with dense urban buildings. Local feature space association descriptors use a certain mathematical method to calculate the spatial correlation characteristics of local features such as gradient and binary [7]. In 2012, Vandergheynst et al. proposed a FREAK (Fast Retina Keypoint) descriptor based on the mechanism of human visual imaging [8], whose descriptors are more reasonable in terms of matching accuracy. In 2018, Yi et al. proposed LIFT [9] descriptor based on convolutional neural network, which can be used to learn descriptors and improve them compared with traditional manual descriptors.

Feature matching is the key to the rapid development of indoor positioning and navigation technology while traditional feature detection algorithms have different performance in different environments. Because indoor images are affected by illumination, angle and scale, a single traditional algorithm is not sufficient to meet the requirements in terms of processing efficiency and large rotation changes. Therefore, we performed feature matching on indoor images from the characteristics of image data, and compared processing speed and matching rate of the three traditional algorithms that of three methods using the improved triple-sample shallow convolutional neural network learning descriptors. Then we proposed an improved algorithm adopting the SURF feature detection, and the triple-sample shallow convolutional neural network learning descriptor, and we verified the performance of the algorithm under rotation changes using three groups of indoor image data in terms of matching rate, repetition rate and correct matching number.

2 Research Foundation

(1) SIFT Algorithm

The SIFT algorithm first constructs a Gaussian scale space through a Gaussian convolution kernel [10], and then performs extreme point detection and extraction on different scale space layers. In the SIFT detection method, after the spatial scale layer is constructed, the stabilized feature points are detected in the scale space by the function DOG (Difference of Gaussian). It is ensured that the SIFT

Algorithm has certain antagonistic effect on the scale change through the detection and calculation of feature points in the scale space. In the research of Prof. David Lowe, in order to reduce the impact of mutations, Gaussian function is also used to smooth the histogram.

(2) SURF Algorithm

The algorithm has been accelerated on the basis of SIFT, which makes it faster and more comprehensive. The SURF algorithm performs Gaussian filtering processing by adding and subtracting the integral image to speed up the construction of the scale space. The integrated of the image can be calculated by simply scanning the pixels on the original image. Simplify the Gaussian second-order differential template and perform a Gaussian convolution operation between the template and the image to convert it into a box filtering operation [11]. When constructing the image pyramid, the size of the box filter template is continuously expanded to obtain a linear scale space. The integral images and different sizes of filter templates are used to generate a response image of the Hessian matrix determinant, using a non-maximum suppression method. The feature point results in different scale spaces are obtained [12]. In order to make the feature points own rotational invariant performance, the Haar wavelet response calculation is used to determine the main direction of the feature points.

(3) ORB Algorithm

The ORB algorithm is currently the most widely used method in real-time image detection matching in the field of computer vision. It uses the OFAST algorithm to quickly perform feature point detection. The basic idea can be divided into two parts: the first part is the FAST corner extraction of the image, and seek the center point of the gray level obviously change; the second part is the construction of the BRIEF descriptor. A directional description of the surrounding area of the extracted feature points is made for subsequent matching of the feature points. The FAST involved in the ORB is a fast corner detection method, which mainly detects the position of the gray range change of the local range, compares the difference between the gray level of the central pixel and the gray level of the surrounding pixels, and determines the potential feature point when the difference is large. However, the detected feature points do not have scale and directionality. Therefore, in the ORB method, by constructing the image pyramid layer and detecting the corner points in each layer of the image pyramid, it is resistant to the scale change. The resistance to the rotation change is realized by the gray centroid theory, and the vector between the geometric center of the image and the center of the gray scale is calculated [13], giving the detection angle a main direction, causing the rotation of the image to change. Have a certain detection ability.

3 Improved Matching Algorithm Based on Neural Network Descriptor

The feature points extracted by the feature detection algorithm find the correspondence between images through local descriptors, which is one of the most widely studied problems in computer vision. Based on the end-to-end learning descriptor of CNN architecture [14], in the training of large data sets of positive and negative sample pairs, the core is to select the appropriate indoor image triple sample data, iterative optimize and update the network parameters through the principle of backpropagation algorithm to build good learning descriptors.

This paper improved the image feature matching based on the local feature descriptor TFEAT [15] based on the triple-sample shallow convolutional neural network learning. TFEAT utilizes training samples based on triple samples, as well as mining related information for difficult unrelated samples of triple samples. Difficult unrelated samples refer to the fact that the uncorrelated samples have relatively small values for the input network calculation output and are difficult to distinguish. In the image data, different objects in the room are selected to correspond to unrelated image blocks, and the parameters can be trained in negative. For example, due to the geometric transformation of image blocks corresponding to different objects, such as certain rotations, scales, etc., it is possible to make their performance in optical images consistent. Image blocks corresponding to the same object are very likely to be completely inconsistent in optical imaging. It is precisely because of the existence of such image blocks that the data set of "difficult negative sample pairs" needs to be fully utilized, and back propagation promotes shallow neural networks. The training makes the learning descriptors perform better.

Training using triple-samples involves samples the form of (a, p, n), where a (anchor) is the reference sample, p (positive) is the relevant sample, and n (negative) is the unrelated sample. In the training samples used in this dissertation, sample a and sample p are samples of different perspectives of the same feature point, and n is a sample of different feature points. Sample a and ample p in the feature space will close when optimizing network parameters, and pushes a and n away. See as Fig. 1.

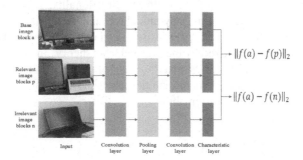

Fig. 1. Schematic diagram of the process of triple sample learning

The learning process of the above three samples can be expressed mathematically as formula (1):

$$\begin{cases} \delta_+ = \|f(a) - f(p)\|_2 \\ \delta_- = \|f(a) - f(n)\|_2 \end{cases} \tag{1}$$

Where δ_+ and δ_- represent similarities between sample features, the minimum value of the loss function is set to 0, there is no upper limit, and the network parameters are optimized to make the distance between a and p tiny. μ is a given parameter. When $\delta_- > \delta_+ + \mu$, the value of the loss function drops to 0, the network parameters are no longer updated, the loss function of the learning training is formula (2), and the difficult unrelated samples in the triple sample are defined as formula (3):

$$\lambda(\delta_+, \delta_-) = max(0, \mu + \delta_+ - \delta_-) \tag{2}$$

$$\begin{cases} \delta_* = min\left(\delta_-, \delta_-'\right) \\ \delta_-' = \|f(p) - f(n)\|_2 \end{cases} \tag{3}$$

When $\delta_* = \delta_-$, exchange the reference sample a and the related sample p in the calculation of the triple sample formula to make the related sample become the reference sample, and the reference sample becomes the relevant sample, which can make the indistinguishable irrelevance in the triple sample The sample is used for backpropagation. Through such a calculation process, the δ_* value will always be a set of sample pairs with a large feature similarity distance, and the mathematical calculation formula of the loss function at this time can be expressed as the formula (4).

$$\lambda(\delta_+, \delta_*) = max(0, \mu + \delta_+ + \delta_*) \tag{4}$$

The learning descriptor effectively mines the difficult unrelated sample pairs to conduct network training, which reduces the total sample input and reduces the computational cost. For the initial time of network training, the network parameters are usually set to a random smaller number to achieve the purpose of initialization. The triple-samples shallow convolution training method was adopted to set the detailed parameters. After each iteration, the learning rate is updated to 0.9 times, the learning rate is set to 0.01, and iteration is continued until the drop is 10^{-6} to stop training. Due to the characteristics of the image data, after using the feature point matching algorithm to detect and match the image, there will be a certain mismatching point, which affects the accuracy of the subsequent data processing. Therefore, it is necessary to perform certain processing on the mismatched point. In this paper, the random sampling consistency algorithm (ie RANSAC algorithm) is adopted to eliminate the mismatched points.

Through experiments, the performance of the matching of the three traditional manual operators SIFT, SURF, ORB mentioned above and the performance matching based on neural network descriptors were verified by time. Two similar images were selected, and the image size was 4608 * 3456. In order to increase the running speed, it was sampled 4 times down to obtain an image of 1154 * 564. The traditional operator is based on windows7 (CPU: i3, graphics card GT-520M, 2G memory) and opencv2.4.9

programming environment implementation code, and the TFEAT descriptor matching was based on the Windows7's pytorch1.0.1 and opencv2.4.9 environment.

Since the shallow convolutional neural network learning of the triple samples in this paper is an improvement on the feature descriptor, the above three algorithms and methods combining the improved descriptor respectively are used to carry out experiments separately to verify the effectiveness of the algorithms with the improved descriptor. The number of feature points extracted by each algorithm was controlled to be about 1000, and the feature points of left and right images were preliminarily matched, then the RANSAC method was used to eliminate the mismatch, and the number of matching points is counted. The time and matching rate of each algorithm for detecting the same number of feature points were calculated and analyzed respectively, which are shown in Table 1.

Table 1. Feature point detection results

Detection operator	Points extracted separately from left and right images		The correct match points	Match time	Match rate
SIFT	923	745	351	6.05 s	42.1%
SURF	1045	1043	430	1.696 s	41.2%
ORB	1000	1000	287	0.878 s	28.7%
SIFT+TFEAT	1000	1000	456	4.758 s	45.6%
SURF+TFEAT	986	965	541	1.485 s	55.5%
ORB+TFEAT	752	718	258	0.644 s	35.1%

It can be seen from Table 1 that the algorithms using the three traditional algorithms for feature detection and the local feature descriptors based on the triple-sample shallow convolutional neural network learning in this paper has a greater processing efficiency and accuracy than the traditional algorithms. It can be seen from the analysis that the matching time through the SIFT operator combining with the TFEAT method to detect the same number of feature points reduced by 1.292 s, and the correct matching rate was increased by 3.5%. The traditional SURF combing with the TFEAT method has the highest correct matching rate, which reached 55.5%, and the matching time also reached by 0.21 s, which showed its obvious relative advantage. The least time-consuming is the ORB operator. Although the operation efficiency is highest but the matching rate is lowest, the matching accuracy is increased by 6.4% and the running time is reduced by 0.234 s after combining with feature descriptor of this paper for matching. Therefore, it can be verified that adopting the descriptor algorithm proposed in this paper based on the traditional feature extraction algorithm can effectively improve the accuracy of image matching and reduce the running time.

In summary, considering the real-time and matching rate, this paper selected the 64 * 64 image block with the feature points extracted by the SURF method in the indoor images as the center, and input the network for parameter calculation, then we obtained a 128-dimensional local learning descriptor after processing through the shallow convolutional neural network layer.

4 Experiment

The following experiment is mainly to verify the effectiveness of the improved algorithm combining the TFEAT descriptor based on the triple-sample shallow neural network for feature matching with the SURF algorithm for feature detection in terms of rotation changes. Aiming at the images with different features, we evaluated the performance of different algorithms including SIFT, SURF, ORB and our improved method in terms of rotation changes respectively, which chose feature point repetition rate and image matching accuracy as evaluation criteria.

4.1 Experimental Data Introduction

In this paper, three different types of indoor image data were used to analyze the performance of four different matching methods in three groups of data, and to compare and analyze the effectiveness of our proposed improved algorithm. The experimental data of the three groups were from different experimental areas in the room as shown in Fig. 2. The region a data were indoor desks, the data feature points were many, but a large number of textures were repeated. The region b data were the wall maps, the data features more but the features were not obvious. The region b data were the door frames, the number of data features were small, and there were a large number of areas such as white walls and almost no texture information.

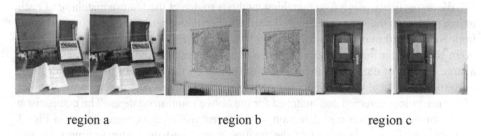

region a   region b   region c

Fig. 2. Experimental image data

4.2 Feature Detection Algorithm Matching Experiment and Analysis

In this paper, four matching methods based on SIFT, SURF, ORB and our improved algorithm were used to carry out feature detection matching experiments in three types of images, and feature point repetition rate, correct matching quantity and image matching accuracy were used as evaluation criteria for performance evaluation and analysis.

(1) Repetition rate: refers to a rate obtained by dividing the number of feature points that can be repeatedly detected by the total number of detected features in an image pair with overlapping degrees. It can be obtained from the definition of repetition rate, which can reflect the adaptability of the detection algorithm on the image to some extent. The mathematical formula for the repetition rate is shown in (5):

$$R = \frac{N}{min(N_1, N_2)} h_{overlap} \tag{5}$$

Where R is the repetition rate, N is the number of feature points from the left image projection transformation to the right image, N_1 and N_2 are the feature points extracted from the left image and the right image respectively, and $h_{overlap}$ is the overlap degree of the left and right images.

(2) Matching accuracy rate: refers to the rate of the number of features matching correctly in the two images to the total number of feature matches. The correct matching number in this paper refers to the matching result of the two images under the homography transformation, and the corresponding difference of the same name image points is less than 1.5 pixels. Therefore, the matching correct number and the matching correct rate also reflect the matching accuracy and accuracy of feature points. The mathematical formula for the accuracy rate is shown in (6):

$$P = \frac{T}{N} \tag{6}$$

Where P is the image matching accuracy rate, T is the correct number of image matching, and N is the total number of image matching.

We respectively using four matching methods to detect the feature matching of each image relative to the reference image. In order to verify the performance of our proposed improved algorithm in the case of rotation, we need to set the data of 3 groups from 0° to 90 in 10° steps for image rotation and then feature extraction and matching, resulting in a large number of data experimental results, limited by the length of the article, we will only show statistical results. Detailed statistical analysis was performed on the number of feature points detected and matched for the above rotation changes. The comparison results of the repetition rate detection of the three groups data were shown in Fig. 3 (the abscissa is the magnitude of the rotation angle, and the ordinate represents the feature point repetition rate). The image matching accuracy was shown in Fig. 4 (the abscissa represents the rotation step and the ordinate represents the number of correct image matching), and the image matching accuracy was shown in Fig. 5 (the abscissa represents the rotation angle and the ordinate represents the correct matching rate). The time it takes for image matching is shown in Fig. 6 (the abscissa represents the rotation angle and the ordinate represents the time it takes to match). In all the graphs in this chapter, region a is represented on the left, region b is represented in the middle and region c is represented on the right.

When the image rotation changes, the feature points extracted by each algorithm were controlled at about 1000. As shown in Fig. 3, the repetition rate of the feature points extracted by each algorithm in region a -with obvious feature is relatively stable, whose

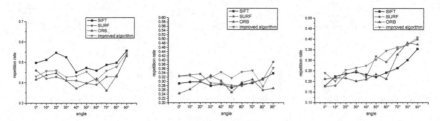

Fig. 3. Repeat rate comparison analysis

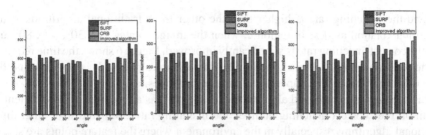

Fig. 4. Correct match quantity comparison

fluctuation range of the repetition rate is about 40%. In region b, the overall repetition rate of the improved algorithm is about 32%. In region c, the repetition rate fluctuation range of all algorithms is relatively large, and it can be seen that the improved algorithm is superior to the other three traditional algorithms. As shown in Fig. 4, the number of correct matches extracted by SIFT, SURF and our improved algorithm respectively is significantly higher than the ORB algorithm. It can be shown that although the number of repeated feature points extracted by the ORB can reach the number of above three algorithms, the number of correct extractions in the texture-like regions is significantly less than the previous two algorithms. In region c, it can be seen that the matching number of the improved algorithm is significantly higher than that of the three traditional methods, and the antagonistic effect on rotation is better. Figure 5 is a comparison of the matching rate of various algorithms. It can be seen that the matching rate of all algorithms in region a fluctuate significantly in the region a, and the improved algorithm performs best when the angles are rotated by 40° and 80°. In region b, it can be seen that our improved algorithm is weaker than the SURF algorithm when the angle is rotated

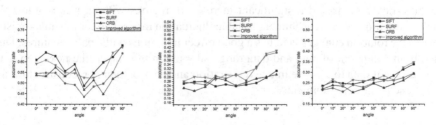

Fig. 5. Matching rate comparison analysis

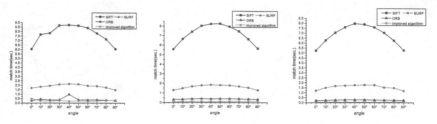

Fig. 6. Matching time comparison analysis

30° and the matching rate is higher than the other three traditional algorithms in the remaining rotation angles. In region c, when the image rotates 10°, 30°, 40°, 80° and 90°, the correct matching rate is significantly improved. Figure 6 shows the time required by the four algorithms when extracting the same feature points. It is obvious that the improved algorithm in this paper has obvious advantages.

In summary, the improved algorithm in this paper has a significant improvement in repetition rate, correct matching number and matching rate compared with other three traditional algorithms, especially in the environment where the feature points are sparse and the texture is weak. Rotational changes have certain antagonistic properties and can guarantee a certain reliability even in the case of large rotation angles.

5 Conclusion

Aiming at the problem that the traditional matching methods are difficult to balance the robustness and real-time of indoor image matching, this paper conducted image matching through three traditional algorithms and the three algorithms with the feature learning descriptor of the triple-sample shallow convolutional neural network respectively. It is verified by experimental comparison that the improved descriptor proposed in this paper can effectively improve the correct matching rate of images and improve the operating efficiency. Considering the requirements of real-time and accuracy of registration results comprehensively, we carried out image matching using SURF for feature detection and the improved feature learning descriptor of the triple-sample shallow convolutional neural network for feature matching, and used the appropriate data sample training method to obtain a better adapted model. We mainly verified the robustness of the algorithm in the case of rotation changes in terms of repetition rate, correct number and correct rate. The experimental results show that the improved algorithm has a smaller increase in feature-rich regions and a significant increase in regions without rich features. In addition, our improved algorithm has a stable fluctuation range, has certain antagonistic effect to the rotation changes, and has a good effect in regions with sparse features. Due to the limited amount of data and data range adopted in this paper, the next step is to use a variety of data to achieve image registration and environmental reconstruction for large scene indoor environments.

References

1. Chai, H.: Data association method for mobile robots in SLAM. Doctor, Dalian University of Technology (2010)
2. Gao, X., Zhang, T., Liu, Y.: Visual SLAM Fourteen Lectures –Form Theory to Practice, 1st edn. China Machine Press, Beijing (2017)
3. Yan, K., Sukthankar, R.: PCA-SIFT: a more distinctive representation for local image descriptors. IEEE Comput. Soc. **2**(2), 506–513 (2004)
4. Mikolajczyk, K., Schmid, C.: A performance evaluation of local descriptors. In: Computer Vision and Pattern Recognition, USA, pp. 257–263 (2003)
5. Tola, E., Lepetit, V., Fua, P.: DAISY: an efficient dense descriptor applied to wide-baseline stereo. IEEE Trans. Software Eng. **32**(5), 815–830 (2010)
6. Geng, Z., Zhang, B., Fan, D.: Digital Photogrammetry. Surveying and Mapping Publishing House, Beijing (2010)
7. Leutenegger, S., Chli, M., Siegwart, R.Y.: BRISK: binary robust invariant scalable keypoints. In: IEEE International Conference on Computer Vision, Spain, pp. 2548–2555 (2011)
8. Vandergheynst, P., Ortiz, R., Alahi, A.: FREAK: fast retina keypoint. In: IEEE Conference on Computer Vision & Pattern Recognition, USA, pp. 510–571 (2012)
9. Yi, K.M., Trulls, E., Lepetit, V., Fua, P.: LIFT: learned invariant feature transform. In: Leibe, B., Matas, J., Sebe, N., Welling, M. (eds.) ECCV 2016. LNCS, vol. 9910, pp. 467–483. Springer, Cham (2016). https://doi.org/10.1007/978-3-319-46466-4_28
10. Morevec, H.P.: Towards automatic visual obstacle avoidance. In: International Joint Conference on Artificial Intelligence, p. 584 (1977)
11. Simard, P.Y., Haffner, P., Lecun, Y.: Boxlets: a fast convolution algorithm for signal processing and neural networks. In: Conference on Advances in Neural Information Processing Systems, USA, pp. 571–577 (1999)
12. Hu, J.: Research on high-resolution aerial image feature matching technology. Doctor, East China University of Technology (2018)
13. Rosin, B.P.L.: Measuring corner properties. Comput. Vis. Image Underst. **73**(2), 291–307 (1999)
14. Fischer, P., Dosovitskiy, A., Brox, T.: Descriptor matching with convolutional neural networks: a comparison to SIFT. Comput. Sci. (2014)
15. Vijay, K.B.G., Carneiro, G., Reid, I.: Learning local image descriptors with deep siamese and triplet convolutional networks by minimizing global loss functions. In: IEEE Conference on Computer Vision & Pattern Recognition, USA, pp. 5385–5394 (2016)

Robust 3D Face Alignment with Efficient Fully Convolutional Neural Networks

Lei Jiang[1,3], Xiao-Jun Wu[1,3(✉)], and Josef Kittler[2]

[1] School of IoT Engineering, Jiangnan University, Wuxi 214122, China
ljiang_jnu@outlook.com, xiaojun_wu_jnu@163.com
[2] Center for Vision, Speech and Signal Processing (CVSSP), University of Surry,
Guildford GU2 7XH, UK
j.kittler@surrey.ac.uk
[3] Jiangsu Provincial Engineering, Laboratory of Pattern Recognition
and Computational Intelligence, Jiangnan University, Wuxi 214122, China

Abstract. 3D face alignment from monocular images is a crucial process in computer vision with applications to face recognition, animation and other areas. However, most algorithms are designed for faces in small to medium poses (below 45°), lacking the ability to align faces in large poses up to 90°. At the same time, many methods are not efficient. The main challenge is that it is time consuming to determine the parameters accurately. In order to address this issue, this paper proposes a novel and efficient end-to-end 3D face alignment framework. We build an efficient and stable network model through Depthwise Separable Convolution and Densely Connected Convolutional, named MobDenseNet. Simultaneously, different loss functions are used to constrain 3D parameters based on 3D Morphable Model (3DMM) and 3D vertices. Experiments on the challenging AFLW, AFLW2000-3D databases show that our algorithm significantly improves the accuracy of 3D face alignment. Model parameters and complexity of the proposed method are also reduced significantly.

Keywords: 3D face alignment · 3D Morphable Model · Computer vision

1 Introduction

Face alignment, which fits a face model to an image and extracts the semantic meanings of facial pixels. Traditional face alignment is to locate the feature points of human face. Such as corners of the eyes, corners of the mouth, tip of the nose, etc. This is a fundamental processing process for many computer vision tasks, e.g., face recognition [3], facial expression analysis [2], facial animation [6, 7] and

Electronic supplementary material The online version of this chapter (https://doi.org/10.1007/978-3-030-34110-7_23) contains supplementary material, which is available to authorized users.

© Springer Nature Switzerland AG 2019
Y. Zhao et al. (Eds.): ICIG 2019, LNCS 11902, pp. 266–277, 2019.
https://doi.org/10.1007/978-3-030-34110-7_23

so on. In view of the importance of this problem, face alignment has been widely studied since the Active Shape Model (ASM) of Cootes in the early 1990s [10].

Despite the continuous improvement on the alignment accuracy, face alignment is still a very challenging problem. Traditional 2D face alignment can achieve satisfactory accuracy in small to medium poses, but this does not meet the changing conditions in real-world applications, non-frontal images, low image resolution, variable illumination and occlusion, etc. 3D face alignment aims to reconstruct 3D face structure through 2D image and estimated the position of 3D and 2D face feature points after 3D face alignment to 2D image.

Motivated by the needs to address the efficient model, pose variation, and the lack of prior work in handling poses, the paper proposes a novel and efficient network structure, and uses different loss functions to optimize the 3D parameters and 3D vertices. The purpose is to calculate the positions of 2D and 3D facial feature points under arbitrary postures. The reason for the efficiency of MobileNet [18] is that the Depthwise Separable Convolution is used in the network structure. Because of the Densely Connected between convolutional layers, DenseNet [19] strengthened the transmission of feature, made more effective use of feature and reduced the number of parameters to a certain extent. Inspired by the above two network structures, our network structure has high efficiency of both Depthwise Separable Convolution and feature reuse of Densely Connected. To achieve a balance between high efficiency and high precision. Finally, extensive experiments are conducted on a large subset of AFLW dataset [23] with a wide range of poses, and the AFLW2000-3D dataset [35] with the comparison with a number of methods. An overview of our method is shown in Fig. 1.

In summary, our contributions are summarized as follows:

(1). *We proposes a novel and efficient network structure (MobDenseNet). To the best of our knowledge, this is the first that Depthwise Separable Convolution and Densely Connected are combined in a network leading to a new structure of DNN.*

(2). *Different loss functions are used to optimize the parameters of 3D Morphable Model and 3D vertices. Meanwhile, face alignment that can estimate 2D/3D landmarks with an arbitrary pose.*

(3). *We experimentally verified that our algorithm has significantly improved performance of 3D face alignment compared to the previous algorithms, The proposed face alignment method can deal with arbitrary pose and it is more efficient.*

2   Related Work

In this section, we will review the prior work in generic face alignment and 3D face alignment.

2.1   Generic Face Alignment

Face alignment has achieved many achievements, including the classic AAM [9,26] and ASM [8] models. This method considers face alignment as an optimization problem to find the best shape and appearance parameters, which make

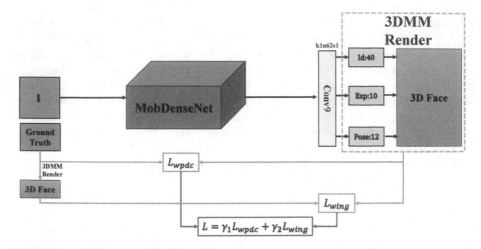

Fig. 1. Overview of the ours method. Efficient full convolutional neural networks (Mob-DenseNet). Figure 2 describes the details of MobDenseNet. The 3D parameters and 3D vertices are constrained using different loss functions.

the appearance model best fit the input face. The basic idea of Constrained Local Model (CLM) [1,11,27] in Discriminative methods is to learn a set of local appearance models, one for each landmark, and the decision from the local models are combined with a global shape model. Cascaded regression gradually refines a specified initial prediction value through a series of regressions. Each regression unit relies on the output of the previous regression unit to perform simple image operations, and the entire system can automatically learn from the training samples [12]. The ESR [7] (Explicit Shape Regression) proposed by Sun et al. includes three methods, namely two-level boosted regression, shape-indexed features and correlation-based feature selection method.

Besides traditional models, deep convolutional neural networks have recently been used for feature point localization of faces. Sun et al. [28] firstly use CNN to regress landmark locations with the raw face image, accurately positioning of 5 key points of faces from coarse to fine. The work of [16] using the human body pose estimation, the boundary information is introduced into the key point regression. In recent years, most of the landmark detections of faces have been studied on "coarse to fine", while Feng et al. [14] have taken a different approach, using the idea of cascaded convolutional neural networks. And [14] compared the commonly used loss functions in face landmark detection, and based on this, the concept of wing loss is proposed.

2.2   3D Face Alignment

Although the traditional method has achieved many achievements in face alignment, it will be affected by non-frontal face, illumination and occlusion in real-life applications. The most common method is the multi-view framework [29], which

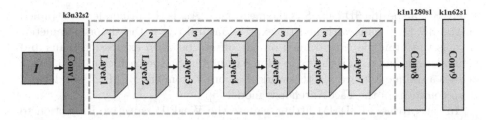

Fig. 2. Details of MobDenseNet. k3n64s1 corresponds to the kernel size(k), number of feature maps(n) and stride(s) of conv1.

uses different landmark configurations for different views. For example, TSPM [34] and CDM [33] use the DPM-like [15] method to align faces of different shape models, and finally select the most probable model as the final result. However, since each view requires testing, the computational cost of the multiview approach is always high.

In addition to multi-view solutions, 3D face alignment is a more common approach. 3D face alignment [16,20], which aims to fit a 3D morphable model (3DMM) [3] from a 2D image. The 3D Morphable Model is a typical statistical 3D face model. It has a clear understanding of the prior knowledge of 3D faces through statistical analysis. Zhu et al. [35] proposed a localization method based on 3D face shape, which solved the problem that some feature points were invisible under extreme postures (such as side faces). Liu et al. [21] used the cascade of 6 convolutional neural networks to solve the problem of locating facial feature points in a large pose by using 3D face modeling. This paper [13] designed a UV position map to achieve 3D shape features of a complete human face in a 2D UV space.

Our approach is also based on convolutional neural networks, but we have redesigned the network structure to make it efficient and robust. At the same time, we use different loss functions for 3D parameters and 3D vertices to constrain the semantic information of 3D parameters and 3D vertices respectively.

3 Proposed Method

In this section we introduce the proposed robust 3D face alignment (R3FA) which fits 3D morphable model with efficient fully convolutional neural networks.

3.1 3D Morphable Model

The 3D Morphable model is one of the most successful methods for describing 3D face space. Blanz et al. [3] proposed a 3D morphable model (3DMM) of 3D face space with PCA. It is expressed as follows:

$$S = \overline{S} + A_{id}\alpha_{id} + A_{exp}\alpha_{exp} \tag{1}$$

where S is a specific 3D face, $\overline{S}$ is the mean face, A_{id} is the principle axes trained on the 3D face scans with neutral expression and α_{id} is the shape parameter, A_{exp} is the principle axes trained on the offsets between expression scans and neutral scans and α_{exp} is the expression parameter. So the coefficient $\{\alpha_{id}, \alpha_{exp}\}$ defines a unique 3D face . In this work A_{id} comes from the BFM [24] model and A_{exp} comes from the FaceWarehouse model [5].

In the process of 3DMM fitting, we use the Weak Perspective Projection to project 3DMM onto the 2D face plane. This process can be expressed as follows:

$$S_{2d} = f * Pr * R * \{S + t_{3d}\} \tag{2}$$

where S_{2d} is the 2D coordinate matrix of the 3D face after Weak Perspective Projection, rotation and translation. f is the scaling factor. Pr is a perspective projection matrix $\begin{pmatrix} 1 & 0 & 0 \\ 0 & 1 & 0 \end{pmatrix}$. R is a rotation matrix constructed according to three rotation angles of pitch, yaw and roll respectively. t_{3d} is the translation transformation matrix of 3D points. Therefore, for the modeling of a specific face, we only need to solve the 3D parameter $P = [f, pitch, yaw, roll, t_{3d}, \alpha_{id}, \alpha_{exp}]$.

3.2   MobDenseNet Structure

The reason MobileNet [18] is effective is the use of Depthwise Separable Convolution technology in the network structure. Based on MobileNetV1 [18], the design of MobileNetV2 [25] combines with the recent popular residual ideas. But the idea of residuals is achieved by the direct addition of elements. [19] a phenomenon that many layers of the ResNet [17] network, the first performer of residual thinking, contribute less and can be randomly discarded during training. This shows that residual ideas are prone to redundant information. In order to solve this problem, DenseNet [19] proposes any layer of the network, the feature map of all the layers in front of the layer is the input of this layer. The feature map of the layer is the input of all the layers behind. However, DenseNet has many parameters and the network structure is not efficient. So combining with MobileNet's efficiency and DenseNet's feature enhancement, we build a new network structure MobDenseNet by combining DenseNet's dense connections on the overall framework of MobileNet. Our network structure includes both MobileNet's high efficiency and enhance feature representation.

The architecture of MobDenseNet is illustrated in Fig. 2. MobDenseNet is a fully convolutional neural network without full connection layer. Conv1 is a convolution layer with kernel size(k) of 3, stride(s) of 2 and number of feature maps(n) of 32 to extract rough features. $Layer1$ to $Layer7$ are 7 dense blocks for extracting depth features. Figure 3 shows the details of one of the Dense-Block, $Layer3$. The convolution layer of a set of $1 \times 1, 3 \times 3, 1 \times 1$ filters in Mob-DenseNet as a basic unit called MobileBlock. As shown in Fig. 3, this set of basic units is consistent with MobileNetV2. DenseLayer3 contains three sets of Mobile Blocks (each MobileBlock output is cascaded as the input of the next Mobile-Block). As such, MobDenseNet retains the simplicity and efficiency of MobileNet.

As shown in Fig. 3, Layer3 contains three sets of MobileBlocks. In order to match the number of channels connected to the Dense connection, we added a transition layer after each MobileBlock (the convolution layer filter is 1×1), the purpose is adjust the number of channels in the preview MobileBlock output feature map. We use both real face images and generated face images to train our MobDenseNet (details can be found in the suppl. material).

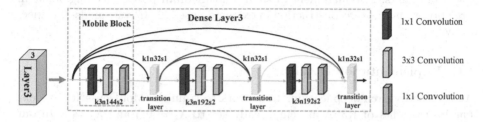

Fig. 3. The details of one of the DenseBlock, *Layer3*. The convolution layer of a set of $1 \times 1, 3 \times 3, 1 \times 1$ filters in MobDenseNet as a basic unit called MobileBlock. The transition layer is the number of channels to match the input and output feature maps.

3.3 Loss Function

We chose two different Loss Functions to jointly train MobDenseNet. For 3D parameters and 3D vertices we use different loss functions for training. We follow the Weighted Parameter Distance Cost (WPDC) of Zhu et al. [35] to calculate the difference between the ground truth of 3D parameters and the predicted 3D parameters. The basic idea is explicitly modeling the importance of each parameter:

$$L_{wpdc} = (P_{gt} - \overline{P})^T W (P_{gt} - \overline{P}) \tag{3}$$

where $\overline{P}$ is the estimation and P_{gt} is the ground truth. The diagonal matrix W contains the weights. For each element of the shape parameter p, its weight is the inverse of the standard deviation that was obtained from the data used in 3DMM training. Because our ultimate goal is to accurately obtain 68 landmarks of human faces. So for 3D face vertices reconstructed with 3D parameters, we use Wing Loss [14] which is defined as:

$$L_{wing}(\Delta V(P)) = \begin{cases} \omega \ln(1 + |\Delta V(P)|/ \in) & if \ |\Delta V(P)| < \omega \\ |\Delta V(P)| - C & otherwise \end{cases} \tag{4}$$

where $\Delta V(P) = V(P_{gt}) - V(\overline{P}), V(P_{gt})$ and $V(\overline{P})$ are the ground truth of the 3D facial vertices and the 3D facial vertices reconstructed using the 3D parameters predicted by the network, respectively. ω and $\in$ are parameters. $C = \omega - \omega \ln(1 + \omega/ \in)$ is a constant that smoothly links the piecewise-defined linear and nonlinear parts.

Overall, the framework is optimized by the following loss function:

$$L_{loss} = \lambda_1 L_{wpdc} + \lambda_2 L_{wing} \tag{5}$$

where λ_1 and λ_2 are parameters, which balance the contribution of L_{wpdc} and L_{wing}. The selection of those parameters will be discussed in the next section.

4   Experiments

In this section, we evaluate the performance of R3FA on three common face alignment tasks, face alignment in small and medium poses, face alignment in large poses, and face reconstruction in extreme poses ($\pm 90°$ yaw angles), respectively.

4.1   Implementation Details

We use the Pytorch deep learning framework to train the MobDenseNet models. The loss weights of R3FA are empirically set to $\lambda_1 = 0.5$ and $\lambda_2 = 1$. In our experiments, we set the parameters of the Wing loss as $\omega = 10$ and $\in = 2$. The Adam solver [22] is employed with the mini-batch size and the initial learning rate set to 128 and 0.01, respectively. There are 680,000 face images in our training data set, including 430,000 real face images and 250,000 synthetic face images. Real face images come from 300W-LP [35] datasets, and various data enhancement algorithms are adopted to expand the datasets. We run the training for a total of 40 epochs. After 15, 25 and 30 epochs, we reduced the learning rate to 0.002, 0.0004 and 0.00008 respectively.

4.2   Evaluation Databases

We evaluate the performance of R3FA on two publicly available face data sets AFLW [23] and AFLW2000-3D [35]. These two data sets contain small and medium poses, large poses and extreme poses ($\pm 90°$ yaw angles). We divide the dataset AFLW and AFLW2000-3D into three intervals of $[0°, 30°]$, $[30°, 60°]$, and $[60°, 90°]$ according to the face absolute yaw angle, and each interval is about 1/3 of the total.

AFLW. AFLW face database is a large-scale face database including multi-pose and multi-view, and each face is marked with 21 feature points. This database has a very large amount of information, including pictures of various poses, expressions, lighting, and ethnicity. The AFLW face database consists of approximately 250 million hand-labeled face images, of which 59% are women and 41% are men. Most of the images are color, images only a few are gray images. We only use part of the extreme pose face images of the AFLW database for qualitative analysis.

AFLW2000-3D. AFLW2000-3D is constructed by [35] to evaluate 3D face alignment on challenging unconstrained images. This database contains the first 2000 images from AFLW and expands its annotations with fitted 3DMM parameters and 68 3D landmarks. We use this database to evaluate the performance of our method on face alignment tasks.

4.3 Evaluation Metric

Given the ground truth 2D landmarks U_i, their visibility v_i, and estimated landmarks $\hat{U}_i$ of N_t testing images. Normalized Mean Error (NME), which is the average of the normalized estimation error of visible landmarks, i.e.,

$$NME = \frac{1}{N_t}\sum_i^{N_t}(\frac{1}{d_i|v_i|_1}\sum_j^N v_i(j)||\hat{U}_i(:,j) - U_i(:,j)||) \qquad (6)$$

where d_i is the square root of the face bounding box size, as used by [37]. Note that normally d_i is the distance of two centers of eyes in most prior face alignment work dealing with near-frontal face images.

4.4 Comparison Experiments

Comparison on AFLW. In the AFLW dataset, 21,080 images were selected as test samples, with 21 landmarks in each sample. During testing, we divide the testing set into 3 subsets according to their absolute yaw angles: $[0°, 30°], [30°, 60°]$ and $[60°, 90°]$ with 11,596, 5,457 and 4,027 samples respectively. Since few experiment has been conducted on AFLW, we choose some baseline methods with released codes, including CDM [33], RCPR [4], ESR [7], SDM [32], 3DDFA [35] and nonlinear 3DMM [30]. Table 1 demonstrates the comparison results. The NME(%) of face alignment results on AFLW with the first and the second best results highlighted. The results of provided alignment models are marked with their references. Figure 4 shows the corresponding CED curves. Our CED curve is only compared to the best method in Table 1. The results show that our R3FA algorithm significantly improves the face alignment accuracy in full pose. The minimum standard deviation of R3FA also proves its robustness to posture changes.

Table 1. The NME(%) of face alignment results on AFLW and AFLW2000-3D.

Method	AFLW DataSet(21 pts)					AFLW2000-3D DataSet(68 pts)				
	$[0°,30°]$	$[30°,60°]$	$[60°,90°]$	Mean	Std	$[0°,30°]$	$[30°,60°]$	$[60°,90°]$	Mean	Std
CDM	8.150	13.020	16.170	12.440	4.040	-	-	-	-	-
RCPR	5.430	6.580	11.530	7.850	3.240	4.260	5.960	13.180	7.800	4.740
ESR	5.660	7.120	11.940	8.240	3.290	4.600	6.700	12.670	7.990	4.190
SDM	4.750	5.550	9.340	6.550	2.450	3.670	4.940	9.760	6.120	3.210
3DDFA(CVPR16)	5.000	**5.060**	6.740	5.600	0.990	3.780	4.540	7.930	5.420	2.210
Nonlinear 3DMM(CVPR18)	-	-	-	-	-	-	-	-	4.700	-
Ours-R3FA	**4.549**	5.427	**6.204**	**5.393**	**0.676**	**3.149**	**4.010**	**5.270**	**4.143**	**0.871**

Table 2. The NME(%) of face alignment results on AFLW and AFLW2000-3D with the different network structures.

Method	Extracting Params Time(ms/pic)		Params	AFLW DataSet(21 pts)					AFLW2000-3D DataSet(68 pts)				
	AFLW(21 pts)	AFLW2000-3D(68 pts)		$[0°, 30°]$	$[30°, 60°]$	$[60°, 90°]$	Mean	Std	$[0°, 30°]$	$[30°, 60°]$	$[60°, 90°]$	Mean	Std
RestNeXt50	0.799ms	2.012ms	90.585M	4.599	5.516	6.297	5.471	0.694	3.122	4.065	5.351	4.179	0.913
MobileNetV2	**0.316ms**	**0.956ms**	**9.487M**	4.643	5.581	6.397	5.540	0.716	3.236	4.080	**5.181**	4.165	0.796
DenseNet121	0.684ms	2.221ms	27.9M	**4.442**	**5.249**	**6.168**	**5.286**	0.705	**3.051**	**3.912**	5.297	**4.087**	0.925
MobDenseNet	0.395ms	1.024ms	10.900M	4.549	5.427	6.204	5.393	0.676	3.149	4.010	5.27	4.143	0.871

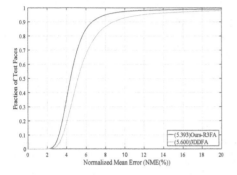

Fig. 4. Comparisons of cumulative errors distribution (CED) curves on AFLW.

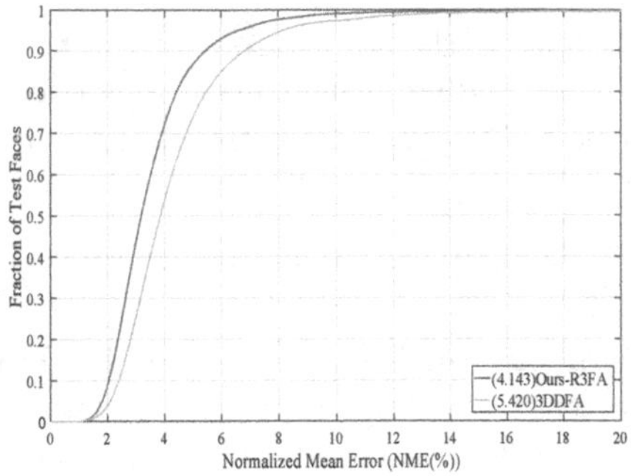

Fig. 5. Comparisons of cumulative errors distribution (CED) curves on AFLW2000-3D.

Comparison on AFLW2000-3D. In the AFLW2000-3D dataset, 2000 images were selected as test samples, with 68 landmarks in each sample. Considering the visible and invisible evaluation, 3D face alignment evaluation can be downgraded to a full landmark evaluation. we divide the testing set into 3 subsets according to their absolute yaw angles: $[0°, 30°], [30°, 60°], [60°, 90°]$ with 1,312, 383 and 305 samples respectively. Table 1 demonstrates the comparison results. The NME(%) of face alignment results AFLW2000-3D with the first and the second best results highlighted. The results of provided alignment models are marked with their references. Figure 5 shows the corresponding CED curves. Our CED curve is only compared to the best method in Table 1. Table1 and Fig. 5 demonstrate that our algorithm also has a significant improvement in the prediction of invisible regions, showing good robustness for face alignment in arbitrary poses.

Comparison on Different Network Structures. We selected a variety of different network structures for comparison during the experiment. The experimental network structure includes ResNeXt [31], MobileNetV2 [25], DenseNet121 [19], and our proposed MobDenseNet. To the best of our knowledge, these three popular and efficient network structures are the first to be used in the field of 3D face alignment. Table 2 demonstrates the comparison results. The NME(%) of face alignment results on AFLW and AFLW2000-3D with the different network structures. The table shows the time when each sample extracts parameters through the network model and the parameter size of the network model. Extracting params time (ms/pic) is calculated on GTX 1080Ti and 64 GB RAM. These three network structures can be divided into two categories, one is the efficient network structure represented by MobileNetV2, and the other is the high-precision network structure of ResNeXt50 and DenseNet121. In order to balance efficiency and high precision, we have designed MobDenseNet independently. The experimental results demonstrate the motivation and expected results of our original design. Our network structure achieves a balance between high efficiency and high precision. Comparison and analysis with MobileNetV2 and DesenNet can be found in suppl. material. The 2D/3D alignment results of our method are shown in Fig. 6.

Fig. 6. The results of 2D/3D face alignment of our method. Result of 2D face alignment (second rows), 3D face alignment (third rows), Align 3D face mesh to 2D image (fourth rows).

5   Conclusions

In this paper, we propose a novel and efficient framework (R3FA), which solves the problem of 2D/3D face alignment with full pose. In order to balance the computational efficiency and alignment accuracy of the model, we propose a new deep network MobDenseNet. We innovatively use two loss functions to jointly optimize 3D reconstruction parameters and 3D vertices. At the same time, we use real and synthetic images to train our network together. We have achieved the best accuracy on both AFLW and AFLW2000-3D datasets compared to existing algorithms. Comparing experiments with several popular networks, our algorithm can achieve a good balance between accuracy and efficiency. In the future, we will further improve the accuracy of 2D/3D face alignment, and at the same time the algorithm will have higher efficiency.

Acknowledgments. The paper is supported by the National Natural Science Foundation of China (Grant No. 61672265,U1836218), the 111 Project of Ministry of Education of China (Grant No. B12018), and UK EPSRC Grant EP/N007743/1, Muri/EPSRC/ Dstl Grant EP/R018456/1,

References

1. Asthana, A., Zafeiriou, S., Cheng, S., Pantic, M.: Robust discriminative response map fitting with constrained local models. In: Proceedings of the IEEE Conference on Computer Vision and Pattern Recognition, pp. 3444–3451 (2013)
2. Bettadapura, V.: Face expression recognition and analysis: the state of the art. arXiv preprint arXiv:1203.6722 (2012)
3. Blanz, V., Vetter, T.: Face recognition based on fitting a 3D morphable model. IEEE Trans. Pattern Anal. Mach. Intell. **25**(9), 1063–1074 (2003)
4. Burgos-Artizzu, X.P., Perona, P., Dollár, P.: Robust face landmark estimation under occlusion. In: Proceedings of the IEEE International Conference on Computer Vision, pp. 1513–1520 (2013)
5. Cao, C., Weng, Y., Zhou, S., Tong, Y., Zhou, K.: Facewarehouse: a 3D facial expression database for visual computing. IEEE Trans. Vis. Comput. Graph. **20**(3), 413–425 (2014)
6. Cao, C., Wu, H., Weng, Y., Shao, T., Zhou, K.: Real-time facial animation with image-based dynamic avatars. ACM Trans. Graph. **35**(4) (2016)
7. Cao, X., Wei, Y., Wen, F., Sun, J.: Face alignment by explicit shape regression. Int. J. Comput. Vis. **107**(2), 177–190 (2014)
8. Cootes, T., Baldock, E.R., Graham, J.: An introduction to active shape models. Image Process. Anal. 223–248 (2000)
9. Cootes, T.F., Edwards, G.J., Taylor, C.J.: Active appearance models. IEEE Trans. Pattern Anal. Mach. Intell. **6**, 681–685 (2001)
10. Cootes, T.F., Taylor, C.J., Lanitis, A.: Active shape models: evaluation of a multi-resolution method for improving image search. In: BMVC, vol. 1, pp. 327–336 (1994)
11. Cristinacce, D., Cootes, T.F.: Feature detection and tracking with constrained local models. In: BMVC, vol. 1, p. 3 (2006)
12. Dollár, P., Welinder, P., Perona, P.: Cascaded pose regression. In: 2010 IEEE Conference on Computer Vision and Pattern Recognition (CVPR), pp. 1078–1085. IEEE (2010)
13. Feng, Y., Wu, F., Shao, X., Wang, Y., Zhou, X.: Joint 3D face reconstruction and dense alignment with position map regression network. arXiv preprint arXiv:1803.07835 (2018)
14. Feng, Z.-H., Kittler, J., Awais, M., Huber, P., Wu, X.-J.: Wing loss for robust facial landmark localisation with convolutional neural networks. In: 2018 IEEE/CVF Conference on Computer Vision and Pattern Recognition, pp. 2235–2245. IEEE (2018)
15. Forsyth, D.: Object detection with discriminatively trained part-based models. Computer **2**, 6–7 (2014)
16. Gu, L., Kanade, T.: 3D alignment of face in a single image. In: Null, pp. 1305–1312. IEEE (2006)
17. He, K., Zhang, X., Ren, S., Sun, J.: Deep residual learning for image recognition. In: Proceedings of the IEEE Conference on Computer Vision and Pattern Recognition, pp. 770–778 (2016)

18. Howard, A.G., et al.: Mobilenets: Efficient convolutional neural networks for mobile vision applications. arXiv preprint arXiv:1704.04861 (2017)
19. Huang, G., Liu, Z., Van Der Maaten, L., Weinberger, K.Q.: Densely connected convolutional networks. In: CVPR, vol. 1, p. 3 (2017)
20. Jourabloo, A., Liu, X.: Pose-invariant 3D face alignment. In: Proceedings of the IEEE International Conference on Computer Vision, pp. 3694–3702 (2015)
21. Jourabloo, A., Liu, X.: Large-pose face alignment via CNN-based dense 3D model fitting. In: Proceedings of the IEEE Conference on Computer Vision and Pattern Recognition, pp. 4188–4196 (2016)
22. Kingma, D.P., Ba, J.: Adam: A method for stochastic optimization. arXiv preprint arXiv:1412.6980 (2014)
23. Koestinger, M., Wohlhart, P., Roth, P.M., Bischof, H.: Annotated facial landmarks in the wild: a large-scale, real-world database for facial landmark localization. In: 2011 IEEE International Conference on Computer Vision Workshops (ICCV Workshops), pp. 2144–2151. IEEE (2011)
24. Paysan, P., Knothe, R., Amberg, B., Romdhani, S., Vetter, T.: A 3D face model for pose and illumination invariant face recognition. In: Sixth IEEE International Conference on Advanced Video and Signal Based Surveillance. AVSS 2009, pp. 296–301. IEEE (2009)
25. Sandler, M., Howard, A., Zhu, M., Zhmoginov, A., Chen, L.C.: Inverted residuals and linear bottlenecks: Mobile networks for classification, detection and segmentation. arXiv preprint arXiv:1801.04381 (2018)
26. Saragih, J., Goecke, R.: A nonlinear discriminative approach to AAM fitting. In: IEEE 11th International Conference on Computer Vision. ICCV 2007, pp. 1–8. IEEE (2007)
27. Saragih, J.M., Lucey, S., Cohn, J.F.: Deformable model fitting by regularized landmark mean-shift. Int. J. Comput. Vis. **91**(2), 200–215 (2011)
28. Sun, Y., Wang, X., Tang, X.: Deep convolutional network cascade for facial point detection. In: Proceedings of the IEEE Conference on Computer Vision and Pattern Recognition, pp. 3476–3483 (2013)
29. Tran, A.T., Hassner, T., Masi, I., Medioni, G.: Regressing robust and discriminative 3D morphable models with a very deep neural network. In: 2017 IEEE Conference on Computer Vision and Pattern Recognition (CVPR), pp. 1493–1502. IEEE (2017)
30. Tran, L., Liu, X.: Nonlinear 3D face morphable model. arXiv preprint arXiv:1804.03786 (2018)
31. Xie, S., Girshick, R., Dollár, P., Tu, Z., He, K.: Aggregated residual transformations for deep neural networks. In: 2017 IEEE Conference on Computer Vision and Pattern Recognition (CVPR), pp. 5987–5995. IEEE (2017)
32. Yan, J., Lei, Z., Yi, D., Li, S.: Learn to combine multiple hypotheses for accurate face alignment. In: Proceedings of the IEEE International Conference on Computer Vision Workshops, pp. 392–396 (2013)
33. Yu, X., Huang, J., Zhang, S., Metaxas, D.N.: Face landmark fitting via optimized part mixtures and cascaded deformable model. IEEE Trans. Pattern Anal. Mach. Intell. **11**, 2212–2226 (2016)
34. Zhu, X., Ramanan, D.: Face detection, pose estimation, and landmark localization in the wild. In: 2012 IEEE Conference on Computer Vision and Pattern Recognition (CVPR), pp. 2879–2886. IEEE (2012)
35. Zhu, X., Lei, Z., Liu, X., Shi, H., Li, S.Z.: Face alignment across large poses: a 3D solution. In: Proceedings of the IEEE Conference on Computer Vision and Pattern Recognition, pp. 146–155 (2016)

MSDNet for Medical Image Fusion

Xu Song, Xiao-Jun Wu$^{(\boxtimes)}$, and Hui Li

Jiangsu Provincial Engineering Laboratory of Pattern Recognition and
Computational Intelligence, School of IoT Engineering,
Jiangnan University, Wuxi 214122, China
xiaojun_wu_jnu@163.com

Abstract. Considering the DenseFuse only works in a single scale, we
propose a multi-scale DenseNet (MSDNet) for medical image fusion. The
main architecture of network is constructed by encoding network, fusion
layer and decoding network. To utilize features at different scales, we
add a multi-scale mechanism which uses three filters of different sizes to
extract features in encoding network. More image details are obtained by
increasing the encoding network's width. Then, we adopt fusion strategy to fuse features of different scales respectively. Finally, the fused
image is reconstructed by decoding network. Compared with the existing methods, the proposed method can achieve state-of-the-art fusion
performance in objective and subjective assessment.

Keywords: Medical image fusion · Multi-scale · Dense block · Deep
learning

1 Introduction

Medical image fusion plays an important role in medical clinical applications.
Recently, medical image fusion mainly concentrates on computerized tomography (CT), magnetic resonance imaging (MRI), positron emission tomography (PET) and single-photon emission computed tomography (SPECT) modalities [1]. Different imaging mechanism leads to different focus on medical images.
For example, the CT has an advantage of dense resolution of denses structures like bones and implants, the MRI is good at soft-tissue details with high-
resolution anatomical information, while the blood flow and metabolic changes
can be supported by PET and SPECT images but with low spatial resolution [2].
Therefore, how to extract the salient features of different modalities and how to
choose proper fusion strategy are main issues in medical image fusion.

Generally speaking, the most common method is multi-scale transform
(MST) in image fusion. MST-based methods consist of decomposition, fusion
and reconstruction. There are many MST-based methods for image fusion, such
as discrete wavelet transform (DWT) [4], contourlet transform [3] and curvelet
transform (CVT) [5] etc. Du et al. [17] presented a multiscale decomposition
method based on local Laplacian filtering (LLF) with an information of interest
(IOI)-based strategy for medical image fusion.

© Springer Nature Switzerland AG 2019
Y. Zhao et al. (Eds.): ICIG 2019, LNCS 11902, pp. 278–288, 2019.
https://doi.org/10.1007/978-3-030-34110-7_24

Representation learning [8, 23, 24] is widely used in image fusion in recent years. In sparse representation, Liu et al. [6] applied adaptive sparse presentation in image fusion and denoising. Yin et al. [7] proposed a novel multi-focus image fusion approach based on sparse representation which used joint dictionary. In low-rank representation (LRR), Li et al. [8] proposed a novel multi-focus image fusion based on dictionary learning and LRR to get a better performance.

With the development of deep learning, many image fusion methods based on deep learning are proposed. Because of the depth of network, we can use many deep features to make fusion. In [9], authors presented a new method based on a deep convolutional neural network (CNN). The two source images are fed to network and the score map will be obtained. In [10], Li et al. considered the features of middle layers of pretrained VGG-network [11] and used l_1-norm and weighted-average strategy to generate several candidates of the fused detail content.

In 2017, Prabhakar et al. [21] proposed an image fusion framework which consists of feature extraction layers, a fusion layer and reconstruction layers. Their feature extraction layers have Siamese network architecture and reconstruction layers consist of three CNN layers. In 2019, Li et al. [12] proposed a DenseFuse whose encoding network is combined with convolutional layers and dense block for infrared and visible images. Although this method achieves better performance, but it still has a drawback because it just considers a single scale to extract image feature in encoding network.

To solve this problem, in this paper, we improve the DenseFuse [12] with a multi-scale mechanism in encoding network. Then, we apply the improved architecture to the medical image fusion. We use three filters of different sizes to extract features of the end of original encoder of DenseFuse respectively. So that we can obtain more features maps of different scales, then, we adopt fusion strategy to fuse them respectively. Finally, we cascade the fused features of different scales into decoder to obtain the fused image.

The structure of the rest paper is organized as follows. In Sect. 2, we will briefly introduce the related work. In Sect. 3, the improved method will be presented in detail. Section 4 shows the experimental results. Finally, Sect. 5 is the conclusion of our paper.

2   Related Works

Recently, many deep learning methods are adopted in the field of image fusion. With the development of deep networks, some issues have arisen, such as the disappearance of gradients and the increase of parameters etc. In CVPR 2017, Huang et al. [13] presented the Dense Convolutional Network (DenseNet) in which the feature-maps of each layer are treated as input into all subsequent layers. This architecture has several advantages: they can make vanishing-gradient problem alleviated, make full use of the features of the middle layers and reduce the number of parameters.

Based on the advantages of DenseNet, In 2019, Li et al. [12] proposed a novel deep learning architecture, which consists of encoding network and decoding network. Their encoding network is constructed by convolutional layers and dense block. Then, the authors fuse them by fusion layer. Finally, the fused image is reconstructed by a decoder. In encoder, they apply dense block [13] to leverage more useful information from middle layers. A unique training strategy was developed in DenseFuse. Then, the output image is reconstructed by decoding network using the extracted features. Therefore, in the fusion phase, the two source images are fed to encoding network. Then, two feature maps are obtained and they are fused by fusion strategy. Ultimately, the fusion maps are transmitted to decoder network and the fused image can be obtained.

In this paper, we propose a multi-scale DenseNet (MSDNet), which is built on DenseFuse. We add multi-scale mechanism in encoder to extract features from different scales. Then, we apply fusion strategy to fuse them respectively. We utilize the decoder of Densefuse which is four CNN layers to reconstructed the fused image. We will introduce the algorithm in detail in Sect. 3.

3   Methodology

In this section, the improved method will be introduced in detail. First of all, we apply our method to medical image fusion. The framework of the method is shown in Fig. 1.

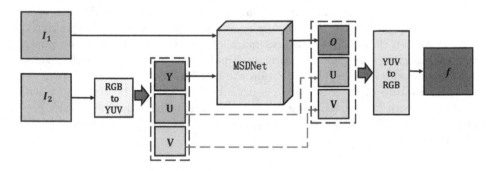

Fig. 1. The framework of the proposed method.

The input medical images are denoted as I_1 and I_2. We adopt the method [18] to convert the color images into YUV color space. If I_1 is grayscale, we convert I_2 to YUV space but we just leverage the Y channels of I_2. We then input the two (converted) images into MSDNet. Finally, combining the output of MSDNet with U and V channels of I_2, the fused image (f) is obtained by converting YUV to RGB color space.

Secondly, considering only a single scale feature is used in DenseFuse, our goal is adding multi-scale mechanism in encoder of DenseFuse. Therefore, our

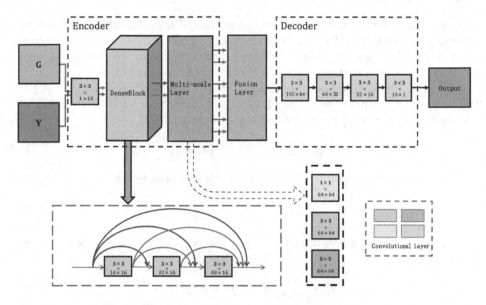

Fig. 2. The architecture of the MSDNet.

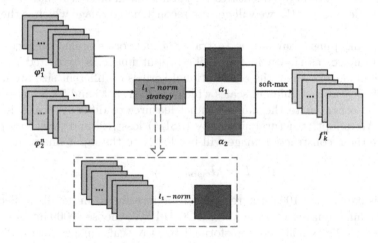

Fig. 3. The diagram of l_1-norm strategy.

new framework is called MSDNet. MSDNet is made of encoder, a fusion layer and decoder as shown in Fig. 2.

The encoder is constructed by a convolutional layer, dense block and a multi-scale layer. We add multi-scale layer whose filters' size are 5×5, 3×3 and 1×1 respectively to extract features from coarse to fine at the end of Denseblock. Why we choose these sizes of filters? Because we adopt 1×1 filters to fuse the information of different channels at the same location and 3×3, 5×5 filters to fuse the information of different channels around the same location. When we choose a larger size of filters, the features extracted from the filters will not be obvious, so larger size of filters is not selected. Through the multi-scale layer, we will get three groups of multi-channel features. Then, we choose l_1-norm strategy [12], which is shown in Fig. 3, to fuse them respectively.

In Fig. 3, the feature maps are denoted as $\varphi_i^{1:n}(x,y)$, where $i \in \{1, \ldots, k\}$ is the number of input images, $n \in \{1, 2, \ldots, N\}$, and $N = 64$ is the number of feature maps. $\varphi_i^{1:n}(x,y)$ are processed by l_1-norm as Eq. 1.

$$\alpha_i(x,y) = \sum_1^n ||\varphi_i^{1:n}(x,y)||_1 \qquad (1)$$

Then the average operator is utilized to calculate the weight map by Eq. 2.

$$w_i(x,y) = \frac{\alpha_i(x,y)}{\sum_{i=1}^k \alpha_i(x,y)} \qquad (2)$$

Finally, $f_k^n(x,y)$, where $k \in \{1,3,5\}$ is the scale of filters, is calculated by Eq. 3.

$$f_k^n = \sum_{i=1}^k w_i(x,y) \times \varphi_i^n(x,y) \qquad (3)$$

The three groups of fused features f_1, f_3 and f_5 will be concatenated together as input to decoder, lastly, we will get the reconstructed image which is the fused image.

In training phase, our aim is to train the network's ability to reconstruct the input image, as shown in Fig. 4. The input image is extracted by dense convolutional layers, then, the convolutional kernels of different size are used to extract the features of different scales which are 1×1, 3×3 and 5×5 respectively. Finally, we concatenate the multi-channel features of different scales into the decoder. We adopt structural similarity (SSIM) loss [12] and pixel loss [12] to guarantee the reconstructed image will be closely to the input image, as Eq. 4.

$$L = \lambda L_{ssim} + L_p \qquad (4)$$

In this paper, $\lambda = 1000$, the reason will be introduced in details in Sect. 4.2.

Our training images are from MS-COCO [14]. We choose 80000 images, which are resized to 256×256 and transformed to gray scale images, are utilized to train the network. Learning rate, batch size and epochs are set as 1×10^{-4}, 2 and 4 respectively.

4   Experiments and Analysis

4.1   Experiment Settings

In our experiment, there are three fusion categories of medical images, which are computerized tomography (CT) and magnetic resonance imaging (MRI), MRI and positron emission tomography (PET), and MRI and single-photon emission computed tomography (SPECT) [20].

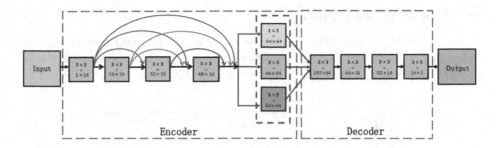

Fig. 4. The framework of training process.

As shown in Fig. 1, in CT and MRI, CT is I_1 and MRI is I_2; in MRI and PET, MRI is I_1 and PET is I_2; in MRI and SPECT, MRI is I_1 and SPECT is I_2. Therefore, we fuse three groups of medical images and analyze them from objective and subjective points of views.

We compare the proposed method with seven prior methods, including a medical image fusion method based on convolutional neural networks (CNN) [2], IHS-PCA method [15] which adopted intensity-hue-saturation (IHS) transform and principal component analysis (PCA) to preserve more spatial feature and more required functional information with no color distortion, LES-DC [16], LLF-IOI [17], medical image fusion with PA-PCNN in nonsubsampled shearlet transform domain (NSST) [18], infrared and visible image fusion using a deep learning framework (VGG) [10], DenseFuse [12].

In order to evaluate our proposed method, we compare our method with seven existing methods and we choose six quality indicators. They are: $SSIM_a$; $PSNR_a$; FMI_{dct}, FMI_w, FMI_{edge} and $FMI_{gradient}$ [19] which calculate mutual information for the discrete cosine, wavelet, edge and gradient features, respectively.

In our experiment, the $SSIM_a$ and $PSNR_a$ are calculated by Eqs. 5 and 6,

$$SSIM_a(F) = (SSIM(F, I_1) + SSIM(F, I_2)) \times 0.5 \qquad (5)$$

$$PSNR_a(F) = (PSNR(F, I_1) + PSNR(F, I_2)) \times 0.5 \qquad (6)$$

where $SSIM(\cdot)$ denotes the structural similarity operation [22], $PSNR(\cdot)$ denotes peak signal-to-noise ratio, F is the fused image and I_1, I_2 are source images. The values of $SSIM_a$ and $PSNR_a$ represent the ability to retain structural information and original information of source images, respectively.

With the increase of all these six measures, the image fusion performance will be improved.

We use Python for all experiments and adopt Tensorflow architecture. Our method was implemented with NVIDIA GTX 1080Ti GPU.

4.2   Loss of Training Phase

In [12], $\lambda \in \{1, 10, 100, 1000\}$, according to the experimental comparison as shown in Fig. 5, we find that the model converges faster and more stable when $\lambda = 1000$. Therefore, in this paper, we choose $\lambda = 1000$.

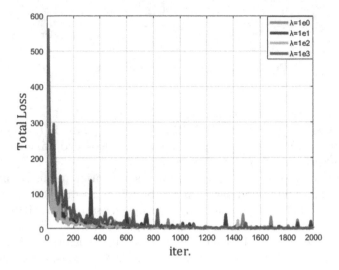

Fig. 5. The graph plot of L.

4.3   Baseline

Firstly, we compare the method with DenseFuse ($\lambda = 1000$), which is a recently developed fusion method, separately. In Table 1, the values are the average results for 60 fused images, including **CT** and **MRI**, **MRI** and **PET** and **MRI** and **SPECT**. The best results are bloded. We can see that it is effective for adding multi-scale mechanism in DenseFuse.

Table 1. The average values of quality metrics for 60 fused images, including **CT** and **MRI**, **MRI** and **PET** and **MRI** and **SPECT**.

Metrics	DenseFuse	Ours
FMI_{dct}	0.4016	**0.4063**
FMI_{w}	**0.4193**	0.4153
FMI_{edge}	0.8739	**0.8749**
$FMI_{gradient}$	0.6632	**0.6646**
$SSIM$	**0.7795**	0.7790
$PSNR$	18.5016	**18.6062**

4.4   Subjective Evaluation

The fused images which are obtained by the seven compared methods and proposed method are shown in Fig. 6.

As we can see from Fig. 6, LES-DC [16] and VGG [10] retain less valid information than other methods because some features are not very clear. The fused images obtained by LLF-IOI [17] are a little sharp and have some artificial noise. Compared with the existing methods, the fused images obtained by our method are more natural. We will leverage objective indicators to analyze the fusion performance.

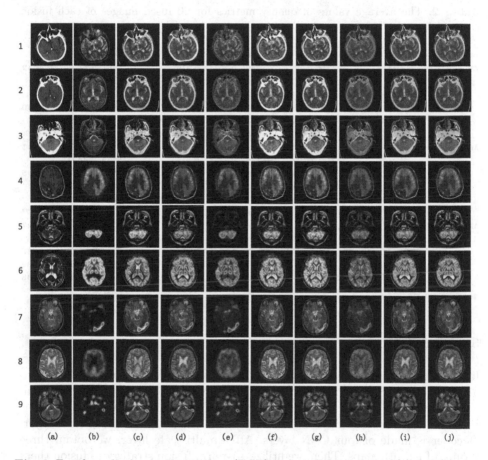

Fig. 6. Fused results for medical images (RGB) images. Rows 1 to 3 of (a) and (b) are CT and MRI images; Rows 4 to 6 of (a) and (b) are MRI and PET images; Rows 7 to 9 of (a) and (b) are MRI and SPECT images; (c) CNN; (d) IHS-PCA; (e) LES-DC; (f) LLF-IOI; (g) NSST with PAPCNN; (h) VGG; (i) DenseFuse; (j) Ours

4.5   Objective Evaluation

We use SSIM, PSNR, FMI_{dct}, FMI_w, FMI_{edge}, $FMI_{gradient}$ to analyze fusion performance. We test three groups of medical images, they are: CT and MRT, MRI and PET and MRI and SPECT. The results are shown in Table 2.

In Table 2, the best results are bloded, the second-best results are marked in red and the third-best results are marked in blue. In Table 2, it can be seen that proposed method's indicators are very high for the most part. It proves that the results of proposed method has more salient features and less artificial noise.

Table 2. The average values of quality metrics for 20 fused images of each fusion categories.

Images	Metrics	CNN	IHS-PCA	LES-DC	LLF-IOI	NSST_PAPCNN	VGG	DenseFuse	Ours
CT and MRI	FMI_{dct}	0.3344	0.2833	0.2739	0.3074	0.3493	0.3161	0.3973	**0.4052**
	FMI_w	0.3216	0.3212	0.3060	0.2830	0.2965	0.3128	**0.4121**	0.4096
	FMI_{edge}	**0.8750**	0.8662	0.8490	0.8642	0.8736	0.8644	0.8709	0.8721
	$FMI_{gradient}$	0.5961	0.5926	0.6070	0.5146	0.5427	0.5929	0.6166	**0.6190**
	$SSIM$	0.7150	0.7314	0.7312	0.6297	0.7092	0.7390	**0.7561**	0.7551
	$PSNR$	15.1231	14.8702	**16.3497**	14.4025	15.0665	15.7063	15.3718	15.5106
MRI and PET	FMI_{dct}	0.3193	0.2691	0.2106	0.3197	0.3274	0.2928	0.4093	**0.4131**
	FMI_w	0.2555	0.3367	0.2873	0.3284	0.3153	0.3173	**0.4441**	0.4357
	FMI_{edge}	0.8735	0.8677	0.8499	0.8452	0.8754	0.8702	0.8787	**0.8795**
	$FMI_{gradient}$	0.6454	0.6640	0.6528	0.6581	0.6546	0.6646	**0.7141**	0.7139
	$SSIM$	0.7443	0.7892	0.7616	0.7363	0.7833	0.7862	**0.8097**	0.8087
	$PSNR$	18.6706	18.6265	**20.6856**	17.9582	18.0490	19.7616	19.0303	19.1675
MRI and SPECT	FMI_{dct}	0.2779	0.2481	0.2164	0.2848	0.2873	0.2559	0.3982	**0.4007**
	FMI_w	0.2466	0.2920	0.2358	0.3175	0.2834	0.2727	**0.4016**	0.4007
	FMI_{edge}	0.8720	0.8591	0.8489	0.8240	0.8724	0.8659	0.8720	**0.8732**
	$FMI_{gradient}$	0.5586	0.5912	0.5574	0.6114	0.5898	0.5847	0.6589	**0.6609**
	$SSIM$	0.6781	0.7570	0.6857	0.6980	0.7506	0.7334	0.7727	**0.7733**
	$PSNR$	20.2285	20.2886	20.7385	19.7199	**21.2716**	19.9470	21.1027	21.1407

5   Conclusion

In this paper, we propose a multi-scale DenseNet by adding multi-scale mechanism into DenseFuse and apply the improved method for medical image fusion.

Our network consists of constructed by encoder, fusion layer and decoder. Encoder is made of a convolutional layer, dense block and multi-scale layer. Decoder is made of four CNN layers. After multi-scale layer, we obtain three groups of feature maps. Then, we utilize L_1-norm fusion strategy to fusion them respectively. We concatenate them as input into decoder. Finally, we obtain the fused image reconstructed by decoder.

We use subjective and objective quality metrics to evaluate the performance of fusion results. The results of experiments indicate that our method is effective for medical image fusion.

References

1. Du, J., Li, W., Lu, K., et al.: An overview of multi-modal medical image fusion. Neurocomputing **215**, 3–20 (2016)
2. Liu, Y., Chen, X., Cheng, J., et al.: A medical image fusion method based on convolutional neural networks. In: 2017 20th International Conference on Information Fusion (Fusion), pp. 1–7. IEEE (2017)
3. Yang, S., Wang, M., Jiao, L., et al.: Image fusion based on a new contourlet packet. Inf. Fusion **11**(2), 78–84 (2010)
4. Li, H., Manjunath, B.S., Mitra, S.K.: Multisensor image fusion using the wavelet transform. Graph. Models Image Process. **57**(3), 235–245 (1995)
5. Guo, L., Dai, M., Zhu, M.: Multifocus color image fusion based on quaternion curvelet transform. Opt. Express **20**(17), 18846–18860 (2012)
6. Liu, Y., Wang, Z.: Simultaneous image fusion and denoising with adaptive sparse representation. IET Image Proc. **9**(5), 347–357 (2014)
7. Yin, H., Li, Y., Chai, Y., et al.: A novel sparse-representation-based multi-focus image fusion approach. Neurocomputing **216**, 216–229 (2016)
8. Li, H., Wu, X.-J.: Multi-focus image fusion using dictionary learning and low-rank representation. In: Zhao, Y., Kong, X., Taubman, D. (eds.) ICIG 2017. LNCS, vol. 10666, pp. 675–686. Springer, Cham (2017). https://doi.org/10.1007/978-3-319-71607-7_59
9. Liu, Y., Chen, X., Peng, H., et al.: Multi-focus image fusion with a deep convolutional neural network. Inf. Fusion **36**, 191–207 (2017)
10. Li, H., Wu, X.J., Kittler, J.: Infrared and visible image fusion using a deep learning framework. In: 2018 24th International Conference on Pattern Recognition (ICPR), pp. 2705–2710. IEEE (2018)
11. Simonyan, K., Zisserman, A.: Very deep convolutional networks for large-scale image recognition. arXiv preprint arXiv:1409.1556 (2014)
12. Li, H., Wu, X.J.: DenseFuse: a fusion approach to infrared and visible images. IEEE Trans. Image Process. **28**(5), 2614–2623 (2019)
13. Huang, G., Liu, Z., Van Der Maaten, L., et al.: Densely connected convolutional networks. In: Proceedings of the IEEE Conference on Computer Vision and Pattern Recognition, pp. 4700–4708 (2017)
14. Lin, T.-Y., et al.: Microsoft COCO: common objects in context. In: Fleet, D., Pajdla, T., Schiele, B., Tuytelaars, T. (eds.) ECCV 2014. LNCS, vol. 8693, pp. 740–755. Springer, Cham (2014). https://doi.org/10.1007/978-3-319-10602-1_48
15. He, C., Liu, Q., Li, H., et al.: Multimodal medical image fusion based on IHS and PCA. Procedia Eng. **7**, 280–285 (2010)
16. Xu, Z.: Medical image fusion using multi-level local extrema. Inf. Fusion **19**, 38–48 (2014)
17. Du, J., Li, W., Xiao, B.: Anatomical-functional image fusion by information of interest in local Laplacian filtering domain. IEEE Trans. Image Process. **26**(12), 5855–5866 (2017)
18. Yin, M., Liu, X., Liu, Y., et al.: Medical image fusion with parameter-adaptive pulse coupled neural network in nonsubsampled shearlet transform domain. IEEE Trans. Instrum. Meas. **99**, 1–16 (2018)
19. Haghighat, M., Razian, M.A.: Fast-FMI: non-reference image fusion metric. In: 2014 IEEE 8th International Conference on Application of Information and Communication Technologies (AICT), pp. 1–3. IEEE (2014)
20. http://www.escience.cn/people/xiaomi/index.html

21. Prabhakar, K.R., Srikar, V.S., Babu, R.V.: DeepFuse: a deep unsupervised approach for exposure fusion with extreme exposure image pairs. In: ICCV, pp. 4724–4732 (2017)
22. Wang, Z., Bovik, A.C., Sheikh, H.R., et al.: Image quality assessment: from error visibility to structural similarity. IEEE Trans. Image Process. **13**(4), 600–612 (2004)
23. Chen, Z., Wu, X.J., Kittler, J.: A sparse regularized nuclear norm based matrix regression for face recognition with contiguous occlusion. Pattern Recogn. Lett. (2019)
24. Chen, Z., Wu, X.-J., Yin, H.-F., Kittler, J.: Robust low-rank recovery with a distance-measure structure for face recognition. In: Geng, X., Kang, B.-H. (eds.) PRICAI 2018. LNCS (LNAI), vol. 11013, pp. 464–472. Springer, Cham (2018). https://doi.org/10.1007/978-3-319-97310-4_53

A Scale Normalization Algorithm Based on MR-GDS for Archaeological Fragments Reassembly

Congli Yin[1], Pengbo Zhou[1(✉)], Mingquan Zhou[1], Zhongke Wu[1],
and Guoguang Du[2]

[1] College of Information Science and Technology,
Beijing Normal University, Beijing, China
coliyin@163.com, {zhoupengbo,mqzhou,zwu}@bnu.edu.cn
[2] Vision AI Group, CloudMinds Technologies, Beijing, China
george.du@cloudminds.com

Abstract. In template-based archaeological fragments reassembly, the fragments and the template usually have scale variances, which needs to be eliminated by scale normalization. Traditional methods need at least two pairs of matched points for scale normalization, which is non-trivial for many fragments. In this paper, a scale normalization algorithm for template-based fragments reassembly is proposed, which solves the reassembly problem for fragments and the template with scale variances. Firstly, one pair of corresponding points between the fragment and the template is selected as the anchor points. Secondly, the Geodesic Disk Spectrum (GDS) of the fragment and the Multi-Radii Geodesic Disk Spectrum (MR-GDS) of the template are computed, respectively. Thirdly, the GDS descriptors are compared to obtain candidates of the scale variances, which will be further verified through an ICP-based strategy. At last, the fragments are registered to the template after scale normalization. Experiments on scale normalization and fragments reassembly all achieved accurate results. The proposed algorithm is suitable for the scale estimation of small fragments, which expands the application scenarios greatly for the template-based fragments reassembly.

Keywords: Scale normalization · Geodesic disk · Fragments reassembly

1 Introduction

The template plays a pivotal role in template-based fragments reassembly tasks. The premise that the template can work lies in that it has the same geometric scale as the fragments. However, the fragments and the template often have scale variances in practical applications. The usual solution to this problem is to conduct scale normalization for the fragments and the template. Existing scale normalization algorithms could be roughly divided into two categories:

© Springer Nature Switzerland AG 2019
Y. Zhao et al. (Eds.): ICIG 2019, LNCS 11902, pp. 289–299, 2019.
https://doi.org/10.1007/978-3-030-34110-7_25

global information-based methods [1,2] and feature point-based methods [3,4]. However, the former is only applicable for full shapes and the latter is strongly dependent on feature points. It is often difficult to obtain correct normalization results when the fragments are small or the features of the shape are not discriminative.

This paper presents a scale normalization algorithm for template-based fragments reassembly, which effectively solves the reassembly problem of fragments and template with scale variances. The Multi-Radii Geodesic Disk Spectrum (MR-GDS) descriptor is firstly proposed which explicitly fuses the geometric scale. The scale variances are computed by comparing the GDS of the fragment and the MR-GDS of the template. The proposed algorithm needs only one pair of matched points and is suitable for fragments with few extremities. Pipeline of our algorithm is illustrated in Fig. 1, which involves the anchor point selection stage, the scale variance estimation stage, and the post verification stage.

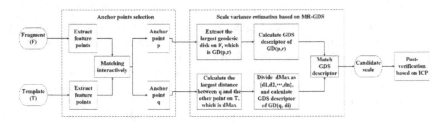

Fig. 1. Pipeline of the proposed algorithm. The anchor point selection stage is on the left, the scale variance estimation stage based on MR-GDS is on the middle, and the post verification stage is on the right.

In summary, main contributions of our work is as follows:

(1) A scale normalization algorithm is proposed, which solves the reassembly problem of fragments and template with scale variances. The Multi-Radii Geodesic Disk Spectrum (MR-GDS) is firstly proposed to conduct scale normalization.
(2) A post-verification strategy based on Interactive Closest Points (ICP), which conducts ICP for geodesic disks with different scale normalization, is proposed to optimize the scale estimation results.

The remainder of the paper is arranged as follows. The related work will be introduced in Sect. 2. In Sect. 3, pipelines of our algorithm are discussed in detail. Next, experimental results and discussions are presented in Sect. 4. Finally, conclusions are summarized in Sect. 5.

2   Related Work

In this section, methods for 3D shape scale normalization are generally summarized. Some methods transform the problem from Euclidean space into another domain and find the scale integrally. Savva et al. [2] address the problem of recovering reliable sizes for a collection of models defined using scales with unknown correspondence to physical units. Their approach provides quite correct size estimates for 3D models by combining category-based size priors and size observations from 3D scenes.

Zaharescu et al. [3] proposed a scale-independent feature point extractor that called MeshDOG and a scale-independent feature descriptor that called MeshHOG, which extract and match feature points on rigid or non-rigid shapes. Bronstein et al. [4] proposed the Scale Invariant Heat Kernel Signature (SI-HKS) descriptor and applied it to the identification of non-rigid shapes, which solves the feature extracting and feature matching problem of different scales.

Some methods find corresponding feature points firstly and then conduct matching. Sahillioğlu and Yemez [5] presents a scale normalization method for isometric shape matching in a combinatorial matching framework, which resolves the scale ambiguity by finding a coarse matching between extremities of shapes based on a novel scale-invariant isometric distortion measure. However, their method needs at least three pairs of points with accurate correspondences. In many cases, it is difficult to find enough corresponding points, especially when the area of the fragment is less than half of the template.

3   Pipeline of Our Algorithm

In this section, pipeline of our algorithm is presented, which contains the anchor points selection, the scale variance estimation based on MR-GDS, and the post verification.

3.1   Anchor Points Selection

A pair of matched points on the fragment and the template is regarded as anchor points. The anchor points are significant since the scale normalization and fragments reassembly are all based on correct anchor points. In order to ensure the accuracy of the corresponding anchor points, we proposed a strategy based on Gaussian curvature to select the anchor points interactively.

Let the fragment and the template be F and T, respectively. The non-boundary points with the top k largest Gaussian curvature on F are selected firstly, and an interval $[g_{min}, g_{max}]$ is obtained according to the sorting k Gaussian curvature. Secondly, the points whose Gaussian curvature are within $[g_{min}, g_{max}]$ are selected on T. Thirdly, a pair of corresponding points is selected interactively as the anchor points. In the experiments, we generally set $k \leq 10$ to reduce the difficulties of interactive selection. Figure 2 illustrates a pair of anchor points (red dots) selected on the fragment and the template.

3.2   Scale Variance Estimation Based on MR-GDS

In this section, we firstly recap the background of Geodesic Disk Spectrum (GDS) and then propose the MR-GDS descriptor. The scale variance are estimated finally.

(a)   (b)

Fig. 2. A pair of anchor points (red dots) on the template (a) and the fragment (b). (Color figure online)

GDS. Shape Index was initially proposed for the graphical visualization of the surface [6]. Dorai et al. [7] employed a modified definition for surface point identifying, which is defined as follows:

$$S_I(p) = \frac{1}{2} - \frac{1}{\pi}\tan^{-1}(\frac{\kappa_1(p) + \kappa_2(p)}{\kappa_1(p) - \kappa_2(p)}) \tag{1}$$

where $S_I(p)$ ranges during $[0, 1]$, $\kappa_1(p)$ is the maximum normal curvature, $\kappa_2(p)$ is the minimum normal curvature and $\kappa_1(p) > \kappa_2(p)$. Shape Index provides a continuous gradation between salient shapes, such as convex, saddle, concave, and it owns a large vocabulary to describe subtle shape variations. Shape Index is appropriate for the description of the distribution of the disk since the value ranges from $[0, 1]$.

Du et al. [8] proposed Geodesic Disk Spectrum (GDS) for the part-in-whole matching task. Let P be a 3D manifold surface of n vertices, a geodesic disk $GD(p, r)$ with center p and radius r is defined as follows:

$$GD(p, r) = \{v, \ gd(v, p) \le r\} \tag{2}$$

where $gd(v, p)$ is the geodesic distance between any point v to the center p. GDS is obtained by counting the distribution of Shape Index for all the points within a geodesic disk. GDS of one geodesic disk is given by:

$$GDS(p, r) = (\frac{n_1}{n}, \frac{n_2}{n}, ..., \frac{n_N}{n}) \tag{3}$$

where N is the number of bins range in $[0,1]$ and $n_1, n_2, ..., n_N$ are the number of points that fall into respective bins.

MR-GDS. The MR-GDS descriptor is proposed in this section. The MR-GDS descriptor of the template T depends on the multi-radii geodesic disks, and the multi-radii geodesic disks center on the anchor point q need to be extracted.

Procedures of computing the MR-GDS descriptor are listed as follows. Firstly, the farthest point s away from q on T is found and the distance between distance s and q is set as $d_{\max}$. Secondly, divide $d_{\max}$ into $n-1$ discrete intervals equally as $\{d_1, d_2, \ldots, d_n\}$, and all the geodesic disks with the center q and the radius d_i are extracted. Figure 3 shows a set of geodesic disks with different radii on T. Note that n is usually set as $d_{\max}/mesh\_resolution$, where $mesh\_resolution$ is the resolution of the template, which is the average point-to-point distance. This configuration ensures enough samplings of geodesic disks and contributes to accurate scale estimation results. Finally, the GDS descriptor is computed for all geodesic disks with different radii, and they combine into the MR-GDS descriptor together.

Fig. 3. A set of geodesic disks with different radii on T. The red regions are geodesic disks and the radii of the geodesic disks are is increasing from left to right. (Color figure online)

Scale Variance Estimation. Scale normalization is actually the calculation of the scale variance between the fragments and the template. Based on the anchor points obtained in Sect. 3.1, the largest enclosed geodesic disk on F with the center of anchor point is extracted firstly to compute the GDS descriptor. Then, the scale variance will be estimated by comparing the GDS of the fragment and the MR-GDS of the template. The specific procedures of scale variance estimation are listed as follows.

Firstly, extract the largest geodesic disk on F and compute the GDS descriptor of the fragment. Aiming at F, the largest enclosed geodesic disk $GD\,(p, r)$ centered on the anchor point p is needed. All geodesic distances between boundary points and p are computed firstly, and the shortest one is set as the radius r of $GD\,(p, r)$. Note that principle curvatures of boundary points are abnormal from the ones on the template, so the two-ring neighbor points of the boundary are deleted, which eliminate the affections of GDS descriptor calculating. Figure 4 illustrates the extracted geodesic disk on the remained fragment regions. The GDS descriptor is then computed.

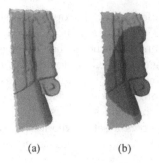

(a)   (b)

Fig. 4. (a) The gray region is two-ring neighbor points of boundary on fragment, which is deleted in order to eliminate the affections of GDS descriptor calculating. (b) The red region is the largest geodesic disk on the remained fragment. (Color figure online)

Secondly, comparing GDS of the fragment and the MR-GDS of the template are conducted. The similarity between $GDS(p, r)$ and $GDS(q, d_i)$ is given as follows:

$$dis = E(GDS(p, r) - GDS(q, d_i)) \tag{4}$$

Note that the similarities are measured as the variance of differences between each value of GDS. The most similar m geodesic disks are selected as candidate disks and their radii d_i are recorded. The scale variance is computed as the ratio between d_i and r, where d_i is one of the candidate disks. At last, m scale variances are obtained. Figure 5 shows the candidate GDS descriptors of the most similar m geodesic disks, where $m = 3$ in this case. We can see that the GDS descriptors between $GD(p, r)$ and the candidate disks are quite similar.

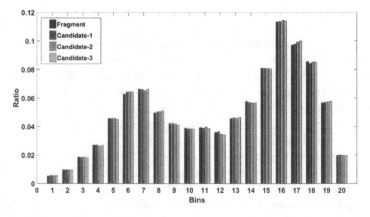

Fig. 5. The three similar GDS compare with $GDS(p, r)$, which will be used for the next post-verification strategy.

3.3   Post-verification Strategy Based on ICP

A post-verification strategy based on ICP [9] is proposed to find the most accurate scale variance. The largest geodesic disk of the fragment is geometrically modified according to the m scale variances. Then, the largest geodesic disk of the fragment is registered with m corresponding geodesic disks on the template, and the registration error is achieved using ICP. Among them, the one with the lowest registration error is selected and the corresponding scale variance is selected as the final scale estimation result. Detailed descriptions of this algorithm is shown in Algorithm 1. The transformations between the fragment and the template are also obtained through ICP and the fragment can be matched to the template. The fragments are thus reassembled when multiple fragments are all matched to the template.

Algorithm 1. A post verification strategy based on ICP

Input: $GD(p, r)$; $GD(q, d_i)$: candidate geodesic disk, $i = 1, 2, \cdots, m$;
Output: matched $GD(q, d_k)$, translation T_T and rotation T_R
1: $for(k = 1; k <= m; k++)$;
2: conduct ICP between $GD(p, r)$ and $GD(q, d_k)$, ε_k is the corresponding error;
3: keep $\varepsilon_{\min} = \min(\varepsilon_k(k = 1, 2, \cdots, m))$;
4: return $GD(q, d)$ with corresponding error $\varepsilon_{\min}$, translation T_T and rotation T_R;

---

4   Experiments

In the section, datasets used in our experiments are firstly introduced. Experimental results and discussions on scale estimation and fragments reassembly are then presented.

4.1   Datasets

We build two datasets to verify the proposed algorithm. Examples of the two datasets are shown in Fig. 6 on the same perspective. Note that, the Ground Truth is obtained manually and all fragments have different translations compared with the template. The first dataset is used to evaluate the effectiveness of the proposed scale normalization algorithm and the second dataset is used to evaluate the effectiveness of the proposed algorithm for fragments reassembly.

Dataset 1: Since there is no existing benchmarks for 3D shape scale normalization, we constructed dataset 1 to verify the effectiveness of the proposed algorithm. The scanned Terracotta Warriors template is randomly segmented. Geomagic Studio 2012 is used to perform random scale transformation on each fragment and the scale transformation are recorded as Ground Truth.

Dataset 2: In order to verify the practicability of the scale normalization algorithm in the fragment reassembly, we use the artificial Terracotta Warriors as a template for the experiment, while the fragments are still in the original sizes.

Fig. 6. The datasets on the same perspective. (a) shows dataset 1, where the template Terracotta Warriors 3D model is segmented into four fragments randomly and the fragments are modified in random scales. These scales are regarded as the Ground Truth. (b) shows dataset 2, where the artificial Terracotta Warriors 3D model is set as the template and five fragments are with real scales.

4.2 Experimental Results

Scale Normalization. Experiments for scale normalization are conducted on dataset 1. The accuracy of scale estimation is evaluated by the error ε and the error ratio δ, which are defined in the follow. Scale is the experimental results and GT is Ground Truth.

$$\varepsilon = scale - GT, \ \delta = \frac{scale - GT}{GT} \tag{5}$$

The scale estimation results of our algorithm are shown in Table 1, where *mesh_resolution* represents the average point to point distance of the template, scale represents our result, respectively. ε and δ in Table 1 are both quite small, which illustrates the effectiveness of the proposed algorithm.

The time costs are shown in Table 2 for the four fragments. The main time costs can be divided into three parts, which are the computation of GDS for fragments, the computation of MR-GDS of the template, and the post verification using ICP. The time costs are all with the milliseconds level, which is quite fast.

Our algorithm is compared with the scale normalization algorithm proposed by Sahillioğlu and Yemez [5]. Their algorithm all failed in estimating the scales of the two datasets we used. Their method failed in finding three pairs of corresponding points, and can not compute the scale variances through proportional constraints. This illustrates the advantage of our algorithm in dealing with relative small fragments.

Table 1. The scale estimation results. Mesh resolution represents the average point-to-point distance of the template, scale represents our result, respectively.

Fragments	$mesh\_resolution$	GT	scale	ε	δ
p1	0.81978	1.30	1.3038	0.0038	0.29%
p2		0.87	0.8675	0.0025	0.28%
p3		1.45	1.4421	0.0079	0.54%
p4		0.92	0.9175	0.0025	0.27%

Table 2. The time costs of the experiments. The main time costs can be divided into three parts, which are the computation of GDS for fragments $t1$, the computation of MR-GDS of the template $t2$, and the post verification using ICP $t3$. The time costs are all with the milliseconds level, which is quite fast.

Fragments	$t1$ (ms)	$t2$ (ms)	$t3$ (ms)	Total (ms)
p1	594	3219	126	3939
p2	640	3609	169	4418
p3	750	3578	184	4512
p4	328	3734	117	4179

Fragment Reassembly. Experiments of fragment reassembly are conducted on dataset 2. The scales of these fragments compared with the template are estimated firstly. Then, the fragments are modified according to the estimated scales in order to conduct the ICP algorithm. At last, using the transformations obtained by ICP, the fragment could be registered to the template. To numerically evaluate reassembly accuracy, the reference error ε_R and the reference error ratio δ_R are defined. Let S, S' be the template model and the reassembled model, respectively. The reference error ε_R is defined as follow

$$\varepsilon_R = \sqrt{\sum_{v \in S, v' \in \widehat{S}} d^2(v, v')/|S|} \tag{6}$$

where $|S|$ represents the number of points of S, $d(;)$ represents the Euclidean distance. The reference error ratio δ_R is measured as a percentage of the diagonal length of bounding box.

The results of fragments reassembly by our algorithm are shown in Fig. 7. The scanned fragments are shown in Fig. 7(a) and (b) shows the reassembly results. The error distribution of each point is shown in Fig. 7(c), where the red color represents a large error and the blue color represents the opposite. It can be intuitively seen that the error is relatively small.

Quantitative results are shown in Table 3, including reference error ε_R and the reference error ratio δ_R. It can be seen that our algorithm obtains a high accuracy of reassembly.

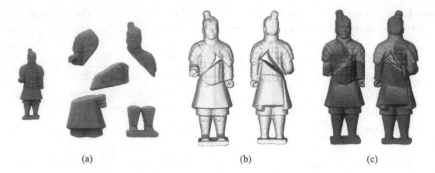

(a)   (b)   (c)

Fig. 7. The fragments reassembly results of Terracotta Warriors. (a) The scanned fragments. (b) Reassembly results. (c) The error distribution of each point, red represents a large error while blue represents the opposite. (Color figure online)

Table 3. Quantitative results of the fragment reassembly. ε_R is the reference error and δ_R is the reference error ratio.

ε_R	δ_R	Bounding box
0.520	0.217%	239.46

5   Conclusions

In this paper, we propose a scale normalization algorithm based on MR-GDS for archaeological fragments reassembly. The MR-GDS descriptor is firstly proposed which integrate the scale information into the descriptor. With only one pair of matched points, the GDS descriptor of the fragment and the MR-GDS descriptor of the template could be computed. The scale variance can thus be estimated by comparing the GDS descriptor and the MR-GDS descriptor. In order to improve the accuracy of scale estimation, a post-verification strategy based on ICP is also proposed. Experiments are conducted for both scale normalization tasks and template-based fragments reassembly tasks, which all achieved accurate results. Compared with other algorithms, our algorithm needs only one pair of matched points and is suitable for fragments with few extremities, which expands the application scenes greatly for template-based archaeological fragments reassembly tasks.

Acknowledgments. Thanks to the financial support of National Natural Science Foundation of China (61731015) and Qingdao Major Special Projects of Independent Innovation (2017-4-3-2-xcl).

References

1. Kobbelt, L., Schrder, P., Kazhdan, M., et al.: Rotation invariant spherical harmonic representation of 3D shape descriptors. In: Eurographics Symposium on Geometry Processing, pp. 156–164 (2003)

2. Savva, M., Chang, A.X., Bernstein, G.: On being the right scale: sizing large collections of 3D models. In: Proceedings of SIGGRAPH Asia Indoor Scene Understanding Where Graphics Meets Vision ACM (2014)
3. Zaharescu, A., Boyer, E., Varanasi, K., et al.: Surface feature detection and description with applications to mesh matching. In: Proceedings of IEEE Computer Society Conference on Computer Vision and Pattern Recognition, pp. 373–380 (2009)
4. Bronstein, M.M., Kokkinos, I.: Scale-invariant heat kernel signatures for non-rigid shape recognition. In: Proceedings of IEEE Computer Society Conference on Computer Vision and Pattern Recognition, pp. 1704–1711 (2010)
5. Sahillioğlu, Y., Yemez, Y.: Scale normalization for isometric shape matching. In: Computer Graphics Forum, pp. 2233–2240 (2012)
6. Koenderink, J.J., Van Doorn, A.J.: Surface shape and curvature scales. Image Vis. Comput. **10**(8), 557–564 (1992)
7. Dorai, C., Jain, A.K.: COSMOS-A representation scheme for 3D free-form objects. IEEE Trans. Pattern Anal. Mach. Intell. **19**(10), 1115–1130 (1997)
8. Du, G., Yin, C., Zhou, M., et al.: Part-in-whole matching of rigid 3D shapes using geodesic disk spectrum. Multimed. Tools Appl. **77**, 1–21 (2017)
9. Besl, P.J., McKay, N.D.: A method for registration of 3-D shapes. IEEE Trans. Pattern Anal. Mach. Intell. **14**(2), 239–256 (1992)

Histogram-Based Nonlinear Transfer Function Edit and Fusion

Min Gao[1], Yuzhe Xiang[1], Lijun Wang[1], Richen Liu[1(✉)], Sitong Fang[1], Siming Chen[2,3], Jingle Jia[1], Genlin Ji[1], and Bin Zhao[1]

[1] School of Computer Science and Technology, Nanjing Normal University, Nanjing, China
richen@pku.edu.cn
[2] Fraunhofer Institute for Intelligent Analysis and Information Systems, Sankt Augustin, Germany
[3] University of Bonn, Bonn, Germany

Abstract. Volume visualization has wide application in science, engineering, biomedicine and other domains to help understand complex observational or simulative data. Transfer function is a traditional volume visualization approach, which is designed to assign different schemes of color and transparency for each voxel in volume data. In this paper, we design a histogram-based nonlinear transfer function editor. The design of nonlinear histogram and non-uniform grids in the background provides visual cues for users to edit transfer function more efficiently. The larger the histogram bin sizes are, the wider the bin widths will be drawn in the background. Then, a wavelet-like short transfer function (we call it TF-let) is designed, which can be serialized and reloaded fast in the subsequent explorations. Furthermore, we design a TF-let fusion approach to fuse multiple TF-lets by simply clicking the corresponding TF-let nodes. Compared with the traditional linear method, two evaluation tests show that the proposed approach is less sensitive and more efficient to edit the control points of the transfer function. Finally, use cases show the proposed approach is capable of achieving some hard-to-find tiny structures and visualizing them much more clearly.

Keywords: Volume visualization · Transfer functions · Histogram-based manipulation

1 Introduction

Volume visualization has been widely used in multiple domains of science and engineering, e.g., oil/gas exploration, atmospheric and oceanic simulations, medical diagnostics, etc. In the field of visualization, how to generate rich image results and provide users with efficient means of interaction is important. With

---

The first two authors are equally contributed.

© Springer Nature Switzerland AG 2019
Y. Zhao et al. (Eds.): ICIG 2019, LNCS 11902, pp. 300–315, 2019.
https://doi.org/10.1007/978-3-030-34110-7_26

the development of graphics hardware and volume visualization algorithms, volume rendering has a tendency towards maturity, which gets faster and more precise. Consequently, the focus of volume rendering has turned into the design of the transfer function (we abbreviated it into TF in this paper), which is designed to assign different schemes of color and opacity for each voxel in volume data.

Volume visualization algorithms will transform the volume voxels into visualization results with different colors and opacities. A transfer function can be defined as:

$$T: \boldsymbol{x} \rightarrow \{\boldsymbol{c}, \alpha\}, \boldsymbol{x} \in \mathbb{R}^n \tag{1}$$

where $\boldsymbol{x}$ is the intensity or the density of volume data, and $\{c, \alpha\}$ usually represents a two-dimensional group including color and opacity, as shown in Fig. 1a. Besides, the term "attribute" in this paper represents some objects in the data, for example, the blood, fat, soft tissues, and skeleton in the medical data. They are different attributes (tissues) as shown in Fig. 1b. In TF editor, An attribute corresponds to a wavelet-like transfer function, we call it a TF-let in our paper.

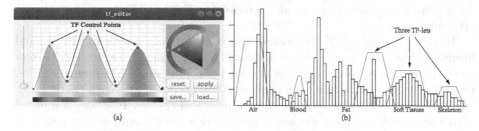

Fig. 1. (a) Traditional linear TF editor, which is implemented in our paper to make comparison with the proposed nonlinear approach. The horizontal axis represents the intensity/density of the volume data while the vertical-axis represents the opacity values. The points on the transfer function curves are control points. The color of each control point decides the color of the volume voxels with the corresponding intensity/density values. (b) The illustration of histogram-based traditional linear TF editor for a medical volume data. A peak in the illustration represents one attribute (tissue) of the data, e.g., the leftmost peak represents air while the rightmost one represents skeleton. Each peak is called a transfer function-let (TF-let) in the paper.

Essentially, TFs classify volume data according to the distribution of them in the feature space when conducting TF editing. Users are forced to edit the data-centric transfer functions in a trial-and-error way. The approach is to assign values of TF control points to define the colors and opacities of each voxel in volume data [8,11]. The TF control points play a significant role in traditional TF editing, which control the final rendering results. The color and transparency of each point between control points can be interpolated by two of the closest control points. Users can adjust the transparency value and the position of each control point by dragging operation. For more information about traditional TFs and the control points, please refer to the literature [2,8,11,22].

In this paper, we design a histogram-based nonlinear transfer function editor. Nonlinear histogram and scales are drawn in the background, providing visual cues about where to place control points and how much their optimal opacity values are. The adjustment sensitivity of each control point in the TF editor are closely related to the histogram bin sizes. A point in the TF editor with a large bin size means there are many voxels within the corresponding ranges of intensity values. Once the control points are moved at a point with a relatively higher histogram bin size, the number of influenced voxels would be more, and the corresponding adjustment sensitivity would be larger. In an extreme case, the values of histogram bin size increase or decrease rapidly, it is difficult for users to specify the expected intensity range for a given attribute. Because it is a classic trial-and-error process. Besides, some insignificant attribute values and ranges, e.g., air in the medical data will disturb the judgments of users.

The proposed nonlinear approach is capable of serializing TF-lets, which enables users reload the single TF-let efficiently in the subsequent explorations. More importantly, users can use a focus + contexts (F+C) TF-let fusion to view multiple focus attributes together with their context environments simultaneously. An arbitrary combination of multiple focus attributes and multiple context attributes (the context tissues in medical data) can be achieved by the TF-let fusion. Besides, they can also remove any focus attributes or any context attributes.

In order to evaluate the proposed approach compared with the traditional linear method, we conduct two evaluation tests, including an sensitivity test and a performance test, to get the sensitivity results and performance results, respectively. The evaluation tests show that the proposed approach is less sensitive and more efficient to edit the control points of transfer function, compared with the traditional linear method. Finally, Some use cases show the proposed method can find some detailed information (e.g., blood vessels in medical data, etc.) which the traditional method can not achieve.

2   Related Work

The design methods of transfer function can be roughly divided into data-centric methods and image-centric methods [25], as shown in Fig. 2. In this paper, we review the related work on the above two aspects to illustrate the background of our work.

2.1   Data-Centric Transfer Functions

In terms of dimensionality, we can classify data-centric transfer functions into one-dimensional, two-dimensional and higher-dimensional. First of all, Yuan et al. [29] introduced fish-eye magnification tool in the horizontal axis of one-dimensional transfer function design interface to facilitate users to observe volume data with complex numerical distribution. Igouchkine et al. [13] implemented an 1-D transfer function which can assign different properties to subregions and their boundaries. Liu et al. [16–20] used 1-D transfer functions to visualize seismic volume data.

Some work [14,15] used two-dimensional transfer functions due to the limitations of one-dimensional transfer function, which can help users define color and

Related Works	Data-centric transfer functions			Image-centric transfer functions		
	One-dimensional Two-dimensional	Higher-dimensional	Multivariate	Parameter optimization	Result optimization	Image quality improvement
Yuan et al. [29]	+	-	-	-	+	-
Igouchkine et al. [13]	+	-	-	-	+	-
Kniss et al. [14] [15]	+	-	-	-	+	-
Sereda et al.[27]	+	-	-	-	-	-
Ma et al. [23]	+	-	-	-	-	-
Ebert et al. [5]	-	-	+	-	-	-
Guo et al. [9] [10]	-	-	+	-	-	-
Blaas et al. [3]	+	-	+	-	-	-
He et al. [12]	-	-	-	+	-	-
Marks et al.[24]	-	-	-	+	-	-
Lu et al.[22]	-	-	-	-	+	-
Ropinski et al.[26]	-	-	-	-	+	-
Guo et al.[8]	-	-	-	-	+	-
Wiebel et al.[28]	-	-	-	-	+	-
Blake et al.[4]	-	-	-	-	-	+
Binyahib et al.[2]	-	-	-	-	-	+
Berger et al.[1]	-	-	-	-	-	+
Fang et al.[6]	-	-	-	+	-	-

Fig. 2. Types of related work with different methods. We categorize the papers into two types according to the basis of the transfer function setting, e.g., data-centric functions and image-centric transfer functions. Data-centric transfer functions include one-dimensional, two-dimensional and higher-dimensional transfer function design. Parameter optimization, result optimization and image quality improvement are based on image-centric transfer functions.

opacity with rectangular and trapezoid shapes. In order to display body data surface information better, Sereda et al. [27] proposed a transfer function design approach based on LH histograms. Ma et al. [23] presented a semi-automatic transfer function design scheme which clusters the entries according to the similarities of one or two dimensional volumetric features.

In addition to these univariate transfer functions, colorful volume data can be regarded as multi-variable volume data. Ebert et al. [5] proposed a transfer function which takes advantage of the color distance gradient dot product to help users find the desired tissue information. Furthermore, the interactive dynamic coordinate system [3] is used to project the high-order multi-variable data into the two-dimensional space, in order to facilitate the user to select features. In addition, Guo et al. [9,10] put forward a multi-variable transfer function design interface based on the combination of dimensional projections and row coordinates.

2.2 Image-Centric Transfer Functions

Compared with data-centric transfer functions, image-centric transfer functions are set to indirectly change the transfer functions by targeting specific image results, it will allow users through some approaches to adjust the result of visualization instead of directly editing the transfer function. The improvement and optimization of volume rendering is actually the optimization of the transfer function parameters. In order to solve this problem, He et al. [12] presented a generation of transfer functions with stochastic search techniques. In this process, the computer could optimize the transfer function according to the requirements of users, and finally got the iterative results which exploited many image processing methods. Similarly, design galleries [24] provided a series of different transfer functions for users to choose and then optimize the final visualization results.

Fang et al. [6] proposed an image-based transfer function design for data exploration in volume visualization. It allows users to adjust the parameters to achieve the desired effect. Example-based volume visualization [21] is also a goal-oriented approach, users can find some visual examples which are defined on the color statistical properties of the image results, and transfer the style of the examples to their approaches. Ropinski et al. [26] proposed a transfer function based on stroke, in which users could extract the feature distribution of the corresponding volume data by specifying foreground and background on the volume rendering image. In addition, WYSIWYG (What You See is What You Get) [8,28] allows users to use a set of tools which are similar to the operations in painting software like Photoshop. It can be used to modify the styles of visualization results.

In recent years, many visualization researchers have proposed a series of methods to improve the image quality of the final visualization results. For example, Lathen et al. [22] proposed an automatic tuning of spatially varying transfer functions, but they just aimed to increase the contrast between the blood vessels and the surrounding tissue. Blake et al. [4] designed a transfer function to categorize each ray to refine the results. Similarly, Binyahib et al. [2] presented an algorithm for parallel volume rendering that was a hybrid between classical object order and image order techniques. Additionally, in order to further improve the visual image effect, a generative model [1] which transformed transfer functions into a view-invariant latent space for users to interact and analyze volume rendering images.

3   Our Methods

Traditional one-dimensional TF editors usually adopt the method of distributing the attribute value evenly. Only one TF or TF-let can be loaded in one exploration time. Repeated editing TFs for an identical data makes the exploration tedious and inefficiently. In order to help users to get optimal visualization results and shorten the time of trial-and-error exploration process, a histogram-based nonlinear TF is designed. Fast loading, reloading and unloading individual single TF-lets are easy to achieve in our method, which makes the TF-let fusion more efficiently.

Figure 3 shows the pipeline of the proposed approach. First, the raw data are processed into volume data. Second, the volume visualization algorithm transforms the volume data into visualization results. Third, users conduct adjustment by nonlinear TF editing. The nonlinear histogram can give users visual cues for

the exploration. It lowers the sensitivity and promotes efficiency. All TF-lets will
be serialized for reloading and the subsequent analytics. Fourth, in the TF-lets
fusion stage, users can get an arbitrary combination of the results rendered by
multiple TF-lets. For example, users can use a focus + contexts technique to
view multiple focus tissues together with their context environments simultaneously. Besides, they can also remove any tissue or corresponding contexts by
double clicking the TF-let node.

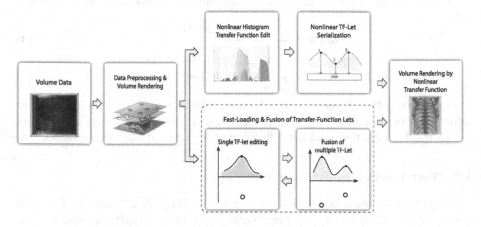

Fig. 3. Pipeline of the proposed approach. The raw data are preprocessed into a vol-
ume. Users adjust nonlinear TFs with visual cues provided by nonlinear histogram. All
TF-Lets are serialized into disks. They will be deserialized for fast reloading. Several
TF-Lets can be fused into a final TF in a focus-and-contexts way.eps

3.1 Histogram-Based Nonlinear Transfer Function

Traditional transfer functions map attribute values and ranges evenly on the
TF editor. The adjustment of TFs especially for the tuning of control points
is time-consuming. Thus, we design a nonlinear TF equipped with non-uniform
histograms to provide some visual cues and decrease the adjustment sensitivity
of control points.

The histogram has 256 bins. To reduce visual clutter, we just render 32
girds for 256 histogram bins. Each grid represents 8 bins. During the process
of preprocessing volume data, we should compute the histogram of the volume
data. The larger the bin size is, the wider the corresponding histogram bin will
be drawn. The bin widths can be computed as follows:

$$binWidth[i] = \frac{b_i}{b_1 + b_2 + \cdots + b_n} * widgetWidth, i \in n \qquad (2)$$

where b_i means the size of each bin.

The vertical axis of nonlinear TF editor stands for opacity, that is α value. Sometimes, the range of one attribute is so small, which make it difficulty getting a reasonable density range values for it when using traditional TF hardly give users visual cues. A nonlinear mapping of the horizontal axis is designed for magnifying the widths where bin size is large.

Furthermore, we also magnify the width of vertical axis at low scale values, because alpha values for most attributes in volume data should be assigned to be a relatively low value, e.g., between 0.0 and 0.1.

The transform between control points and nonlinear coordinates are as shown below:

$$coord = \frac{e^{-a*(1-control\ point)} - e^{-a}}{1 - e^{-a}} \tag{3}$$

$$control\ point = 1.0 + \frac{1.0}{a} * \lg\left((1 - e^{-a}) * mouse + e^{-a}\right) \tag{4}$$

where a means the degree of magnification. The higher a is, the wider the low value parts of nonlinear TFs will be. In this way, the workspace of low opacity values will be amplified, and the efficiency of adjustment will be improved.

3.2   Fast Loading of Transfer Functions

Users often need some fast serialization and deserialization function of control points to help them to explore the volume data. For example, medical experts need to shift among the rendering results of different tissues. With the traditional TF editor, users can only load one TF at a time, and cannot shift among the different visualization results. We notice that many tissues in medical data can be extracted by a wavelet-like TF, we call it TF-let.

When users get optimal rendering results by a TF-let, they can serialize all color schemes into disks for the subsequent loading with the aid of the functionalities of fast loading and reloading. The interface for the fast loading function is designed to be a two-dimension region, which is designed in the bottom part of TF editor, as shown in Fig. 4. One TF-let node appears when the user decides to serialize the TF control points data and load it, and the vertical coordinates (with absolute values) of each node represents the maximum opacity of the control points in the corresponding TF-let.

3.3   Fusion of Multiple TF-lets

We also design a focus and contexts visualization technique to explore the volume data by TF-lets fusion. We take medical data as an example. If users want to explore the neighboring soft tissues (contexts) when they view the blood vessel (focus attribute), they can click the corresponding TF-let node to add it into the final fused TF, as shown in Fig. 4.

Besides, they can also double-click one of multiple TF-let nodes to remove it from the final fused TF when users do not want to see the corresponding

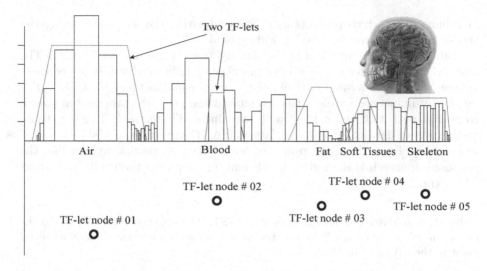

Fig. 4. The illustration of histogram-based nonlinear TF editor. The bin widths of the histogram are computed by the corresponding bin sizes. A TF-let in the illustration can represent one attribute (e.g., one tissue) of the volume data. The leftmost TF-let represents air while the rightmost one represents skeleton. The nonlinear scheme makes the TF adjustment less sensitive and more efficient. Each TF-let has its own TF-node for fast loading and fusion.

attribute in the final rendering results. The fusion process including adding TF-let node and removing TF-let node is efficient in our nonlinear TF editor because the individual single TF-lets are serialized and saved in advance.

4   Evaluation

We evaluate the proposed approach by sensitivity test and performance test for three different datasets. Furthermore, we also find that, the proposed approach can get more detailed and accurate results in some occasions, compared with the traditional linear TF methods [7–10,16].

In our experiments, we test our method on three different medical datasets, including dataset CHEST, dataset HEAD and dataset HAND. The resolution of the dataset CHEST is $120 \times 192 \times 192$, the dataset HEAD is $256 \times 256 \times 255$, and the dataset HAND is $244 \times 124 \times 257$, respectively.

4.1   Sensitivity Test

We conducted three sensitivity tests to measure the sensitivity of control points assignment. As mentioned above, the sensitivity refers to the average number of influenced voxels, when users move control points to left/right equal-distantly. It reveals the sensitivity to the perturbations of control point's position. In the dataset HEAD, attribute values and ranges of air account for a great proportion of volume data, which prevents users from adjusting the TF. Thus, we ignore the air parts by narrowing the bin widths of air.

Table 1 shows the result of the sensitivity test for the dataset CHEST. The sensitivity values refer to the average number of influenced voxels in the chest volume when users move a control point a given equal-distance to the left. The number of influenced voxels is much smaller when using the proposed approach compared with that using the traditional linear TF method. The sensitivity test results of dataset HEAD and dataset HAND are shown in Tables 2 and 3, respectively. From the three groups of sensitivity test results, we can find the proposed approach is insensitive to TF editing compared the traditional linear TF method.

Table 1. Sensitivity test for the dataset CHEST. The sensitivity values refer to the average number of influenced voxels in the chest volume data when users move a control point to the left equal-distantly.

Control points	Control point #01	Control point #02	Control point #03
Traditional linear TF	2.87	5.57	2.53
Our approach	0.77	0.78	0.76

Table 2. Sensitivity test for the dataset HEAD. The sensitivity values refer to the average number of influenced voxels in the head volume data when users move a control point to the left equal-distantly.

Control points	Control point #01	Control point #02	Control point #03
Traditional linear TF	0.02	0.03	0.03
Our approach	0.01	0.02	0.01

Table 3. Sensitivity test for the dataset HAND. The sensitivity values refer to the average number of influenced voxels in the hand volume data when users move a control point to the left equal-distantly.

Control points	Control point #01	Control point #02	Control point #03
Traditional linear TF	0.34	1.44	0.18
Our approach	0.13	0.13	0.13

4.2 Performance Test

We have also conducted the performance tests for the proposed approach compared with the traditional linear TF method. We obtain the comparative timing results of both methods. We take the dataset HAND as an example. First, we test the time to get the rendering results of bones and vessels separately by the traditional linear TF for comparison. Second, for the reason that the editing of each single TF-let in our method needs to be done only once, we test the time of the two TF-lets editing, respectively. The two TF-lets are the TF-let of bones and the TF-let of vessels. Then, the timing results of the fusion process based on the two single TF-lets are obtained. Third, we calculate the total editing time of two single TF-lets and compare it with the time of the traditional linear TF method.

We find that the traditional linear TF method takes almost twice as long as our method, as shown in Table 4. Using traditional linear TF method, the average time of five users took is 98.8 s. The average time of the proposed approach is 57.2 s. The time of the traditional method is about 1.7 times of the proposed approach. Additionally, the average time of TF fusion process is 2.1 s.

Table 4. Performance comparison (in seconds) between traditional linear TF methods [7–10,16] and the proposed approach. The exploration of the TF-lets needs to be done only once. Next time users can just load the TF-lets saved before and do some minor adjustments. In this case, users can get the fusion done in seconds without editing once again. Therefore, the whole progress is accelerated greatly. The "T_s" means the total time of two single TF-lets editing, which is the sum of "TF-Let of Bone" and "TF-Let of Vessel".

Users	Traditional linear TF	TF-let of bones	TF-let of vessels	T_s	TF fusion
User #01	96.62	25.16	40.22	65.38	1.83
User #02	97.45	27.14	20.72	47.86	2.37
User #03	95.76	21.18	28.25	49.43	1.93
User #04	87.20	20.40	22.04	42.44	2.28
User #05	116.90	25.72	44.73	70.45	2.28

4.3 Case Study

In our performance test, the proposed approach performs better in fine-tuning than the traditional linear TF method. It is hard for users to find the outlines of some tissues of the dataset HEAD, such as the nose, mouth, etc. The corresponding results rendered by the traditional linear TF method and the proposed approach are show in Fig. 5(a) and (b). Similarly, it is hard to find the clumps which are probably some lesions on the surface of the chest in the dataset CHEST, because the attribute ranges of these tissues are quite small, as shown in Fig. 5(c) and (d).

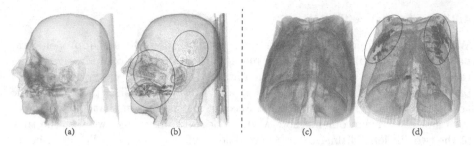

Fig. 5. Evaluation cases for dataset HEAD and dataset CHEST. It is easy to get some interesting results by the proposed approach, while it is quite hard for users to get the similar results by the linear method. (a) The rendering result of the dataset HEAD using the traditional linear TF method. (b) The rendering result of the dataset HEAD using the proposed approach. The outline of the various tissues in the red circles are much more clear. (c) The rendering result of the dataset CHEST using the linear method. (d) The rendering result of the dataset CHEST using the proposed approach. Users can find some clumps which are probably some lesions in the red circles on the surface of the chest. (Color figure online)

Furthermore, it is difficult to get the blood vessels by the traditional linear TF method in dataset HAND because the attribute range of blood vessels is quite small. The results of the blood vessels rendered by two users through the traditional linear TF method, as shown in Fig. 6(a) and (b). In our approach, users can get the TF-lets of the blood vessels first. Then, they can add the

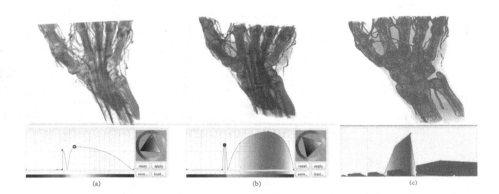

Fig. 6. Evaluation case for dataset HAND. (a)–(b) The traditional linear TF editing results illustrated by two users for the dataset HAND. They tried to get the blood vessels in try-and-error way. They find it difficulty to get an optimal result. It is time-consuming for them to get these two results. (c) The proposed approach are used by users to find the blood vessels. It is easy for all of the five users to get such a much more clear result compared with that extracted by the traditional method. Besides, we can also find the contexts of blood vessels are more clear, i.e., the contours and structures of the bones.

TF-let to the fusion result. Therefore, users can see the tissue of the blood vessels clearly in the final result. The result rendered by the proposed approach is shown in Fig. 6(c).

5   Results

The experiments are performed on a workstation. The workstation is with the configuration of Intel Core i7-6700 CPUs operating at 2.70 GHz and 16 GB RAM. In Sect. 5.1, we will see how the so-called TF-let works. The results achieved by fusing multiple TF-lets will be shown in Sect. 5.2.

5.1   Results of Fast-Loading of Single TF-Let

Users can get a rendering result rendered by serialized TF-lets if they saved the corresponding TF-lets before. We take medical data as an example. The TF-lets of all tissues can be serialized and saved to disk individually. Users can view any tissue in the dataset efficiently by clicking the TF-let node. However, when users load a new dataset, it needs users to explore the data and find the individual TF-lets for all tissues. In our evaluation, we find the time to obtain multiple TF-lets is about 59% of that spent on the traditional method when finding the same tissues, because the traditional method needs to explore multiple tissues simultaneously.

Figure 7(a) shows the single TF-let of the thorax in the dataset CHEST. By clicking the corresponding TF-let node, the rendered result shown in Fig. 7(b) is loaded. The three single TF-lets of the chest bones, the hand bones, and the skull are shown in Fig. 7(c), (e), and (g), respectively. The corresponding rendering results are shown in Fig. 7(d), (f), and (h).

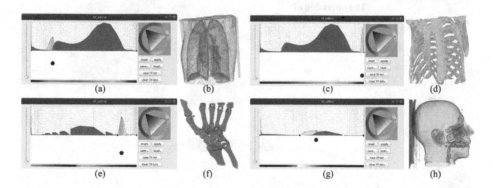

Fig. 7. (a) The single TF-Let of the thorax in the dataset CHEST. (b) The rendering result of the thorax by TF-let in (a). (c) The single TF-Let of the chest bones in the dataset CHEST. (d) The rendering result of the chest bones by TF-let in (c). (e) The single TF-Let of the hand bones in the dataset HAND. (f) The rendering result of the hand bones by TF-let in (e). (g) The single TF-Let of the skull in the dataset HEAD. (h) The rendering result of the skull by TF-let in (g).

5.2   Results of TF-Lets Fusion

In the TF-lets fusion stage, users can get an arbitrary combination of the results rendered by multiple TF-lets. For example, users can use a focus + contexts technique to view multiple focus tissues together with their context environments simultaneously. Furthermore, they can also remove any tissue or corresponding context by double clicking the TF-let node. Therefore, it is efficient to perform the fusion steps due to the fast click and double click actions.

In our experiment, we test the proposed fusion approach on all the three datasets. Figure 8 shows the fusion result of the skin, the blood vessels, and the bones of the dataset HAND. The three single results on the left of Fig. 8 refer to the tissues of the skin, the blood vessels, and bones of the hand. If users want to see the bones (focus) with the blood vessels (contexts) and except for the skin, they can remove the attribute (the skin) by simply clicking the corresponding TF-let node in the transfer function editor. Then they can get the final fusion result of the blood vessels and the bones. The fusion result of the skin and bones of the dataset HEAD is shown in Fig. 9(a), while the fusion result of the thorax and chest bone of the dataset CHEST is shown in Fig. 9(b).

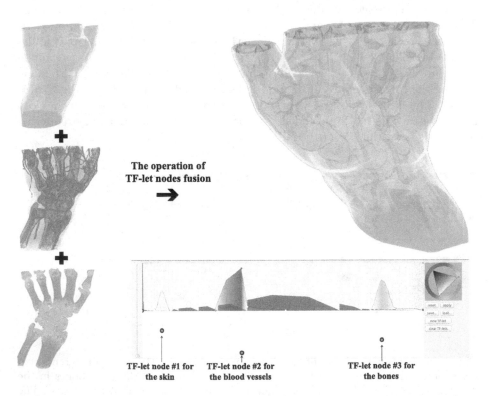

The operation of
TF-let nodes fusion

→

TF-let node #1 for
the skin

TF-let node #2 for
the blood vessels

TF-let node #3 for
the bones

Fig. 8. The fusion result of the skin, blood vessels, and bones of the dataset HAND. Users just need to click the three TF-let nodes for the skin, blood vessels and bones to achieve the final fusion results.

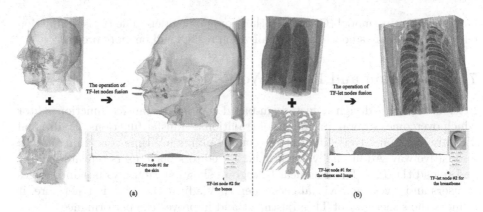

Fig. 9. (a) The fusion result of skin and bones of the dataset HEAD. Users just need to click the two TF-let nodes for the skin and bones to achieve the final fusion results. (b) The fusion result of thorax (together with lungs) and breastbone of the dataset CHEST. Users also just need to click the two TF-let nodes for the thorax and chest bone to achieve the final fusion results.

Actually, users can get an arbitrary fusion combination by specifying multiple focus tissues and multiple context tissues efficiently, because they just need to click the corresponding TF-let nodes to achieve it.

6   Discussion

The proposed nonlinear TF is capable of satisfying users' editing requirements. Fast loading and Fusion of multiple TFs save users' time and improve efficiency. However, there are still some limitations in our approach.

First, the background histogram in our transfer function design is just to provide users with visual cues about the sensitivity. The higher the histogram bin value is, the more sensitive the TF editing will be. The problem is every single model (i.e., a peak) of the histogram is inconsistent with an attribute (e.g., a tissue) in the volume data in general. That is to say, we can not get the TF-let range of one attribute directly according to the background histogram.

Second, although we can save much time when users use single TF-let, it still needs users to get each optimal TF-let for a new dataset in a trial-and-error way. For a given dataset, users can serialize the satisfied TF-lets after the trial-and-error editing, which can be used to fast reload the TF-lets in a new exploration process. In the future, we plan to use the machine learning methods to provide a visual guidance about how to get the range of a TF-let efficiently for a new dataset, or recommend several TF-let range choices for users.

Third, the current TF fusion is a little bit straight-forward because we use a simple adding scheme, which just adds the control points from one TF-let into another. Although the simple adding scheme can achieve greatest rendered results, some detailed information may be missing especially for the overlapping area between two TF-lets. In the future, we plan to implement the TF fusion based on

Gaussian mixture model (GMM) or other complex models. The transfer function curves can be more smooth, and visualization results will be more precise.

7   Conclusion and Future Work

In this work, we design a histogram-based nonlinear transfer function editor which overcomes several limitations of traditional transfer functions. Traditional TFs are linear and the editing of the control points are time-consuming and in a sensitive way. Additionally, traditional TF editors make users repeatedly load and reload the TFs. The nonlinear histogram shows attribute values and ranges to users and gives them visual cues when they adjust the TFs. Furthermore, it reduces the sensitivity of TF adjustment and improves the performance.

The single TF-let is proposed for fast loading and fusion of multiple TF-lets. Users can switch between different transfer functions without repeated loading. The fusion of TFs enables to visualize multiple focus tissues and multiple contexts (neighbouring tissues) in an arbitrary combination. In the future, we plan to introduce machine learning method and Gaussian mixture model (GMM) in our TF editor to boost TF adjustment efficiency and get more accurate visualization results.

Acknowledgments. This work was supported by the National Nature Science Foundation of China (NSFC) Grant Nos. 61702271, 41971343, and 61702270. The authors would like to thank Lei Xiao, Zhiqi Zhang and Yelai Sun for participating in the contrast experiment and giving feedbacks. The authors also would like to thank Rongtao Qian who helped to proofread the paper.

References

1. Berger, M., Li, J., Levine, J.A.: A generative model for volume rendering. IEEE Trans. Vis. Comput. Graph. **25**(4), 1636–1650 (2019)
2. Binyahib, R., Peterka, T., Larsen, M., Ma, K.L., Childs, H.: A scalable hybrid scheme for ray-casting of unstructured volume data. IEEE Trans. Vis. Comput. Graph. **25**(7), 2349–2361 (2018)
3. Blaas, J., Botha, C.P., Post, F.H.: Interactive visualization of multi-field medical data using linked physical and feature-space views. In: EuroVis, pp. 123–130 (2007)
4. Blake, N., Kirby, R.M., Robert, H.: GPU-based volume visualization from high-order finite element fields. IEEE Trans. Vis. Comput. Graph. **20**(1), 70–83 (2014)
5. Ebert, D., Morris, C., Rheingans, P., Yoo, T.: Designing effective transfer functions for volume rendering from photographic volumes. IEEE Trans. Vis. Comput. Graph. **8**(2), 183–197 (2002)
6. Fang, S., Biddlecome, T., Tuceryan, M.: Image-based transfer function design for data exploration in volume visualization. In: IEEE Visualization, pp. 319–326, October 1998
7. Gao, M., et al.: Interactive geological visualization based on quadratic-surface distance query. J. Electron. Imaging **28**(2), 021009 (2019)
8. Guo, H., Mao, N., Yuan, X.: WYSIWYG (what you see is what you get) volume visualization. IEEE Trans. Vis. Comput. Graph. **17**(12), 2106 (2011)

9. Guo, H., Xiao, H., Yuan, X.: Multi-dimensional transfer function design based on flexible dimension projection embedded in parallel coordinates. In: IEEE Pacific Visualization Symposium, pp. 19–26, March 2011
10. Guo, H., Xiao, H., Yuan, X.: Scalable multivariate volume visualization and analysis based on dimension projection and parallel coordinates. IEEE Trans. Vis. Comput. Graph. **18**(9), 1397–1410 (2012)
11. Guo, H., Yuan, X.: Survey on transfer function in volume visualization. J. Comput.-Aided Des. Comput. Graph. **24**(10), 1249–1258 (2012)
12. He, T., Pfister, L.H.A.K.H.: Generation of transfer functions with stochastic searchtechniques. In: The 7th Annual IEEE Visualization (1996)
13. Igouchkine, O., Zhang, Y., Ma, K.L.: Multi-material volume rendering with a physically-based surface reflection model. IEEE Trans. Vis. Comput. Graph. **24**(12), 3147–3159 (2018)
14. Kniss, J., Kindlmann, G., Hansen, C.: Interactive volume rendering using multi-dimensional transfer functions and direct manipulation widgets. In: IEEE VIS (2001)
15. Kniss, J., Kindlmann, G., Hansen, C.D.: 9-multidimensional transfer functions for volume rendering. Vis. Hand. **8**(3), 189–209 (2005)
16. Liu, R., Chen, S., Ji, G., Zhao, B., Li, Q., Su, M.: Interactive stratigraphic structure visualization for seismic data. J. Vis. Lang. Comput. **48**(2018), 81–90 (2018)
17. Liu, R., Guo, H., Yuan, X.: Seismic structure extraction based on multi-scale sensitivity analysis. J. Vis. **17**, 157–166 (2014)
18. Liu, R., Guo, H., Yuan, X.: A bottom-up scheme for user-defined feature comparison in ensemble data. In: ACM SIGGRAPH Asia 2015 Symposium on Visualization in High Performance Computing (2015)
19. Liu, R., Guo, H., Yuan, X.: User-defined feature comparison for vector field ensembles. J. Vis. **20**, 217–229 (2017)
20. Liu, R., Guo, H., Zhang, J., Yuan, X.: Comparative visualization of vector field ensembles based on longest common subsequence. In: IEEE Pacific Visualization Symposium (2016)
21. Lu, A., Ebert, D.S.: Example-based volume illustrations. In: IEEE VIS (2005)
22. Läthén, G., Lindholm, S., Lenz, R., Persson, A., Borga, M.: Automatic tuning of spatially varying transfer functions for blood vessel visualization. IEEE Trans. Vis. Comput. Graph. **18**(12), 2345–2354 (2012)
23. Ma, B., Entezari, A.: Volumetric feature-based classification and visibility analysis for transfer function design. IEEE Trans. Vis. Comput. Graph. **24**(12), 3253–3267 (2018)
24. Marks, J., et al.: Design galleries: a general approach to setting parameters for computer graphics and animation. In: ACM SIGGRAPH (1997)
25. Pfister, H., et al.: The transfer function bake-off. IEEE Comput. Graph. Appl. **21**(3), 16–22 (2001)
26. Ropinski, T., Praßni, J., Steinicke, F., Hinrichs, K.: Stroke-based transfer function design. In: The IEEE/EG Symposium on Volume and Point-Based Graphics, pp. 41–48 (2010)
27. Sereda, P., Bartroli, A., Serlie, I., Gerritsen, F.: Visualization of boundaries in volumetric data sets using lh histograms. IEEE Trans. Vis. Comput. Graph. **12**(2), 208 (2006)
28. Wiebel, A., Vos, F.M., Foerster, D., Hege, H.C.: WYSIWYP: what you see is what you pick. IEEE Trans. Vis. Comput. Graph. **18**(12), 2236–2244 (2012)
29. Yuan, X., Nguyen, M.Z., Chen, B., Porter, D.H.: High dynamic range volume visualization. In: IEEE VIS (2005)

Realistic Modeling of Tree Ramifications from an Optimal Manifold Control Mesh

Zhengyu Huang[1], Zhiyi Zhang[1], Nan Geng[1], Long Yang[1],
Dongjian He[2], and Shaojun Hu[1(✉)]

[1] College of Information Engineering,
Northwest A&F University, Yangling, China
hsj@nwsuaf.edu.cn
[2] College of Mechanical and Electronic Engineering,
Northwest A&F University, Yangling, China

Abstract. Modeling realistic branches and ramifications of trees is a challenging task because of their complex geometric structures. Many approaches have been proposed to generate plausible tree models from images, sketches, point clouds, and botanical rules. However, most approaches focus on a global impression of trees, such as the topological structure of branches and arrangement of leaves, without taking continuity of branch ramifications into consideration. To model a complete tree quadrilateral mesh (quad-mesh) with smooth ramifications, we propose an optimization method to calculate a suitable control mesh for Catmull–Clark subdivision. Given a tree's skeleton information, we build a local coordinate system for each joint node, and orient each node appropriately based on the angle between a parent branch and its child branch. Then, we create the corresponding basic ramification units using a cuboid-like quad-mesh, which is mapped back to the world coordinate. To obtain a suitable manifold initial control mesh as a main mesh, the ramifications are classified into main and additional ramifications, and a bottom-up optimization approach is applied to adjust the positions of the main ramification units when they connect their neighbors. Next, the first round of Catmull–Clark subdivision is applied to the main ramifications. The additional ramifications, which were selected to alleviate visual distortion in the preceding step, are added back to the main mesh using a cut-paste operation. Finally, the second round of Catmull–Clark subdivision is used to generate the final quad-mesh of the entire tree. The results demonstrated that our method generated a realistic tree quad-mesh effectively from different tree skeletons.

Keywords: Tree quad-mesh · Construction optimization · Catmull–Clark subdivision · Manifold tree modeling

1 Introduction

In computer graphics, tree modeling and animation have wide applications in the fields of film production, video games, and virtual reality because plants increase

© Springer Nature Switzerland AG 2019
Y. Zhao et al. (Eds.): ICIG 2019, LNCS 11902, pp. 316–332, 2019.
https://doi.org/10.1007/978-3-030-34110-7_27

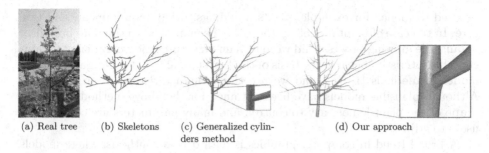

(a) Real tree   (b) Skeletons   (c) Generalized cylin-   (d) Our approach
                                   ders method

Fig. 1. Prevailing apple tree modeling using our approach. In comparison with (a), the tree model in (d) with (b) is a manifold quad-mesh that takes the continuity of branch ramifications into consideration, inherently compensating for the disadvantages of (c).

the realism of virtual scenery. In the past three decades, many approaches have been presented to achieve the realistic modeling and animation of trees. Tree modeling methods can be categorized into rule-based methods [13,21,23,24], sketch-based methods [17], image-based method [10,26], and modeling methods from point clouds [9,14]. However, most of these studies concentrated on modeling the global morphology of trees, including the complex branch structures and botanical arrangement of leaves. A typical simplified structure to represent tree branches is a generalized cylinder. Many studies in the animation of tree growth [19] and swaying in wind fields [7,8,13,20] also use the same simplified structure to represent bending branch joints.

Although generalized cylinders are efficient and superior in terms of realism in tree modeling, the discontinuity between branches for generalized cylinder representation is obvious, as shown in the close-up in Fig. 1(c). This discontinuity of branches is easy to solve if implicit surface representation is adopted, but this is difficult to control interactively.

The motivation of our work is to create a complete manifold quadrilateral mesh (quad-mesh) effectively, as shown in Fig. 1(d), from user-defined skeletons of a tree (Fig. 1(b)) using Catmull–Clark subdivision for continuous ramification construction, thereby overcoming the drawbacks of both generalized cylinders and implicit surfaces. This study makes two main contributions:

- We propose a method to generate a tree model effectively with smooth ramifications that combines subdivision surface construction with parametric surface construction.
- We propose an optimization algorithm for a tree's control mesh construction using user-defined skeletons.

2 Related Work

The earliest developed plant models were procedural models, which generate content using a procedure that has the function of database amplification and can be used to model, for example, plants, buildings, urban environment, and texture. In the case of plant modeling, they have been applied to simulate botanical organs, the growing process, and various plant structures. Self-organizing parameter characteristics became the basis of the L-system [22] and self-organizing tree modeling methods [18,28], and we use those characteristics in our approach. Although plausible models have been obtained for the above methods, the final shape of the plant is not easy to control, and many parameters are complex for users to adjust.

A broad trend in computer graphics is data-driven synthesis, where models are created based on real-world measurements, such as those in images or laser scans of geometry. Tan et al. [26] proposed a method of combining input images with user interaction in the construction of trees. Hu et al. [10] modeled trees based on two images from different views with polar constraints for animation using a physical model. Livny et al. [15] reconstructed multiple overlapping trees from point clouds simultaneously without pre-segmentation by applying a series of global optimization-based biologically derived heuristics. Such methods can be extremely effective; however, they are often intended for geometric reconstruction. Hence, maintaining the continuity of ramifications is beyond their scope.

Implicit surface tree modeling is other popular method, which began with an idea presented by Bloomenthal [3]. Compared with parametric surfaces, implicit surfaces are difficult to control and time-consuming, but owing well continuity, noise-resistant, performing Boolean operation easily. There are many types of implicit surfaces, including the convolution surface, which is defined as an iso-surface in a scalar field that convolves a geometric skeleton using a kernel function [4]. An interesting application of the convolution surface is modeling sketch-based models [1,25,32], which takes advantage of the rotundity and smoothness of convolution surfaces, which is suitable for tree branches. Another type of typical implicit surface is the Poisson surface [12], which concludes surface reconstruction using Poisson's equation.

There has also been some effort to model smooth joint structures on both parametric surfaces and implicit surfaces for trees (not for botanical trees only). Tobler et al. [27] combined generalized subdivision with mesh-based parameterized L-systems to generate smooth ramification structures. Felkel et al. [5] generated topologically correct surfaces of branching tubular structures for a vessel tree using the maximal-disc interpolation method. Galbraith et al. [6] built implicit surfaces as hierarchical BlobTrees [30] and combined surface components in both smooth and non-smooth configurations. Angles et al. [2] proposed an interactive method to refine the joint shape using a user-defined sketch.

Zhu et al. [31] proposed a method of modeling high-quality quad-only tree shapes efficiently based on local convolution surface approximation, which offer credible for our idea of modeling manifold trees with smooth ramifications. However, they focused on remeshing a given triangle mesh of a tree into a quad-mesh. Another solution for continuous vascular structure reconstruction was proposed by [29]. The resulting meshes were not manifold because of the bifurcation tiling scheme in their method, whereas our meshes are manifold because we adopt the cut-paste process.

Although the works of [5] and [29] are similar to our work, the ramifications of botanical trees we attempt to reconstruct possess their own features.

3   Overview

The final aim of our work is to create a manifold tree quad-mesh with tolerable visual distortion and smooth ramifications, which is described by the following objective function:

$$f(Rems) = \sum_{i=1}^{N} RU(Rems_i) + \sum RC(Rem_{i,j}) + \sum CP(Rem_{i,k}), \quad (1)$$

where $Rems$ denotes the set of all ramifications in a tree extracted from the skeleton information of branches, and is regarded as an independent variable in the objective function. Sub-objective function RU is the distortion function of the ramification unit for Catmull–Clark subdivision. $Rems_i$ is the i-th ramification in the set $Rems$. Sub-objective function RC is the distortion function of the ramification connection between two neighbor ramifications. $Rem_{i,j}$ is the connection between the i-th ramification and j-th ramification. Sub-objective function CP (cut-paste) is the fitness function of the pasted ramification between two overlapping ramifications. $Rem_{i,k}$ is the i-th ramification merged with the k-th ramification.

Hence, we convert the problem into creating a tree model with minimum $f(Rems)$. Figure 2 shows the workflow of our tree modeling system, which consists of three parts.

First, skeletons of a tree are defined by the user. Then, basic ramification units, which can represent continuous ramification structures after Catmull–Clark subdivision, are created with an RU value equal to zero as the initial state using the skeleton information of branches in the local coordinate system, thereby

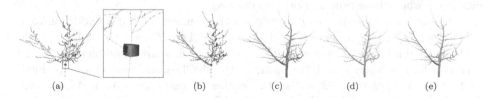

(a)   (b)   (c)   (d)   (e)

Fig. 2. Overview of our tree modeling approach. (a) Users define the skeleton information of branches. Extract the close-up of one ramification skeleton and create a basic ramification unit. (b) Propagate ramifications for a single ramification unit. (c) Connect ramification units using an optimization algorithm and distinguish the additional ramifications from the main mesh simultaneously. (d) Subdivide the main mesh to which the additional ramifications are pasted back. (e) Obtain the final mesh with one more subdivision.

setting their parent node as the origin. The ramification units are mapped back to the world coordinate system. This part of the procedure is described in Sect. 4.

Once all ramifications are arranged, they can be easily sorted according to the order of their parent nodes and checked to determine whether they are connectable ramifications or additional ramifications. A bottom-up optimization algorithm is applied recursively to adjust all connections among connectable ramifications, thereby striking a balance between the RU and RC functions in addition to making the ramification propagate. We obtain the main mesh of the tree at the end of this step. The details of this part of the procedure are described in Sect. 5.

If there exist any additional ramifications, then this means that some child branches that could destroy the manifold of the tree mesh have been detected. They should be cut and pasted into the main mesh after its first Catmull–Clark subdivision. The CP function indicates the distortion in this operation as discussed in Sect. 6. In addition, the reason why we select Catmull–Clark subdivision scheme is that Catmull–Clark subdivision can generate smooth surface for trees with keeping the symmetry from its control meshes, which means it would not introduce extra distortion into tree models. The details of discussion about subdivision scheme selection are discussed in the appendix.

4   Basic Branch Unit Creation

Figure 3 shows two typical basic ramification units: the connection unit shown in Fig. 3(a) is for those segments of branches that do not have any child branches, whereas the ramification unit in Fig. 3(b) is for a child branch that has start direction $(cv_1 - cv_0)$ located in the i-th node bv_i of its parent branch, counted from the root node.

For the connection unit between bv_i and bv_{i+1}, DS_i is the unit start direction that is the same as $(bv_{i+1} - bv_i)$, and DE_i is the unit end direction. Additionally, $S_j(j = 0, 1, 2, 3)$ denotes the vertices of the start boundary and E_j denotes the vertices of the end boundary. They are created by basis $\{B, N, DS_i\}$. Both the start and end boundaries of ramifications are sorted clockwise when these ramifications are created.

The ramification unit is an expansion of the connection unit, in addition to a sub-branch. Q is the intersection of main face $ABCD$ and the child branch skeleton. Subface $abcd$ is also called a sub-branch start boundary, which is recorded for boundary calculation using Catmull–Clark subdivision as explained in Sect. 6. At this step, Q is also the center of main face $A_0A_1A_2A_3$, and Q', which superposes Q, is the center of subface $a_0a_1a_2a_3$. The sum of cosine distances between the pairs of vectors is selected as the RU function, that is,

$$RU(Rems_i) = \sum_{k=0}^{3} CosDistance(QA_k, Q'a_k) = \sum_{k=0}^{3} \frac{QA_k \cdot Q'a_k}{\|QA_k\| \cdot \|Q'a_k\|}. \quad (2)$$

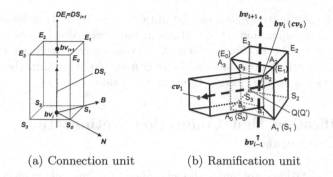

(a) Connection unit   (b) Ramification unit

Fig. 3. Two typical basic branch units created according the skeleton

4.1 Criteria

A suitable basic ramification unit plays a large role in ramification representation. Taking the properties of Catmull–Clark subdivision into consideration, the following criteria should be satisfied naturally for high-quality tree quad-mesh construction.

1. A ramification unit is created corresponding to a subbranch.
2. Each RU value of the ramification unit when it is built is zero (the minimum value) initially because this value will be increased in the subsequent connection optimization step, so a zero value simplifies the calculation.
3. The diameter of a branch should be multiplied by correction factor α to counteract the shrinkage caused by Catmull–Clark subdivision (particularly the first two subdivisions).

4.2 Ramification Unit in the Local Coordinate System

Let $\{\boldsymbol{X}, \boldsymbol{Y}, \boldsymbol{Z}\}$ denote the basis of the world coordinate system in $\boldsymbol{R}^3$, in which the skeletons of all branches from a tree are user-defined. Local coordinate systems with basis $\{\boldsymbol{x}, \boldsymbol{y}, \boldsymbol{z}\}$ can be built for each child branch, and their mapping to the world coordinate system is decomposed into one 1×3 translation vector $\boldsymbol{T}_0$, and two 3×3 rotation matrices $\boldsymbol{Rot1}$ and $\boldsymbol{Rot2}$. Given a vector in the world coordinate system, $\boldsymbol{P}$, and a vector in a local coordinate system, $\boldsymbol{p}$, we have the following surjective mapping equations:

$$p = \boldsymbol{Rot2} \cdot \boldsymbol{Rot1} \cdot (\boldsymbol{P} - \boldsymbol{T}_0) \qquad (3)$$

$$P = \boldsymbol{Rot1}^T \cdot \boldsymbol{Rot2}^T \cdot \boldsymbol{p} + \boldsymbol{T}_0, \qquad (4)$$

where $\boldsymbol{T}_0$ is $\boldsymbol{bv}_i$ in Fig. 3; $\boldsymbol{Rot1}$ is the rotation matrix calculated by the Rodrigues rotation formula to make the parent branch direction $(\boldsymbol{bv}_{i+1} - \boldsymbol{bv}_i)$ aligned to the $\boldsymbol{y}$ axis, whereas $\boldsymbol{Rot2}$ makes $\boldsymbol{y} \times (\boldsymbol{cv}_1 - \boldsymbol{cv}_0)$ aligned to $\boldsymbol{x}$. Then ramification unit Rem_i, such as that in Fig. 3(b), contains set of vertices V_{local}, and set of faces F is built in this local system. Then, according to Eq. 4, Rem_i

in the world coordinate system can be obtained easily by translating V_{local} to V, which is a corresponding set of vertices in the world coordinate system. With the help of the local coordinate system, it becomes trivial to check whether the neighbor ramifications are connectable by converting them into the same local coordinate system and projecting them into the same plane.

5   Ramification Unit Connection Optimization and Propagation

After all ramifications are built and classified, we link all connectable ramifications first using a connection optimization algorithm to alleviate distinct distortion among ramifications. Thus, we should first distinguish connectable ramifications from additional ramifications.

If a node has more than one child branch, then one child branch is selected to create a ramification as the "current ramification", and the other branches are checked to determine whether they are additional ramifications, as shown in Fig. 4. According to the shape of the ramification unit, there are two cases in which a child branch can be considered as an additional ramification:

1. The absolute value of the angle between two projected vectors of the child branch in the current ramification modulo 45° is smaller than 10° (Fig. 4(a)).
2. Q and Q', which are the intersection points of two child branches on the current ramification, are not on the same face (Fig. 4(b)).

In this section, sub-objective functions RU and RC must be considered simultaneously. Thus, f_2, which is the objective function in this step, is

$$f_2(Rems) = \sum_{i=1}^{N} RU(Rems_i) + \sum RC(Rem_{i,j}). \tag{5}$$

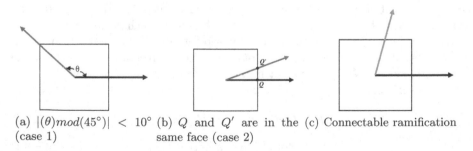

(a) $|(\theta)mod(45°)| < 10°$ (b) Q and Q' are in the (c) Connectable ramification
(case 1)   same face (case 2)

Fig. 4. Distinguishing the ramification type in the transverse view of the ramification unit cross section (black square). The black arrow is the projected vector of the child branch in the current ramification. The red arrow is that in the additional ramification. The blue arrow is that in the connectable ramification, which can be attached to the current ramification trivially before the subdivision step. (Color figure online)

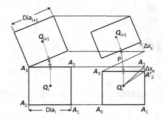

Fig. 5. Axial equilibrium between two connectable ramifications

To determine the minimum value, we divide this task into two independent parts: a radial neighbor ramification connection and axial connection calibration with repulsion equilibrium.

The radial neighbor ramification connection attempts to determine corresponding adjacent start and end boundaries between neighbor ramifications along the directions of skeletons:

$$Idx = argmin \sum_{k=0}^{m-1} CosDistance(CE_k^{(i)}, CS_{(k+Idx)mod(m)}^{(i+1)}), \tag{6}$$

where $CE_k^{(i)}$ is the end boundary in Rem_i and $CS_k^{(i+1)}$ is the start boundary in Rem_{i+1}. When the ramifications on one branch connect correctly, axial connection calibration is applied to expand the connection space between neighbor ramifications, which is described as

$$\begin{cases} S_i^{(k)} = argmax(\sum_{i=0}^{3} \left\| E_i^{(k-1)} - S_i^{(k)} \right\|), s.t. \left\| Q^{(k)} - S_i^{(k)} \right\| \geq \alpha \cdot Dia_{max} \\ E_i^{(k)} = argmax(\sum_{i=0}^{3} \left\| E_i^{(k)} - S_i^{(k+1)} \right\|), s.t. \left\| E_i^{(k)} - Q^{(k)} \right\| \geq \alpha \cdot Dia_{max} \end{cases} \tag{7}$$

For a pair of neighbor ramifications, the solution of Eq. 7 can be explained by Fig. 5. Δx_e is the axial movement of the end boundary in Rem_i, and based on the law of cosines, the increment of RU is

$$\Delta RU = 4 \cdot cos(\angle A_2 Q_i A_2') = 2 \frac{\|Q_i A_2\|^2 + \|Q_i A_2'\|^2 - \|A_2 A_2'\|^2}{\|Q_i A_2\| \cdot \|Q_i A_2'\|} \tag{8}$$

where Δx_e equals $\|A_2 A_2'\|$. $\|Q_i A_2\|$ is the radius of the sphere tangent to edges of the cube with an edge length of Dia_i before axial connection calibration. The constant 4 results from the symmetry of the cube. Simultaneously, the increment of RC is

$$\Delta RC = \begin{cases} -(1 - \frac{P}{T}) \cdot CosDistance(CE_k^{(i)}, CS_{(k+Idx)mod(m)}^{(i+1)}) & 0 \leq P < T \\ 0 & P \geq T \end{cases}, \tag{9}$$

where P is the distance between the center of the end boundary in Rem_i and that of the start boundary in Rem_{i+1}, which can also be regarded as the repulsion

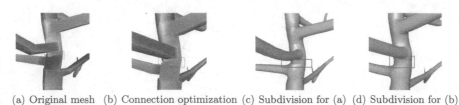

(a) Original mesh   (b) Connection optimization   (c) Subdivision for (a)   (d) Subdivision for (b)

Fig. 6. Effect of connection optimization

between the neighbor ramifications because ΔRC is only valid for a sufficiently close distance. Threshold T is set to Dia_i. When ΔRC is negative, this means that axial movement Δx_e is helpful for reducing the visual distortion of the connection.

The solution retrieval of Δx_s and Δx_e for $min(\Delta RU + \Delta RC)$ is conducted iteratively, and the effect of connection optimization is shown in Fig. 6. The figure shows that connection optimization avoids the overlap between the neighbor ramifications (Fig. 6(a)). Moreover, the subdivision surface of the ramification connection (in the red box) after optimization (Fig. 6(d)) is smoother than that without optimization (Fig. 6(c)).

By contrast, for any Δx_e, if $min(\Delta RU + \Delta RC)$ is always larger than given additional ramification threshold T_{add}, then Rem_i is considered as an additional ramification and should not be connected into main mesh in this step; it is also the last case to obtain an additional ramification.

After all additional ramifications for the next step have been picked up, we also obtain connectable ramification set $Rams_c$. Then, the connection optimization algorithm is applied from bottom to top in $Rams_c$ recursively for sub-branch propagation, as shown in Fig. 2(b), which can be described by the propagation Algorithm 1. The main idea of this algorithm is to search all child branches along a branch's node list (skeleton) and connect corresponding connectable ramifications successively. When this algorithm is applied from the root node of a tree, we can obtain the main mesh of the tree, and the remaining task is a cut-paste operation for additional ramifications.

6   Additional Ramification Cut-Paste

As all basic ramifications are constructed first, our modeling method has a local priority. Distortion accumulates if all basic ramifications are connected, and the two-manifold structure of the tree modeling surface is distorted by the overlap of ramifications. If a ramification can cause high distortion or overlaps with other ramifications, then we select it as an additional ramification before the ramification connection optimization step to avoid it having a bad effect on the entire tree. To merge those additional ramifications back into the main mesh created in the ramification connection optimization step, cut-paste is performed.

Only when additional ramifications exist can this operation be implemented to merge those additional ramifications into the main mesh after the first

---

Algorithm 1. Sub-branch propagation

Input: Current ramification that needs to grow up $CurrentRam$,
           connectable ramification set $Rams_c$,
           all node lists' (skeletons') set $Branches$;
Output: Grown up ramifications $CurrentRam'$;
1: Define an empty sub-branch's ramification queue, $qRam$;
2: Define array Ram_array to record the current branch's child branch identifier (ID)
   using its node list with initial value -1;
3: Define $CurrentBranch = Branches[CurrentRam.ChildNodeID]$;
4: Define current child ID $CurrentCid = 0$;
5: **for** $i > CurrentBranch.Cid.size$ **do**
6:     $SubBranch = Branches[CurrentBranch.Cid[CurrentCid]]$;
7:     $Ram\_array[SubBranch.sid] = SubBranch.Cid[CurrentCid]$;
8:     i=i+1;
9: **end for**
10: $CurrentCid = 0$;
11: **while** $j < CurrentBranch.NodeList.size$ **do**
12:    **if** $Ram\_array[CurrentCid] \neq -1$ **then**
13:       $SubBranch = Branches[CurrentBranch.Cid[CurrentCid]]$;
14:       Define temporary ramification
          $Ram = Rams_c[SubBranch.RamID]$;
15:       Run this algorithm recursively for Ram and obtain grown up ramification
          $RamG$;
16:       $qRam$.push($RamG$);
17:    **end if**
18: **end while**
19: Define temporary ramification Ram'
20: **while** $iRam.size > 0$ **do**
21:    $Ram' = iRam$.pop()
22:    **if** $iRam.size > 0$ **then**
23:       Define the next ramification that needs to be connected, $Ram2 = iRam$.pop()
24:       Connect Ram' with $Ram2$ according to Eq. 5 and obtain new Ram' ;
25:       Update the end boundary indices of Ram';
26:    **else**
27:       Create a connection unit along the remainder of CurrentBranch.NodeList
28:    **end if**
29: **end while**
30: return Ram'.

Catmull–Clark subdivision. Each additional ramification grows up according to Algorithm 1, and is cut alone with the sub-branch boundary after the first subdivision. Then, according to the Catmull–Clark subdivision process, the original sub-branch boundary is determined by recording the new edge vertices that were generated from vertices that belong to the original sub-branch boundary. This method stably calculates the current sub-branch boundary shown in Fig. 7. As the sub-branch boundary is known, we can extract the vertex set and corre-

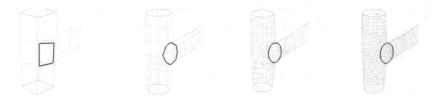

Fig. 7. Boundary calculation after Catmull–Clark subdivision. From left to right: Original boundary, boundary after 1st, 2nd and 3rd subdivision.

sponding face set of the grown sub-branch beginning with any seed vertex in this sub-branch.

Then, a segment-quad-face intersection test based on segment-triangle one [16] is implemented to determine the intersection face in the main mesh in addition to the closest vertex. To save time, we limit the intersection test scope to a sphere, with the joint node of the additional ramification as the center point and 1.5 times its diameter as the radius. The one-ring neighbor of the closest vertex constitute the paste-destination boundary. The sub-branch boundary can match the paste destination boundary using an equation similar to Eq. 6:

$$Idx = argmin \sum_{k=0}^{m-1} CosDistance(\boldsymbol{SB}_k, \boldsymbol{PB}_{(k+Idx)mod(m)}), \qquad (10)$$

where $\boldsymbol{SB}$ and $\boldsymbol{PB}$ are the sub-branch boundary and paste destination boundary, respectively, which were projected into same plane following their center point alignment. Additionally, $m = 8$, in this case.

When merging the two boundaries, sub-objective function CP between Rem_i and Rem_k is described as

$$CP(Rem_{i,k}) = \beta \sum_{j=0}^{m-1} CosDistance(\boldsymbol{SB}_j^{(i)}, \boldsymbol{PB}_j^{(k)})$$

$$+ (1-\beta) \sum_{j=0}^{m-1} \|\boldsymbol{SB}_j^{(i)} - \boldsymbol{PB}_j^{(k)}\|, \qquad (11)$$

where β is a weight factor for the boundary merge, $\boldsymbol{SB}^{(i)}$ is the sub-branch boundary in Rem_i, and $\boldsymbol{PB}^{(k)}$ is the paste destination boundary close to Rem_k, which is regarded as an additional ramification. As we can see, two factors contribute to cut-paste distortion: the angle deflection between $\boldsymbol{PB}$ and $\boldsymbol{SB}$, and the Euclidean distance between them. Thus, we need to rotate and translate $\boldsymbol{PB}$ and $\boldsymbol{SB}$ to determine the minimum CP. Figure 8(a) to (d) show the entire cut-paste process as an example. The additional ramifications' cut-paste process is described as follows:

1. Calculate the intersection point between the skeleton in an additional ramification and main mesh after the first Catmull–Clark subdivision.

2. Determine the closest vertex to the intersection point in the main mesh.
3. Delete the face that contains the closest vertex and its one-ring neighbor in the main mesh, and obtain the entire boundary as a paste destination boundary.
4. Extract a sub-branch from the additional ramification along with its sub-branch boundary.
5. Merge the sub-branch boundary and paste the destination boundary with minimizing Eq. 11 using the rotation and translation operation.
6. After all additional ramifications are cut and pasted, apply the Catmull–Clark subdivision to obtain the final modeling of the tree.

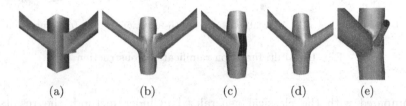

(a)   (b)   (c)   (d)   (e)

Fig. 8. Cut-paste process for an additional ramification. (a) Merge the sub-branch at the right-hand side, which is an additional ramification, with the main mesh. (b) Extract the additional ramification with its sub-branch boundary after the first Catmull–Clark subdivision. (c) Determine the closest vertex in the main mesh in addition to its one-ring neighbor as the paste-destination boundary, which is used to delete the overlapping face when implementing the paste operation. (d) Match the sub-branch boundary of the additional ramification to the paste-destination boundary and merge the two branches using one more subdivision. (c) Another ramifications' cut-paste result for an additional branch with a different diameter, rotation and position.

Figure 8(e) shows the generality of our cut-paste process by pasting another additional ramification into the main mesh with a different position, rotation, and diameter.

7   Results and Discussion

In this section, we present the results of our method using a sketching tree modeling interface. To obtain the 3D skeleton of branches for our method, we drew and adjusted our tree from both the front view and side view, adopting the same method as that in [10]. The main user interfaces of the tree modeling system are shown in Fig. 9(a), which denote two 2D views. We input two pictures of a tree with its camera parameters and sketched the 2D skeletons along the pictures so that the 3D skeletons of branches could be calculated.

In our first experiment, as Fig. 9 shows, we attempted to reconstruct a simple binary tree whose point cloud in Fig. 9(b) was obtained using structure from motion as ground truth from photographs that covered the tree fork 360°.

(a) Pictures in two views   (b) Point cloud   (c) Generalized cylinders (d) Our approach   (e) Poisson surface

Fig. 9. Examples of a model for a ramification of a real-tree

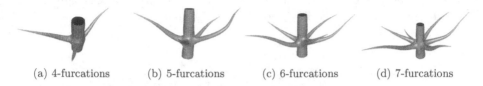

(a) 4-furcations   (b) 5-furcations   (c) 6-furcations   (d) 7-furcations

Fig. 10. Multi-furcation ramification construction

Compared with the classical generalized cylinder method, the results in Fig. 9(c) and (d) demonstrate that our approach modeled tree ramifications as a manifold, preserving the shape and features expressed by generalized cylinders faithfully. The gray parts of the point cloud indicate the difference between the modeling surface and real surface. Without any special approximate algorithm to fit the point cloud, our result in Fig. 9(d) had fewer gray parts than that for the generalized cylinders in Fig. 9(c), particularly around the ramification part, which means that our method was more suitable for describing the tree structure than generalized cylinders.

This experiment also demonstrated that our result, which was available by drawing simple skeletons, was a suitable summary and simplification of that created by screened Poisson surface reconstruction [11] from a dense point cloud. Although the Poisson surface in Fig. 9(e) had more details, our result in Fig. 9(d) demonstrated a similar global geometric impression to its result. By contrast, the Poisson surface could not express the texture of bark well geometrically because it was limited by the density of the point cloud obtained from pictures. In this case, texture mapping for a bump map may be a better choice to represent tree bark, and our surface could be smoother and easily parameterized for texture mapping.

Another experiment was conducted to verify whether the cut-paste step was suitable for multi-furcation ramifications. In this experiment, we set all the ramifications as additional ones manually for verification. We present the results for ramifications with a furcation number from 4 to 7 (additional ramification numbers were 3 to 6) in Fig. 10. The two-manifold property for the meshes were maintained well as the furcations increased, which means that the cut-paste process that we adopted decreased distortion and avoided overlap for multi-ramifications. Table 1 records the face number for the final mesh, and the time cost for cut-paste and subdivision; the furcation number is in proportion to all of other items.

Table 1. Time cost for multi-furcation ramification construction

Furcation number	Face number	Cut-paste (ms)	Twice subdivison (ms)
4	1104	82	41
5	1408	121	49
6	1904	179	76
7	2208	259	98

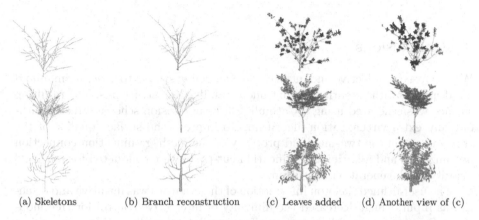

(a) Skeletons   (b) Branch reconstruction   (c) Leaves added   (d) Another view of (c)

Fig. 11. Variety of results generated from user-defined skeletons of different trees. From top to bottom: cherry tree (Tree1), maple tree (Tree2), and manual apple tree (Tree3).

As the results of the experiments have demonstrated, our method was suitable for tree ramification modeling. Our method was applied in the next experiment to some complete trees. Figure 11 shows a variety of results generated from skeletons of different trees. The complexity of the skeletons ranged from a small number to a large number. All the meshes of trees were manifold, with continuous ramifications, which increased the realism of the trees. Our method obtained a complete tree model for different types of trees, and maintained the two-manifold property of their ramifications.

The corresponding time cost of these trees in each step is shown in Table 2. The additional ramifications were recognized automatically according the Sect. 5. The table shows that, in our method, a complete tree was modeled in a short time. Taking Table 1 into consideration, we can found that the average time consumed in the cut-paste step per additional ramification was far longer than that in Table 2. Thus, this also demonstrated that the most time-consuming step was cut-paste because of the intersection test between additional ramifications and the main mesh, which is why we limited the search scope in this step. Further research is necessary to reduce the time of the cut-paste step.

Table 2. Time cost in each step of modeling for different trees

Tree no.	Branches number	Connection optimization (ms)	Additional ramifications number	Cut-paste (ms)	1st subdivison (ms)	2nd subdivison (ms)
Tree1	85	1572	5	4991	361	3601
Tree2	200	2101	4	8486	547	4632
Tree3	42	242	0	0	194	414

8   Conclusions

We proposed an effective and intuitive tree modeling system to generate manifold quad-meshes with smooth and continuous ramification structures. The resulting surface was generated using a Catmull–Clark subdivision scheme directly without any extra virtualization algorithm. To improve the surface quality of the tree and retain the two-manifold property of the mesh, ramification connection optimization and additional ramification cut-paste were conducted for our local priority mesh generation algorithm.

The user-defined skeleton information of the branches was intuitive and essential as input, which decreased the difficulty of interactive control for tree modeling. Our resulting meshes were purely quadrilateral with continuous ramifications, which makes them similar to those that adopt generalized cylinders, and can be a reasonable summary of the Poisson surface in a short time.

Acknowledgements. We thank the ICIG2019 reviewers for their thoughtful comments. The work is supported by the NSFC (61303124), NSBR Plan of Shaanxi (2019JM-370), Key Research and Development Program of Shaanxi (2018NY-127) and the Fundamental Research Funds for the Central Universities (2452017343).

References

1. Alexe, A., Barthe, L., Cani, M., Gaildrat, V.: Shape modeling by sketching using convolution surfaces. In: Pacific Graphics (Short Papers), p. 39 (2007)
2. Angles, B., Tarini, M., Wyvill, B., Barthe, L., Tagliasacchi, A.: Sketch-based implicit blending. ACM Trans. Graph. **36**(6), 181:1–181:13 (2017)
3. Bloomenthal, J.: Skeletal design of natural forms. Computer Science University of Calgary (1995)
4. Bloomenthal, J., Shoemake, K.: Convolution surfaces. In: SIGGRAPH 1991, Providence, RI, USA, 27–30 April 1991, pp. 251–256 (1991)
5. Felkel, P., Wegenkittl, R., Buhler, K.: Surface models of tube trees. In: 2004 Computer Graphics International Conference (CGI 2004), Crete, Greece, pp. 70–77 (2004)
6. Galbraith, C., Mündermann, L., Wyvill, B.: Implicit visualization and inverse modeling of growing trees. Comput. Graph. Forum **23**(3), 351–360 (2004)
7. Habel, R., Kusternig, A., Wimmer, M.: Physically guided animation of trees. Comput. Graph. Forum **28**(2), 523–532 (2009)

8. Hu, S., Chiba, N., He, D.: Realistic animation of interactive trees. Vis. Comput. **28**(6–8), 859–868 (2012)
9. Hu, S., Li, Z., Zhang, Z., He, D., Wimmer, M.: Efficient tree modeling from airborne lidar point clouds. Comput. Graph. **67**, 1–13 (2017)
10. Hu, S., Zhang, Z., Xie, H., Igarashi, T.: Data-driven modeling and animation of outdoor trees through interactive approach. Vis. Comput. **33**(6), 1017–1027 (2017)
11. Kazhdan, M., Hoppe, H.: Screened poisson surface reconstruction. ACM Trans. Graph. **32**(3), 1–13 (2013)
12. Kazhdan, M.M., Bolitho, M., Hoppe, H.: Poisson surface reconstruction. In: Proceedings of the Fourth Eurographics Symposium on Geometry Processing, Cagliari, Sardinia, Italy, 26–28 June 2006, pp. 61–70 (2006)
13. Li, C., Deussen, O., Song, Y.Z., Willis, P., Hall, P.: Modeling and generating moving trees from video. ACM Trans. Graph. **30**(6), 127 (2011)
14. Livny, Y., et al.: Texture-lobes for tree modelling. ACM Trans. Graph. **30**(4), 53:1–53:10 (2011)
15. Livny, Y., Yan, F., Olson, M., Chen, B., Zhang, H., El-Sana, J.: Automatic reconstruction of tree skeletal structures from point clouds. ACM Trans. Graph. **29**(6), 151:1–151:8 (2010)
16. Möller, T., Trumbore, B.: Fast, minimum storage ray/triangle intersection, pp. 21–28 (1997)
17. Okabe, M., Owada, S., Igarashi, T.: Interactive design of botanical trees using freehand sketches and example-based editing. Comput. Graph. Forum **24**(3), 487–496 (2005)
18. Palubicki, W., Horel, K., Longay, S., Runions, A., Lane, B.: Self-organizing tree models for image synthesis. ACM Trans. Graph. **28**(3), 1–10 (2009)
19. Pirk, S., Niese, T., Deussen, O., Neubert, B.: Capturing and animating the morphogenesis of polygonal tree models. ACM Trans. Graph. **31**(6), 169:1–169:10 (2012)
20. Pirk, S., Niese, T., Hädrich, T., Benes, B., Deussen, O.: Windy trees: computing stress response for developmental tree models. ACM Trans. Graph. **33**(6), 1–11 (2014)
21. Pirk, S., et al.: Plastic trees: interactive self-adapting botanical tree models. ACM Trans. Graph. **31**(4), 50:1–50:10 (2012)
22. Prusinkiewicz, P., Lindenmayer, A.: The Algorithmic Beauty of Plants (1990)
23. Runions, A., Lane, B., Prusinkiewicz, P.: Modeling trees with a space colonization algorithm. In: Proceedings of the Third Eurographics Conference on Natural Phenomena, NPH 2007, Eurographics Association, Aire-la-Ville, Switzerland, pp. 63–70 (2007)
24. Stava, O., et al.: Inverse procedural modelling of trees. Comput. Graph. Forum **33**(6), 118–131 (2014)
25. Tai, C., Zhang, H., Fong, J.C.: Prototype modeling from sketched silhouettes based on convolution surfaces. Comput. Graph. Forum **23**(1), 71–84 (2004)
26. Tan, P., Zeng, G., Wang, J., Kang, S.B., Quan, L.: Image-based tree modeling. ACM Trans. Graph. **26**(3), 87 (2007)
27. Tobler, R.F., Maierhofer, S., Wilkie, A.: Mesh-based parametrized l-systems and generalized subdivision for generating complex geometry. Int. J. Shape Model. **8**(2), 173–191 (2002)
28. Wang, Y., Xue, X., Jin, X., Deng, Z.: Creative virtual tree modeling through hierarchical topology-preserving blending. IEEE Trans. Vis. Comput. Graph. **1**(99), 2521–2534 (2017)

29. Wu, X., Luboz, V., Krissian, K., Cotin, S., Dawson, S.: Segmentation and reconstruction of vascular structures for 3D real-time simulation. Med. Image Anal. **15**(1), 22–34 (2011)
30. Wyvill, B., Guy, A., Galin, E.: Extending the CSG tree - warping, blending and boolean operations in an implicit surface modeling system. Comput. Graph. Forum **18**(2), 149–158 (1999)
31. Zhu, X., Jin, X., You, L.: High-quality tree structures modelling using local convolution surface approximation. Vis. Comput. **31**(1), 69–82 (2015)
32. Zhu, X., Jin, X., Liu, S., Zhao, H.: Analytical solutions for sketch-based convolution surface modeling on the GPU. Vis. Comput. **28**(11), 1115–1125 (2012)

Computational Imaging

A New Method to Expand the Showing Range of a Virtual Reconstructed Image in Integral Imaging

Lizhong Zhang, Shigang Wang[✉], Wei Wu, Jian Wei, and Tianshu Li

Jilin University, Changchun, Jilin Province 130012, China
2289154372@qq.com, wangshigang@vip.sina.com

Abstract. In studies of virtual image reconstruction in integral imaging, increasing the resolution and broadening the display range of the reconstructed image have become major concerns. The resolution of the reconstructed image can be improved by using a reconstruction technique based on a lens array model. However, we have to discard some pixels in the reconstructed image generated by this technique; otherwise, the display quality may suffer from stripe distortions caused by this method. We propose a novel reconstruction technique that provides an explicit analysis of the distortion and that uses matching blocks to replace the distortion area. The display range is greatly broadened and the display quality is improved, thus improving the integral imaging.

Keywords: Integral imaging · Image reconstruction · Ray-tracing

1 Introduction

Integral imaging has attracted attention as a new type of true 3D display technique because of its excellent display quality, equipment-free characteristic, and lack of fatigue [1–3]. Studies on integral imaging have focused on the acquisition of the elementary image array [4–10], reconstruction of displayed images [11, 12], and applications in display devices [13]. Integral imaging can be of three main types: total optical integral imaging, computer-assisted integral imaging, and virtual reconstruction integral imaging. In virtual reconstruction integral imaging, we simulate an optical lens array and a charge-coupled device (CCD) to pick up an elementary image array, and then, we reconstruct virtual images based on this array. Through this procedure, we can obtain images of different depths or from different viewing points. In recent years, ray-tracing techniques [14, 15] have been widely used for virtual reconstruction owing to their excellent reconstruction quality. However, we can only trace a light ray that goes through the center of each microlens and obtain the pixels produced by the light ray. Thus, the resolution of the reconstructed image remains very low and is at most the same as that of the microlens.

Therefore, many studies have tried to improve the resolution of the reconstructed image. One study [16] proposed a novel reconstruction technique based on lens array

© Springer Nature Switzerland AG 2019
Y. Zhao et al. (Eds.): ICIG 2019, LNCS 11902, pp. 335–346, 2019.
https://doi.org/10.1007/978-3-030-34110-7_28

models that is similar to the traditional ray-tracing technique. Instead of picking up one pixel from each elementary image, a square block of a certain size that contains an accurate pixel is picked up from each elementary image to constitute a reconstructed image from different viewing points. Thus, the resolution can be increased by a factor of the length of the square block. However, because of interference from stray light in the process of picking up and discarding the distortion area, the quality of the reconstructed image is greatly degraded. Therefore, eliminating stray light and correcting the distortion area remain major unsolved problems in virtual reconstruction.

Instead of using optical devices such as a lens array and CCD for pickup, we use the MAYA software to create a virtual camera array to simulate an actual picking-up system by properly adapting the parameters of virtual cameras. In other words, we use a virtual picking-up process instead of an optical one to effectively eliminate the interference of stray light, as shown in Fig. 1. After we eliminate the interference caused by stray light, we analyze how stripe distortion is produced, and we propose a method to find the matching block for the distortion area. Then, we substitute the distortion area with its matching block rather than directly discarding this area; doing so helps greatly expand the display range of the reconstructed image.

2   Simulating Optical Lens Array Using Virtual Camera Array

We develop a virtual picking-up system in MAYA to eliminate stray light. This implies that the elementary image can only contain objects from the nearest microlens, as shown in Fig. 1(a). To set the parameters of the virtual camera array correctly, it is necessary to first understand the picking-up procedure.

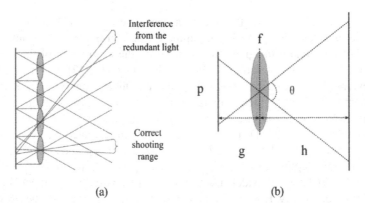

(a)   (b)

Fig. 1.   (a) The analysis of the generation of the distortion. In virtual picking-up system, it mainly derived from the interference of redundunt light; (b) Picking-up range of a single lens.

Figure 1(b) shows a part of the picking-up system; this, in turn, is a part of a complete optical system established according to the Gaussian formula. In the figure, we define h as the object distance, g as the image distance, p as the pitch between the microlens, and p also means the size of the microlens. If a virtual camera array is used in an analog optical picking-up system, we need to keep the viewing angle in the virtual condition identical to that in the optical system by altering the horizontal and vertical aperture values of the virtual camera while keeping the focal length of the virtual camera equal to that of the lens array. Therefore, we alter the aperture value to change the value of the camera's negative to guarantee that the shooting range of one camera is the same as that of its matching microlens, as shown in Eq. (1).

$$\tan \frac{\theta}{2} = \frac{p}{2g} = \frac{d}{2f} \tag{1}$$

In Eq. (1), θ is the horizontal or vertical angle and d is the focal length of the virtual camera. In the experiment, we use a camera array of size 50×50 to simulate a lens array of size 50×50. Figure 2(a) shows the setup of the picking-up system in MAYA, and Fig. 2(b) shows an elementary image array of size 10000×10000. We can eliminate the interference caused by stray light and also adjust the resolution of the elementary image flexibly in the virtual environment, thus obtaining a better image than the low-resolution one obtained using the optical system. In the experiment, we set the resolution of the elementary image as 200×200, which is a little too high for the optical picking-up system, and we obtained an elementary image array of 10000×10000 resolution.

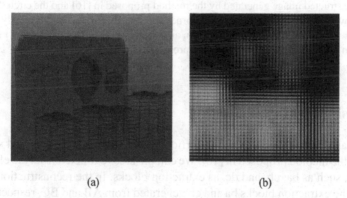

(a)   (b)

Fig. 2. (a) Virtual setup and elementary image generation. The green part is camera array whose size is 50 * 50 in this virtual picking-up system and the front objects are virtual buildings and balloons. The picking-up system is built in MAYA and parameters of cameras are set according to the lens array to simulate; (b) Elementary image array generated by virtual system. The resolution of the element images generated by each virtual camera is 200 * 200 in the experiment, we joint these element images and get the elementary image array whose resolution is 10000 * 10000. (Color figure online)

Then, we apply the method proposed in [16] to reconstruct images from different viewing points. Figure 3 reconstructed image whose viewing point is at top left corner.

We can clearly identify a striped distortion area, which is circled in the figure. A small display error may arise owing to the use of traditional image filters. Therefore, we have to discard the distortion area that causes a decrease in the display range. The building in the bottom right corner will be totally unseen in Fig. 3 if we discard the circled distortion area. Figure 3 shows that the distortion area does not have a total display error, indicating that we can correct these areas instead of discarding them directly. After we eliminate the interference of stray light, we can conclude from further analysis that the distortion arises from improper pixel extraction. We can fix it by obtaining correct pixel blocks to substitute for the distortion area to improve the image quality.

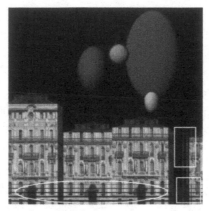

Fig. 3. Reconstructed image generated by the method proposed in [16] and the circled distortion area. The viewing point is set at the top left corner and the distortion area are mainly located in circled area, we have to discard these distortion area which will hamper the display range of the reconstruction image according to the method proposed in document [16].

3   Analysis of Distortion

We need to analyze the origin of the distortion before we correct it. Figure 4 shows the principle of the method proposed in [16]. We call the areas extracted from the elementary image array, such as ba, cb, and dc, as extraction blocks. In the reconstruction process, we see that the extraction blocks ba and cb generated from AB and BC, respectively, are still in their own single elementary image because these areas are close to the viewing point O. By contrast, the extraction block dc goes across two elementary images because it is far from the viewing point. This block is not generated from the same elementary image, and thus, the object picked up in this area is discontinuous, thereby generating distortion.

As shown in Fig. 4, the correct extraction area is area 1. Area 2 is discrete from area 1, thus causing the generation of distortion. If we substitute area 2 by its matching area to make extraction block dc continuous, we can eliminate the distortion and expand the display range of the reconstructed image. Therefore, our next step is to locate the distortion area and search for its matching block. If we set the viewing point on the

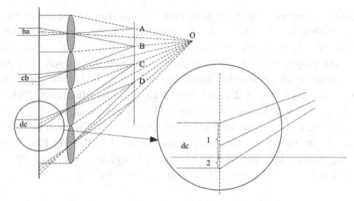

Fig. 4. Principle of generation of distortion. The background picture is elementary image array, in the element image which is far from the viewing point O, the extraction is not only located in a single element image and the area 2 is distortion area which need to be modified. Merely discarding this extraction area will not only hamper the display range of the reconstruction image but also reduce the using efficiency of the elementary image array because area 1 is correctly picked up.

optical axis of the first camera at the top left corner, as shown in Fig. 5, we use virtual reconstruction to clarify the position of the viewing point rather than building an optical reconstruction system. We classify the distortion into three types.

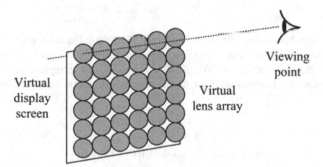

Fig. 5. Position of virtual viewing point. The viewing point and its position is simulated according to parameters of the picking-up system, it can be set anywhere and after it is set we can calculate the size of the extraction area and their position in elementary image array to get the reconstruction image at this viewing point.

3.1 Distortion in Bottom Left Corner

First, we analyze the distortion at the bottom left corner, as shown in Fig. 6. The reconstructed image is shown in the left-hand side of Fig. 6. M and N are extraction blocks in the same column that contain the distortion area. The colored area is the distortion area, and it grows wider as we approach the bottom of the image, we have to discard the extraction area with colored area which will reduce the display range of the reconstruction image. We amplify this area in the top of Fig. 6 to clearly analyze this area. From the reconstructed image, it can be inferred that plane light arrays AA' and BB' match AA" and BB", respectively. Distortion area 2 should be searched in the upper elementary image and its matching block is 2'; distortion area 1 and its matching block 1' can be searched in the same way. We use the matching block to replace the distortion area in the image reconstruction process to correct the distortion in the bottom left corner. If the coordinate of the first pixel that we extract is (m, n) in the top left corner of the elementary image array, the size of the elementary image is a × a, and the size of the extraction block is s × s. Then, we define parameter u in Eq. (2):

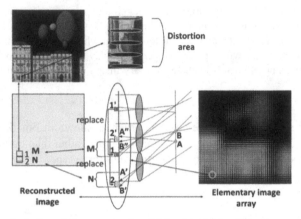

Fig. 6. Distortion in bottom left corner and matching blocks for distortion area. The blue stripe and the red stripe is distortion area which need to be modified, their matching block should be searched in adjacent element images. We use the matching block to replace the distortion area and joint all the corrected extraction block to generate reconstruction images based on different viewing points.

$$u = m + s + (a + \Delta)(i - 1) - ai$$
$$= m + s + \Delta(i - 1) - a \tag{2}$$

$$\Delta = \frac{pg}{h + l} \tag{3}$$

where i is the rank number of the extraction block in the vertical direction, l is the distance between the viewing point and the reconstruction plane, and Δ is the nonperiodic extraction distance mentioned in [16]. When i is small, u < 0; in this case, there will be no distortion in the extraction block; with an increase in i, the extraction block moves further away from the viewing point. Therefore, u will eventually become positive, and distortion will emerge in the extraction block. After the calculation, we can obtain the size of the distortion in the extraction block, which is u × s.

According to the above method, we can determine the position and size of the distortion area. We still have to consider one more condition. As shown in Fig. 6, we need to search for the matching block of the area in the nearest elementary image to reduce the deviation in the reconstructed image. This means that we need to set proper parameters for the system to make the matching system not go across two elementary images. Once it happens, we need to search for the matching block in the second-nearest elementary image. The searching method is the same as that used previously.

3.2 Distortion in Top Right Corner

Figure 7 shows the distortion in the top right corner. The reconstructed image is in the left-hand side of the figure, and extraction blocks M and N contain colored distortion areas. Therefore, the distortion will grow wider when approaching the right-hand side of the image. We also amplify this area to analyze the distortion. Based on the reconstruction plane, we conclude that light arrays AA' and BB' match AA" and BB", respectively. For distortion area 2, we can find the matching block in the elementary image at the left, which is marked as area 2'. Other matching blocks are searched in the same way. We also replace the distortion area with its own matching block when reconstructing the image to improve the display quality of the top right corner. We define o in Eq. (4):

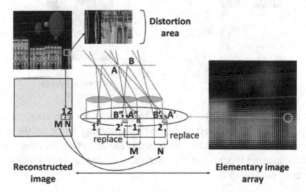

Fig. 7. Distortion in top right corner and matching blocks for distortion area. The distortion area is still in stripe shape and according to the method in Fig. 6, we can get corrected extraction block and generate reconstruction images.

$$o = n + s + (a + \Delta)(j - 1) - aj = n + s + \Delta(j - 1) - a \qquad (4)$$

where j is the rank number of the extraction block in the horizontal direction. We make the following observations: When j is small, o < 0; in this case, there will be no distortion area in the extraction block; as j increases, the extraction block moves away from the viewing point. o will eventually become positive, and distortion emerges in the extraction block. After the calculation, we can obtain the size of the distortion in its extraction block as s × o. By using this method, we can obtain the position and size of the distortion area.

3.3 Distortion in Bottom Right Corner

This distortion area can still be divided into three parts, marked as 1, 2, and 3 in Fig. 8. The matching blocks for distortion areas 1 and 2 can be searched in the upper and left elementary images, respectively. Distortion area 3 is a special case. As shown in Fig. 8, block 3' is the matching block of area 3; however, block 3' is still located in the distortion area, so we have to search the matching block of area 3 in the elementary image that is at its top left corner. If we continue to use the parameters that have been set before, we can conclude that with increasing i and j, the distortion area will eventually emerge. The size of distortion area 1 is u × (s − o), the size of distortion area 2 is (s − u) × o and the size of distortion area 3 is u × o.

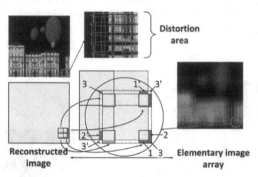

Fig. 8. Distortion at bottom right corner and matching blocks for distortion area. The distortion area is not in stripe shape and the method of finding matching block of the distortion area is different from the method in Figs. 6 and 7. We separate the distortion into three small blocks and find their individual matching blocks, the we joint these three matching blocks and correct area together to get the corrected block.

Thus far, we have corrected the distortion area. When the viewing points are at other positions, the analysis and substitution can be performed in the same way. By using this method, we can reconstruct images based on different viewing points with a larger display range.

4 Experiment Result

The virtual optical system is set according to the formula (5), we set the distance between the viewing point at the top left corner and the elementary image array as 3.5 mm + 21 mm + 329 mm = 353.5 mm. Therefore, the distance l between the viewing point and the reconstructed image plane is 329 mm. According to Eq. (1), we set the size of the virtual cameras' aperture as 0.034 × 0.034 in MAYA. This means that the size of the cameras' negatives is 1 mm × 1 mm. Furthermore, we set the focal length as 3 mm, distance between each camera as 1 mm, and the size of the camera array as 50 × 50. We use this camera array to simulate the lens array whose focal length is 3 mm, size is 50 × 50, and interval between microlens is 1 mm. We set the resolution of the elementary image as 200 × 200 to obtain an elementary image array whose resolution is 10000 × 10000, as shown in Fig. 2.

$$\frac{1}{3} = \frac{1}{3.5} + \frac{1}{21} \tag{5}$$

In this reconstruction procedure, we set the pixel as the unit, size of extraction block as 31 × 31 pixels, and coordinate of first pixel in elementary image array as (84, 84). According to [16], the interval of the extraction block is 202 pixels; this means that Δ is $202 - 200 = 2$. After the above calculation, we can conclude that the distortion emerges after the 45th extraction block in both the vertical and the horizontal directions, and the width of the distortion area increases by 2, 4, 6, 8, … pixels. Accordingly, we can search for the matching block of the distortion area and replace the distortion area with its matching block in the reconstruction process. Figure 9 shows the contrast between before and after the correction.

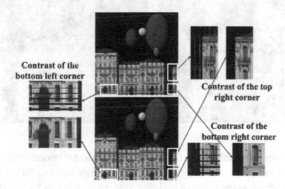

Fig. 9. Contrast between before and after the correction of the reconstructed image.

Figure 9 shows the evident improvement in the reconstructed image and the expansion of the display range, which is important for the overall improvement of the display quality. The display range of the reconstruction image can be improved by 29.1% according to formula (6). Figures 10, 11 and 12 show the contrast of the reconstructed image based on the other three viewing points, the method we applied to acquire these

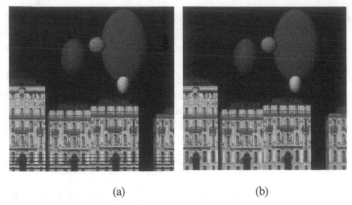

(a)   (b)

Fig. 10. Contrast of reconstructed images based on viewing point at top right corner. (a) before remediation; (b) after remediation. In the pic the distortion area is correctly replaced by their own matching blocks and the display range of the reconstruction image is expanded.

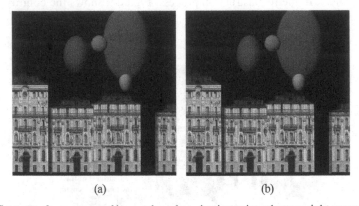

(a)   (b)

Fig. 11. Contrast of reconstructed images based on viewing point at bottom right corner. (a) before remediation; (b) after remediation. The position of the viewing point is different from which in Fig. 10, as we can see the showing range of building roof is larger in this pic than which in Fig. 10. The distortion area is mainly located in the black background which makes the contrast of (a) and (b) less obvious.

reconstruction images obeys the principle we used before. Although there are still some evident mistakes in the remedied reconstruction pictures, the general dispaly qualities are greatly improved and the showing range is expanded.

$$\frac{(50*31*51*31)-(44*31*44*31)}{44*31*44*31}=29.1\% \qquad (6)$$

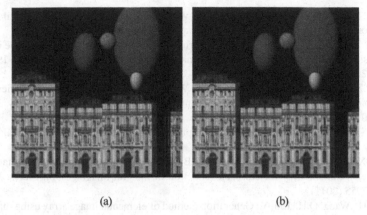

(a)   (b)

Fig. 12. Contrast of reconstructed images based on viewing point at bottom left corner. (a) before remediation; (b) after remediation. According to the position of this viewing point, we can see more right side of each building. The distortion area is mainly located at right side of the image, as we can see, after processing the distortion is eliminated and the right side of the images is completely reconstructed.

The above figures show the excellent improvement in the display range and display quality, especially when the distortion area is evident to viewers. However, this method still has some limitations in that the number of calculations is large and it is a little complicated to implement in a program. Furthermore, the procedure is time-consuming, and the viewing angle is narrow and still needs to be optimized.

5 Summary

We devise a setup for a virtual picking-up system in which a virtual camera array is used to simulate an optical picking-up system and to expand the display range of the reconstructed image by analyzing the generation of the distortion area and substituting it with its matching block. In this way, we improve the display quality of the reconstructed image and increase the usage efficiency of the elementary image array. We assume that in a practical integral imaging application, we can orient the position of the viewer's viewing point by using sensor equipment. Simultaneously, we can correct the elementary image array to avoid the generation of distortion to achieve better display quality and to make this method valuable and practical.

References

1. Lippmann, G.: Epreuves reversibles donnant la sensation du relief. J. Phys. Theor. Appl. **7**, 821–825 (1908)
2. Ives, H.E.: Optical properties of a Lippmann lenticulated sheet. JOSA **21**, 171–176 (1931)
3. Javidi, B., Sola-Pikabea, J., Martinez-Corral, M.: Breakthroughs in photonics 2014: recent advances in 3-D integral imaging sensing and display. IEEE Photonics J. **7**, 0700907 (2015)

4. Jiao, T.T., Wang, Q.H., Deng, H., Zhou, L., Wang, F.: Computer-generated integral imaging based on 3DS MAX. Chin. J. Liq. Cryst. Disp. **23**, 621–623 (2008)
5. Jiao, X.X., Zhao, X., Yang, Y., Fang, Z.L., Yuan, X.C.: Optical acquiring technique of three-dimensional integral imaging based on optimal pick-up distance. Opt. Precis. Eng. **19**, 2805–2811 (2011)
6. Lyu, Y.Z., Wang, S.G., Ren, G.X., Yu, J.Q., Wang, X.Y.: Two dimensional multiview image array pickup and virtual viewpoint image synthesis algorithm. J. Harbin Eng. Univ. **34**, 763–767 (2013)
7. Yang, S.W., et al.: Influences of the pickup process on the depth of field of integral imaging display. Opt. Commun. **386**, 22–26 (2017)
8. Yuan, X.C., Xu, Y.P., Yang, Y., Zhao, X., Bu, J.: Design parameters of elemental images formed by camera array for crosstalk reduction in integral imaging. Opt. Precis. Eng. **19**, 2050–2055 (2011)
9. Deng, H., Wang, Q.H., Liu, Y.: Generation method of elemental image array using micro-lens array with different specifications. Optoelectron. Technol. **34**, 73–77 (2014)
10. Jang, J., Cho, M.: Fast computational integral imaging reconstruction by combined use of spatial filtering and rearrangement of elemental image pixels. Opt. Lasers Eng. **75**, 57–62 (2015)
11. Fan, J., Wu, F., Lyu, G.J., Zhao, B.C., Ma, W.Y.: One-dimensional integral imaging display with large viewing angle. Optik **127**, 5219–5220 (2016)
12. Lyu, Y.Z., Wang, S.G., Zhang, D.: Elemental image array generation and sparse viewpoint pickup in integral imaging. J. Jilin Univ. (Eng. Technol. Ed.) **43**, 1–5 (2013)
13. Li, D., Zhao, X., Yang, Y., Fang, Z.L., Yuan, X.C.: Non-flipping reconstruction system design implementation in three dimension integral imaging. J. Optoelectron. Laser **23**, 35–40 (2012)
14. Xing, S.J., et al.: High-efficient computer-generated integral imaging based on the backward ray-tracing technique and optical reconstruction. Opt. Express **25**, 330–338 (2017)
15. Piao, Y., Wang, Y.: Non-periodic reconstruction technique of computational integral imaging. J. Inf. Comput. Sci. **5**, 1259–1264 (2008)
16. Piao, Y., Wang, Y.: Technique of Integral Imaging, 1st edn. Publishing House of Electronics Industry, Beijing (2005)

Light Field Retrieval via Focus Variation

Runnan Zhang[1,2,3], Jiasong Sun[1,2,3], and Chao Zuo[1,2,3]($\boxtimes$)

[1] School of Electronic and Optical Engineering, Nanjing University of Science and Technology,
No. 200 Xiaolingwei Street, Nanjing 210094, Jiangsu, China
zuochao@njust.edu.cn
[2] Smart Computational Imaging (SCI) Laboratory, Nanjing University of Science
and Technology, Nanjing 210094, Jiangsu, China
[3] Jiangsu Key Laboratory of Spectral Imaging and Intelligent Sense, Nanjing University
of Science and Technology, Nanjing 210094, Jiangsu, China

Abstract. Light field imaging is a new computational imaging method in recent years, which is a representation of full four-dimensional (4D) radiance of all rays with spatial and angular information in free space. However, most current light field imaging systems are limited by the contradiction between spatial resolution and angular resolution, that is, trading spatial resolution for angular resolution. In this paper, we present a full resolution light field microscopy technique based on 3D intensity transport. The advantage of our method is that it does not sacrifice spatial resolution, and the reconstructed light field is of full resolution, comparable to that of the image sensor itself. First, a non-linear iterative reconstruction algorithm is proposed to reconstruct the full resolution light field from the 3D intensity stack which is captured by axial scanning. Then, we investigate the key factors that influence the quality of the reconstructed 4D light field, which is proved to be related to the number of reconstructed viewing angles and the number of captured images of each stack. Finally, experiments are carried out with real 3D samples, and the above methods are tested and evaluated with simple two-layer samples and complex multi-layer samples as *Cyclops* and *Drosophila*. The reliability and accuracy of our method are verified by simulation and experimental results.

Keywords: Light field microscopy imaging · Three-dimensional intensity transport · Nonlinear optimization

1 Introduction

Light field (LF) imaging technique is developing rapidly during the past decades, and many researchers have made contributions to the improvement of the theory [1–3]. It plays an important role in many fields such as security surveillance, photographic media, aerial photography, stereo display, scientific instruments, animation rendering and so on. Nowadays, there are three main approaches to obtain light field: (1) Inserting a microlens array between main lens and image plane. The plane of microlens array is considered as spatial information and the plane of image sensor records angular information. There are some application such as plenoptic camera [4], light field microscopy

© Springer Nature Switzerland AG 2019
Y. Zhao et al. (Eds.): ICIG 2019, LNCS 11902, pp. 347–358, 2019.
https://doi.org/10.1007/978-3-030-34110-7_29

(LFM) [5], hand-held camera Lytro [6] and Adobe Systems Inc light field camera [7]. (2) Arranging large camera arrays. It refers to the method of reconstructing the light field by capturing a series of images with slightly different angles of view through a certain arrangement of the cameras in space. Such as 128 camera arrays in Stanford [8], with different spatial layouts of cameras, some features that are different from ordinary cameras, including spatial resolution, dynamic range, depth of field, frame rate and spectral sensitivity can be achieved. (3) Using programmable masks. This method process the aperture of the camera by programmable masks to reconstruct the light field. For example, programmable aperture microscopy (PAM) [9], compressive light field photography [10] and programmable aperture photography (PAP) [11]. However, there are some disadvantages of these approaches to obtain light field. Microlens array sacrifices spatial resolution for angular resolution. While the scale of camera arrays is very large, the hardware cost is really high and it is difficult to apply widely. The programmable masks may bring in noise and longtime cost. The way to obtain the light field data indirectly contain the light field reconstruction from the focal stack [12, 13].

The transport of intensity equation (TIE) allows the phase of a coherent field to be retrieved non-interferometrically given positive defined intensity measurements and appropriate boundary conditions. However, in microscopy system, the partial coherence of extended source is nonnegligible. Inspired by some former researches about phase retrieval under partially coherent illumination [14, 15], in this paper, a non-liner iterative reconstruction algorithm to obtain full resolution light field from three-dimensional (3D) intensity stack is proposed. Then, the captured images are processed to reconstruct full resolution light field using proposed method. Moreover, we analyze the key factors that influence the quality of reconstructed light field, that is, the number of reconstructed viewing angles and the number of captured images. Finally, experiments are carried out with real 3D samples.

2 Method

2.1 Principle and Mathematic Modulation

In this section, the principle and mathematic modulation of traditional light field imaging are introduced. Figure 1 shows the relationship between light field and the images captured by a CCD. Four-dimensional light field $L(x, y, \theta_x, \theta_y)$ is represented by the reference plane distribution of two spatial variates x, y and two angular variates θ_x, θ_y. This figure only shows 2D cross section $x - \theta_x$ of the 4D light field L for clarity. Each point in the $x - \theta_x$ space represents an individual light ray.

As is shown in Fig. 1(a), when the focal plane of the microscopy system is in line with the reference plane of light field, rays coming from this plane share the same position but with different directions, so they are distributing vertically in 2D cross section $x - \theta_x$. Each pixel of the captured image is the integration of light ray intensity along a direction, giving a vertical projection of the light field. As is shown in Fig. 1(b), when focal plane of the microscopy system deviate from the reference plane by Δz, rays arriving at the reference plane which coming from the focal plane have different positions and different directions due to the Δz deviation, therefore the 2D cross section $x - \theta_x$ of light field is slanted. Each camera pixel records integration of light ray intensity along slanted line, giving a slanted projection of light field:

$$I_{zr} + \Delta z(x_c, y_c) = \iint\limits_{NA} L\big(x_c m - \Delta z\theta_x, x_c m - \Delta z\theta_x, \theta_x, \theta_y\big) d\theta_x d\theta_y \qquad (1)$$

where $I_{zr} + \Delta z(x_c, y_c)$ is the captured image with focal plane located at $zr + \Delta z$, m is the magnification of objective lens. Noted that the captured image not only records the information of a slice of object at a focal plane, but also information from the whole 3D surface of object in a corresponding range. The spatial and angular range of light field is decided by field-of-view (FOV) of CCD and numerical aperture (NA) of objective lens.

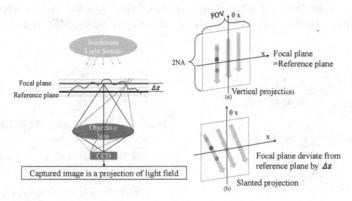

Fig. 1. Relationship between light field and the captured images

2.2 Non-linear Iterative Reconstruction Algorithm

In this section, an algorithm to reconstruct light field from different focal plane images is explained. By capturing 3D intensity stack from different focal plane, different 2D projections of 4D light field are obtained. According to the back-projection [16] algorithm, the captured projected images can be back-projected to the light field. The light field is computed by:

$$L_{rec}\big(x, y, \theta_x, \theta_y\big) = \frac{1}{N} \sum_n I_{zr} + \Delta z_n\left(\frac{x + \Delta z_n \theta_x}{m}, \frac{y + \Delta z_n \theta_y}{m}\right) \qquad (2)$$

where N is the number of captured images.

While Eq. 2 is an initialization of light field, a non-linear iterative reconstructing algorithm is proposed to obtain 4D light field. The reconstruction steps are as following, the flow chart is shown in Fig. 2:

Step 1: Capturing 3D intensity stack $I_1, I_2, \ldots, I_N$ of different focal plane by axial scanning.

Step 2: Initializing a 4D light field $LF\big(x, y, \theta_x, \theta_y\big)$ according to Eq. 2.

Step 3: Propagating L_F to L_{Fk} according to Eq. 1.

Step 4: Updating L_{Fk} by I_k. First integrate L_{Fk} by angles and achieved I_{sum}, then use I_k to constrain I_{sum} and obtain a coefficient matrix C_k, finally use C_k to update L_{Fk} for every angle.

Step 5: Propagating L_{Fk} back to L_F.

Step 6: For N intensity images $I_1, I_2, \ldots, I_N$, propagating LF to each focal plane, the same methods as steps 2–5 are adopted.

Step 7: Repeating steps 2–6 until the value of cost function of the reconstructed light field is at a minimum, and then complete the reconstruction of the full resolution light field from N images.

Noted that the calculation method of the cost function in Step 7 is: integrating the reconstructed light field by angles and normalizing it to obtain an intensity image I_n' at a certain z plane, and make a subtraction with the original I_n taken at the corresponding z. The square error MSE of I_n' and I_n ends the iteration where the MSE is at a minimum.

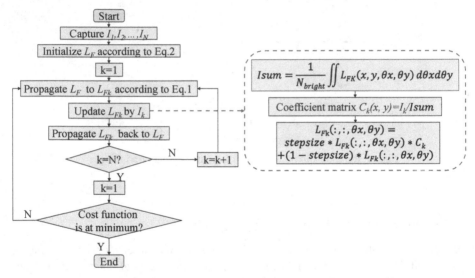

Fig. 2. Flow chart of non-liner iterative reconstruction algorithm

2.3 Algorithm Verification and Simulation Results

Supposing there are three objects O, S, and A locate at different Z planes in free space, as shown in Fig. 3. The 3D intensity stack of three planes are captured through axial scanning. O is located at z = −2 mm, S is located at z = 0 mm and A is located at z = 2 mm, and the viewing angles range from −10° to +10° with 0.5° interval. The captured images are focused on three planes of O, S, and A respectively, and the 3D intensity stack is obtained as shown in Fig. 4(a). The ideal light field distribution of the three planes is shown in Fig. 4(b).

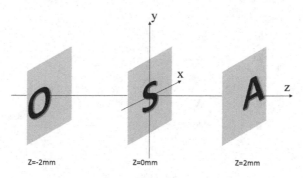

Fig. 3. Objects in space

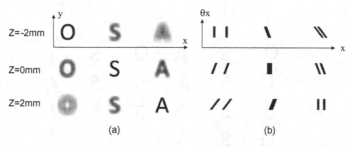

Fig. 4. Captured intensity stack and ideal light field (a) intensity stack (b)ideal light field

The non-linear iterative algorithm is used to reconstruct light field from the 3D intensity stack, and the quality of the reconstructed light field is related to iterative times. It can be seen from the iterative results that the blurring of light field in the $x - \theta_x$ cross section decreases with the increasing times of iteration. The shadow is reduced, and the reconstructed light field becomes more and more clear and approaching the ideal light field. Figure 5 shows the $x - \theta_x$ cross-sections of the light field, which are reconstructed after 5, 10, 20, 30 iterations respectively.

The cost function is used to judge the stop of iteration. The calculation method of the cost function has been explained in Sect. 2.2. Figure 5(f) is the relationship between the MSE and iteration times. It is shown that the value of MES decreases with iteration going on. When the iteration time is more than 30, it is seen that the reconstructed light field has converged, and thus iteration can be stopped.

Take out $(-10°, -10°)$, $(-10°, 10°)$, $(10°, -10°)$, $(10°, 10°)$ four angles of view, comparing the ideal light field (Fig. 6(b)) with the reconstructed light field (Fig. 6(a)) at 30 iteration times. It can be seen that except for some weak shadows which result from reconstruction errors, the reconstructed light field is almost identical to the ideal light field. We can say that the accurate reconstruction of full-resolution 4D light field is realized by 3D intensity stack.

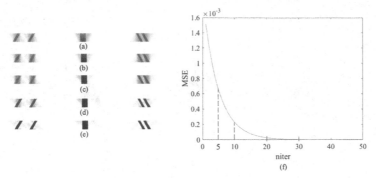

Fig. 5. Light field recovered using non-liner iterative reconstruction algorithm. (a) initialized light field (b)-(e) Reconstructed results after 5, 10, 20, 30 iterations (f) Relationship between MES and iteration times

$(-10°, 10°)$	O	S	A	O	S	A
$(10°, 10°)$	O	S	A	O	S	A
$(-10°,-10°)$	O	S	A	O	S	A
$(10°, -10°)$	O	S	A	O	S	A
	(a)				(b)	

Fig. 6. Comparison between reconstructed and ideal light field (a) reconstructed light field after 30 iteration times (b) ideal light field

3 Experiment Results and Analyze

3.1 System Setup

The whole light field microscopy system is setup based on an inverted microscope (OLYMPUS IX81) equipped with motorized stage. As is shown in Fig. 7, the microscopy is composed of a collector lens, a condenser lens associated with aperture diaphragm, objective, reflective mirror, and tube lens, producing a magnified image of the specimen at the image plane. The sample is illuminated by the incoherent light source (NA = 0.55) and imaged by an objective (OLYMPUS Plan Objective, 10x/0.25NA). A monochrome industrial camera (IMAGINGSOURCE, DMK 33UP1300, pixel size 4.8 μm, frame rate 30 fps) is placed at the image plane. The microscopy is connected to PC through serial port RS232, and the motorized stage can be controlled by PC software Micro-Manager.

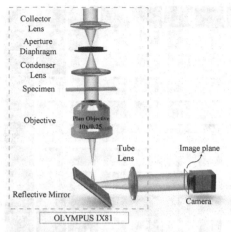

Fig. 7. Schematic setup for microscopy system

3.2 Light Field Reconstruction for a Simple Two-Layer Sample

Stacking the USAF target and the ruler target together as a simple two-layer 3D sample to be tested. The USAF target is placed at $z1 = -80$ μm and the ruler target is placed at $z2 = 80$ μm. The captured images are shown in Fig. 8.

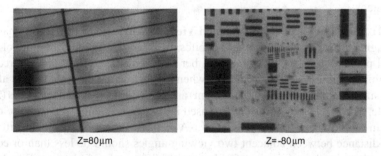

Fig. 8. Captured intensity stack focused at z1 and z2

After obtaining two different focal plane images, the light field can be reconstructed by a non-linear iteration algorithm proposed in Sect. 2.2. The reconstructed light field is shown in Fig. 9, each intensity image is from a viewing angle (θ_x, θ_y), and every point (x, y) in an image represents spatial information. The relative position of the two layers changes under different viewing angles.

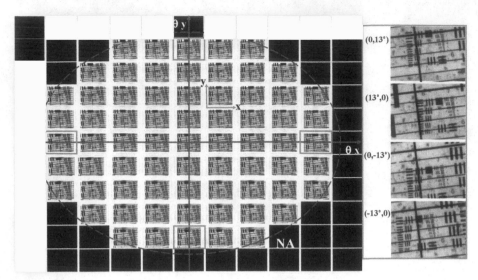

Fig. 9. Reconstructed light field

3.3 Influencing Factors of Reconstructed Light Field Quality

In this section, two influencing factors of reconstructed light field quality are analyzed, that is, the number of reconstructed viewing angles and the number of captured images of each stack.

Factor 1: The Number of Reconstructed Viewing Angles. In the traditional light field imaging model based on geometric optics, in order to meet the continuity of different focal plane objects, the minimum number of reconstructed light fields is required. The minimum number of viewing angles when reconstructing the light field is affected by pixel size of camera (d), magnification (m) and NA of objective, and thickness (Zmax) of sample. The pixel sizes of the camera used in this experiment is 4.8 μm, the magnification m of the objective lens is 10, and NA = 0.25. When the image is shifted, the shifting distance between adjacent two viewing angles should be less than or equal to 4.8 μm, otherwise the continuity of objects with different focal planes will be broken. In this experiment, the distance between the upper and lower layers of the sample is Zmax. Therefore, the minimum interval of viewing angle is $\Delta\theta = \mathrm{d}/(m Z_{\max})$, and the minimum number of viewing angles in vertical and horizontal directions is calculated by Eq. 3:

$$N \propto 2\frac{N A m Z_{\max}}{d} \tag{3}$$

That is, the number of reconstructed views is proportional to NA, m, and inversely proportional to d. In this experiment, 5×5, 9×9, 15×15 and 21×21 viewing angles were reconstructed respectively. The number of reconstruction views can be achieved by expanding the viewing angle sampling reconstruction density during iteration. The result of reconstructed light field under different numbers of viewing angles are shown in Fig. 10:

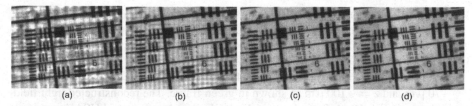

Fig. 10. Reconstructed light field with different number of viewing angles (a) 5 × 5 (b) 9 × 9 (c) 15 × 15 (d) 21 × 21

As is depicted in Fig. 10, with the growing number of reconstructed viewing angles, the grid shadow in the reconstructed light field is decreasing, and the quality is improved. However, there is no single pixel point in FOV restricted by microscopy imaging resolution, and the object is not intermittent, so that 21 × 21 viewing angles are sufficient to reconstruct a satisfactory quality of light field.

Factor 2: The Number of Captured Images. In addition, in order to further analyze the influencing factors of reconstructing the light field quality under incoherent illumination, the following three series of comparative experiments are carried out: (1) using three defocused images; (2) using one focused image and one defocused image; (3) using two focused image and three defocused images. The intensity stack used here are shown in Fig. 11.

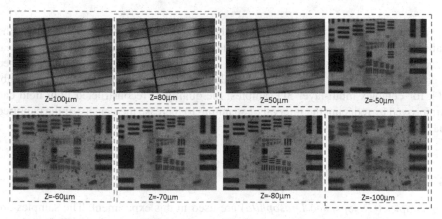

Fig. 11. Captured intensity stack

1. Using three defocused images located at $z = 50$ μm, $z = -50$ μm and $z = -100$ μm (in red frame). The reconstructed light field (selecting one view) is shown in Fig. 12(a). It can be seen that the reconstructed light field using two defocused images is blurred in both layers.
2. Using a focused image (focused at the ruler target $z = 80$ μm), a defocused image (USAF target is defocused at $z = -60$ μm), as shown in blue frame. The reconstructed

light field is shown in Fig. 12(b). It can be seen that the ruler target in the reconstructed light field is clear and the USAF target is blurred. This is because the quality of the reconstructed light field is affected by the quality of the captured intensity stack.

3. Using two focused image, including USAF target located at $z = -80\ \mu m$ and ruler target located at $z = 80\ \mu m$, and three defocused images located at $z = 100\ \mu m$, $z = -70\ \mu m$ and $z = -100\ \mu m$ as shown in green frame. The reconstructed light field is shown in Fig. 12(c). It can be seen that both the ruler target and USAF target are clear in reconstructed light field. Noted that compared with Fig. 10(d), the quality of reconstruction is slightly lower. This may be because 21×21 viewing angles still cannot fully meet the requirements.

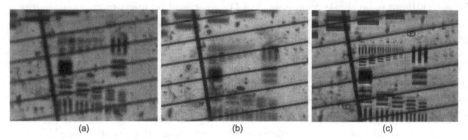

Fig. 12. Reconstructed results (a) three defocused images (b) one focused image and one defocused image (c) two focused image and three defocused images.

From these three experimental results, the following conclusion can be drawn: the quality of the reconstruction of the light field is determined by the clearest original images. For this simple two-layer object, the clearest two-layer intensity images focused on the upper and lower layer need to be taken for reconstructing a high-quality light field; for complex multi-layer 3D samples, the quality of reconstructed light field can be improved by reducing the interval of scanning to increase the density of the captured axial intensity stack.

3.4   Experiment on Multi-layer Samples

Two samples (*Cyclops*, and *Drosophila*) are used in this experiment. The samples are scanned axially, and two 3D intensity stacks are taken at intervals and the light field are reconstructed with 21×21 viewing angles. The intensity stacks are shown in Fig. 13. The full-resolution light field reconstruction results [selecting $(0°, 13°)$ $(0°, -13°)$ $(-13°, 0°)$ $(13°, 0°)$ four views] are shown in Fig. 14(a),(c), and the $x - \theta x$ cross section of light field is shown in Fig. 14(b),(d). It can be seen that the relative position of different layers is changing under different viewing angles. Through the experiments on multi-layer 3D samples, it can be confirmed that different horizontal and vertical parallax views are synthesized successfully from the light field which was reconstructed from the stack of the focal images captured by axial scanning.

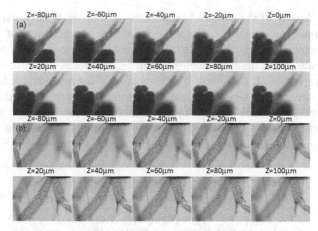

Fig. 13. Captured intensity stacks (a) *Cyclops* (b) *Drosophila*

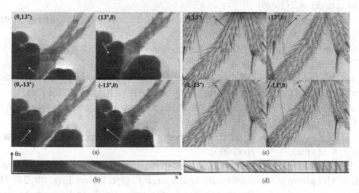

Fig. 14. Reconstructed light field (a)(c) four viewing angles of reconstructed light field (b)(d) $x - \theta_x$ cross section of reconstructed light field

4 Conclusion

In this paper, a non-liner iterative reconstruction algorithm to obtain full resolution light field from 3D intensity stack is proposed. A serial of intensity images located at different focal plans are captured by axial scanning. Compared with microlens array, our method does not sacrifice spatial resolution. Compared with camera arrays, our method is easily set up and does not need to transform microscopy by extra hardware. Compared with programmable masks which can only open a small amount of aperture through each frame, the aperture of our method is fully open for incoherent imaging. Furthermore, the number of reconstructed viewing angles and the number of captured images of each stack will influence the quality of reconstructed light field, that is, the minimum number of reconstructed viewing angles should be calculated to avoid breaking the continuity of different focal plane objects. Apart from this factor, the number of captured images also influences the reconstructed quality. For real multi-layer samples, the quality of the reconstructed light field can be improved by reducing the interval of the scanning to increase the density of the captured axial intensity images. Finally, experiments on multi-layer samples are carried out to prove reliability and accuracy of our method. Under the objective lens with NA $= 0.25$, 10 intensity images with axial interval of 20 μm are measured. The iterative reconstruction algorithm effectively reconstructs the light field sub-image of 21×21 view. The resolution of the reconstructed light field is comparable to native image sensor, and the reconstructed light field effectively displays the detailed features of thick objects under different viewing angles. It is confirmed that images under different viewing angles from the full resolution light field can be reconstructed from 3D intensity stack.

References

1. Lippmann, G.: Reversible prints integral photographs. Acad. Sci. **7**, 821–825 (1908)
2. Gershun, A.: The light field. J. Math. Phys. **18**, 51–151 (1939)
3. Levoy, M., Hanrahan, P.: Light field rendering. In: Proceedings of SIGGRAPH. ACM Press, New York, pp. 31–42 (1996)
4. Adelson, E., Wang, Y.A.: Single lens stereo with a plenoptic camera. IEEE Trans. Pattern Anal. Mach. Intell. **14**(2), 99–106 (1992)
5. Levoy, M., Ng, R., Adams, A.: Light field microscopy. Proc. SIGGRAPH **25**(3), 924–934 (2006)
6. Ng, R., Levoy, M., Bredif, M.: Light field photography with a hand-held plenoptic camera. Technical Report CSTR. Stanford Computer Science Tech Report CSTR (2005)
7. Georgiev, T., Intwala, C., Goma, S.: Light field camera design for integral view photography. Adobe Technical Report (2006)
8. Wilburn, B., Joshi, N., Vaish, V., et al.: High performance imaging using large camera arrays. Proc. SIGGRAPH **05**, 765–776 (2005)
9. Zuo, C., Sun, J., Feng, S., et al.: Programmable aperture microscopy: a computational method for multi-modal phase contrast and light field imaging. Opt. Lasers Eng. **80**, 24–31 (2016)
10. Marwah, K., Wetzstein, G., Bando, Y., et al.: Compressive light field photography using overcomplete dictionaries and optimized projections. ACM Trans. Graph. **32**(4), 1–12 (2013)
11. Liang, C.K., Liu, G., Chen, H.: Light field acquisition using programmable aperture camera. In: Proceedings of IEEE International Conference on Image Processing. IEEE Press, Washington DC, vol. 5, pp. 233–236 (2007)
12. Yin, X., Wang, G., Li, W., Liao, Q.: Iteratively reconstructing 4D light fields from focal stacks. Appl. Opt. **55**(30), 8457–8463 (2016)
13. Liu, C., Qiu, J., Jiang, M.: Light field reconstruction from projection modeling of focal stack. Opt. Express **25**(10), 11377–11388 (2017)
14. Zuo, C., Chen, Q., Tian, L., et al.: Transport of intensity phase retrieval and computational imaging for partially coherent fields: The phase space perspective. Opt. Lasers Eng. **71**, 20–32 (2015)
15. Zuo, C., Chen, Q., Asundi, A.: Light field moment imaging: comment. Opt. Lett. **39**, 3 (2014)
16. Chen, N., Ren, Z., Li, D., et al.: Analysis of the noise in back projection light field acquisition and its optimization. Appl. Opt. **56**(13), 20–26 (2017)

Image Reconstruction of an Emerging Optical Imager

Gang Liu[1,2(✉)], Desheng Wen[1], Zongxi Song[1], Weikang Zhang[1,2],
Zhixin Li[1,2], Xin Wei[1,2], and Tuochi Jiang[1,2]

[1] Xi'an Institute of Optics and Precision Mechanics,
Chinese Academy of Sciences, Xi'an 710119, Shaanxi, China
`liugang@opt.cn`
[2] University of Chinese Academy of Sciences, Beijing 100049, China

Abstract. The emerging optical imager can reduce the system weight, size and power consumption by an order of magnitude compared to conventional optical telescopes at the same resolution. It utilizes Fourier-domain interferometry and samples by radial scheme. To date, there is little research on efficient image reconstruction algorithm of it. In this paper, we analyze the sampling properties of the imager and propose a compressive sensing (CS) based image reconstruction method for it. We also discuss the accurate and fast transform from the radial sampling scheme to Cartesian coordinate. The simulations of the proposed method have achieved good performance.

Keywords: Interference · Image reconstruction · Compressive sensing

1 Introduction

In the field of astronomy and remote sensing, it is important to obtain the high resolution image of remote target. However, a high resolution telescope requires a large aperture, which comes with a large size, heavy weight and high power. In addition, launching heavy and large objects into space is expensive. These factors restrict the development of large aperture telescope in aerospace. The emerging imaging technology called compact passive coherent imaging technology with high resolution (CPCIT) provides a way to solve this problem.

CPCIT utilizes interference and photonic integrated circuit (PIC) technology to imaging. It can reduce the system weight, size and power consumption by an order of magnitude compared to conventional optical telescopes at the same resolution. In 2010, Fontaine et al. [18] outlined the possibility of amplitude- and phase-accurate measurements. In 2013, researchers at UC Davis and LM Advanced Technology Center developed the segmented planar imaging detector for EO reconnaissance (SPIDER) [13–15,20]. The research was developed by funding from National Aeronautics and Space Administration (NASA) and applied this technology for the first time. To date, only SPIDER has made imaging verification tests [3]. SPIDER is made up of many lenslets arranged

© Springer Nature Switzerland AG 2019
Y. Zhao et al. (Eds.): ICIG 2019, LNCS 11902, pp. 359–372, 2019.
https://doi.org/10.1007/978-3-030-34110-7_30

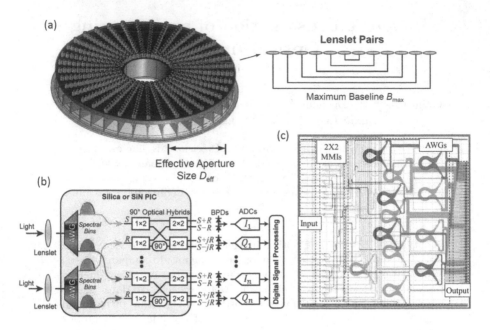

Fig. 1. The SPIDER imager concept. Figures are taken from [3]. (a) Lenslet array arrangement of SPIDER. (b) Schematic view of first generation PIC. (c) Schematic view of second generation PIC

in a radial-spoke pattern, each spoke is a 1D lenslets array composing of a set of lenslets. These lenslets comprise different baselines (lenslet pair) and couple light into PIC. PIC is behind the lenslets array and contains optical components for complex visibility (amplitude and phase) measurement. These optical components include arrayed waveguide gratings (AWG), spectral separation, beam combination and 90° optical hybrids, etc. Various lenslet pairs are equivalent to many small Michelson stellar interferometers. The SPIDER samples a target that is imaged in the Fourier domain and uses an inverse Fourier transform to reconstruct an image. The schematic diagram of the lenslets arrangement of SPIDER is illustrated in Fig. 1(a). Figure 1(b) and (c) are the first and second generation schematics of PIC. An example set of SPIDER parameters is shown in Table 1.

As discussed above, CPCIT samples in Fourier domain and requires image reconstruction. To date, there is little research work on image reconstruction for CPCIT. In the paper, we analyze the sampling structure and characteristics of CPCIT and propose an image reconstruction algorithm suitable for CPCIT. The paper is organized as follows. Section 2 discusses the sampling properties of CPCIT and describes the emerging direct and fast Polar Fourier transform, which is suitable for CPCIT. Section 3 presents the compressive sensing based image reconstruction method. The experimental simulations for verifying the

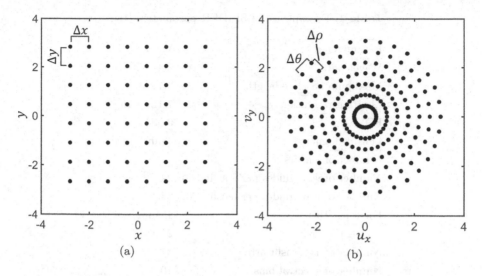

Fig. 2. Illustration of (a) the Cartesian sampling scheme and (b) the Polar scheme.

proposed method are shown in Sect. 4. Finally we provide a summary and a discussion in Sect. 5.

2   Radial Sampling Scheme

The characteristics of imaging system are greatly influenced by point spread function (PSF), which is closely related to the sampling trajectory. Therefore, studying the sampling scheme of imaging system is very important for image reconstruction. As shown in Fig. 1, CPCIT is sampling in radial scheme, which suits to be described in Polar coordinate system. Besides, there are Cartesian scheme (e.g., most of cameras), spiral scheme (e.g. radio interferometry), etc. Figure 2 shows a Cartesian grid and a Polar grid. The general CPCIT equation for imaging reads as:

$$K(\mathbf{u}) = \int_{\mathbb{R}^2} I(\mathbf{a}) exp(i2\pi\mathbf{a} \cdot \mathbf{u}) d\mathbf{a} = \mathcal{F}\{I(\mathbf{a})\}. \tag{1}$$

Here $\mathcal{F}\{\cdot\}$ is the usual Fourier transform. $K(\mathbf{u})$ is the complex visibility measurement. $I(\mathbf{a})$ is the intensity distribution of an incoherent optical source, $\mathbf{a} = (a_1, a_2) \in R^2$ denotes a location lies in the optical source region. $\mathbf{u} = (u, v) \in R^2$ are the corresponding Fourier coordinates defined by $\mathbf{u} = \mathbf{b}/\lambda$, where $\mathbf{b}$ is the baseline separating the two lenslets. Writing the frequency $\mathbf{u} = (u, v)$ in Polar coordinates as

$$u = \rho cos(\theta), v = \rho sin(\theta), \tag{2}$$

where ρ represents the radius and θ is the angle. Then Eq. 1 can be represented as

$$K(\rho, \theta) = \mathcal{PF}\{I(\mathbf{a})\}. \tag{3}$$

Table 1. Example set of SPIDER parameters [16].

Parameter	Value
Wavelength	500–900 nm
Maximum baseline length	0.12 m
Limiting resolution	7.12 μrad
FOV	0.58°
Lenslit diameter	5 mm
Number of lenslits	12
Number of waveguides per lenslit (X)	24
Number of waveguides per lenslit (Y)	24
Focal length	18 mm
Waveguide size	25 μm
Number of 1D lenslit arrays	37
Number of spectral bins	10
Spectral bin bandwidth	40 nm

Here $K(\rho, \theta)$ is defined with Polar variables and $\mathcal{PF}\{\cdot\}$ presents the Polar Fourier transform.

There are some unique properties of radial trajectory that is worth paying attention to [7].

Firstly, when ignoring other effects for simplicity, the PSF can be obtained by setting all sample values to one and zero otherwise and processing the data with the usual image reconstruction procedure. In radial trajectory, the center of the PSF is basically unaffected by changes of the radial count. Most target information remains visible even for a significant amount of streaking artifacts. For this reason, radial sampling offers an attractive under-sampling behavior. In contrast, in Cartesian sampling a reduction of the Fourier domain rows leads to either a resolution decline or the occurrence of aliasing effects that render the image useless.

Secondly, each ray of the radial trajectory carries an equal amount of low and high spatial frequencies. In contrast, for Cartesian sampling the important low spatial frequencies are concentrated in a small number of rows, which creates a difficulty in balancing the acquisition of low and high spatial frequencies in under-sampling scheme. In addition, the aliasing artifacts of a radial under-sampling are scattered to different directions. Thus the incoherence of its PSF masks the artifacts inconspicuous and more noise-like. As all radials pass the center of Fourier domain, the number of sample points is much higher for the low frequencies than for high frequencies. This is essentially different to the Cartesian scheme, where all frequencies are equally covered. Although the radial sample distribution increased complications for the image reconstruction, it is actually a reasonable strategy for typical objects that sampling the low frequencies more densely. In fact, many natural images are characterized by an energy concentration in the center region of the Fourier domain.

We can use these properties to study image reconstruction algorithms that is suitable for CPCIT. The algorithms are detailed in Sect. 3. Here we discuss the first step of image reconstruction, transforming the samples from Polar coordinate to Cartesian coordinate. The traditional method from Polar coordinate to Cartesian coordinate is interpolation. Typically, it is implemented either in the frequency domain (e.g. the regridding method [21]) or in the image domain (e.g. the filtered back projection method [23]). The regridding method interpolates the radial data onto a Cartesian grid by convolution in the Fourier domain, and the approximated Cartesian data can be processed by the standard fast Fourier transform afterwards. However, regridding methods involve significant computation. In order to obtain accurate and fast discrete Fourier transform for Polar grids, we use the direct Polar Fourier transform (PFT) in CPCIT, As discussed in literature [1]. The PFT can accomplish direct and exact computational procedure for the true Polar FT (2D). It is fast, devoid of any oversampling (e.g. PPFFT [2]) or interpolations (e.g. USFFT [17]), and no design on parameters (e.g. MLFFT [24]).

The algorithm of PFT is shown as follows. Consider an image $g(r,c)$ of size $(N+1) \times (N+1)$, where N is even, and r, c are row and column indices respectively. The Polar grid of frequencies $u_x(p,q)$, $v_y(p,q)$ is defined in the circle inscribed in the fundamental region, $\{u,v\} \in [N+1, N+1]^2$. The Polar Fourier transform is defined by

$$G(p,q) = \sum_{c=-N/2}^{N/2} \sum_{r=-N/2}^{N/2} g(r,c) exp(-i\frac{2\pi q}{N+1}(r\cos\theta_p + c\sin\theta_q)), \qquad (4)$$

where $-N/2 \leq q \leq N/2$ represent the points on a radial ray, $\theta_p = p\Delta\theta, 0 \leq p \leq P-1$ are the angles. $\Delta\theta = 180°/P$ is the angular spacing and P is the total number of radial rays. PFT uses 1D fractional Fourier Transform (FrFT) for the computation of Fourier coefficients on radial rays of the Polar grid [4]. 1D FrFT, also known as the Chirp-Z transform, is given by

$$G^\eta(k) = \sum_{q=-N/2}^{N/2} g(q) exp(-i\frac{2\pi k\eta q}{N+1}), -N/2 \leq k \leq N/2, \qquad (5)$$

where η is an arbitrary scalar value, $g(q)$ is a discrete 1D signal, $-N/2 \leq q \leq N/2$ and N is an even integer. Here we require few definitions. The 1D Fourier domain scaling of an image along the X axis can be computed by a 1D FrFT along each row using

$$G^\eta_x(r,c) = \sum_{q=-N/2}^{N/2} g(r,q) exp(-i\frac{2\pi c\eta q}{N+1}), \qquad (6)$$

and the Fourier domain scaling along the Y axis is computed along each column using

$$G_y^\eta(r, c) = \sum_{q=-N/2}^{N/2} g(q, c) exp(-i\frac{2\pi r\eta q}{N+1}). \tag{7}$$

Here $-N/2 \le r, c \le N/2$.

Consider the level one scaling with $\eta = cos(\Delta\theta)$, which is composed of two solutions achieved using Eqs. 6 and 7. We take another 1D FrFT which with a variable scale for each column to compute the 2D Fourier domain radial date on the X axis scale grid. For the column c, we scale it by a factor $|c|\xi$ where $\xi = sin(\Delta\theta)$,

$$G_x^{\eta,\xi}(r, c) = \sum_{q=-N/2}^{N/2} g_x^\eta(q, c) exp(-i\frac{2\pi r|c|\xi q}{N+1}). \tag{8}$$

Similarly, for each row r of the Y axis scaled grid situation, we use the same scale factor $|r|\xi$,

$$G_y^{\eta,\xi}(r, c) = \sum_{q=-N/2}^{N/2} g_x^\eta(r, q) exp(-i\frac{2\pi c|r|\xi q}{N+1}). \tag{9}$$

Here $-N/2 \le r, c \le N/2$.

We can observe that only the desired points which accurately overlap with the radial points on the Polar grid rays need to be evaluated. There are four symmetrical radial rays, two at an angle $\Delta\theta$ and $180° - \Delta\theta$ from the X axis scaled grid (or basically the horizontal lines), and the other two at angles $90° \pm \Delta\theta$ from the Y axis scaled grid (or the basically vertical lines). The orthogonal rays at $0°$ and $90°$ are not included. Then the complete level one solution of the Fourier data on four radial rays is given: $G(1, q), G(P-1, q), G(P/2-1, q)$ and $G(P/2+1, q)$, which is denoted by G_1. For a Polar grid with P is even, the different radial rays oriented in X axis and Y axis are given by $\theta_l = l \times \Delta\theta, l \ge 0$. The corresponding scale factors are $\eta_l = cos\theta_l$ and $\xi_l = sin\theta_l$. Consequently, the solutions of all levels can be written as

$$G_x^{\eta_l,\xi_l}(r, c) = \sum_{q=-N/2}^{N/2} g_x^{\eta_l}(q, c) exp(-i\frac{2\pi r|c|\xi q}{l(N+1)}), \tag{10}$$

and

$$G_y^{\eta_l,\xi_l}(r, c) = \sum_{q=-N/2}^{N/2} g_y^{\eta_l}(r, q) exp(-i\frac{2\pi c|r|\xi q}{l(N+1)}), \tag{11}$$

where $-N/2 \le r, c \le N/2$ and $1 \le l \le L$. The set of scales $S = [\eta_l, \xi_l; 1 \le l \le L]$ has the cardinality of $2L$. The complete Polar Fourier transform is given by

$$G = \bigcup_{l=1}^{L} G_l. \tag{12}$$

Here G_l are the solutions for different levels l, $1 \leq l \leq L$.

There is no direct inverse Polar Fourier transform. The proposed PFT can be written as a linear operator T_{PF}, then the inverse transform can be approached by solving an optimization problem

$$\min_x \| T_{PF}x - y \|_2^2, \tag{13}$$

where x is real vector of size $(N+1)^2 \times 1$ representing the signal, y is a complex valued vector of size $P(N+1) \times 1$ representing the transformed signal. T_{PF} is a complex valued matrix of size $P(N+1) \times (N+1)^2$.

As the local sampling density of points in the Polar grid is varied, weights Ω are introduced to compensate for its effects. Then we have

$$\min_x \| \Omega \circ T_{PF}x - \Omega \circ y \|_2^2, \tag{14}$$

and we solve it iteratively using the relation of least squares (LS) solution

$$x_{j+1} = x_j - \mu T_{PF}^H \Omega^2 \circ (T_p x - y), \tag{15}$$

where μ is the step size and j is the iteration number. T_{PF}^H is the adjoin operator of T_{PF}. For details, see [1].

In this section, we introduce a direct discrete Polar Fourier transform, which is suitable for CPCIT. AS CPCIT samples in Polar scheme in spatial frequency domain, it is necessary to interpolate into Cartesian coordinate and then inverse Fourier transform, or directly Polar Fourier transform. Because interpolation may cause inaccuracy and high complexity, the PFT introduced in this section is a good choice.

3   Image Reconstruction

As discussed in Sect. 2, the aliasing artifacts of a radial under-sampling are scattered to different directions. Thus the incoherence of its PSF masks the artifacts inconspicuous and more noise-like. In addition, each ray of the radial trajectory carries an equal amount of low and high spatial frequencies. These characteristics of radial sampling are very suitable for CS reconstruction. In this section, we propose a CS-based image reconstruction method for CPCIT.

3.1   Compressive Sensing

The basic principle of CS is that the compressible or sparse signal can be reconstructed from a small amount of measurements, which can even fewer than the number of the Nyquist theory required [11,12]. CS has important applications in many areas, such as radio interferometry [28], medical imaging [22], etc. Consider a finite signal $x \in R^N$, a real basis $\Psi \in R^{N \times T}$, the signal can be decomposed as

$$x = \Psi \alpha, \tag{16}$$

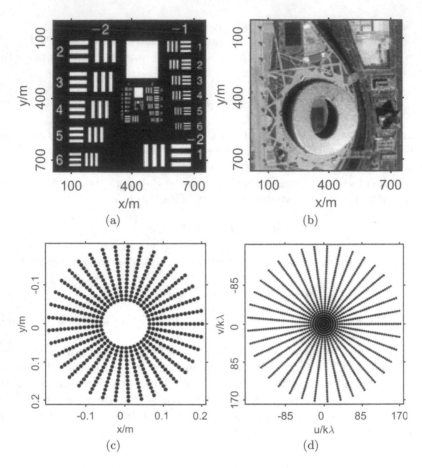

Fig. 3. The test images used in simulations and the sampling arrangement of CPCIT. (a) 1951 USAF. (b) Brid's Nest. (c) 2D arrangement of lenslet array. (d) corresponding spatial frequency coverage.

where α is a sparse representation of x in Ψ. Ψ could be wavelet transform or Fourier transform, etc. The linear measurement of x can be expressed as

$$y = \Phi x = \Gamma \alpha, \tag{17}$$

where $\Phi \in R^{M \times N}$ represents measurement matrix, $\Gamma \in R^{M \times N}$ represents sensing matrix, $y \in R^{M}$ represents the observation vector. If $M \ll N$, then the system is highly ill-posed. In the framework of CS theory, x can be exactly reconstructed with a high probability when G satisfies the restricted isometry property (RIP) [5]. Various basises satisfy RIP condition, such as Gaussian random basis [9], Toplit basis [8], Bernoulli basis [10], etc.

From the CS perspective, the ill-posed problem can be solved by minimization the L_1-norm of the sparse coefficient α

$$\min_x \| \alpha \|_1 \ such \ that \ \| y - \Gamma\alpha \|_2 < \epsilon, \tag{18}$$

where the L_1-norm is given by $\| \alpha \|_1 = \sum_i | \alpha_i |$, while the L_2-norm is given by $\| \alpha \|_2 = (\sum_i | \alpha_i |^2)^{1/2}$. The constraint ϵ is related to the residual noise level.

3.2   CS-Based Method in CPCIT

The linear representation of the image reconstruction process of CPCIT can be expressed as

$$y = Ax + n, \tag{19}$$

with

$$A = CF, \tag{20}$$

where x is the original image with size $N = N^{1/2} \times N^{1/2}$, $y \in R^M$ is the M visibility samples. $A \in R^{M \times N}$ represents sensing matrix, $F \in R^{N \times N}$ represents the Fourier transform, which could be fast FT or PFT. $C \in R^{M \times N}$ is the rectangular binary matrix implementing the mask characterizing visibility coverage. The vector n represents noise corrupting the measurements. The Total Variation (TV) minimization problem can also be applied because that many natural signals are also compressible or sparse in the magnitude of their gradient. Replacing the L_1-norm sparsity prior with the TV-norm of the signal itself

$$\min_x \| x \|_{TV} \ such \ that \ \| y - CFx \|_2 < \epsilon. \tag{21}$$

Here the TV-norm is defined by the L_1-norm of the gradient of the signal $\| x \|_{TV} = \| \nabla x \|_1$. We also could pose an enhanced $TV+$ problem with the prior knowledge of the positivity of the signal as

$$\min_x \| x \|_{TV} \ such \ that \ \| y - CFx \|_2 < \epsilon \ and \ x \geq 0. \tag{22}$$

The basic algorithms in radio telescope research, such as CLEAN [19], MEM [25], can also be used for image reconstruction of CPCIT. But the performances of these algorithms are inferior to CS based algorithms [28], so they are no longer detailed here. Compared to the spiral sampling of radio telescope, the radial sampling of CPCIT is more suitable for CS algorithm. It is worth noting that there are many other recovery algorithms, such as orthogonal matching pursuit (OMP) [26], fast iterative shrinkage-thresholding (FIST) [6], etc. We have only discussed several common ones.

4   Experimental Simulation

In this section, we simulate the reconstructed images based on direct Fourier transform and the proposed CS methods. One of the test images is the 1951

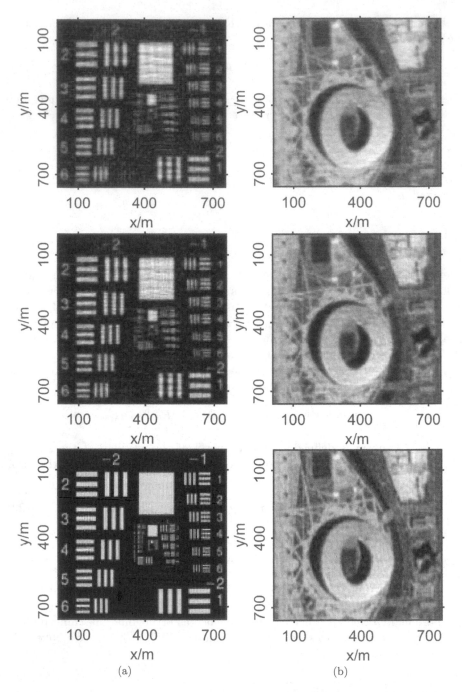

Fig. 4. The reconstructed images of USAF and Nest using various methods. (a) The reconstructed images (from top to bottom) of USAF using direct FT, BP, TV+, respectively. (b) The reconstructed images (from top to bottom) of Nest using direct FT, BP, TV+, respectively.

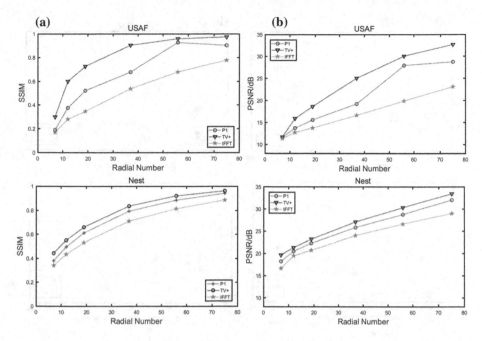

Fig. 5. The performances of different methods with radial number changed on the (a) USAF and (b) Nest.

USAF resolution test chart (called USAF for simplicity) and the other one is the remote sensing image of the Beijing National Stadium, also known as the Bird's Nest (called Nest for simplicity). They are shown in Fig. 3(a) and (b), respectively. Both of them have same size of 128×128 pixels. Figure 3(c) is the 2D arrangement of lenslet array and Fig. 3(d) is the corresponding spatial frequency coverage. We use the system parameters in Table 1 for the simulations. The radial number is 37. The peak signal-to-noise ratio (PSNR) and the structural similarity index (SSIM) are introduced as performance metrics to quantitatively evaluate the reconstructed image quality of these methods [27].

Figure 4 shows the reconstructed images using direct FFT and CS methods which include basis pursuit (BP) (Eq. 18) and TV+ (Eq. 22) approaches. The TV+ method has been shown to achieve good reconstruction quality. Figure 5 shows the reconstruction performance of different approaches with various radial numbers. Figure 6 shows the reconstruction performance of different approaches with various sampling number on a single radial. It can be seen that the reconstruction quality become better when the radial number and the sampling number of a single radial are increasing and the TV+ method achieves a good performance. As the number of sample points is much higher for the low frequencies than for high frequencies in radial sampling scheme, the performance of Direct FFT is acceptable and avoiding the influence of the aliasing effect.

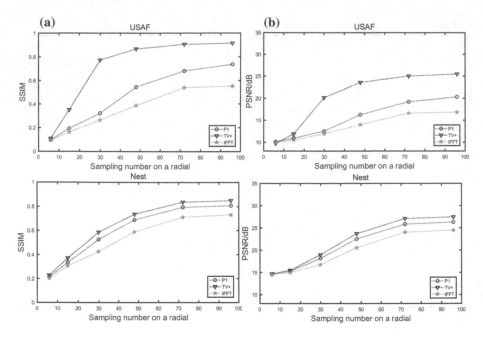

Fig. 6. The performances of different methods with sampling number on a single radial changed on the (a) USAF and (b) Nest.

5   Discussion and Conclusions

In this paper, we present a new imaging technology named CPCIT. We analyze the sampling properties of it and then propose a CS based image reconstruction method. CPCIT can reduce the system weight, size and power consumption by an order of magnitude compared to conventional optical telescopes at the same resolution. As sampling scheme is an important part of image reconstruction, we discuss the radial sampling scheme of CPCIT and use PFT to transform the radial Fourier samples of CPCIT into Cartesian coordinate. However, due to the computation of PFT is rather complicated, we have not succeeded in combining it with CS. The combination of PFT and CS is an important part of future work. In addition, we also consider processing the samples in Polar coordinate, and transforming them to Cartesian coordinates at the end. CPCIT is still in the initial stage of research at present. There is little study of image reconstruction algorithm for it. However, the mature application of CPCIT will have a remarkable impact on the development of astronomical observation and remote sensing.

References

1. Abbas, S.A., Sun, Q., Foroosh, H.: An exact and fast computation of discrete Fourier transform for polar and spherical grid. IEEE Trans. Signal Process. **65**(8), 2033–2048 (2017)
2. Averbuch, A., Coifman, R.R., Donoho, D.L., Elad, M., Israeli, M.: Fast and accurate polar Fourier transform. Appl. Comput. Harmon. Anal. **21**(2), 145–167 (2006)
3. Badham, K., et al.: Testbed experiment for SPIDER: a photonic integrated circuit-based interferometric imaging system. In: Advanced Maui Optical and Space Surveillance (AMOS) Technologies Conference (2017)
4. Bailey, D.H., Swarztrauber, P.N.: The fractional Fourier transform and applications. SIAM Rev. **33**(3), 389–404 (1991)
5. Baraniuk, R.G.: Compressive sensing [lecture notes]. IEEE Signal Process. Mag. **24**(4), 118–121 (2007)
6. Beck, A., Teboulle, M.: A fast iterative shrinkage-thresholding algorithm for linear inverse problems. SIAM J. Imaging Sci. **2**(1), 183–202 (2009)
7. Block, K.T.: Advanced methods for radial data sampling in magnetic resonance imaging. SUB University of Goettingen (2008)
8. Candes, E.J., Romberg, J.K., Tao, T.: Stable signal recovery from incomplete and inaccurate measurements. Commun. Pure Appl. Math. **59**(8), 1207–1223 (2006)
9. Candes, E.J., Tao, T.: Decoding by linear programming. IEEE Trans. Inf. Theory **51**(12), 4203–4215 (2005)
10. Candes, E.J., Tao, T.: Near-optimal signal recovery from random projections: universal encoding strategies? IEEE Trans. Inf. Theory **52**(12), 5406–5425 (2006)
11. Candès, E.J., Wakin, M.B.: An introduction to compressive sampling. IEEE Sig. Process. Mag. **25**(2), 21–30 (2008)
12. Cands, E.J., Romberg, J., Tao, T.: Robust uncertainty principles: exact signal frequency information. IEEE Trans. Inf. Theory **52**(2), 489–509 (2006)
13. Duncan, A., et al.: SPIDER: next generation chip scale imaging sensor update. In: Advanced Maui Optical and Space Surveillance Technologies Conference (2016)
14. Duncan, A., et al.: SPIDER: next generation chip scale imaging sensor. In: Advanced Maui Optical and Space Surveillance Technologies Conference (2015)
15. Duncan, A., et al.: Experimental demonstration of interferometric imaging using photonic integrated circuits. Opt. Express **25**(11), 12653 (2017)
16. Duncan, A.L., Kendrick, R.L., Stubbs, D.M.: Interferometer array imaging system using photonic integrated circuit cards, 5 September 2017. US Patent 9,754,985
17. Fenn, M., Kunis, S., Potts, D.: On the computation of the polar FFT. Appl. Comput. Harmon. Anal. **22**(2), 257–263 (2007)
18. Fontaine, N.K., Scott, R.P., Zhou, L., Soares, F.M., Heritage, J.P., Yoo, S.J.B.: Real-time full-field arbitrary optical waveform measurement. Nat. Photonics **4**(4), 248–254 (2010)
19. Gull, S.F., Daniell, G.J.: Image reconstruction from incomplete and noisy data. Nature **272**(5655), 686–690 (1978)
20. Kendrick, R., Duncan, A., Wilm, J., Thurman, S.T., Stubbs, D.M., Ogden, C.: Flat panel space based space surveillance sensor. In: Advanced Maui Optical and Space Surveillance Technologies Conference (2013)
21. Liu, Q., Nguyen, N.: An accurate algorithm for nonuniform fast Fourier transforms (NUFFT's). IEEE Microw. Guided Wave Lett. **8**(1), 18–20 (1998)
22. Lustig, M., Donoho, D., Pauly, J.M.: Sparse MRI: the application of compressed sensing for rapid MR imaging. Magn. Reson. Med. **58**(6), 1182 (2007)

23. Natterer, F.: The Mathematics of Computerized Tomography, vol. 32. SIAM, Philadelphia (1986)
24. Pan, W., Qin, K., Chen, Y.: An adaptable-multilayer fractional Fourier transform approach for image registration. IEEE Trans. Pattern Anal. Mach. Intell. **31**(3), 400–414 (2009)
25. Schwarz, U.: Mathematical-statistical description of the iterative beam removing technique (method clean). Astron. Astrophys. **65**, 345 (1978)
26. Tropp, J.A., Gilbert, A.C.: Signal recovery from random measurements via orthogonal matching pursuit. IEEE Trans. Inf. Theory **53**(12), 4655–4666 (2007)
27. Wang, Z., Bovik, A.C., Sheikh, H.R., Simoncelli, E.P.: Image quality assessment: from error visibility to structural similarity. IEEE Trans. Image Process. **13**(4), 600–612 (2004)
28. Wiaux, Y., Jacques, L., Puy, G., Scaife, A.M.M., Vandergheynst, P.: Compressed sensing imaging techniques for radio interferometry. Mon. Not. R. Astron. Soc. **395**(3), 1733–1742 (2009)

Speckle Reduction for Fourier Ptychographic Reconstruction Using Gamma-Correction and Reshaped Wirtinger Flow Optimization

Zhixin Li[1,2]($\boxtimes$), Desheng Wen[1], Zongxi Song[1], Gang Liu[1,2], Weikang Zhang[1,2], Xin Wei[1,2], and Tuochi Jiang[1,2]

[1] Xi'an Institute of Optics and Precision Mechanics, Chinese Academy of Sciences, Xi'an 710119, China
lizhixin2015@opt.cn
[2] University of Chinese Academy of Sciences, Beijing 100049, China

Abstract. Fourier ptychography is a newly reported computational imaging technique, which is used for long-distance, sub-diffraction imaging recently. Compared to conventional Fourier ptychographic microscopy, there is pronounced laser speckle noise in captured images. In this work, a new framework is proposed to suppress speckle noise and reconstruct the high-resolution image for diffuse object. We introduce a random phase to simulate the effects of rough surface during imaging process, and then recover the high-resolution spectrum following two steps: the first is to promote the noisy captured images using Gamma-correction, and the second step is to recover the Fourier spectrum using reshaped Wirtinger flow optimization. Experiments on both simulation and real data demonstrate that the proposed method incorporates speckle noise reduction into reconstruction process, which can achieve better results on both visual and quantitative metrics compared to previous work.

Keywords: Speckle reduction · Fourier Ptychography · Phase retrieval · Computational imaging

1 Introduction

Fourier Ptychography (FP) is a novel method to improve spatial resolution in microscopy, which can beyond the diffraction-limit of objective lens. This technique illuminates the target with different angels, and correspondingly captures multiple low-resolution images describing different spatial spectrum bands of the target. By stitching these spectrum bands together in the Fourier space, the entire high-resolution spatial spectrum can be reconstructed, including both phase and amplitude [1, 2]. Recently, initial work in macroscopic imaging suggests that FP has potential benefits in improving spatial resolution for long-distance imaging [3]. Holloway et al. demonstrate that Fourier ptychography can dramatically improve the resolution of stand-off scenery and their experiments show resolution gains of are achievable [4]. The following research of them proposes FP for diffuse objects could produce speckle on the image plane, which deteriorates

© Springer Nature Switzerland AG 2019
Y. Zhao et al. (Eds.): ICIG 2019, LNCS 11902, pp. 373–383, 2019.
https://doi.org/10.1007/978-3-030-34110-7_31

perceptual quality of the recovered high-resolution image [5]. There are two methods to suppress speckle noise including optical processing and digital image processing. Optical processing reduces the speckle noise by reducing the spatial coherence of laser beams or diversifying the wavelength and angle [6, 7]. Digital image processing is also important for the suppression of speckle. Several algorithms have been proposed for reducing speckle such as wavelet-based transformations [8], Lee-filter [9], nonlocal means algorithm [10], etc. Besides, the recent research [11] shows that gamma-correction of noisy hologram can affect the speckle noise reduction effect, which does not introduce a lot of computational complexity.

In fact, Fourier ptychography can reduce the speckle size by reducing diffraction blur. Thus, an effective reconstruction algorithm is also important for suppressing speckle noise. Mathematically, FP can be considered as a typical phase retrieval optimization process, which aims to recover the complex high-resolution spatial spectrum. Alternating projection (AP) [12] is a phase retrieval algorithm, which has been widely used in conventional Fourier ptychography including the latest macroscopic Fourier ptychography. AP algorithm is easy to use and converges quickly, but is sensitive to measurement noise. Wirtinger flow optimization for Fourier Ptychography (WFP) is a novel application of Wirtinger Flow optimization proposed by Bian [13, 14], which minimizes the intensity error between estimated low-resolution images and corresponding measurements using the gradient scheme and Wirtinger calculus [15]. Zhang et al. propose a reshaped Wirtinger flow approach for solving quadratic system of equations [16]. The experiments demonstrate this lower-order loss function based on absolute magnitude has great advantages in statistical and computational efficiency compared to Wirtinger Flow optimization. Here this optimization algorithm is first used for Fourier ptychographic reconstruction and we call it Reshaped-WFP (reshaped Wirtinger flow optimization for Fourier Ptychography).

Based on previous work, a new framework is proposed to reduce the effects of speckle noise and improve quality of the reconstructed high-resolution image. The advantages of our work are three aspects: A random optical phase is introduced to simulate the effects of rough surface toward long-distance imaging using FP; Gamma-correction is used as data preprocessing for captured low-resolution images to suppress the speckle noise; Reshaped Wirtinger flow optimization for Fourier Ptychography (Reshaped-WFP) is implemented as the reconstruction algorithm to retrieval the high-resolution spatial spectrum, which can increase peak signal to noise ratio (PSNR) and reduce relative error (RE).

2   Methods

2.1   Image Formation Model for Diffuse Objects

Most real-world objects are 'optically rough' on the scale of optical wavelength. The surface of them has many microscopic scattering points fluctuating randomly. Each point along the surface acts as a secondary source when coherent light illuminates the object. These secondary light sources scattering from the points interfere with each other to produce speckle on the image plane [17]. The speckle overlaps with the image and distorts the recovered results, which should be suppressed for laser illumination imaging.

The roughness of object's surface plays a decisive role in speckle phenomenon. It can be described by three important parameters including root mean square (rms) height, correlation length of surface height and rms slope. These parameters depict statistical characteristics of the surface height, which can uniquely determine the roughness of surface. As a preliminary simulation study, only rms height and rms slope are taken into consideration to simulate the rough surface here. Besides, the Gaussian distribution is important to describe surface scattering models because it is suitable for most scenarios. The target is considered as an ideal smooth model with a rough surface following Gaussian distribution, as shown in Fig. 1. The laser beam with center λ wavelength illuminates the object located at the coordinate plane r_0 and scatters. The complex amplitude of optical field in the Fraunhofer plane r' can be described as

$$U(r') = \int \psi(r_0) \exp(\frac{-i4\pi z(r_0)}{\lambda}) \exp(\frac{-i2\pi r_0 \cdot r'}{\lambda z}) dr_0 \qquad (1)$$

where $\psi(r_0)$ denotes illuminated field emerging from the smooth object, $z(r_0)$ is the height function of random surface following Gauss distribution, $4\pi z(r_0)/\lambda$ is the optical phase and is the distance between observation plane and scattering surface. Specially, a phase function $\exp(-i4\pi z(r_0)/\lambda)$ is introduced to simulate the scattering for random rough surface. We could change the variance σ_z^2 of height function to control the roughness of objects.

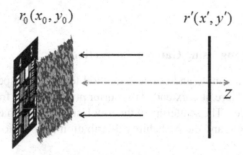

$r_0(x_0, y_0)$ $r'(x', y')$

Fig. 1. The schematic diagram of speckle field produced by surface scattering in the Fraunhofer plane.

We describe our camera aperture using the pupil function $P(x', y')$, which can be considered as an ideal low-pass filter. (x', y') are the 2D spatial frequency coordinates in the Fraunhofer plane. Since optical field is limited by camera aperture, the light field immediately after the aperture is given by product $U(r')P(x', y')$. This band limited optical field then propagates to the image plane and is recorded by camera sensor.

$$I(x, y) = \left| F^{-1}[U(r')P(x', y')] \right|^2 \qquad (2)$$

where $I(x, y)$ is a simulated image with laser speckle noise, (x, y) are the 2D spatial frequency coordinates in the image plane, and F^{-1} denotes the inverse Fourier transform.

Then we recenter the camera in Fourier plane at m different locations $(c_{x'}(i), c_{y'}(i)), i = 1, 2, \cdots m$. From previous work, adequate reconstruction results can be achieved when two adjacent positions satisfy the overlap ratio of 65% or more [1]. The final series of low-resolution images can be given as

$$I_i(x, y) = \left| F^{-1} \left[U(r') P(x' - c_{x'}(i), y' - c_{y'}(i)) \right] \right|^2 \tag{3}$$

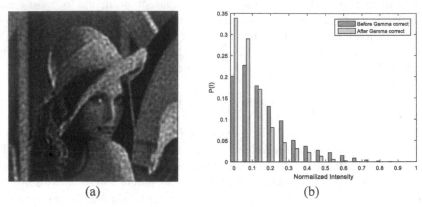

(a)   (b)

Fig. 2. (a) A simulated image with laser speckle noise. (b) Normalized intensity distribution of (a) using Gamma-correction.

2.2 Data Preprocessing Using Gamma-Correction

Gamma-correction is a simple and efficient method to suppress speckle noise in holographic imaging [11]. Here, it is extended to fourier ptychography framework to preprocess the captured images. The scattering of the rough surface can change the polarization state of the incident light and the probability distribution of speckle image's intensity is described as

$$p(I_i) = 4 \frac{I_i}{\mu^2} \exp(-2 \frac{I_i}{\mu}) \qquad for \ I_i \geq 0 \tag{4}$$

where μ is the mean intensity. Equation (5) is the Fourier transform of Eq. (4)

$$F(\omega) = \frac{1}{2 + j\mu\omega} \tag{5}$$

From the Eq. (5), it is clear that the Fourier transform curve becomes smooth with decrease of μ. The Gamma-correction used to suppress the intensity of speckle noise can be given as

$$I_{pi} = c I_i^\Gamma \tag{6}$$

where I_i is the normalized intensity of original captured image, I_{pi} is the image after Gamma-correction and c is a positive constant. We use a $512px \times 512px$ 'Lena' image shown in Fig. 2(a) as the measured images with strong speckle noise $\sigma_z^2 = 0.14$. Figure 2(b) is the normalized intensity distribution after gamma-correction with $\Gamma = 1.2$. It can be seen that the intensity distribution of target becomes steeper using gamma-correction, which means the number of low gray values increased and the number of high gray values reduced. Thus, the mean intensity μ of noisy image is also reduced in this transformation. The Fourier transform function curve after gamma-correction becomes smoother, so the contrast of the FFT transformation is lower than before. It's very beneficial for reconstruction which can be verified by following experiments.

However, the imaging objects and noise intensity are unknown for most applications. Obtaining the reasonable value of Γ which can fit most real situations is crucial for the preprocessing step. To address this problem, we first estimate the variance of captured images and then calculate the Γ based on it. From the Subsect. 2.1, it can be seen that I_i is a series of low resolution images corrupted with diffraction blur and speckle noise. Estimating the variance of all images is inapplicable because it requires high computation cost. Then the center image is selected to estimate the value of Γ. Speckle can be regarded as multiplicative noise following negative exponential distribution [17]. To estimate speckle noise level, the natural logarithm of the captured center image is taken to convert the noise into a more convenient additive model $\xi_c = \ln(I_c)$. Here the new variable ξ_c is modeled as a noise-free signal ξ_c' corrupted by additive noise η, which can be described as $\xi_c = \xi_c' + \eta$. Specifically, η is signal-independent additive noise with zero mean and σ_η^2 variance. A novel method to estimate the noise level of ξ_c is based on principal component analysis (PCA) of image blocks, which has higher computational efficiency and better accuracy compared with other methods. From the previous research [18], the m smallest eigenvalues of Σ_{ξ_c} equal σ_η^2 if the information in noise-free image ξ_c' is redundant. Where Σ_{ξ_c} is the population covariance matrices of ξ_c. Then the value of Γ can be computed by

$$\Gamma = k\sigma_\eta^2 + b \tag{7}$$

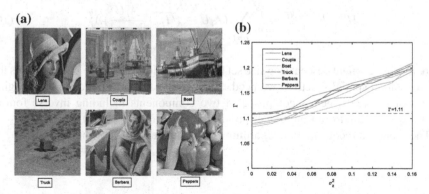

Fig. 3. (a) Six test images. (b) The estimated Γ value for test images with different speckle noise level.

A large number of experiments indicate that the reasonable value of ranges from 1 to 1.25. In this work, $k = 1$ and $b = 1.07$ can fit the most scenes. Figure 3(a) provides six test images and Fig. 3(b) provides Γ value of them under different speckle noise level.

2.3 Reshaped-WFP Optimization

To obtain the high-resolution image, we use Reshaped-WFP optimization to recover the high resolution complex field in the aperture plane. Reshaped Wirtinger flow is a recently reported algorithm to recover a vector x based on the magnitude measurements $y = \{|\langle a_i, x \rangle|\}_{i=1}^{m}$ and the design vectors $\{a_i\}_{i=1}^{m}$. It solves the problem by minimizing the nonconvex loss function via a gradient algorithm, and enjoys geometric convergence to a global optimal as long as the number of measurements is at the order of $O(n)$, where n is the dimension of x. In this work, we extend the Reshaped Wirtinger flow optimization to fourier ptychographic reconstruction algorithm. Here the high resolution spectrum of target is considered as the vector of interest, fourier ptychographic imaging process is considered as the design vectors, and the captured images after gamma-correction are taken as the magnitude measurements. Then the loss function is given as

$$\min f(\hat{U}) = \frac{1}{2m} \sum_{i=1}^{m} \left(\left| A_i \hat{U} \right| - \sqrt{I_{pi}} \right)^2 \tag{8}$$

the gradient of the loss function is

$$\nabla f(\hat{U}) = \frac{1}{m} \sum_{i=1}^{m} (A_i \hat{U} - \sqrt{I_{pi}} \cdot \mathrm{sgn}(A_i \hat{U})) A_i^T = \frac{1}{m} \sum_{i=1}^{m} (A_i \hat{U} - \sqrt{I_{pi}} \cdot \frac{A_i \hat{U}}{\left| A_i \hat{U} \right|}) A_i^T \tag{9}$$

In implementation, $\hat{U}$ can be solved in a descending manner as

$$\hat{U}^{(t+1)} = \hat{U}^{(t)} - \frac{\mu}{m} \sum_{i=1}^{m} (A_i \hat{U} - \sqrt{I_{pi}} \cdot \frac{A_i \hat{U}}{\left| A_i \hat{U} \right|}) A_i^T \tag{10}$$

where μ is the gradient descent step size set by user and plural vector $\hat{U} \in \mathbb{C}^n$ denotes the high resolution spatial spectrum we need. Specifically, A_i corresponds to the imaging process of Eq. (3) which is composed of two components including inverse fourier transform F^{-1} and down sampling of pupil $P(x' - c_{x'}(i), y' - c_{y'}(i))$.

The proposed reconstruction algorithm is summarized as Algorithm 1.

Algorithm 1:Our reconstruction algorithm

Input : Measured images $\sqrt{I_i} = \left\{ \sqrt{I_i} \right\}_{i=1}^{m}$, sampling matrix $\left\{ A_i \right\}_{i=1}^{m}$;

Parameters: Step size μ ,the positive constant c and Γ

Preprocessing: $I_{pi} = cI_i^{\Gamma}$

Initialization: $\hat{U}^{(0)} = F(\frac{1}{m}\sum_{i=1}^{m}\sqrt{I_{pi}}), t = 0$

While not converged **do**

    Update $\hat{U}^{(t+1)}$ according to Eq. (9);

      $t := t+1$;

    end

end

output: $\hat{U}^{(t)}$;

---

3 Experiments

In this section, a series of experiments are conducted on both simulation and real data, to demonstrate the performance of proposed algorithm.

3.1 Experiment on Simulation Data

In order to better fit the real situation, the sub-imaging setup parameters are set as follows. The illumination wavelength is 632.8 nm, the focal length of the lens is 75 mm and the aperture diameter is 2.3 mm which corresponds to an ideal pupil function (all ones in the pupil circle and all zeros outside). Similar to the research [14], the overlap ratio between two adjacent pictures is set to be $\xi = 65\%$. We use the $512px \times 512px$ 'Lena' image from the USC-SIPI image database [19] as ground truth and the pixel size of captured images is 2.2 um. The number of horizontal and vertical measurements is $m = 15 \times 15$. The captured LR images' pixel numbers are set to be one fifth of the reconstruction image along both dimensions, and are obtained according to Eq. (3).

Based on the above parameter settings and Fourier ptychography imaging method, the simulation of our sub-diffraction imaging process is synthesized by the following steps: (1) Adding rough surface to the ground truth image to simulate a diffuse object. (2) We perform the FFT transformation on the obtained image and pick out the corresponding sub-region by multiplying it with the pupil function. (3) Translating the pupil to capture different regions of the Fourier domain and get a series of noisy images with limited spectrum. (4) Gamma-correction of these low resolution images to initially suppress the intensity

In addition to visual effects, two quantitative evaluation criteria are adopted to objectively evaluate the quality of algorithms. The first one is peak signal to noise ratio (PSNR), which is widely used to assess the image quality after processing. It can intuitively describe the intensity difference between two images, and would be greater for higher quality image. Another criterion is relative error (RE) [20], which is given as

$$RE(z, \hat{z}) = \frac{\min_{\phi \in [0, 2\pi)} \left\| e^{-j\phi} z - \hat{z} \right\|^2}{\left\| \hat{z} \right\|^2} \tag{11}$$

It is mainly used to measure the difference between two complex functions z and $\hat{z}$, here to compare the recovered spectrum with original spectrum. The RE scores range from 0 to 1, and is smaller for higher quality recovery.

To demonstrate the performance and advantages of proposed algorithm, a series of experiments are simulated on synthetic data. We compare our algorithm with the AP algorithm, which is also used in research [4, 5] to recover the image with speckle noise for long-distance, sub-diffraction imaging. Here the update of pupil function does not be considered for simplicity. The fluctuation of object's surface follows Gaussian distribution, and the variance σ_z^2 of height function ranges from 0.08 to 0.16. With the increase of variance σ_z^2, the surface roughness of object increases and the speckle noise becomes more pronounced. By algorithm testing, the number of iterations is set to 300 to ensure the convergence of proposed algorithm.

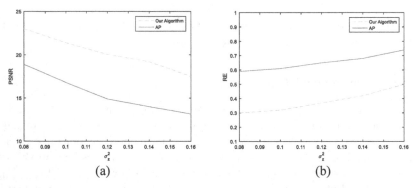

(a)   (b)

Fig. 4. (a) Quantitative comparison for the PSNR (dB) at different speckle noise levels. (b) Quantitative comparison for the RE at different speckle noise levels.

The quantitative results are shown in Fig. 4(a) and (b). It is clear that the qualities of reconstructed images degrade with the increase of surface roughness, the PSNR becomes smaller and the RE becomes larger. However, the proposed algorithm has obvious advantages in PSNR and RE for different levels of speckle noise compared to AP. It can raise PSNR by almost 5 dB and reduce RE by almost 0.3, even in strong noise levels. Besides, the reconstruction quality of our algorithm does not degenerate a lot with the increase of surface roughness. This demonstrates the robustness of proposed method to laser speckle noise, and thus it has a wider application value toward long-distance Fourier Ptychography reconstruction. Figure 5 provides the visual reconstruction results, and the variance is fixed at 0.10. Figure 5(a) is one of the captured images simulated by the proposed framework, which is hardly to recognize due to speckle noise corruption. Figure 5(b) and (c) are recovered high-resolution amplitude images using AP and the proposed algorithm, respectively. There is a lot of speckle in Fig. 5(b) because AP is sensitive to measurement noise. Figure 5(c) is of higher quality than Fig. 5(b), which can remove most of noise without losing crucial high frequency details. This is because the proposed algorithm incorporates speckle noise reduction into the reconstruction process. The convergence rate of above methods is shown in Fig. 5(d) and (e). It demonstrates that our proposed algorithm could obtain a good result in the fiftieth iteration, and converge within 200 iterations. There is no great difference in convergence speed compared with AP. Therefore, the proposed algorithm could obtain satisfying reconstruction quality with less speckle noise and more image details, which outperform the AP on both visual and quantitative results.

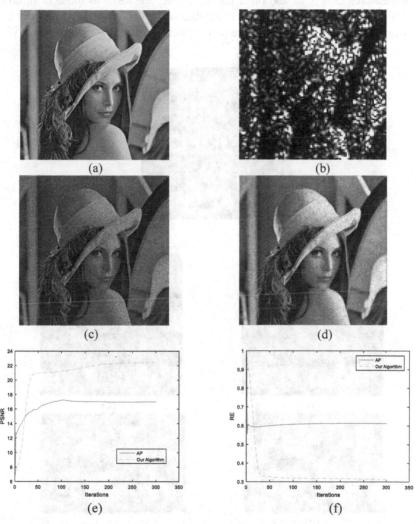

Fig. 5. Comparison of the reconstruction results. (a) Original image (b) Simulated acquisition image. (c) The reconstructed image using AP. (d) The reconstructed image using proposed algorithm. (e) The convergence rate of different methods for PSNR. (f) The convergence rate of different methods for RE

3.2 Experiment on Real Data

To further verify the performance of proposed algorithm, we use the real data set from research [4] as initial input images (http://jrholloway.com/projects/towardCCA). The scene is a translucent Dasani water bottle label and we only intercept part of them, as shown in Fig. 6. Due to the roughness surface, this diffuse water bottle label has a random phase which can produce a highly varying optical field at the image plane, and thus the captured images contain laser speckle noise. The real data set is captured by the setup with 81% overlap between adjacent images. The number of horizontal and vertical measurements is 17 and other parameters are the same as those in simulation process. Figure 6(a) is the center image of the data set, which is degraded by speckle and diffraction blur. Figure 6(b) and (c) are reconstruction intensity images using AP and

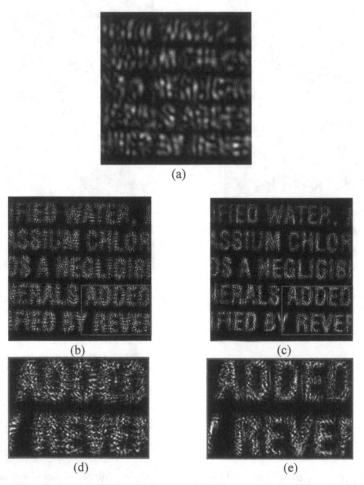

Fig. 6. Reconstruction comparison on real data set. (a) The center image of real data set. (b) The recovered intensity image using AP. (c) The recovered intensity image using proposed algorithm. (d) The detail region of (b). (e) The detail region of (c).

the proposed algorithm respectively. Compared to AP, our algorithm can remove some of the artifacts and reduce the contrast of speckle as shown in Fig. 6(c). Figure 6(d) and (e) are detail regions of Fig. 6(b) and (c), which can be seen that the proposed algorithm has lower speckle compared to AP in visual.

4   Conclusions and Discussions

This paper proposes a new reconstruction framework for long-distance, sub-diffraction imaging using Fourier ptychography, which aims to reduce the speckle noise produced by diffuse objects. Compared to previous FP implementations, a randomly distributed phase is introduced to obtain noisy images with different levels of speckle. Then we use Gamma-correction as data preprocessing, which can preliminary suppress speckle noise without large computational complexity. Based on the recently reported reshaped Wirtinger flow optimization, we recover the high resolution spectrum as solving quadratic system of equations, and present a solution utilizing the gradient descent scheme. The results demonstrate that proposed algorithm can get better quantitative and visual effects compared to AP algorithm which is mainly used in this field now. Specially, the recovered image with less noise and more details can be achieved because no filter is used during the reconstruction. From the previous research, Fourier ptychographic imaging for long distance has potential significance in many computer vision and imaging applications including remote sensing and surveillance. However, Speckle noise and the robustness of reconstruction algorithm are main barriers to build a real system. This work solves these problems and will help a lot to realize a full-scale implementation.

References

1. Zheng, G., Horstmeyer, R., Yang, C.: Nat. Photonics **7**, 739 (2013)
2. Ou, X., Horstmeyer, R., Zheng, G., Yang, C.: Opt. Express **23**, 3472 (2015)
3. Dong, S., et al.: Opt. Express **22**, 13586 (2014)
4. Holloway, J., et al.: IEEE Trans. Comput. Imaging **2**, 251 (2016)
5. Holloway, J., Wu, Y., Sharma, M.K., Cossairt, O., Veeraraghavan, A.: Sci. Adv. **3**, e1602564 (2017)
6. Caprio, G.D., et al.: Biomed. Opt. Express **5**, 690 (2014)
7. George, N., Jain, A.: Appl. Opt. **12**, 1202 (1973)
8. Sharma, A., Sheoran, G., Jaffery, Z.A.: Opt. Lasers Eng. **46**, 42 (2008)
9. Leng, J., Zhou, J., Lang, X., Li, X.: Opt. Rev. **22**, 844 (2015)
10. Buades, A., Coll, B., Morel, J.M.: Proceedings IEEE Computer Society Conference on Computer Vision and Pattern Recognition, vol. 2, p. 60 (2005)
11. Huang, X., Jia, Z., Zhou, J., Yang, J., Kasabov, N.: IEEE Access **6**, 5227 (2018)
12. Ou, X., Horstmeyer, R., Yang, C., Zheng, G.: Opt. Lett. **38**, 4845 (2013)
13. Candes, E.J., Li, X., Soltanolkotabi, M.: IEEE Trans. Inf. Theory **61**, 1985 (2015)
14. Bian, L., Suo, J., Zheng, G., Guo, K., Chen, F., Dai, Q.: Opt. Express **23**, 4856 (2015)
15. Bian, L., et al.: Sci. Rep. **6**, 27384 (2016)
16. Zhang, H., Liang, Y.: arXiv:1605.07719
17. Goodman, J.W.: Speckle Phenomena in Optics: Theory and Application, p. 7. Roberts and Company Publishers, Colorado (2007)
18. Deledalle, C.A., Salmon, J., Dalalyan, A.: BMVC **81**, 425 (2011)
19. Weber, A.G.: USC-SIPI Rep. **315**, 1 (1997)
20. Chen, Y., Candes, E.J.: arXiv:1505.05114

Color and Multispectral Processing

Adaptive and Rotating Non-local Weighted Joint Sparse Representation Classification for Hyperspectral Images

Jingwen Yan[1], Hongda Chen[1], Zixin Xie[1], and Lei Liu[2]([✉])

[1] Engineering College, Shantou University, Shantou 515063, China
jwyan@stu.edu.cn
[2] Medical College, Shantou University, Shantou 515063, China
wliulei@stu.edu.cn

Abstract. In this paper, we propose an adaptive and rotating non-local weighted joint sparse representation classification (ARW-JSRC) method for hyperspectral image (HSI). The proposed method aims at avoiding misclassification of the HSI pixels located around the boundaries of class and over-smoothed classification performance caused by the window-based technique used in joint sparse representation classification (JSRC). Since the window-based technique leads to the undesired classification result, an adaptive threshold based on the spectral angle between different classes and the rotated similar window replaced the traditional rectangular window are applied to sufficiently utilize the rich spectral-spatial signatures and alleviate this problem. Furthermore, a new weight formula that accurately reflects the spectral-spatial feature in HSI is applied to obtain more appropriate weights for HSI pixels in search window. Experimental results indicate that our method achieves great improvement in HSI classification, comparing to several widely used classification methods.

Keywords: Hyperspectral image classification · Adaptive threshold · Rotated similar window · Non-local weighted

1 Introduction

Since hyperspectral image (HSI) has hundreds of spectral bands, it has a higher spectral resolution comparing to other kinds of images, which improves its ability to distinguish different materials [1, 2]. Due to the each pixel in HSI corresponds to a spectral curve, it means that HSI classification is to assign each pixel a land-cover class based on their respective spectral information [3]. However, the high dimensional characteristic existing in HSI may cause the Hughes phenomenon [4], which poses a big challenge to the HSI classification.

Supported by the NSF of China (No. 61672335 and 61601276), and by Department of Education of Guangdong Province (No. 2016KZDXM012 and 2017KCXTD015).

Sparse representation (SR), a useful tool for high-dimensional signal processing, has been applied to HSI classification last few years. Related studies shown in [7–10] have displayed the achievement the SR based methods made. In 2011, Yi chen firstly applied the sparse representation classification (SRC) approach from other fields to HSI classification [5]. Meanwhile, the author proposed a joint sparse representation classification (JSRC) method rooting in the assumption that HSI pixels in a small area consist of similar material (same class). Though the JSRC has a better performance than SRC, there is a situation that not all HSI pixels can meet the assumption of JSRC. When the HSI pixel locates at regional edge, its neighboring pixels can not be guaranteed homogeneity. In order to reduce the interference of heterogenous pixels in the neighborhood, Zhang in [6] proposed a non-local weighted joint sparse representation classification (NLW-JSRC) method. By assigning different weights to HSI pixels in search window according to the similarities between neighboring pixels and central pixel, the NLW-JSRC can improve the problem existing in JSRC. However, its calculation of weights can not fully consider the spatial information of the HSI and can not assign appropriate weights for pixels in search window.

In order to effectively reduce the interference of the heterogeneous pixels in the search window, we propose an adaptive and rotated non-local weighted sparse representation classification (ARW-JSRC) method. Compared with NLW-JSRC, our proposed method can provide more appropriate weight to every pixel in the search window. It uses a rotation transformation strategy to measure the similarity between the pixels in the search window, so as to make full use of the spatial information of the image. Then, a new weight calculation method is used to give more appropriate weight to each pixel in the search. The adaptive threshold involved in the weight formula is obtained by calculating the median of the maximum and minimum spectral angles of various training samples.

The remainder of this paper is organized as follows. The non-local weighted joint sparse representation classification is described in Sect. 2. Then, the adaptive and rotated non-local weighted joint sparse representation classification is introduced in Sect. 3. The experimental results and discussion are presented in Sect. 4. The conclusion is shown in Sect. 5.

2   Related Works

2.1   JSRC

In the JSRC, it is assumed that all neighboring HSI pixels in a small area can be approximately represented by the linear combination of a few common atoms with different coefficients. For any test HSI pixel $x_i(i = 1, 2, \cdots, N)$, let its search window size be set as $\sqrt{S} \times \sqrt{S}$, then the joint signal matrix $X = [x_1, x_2, \ldots, x_S]$ can be represented as

$$X = [x_1 \ x_2 \ \dots \ x_S]$$
$$= [D\alpha_1 \ D\alpha_2 \ \dots \ D\alpha_S]$$
$$= D \underbrace{[\alpha_1 \ \dots \ \alpha_i \ \dots \ \alpha_S]}_{\Phi}$$
$$= D\Phi, \tag{1}$$

where Φ is the sparse coefficient matrix with few nonzero rows and N is the number of test pixels in HSI. D is the over-complete dictionary consist of training pixels randomly selected from all classes in HSI with a certain proportion. Given the over-complete dictionary D and the joint signal matrix X, the sparse matrix Φ can be obtained as follow:

$$\Phi = \arg\min \|X - D\Phi\|_F \quad \text{s.t.} \ \|\Phi\|_{row,0} \leq K, \tag{2}$$

where $\|\Phi\|_{row,0}$ denotes the number of nonzero rows of Φ. Besides, the objective function (2) can be solved by the simultaneous orthogonal matching pursuit (SOMP) algorithm [11,12]. Once the sparse matrix Φ is obtained, the test pixel x can be labeled as follow

$$Class(x_i) = \arg \min_{m=1,2,\dots,M} \|X - D^m \Phi^m\|_F,$$
$$i = 1, 2, \dots, N, \tag{3}$$

where M is the number of classes in HSI. D^m is the sub-dictionary constructed by HSI pixels randomly selected from mth class.

2.2 NLW-JSRC

The author in [6] proposed the NLW-JSRC method that assigns appropriae weights to all neighboring pixels in search window based on the similarities between neighboring pixels and the central test pixel. The weight w_{ij} can be obtained mathmatically by

$$w'_{ij} = (1 - (\frac{\|J(x_i) - J(x_j)\|}{\rho})^2)^2, \tag{4}$$

where $\|J(x_i) - J(x_j)\|$ denotes the similarity measure (euclidean distance) between the two HSI patches, which are sized as $so \times so$ and centered at the test pixel x_j and the neighboring pixel x_j, respectively. Parameter ρ is the $\max(\|J(x_i) - J(x_j)\|)$. Then, the weight scheme w'_{ij} is modificated as follow:

$$w_{ij} = \begin{cases} 0 & 0 < w'_{ij} < w'_1 \\ w'_{ij} & w'_1 < w'_{ij} < w'_2 \\ 1 & w'_2 < w'_{ij} < 1 \end{cases}, \tag{5}$$

where w'_1 and w'_2 are two parameters applied to judge valid and invalid neighboring pixels.

With the joint consideration of (2) and (5), we get:

$$\boldsymbol{\Phi}_{NLW} = \arg\min \|\boldsymbol{XW}_{NLW} - \boldsymbol{D\Phi}\|_F,$$
$$s.t. \|\boldsymbol{\Phi}\|_{row,0} \leq K, \tag{6}$$

where $\boldsymbol{W}_{NLW} = diag(w_{i1}, w_{i2}, \ldots, w_{im})$ is the non-local weighted matrix, and each weight can be get by (5). The sparse coeffiecent matrix $\boldsymbol{\Phi}_{NLW}$ can be obtained as similar as the JSRC. Finaly, the label fo the test pixel $\boldsymbol{x}_i$ is given by minimizing the residual:

$$Class(\boldsymbol{x}_i) = \arg \min_{m=1,2,\ldots,M} \|\boldsymbol{XW}_{NLW} - \boldsymbol{D}^m\boldsymbol{\Phi}_{NLW}^m\|_F,$$
$$i = 1, 2, \ldots, N. \tag{7}$$

3   Adaptive and Rotated Weighed Joint Sparse Representation Classification

Due to the NLW-JSRC can not consider the directionality of HSI spatial structure and the Turkey function failed to give appropriate weights. To make up for the deficiency of NLW-JSRC, the adaptive and rotated weighed joint sparse representation classification (ARWJSRC) is proposed. The proposed method can be divided into three parts, containing spectral angle, rotated similar window, weighed function.

3.1   Spectral Angle

In this paper, the spectral angle is used to measure the similarity between HSI pixels. Suppose that there is a search window centered at HSI pixel $\boldsymbol{x}_i(i = 1, 2, \cdots, N)$ with the size of $\sqrt{S} \times \sqrt{S}$ and pixel $\boldsymbol{x}_j(j = 1, 2, \cdots, S)$ is one of HSI pixels in search window, then the similarity between $\boldsymbol{x}_i$ and $\boldsymbol{x}_j$ can be written as

$$\theta_{ij} = \theta(\bar{\boldsymbol{x}}_i, \bar{\boldsymbol{x}}_j) = \frac{180°}{\pi} \arccos \frac{\bar{\boldsymbol{x}}_i \cdot \bar{\boldsymbol{x}}_j}{\|\bar{\boldsymbol{x}}_i\|_2 \|\bar{\boldsymbol{x}}_j\|_2}, \theta_{ij} \in [0°, 90°], \tag{8}$$

where $\bar{\boldsymbol{x}}_i$ denotes the average of HSI pixels in similar window centered at $\boldsymbol{x}_i$ with the size of $\sqrt{s} \times \sqrt{s}$. It can be written as $\bar{\boldsymbol{x}}_i = \frac{1}{s}\sum_{n=1}^{s} \boldsymbol{x}_n(i = 1, 2, \cdots, N)$. $\boldsymbol{x}_n$ is one of HSI pixels in similar window. Besides, $\bar{\boldsymbol{x}}_j$ is the average of HSI pixels in similar window centered at $\boldsymbol{x}_j$ with the size of $\sqrt{s} \times \sqrt{s}$.

The deficiency exiting in NLW-JSRC can not be solved if the similarity between $\boldsymbol{x}_i$ and $\boldsymbol{x}_j$ is measured directly as above. Because the calculation introduced above dose not consider the directionality of HSI spatial structure. Thus, the rotated similar window strategy is introduced in next subsection.

3.2 Rotated Similar Window Strategy

NLW-JSRC dose not consider the directionality of HSI spatial structure and only calculate the Euclidean distance between two HSI patches. As considering the redundancy of image spatial information, we apply the rotated similar window technology instead of the traditional window technology to measure the similarity between neighboring pixel and the central. The rotated window method looks for the most similar structure through the rotation of the HSI patches so that the similarity between neighboring pixel and the central can be more accurately estimated. The Fig. 1 illustrates the process.

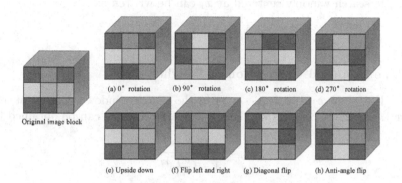

Fig. 1. The rotation measurement of similarity. The rotated similar window consists of the central pixel and its 8 neighboring pixels. Suppose that (a)–(d) are the HSI blocks obtained by rotating the original HSI block 0°, 90°, 180°, 270°, respectively. Besides, (e)–(h) are obtained by flipping the original HSI block upside down, left and right, diagonally, anti-diagonally, respectively. It is obvious that they have low similarities with it although (b)–(h) have the same spatial structure with the original HSI block. Because their directionality of HSI block are different from the original HSI block unless the (a). Thus, to find the most similar structure by rotating the HSI block is important to get a more accurate similarity measurement.

The following passage will mathematical introduce the specific process. Suppose that $\phi(\boldsymbol{x}_i)$ and $\phi(\boldsymbol{x}_j)$ respectively denotes the similar window centered at test HSI pixel $\boldsymbol{x}_i$ and $\boldsymbol{x}_j$ that is one of HSI pixels in the search window centered at $\boldsymbol{x}_i$. Then, the most similar structure $\hat{\phi}(\boldsymbol{x}_j)$ of $\boldsymbol{x}_j$ with $\phi(\boldsymbol{x}_i)$ can be obtained by

$$\hat{\phi}(\boldsymbol{x}_j) = R_k[\phi(\boldsymbol{x}_j)] = \arg\min_{k=0,1,\cdots,7} \|\phi(\boldsymbol{x}_i) - R_k[\phi(\boldsymbol{x}_j)]\|_F, \qquad (9)$$

where $R_k[\bullet]$ denotes kth rotation or flip operation.

By getting $\hat{\phi}(\boldsymbol{x}_j)$ and $\phi(\boldsymbol{x}_j)$, their residual r_{min}, r_o with $\phi(\boldsymbol{x}_i)$ can be respectively expressed as

$$r_{min} = \|\hat{\phi}(\boldsymbol{x}_j) - \phi(\boldsymbol{x}_i)\|_F, \qquad (10)$$

$$r_o = \|\phi(\boldsymbol{x}_j) - \phi(\boldsymbol{x}_i)\|_F. \tag{11}$$

Once the residuals r_{min}, r_o are obtained, a direction coefficient O can be got. The coefficient O can revise the spectral angle obtained by (9), which improve the measurement of similarity between HSI pixels. The coefficient O can be got by

$$O = \frac{r_{min}}{r_o}. \tag{12}$$

Then the revised spectral angle $\hat{\theta}_{ij}$ between the test pixel $\boldsymbol{x}_i$ and any HSI pixel $\boldsymbol{x}_j$ in search window centered at $\boldsymbol{x}_i$ can be written as

$$\hat{\theta}_{ij} = \hat{\theta}(\bar{\boldsymbol{x}}_i, \bar{\boldsymbol{x}}_j) = \theta(\bar{\boldsymbol{x}}_i, \bar{\boldsymbol{x}}_j) \times O. \tag{13}$$

3.3   The Proposed Calculation of Weights

For any HSI pixel $\boldsymbol{x}_j(j = 1, 2, \cdots, S)$ in the search window centered at a test pixel $\boldsymbol{x}_i(i = 1, 2, \cdots, N)$, its weight w_{ij} in search window can be obtained by

$$w_{ij} = \frac{1}{1 + (\frac{\hat{\theta}_{ij}}{\theta_{th}})^G}, \tag{14}$$

where G is the order that determined the decay rate of weight. The larger weight is, the more similar HSI pixels are. Vice versa. θ_{th} is a adaptive threshold which is got by calculating the median between the maximum and minimum of spectral angle between training samples. Here is its detailed process.

Given the training samples $\boldsymbol{X}_{train} = [\boldsymbol{X}_1, \cdots, \boldsymbol{X}_i, \cdots, \boldsymbol{X}_M]$, where $\boldsymbol{X} \in \mathbb{R}^{B \times N_i}$ is class ith training samples and N_i denotes the number of training samples in ith class. Then the average $\bar{X}_i$ of class i can be written as

$$\bar{X}_i = \frac{1}{N_i} \sum_{n=1}^{N_i} x_i^n, i = 1, 2, \cdots, M. \tag{15}$$

After getting averages of all classes according to (15), their spectral angles $\theta_{ij} = \theta(\bar{X}_i, \bar{X}_j)$ can be obtained by (8) and sorted. The adaptive threshold θ_{th} is the median between the maximum θ_{max} and minimum θ_{min} selecting from the sorted spectral angles.

$$\theta_{th} = \frac{\theta_{max} + \theta_{min}}{2}. \tag{16}$$

3.4   Reconstruction and Classification

Suppose that there is a search window centered at test pixel $\boldsymbol{x}_i$ with the size of $\sqrt{S} \times \sqrt{S}$ and all pixel in search window construct a joint signal matrix $\boldsymbol{X} = [\boldsymbol{x}_i^1, \boldsymbol{x}_i^2, \cdots, \boldsymbol{x}_i^S]$, then a rotating weighted matrix $\boldsymbol{W}_{OW} =$

$diag(w_{i1}, w_{i2}, \cdots, w_{iS})$ according to (14). Similar to (7), the sparse coefficient matrix Φ_{OW} can be obtained by

$$\Phi_{OW} = \arg\min \|XW_{OW} - D\Phi\|_F, s.t. \|\Phi\|_{row,0} \leq K, \tag{17}$$

In this paper, the SOMP algorithm is used to solve (17). Once the sparse coefficient matrix Φ_{OW} is got, the class of test HSI pixel x_i can be determined by

$$Class(x_i) = \arg\min_{n=1,2,\ldots,M} \|XW_{OW} - D_n\Phi_{OW}^n\|_F,$$

$$i = 1, 2, \ldots, N. \tag{18}$$

4   Experiment and Discussion

In this paper, two data sets containing Indian Pines and Pavia University are used to evaluate the performance of the proposed method. Besides, several classical HSI classification algorithms are also used as contrasting methods to prove the superiority of our proposed method. The section can be divided into two parts: 1) experimental data; 2) experimental result and discussion.

In this paper, four evaluating indicators including the average accuracy (AA), the overall accuracy (OA), the kappa coefficient, and time were used to judge the classification results. In order to display superiority of the proposed method, several classical algorithms including SVM [14], SRC [5], JSRC [5], NLW-JSRC [6] are applied to compare with our method. Among those methods, SVM and SRC are pixel-wise classification algorithms which only takes into account the spectral information, whereas the rest is the spectral-spatial classification method.

The parameters of SVM are obtained by the 5-fold cross-validation technique. According to [5,15], the sparsity level of all the sparse representation-based method mentioned in this paper was set to 3. If rising in sparsity level, it not only causes higher computational cost but also mislead the dictionary atoms from wrong classes to be selected, which leads to the worse classification performance. For Indian Pines and Pavia University, the window sizes in JSRC were 7×7 and 11×11, respectively. As for the NLW-JSRC, the window sizes were set as 9×9 and 13×13, respectively. Besides, the size of the nonlocal weighting patch was 7×7. The parameters w_1, w_2 for the thresholds of nonlocal weights were 0.14 and 0.88, respectively. More detail was shown in [6]. All the experiments were conducted using MATLAB R2014a on a 3.2 GHz computer with 64.0 Gb RAM.

4.1   Indian Pines

The Indian Pines has 220 spectral bands ranging from 0.4-2.5um where each band consists of 145×145 pixels with a spatial resolution of 20m. Due to serious water absorption [13], we remove 20 absorption bands (no. 104-108, 150-163, 220) and retain only the remaining 200 bands. For this data set with 16 classes

Table 1. Sixteen classes in the AVIRIS Indian Pines data and the training and test sets for each class.

Class	Name	Train	Test
1	Alfalfa	6	40
2	Corn-notill	129	1299
3	Corn-mintill	83	747
4	Corn	24	213
5	Grass-pasture	48	435
6	Grass-trees	73	657
7	Grass-pasture-mowed	5	23
8	Hay-windrowed	48	430
9	Oats	4	16
10	Soybean-notill	97	875
11	Soybean-mintill	196	2259
12	Soybean-clean	59	534
13	Wheat	21	184
14	Woods	114	1151
15	Blgs-grass-trees-drives	39	347
16	Stone-steel-towers	12	81
	Total	958	9291

Table 2. Nine classes in the ROSIS Urban Pavia University data and the training and test set for each class.

Class	Name	Train	Test
1	Asphalt	332	6299
2	Meadows	933	17716
3	Gravel	105	1994
4	Trees	154	2910
5	Painted metal sheets	68	1277
6	Bare Soil	252	4777
7	Bitumen	67	1263
8	Self-Blocking Bricks	185	3497
9	Shadows	48	899
	Total	2144	40632

of land cover, we randomly select 10% of each class of samples for training and the remaining is used for testing. The reference contents are shown in Table 1 and the label map of ground truth is shown in Fig. 4(a).

The classification map was shown in Fig. 2(b)–(h) and the classification results including OA, AA, Kappa, and time were displayed in Table 3. As it shown in Table 3, all the pixel-wise methods (KNN, SVM, and SRC) had worse performance than the spectral-spatial classification methods (JSRC, NLW-JSRC, SAJSRC, and ARW-JSRC). The reason is that those pixel-wise methods can not take advantage of spatial information in HSI and avoid the "Houghes" phenomenon. HSI pixels belong to same class may have different spectral characteristic and those are same class may have the similar spectral characteristic, which brings great difficulties to those pixel-wise classification methods. Among all approaches listed at Table 3, the proposed method ARW-JSRC displays the best classification performance comparing with other methods in terms of OA, AA, $Kappa$. Especially, the improvement brought by ARW-JSRC on JSRC is significantly obvious in terms of various evaluation metrics. For instance, the OA

Table 3. Classification results of the Indian Pines and Pavia University, including classification accuracies for every class, *AA*, *OA*, *Kappa*, and *Time* obtained by SVM, SRC, JSRC, NLW-JSRC, and ARW-JSRC

Class	Indian Pines					Pavia University				
	SVM	SRC	JSRC	NLW-JSRC	ARW-JSRC	SVM	SRC	JSRC	NLW-JSRC	ARW-JSRC
1	26.83	17.07	92.50	97.56	**100.00**	91.97	74.31	91.03	93.90	97.27
2	68.40	54.86	94.55	93.39	97.82	96.46	94.12	99.79	99.32	**100.00**
3	54.75	51.14	91.15	91.30	95.72	71.01	60.33	94.88	98.80	98.85
4	34.27	41.31	90.61	84.98	**100.00**	92.54	80.07	90.31	94.54	94.19
5	88.71	83.87	94.69	94.70	99.08	99.22	99.53	99.69	100.00	**100.00**
6	94.67	90.11	96.18	99.24	99.24	75.47	55.70	99.46	87.06	99.94
7	28.00	80.00	84.00	92.00	**100.00**	74.43	76.33	98.89	98.42	99.92
8	99.07	98.37	97.20	99.07	**100.00**	85.62	74.21	95.00	98.23	99.66
9	5.56	16.67	66.67	55.56	61.11	97.55	94.99	55.73	86.43	52.50
10	62.24	68.08	89.14	93.36	96.34					
11	83.34	73.25	96.42	94.84	98.82					
12	74.86	40.15	80.04	88.18	99.25					
13	95.11	90.22	91.26	97.28	99.46					
14	95.96	91.12	99.82	98.77	**100.00**					
15	57.93	44.96	85.63	96.54	96.83					
16	93.98	93.98	92.77	100.00	96.39					
OA	77.49	69.95	93.67	94.67	**98.34**	90.26	81.79	96.05	96.29	**98.01**
AA	66.48	64.70	90.16	92.30	**96.25**	87.14	78.84	91.64	95.19	**93.59**
Kappa	74.08	65.62	92.77	93.90	**98.11**	86.98	75.50	94.76	95.05	**97.36**
Time(s)	831.80	5.12	22.97	107.70	**193.99**	1403.50	26.37	190.51	574.33	**1990.33**

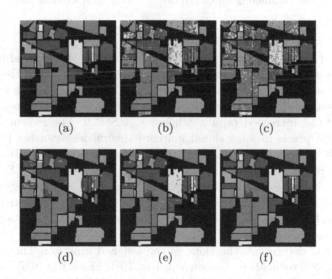

Fig. 2. Classification map for the Indian Pines image. (a) Label map; (b) SVM (*OA* = 77.49%); (c) SRC (*OA* = 69.95%); (d) JSRC (*OA* = 93.67%); (e) NLW-JSRC (*OA* = 93.26%); (f) ARW-JSRC (*OA* = 98.34%).

has increased from 93.67% to 98.34%. Though the NLW-JSRC and SAJSRC also has improved the classification result of JSRC, the ARW-JSRC makes the great improvement on the JSRC about 5%, which is more efficient than the NLW-JSRC and SAJSRC. Moreover, the ARW-JSRC has the 100% classification accuracy in class 1, 4, 7, 8, and 14. The reason why the ARW-JSRC can make such a great improvement is that it considers the directionality of spatial structure in HSI and assigns more appropriate weights for HSI pixels in search window. However, using the rotated similar window and the nonlocal weighted based method leads to the large computation consumption for the ARW-JSRC.

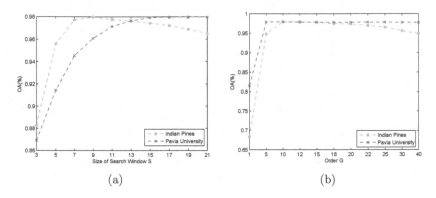

Fig. 3. Influence of parameters on classification. (a) Search window size S; (b) Order G.

The size of search window S directly determines the size of neighborhood of the test pixel, which finally influences the joint signal matrix and the classification. The influence of search window on the classification has shown in Fig. 3(a). The size of search window S ranged from 3×3 to 21×21. As it can be seen in Fig. 3(a), the OA increased rapidly when $3 < \sqrt{S} < 9$. The reason is that the number of HSI pixels in joint signal matrix is insufficient causing the unsatisfactory result at first. When $\sqrt{S} = 4$, the OA reaches its peak. However, the heterogenous pixels in search window will be more and more when $\sqrt{S} > 4$, which brings great challenges to the classification. Thus, once $\sqrt{S}$ is larger than the optimal threshold, the ARW-JSRC can not solve efficiently all the heterogenous pixels in search window. In order to have the good classification performance, the size of search window S can be set as 9×9.

The order G determines the slope of the weighed function. The influence of order G on the classification is shown in Fig. 3(b). From Fig. 3(b), it is known that the ARW-JSRC got its best OA when $G = 12$. When $1 < G < 12$, the OA rose quickly because more appropriate weights can be given by the weighed function as G grew. However, the OA decreases slow when $G > 12$. The reason is that those have small similarity may be given large weights when G is too large. Therefore, the optimal order of weighed function can be set as $G = 12$.

4.2   Pavia University

The geometric resolution of Pavia University image is 1.3 m and it has 115 bands ranging from 0.43 to 0.86μm. Some of bands in the HSI data are noisy and we only preserve 103 bands for the experiment. For this data with 9 classes of ground truth, we randomly select 5% of each class of samples for training and the remaining is used for testing. The specific information can be seen in Table 2 and the label map of ground truth shown in Fig. 4(a).

The classification map is shown in Fig. 4(b)–(h) and the classification results can be seen in Table 3. Due to the more adequate samples than the Indian Pines, most classification algorithms have the higher OA, especially for the pixel-wise methods. Though the ARW-JSRC has the best classification performance in terms of OA, AA, and $Kappa$, it cost most time to obtain the better results. It means that the ARW-JSRC obtains the better classification result ($OA = 98.05\%$) than the JSRC ($OA = 96.05\%$) by consuming more time. As for the size of search window S and order of weighed function G, their optimal value can be set as $\sqrt{S} = 7$ and $G = 3$ from Fig. 3(a) and (b).

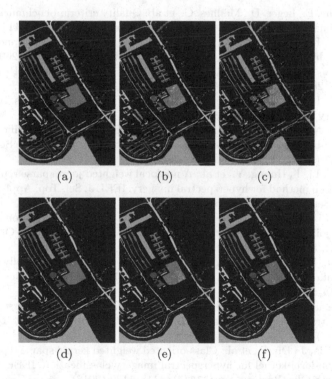

Fig. 4. Classification map for the Pavia University image. (a) Label map; (b) SVM ($OA = 90.26\%$); (c) SRC ($OA = 81.79\%$); (d) JSRC ($OA = 96.05\%$); (e) NLW-JSRC ($OA = 95.99\%$); (f) ARW-JSRC ($OA = 98.05\%$).

5   Conclusion

Aiming at the problem that JSRC can not deal with the interference of heterogeneous pixels in the search window, a joint sparse representation classification algorithm based on adaptive rotation weighting is proposed. The algorithm mainly uses the strategy of rotating similar window to measure the similarity between pixels, and uses a new method of weight calculation to assign weight to each pixel in the search window. In addition, the median of the maximum and minimum spectral angles of various training samples are used as the adaptive threshold of the weight formula. Experiments show that the proposed algorithm achieves remarkable improvement in classification accuracy.

Although the proposed method achieves good classification accuracy, it takes a heavy computation. In the future, we will start with reducing the time complexity of the algorithm and improve the efficiency of the algorithm.

References

1. Christophe, E., Leger, D., Mailhes, C., et al.: Quality criteria benchmark for hyperspectral imagery. IEEE Trans. Geosci. Remote Sens. **43**(9), 2103–2114 (2005)
2. Plaza, A., Benediktsson, J.A., Boardman, J.W., et al.: Recent advances in techniques for hyperspectral image processing. Remote Sens. Environ. (2009)
3. Landgrebe, D.: Hyperspectral image data analysis. IEEE Signal Process. Mag. **19**(1), 17–28 (2002)
4. Hughes, G.P.: On the mean accuracy of statistical pattern recognizers. IEEE Trans. Inf. Theory **14**(1), 55–63 (1968)
5. Chen, Y., Nasrabadi, N.M., Tran, T.D.: Hyperspectral image classification using dictionary-based sparse representation. IEEE Trans. Geosci. Remote Sens. **49**(10), 3973–3985 (2011)
6. Zhang, H., Li, J., Huang, Y., et al.: A nonlocal weighted joint sparse representation classification method for hyperspectral imagery. IEEE J. Sel. Top. Appl. Earth Obs. Remote. Sens. **7**(6), 2056–2065 (2014)
7. Fu, W., Li, S., Fang, L., et al.: Hyperspectral image classification via shape-adaptive joint sparse representation. IEEE J. Sel. Top. Appl. Earth Obs. Remote. Sens. **9**(2), 556–567 (2016)
8. Ni, D., Ma, H.: Fast classification of hyperspectral images using globally regularized archetypal representation with approximate solution. IEEE Trans. Geosci. Remote Sens. **55**(4), 2414–2430 (2017)
9. Bai, J., Zhang, W., Gou, Z., et al.: Nonlocal-similarity-based sparse coding for hyperspectral imagery classification. IEEE Geosci. Remote Sens. Lett. **14**(9), 1474–1478 (2017)
10. Gan, L., Xia, J., Du, P., et al.: Class-oriented weighted kernel sparse representation with region-level kernel for hyperspectral imagery classification. IEEE J. Sel. Top. Appl. Earth Obs. Remote. Sens. **11**(4), 1118–1130 (2018)
11. Leviatan, D., Temlyakov, V.N.: Simultaneous approximationby greedy algorithms. Adv. Comput. Math. **25**(13), 73–90 (2006)
12. Tropp, J.A., Gilbert, A.C., Strauss, M.J., et al.: Algorithms for simultaneous sparse approximation. Part I: Greedy pursuit. Signal Process. **86**(3), 572–588 (2006)

13. Gualtieri, J.A., Cromp, R.F.: Support vector machines for hyperspectral remote sensing classification. In: Applied Imagery Pattern Recognition Workshop, vol. 3584, pp. 221–232 (1999)
14. Melgani, F., Bruzzone, L.: Classification of hyperspectral remote sensing images with support vector machines. IEEE Trans. Geosci. Remote Sens. **42**(8), 1778–1790 (2004)
15. Fang, L., Wang, C., Li, S., et al.: Hyperspectral image classification via multiple-feature-based adaptive sparse representation. IEEE Trans. Instrum. Meas. **66**(7), 1646–1657 (2017)

Separating Skin Surface Reflection Component from Single Color Image

Shuchang Xu[1（✉）], Zhengwei Yao[1], and Yiwei Liu[2]

[1] College of Information Science and Engineering,
Hangzhou Normal University, Hangzhou 311121, China
xusc@hznu.edu.cn
[2] www.Learnings.ai, Beijing 100080, China

Abstract. Due to the complex structure and rough surface of human skin, obtaining skin surface reflection is often difficult. To our knowledge, existing methods for measuring skin surface reflection are mostly device dependent. In this paper, we describe an approach that, unlike all previous methods, is able to extract the skin surface reflection component from a single color image without the need for any special device or prior information. First, we introduce a complete model for skin imaging incorporating Lambert-Beer law with the Dichromatic Reflection Mode, followed by extracting a pigment concentration map using the ICA algorithm. Finally we estimate the surface reflectivity in each color channel, and calculate the overall surface reflection component. Experiments are designed to verify the proposed algorithm and show good agreement with the ground truth obtained by special device.

Keywords: Surface reflection · Dichromatic Reflection Mode · Skin pigments

1 Introduction

Surface reflection, also known as specular reflection, always leads to the presence of highlights in images and is widely involved topic in various research areas such as computer vision, image processing and pattern recognition. Many algorithms have been developed to detect and remove surface reflection during the previous decades. Early in the 90's, researchers had tried to remove surface reflection by using polarizer filters [1, 2]. Based on the Dichromatic Reflection Model (DRM) proposed by Shafer [3], which define reflection as a linear combination of a surface reflection component and a body reflection component, Tan [4] et al. develop a diffuse-to-specular mechanism to separate surface reflection from a single image. Unfortunately, all these algorithms perform poorly on skin images due to the multi-layer structure of the human skin and complex interaction of light beneath skin.

1.1 Related Work

Considered the largest organ of the human body, skin is actually a turbid media which consists of several layers. The outermost skin layer is non-flat and definitely cannot be

© Springer Nature Switzerland AG 2019
Y. Zhao et al. (Eds.): ICIG 2019, LNCS 11902, pp. 400–409, 2019.
https://doi.org/10.1007/978-3-030-34110-7_33

treated as a Lambertian surface. To simulate and obtain the surface reflection of the skin, many models as well as measurements have been developed.

Surface Reflection Models: As the most popular reflection models, BRDF (Bidirectional Reflectance Distribution Function) and BSSRDF (Bidirectional Surface Scattering Reflectance Distribution Function) describe how light travels when it hits a surface. BSSRD is proven to be a more reasonable choice for the translucent human skin, which involves significant subsurface scattering [5, 6]. In addition, many multi-layer models [7–11], including Monto Carlo simulations [9], the K-M theory [10], and the dipole diffusion theory [11] have been developed to accurately simulate possible skin reflections and interactions between incident light and skin.

Surface Reflection Measurements: Generally, it is difficult to measure the parameters of each skin layer despite fine theoretical foundation provided by the BSSRDF. Therefore, researchers have set up 3D environments to measure surface reflection [12, 13]. More specifically, Angelopoulou [14] reveals that skin reflectance exhibit a local "W" pattern regardless of race and gender by using a high resolution, high accuracy spectrograph. We call the measurement method above 3D measurement and 1D measurement respectively. In the cosmetic industry, exclusive equipments are developed to carry out image difference based 2D measurement to quantitatively evaluate the effect of product [15]. In summary, measuring skin surface reflection seems difficult without help from special instruments.

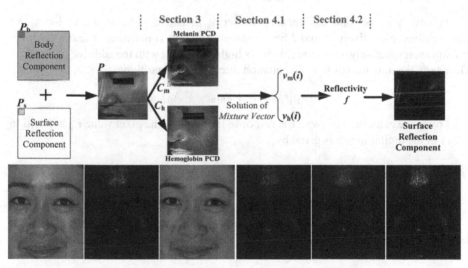

Fig. 1. The surface reflection component is separated based on a single image. (Top): flowchart of proposed algorithm. (Bottom) (From left to right): Input image, surface reflection component obtained by proposed algorithm, resultant image after removing surface reflection, R-channel component, G-channel component and B-channel component of surface reflection. (Color figure online)

In this paper, a method which does not require hardware, segmentation and any prior information is proposed to globally estimate skin surface reflection component using only a color image, as shown in Fig. 1. We construct a complete skin imaging model by combining the Lambert Beer law with the DRM, followed by measuring independent pigment concentration distributions to separate skin surface reflection, which can then be decomposed into its corresponding RGB components, as shown in bottom of Fig. 1.

2 Skin Reflection Model

2.1 Sub Surface Reflection Model

The traditional Lambert Beer law is usually defined as:

$$A = -\log(I/I_0) = \varepsilon * l * c \tag{1}$$

Where A is absorbance, and can also be written as a product of extinction coefficient ε, path length l and absorbing species concentration c. I and I_0 are the power of transmitted illumination and incident illumination respectively. Incorporating Lambert Beer law with Dawson's experiments [16]: skin absorbance can be represented by the linear combination of dominant pigments (melanin and hemoglobin) absorbance, skin absorbance can be denoted as follows taking the skin baseline absorption and the residual pigment contribution A_0 into account.

$$A = \varepsilon_m l_m c_m + \varepsilon_h l_h c_h + A_0 \tag{2}$$

Where A is the skin absorbance. Subscript m and h indicate the melanin and hemoglobin respectively. c and l here indicate pigment concentration and skin layer thickness, respectively. Equation (2) shows high consistent with the additive of Lambert Beer law. We now have following equation after taking logarithm:

$$I = -\exp\{\varepsilon_m l_m c_m + \varepsilon_h l_h c_h + A_0\} * I_0 \tag{3}$$

Given the camera sensor spectral response function Ψ, the pixel value P_b at position (x, y) in the digital image is given by

$$P_b(x, y) = k \int I\psi(\lambda)d\lambda = -k \int \exp\{\varepsilon_m l_m c_m(x, y) + \varepsilon_h l_h c_h(x, y) + A_0(\lambda)\} * I_0 * \psi(\lambda)d\lambda \tag{4}$$

Here k is a camera gain constant. Under reasonable assumption, camera sensors can be considered as narrowband and treated as a delta function [17, 18]. Therefore, we have $(x, y$ and λ are omitted for simplicity):

$$P_b = -k \exp\{v_m c_m + v_h c_h + A_0\} * I_0 \tag{5}$$

Where $v = l * \varepsilon$. Generally, light in real word can be separated into different planckian type illuminators and planckian SPD (Spectral Power Distribution) provides good approximation of common illumination, such as sunset light, halogen lamps and tungsten lamps. Incident illumination is then written as simplified planckian radiator:

$$I_0 \approx g_1 \lambda^{-5} \exp(-g_2/T\lambda) \tag{6}$$

Where g_1 and g_2 are constant, the term T is called correlated colour temperature. Taking logarithm after combining (5) and (6) arrives at:

$$-\log P_b = K + \{v_m c_m + v_h c_h + A_0\} \tag{7}$$

Where $K(\lambda) = \log k - 5\log\lambda + \log g_1 - g_2/T\lambda$. More specifically, the sub surface model for every pixel in i ($i = RGB$) channel of skin image can be given by:

$$-\log P_b(x, y, i) = K(i) + \{v_m(i)c_m(x, y) + v_h(i)c_h(x, y) + A_0(i)\} \tag{8}$$

2.2 Complete Reflection Model

Small portion of incident light is reflected on surface and the rest penetrates into the sub surface. Most of visible light that reaches subcutis if reflected back to the upper layers due to the presence of fat after experiencing absorption, scattering and transmission in epidermis and dermis.

As illustrated in Fig. 2, the complete skin reflection is composed of surface reflection and body reflection. Considering as a quasi-transparent medium, skin can be well modeled by the Dichromatic Reflection Model. We then define pixel P in skin image as follows taking surface reflection pixel P_s into account:

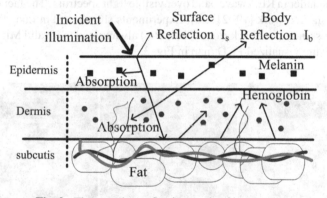

Fig. 2. The complete reflection mode of human skin.

$$P(x, y, \lambda) = m_b(x, y)P_b(\lambda) + m_s(x, y)P_s(\lambda) \tag{9}$$

Where m_b and m_s are the geometrical factors which encode information about incident angle, shadow etc. Plugging Eqs. (9) into (8) gives:

$$-\log P = K + \{v_m c_m + v_h c_h + A_0\} + \log\{(1 - f m_s)/m_b\} \tag{10}$$

Where $f(x, y, i) = P_s(x, y, i)/P(x, y, i)$ is defined to be surface reflectivity. K in above equation can be set to zero by normalizing each channel to zero-mean. Therefore, defining $Z(x, y, i) = \log P(x, y, i)$, we can rewrite Eq. (11) as follows:

$$-\overline{Z} = \{v_m c_m + v_h c_h + A_0\} + \log\{(1 - f m_s)/m_b\} \tag{11}$$

3 Extracting Pigment Concentration Distribution

Potential inconsistent illumination may lead to unexpected error. We then use the channel difference (B-R) and (G-R) to minimize the log item in Eq. (11) to build 2-D mixture signals with noise:

$$\Delta Z = [\Delta \mathbf{V_m} \ \Delta \mathbf{V_h} \ \Delta N][\mathbf{c}_m \ \mathbf{c}_h \ \mathbf{1}]^T \tag{12}$$

Where,

$$\Delta Z = [\overline{Z}(R)/\overline{Z}(B), \ \overline{Z}(R)/\overline{Z}(G)]^T$$
$$\Delta \mathbf{V_m} = [v_m(B) - v_m(R), \ v_m(G) - v_m(R)]^T$$
$$\Delta \mathbf{V_h} = [v_h(B) - v_h(R), \ v_h(G) - v_h(R)]^T$$
$$\Delta N = [\log \frac{1-f(R)m_s}{1-f(B)m_s}, \ \log \frac{1-f(R)m_s}{1-f(G)m_s}]^T$$

ΔA_0 is negligible and eliminated since research shows A_0 make marginal contribution to skin absorption [16, 19]. Pigment Concentration Distribution (PCD) c is then obtained by carrying out ICA algorithm based on Eq. 12, with the knowledge that the presence of melanin in epidermis and hemoglobin in dermis are mutually independent [18, 20]. Recalling the definition of v in Sect. 2.1, every member in Mixture Vector should be positive given the fact that the extinction coefficient ε of both melanin and hemoglobin are relatively smaller in RED wave band over visible light spectrum. The fact is supported by numerous in-vivo work [19, 21, 22]. Experiments show the skin images containing dominant non-skin region (background, hair etc.) always lead to invalid Mixture Vector. Here we show the visualized PCD map in Fig. 3.

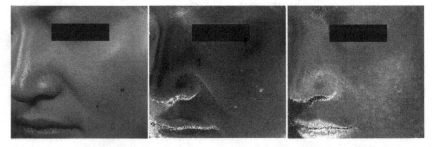

Fig. 3. Visualized PCD map. **Left**: Input image, **Center**: Melanin PCD map. **Right**: Hemoglobin PCD map. Notice that freckles in cheek only appear in melanin PCD map, and lip region shows highest value in hemoglobin PCD map. Refer to Sect. 3 in [23] to find alternative ways for verification. (Color figure online)

4 Surface Reflection Component

4.1 Solution of Mixture Vector

Considered the items A_0 and $\log\{(1 - fm_s)/m_b\}$ in Eq. 11 are wavelength dependent, as well as maybe be additionally location dependent, we design neighboring difference in single channel to minimize dependent effect of wavelength and location to solve v:

$$\Delta P(x, y) = \overline{Z}(x, y) - \overline{Z}(x + 1, y) = v_m \Delta c_m + v_h \Delta c_h + RES \tag{13}$$

Where $\Delta c = c(x + 1, y) - c(x, y)$, RES represent the combined residual differential value of A_0 and f etc., whose value could be close to zero under relaxed assumption that incident illumination at neighboring pixels are quite similar at same wavelength. So far, v can be given by typical linear regression, followed by vector normalization. Our experiments have supported our assumption: RES is always either close or equal to zero.

4.2 Reflectivity Calculation

Equation 11 can be rewritten as follows:

$$F = -Z - \{v_m c_m + v_h c_h\} \tag{14}$$

Where $F(i) = A_0(i) + \log\{(1 - f(i)m_s)/m_b\}$, we then have:

$$f = (1 - m_b \exp(F - A_0(i)))/m_s \tag{15}$$

A_0 is negligible compared with dominant pigments absorption and can be reasonably treated as constant in each channel respectively and removed by zero mean normalization. Using $\bar{F}$ to represent normalized F, and surface reflectivity f can be simply estimated by:

$$f \propto -m_b/m_s \exp(\bar{F}) \tag{16}$$

We take the extreme situation and approximately eliminate the ratio mb/ms by unit standard deviation normalization. Now, it's quite straightforward to give f since P, v and c are already known after combining Eqs. 14 and 16. Following flowchart demonstrate the detailed step to calculate reflectivity f and final SRC.

Algorithm 1: Flowchart of solving reflectivity f

1. Apply ICA algorithm to get PCD c
2. Solve v by neighboring difference in each channels respectively
3. for each channel i (i = R, G, B)
4.   Calculate F according to Eq. 13
5. $\bar{F}$ = ZERO_MEAN(F)
6. f = -exp($\bar{F}$)
7. f = UNIT_STD(f)
8.   SRC(i) = f(i) * P(i)
9. end for

---

5 Experiments and Discussion

5.1 Experimental Setup

According to Sect. 2.2, Surface Reflection Component (SRC) can be obtained if both overall reflection and Body Reflection Component (BRC) are known. It is impossible to capture BRC by household digital camera. However, polarizer is a well option to separate surface reflection under polarized illumination with a pair of orthogonally-polarized filters placed over the light source and on the camera lens respectively. Cross polarization technology is widely used in industry to capture specular-free skin image. We hereby denote crossed polarized image as XPOL, parallel polarized image as PPOL and define SURF as deference between PPOL and XPOL [14, 23], which is then treated as ground truth of surface reflection. TRUVU®, device for imaging skin for cosmetic analysis of the skin, developed by Johnson & Johnson, is used to capture PPOL and XPOL. Figure 4 shows the final experimental setup.

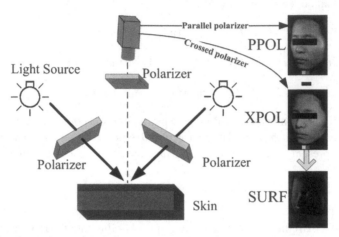

Fig. 4. Schematic diagram of defining ground truth of SRC. Two light sources are placed at both sides of the object with fixed angle. The camera captures PPOL and XPOL at parallel and perpendicular polarization status, according to change of polarization orientation.

5.2   Algorithm Verification

The original image captured by our system is 24-bit, color image with resolution 2592 × 2888. Skin-dominant region is select as ROI to analyze since non-skin region (background, eyebrow, eyelash, hair etc.) are not subject to Lambert-beer law and DRM. It is easy to extend in the case of original image as input after locating skin regions. The SRC in Fig. 5 show the estimated reflectance distribution is consistent with the ground truth except for non-skin regions. In Fig. 5, columns (d–f) show the triple channel component of SRC. The perceivable difference of SRC in RGB channels indicates that surface reflection is wave dependent. However, the proposed algorithm still cannot well estimate the chromaticity of illumination, according to the obvious color difference between SRC and the ground truth.

Figure 6 demonstrates another example of application in cosmetic industry. To test how the SRC varies after applying cosmetic product which helps skin brighten, two images are taken before and after applying skin care product under identical illumination. Obvious increase of surface reflection can be observed on cheek. Therefore, we can design image-based tools to quantitatively evaluate cosmetic product and, more specifically, accurately locate skin region which takes significant effect after application.

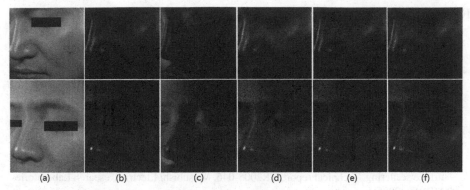

Fig. 5. Algorithm verification by comparing with ground truth. (a) Input image. (b) SRC obtained by our algorithm. (c) Ground truth SURF, difference between PPOL and XPOL. (d–f) R, G and B channel component of SRC. Notice each SRC of R, G and B channel is different. (Color figure online)

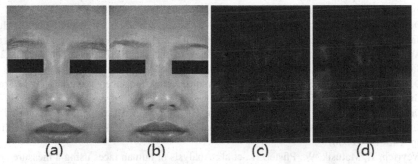

Fig. 6. Experiment shows how the SRC varies before and after cosmetic product. (a) Image taken before applying skin care product. (b) Image taken after applying skin care product in 8 weeks. (c–d) SRC of a and b respectively. (Color figure online)

6 Conclusions

We have introduced a method to extract the skin surface reflection using only a single image. This is achieved by first introducing an inter-channel quotient in log space to estimate the PCD maps. Next, we used neighboring pixel difference to solve mixture vectors. Finally we determined surface reflectivity in every color channel to give the overall surface reflection component. The experiments in Sect. 5 show high correlation between estimated results and ground truth. However, the proposed algorithm cannot well estimate the illumination chromaticity yet. In addition, shadow and non-skin regions in estimated SRC remain little consistent with real image. Recently, we are planning to work on the above problems.

References

1. Nayar, S.K., Fang, X.S., Boult, T.: Separation of reflection components using color and polarization. Int. J. Comput. Vis. **21**(3), 163–186 (1996)
2. Shafer, S.A.: Using color to separate reflection components. Color Res. Appl. **10**, 210–218 (1985)
3. Tan, R.T., Nishino, K., Ikeuchi, K.: Separating reflection components based on chromaticity and noise analysis. IEEE Trans. Pattern Anal. Mach. Intell. (PAMI) **26**(10), 1373–1379 (2004)
4. Krishnaswamy, A., Baranoski, G.: A biophysically-based spectral model of light interaction with human skin. Comput. Graph. Forum **23**, 331–340 (2004)
5. Weyrich, T., Matusik, W., Pfister, H., Ngan, A., Gross, M.: Measuring skin reflectance and subsurface scattering. Technical report. TR2005-046, Mitsubishi Electric Research Laboratories (MERL) (2005)
6. Pat, H., Wolfgang, K.: Reflection from layered surfaces due to subsurface scattering. In: SIGGRAPH, pp. 165–174 (1993)
7. So Ling, C., Ling, L.: A multi-layered reflection model of natural human skin. In: Proceedings of Computer Graphics, pp. 249–256 (2001)
8. Wang, L., Jacques, S.L., Zheng, L.: Monte Carlo modeling of light transport in multi-layered tissues. Comput. Methods Programs Biomed. **47**(2), 131–146 (1995)
9. Doi, M., Tominaga, S.: Spectral estimation of human skin color using the Kubelka-Munk theory. In: Eschbach, R., Marcu, G.G. (eds.), Color Imaging VIII: Processing, Hardcopy, and Applications, Proceedings of SPIE-IS&T Electronic Imaging, SPIE, vol. 5008, pp. 221–228, Santa Clara, California, USA, January (2003)
10. Donner, C., Jensen, H.W.: Light diffusion in multilayered translucent materials. ACM Trans. Graph. **24**(3), 1032–1039 (2005)
11. Debevec, P., Hawkins, T., Tchou, C., Duiker, H.-P., Sarokin, W., Sagar, M.: Acquiring the reflectance field of a human face. In: Computer Graphics, SIGGRAPH 2000 Proceedings, pp. 145–156 (2000)
12. Weyrich, T., Matusik, W., Pfister, H., et al.: Analysis of human faces using a measurement-based skin reflectance model. ACM Trans. Graph. **25**, 1013–1024 (2006)
13. Angelopoulou, E.: Understanding the color of human skin. In: SPIE Conference on Human Vision and Electronic Imaging VI, SPIE, vol. 4299, pp. 243–251 (2001)
14. Matsubara, A.: Differences in the surface and subsurface reflection characteristics of facial skin by age group. Skin Res. Technol. **18**, 29–35 (2011)
15. Dawson, J.B., Barker, D.J., Ellis, D.J., et al.: A theoretical and experimental study of light absorption and scattering by in vivo skin. Phys. Med. Biol. **25**, 695–709 (1980)
16. Finlayson, G.D., Drew, M.S., Lu, C.: Intrinsic images by entropy minimization. In: Pajdla, T., Matas, J. (eds.) ECCV 2004. LNCS, vol. 3023, pp. 582–595. Springer, Heidelberg (2004). https://doi.org/10.1007/978-3-540-24672-5_46
17. Tsumura, N., Ojima, N., Sato, K., et al.: Image-based skin color and texture analysis/synthesis by extracting hemoglobin and melanin information in the skin. In: Proceedings of SIGGRAPH, pp. 770–779 (2003)
18. Krishnaswamy, A., Baranoski, G.V.G.: A study on skin optics. Technical report CS-2004-01, University of Waterloo, Canada, January (2004)
19. Tsumura, N., Haneishi, H., Miyake, Y.: Independent component analysis of skin color image. J. Opt. Soc. Am. **16**(9), 2169–2176 (1999)

20. Anderson, R.R., Pappish, J.A.: The optics of human skin. J. Invest. Dermatol. **77**(1), 13–19 (1981)
21. Zijlstra, W.G., Buursma, A., Meeuwsen-van der Roest, W.P.: Absorption spectra of human fetal and adult oxyhemoglobin, de-oxyhemoglobin, carboxyhemoglobin, and methemoglobin. Clin. Chem. **37**(9), 1633–1638 (1991)
22. Xu, S., Ye, X., Wu, Y., et al.: Automatic skin decomposition based on single image. Comput. Vis. Image Underst. **110**(1), 1–6 (2008)
23. Clemenceau, P., Breugnot, S., Pounet, B.: In vivo quantitative evaluation of gloss. Cosmet. Toiletries **119**, 71–78 (2004)

Parallel Spectrum Reconstruction in Fourier Transform Imaging Spectroscopy Based on the Embedded System

Weikang Zhang[1,2(✉)], Desheng Wen[1], Zongxi Song[1], Xin Wei[1,2], Gang Liu[1,2], Zhixin Li[1,2], and Tuochi Jiang[1,2]

[1] Xi'an Institute of Optics and Precision Mechanics, Chinese Academy of Sciences, Xi'an, China
zhangweikang@opt.cn
[2] University of Chinese Academy of Sciences, Beijing, China

Abstract. In this paper, we design a parallel-processing pipeline for spectrum reconstruction in Fourier transform imaging spectroscopy (FTIS), which works well with the embedded system, NVIDIA Jetson TX2. This embedded system has great performance in parallel computing and can be developed easily by programmers using CUDA C in a single development board. This is very important for data processing on satellite and mobile devices. On the other hand, because of the huge amount of interference data acquired by the Fourier transform spectrometer, traditional interference data processing mechanism is not efficient and time-saving. These data should be processed in a fast way for real time, especially on satellite, to save memory and bandwidth. We take advantage of parallel computing to enable higher efficiency and reduced operation time. Furthermore, traditional serial algorithms for processing interferograms on the ARMs are introduced for comparison. The experimental results show that our parallel spectrum reconstruction pipeline has much higher performance than the serial one, and for huge data, our parallel mechanism also achieves great result in high performance.

Keywords: Spectrum reconstruction · GPU · Embedded system · High performance

1 Introduction

In recent years, benefiting from the rapid development of imaging spectroscopy, the Fourier transform spectrometer [1–6] has played an important role in both space exploration and component analysis. Compared with other spectrometer, it has many advantages in high throughput, multi-channel operation, and high resolution.

© Springer Nature Switzerland AG 2019
Y. Zhao et al. (Eds.): ICIG 2019, LNCS 11902, pp. 410–419, 2019.
https://doi.org/10.1007/978-3-030-34110-7_34

Fourier transform spectroscopy obtains abundant data containing space and spectral information of the target simultaneously. The core device of the spectrometer is the interferometer. The light from the target is separated into two coherent beams, and with the change of the optical path difference, the two interfere beams will interfere on the sensors so as we can obtain a series of interference patterns.

Generally, spectral reconstruction [7,8] mainly includes preprocessing, apodization, phase correction and Fourier transform. An important step in preprocessing is detrending, which is to remove the slowly varying trends from the interfering signals. The purpose of apodization technique is to reduce spectrum leakage by selecting some appropriate functions. To ensure the symmetry of interferogram, phase correction is performed to correct the phase error caused by sampling position offset. Then, we would obtain the spectrum by Fourier transform.

In order to process the obtained interferograms as quickly as possible, we usually simplify the process by omitting some steps, resulting in low spectral quality and poor resolution. Specially, the fast intelligent processing system on satellite requires real-time spectrum reconstruction to save memory and bandwidth, which requires a high-speed method to replace the traditional pipeline.

Comparing with the traditional data-process pipeline, it is a new way to perform general computing on the graphics processing unit (GPU). It is particularly suitable for solving problems that can be represented as data parallel computing, i.e. the parallel execution of the same program on many data elements. Meanwhile, NVIDIA provide Compute Unified Device Architecture (CUDA) as a general-purpose parallel-computing platform and programming model to solve many computational problems more efficiently [9 11].

Fortunately, in the embedded field, NVIDIA also makes great contribution and it provides an embedded development kit, suitable for NVIDIA Jetson series. NVIDIA Jetson represents a series of computing processor boards from NVIDIA. All Jetson boards are carrying a Tegra processor, including Jetson TK1, TX1 and TX2 models. NVIDIA claims that it is a AI supercomputer on a module, powered by the NVIDIA Pascal architecture. Best of all, it packages this performance into a small, power-efficient form factor that is ideal for intelligent edge devices like robots, drones, smart cameras and portable medical devices. The Jetson TX2 supports all the features of the Jetson TX1 module, and enables a larger, more complex deep neural network (DNN).

In this paper, the embedded board, NVIDIA Jetson TX2, is used for our real-time embedded platform, on which our parallel interferogram processing algorithms are performed. The rest of this paper is structured as follows: Sect. 2 briefly explains the characteristics and advantages of the board. Section 3 depicts the algorithms of parallel processing running on the GPU of the embedded board. The experiments are arranged in Sect. 4. At the end of this paper, we make an analysis and draw conclusions.

2 Embedded System

NVIDIA Jetson with GPU-accelerated parallel processing is a leading embedded computing platform. The most important feature is that the Jetson series provide CUDA for developers to improve the performance of algorithms.

Jetson TX2 is a fast, power-efficient embedded AI computing device. This 7.5-watt supercomputer on a module is built around an NVIDIA Pascal-family GPU. In addition to being loaded 8 GB of memory and 59.7 GB/s of memory bandwidth, it has a variety of standard hardware interfaces that make it easy to integrate into a wide range of products and form factors. Some other parameters about TX2 is as follows (Table 1).

Table 1. Details about TX2

Item	Jetson TX2
GPU	NVIDIA Pascal, 256 CUDA cores
CPU	HMP Dual Denver 2/2 MB L2 Quad ARM® A57/2MB L2
Memory	8 GB 128 bit LPDDR4 59.7 GB/s
PCIE	Gen 2 — 1x4 + 1x1 OR 2x1 + 1x2
Data storage	32 GB eMMC, SDIO, SATA
USB	USB 3.0 + USB 2.0
Connectivity	1 Gigabit Ethernet, 802.11ac WLAN, Bluetooth
Other	CAN, UART, SPI, I2C, I2S, GPIOs

From the table, we could see the embedded system is running on two types of ARM with a high-performance GPU. The CPU and GPU differ in frequency in different working modes. Their work frequency is not all the same. The performance of algorithms is also different in different mode. These modes are listed in the following.

- Mode 0: Denver 2 (2.0 GHz), ARM A57 (2.0 GHz), GPU (1.30 GHz);
- Mode 1: ARM A57 (1.2 GHz), GPU (0.85 GHz);
- Mode 2: Denver 2 (1.4 GHz), ARM A57 (1.4 GHz), GPU (1.12 GHz);
- Mode 3: ARM A57 (2.0 GHz), GPU (1.12 GHz);
- Mode 4: Denver 2 (2.0 GHz), GPU (1.12 GHz);

3 Theory

According to the basic principle of Fourier transform spectroscopy [12], spectral recovery can be achieved by Fourier transform of the interferogram. This principle could be described by the following equation:

$$I(\Delta) = \int_{-\infty}^{+\infty} B(\sigma)e^{j2\pi\sigma\Delta}d\sigma, \tag{1}$$

$$B(\sigma) = \int_{-\infty}^{+\infty} I(\Delta)e^{-j2\pi\sigma\Delta}d\Delta, \tag{2}$$

where I is the interferogram, B is the spectrum, and Δ and σ mean the path difference and the wave number, respectively. We can use fast Fourier transform (FFT) instead, whose complexity is $O(NlogN)$.

In this paper, the data-parallel-process pipeline of spectrum reconstruction is divided into three part: detrending, apodization, phase correction and Fourier transform. These parallel algorithms are similar with [13].

3.1 Detrending

Usually, the interference signal $x(t)$ consists of a slowly varying trend superimposed on a fluctuating process $y(t)$. It should take measures to eliminate the trend term, containing the low-frequency part. The trend term could be solved by the least square method, searching for the most appropriate function by minimizing the square errors.

For a linear model that is described by the following equation,

$$y = A\beta + b, \tag{3}$$

the parameters could be solved by the least square method, which can be estimated by

$$\hat{\beta} = (X^T X)^{-1} X^T y. \tag{4}$$

If X is a full-rank matrix,

$$rank(X) = n, m \geq n, X \in R^{m \times n} \tag{5}$$

X can be decomposed by QR decomposition (QRD), that is,

$$X = QR, \tag{6}$$

where Q is an orthogonal matrix meaning and R is an upper triangular matrix. $\hat{\beta}$ could be written by the following form,

$$\hat{\beta} = R^{-1}Q^T y. \tag{7}$$

That is, the detrending is converted to QR decomposition and matrix inversion. For parallel computing, parallel QRD and parallel matrix inversion are performed in our embedded board. These parallel algorithms in [13] could be used for our experiments.

3.2 Apodization

The ideal range of optical path difference is from negative infinity to positive infinity, which in reality is not satisfied by detectors to collect infinite data. That is, the signals we obtain are truncated. According to the Fourier theory, these truncated signals that can be seen as the multiplication of a sequence and a rectangular window, are equivalent to the convolution of the original spectrum of the signal with a sinc function in frequency domain [14]. For a continuous spectrum, the spectral resolution is limited by the sidelobe of the rectangular window due to the discontinuity of the interferogram near the maximum OPD.

Apodization is based on the point-to-point multiplication of interference sequence and a certain apodizing function to suppress the sidelobe effect in the recovery spectrum. In parallel computing, the apodization function using multi-thread can be expressed by

$$y(tid) = w(tid)x(tid), \tag{8}$$

where tid is the current index of the thread and w is the apodization function. Some functions for apodization include the triangular function, Happ-Genzel function, Hamming function, and Bessel function.

3.3 Phase Correction and Fourier Transform

Generally phase is corrected by using Fourier transform so that phase correction are performed together with Fourier transform.

In our experiment, our interferogram is provided by our interferometer. It is a single-sided interference signal, which contains a double-sided interferogram around the zero OPD, and Mertz method is used for the phase by this double-sided interferogram. Suppose the interferogram is asymmetrical because the detector does not pick up the value at the zero OPD and this would introduce a new optical path difference $\phi(\sigma)$, so

$$I(\Delta) = \int_{-\infty}^{+\infty} B(\sigma)e^{-j(2\pi\sigma\Delta+\phi(\sigma))}d\sigma. \tag{9}$$

And

$$B(\sigma)e^{-j\phi(\sigma)} = m_r(\sigma) + jm_i(\sigma), \tag{10}$$

where $m_r(\sigma)$ is the real part of $B(\sigma)e^{(\sigma)}$ and $m_i(\sigma)$ is the imaginary part.

In Mertz method [15], the phase is in a low resolution so that it could be acquired to fit the low phase spectrum based on the least square method by using a high-order polynomial for high-resolution phase spectrum $\phi_0(\sigma)$. The difference between the original phase information $\phi(\sigma)$ and the high-resolution phase spectrum can be calculated,

$$\Delta\phi = \phi(\sigma) - \phi_0(\sigma). \tag{11}$$

The final spectrum through phase correction is given by

$$B(\sigma) = \sqrt{m_r^2(\sigma) + m_i^2(\sigma)}cos(\Delta\phi(\sigma)). \tag{12}$$

In phase correction, we use improved Mertz method [16] in which the high-resolution phase spectrum is obtained by zero filling for the double-sided interferogram to guarantee the same length as the original signal. Furthermore, it is more efficient than Mertz method in parallel computing.

4   Experiments

Our experiments are implemented in C++ and CUDA C on the NVIDIA Jetson TX2 board. Our embedded system is shown in Fig. 1. The white light interferogram is provided by our interferometer for our experiments, as shown in Fig. 2.

Fig. 1. The NVIDIA Jetson TX2 board

4.1   Reconstruction

Figure 3 is the reconstruction result from the Fig. 2. From the figure, our algorithms for interferogram processing has a great result.

4.2   Batch Processing in Different Work Mode

The performance in the Jetson TX2 in all working mode is listed in Tables 2, 3, 4, 5 and 6, respectively. In these tables, Nor. means the QRD and matrix inversion are included and Opt. represents a simplified process, where we record the results of QRD and matrix and use them directly for the batch processing. The Groups are the number of batches we process.

From these tables, Mode 0 has the best performance because of the board working frequency is highest between the five modes. However, the board working in other modes may save more power.

A frame of interferogram

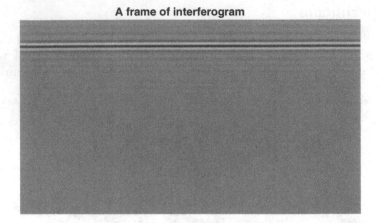

Fig. 2. The white light interferogram

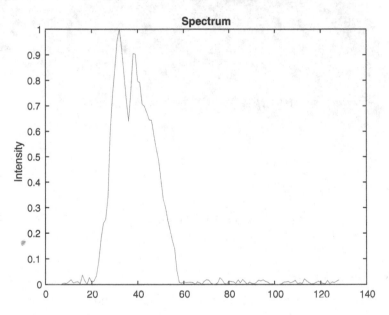

Fig. 3. Result of spectrum reconstruction

Table 2. Performance in Mode 0

Mode 0		Runtime (ms)		
Group		100	500	1000
Nor.	CPU	137.224	696.634	1224.067
	GPU	2.339	9.536	18.289
Nor.	CPU	14.692	70.040	143.701
	GPU	0.604	1.871	3.331

Table 3. Performance in Mode 1

Mode 0		Runtime (ms)		
Group		100	500	1000
Nor.	CPU	312.940	1558.225	3111.297
	GPU	3.078	13.210	25.701
Nor.	CPU	29.172	148.442	290.536
	GPU	0.710	2.541	4.732

Table 4. Performance in Mode 2

Mode 0		Runtime (ms)		
Group		100	500	1000
Nor.	CPU	182.069	952.961	1918.251
	GPU	2.735	10.783	20.869
Nor.	CPU	22.431	105.147	203.572
	GPU	0.735	2.437	4.314

Table 5. Performance in Mode 3

Mode 0		Runtime (ms)		
Group		100	500	1000
Nor.	CPU	191.65	958.99	1919.461
	GPU	2.518	10.612	20.779
Nor.	CPU	18.304	91.617	183.961
	GPU	0.622	2.012	3.716

Table 6. Performance in Mode 4

Mode 0		Runtime (ms)		
Group		100	500	1000
Nor.	CPU	142.648	701.167	1394.146
	GPU	2.579	10.769	20.832
Nor.	CPU	16.194	76.792	153.869
	GPU	0.662	2.192	4.609

4.3   Application

For the actual collected scanning data by the LASIS, as shown in Fig. 4, the size of an image is 256×1024. The interference sequence length is 128 with 16 single-sided zero-crossing samples. The wavelength is from 450 to 900 nm. For a frame of real scene, there are about 200,000 interference fringes to process. On the development board, the spectrum is reconstructed within about 47 ms. The result of spectrum reconstruction is shown in Fig. 5.

Fig. 4. The actual scanning scene

Fig. 5. The spectral cube

5   Conclusions

In this paper, the pipeline of the interferogram processing in spectrum reconstruction have been explored on the embedded NVIDIA Jetson TX2. The construction result reaches great success on the development board. For batch processing, the GPU has given obvious performance improvement, compared with the other ARMs. The processing pipeline we designed is well tested on our board. In the spectrum reconstruction, for detrending, we use parallel QRD and matrix inversion algorithms; for phase correction, an improved Mertz method has been performed for a fast phase correction. These parallel algorithms also has high performance. Especially, the more data, the higher the performance.

As high-performance processing pipeline on the embedded system, it could be considered fast and effective calculations for the interferogram process to meet actual requirements.

References

1. Grandmont, F., Drissen, L., Joncas, G.: Development of an imaging Fourier transform spectrometer for astronomy. Int. Soc. Opt. Photonics **4842**, 392–402 (2003)
2. Lacan, A., et al.: A static Fourier transform spectrometer for atmospheric sounding: concept and experimental implementation. Opt. Express **18**(8), 8311–8331 (2010)
3. Rafert, J.B., Sellar, R.G., Blatt, J.H.: Monolithic Fourier-transform imaging spectrometer. Appl. Opt. **34**(31), 7228–7230 (1995)
4. Dierking, M.P., Karim, M.A.: Solid-block stationary Fourier-transform spectrometer. Appl. Opt. **35**(1), 84–89 (1996)
5. Zhang, C., Zhao, B., Xiangli, B.: Wide-field-of-view polarization interference imaging spectrometer. Appl. Opt. **43**(33), 6090–6094 (2004)
6. Zhang, C., Xiangli, B., Zhao, B.C., Yuan, X.J.: A static polarization imaging spectrometer based on a Savart polariscope. Opt. Commun. **203**(1–2), 21–26 (2002)
7. Su, L., et al.: Spectrum reconstruction method for airborne temporally-spatially modulated Fourier transform imaging spectrometers. IEEE Trans. Geosci. Remote Sens. **52**(6), 3720–3728 (2014)
8. Zhang, C., Jian, X.: Wide-spectrum reconstruction method for a birefringence interference imaging spectrometer. Opt. Lett. **35**(3), 366–368 (2010)
9. Cook, S.: CUDA Programming: A Developer's Guide to Parallel Computing with GPUs. Newnes (2012)
10. Sanders, J., Kandrot, E.: CUDA by Example: An Introduction to General-Purpose GPU Programming. Addison-Wesley Professional (2010)
11. Nvidia, C.: NVIDIA CUDA C programming guide. Nvidia Corporation **120**(18), 8 (2011)
12. Griffiths, P.R., De Haseth, J.A.: Fourier Transform Infrared Spectrometry. Wiley, Hoboken (2007)
13. Zhang, W., Wen, D., Song, Z., et al.: Spectrum reconstruction in Fourier transform imaging spectroscopy based on high-performance parallel computing. Appl. Opt. **57**(21), 5983–5991 (2018)
14. Stoica, P.: Moses R L. Spectral analysis of signals (2005)
15. Mertz, L.: Auxiliary computation for Fourier spectrometry. Infrared Phys. **7**(1), 17–23 (1967)
16. Ting, X.: A method to improve the computing efficiency of mertz method in fourier transform spectroscopy. Acta Optica Sinica **3** (1999)

A Novel Multi-focus Image Fusion
Based on Lazy Random Walks

Wei Liu[1,2] and Zengfu Wang[1,2(✉)]

[1] Institute of Intelligent Machine, Chinese Academy of Sciences, Hefei, China
zfwang@ustc.edu.cn
[2] Department of Automation, University of Science and Technology of China, Hefei, China

Abstract. Most existing fusion methods usually suffer from blurred edges and introduce artifacts (such as blocking or ringing). To solve these problems, a novel multi-focus image fusion algorithm using lazy random walks (LRW) is proposed in this paper. Firstly, the sum of the modified Laplacian (SML) of each source image and a maximum operation rule are used to obtain the highly believable focused regions. Then, a lazy random walks based image fusion algorithm is presented to precisely locate the boundary of focused regions from the above highly believable focused regions in each source image. Experimental results demonstrate that the proposed algorithm can generate high quality all-in-focus images, avoid annoying artifacts and well preserve the sharpness on the focused objects. Our method is superior to the state-of-the-art methods in both subjective and objective assessments.

Keywords: Multi-focus image fusion · Lazy random walks · Sum of the modified Laplacian

1 Introduction

Image quality improvement is an important task in computer vision. Due to the finite depth of field of optical lenses, objects of different distances in the same scene cannot be fully focused. However, in practice, we may need an image with all objects clearly visible, which requires every part of the image is in focus. Multi-focus image fusion, which merges the focus regions from a series of images of the same scene to construct a single image, is a popular way to solve this problem.

The existing multi-focus image fusion methods can be roughly classified into two categories: spatial domain based methods and transform domain based methods. Since the multi-scale decomposition can effectively extract the salient features of the image, the transform domain based methods can achieve good fusion effect [1, 2]. However, transform domain based methods have some disadvantages [3]: the first one is the selection of the decomposition tool. The second drawback is some information in low-contrast areas can be easily lost. Furthermore, slight image mis-registration will result in undesirable artifacts. Different from transform domain based methods, spatial domain based methods directly handle the intensity values of source images, and it selects pixels with more obvious features as the corresponding pixels of the fusion image. This kind of method is simple and effective, and sharpness information of source images can be well preserved in the fused image. The core issue of spatial domain based methods is the evaluation of sharpness. In order to effectively distinguish between the focus areas and the defocus areas, researchers have proposed a number of focus measures, such as sum of the modified Laplacian (SML) [4], multi-scale morphological gradient (MSMG) [5], etc. These focus measurement techniques usually perform well for focus region detection. However, the robustness of focus areas detection is insufficient for smooth areas, image noise and mis-registration, etc. Therefore, the spatial domain based methods often suffer from blocking artifacts and erroneous results at the smooth areas and the boundary of focused areas.

To detect focused areas well, some novel image fusion methods have been presented recently. These image fusion methods can be divided into two categories: the first one is using the "hole-filling" or morphology filter to filter the initial decision map. Firstly, this type of method uses some novel focus measures (LBP [3], surface area [6], convolutional neural network (CNN) [7], etc.) to obtain the initial decision map. Then the "hole-filling" or morphology filter is used to eliminate the noise in the initial decision map. Finally, the final decision map is obtained by the guided filtering to optimize the filtered decision map. These multi-focus image fusion methods can effectively alleviate the impact of noise in decision maps. Most of the focused regions of the source image are merged into the composite image, and the visual effect of the fused image is significantly improved. However, the robustness of the post-processing methods is insufficient, which will result in incomplete filling of larger "hole" or false filling of smaller focused regions and inaccurate locating of the position of boundary. The second one is using some optimization techniques (such as image matting method [8], random walk (RW) algorithm [9], etc.) to obtain the final fusion weight maps. These approaches can be impressively useful. The RW algorithm uses the first arrival probability to decide the label of each pixel. RW-based image fusion algorithms have the advantages of simple model and fast computation speed. However, the first arrival probability ignores the global relationship between the current pixel and other seeds. Therefore, the RW algorithm has the disadvantages that it cannot guarantee convergence to a stable state and the image processing results are not robust. In order to make full use of the whole relationship between the pixel and all seeds, Shen et al. proposes the LRW algorithm through adds the self-loop over the graph vertex to make the RW process lazy [10]. LRW-based superpixel algorithm obtains good boundary adherence in the weak boundary and complicated texture regions. Compared with the traditional RW algorithm, the LRW algorithm has two advantages. Firstly, the LRW algorithm effectively overcomes the problem of RW algorithm which cannot guarantee convergence to a stable state, so it improves the applicability of the algorithm. Secondly, the LRW algorithm uses the commute time of visual transition to depict the difference between pixels, which is more reasonable and appropriate in the simulation of biological vision, thus the LRW algorithm is more robust. On account of these advantages, the LRW algorithm is adopted in the proposed fusion method.

To address the weaknesses of existing multi-focus image fusion methods (such as spatial inconsistency, blurred edges, and vulnerability to mis-registration, etc.), we propose a novel method for multi-focus image fusion in this paper. The schematic diagram of our multi-focus image fusion method is shown in Fig. 1. The proposed method consists of four steps. Firstly, the SML is used to evaluate the focus score of each pixel locally for each source image. Secondly, the focus scores are forwarded to LRW to obtain the global probability maps. Then, we can find the accurate focused map of each source images by the probability maps. At last, the focused maps are used to fuse source images to obtain the all-in-focus image. Unlike many existing methods, the proposed method does not need post-processing to suppress the noise of decision map. This paper provides two contributions: (1) No parameters need to be adjusted during the highly believable focused regions detection. (2) We introduce the LRW algorithm into multi-focus image fusion. The remainder of this paper is organized as follows. In Sect. 2, we briefly review the LRW theory. Section 3 describes the proposed image fusion method in detail. The experimental results and discussions are presented in Sect. 4. Section 5 summarizes this paper.

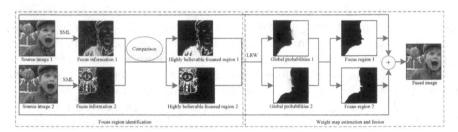

Fig. 1. Schematic diagram of the proposed multi-focus image fusion method

2   Lazy Random Walk Algorithm

The RW algorithm is a very popular approach for image segmentation [11], image fusion [9]. The RW algorithm uses the first arrival probability to decide the label of each pixel. However, the first arrival probability ignores the global relationship between the current pixel and other seeds. In 2014, Shen et al. proposes the LRW based superpixel algorithm and achieves good results [10]. Compared with the traditional RW algorithm, the LRW algorithm can guarantee convergence to a stable state, thus the LRW algorithm is more robust. Therefore, the LRW algorithm is used for multi-focus image fusion in this paper. In the LRW algorithm, we define an undirected graph $G = (V, E)$ on a given image, where V is the set of nodes and $E \subseteq V \times V$ is the set of edges. The LRW graph has the property that there is a non-zero likelihood that a lazy random walk remains at the original node through adds a self-loop over each vertex v_i. Then the adjacency matrix is defined as:

$$W_{i,j} = \begin{cases} 1 - \alpha & \text{if } i = j \\ \alpha \cdot w_{i,j} & \text{if } v_i \text{ and } v_j \text{ are the adjacent nodes} \\ 0 & \text{otherwise} \end{cases} \quad (1)$$

where $\alpha \in (0, 1)$ is lazy factor, $w_{i,j}$ is a function defined on E that models the similarity between nodes v_i and v_j. Since the Gaussian function has the property of geodesic distance, thus the edge-weight $w_{i,j}$ is defined as:

$$w_{i,j} = \exp(-\frac{\|g_i - g_j\|^2}{2\sigma^2}) \quad (2)$$

where g_i and g_j denote the image intensity values at two nodes v_i and v_j, and σ is the user defined parameter to control the sensitivity of the compatibility function to the difference of pixel values.

According to the adjacency matrix W on the graph, the graph Laplacian matrix is defined as:

$$L_{ij} = \begin{cases} d_i & \text{if } i = j \\ -\alpha \cdot w_{i,j} & \text{if } v_i \text{ and } v_j \text{ are the adjacent nodes} \\ 0 & \text{otherwise} \end{cases} \quad (3)$$

where $d_i = \sum_{v_j \in N_i} w_{i,j}$ is the degree of node v_i defined on its neighborhood N_i. We can also write Eq. (3) as $L = D - \alpha W$, $D = diag(d_1, d_2, \cdots d_S)$, S is the size of image I.

Duo to the normalized Laplacian matrix is to be more consistent with the eigenvalues of adjacency matrices in spectral geometry and in stochastic process [12], so we use the normalized Laplacian matrix in this paper. The normalized Laplacian matrix is $NL = I - \alpha D^{-1/2} W D^{-1/2}$. The normalized commute time NCT_{ij} of LRW denote the expected time for a lazy random walk that starts at one node v_i to reach node v_j and return to the node v_i, which is inversely proportion to the probability, so the closed-form of likelihoods probabilities of label l is:

$$f^l = 1 - NCT_{ij} = (I - \alpha D^{-1/2} W D^{-1/2})^{-1} y^l \quad (4)$$

where I is the identity matrix, y^l is a $S \times 1$ vector where all the elements are zero except the seed pixels as 1.

3 Multi-focus Image Fusion Based on LRW

The problem of multi-focus image fusion is the problem of assigning larger weights to focused pixels and smaller weights to defocus pixels. To compute the fusion weight using LRW, we model the fusion problem into a graph. In the LRW algorithm, the commute time is a proper probability measurement of the similarity between the current pixel and the seed pixel. The shorter the commute time, the higher the similarity is, so the fusion weight is inversely proportion to the commute time. In the following subsections, the LRW based image fusion method will be explained in detail.

3.1 Focus Measure

The first step of the proposed method is to get the focus information of source image. In the literature [4], Huang performed a comparison of several focus measures in multi-focus image fusion and showed that SML generally outperform variance, energy of image gradient (EOG), and spatial frequency (SF). In the experiment, we found that accurate decision maps can be obtained by choosing different focus measures, and the difference between the decision maps is small. In this paper, the SML is chosen as the focus measure. More specifically, the SML [4] is defined as:

$$
\mathbf{ML}(x, y) = |2\mathbf{gf}(x, y) - \mathbf{gf}(x - 1, y) - \mathbf{gf}(x + 1, y)| \\
+ |2\mathbf{gf}(x, y) - \mathbf{gf}(x, y - 1) - \mathbf{gf}(x, y + 1)| \tag{5}
$$

$$
\mathbf{SML}(x, y) = \sum_{m=-r}^{r} \sum_{n=-r}^{r} \mathbf{ML}^2(x + m, y + n) \tag{6}
$$

where r is the radius of local patch and $\mathbf{gf}(x, y)$ is the intensity value of gray image.

3.2 Highly Believable Focused Region Detection

This part comprises of three steps to detect the highly believable focused regions.

Step 1: We use Eq. (6) to calculate the focus measure map $\boldsymbol{FM}_n, n = 1, 2, \cdots N$ for each source image $\boldsymbol{I}_n$, where N is the number of source images.
Step 2: According to the focus measure maps of the source images obtained in step 1, a maximum focus measure map $\boldsymbol{mFM}$ is calculated:

$$
\boldsymbol{mFM}(x, y) = \max_n \{\boldsymbol{FM}_n(x, y)\} \tag{7}
$$

Step 3: The highly believable focused region of the nth source image HFR_n is calculated:

$$HFR_n(x, y) = \begin{cases} 1 & \text{if } FM_n(x, y) > \max_{m, m \neq n} \{FM_m(x, y)\} \\ & \& FM_n(x, y) > T \\ 0 & \text{otherwise} \end{cases} \tag{8}$$

The threshold T is set to the average value of image mFM. $HFR_n(x, y) = 1$ indicates that the pixel at (x, y) is considered as a highly believable focus position in the nth source image.

3.3 Image Fusion Based on LRW

The focused regions of the source images are sparse obtained according to Eq. (8). In the final fusion part, the weight map obtained by the HFR_n is meaningless (the values of all weight maps' partial corresponding positions are zero). Therefore, we need to generate a dense weight map based on the sparse HFR_n. The LRW algorithm described in Sect. 2 is particularly applicable to solve this problem. We can regard the highly believable focused region as the seed points of LRW algorithm then use the LRW algorithm to obtain the likelihoods probabilities between the pixels and seed points in each position of the source images. Thereby we can obtain the accurate focus areas of each source image. For the source image I_n, we obtain the positions of seed points of focus areas fp_n and defocus areas dfp_n according to the highly believable focused regions obtained in Sect. 3.2, respectively:

$$fp_n = \{(x, y) | HFR_n(x, y) = 1\} \tag{9}$$

$$dfp_n = \{(x, y) | HFR_{m, m \neq n}(x, y) = 1\} \tag{10}$$

After obtaining the position sets fp_n and dfp_n, we use Eq. (4) to calculate the likelihood probability map $p_n^{fp}(x, y)$ of focus areas and the likelihood probability map $p_n^{dfp}(x, y)$ of defocus areas for each position of source image I_n. So we can get the final decision map of the nth source image by:

$$W_n(x, y) = \begin{cases} 1 & \text{if } p_n^{fp}(x, y) > p_n^{dfp}(x, y) \\ 0 & \text{if } p_n^{dfp}(x, y) \geq p_n^{fp}(x, y) \end{cases} \tag{11}$$

Finally, we obtain the fused image F as follows:

$$F = \sum_{n=1}^{N} W_n I_n \tag{12}$$

4   Experimental Results and Analysis

4.1   Experimental Settings

Experiments are performed on 26 pairs of multi-focus source images. 20 sets of them come from a new multi-focus dataset called "Lytro" [13], and another 6 sets which are widely used in multi-focus fusion research. A portion of source image pairs are shown in Fig. 2. We compare the proposed method with three representative fusion methods which are image matting based image fusion (IM) [8], boundary finding based image fusion algorithm (BF) [5] and convolution neural network based method (CNN) [7]. In our experiments, the parameters of LRW are set to $\sigma = 0.01$ and $\alpha = 0.9992$, respectively. To quantitatively assess the performances of different methods, five widely recognized objective fusion metrics are applied in our experiments. They are the normalized mutual information (Q_{NMI}) [14], image feature based metrics (Q_G) [15], image structural similarity based metric (Q_Y) [16], human perception-based metric (Q_{CB}) [17] and the visual information fidelity fusion (Q_{VIFF}) [18]. For all the five evaluation metrics, a larger value indicates a better fusion performance.

Fig. 2. A portion of source image sets used in our experiments

4.2   Qualitative and Quantitative Comparison

The decision maps and their corresponding fused images obtained by different methods are shown in Figs. 3, 4 and 5, respectively. For clearer comparison, the local magnified regions of fused images are presented in the third row of each figure. It can be seen from the fusion results that the IM method made noticeable artifacts in the transitional regions (the boundaries between focused and defocused regions) and partial defocus regions are also selected in the fused image (Stadium's steel mesh), which owing to the image matting algorithm is difficult to completely accurate extract the focus areas of the source image. The BF method selected many blurred regions of source image into the fused image (golf club). In Fig. 5(b), the BF method failed to fuse the stadium images that captured at complex scenes, and the steel mesh in the fused image is completely taken from the defocus regions. The CNN and the proposed method obtained clearer fused images with high contrast. The visual effects of fusion results are very good. The CNN method performs some post-processing on decision maps (such as "hole-filling" and guided filtering), which will cause the fused image obtained by the CNN method to appear slightly blurred at the focus boundary and misjudge the isolated small focused region in the source images (red box in the "Golf" fused image). Figures 3, 4 and 5(d) shows the result of our method. We can see that our method is able to accurately identify the focused regions and produces the clearest fused images.

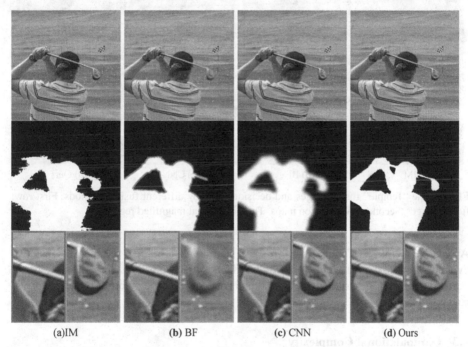

(a)IM	(b) BF	(c) CNN	(d) Ours

Fig. 3. The "Golf" fused images and decision maps by different fusion methods. First row: fused images. Second row: decision maps. Third row: local magnified regions. (Color figure online)

The average objective assessment values of 26 pairs testing images are listed in Table 1. Each bold value in Table 1 indicates the highest value in the corresponding row.

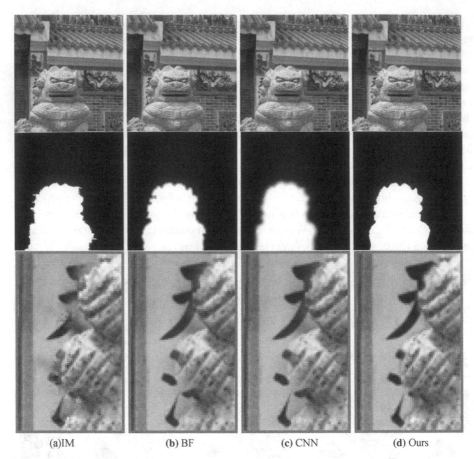

    (a)IM   (b) BF   (c) CNN   (d) Ours

Fig. 4. The "Temple" fused images and decision maps by different fusion methods. First row: fused images. Second row: decision maps. Third row: local magnified regions.

As can be seen from Table 1, the proposed method has obtained the highest objective evaluation value in all five metrics which indicates that the proposed method has better performance in comparison to other methods and reflects the stability of the proposed fusion method.

4.3 Computational Complexity

In the initialization step, the source images are converted to gray scale for calculating SML. The complexity of this step is $O(NK)$, where K is the number of pixels in source image and N is the number of source images. The complexity for computing the SML feature is approximately $O(NK)$. We use the symmetric and highly sparse Laplacian graph to compute the LRW algorithm by solving the large sparse linear system. The complexity of the LRW algorithm is about $O(NK^2)$. With only linear operations involved, the complexity of the fusion step is $O(NK)$. Therefore, the total complexity

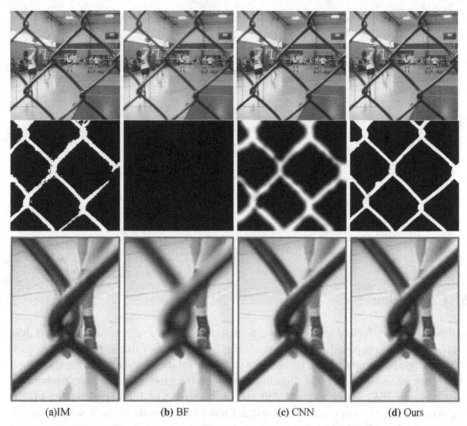

(a)IM   (b) BF   (c) CNN   (d) Ours

Fig. 5. The "Stadium" fused images and decision maps by different fusion methods. First row: fused images. Second row: decision maps. Third row: local magnified regions. (Color figure online)

of our algorithm is $O(NK^2)$. The average computational time for processing all the 26 pairs testing images by different fusion methods is listed in Table 2. All the fusion methods Matlab implementations were executed on the same computer with a 2.20-GHz CPU and 12-GB memory available for Matlab. As can be seen from Table 2, the BF and the proposed method are the two most efficient methods compared with other methods. The IM method uses the image matting technique to obtain the final fusion weight maps, so the running time of IM method is slightly slower than the one of our method. Although CNN can quickly produce fused image using GPU, the running time with CPU is too long and up to about 225 s.

Table 1. The average objective assessments of different image fusion methods

Method	IM	BF	CNN	Ours
Q_{NMI}	1.1243	1.1636	1.1388	**1.1837**
Q_G	0.7087	0.7235	0.7228	**0.7277**
Q_Y	0.9715	0.9893	0.9879	**0.9907**
Q_{CB}	0.7872	0.8074	0.8073	**0.8088**
Q_{VIFF}	0.9139	0.9070	0.9182	**0.9185**

Table 2. The average running time of different fusion methods

Method	IM	BF	CNN	Ours
Time(s)	5.0211	3.6845	225.8157	3.9260

5   Conclusion

In this paper, an effective and robust multi-focus image fusion algorithm based on LRW is proposed. The proposed method first obtains a highly believable focus region in each source image by comparing the focus score of each pixel then forwards the highly believable focus information to LRW algorithm to obtain the global optimization probability maps. Since LRW is able to make full use of the strong correlations between pixels, the proposed method can accurately extract the focus regions of each source image. Experimental results show that the proposed method achieves better performance than the compared fusion methods, both in visual effects and objective evaluations.

References

1. Tian, J., Chen, L.: Multi-focus image fusion using wavelet-domain statistics. In: 17th IEEE International Conference on Image Processing, pp. 1205–1208. IEEE, Hong Kong (2010)
2. Zhang, Q., Guo, B.: Multifocus image fusion using the nonsubsampled contourlet transform. Signal Process. **89**, 1334–1346 (2009)
3. Yin, W.L., Zhao, W.D., You, D., Wang, D.: Local binary pattern metric-based multi-focus image fusion. Opt. Laser Technol. **110**, 62–68 (2019)
4. Huang, W., Jing, Z.L.: Evaluation of focus measures in multi-focus image fusion. Pattern Recogn. Lett. **28**, 493–500 (2007)
5. Zhang, Y., Bai, X.Z., Wang, T.: Boundary finding based multi-focus image fusion through multi-scale morphological focus-measure. Inf. Fusion **35**, 81–101 (2017)
6. Nejati, M., et al.: Surface area-based focus criterion for multi-focus image fusion. Inf. Fusion **36**, 284–295 (2017)
7. Liu, Y., Chen, X., Peng, H., Wang, Z.: Multi-focus image fusion with a deep convolutional neural network. Inf. Fusion **36**, 191–207 (2017)
8. Li, S.T., Kang, X.D., Hu, J.W., Yang, B.: Image matting for fusion of multi-focus images in dynamic scenes. Inf. Fusion **14**, 147–162 (2013)

9. Ma, J.L., Zhou, Z.Q., Wang, B., Miao, L.J., Zong, H.: Multi-focus image fusion using boosted random walks-based algorithm with two-scale focus maps. Neurocomputing **335**, 9–22 (2019)
10. Shen, J.B., Du, Y.F., Wang, W.G., Li, X.L.: Lazy random walks for superpixel segmentation. IEEE Trans. Image Process. **23**, 1451–1462 (2014)
11. Grady, L.: Random walks for image segmentation. IEEE Trans. Pattern Anal. Mach. Intell. **28**, 1768–1783 (2006)
12. Chung, F.R.K.: Spectral Graph Theory. American Mathematical Society, Providence (1997)
13. Nejati, M.: http://mansournejati.ece.iut.ac.ir/content/lytro-multi-focus-dataset
14. Hossny, M., Nahavandi, S., Vreighton, D.: Comments on 'information measure for performance of image fusion'. Electron. Lett. **44**(18), 1066–1067 (2008)
15. Zhao, J., Laganiere, R., Liu, Z.: Performance assessment of combinative pixel-level image fusion based on an absolute feature measurement. Int. J. Innov. Comput. Inf. Control **3**(6), 1433–1447 (2007)
16. Wang, Z., Bovik, A.C., Sheikh, H.R., Simoncelli, E.P.: Image quality assessment: from error visibility to structural similarity. IEEE Trans. Image Process. **13**(4), 600–612 (2004)
17. Chen, Y., Blum, R.S.: A new automated quality assessment algorithm for image fusion. Image Vis. Comput. **27**(10), 1421–1432 (2009)
18. Han, Y., Cai, Y., Cao, Y., Xu, X.: A new image fusion performance metric based on visual information fidelity. Inf. Fusion **14**, 127–135 (2013)

Biological and Medical Image Processing

Joint Multi-frame Detection and Segmentation for Multi-cell Tracking

Zibin Zhou[1], Fei Wang[1(✉)], Wenjuan Xi[1], Huaying Chen[2], Peng Gao[1], and Chengkang He[1]

[1] School of Electronics and Information Engineering, Harbin Institute of Technology, Shenzhen 518055, China
{zhouzibin,xiwenjuan,pgao,hechengkang}@stu.hit.edu.cn,
wangfeiz@hit.edu.cn
[2] School of Mechanical Engineering and Automation, Harbin Institute of Technology, Shenzhen 518055, China
chenhuaying@hit.edu.cn

Abstract. Tracking living cells in video sequence is difficult, because of cell morphology and high similarities between cells. Tracking-by-detection methods are widely used in multi-cell tracking. We perform multi-cell tracking based on the cell centroid detection, and the performance of the detector has high impact on tracking performance. In this paper, UNet is utilized to extract inter-frame and intra-frame spatio-temporal information of cells. Detection performance of cells in mitotic phase is improved by multi-frame input. Good detection results facilitate multi-cell tracking. A mitosis detection algorithm is proposed to detect cell mitosis and the cell lineage is built up. Another UNet is utilized to acquire primary segmentation. Jointly using detection and primary segmentation, cells can be fine segmented in highly dense cell population. Experiments are conducted to evaluate the effectiveness of our method, and results show its state-of-the-art performance.

Keywords: Multi-frame · Segmentation · Joint · Multi-object · Cell tracking

1 Introduction

Multi-cell tracking in image sequence is valuable for stem cell research, tissue engineering, drug discovery and proteomics [1]. Researchers can construct cell lineage trees and analyze cell morphology based on cell tracking results [2].

Cell tracking is more challenging than general object tracking. Firstly, cells may be deformed, such as elongation, contraction, and swelling [3]. Secondly, there is a very high similarity between cells. Cells of same kind have the same internal structure, and they are difficult to be distinguished through their appearance. In addition, the irregular motion of cells, the mitotic behavior, the complexity of the background, and the interference of other impurities also increase the challenge.

Y. Zhao et al. (Eds.): ICIG 2019, LNCS 11902, pp. 435–446, 2019.
https://doi.org/10.1007/978-3-030-34110-7_36

The development of deep learning in recent years has greatly promoted the progress in computer vision. For example, the performance of ResNet [4] exceeded the performance of humans on the ImageNet test set. Cell tracking has evolved from contour evolution, filtering templates, to tracking-by-detection methods [2]. Researchers continue to improve the robustness of algorithms.

There is no such a multi-cell tracking algorithm that can perform well in all varieties of video sequences. For example, Ref. [5] can perform segmentation and tracking very well when cells are large, but not well when cells are small. Highly dense small cells are apt to be missed during tracking, and lead to tracking errors. To solve this challenge, we propose an algorithm that jointly using detection and segmentation for multi-cell tracking. Our method is composed of four portions: cell centroid detection with multi-frame images, primary multi-cell tracker, primary cell segmentation, fine segmentation. Each portion will be detailed in Sect. 3. The contributions of our work can be summarized as follows:

- Multi-frame as input to UNet [6] is proposed, which helps the network to extract spatio-temporal information. Detection performance of mitotic cells is improved, therefore detection performance of mitosis is improved by the mitosis detection algorithm when tracking.
- A fine cell segmentation algorithm is proposed for tracking highly dense small cells. By jointly using primary tracking results of cell centroid detection and primary cell segmentation results, we achieve a new state-of-the-art performance on dataset Fluo-Hela [7].

Effectiveness of our method is evaluated with Cell Tracking Benchmark [7] of Cell Tracking Challenge (www.celltrackingchallenge.net). Performance metrics include tracking accuracy, segmentation accuracy, and a combination performance of both.

2   Related Works

Tracking-by-detection methods are widely used in multi-object tracking [8,9], as well as in multi-cell tracking. Starting with detecting or segmenting cells in a video sequence, these methods establish temporal associations for cells in frames to frames. Detection performance has high impact on tracking performance [10]. As long as good detection results are available, the tracking problem can be simplified [8]. This paper proposes a tracking-by-detection method, which focuses on detection and segmentation. Detection or segmentation in tracking-by-detection methods will be briefly reviewed as below.

Ciresan et al. [11] proposed to use neural networks for segmentation of microbial images in the early days. They use a neural network as a pixel classifier to segment the biological neuron membrane. The network inference must be run on patch-by-patch separately. Unfortunately patches overlap each other, a large amount of computation redundancy occurs, therefore calculation is quite slow.

Ronneberger et al. [6] proposed the semantic segmentation network, i.e. UNet, cell segmentation was further developed. The network is of the encoder-decoder structure, its input is first be downsampled and then upsampled.

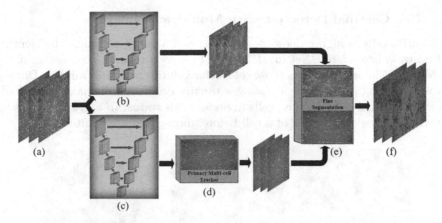

Fig. 1. Overview of our proposed tracking framework. (a) Input. (b) UNet for primary cell segmentation. (c) UNet for cell centroid detection with multi-frame images. (d) Primary multi-cell tracker. (e) Fine segmentation. (f) Final tracking results.

In the upsampling process, low-layer features corresponding to the downsampling layer are connected to the corresponding upsampling layer. The network gets high-level semantics without losing much low-level information and works well with only small amount of training data. Zhou et al. [12] redesigned the skip-connection of UNet and improved segmentation performance by reducing semantic differences of feature maps in encoder and decoder subnetworks.

Payer et al. [5] integrated ConvGRU into a stacked hourglass network for instance segmentation and tracking of cells. ConvGRU not only extracts local features, but also memorizes inter-frame information [13]. The stacked hourglass network is similar to UNet, its input is first be downsampled and then upsampled [14]. This integrated structure can perform cell segmentation well even in the case of a very close membrane. However, when cells are small, it does not perform well. Arbelle et al. [15] proposed a network structure for inter-frame segmentation combining ConvLSTM and UNet. Like ConvGRU, ConvLSTM has spatio-temporal characteristics [16]. The integrated structure can perform excellent segmentation even in the case of partial disappearance of cells, but does not perform well in the case of less training data. The works of Payer et al. [5] and Arbelle et al. [15] are similar.

As long as cells are accurately detected or segmented, tracking will be largely simplified. In Ref. [5], although only the intersection over union is used for inter-frame cell associations, it achieves desired tracking performance.

3   Method

In this section our proposed method is detailed. As shown in Fig. 1, it has four portions: cell centroid detection with multi-frame images, primary multi-cell tracker, primary cell segmentation, fine segmentation.

3.1   Cell Centroid Detection with Multi-frame Images

To identify cells in highly dense population, it is a useful technique to identify cell centroid first. Here UNet [6] (UNet-DET) is used to locate cell centroid.

Mitotic cells are defined as those cells before, during and after mitosis. During mitosis, obvious morphological changes usually occur, which make them look different from normal cells, i.e., cells in non-mitosis status. In Fig. 2, from left to right, morphological changes of a cell before, during and after mitosis.

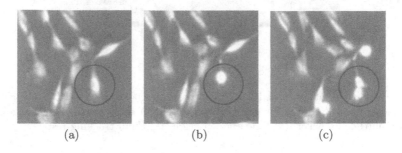

(a)   (b)   (c)

Fig. 2. Morphological changes in mitosis.

Pixels are categorized into three categories: mitotic cells, normal cells and backgrounds. If information in previous nearby frames is included, network can more accurately learn to identify mitotic cells [17].

Different from usual single-frame input method, we feed incorporative consecutive pre-N_{input} frames into the network. This approach does improve cell centroid detection a lot. Combined with past image information, the network can extract living cell behavioral features, and then screen out impurities that do not change shape.

Compared with Ref. [5,15], the overall network complexity based on UNet-DET does not increase much. Only the number of weight parameters in the first layer of the network increases.

A cross-entropy loss function is used to train the network. Mitotic cells are few, and more attention should be paid to them by setting a weight map. The network loss function is defined as in Ref. [6]:

$$L = -\frac{1}{T} \sum_{i=1}^{T} w(i) \log \frac{\exp(h(i, g(i)))}{\sum\limits_{j=1}^{C} \exp(h(i,j))} \tag{1}$$

where T denotes the total number of pixels. $w(\cdot)$ is a weight map. $g(\cdot)$ is the real category corresponding to the input pixel. $h(i, j)$ denotes the final output of category j when input pixel i.

Thresholding inference results, using the flood-fill algorithm [18] to fill internal holes of connected area. Extracting contour of connected area, computing its centroid as cell centroid. High-precision cell centroid detection and classification are acquired without increasing much network overhead.

3.2   Primary Multi-cell Tracker

Different from common object tracking, cell lineage needs to be built up during tracking. If a cell is categorized as a mitotic cell in multiple consecutive frames, it is highly likely to undergo mitosis. A mitosis detection algorithm, using a local cell status matrix, is proposed. The matrix is created in the beginning of new trajectory. Elements of the matrix record the status of a cell: the centroid position (X, Y), its sequence number (Z), whether it is a normal or mitotic cell. When the number of mitotic cells is larger than a given threshold, it can be concluded that mitosis occurs.

As long as images are captured in high frame rate and cells are precisely detected, it is possible to use overlap intersection-over-union (IOU) to build inter-frame object associations [8,19], and then ideal tracking is performed.

When the cell centroid is located, a bounding box with a size of $N_{size} \times N_{size}$ is created around the centroid, where N_{size} is the average length of cells scaled in number of pixels. With the assumption that sequences have the high enough frame rate, inter-frame cells can be associated by only using the IOU of bounding boxes. Each newly detected cell is needed to be associated with an existing trajectory. The association strategy is computed as:

$$\Theta(t, D) = \underset{d \in D}{arg\,ma\,x}(\Lambda(d,t)) \tag{2}$$

$$d(t, D) = \begin{cases} \Theta(t, D), & \Lambda(\Theta(t, D), t) \geq \alpha \\ N, & \Lambda(\Theta(t, D), t) < \alpha \end{cases} \tag{3}$$

where t denotes the cell at the end of the trajectory to be associated with, D the set of candidate detected cells in the current frame, $\Lambda(\cdot, \cdot)$ the IOU of both. α is the minimum overlapping intersection that allows to associate. N denotes that there are no associating candidate cells.

If the largest IOU that is less than α, the candidate cell will be discarded.

The trajectory is terminated when it has no associated cells. For a candidate cell that has no existing trajectory to associate, a temporary new trajectory is created. Short trajectories are most likely pseudo trajectories caused by impurity interference, and therefore are discarded.

If a mitosis event is detected, the original trajectory is terminated. At the same time, cell lineage is established between the mitotic mother cell and its two newborn daughter cells. This distinguishes normal cells which newly enter the field of view from newborn daughter cells.

Primary tracking results of cell centroid detection are acquired, cell IDs of the same trajectory are same.

3.3   Primary Cell Segmentation

UNet [6] (UNet-SEG) is used for primary segmentation of cells. During this stage, image pixels are categorized into cell boundaries, cell interiors, and backgrounds. The cross-entropy loss function is used to train the network. More attention is paid on cell boundaries by setting a weight map.

(a)   (b)   (c)

Fig. 3. Dense cell segmentation results. Cross: mitotic cells. Dot: normal cells. (a) Original image and cell centroid detection results. (b) Primary cell segmentation results. (c) Fine segmentation results.

Threshold is performed to acquire cell segmentation by using inference results of cell boundaries and cell interiors. There may be holes inside segmented cells and the flood-fill algorithm [18] is used to fill these internal holes.

When many cells are close each other, each cell is not separated at this stage. When primary segmentation is finished, as shown in Fig. 3(b), cells close each other may be segmented as a blob, a piece of connected area.

3.4   Fine Segmentation

Results from primary segmentation may contain many connected area as shown in Fig. 3(b). When cells are dense, multiple cells are segmented together. In this section, fine segmentation is conducted to separate each cell individually, which jointly use primary tracking results of cell centroid detection from Sect. 3.2 and primary cell segmentation results from Sect. 3.3.

Assuming cell boundary is closest to its centroid for non-overlapping small cells of similar size, each pixel in a connected area is assigned to a cell centroid contained in this connected area according to the following formulation:

$$P(p_{pixel}) = \arg\min_{p \in P_{det}}(d(p_{pixel}, p)) \tag{4}$$

where P_{det} is a set of cell centroid contained in a connected area, and p_{pixel} denotes pixels in the connected area, $d(\cdot, \cdot)$ denotes the Euclidean distance.

However, it would be a very time-consuming task to calculate Euclidean distance from each pixel to each cell centroid. Therefore, Voronoi [20] is used to accelerate pixel assignment. Pixel assignment is shown as Algorithm 1. Figure 3(c) shows fine segmentation results.

4   Experiment

The effectiveness of our method is evaluated with datasets of Cell Tracking Challenge [9]. The dataset for each kind of cells provides two training sequences

---

Algorithm 1. Fine Segmentation

Input:
 Primary cell segmentation $SEG = SEG_1, SEG_2, ..., SEG_M$;
 Primary tracking results of cell centroid detection $P_{det} = P_1, P_2, ..., P_N$;
Output:
 Fine segmentation result SEG_RES;
 1: Initialize a zero matrix SEG_RES;
 2: Calculate the Voronoi diagram according to P_{det};
 3: Label the connected area of Voronoi diagram, acquire LAB_VOR;
 4: **for** seg in SEG **do**
 5: P_{inside} = cell centroid contained by seg;
 6: **if** len(P_{inside})==1 **then**
 7: SEG_RES += seg;
 8: **else**
 9: **if** len(P_{inside})>1 **then**
 10:   **for** p in P_{inside} **do**
 11:    SEG_RES += $seg \cap LAB\_VOR(p)$;
 12:   **end for**
 13: **end if**
 14: **end if**
 15: **end for**

---

with GT (ground truth) and two test sequences without GT. GT includes TRA (tracking) GT and SEG (segmentation) GT. TRA GT essentially contains cell centroid of all sequences. SEG GT is few, which makes cell segmentation more difficult.

4.1   Training

UNet-DET and UNet-SEG both are composed of 5 downsampling layers and 5 upsampling layers. Adam optimizer [21] is used and the learning rate is set as *0.001*. The exponential decay rate of learning rate is set as *0.95*, the global step size of the decay is set as *4* times of the number of sample set. A weighted cross-entropy loss function is used for training to pay more attention on mitotic cells or cell boundaries. To augment samples, we apply horizontal and vertical flips, and randomly add Gaussian noise or salt and pepper noise on sample set.

For UNet-DET, incorporative consecutive pre-N_{input} frames are fed into the network. The dimension of input is (H, W, N_{input}), here $N_{input} = 3$. The label is TRA GT of last frame. We have modified TRA GT. Mitotic cells are defined as cells of $N_{mitisis}$ frames before and after mitosis, here $N_{mitosis} = 2$. Weight of each category is set as: *0.5*-mitotic cells, *0.3*-normal cells, *0.2*-backgrounds.

For UNet-SEG, SEG GT are categorized into cell boundaries and cell interiors. When the amount of SEG GT is scarce, original images and SEG GT are cropped centered on each cell centroid. N_{cell} training samples with a size of $S_{crop} \times S_{ceop}$ are cropped from each original image. Here S_{crop} is set as *5* times of the mean size of cells, N_{cell} denotes the number of cells in the image. Weight of each category is set as: *0.5*-cell boundaries, *0.3*-cell interiors, *0.2*-backgrounds.

4.2 Comparison of Multi-frame Input and Single-Frame Input

The advantage of multi-frame input over single-frame input is evaluated with Cell Tracking Challenge datasets PhC-PSC and Fluo-HeLa [7], which have more mitosis. The first half of the two training sequences are used as training samples and the other half are used as test samples. Performance of cell centroid detection is scaled with three metrics, i.e., Precision, Recall, F1-score. These metrics on normal cells and mitotic cells are shown in Table 1 respectively.

From Table 1, three metrics are improved 15% with mitotic cells, while slightly improved with normal cells. Inter-frame morphological changes of mitotic cells are obvious, retaining the historical information can improve detection performance.

In our multi-cell tracking algorithm, the improved mitotic cells detection performance will improve the mitosis event detection performance. Table 2 shows the mitosis event detection performance compared with different input modes. Due to our mitosis detection algorithm is strict to determine whether mitosis has occurred, Precision is high of both. The other two metrics of multi-frame input are improved about 20%. Therefore, the reconstruction of the cell lineage will be improved.

Table 1. Detection performance of normal cells and mitotic cells

Status	Input frame	Precision (%)	Recall (%)	F1 score (%)
Mitotic cells	1	44.3	49.7	46.8
	3	**60.1**	**65.3**	**62.6**
Normal cells	1	93.2	91.6	92.4
	3	**94.3**	**93.7**	**94.0**

Table 2. Detection performance of mitosis event

Dataset	Input frame	Precision (%)	Recall (%)	F1 score (%)
Phc-PSC	1	**87.6**	26.8	41.1
	3	86.0	**47.8**	**61.5**
Fluo-Hela	1	77.3	37.2	50.2
	3	**87.7**	**63.6**	**73.7**

4.3 Evaluations on Cell Tracking Benchmark

Cell tracking performance is evaluated in Cell Tracking Benchmark with 2D datasets of Cell Tracking Challenge [7]. Performance of tracking is scaled in TRA (tracking accuracy), SEG (segmentation accuracy), and OP_{CTB} (the mean of both) [7].

Based on the ranking announced on the day April 30th, 2019, which can be seen at the web of Cell Tracking Challenge [9], performance metrics of our proposed method are listed in Table 3. For each dataset, generally performance metrics of more than 20 methods are ranked [9], including the original UNet (FR-Ro-GE) [6], the globally trained UNet (FR-Fa-GE) [22], the method of ConvLSTM integrated into UNet (BGU-IL) [15], the method of ConvGRU integrated into the stacked hourglass network (TUG-AT) [5], and the method of global threshold and global associations with spatio-temporal (KTH-SE) [9].

Table 3. Quantitative comparison of Cell Tracking Benchmark (%)

		Phc-PSC	Fluo-Hela	Fluo-SIM+	Fluo-GOWT1	
OP_{CTB}	1st	80.4	95.3	88.2	95.1	
	2nd	80.4	94.4	88.1	93.4	Ours
	3rd	80.1	94.2	87.8	92.3	KTH-SE(1-4)
				7th 86.0	12th 87.0	HD-Hau-GE
SEG	1st	68.2	91.9	80.7	92.7	CVUT-CZ
	2nd	66.5	90.3	80.2	92.1	RWTH-GE
	3rd	65.3	90.2	79.2	89.4	FR-Ro-GE
				4th 78.4	16th 79.0	FR-Fa-GE
TRA	1st	95.9	99.1	97.5	97.9	BGU-IL(1-4)
	2nd	95.0	99.1	97.3	97.6	TUG-AT
	3rd	94.3	98.8	96.6	96.7	
				4th 98.7	9th 93.6	4th 94.9	

Experiments show excellence of our method on datasets Phc-PSC and Fluo-Hela, highly dense cell datasets. Our method achieves new state-of-the-art performance on SEG and OP_{CTB} of dataset Fluo-Hela. 2nd on TRA of dataset Phc-PSC is achieved. Though these two datasets have very few SEG GT, our method performs excellent.

Our method does not perform very well on datasets Fluo-SIM+ and Fluo-GOWT1. A possible solution to this problem is fully taking advantage of image information when making primary cell segmentation split.

Figure 4 shows multi-cell tracking performance of our method on multiple datasets. For the consideration of clarity, only a portion of field of view is selected and enlarged. Different kind of cells have different morphology. We track trajectories of cells and get each cell segmentation. Fine segmentation results on highly dense cell population is shown as in Fig. 4(a). As shown in Fig. 4(c), cells can be segmented accurately even when partly disappeared. Cells can be segmented accurately when their gray level is similar to that of background.

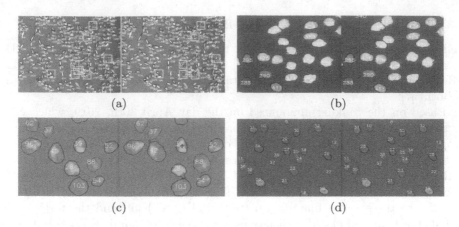

(a)   (b)

(c)   (d)

Fig. 4. Cell tracking results. For each pair of images, the left one is the previous frame, and the right one is the current frame. White numbers: trajectory IDs. Yellow boxes: detected mitosis. Red crosses: mitotic cells. Datasets: (a) Phc-PSC. (b) Fluo-Hela. (c) Fluo-SIM+. (d) Fluo-GOWT1. (Color figure online)

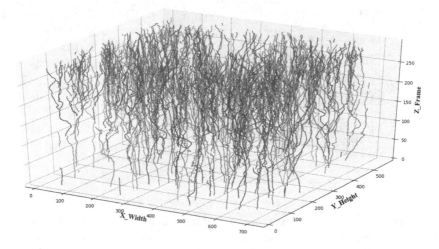

Fig. 5. Cell spatio-temporal trajectories of Phc-PSC.

Figure 5 shows cell spatio-temporal trajectories of our method on dataset Phc-PSC. It shows trajectories of all cells, as well as evolution of cell lineage. Cells will undergo mitosis over time or leave the field of view. As the frame number increases, cell trajectories become dense.

5   Conclusion

We propose a multi-cell tracking framework, which jointly use detection and segmentation. Cell centroid detection is conducted using a UNet with multi-frame input images. Detection of mitotic cells is improved without increasing much network overhead, and therefore improve the detection performance of mitosis event by our mitosis detection algorithm. With our method, normal cells newly entering the field of view can be distinguished from newborn daughter cells. Another UNet is utilized to acquire primary cell segmentation. Fine segmentation is conducted to separate each cell individually, which jointly use primary tracking results of cell centroid detection and primary cell segmentation results.

Evaluations are conducted to compare our method with other methods with datasets in Cell Tracking Challenge. Due to jointly use detection and segmentation, our method performs excellent and achieves a new state-of-the-art performance on dataset Fluo-Hela.

Performance on some datasets is still not very ideal. In future works, fine segmentation will be further optimized, and more image information will be used for more accurately segmentation and tracking.

References

1. Ren, Y., Xu, B., Zhang, J., et al.: A generalized data association approach for cell tracking in high-density population. In: 2015 International Conference on Control, Automation and Information Sciences (ICCAIS), pp. 502–507. IEEE (2015)
2. He, T., Mao, H., Guo, J., et al.: Cell tracking using deep neural networks with multi-task learning. Image Vis. Comput. **60**, 142–153 (2017)
3. Yang, F., Mackey, M.A., Ianzini, F., Gallardo, G., Sonka, M.: Cell segmentation, tracking, and mitosis detection using temporal context. In: Duncan, J.S., Gerig, G. (eds.) MICCAI 2005. LNCS, vol. 3749, pp. 302–309. Springer, Heidelberg (2005). https://doi.org/10.1007/11566465_38
4. He, K., Zhang, X., Ren, S., et al.: Deep residual learning for image recognition. In: Proceedings of the IEEE Conference on Computer Vision and Pattern Recognition (CVPR), pp. 770–778 (2016)
5. Payer, C., Štern, D., Neff, T., Bischof, H., Urschler, M.: Instance segmentation and tracking with cosine embeddings and recurrent hourglass networks. In: Frangi, A.F., Schnabel, J.A., Davatzikos, C., Alberola-López, C., Fichtinger, G. (eds.) MICCAI 2018. LNCS, vol. 11071, pp. 3–11. Springer, Cham (2018). https://doi.org/10.1007/978-3-030-00934-2_1
6. Ronneberger, O., Fischer, P., Brox, T.: U-Net: convolutional networks for biomedical image segmentation. In: Navab, N., Hornegger, J., Wells, W.M., Frangi, A.F. (eds.) MICCAI 2015. LNCS, vol. 9351, pp. 234–241. Springer, Cham (2015). https://doi.org/10.1007/978-3-319-24574-4_28
7. Maška, M., Ulman, V., Svoboda, D., et al.: A benchmark for comparison of cell tracking algorithms. Bioinformatics **30**(11), 1609–1617 (2014)
8. Bochinski, E., Eiselein, V., Sikora, T.: High-speed tracking-by-detection without using image information. In: 2017 14th IEEE International Conference on Advanced Video and Signal Based Surveillance (AVSS), pp. 1–6. IEEE (2017)
9. Ulman, V., Maška, M., Magnusson, K.E.G., et al.: An objective comparison of cell-tracking algorithms. Nat. Methods **14**(12), 1141 (2017)
10. Luo, W., Xing, J., Milan, A., et al.: Multiple object tracking: a literature review. arXiv preprint arXiv:1409.7618v4 (2017)

11. Ciresan, D., Giusti, A., Gambardella, L.M., et al.: Deep neural networks segment neuronal membranes in electron microscopy images. In: Advances in Neural Information Processing Systems, pp. 2843–2851 (2012)
12. Zhou, Z., Rahman Siddiquee, M.M., Tajbakhsh, N., Liang, J.: UNet++: a nested U-Net architecture for medical image segmentation. In: Stoyanov, D., et al. (eds.) DLMIA/ML-CDS -2018. LNCS, vol. 11045, pp. 3–11. Springer, Cham (2018). https://doi.org/10.1007/978-3-030-00889-5_1
13. Ballas, N., Yao, L., Pal, C., et al.: Delving deeper into convolutional networks for learning video representations. arXiv preprint arXiv:1511.06432 (2015)
14. Newell, A., Yang, K., Deng, J.: Stacked hourglass networks for human pose estimation. In: Leibe, B., Matas, J., Sebe, N., Welling, M. (eds.) ECCV 2016. LNCS, vol. 9912, pp. 483–499. Springer, Cham (2016). https://doi.org/10.1007/978-3-319-46484-8_29
15. Arbelle, A., Raviv, T.R.: Microscopy cell segmentation via convolutional LSTM networks. arXiv preprint arXiv:1805.11247 (2018)
16. Xingjian, S.H.I., Chen, Z., Wang, H., et al.: Convolutional LSTM network: a machine learning approach for precipitation nowcasting. In: Advances in Neural Information Processing Systems, pp. 802–810 (2015)
17. Sadeghian, A., Alahi, A., Savarese, S.: Tracking the untrackable: learning to track multiple cues with long-term dependencies. In: Proceedings of the IEEE International Conference on Computer Vision (ICCV), pp. 300–311 (2017)
18. Khudeev, R.: A new flood-fill algorithm for closed contour. In: 2005 Siberian Conference on Control and Communications, pp. 172–176. IEEE (2005)
19. Bochinski, E., Senst, T., Sikora, T.: Extending IOU based multi-object tracking by visual information. In: 2018 15th IEEE International Conference on Advanced Video and Signal Based Surveillance (AVSS), pp. 1–6. IEEE (2018)
20. Okabe, A., Boots, B., Sugihara, K., et al.: Spatial Tessellations: Concepts and Applications of Voronoi Diagrams. Wiley, Hoboken (2009)
21. Kingma, D.P., Ba, J.: Adam: a method for stochastic optimization. arXiv preprint arXiv:1412.6980 (2014)
22. Falk, T., Mai, D., Bensch, R., et al.: U-Net: deep learning for cell counting, detection, and morphometry. Nat. Methods **16**(1), 67 (2019)

Noninvasive Epicardial and Endocardial Extracellular Potentials Imaging with Low-Rank and Non-local Total Variation Regularization

Lide Mu and Huafeng Liu[(⊠)]

State Key Laboratory of Modern Optical Instrumentation, Department of Optical Engineering, Zhejiang University, Hangzhou 310027, China
Lidemu@foxmail.com, liuhf@zju.edu.cn

Abstract. Epicardial and endocardial extracellular potentials imaging has significant implications for diagnosing cardiac diseases. In this paper, we propose a novel noninvasive epicardial and endocardial potentials (EEP) reconstruction method based on low rank and non-local total variation regularization (LRNLTV). The low rank constraint retains the spatiotemporal correlation of EEP and the nonlocal TV constraint make use of the non-local similarity. The constrained optimization problem is solved by augmented Lagrangian multiplier (ALM) method. The simulated PVC data, intervention premature data and clinical PVC data while both EEP map and activation map together with the correlation coefficient (CC), structural similarity (SSIM) and locating error are used to evaluate the proposed method. We also compare LRNLTV method with TV method (L1-norm based) and low rank method, and the proposed framework achieves better results both in reconstruction accuracy and the boundary.

Keywords: Inverse problem of electrocardiography · Low rank · Nonlocal TV · Sparsity

1 Introduction

Reconstructing epicardial and endocardial extracellular potentials from the records of the cardiac electric events by body surface ECG has significant values for better understanding and diagnosis of cardiac disease. However, even with many efforts from noninvasive electrophysiological imaging community, it remains one of open key issues comparing with locating the arrhythmia site accurately by place the catheter on the surface of the heart [1], while is invasive and poses a certain threat to human health.

Improving the reconstruction quality of epicardial and endocardial potentials (EEP) imaging is essential, especially in applications like location of ventricular tachycardia (VT) [2] and premature ventricular contraction (PVC). With the wide adoption of regularizations to achieve unique solution, various approaches have been proposed, including the use of L2-norm based method, L1-norm based method and the use of method based on the rank of the matrix and L0-norm.

Y. Zhao et al. (Eds.): ICIG 2019, LNCS 11902, pp. 447–458, 2019.
https://doi.org/10.1007/978-3-030-34110-7_37

Generalized minimum residuals (GMRes) which is a L2-based method has been employed in [3] to reconstruct the epicardial potential during activation and repolarization of ventricular pacing. However, the shortcoming of L2-norm that the reconstruction results are too smooth and the accuracy is low have been pointed out in [4], and the total variation regularization (L1-based method) was proposed to improve the reconstruction accuracy. However, TV method only take use of the local similarity of the heart surface potential and compute frame by frame, the computing time is too long, the spatiotemporal correlation get lost as well, and a low rank and sparse decomposition method based on sparsity theory was presented in [5], the spatiotemporal correlation is aggregated in the method to improve the reconstruction accuracy, but the noise in ECG still have a great impact on the result.

In this study, we introduce a novel low rank and non-local total variation regularization (LRNLTV) method to solve the ill-posed inverse problem of EEP imaging. Base on the sparsity of EEP, it can be decomposed into two parts: the low rank background part and the sparse time-variant part, and the non-local total variation regularization is applied to the low rank background part to retain the boundary information. The innovations of the method is as follows: (1) spatiotemporal correlation of the EEP can be extract by low rank and sparse decomposition to get the dynamic potential of each node on heart surface; (2) non-local TV constraint take advantage of the nonlocal similarity to obtain better performance on the boundary.

2 Methodology

In this section, a low rank with non-local total variation (LRNLTV) framework is present for solving the inverse problem of EEP imaging. At first, we use the boundary element model (BEM) to obtain the relationship between the EEP and body surface potential (BSP) in the forward model of EEP imaging problem [6]. Then, we introduce the LRNLTV framework to reconstruct the EEP from BSP. At last, the optimization problem is solved by the augmented lagrangian multiplier method, singular value thresholding [7] (SVT) and the gradient descent algorithm.

2.1 BEM-Based Dynamic Electrocardiography Model

In this part, we introduce the dynamic forward model for the relationship between BSP and EEP. Different from the traditional standard "capped" full heart epicardial model, our heart surface model is a union of the endocardium and epicardium, where the heart surface denotes both the endocardium and epicardium surface. According to the previous work, we assume that the potential of cardiac electrical source distributed on a closed surface, and the potential distribution can be considered as an equivalent source. Thus, the relationship between cardiac electrical source and body surface can be expressed by,

$$\sigma_e \nabla^2 \phi_e(r) = \nabla \cdot (-D_i(r) \nabla \varphi(r)) \quad r \ in \ \Omega_h \tag{1}$$

In which, σ_e denotes the body conductivity in cardiothoracic cavity, $\phi_e(r)$ represent the value of extracellular potential at spatial coordinate r, D_i is the intracellular conductivity tensor of myocardial cells, $\varphi(r)$ is transmembrane potential of cardiac myocytes and Ω_h denotes the interior space of myocardial tissue. In order to simplify the forward model, we suppose that there is no other power electrical source in the volume between the heart surface and the body surface and it is an isotropic homogeneous medium, then the cardiac electric field can be represented as a Laplace equation, unify the boundary condition, it can be solved by BEM as,

$$\phi = Hu \tag{2}$$

where $\phi \in R^{J \times 1}$ denotes the potentials measured on the body surface with J-lead electrodes at a particular moment, $u \in R^{I \times 1}$ is the EEP to be reconstructed and $H \in R^{I \times J}$ is a time invariant transfer matrix for specific patients which can be get from the heart-torso model built with the thoracic CT scan or MRI scan data.

However, electrocardiogram signal is a time sequence signal include temporal and spatial information, and the above ϕ is only one frame of the ECG data with spatial information, the single frame forward model can be extended to a multi-frame one,

$$\Phi = HU \tag{3}$$

$$U \in R^{I \times C}, \ \phi \in R^{J \times C}$$

where $\Phi = \begin{bmatrix} \phi_1 \ \phi_2 \ \dots \ \phi_c \end{bmatrix}$, ϕ_c is the c-th frame of body surface and $U = \begin{bmatrix} u_1 \ u_2 \ \dots \ u_c \end{bmatrix}$, U_c is the c-th frame of EEP.

2.2 Low Rank and Sparse Decomposition

The epicardial and endocardial potential is inherent sparse. Therefore, EEP can be decomposed into two parts [8], while the first one is the background part that almost never change with time. And the second part is the time-variant part that changes rapidly over time. The background part represents the highly relevant information between frames and the time-variant part refers to the potential or activation propagation. Thus, we apply the low rank and sparse decomposition approach to reconstruct the EEP, and the EEP matrix can be written as,

$$U = L + S \tag{4}$$

where L is the background part and S is the time-variant part. When measuring the body surface potential information, noise will inevitably be introduced while small noise might cause large error in U. However, if the rank of background part L is as small as possible and the time-variant part is as sparse as possible, the effect of the noise will be effectively eliminated, and the inverse problem becomes a constrained minimization problem,

$$\min rank(L) + \lambda \|S\|_0 + \mu \|\Phi - HU\|_F \quad s.t. \ U = L + S \tag{5}$$

In which $rank(L)$ is the rank of L, $\|S_0\|$ indicates the number of nonzero elements in S, μ is the weight parameter of the fidelity item, and $\|\Phi - HU\|_F$ is Frobenius norm of the matrix, which is defined quadratic sum of the elements in the matrix. However, the minimization problem in Eq. (5) is a nonconvex problem, we need to relax the above equation to a convex form as nuclear norm is a convex approximation of rank and L1 norm is a convex relaxation of L0 norm [9], and the objective function can be expressed by,

$$\min_{L,S} \|L\|_* + \lambda \|S\|_1 + \mu \|\Phi - HU\|_F \quad s.t. \, U = L + S \tag{6}$$

where $\|L\|_*$ denotes the nuclear norm of L, which is the sum of singular values of L, and $\|S\|_1$ represents the L1 norm of S, which is defined as the sum of all the element in matrix S. The background part L and the time-variant part S can be obtained by solving the Eq. (6), and then we can get the solution U which we are interested. The detailed solving process will be introduced in Sect. 2.4.

2.3 Nonlocal TV Constraint

Although the presented low rank and sparse decomposition can eliminate the influence of noise to a certain extent, the remaining noise in the background part L will cause the unsmooth solution, therefore, non-local total variation constraint is adopted to background part L to ensure the non-local smoothness of the solution and better details. According to the work in [10], we define the nonlocal gradient as,

$$\nabla_{NLTV} L(a, b) = (L(b) - L(a))\sqrt{w(a, b)} \tag{7}$$

where $L(a)$ and $L(b)$ denotes the value of position a and b in the background matrix L, and $w(a, b)$ indicates the weights between voxel a and voxel b that is non-negative and symmetric. $w(a, b)$ can be formulated as,

$$w(a, b) = \exp\left(-\frac{\sum_{k=-i}^{i} G(k) \cdot |L(a + i) - L(b + i)|^2}{2h^2}\right) \tag{8}$$

where $G(k)$ is Gaussian kernel with patch size $((2i + 1) \times (2i + 1))$ and h denotes the filtering parameter. Then, the NLTV constraint term for background matrix L can be given as,

$$J(L) = \|\nabla_{NLTV} L\|_1 = \sum_a \sqrt{\sum_{b \in \Omega} (L(b) - L(a))^2 w(a, b)} \tag{9}$$

Thus, the low rank and non-local TV framework for the EEP imaging problem is present below,

$$\min_{L,S,U} \|L\|_* + \lambda \|S\|_1 + \mu \|\Phi - HU\|_F + \alpha J(E) \quad s.t. \, U = L + S, L = E \tag{10}$$

2.4 Optimization Method

We apply the Augmented Lagrange Multiplier method (ALM) [11] to the above optimization problems so that the problem becomes an unconstrained problem, and the augmented Lagrange function is present below,

$$\mathcal{L}(L, S, U, E) = \|L\|_* + \lambda \|S\|_1 - \langle Z, U - (L + S) \rangle + \frac{\beta}{2} \|U - (L + S)\|_F^2 +$$

$$\frac{\mu}{2}\|HU - \Phi\|_F^2 + \alpha J(E) + \langle Z_L, L - E \rangle + \frac{\beta_L}{2}\|L - E\|_F \quad (11)$$

where β and β_L are penalty parameters, Z and Z_L denotes the Lagrange multipliers. However, it is difficult to solve the above function directly, thus we divide it into three sub-problems and solve the sub problems separately.

L, S Subproblem

Separate all the terms with L, we can formulate the L subproblem as,

$$\min_L \|L\|_* + \frac{\beta + \beta_L}{2}\left\|L - \frac{\beta\left(U - S - \frac{Z}{\beta}\right) + \frac{\beta_L}{2}\left(E + \frac{Z_L}{\beta_L}\right)}{\beta + \beta_L}\right\|_F^2 \quad (12)$$

The problem in (12) can be solved by singular value thresholding (SVT) as,

$$L = F_{\frac{1}{\beta + \beta_L}}(X) \quad s.t. \ X = \frac{\beta\left(U - S - \frac{Z}{\beta}\right) + \frac{\beta_L}{2}\left(E + \frac{Z_L}{\beta_L}\right)}{\beta + \beta_L} \quad (13)$$

where $F_\varepsilon(X) = US_\varepsilon(s)V^T$, and UsV^T is the singular value decomposition of X. The S subproblem can be solved in the same way,

$$S = S_{\frac{\lambda}{\beta}}(Y_S) \quad s.t. \ Y_S = U - L + \frac{\beta}{Z} \quad (14)$$

U Subproblem

Combine the terms related to U from the augmented Lagrange function, we have the U subproblem,

$$\min_U \frac{\beta}{2}\left\|U - \left(L + S + \frac{Z}{\beta}\right)\right\|_F^2 + \frac{\mu}{2}\|HU - \Phi\|_F^2 \quad (15)$$

Equation (15) can be solved directly as it is a convex problem,

$$U = \left(\mu H^T H + \beta\right)\left[\beta\left(L + S + \frac{Z}{\beta}\right) + \mu H^T \Phi\right] \quad (16)$$

E Subproblem

Similarly, combine all the E-related term, we can formulate the E subproblem,

$$\min_E \alpha J(E) + \frac{\beta_L}{2}\left\|E - \left(L - \frac{Z_L}{\beta_L}\right)\right\|_F^2 \quad (17)$$

The above problem can be solved by gradient descent algorithm as shown below,

$$E = E - dx\left(\alpha \xi_{NLTV}(E) + \beta_L\left(E - L + \frac{Z_L}{\beta_L}\right)\right). \quad (18)$$

where ξ_{NLTV} denotes the Euler-Lagrange of $J(E)$ as shown in Eq. (19), dx is the step length in the gradient descent algorithm,

$$\xi_{NLTV}(E) = \sum_{a,b \in \Omega} (E(a) - E(b))w(a,b)\left[\frac{1}{|\nabla_{NLTV}E(a)|} + \frac{1}{|\nabla_{NLTV}E(b)|}\right] \tag{19}$$

The Lagrange multipliers are updated by,

$$Z^{k+1} = Z^k - \beta(U - S - L) \tag{20}$$

$$Z_L^{k+1} = Z_L^k - \beta(L - E) \tag{21}$$

3 Experiments

Our experiment consists of three parts based on three types of the datasets. Firstly, we apply the proposed algorithm to the simulated ventricular pacing dataset provided by Karlsruhe Institute of Technology (KIT), the simulation dataset include pacing at eight different pacing positions on the left ventricle (LV) and the right ventricle (RV). After that, the LRNLTV algorithm is used to reconstruct the real intervention pace data including two healthy hearts paced with a catheter device which have 21 cases of 551 different heartbeats shared in the online database EDGAR. Finally, we tried the LRNLTV algorithm on 5 real patients with PVC, and the data was collected by the ethical committee of Zhejiang Provincial Hospital. In the three experiment, we compare the reconstruction result of EEP map and activation sequence map by low rank algorithm, TV algorithm and LRNLTV algorithm.

3.1 Simulation Experiments

As we can locate the disease from the potential distribution on EEP map and the activation time distribution on activation map, and accurately determining the location of heart disease is very important for subsequent treatment, we reconstruct the EEP map and activation map in this experiment. The EEP ground truth and transfer matrix is given in the simulated dataset and we compute the EEP by $\Phi = HU$. However, the measured body surface potentials are accompanied by a certain degree of noise in real situation, we add 30 dB Gaussian white noise M to the BSP as $\Phi = HU + M$.

3.1.1 Spatial EEP Reconstruction

In order to compare the reconstruction performance of the three methods (LR, TV and LRNLTV), we use these three methods to reconstruct EEP maps respectively. Take a pacing site at left ventricle apex as an example, we reconstructed the spatial EEP distribution at four moments (20 ms, 60 ms, 100 ms, 160 ms) as shown in Fig. 1, all three methods reconstructed the pacing point at the apex of left ventricle and spreading to the remote area of the lateral left ventricle. However, for the boundary region of low potential and high potential, the reconstruction result of TV for edge information is poor, while LR algorithm have a better result but the boundary is not particularly clear yet. It is worth mentioning that the proposed LRNLTV algorithm have the best performance that we can clearly see the boundary in the reconstructed EEP map at four moment.

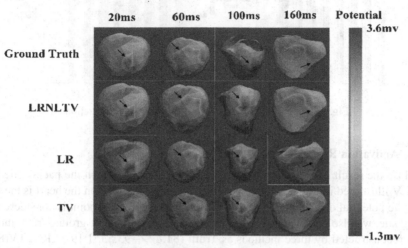

Fig. 1. The reconstruction of EEP at four moments (20 ms, 60 ms, 100 ms, 160 ms) using LRNLTV, LR and TV, the pacing site is at apex LV.

Correlation coefficient (CC) [12] and structural similarity (SSIM) is used to analyze the results quantitatively, while CC and SSIM is defined as,

$$CC_i = \frac{Cov(u_{ri}, u_{ti})}{\sqrt{D(u_{ri})}\sqrt{D(u_{ti})}} \tag{22}$$

$$SSIM_i(x, y) = \frac{(2v_x v_y + c_1)(2Cov(x, y) + c_2)}{\left(v_x^2 + v_y^2 + c_1\right)\left(D(x)^2 + D(y)^2 + c_2\right)} \tag{23}$$

where u_{ri} and u_{ti} are the i-th frame of the truth and the reconstructed result, $Cov(u_{ri}, u_{ti})$ is the covariance, $D(\ldots\ldots)$ denotes the variance, v_x and v_y represent the mean value which are constant avoiding denominator be 0. Error histogram of 8 pacing sites is shown in Fig. 2, the proposed LRNLTV algorithm has the highest CC and SSIM which represent the best reconstruction performance in three methods.

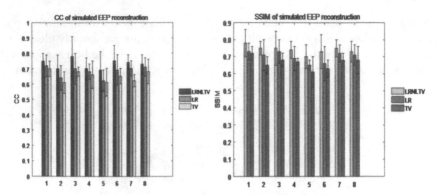

Fig. 2. The CC and SSIM of simulated EEP reconstruction

3.1.2 Activation Reconstruction

Based on the result of EEP map, we get the activation map which the pacing site is at apex LV illustrated in Fig. 3, while the activation time of a node on the heart is the time when the potential drop at maximum. And the earliest activated point is considered the pacing site, we also calculate the coordinate of the pacing site of ground truth and the result reconstructed by three methods as Truth (81.82, −93.53, 1.19), LRNLTV(81.5, −94.6, 0.19), LR(81, −92.1, 0.09), TV(80.13, −92.13, 0.28), and the locating error of the methods are 1.5 mm, 1.98 mm and 2.37 mm.

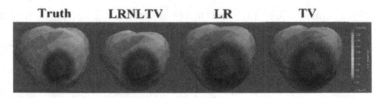

Fig. 3. The ground truth and the reconstruction of activation using LRNLTV, LR and TV, the earliest activated point is at apex LV.

As illustrated in Fig. 3, all three methods suggest that the earliest activated point at apex LV, but LR and TV are less effective in reconstructing details and boundary information, and Table 1 also indicates that the proposed LRNLTV have the highest CC, SSIM and the lowest locating error at different pacing sites.

3.2 Real Experiments

3.2.1 Interventional Premature Data

In this part of the experiment, we reconstruct the activation map of interventional premature data which include BSP measured by 120 electrodes sampled at 2 kHz, transfer matrix and the gold standard Carto System measured pacing site coordination (x, y, z) of 21 cases of 551 heartbeats. We apply the aforementioned 3 methods to the reconstruction

Table 1. CC, SSIM and locating error between reconstructed activation results and ground truth

Pacing sites	LRNLTV			LR			TV		
	CC	SSIM	Err	CC	SSIM	Err	CC	SSIM	Err
Septum center	0.76	0.75	6.75	0.62	0.63	25.68	0.61	0.62	29.32
LV lateral	0.76	0.75	8.63	0.73	0.74	10.76	0.68	0.70	12.31
LV apex	0.85	0.82	1.50	0.80	70.79	1.98	0.78	0.79	2.37
LV anterior	0.76	0.76	5.53	0.69	0.67	15.73	0.60	0.61	29.14
RV posterior	0.73	0.74	10.37	0.68	0.69	15.12	0.63	0.61	25.17
RV anterior	0.75	0.76	8.75	0.73	0.75	10.30	0.65	0.67	17.65
LV lateralepi	0.85	0.81	1.60	0.79	0.77	4.97	0.77	0.76	5.85
LV lateralendo	0.83	0.80	2.10	0.78	0.77	4.96	0.76	0.74	8.71

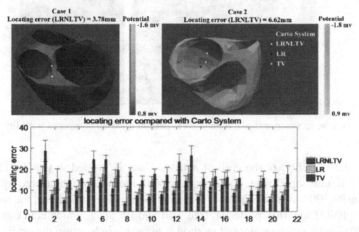

Fig. 4. Location error of LRNLTV, LR, TV compared with Carto System. (Color figure online)

process, two cases of reconstructed EEP map and 14 locating errors of LV and 7 locating errors of RV are displayed in Fig. 4.

As illustrated in Fig. 4, the position of red point is the ground truth record by Carto System, the white point is the pacing site reconstructed by LRNLTV method, the black point is the location result of LR method and the yellow point is the result of TV method. In the two examples shown in Fig. 4, all the three method indicates that the pacing site at RVOT anterior in case 1 and the LV apex in case 2 while the LRNLTV method has the smallest locating error of 3.78 mm and 6.62 mm. Besides, the error histogram also points out that the proposed LRNLTV method have the highest locating accuracy while the mean value of the locating error is 8.6 mm Owning to the nonlocal similarity in the whole map, details are retained, as TV and LR have larger locating errors.

3.2.2 Clinical PVC Data

To verify the feasibility of the proposed LRNLTV algorithm for clinical data, we apply the algorithm to data of 5 real patients with PVC which consist of the thoracic CT scan whose axial spatial resolution is 0.6–1 mm and the 64-lead ECG signal with a sample frequency of 2 kHz, while CT scan also recorded the location of 64-lead electrodes. Before reconstruction, the relationship between torso and heart is needed, the heart model can be obtained by the segmentation of CT slices, and we can also get the coordinates of the 64-lead ECG electrodes from CT scan to build the torso model. By matching the torso model and the heart model, we can get the transfer matrix.

Figure 5 shows the activation map reconstruction of a male PVC patient aged 33. ECG of 3000 ms to 4000 ms is used to the reconstruction. Because the ECG signal contains a lot of noise, the signal is preprocessed by wavelet transform before reconstruction.

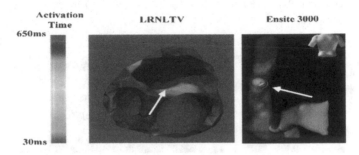

Fig. 5. Activation reconstruction of a male PVC patient aged 33 compared with Ensite 3000

As illustrated in Fig. 6, the earliest activated site is located at the RVOT septum near the ventricular septal side, it is consistent with the position measured by the gold standard Ensite 3000 System which is invasive. For the other 4 patients, the pacing site is located at RVOT anterior, posterior, free wall and LV apex, which is in concert with Ensite 3000 results and the proposed method is effective in locating the origin of PVC.

4   Discussion

We have presented a novel low rank and non-local TV method for EEP reconstruction. By taking advantage of the spatiotemporal information and the nonlocal similarity of EEP, LRNLTV perform better both in locating accuracy and the boundary compared with the LR and TV method, while the background part of LR method have noise inevitably, and the TV method only uses the local similarity of EEP, the temporal correlation between frames get lost. ALM is applied to solve the optimization problem, many parameters are introduced due to the number of constraints, the parameter adjustment is quite important for results, and the computing time is also significant for application of the proposed method.

4.1 Parameter Adjustment

In this paper, the main parameters are λ, μ, α, β, β_L. λ is the weight coefficient fixed at $1/\sqrt{\max(I, J)}$ where (I, J) is the size of solution [13]. μ, β, β_L are the weight coefficient of fidelity term, Fig. 7 shows the locating error and mean value of SSIM change for a case of LV lateral-epi pace, and μ is fixed at [0.03, 0.1], β, β_L is in the range of [0.0002, 0.03], and α is the weight coefficient of NLTV constraint fixed at 5.

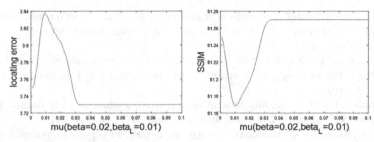

Fig. 6. Locating error and SSIM of different μ and $\beta = 0.02$, $\beta_L = 0.01$

4.2 Program Running Time

All the process of optimization and solution is computed by MATLAB 2018a of windows version with 32 GB RAM and a 10 core 3.3 GHz processor. As shown in Table 2, we record the computing time of 3 different datasets, LR method have the lowest computing time. In particular, LRNLTV method have the highest reconstruction accuracy, while the time cost is acceptable compared with the other two methods.

Table 2. The computing time of three different datasets with LRNLTV, LR and TV method

Frames	LRNLTV	LR	TV
230	175 s	120 s	273 s
323	241 s	165 s	363 s
1000	621 s	350 s	935 s

5 Conclusion

In this paper, we have presented an innovative LRNLTV method for reconstructing EEP from BSP while both spatiotemporal correlation and nonlocal similarity of EEP are considered. The proposed method can improve the reconstruction accuracy with moderate computing time compared with LR and TV method when applied to simulated and real data, and the reconstruction of clinic data proves the effectiveness of the method.

Acknowledgement. This work is supported in part by Shenzhen Innovation Funding (No: JCYJ20170818164343304, JCYJ20170816172431715), by the National Natural Science Foundation of China (No: 61525106, 61427807, U1809204, 61701436), and by the National Key Technology Research and Development Program of China (No: 2017YFE0104000, 2016YFC1300302).

References

1. Paul, T.: Atrial reentrant tachycardia after surgery for congenital heart disease: endocardial mapping and radiofrequency catheter ablation using a novel, noncontact mapping system. Circulation **103** (2001)
2. Wang, L., Gharbia, O.A., Nazarian, S., et al.: Non-invasive epicardial and endocardial electrocardiographic imaging for scar-related ventricular tachycardia. J. Electrocardiol. **49**(6), 887–893 (2016)
3. Ramanathan, C.: Electrocardiographic imaging (ECGI): application of an iterative method and validation in humans. Sanno Coll. Jiyugaoka Bull. **31**(1), 1–17 (2004)
4. Ghosh, S., Rudy, Y.: Application of L1-norm regularization to epicardial potential solution of the inverse electrocardiography problem. Ann. Biomed. Eng. **37**(5), 902–912 (2009)
5. Fang, L., Xu, J., Hu, H., et al.: Noninvasive imaging of epicardial and endocardial potentials with low rank and sparsity constraints. IEEE Trans. Biomed. Eng. (2019)
6. Erem, B., Coll-Font, J., Martinez Orellana, R., et al.: Using transmural regularization and dynamic modeling for noninvasive cardiac potential imaging of endocardial pacing with imprecise thoracic geometry. IEEE Trans. Med. Imaging **33**(3), 726–738 (2014)
7. Cai, J.F., Candès, E.J., Shen, Z.: A singular value thresholding algorithm for matrix completion. SIAM J. Optim. **20**(4), 1956–1982 (2010)
8. Otazo, R., Candès, E., Sodickson, D.K.: Low-rank plus sparse matrix decomposition for accelerated dynamic MRI with separation of background and dynamic components. Magn. Reson. Med. **73**(3), 1125–1136 (2015)
9. Yang, J., Yuan, X.: Linearized augmented lagrangian and alternating direction methods for nuclear norm minimization. Math. Comput. **82**(281), 301–329 (2013)
10. Lou, Y., Zhang, X., Osher, S., et al.: Image recovery via nonlocal operators. J. Sci. Comput. **42**(2), 185–197 (2010)
11. Lin, Z., Chen, M., Wu, L., et al.: The augmented lagrange multiplier method for exact recovery of corrupted low-rank matrices. Eprint Arxiv, September 2010
12. Fang, L., Zhuang, Q., Mao, W., Chen, Y., Liu, H.: TV regularized low-rank framework for localizing premature ventricular contraction origin. IEEE Access **7**, 27802–27813 (2019)
13. Candes, E.J., Li, X., Ma, Y., Wright, J.: Robust principal component analysis? J. ACM (JACM) **58**(3), 11 (2011)

ISDNet: Importance Guided Semi-supervised Adversarial Learning for Medical Image Segmentation

Qingtian Ning[1], Xu Zhao[1(✉)], and Dahong Qian[2]

[1] Department of Automation, Shanghai Jiao Tong University, Shanghai, China
zhaoxu@sjtu.edu.cn
[2] Institute of Medical Robotics, Shanghai Jiao Tong University, Shanghai, China

Abstract. Recent deep neural networks have achieved great success in medical image segmentation. However, massive labeled training data should be provided during network training, which is time consuming with intensive labor work and even requires expertise knowledge. To address such challenge, inspired by typical GANs, we propose a novel end-to-end semi-supervised adversarial learning framework for medical image segmentation, called "Importance guided Semi-supervised Deep Networks" (ISDNet). While most existing works based on GANs use a classifier discriminator to achieve adversarial learning, we combine a fully convolutional discriminator and a classifier discriminator to fulfill better adversarial learning and self-taught learning. Specifically, we propose an importance weight network combined with our FCN-based confidence network, which can assist segmentation network to learn better local and global information. Extensive experiments are conducted on the LASC 2013 and the LiTS 2017 datasets to demonstrate the effectiveness of our approach.

Keywords: Medical image segmentation · Semi-supervised · GAN

1 Introduction

Medical image segmentation is a fundamental yet challenging problem in medical image analysis, which aims to segment organs or pathological area (e.g. left atrium or liver lesion) in medical images. Recently, a typical Fully Convolutional Network (FCN) [20] based methods of encoder-decoder structure have achieved considerable success in semantic image segmentation, such as U-Net [21] and deeplabv3+ [5]. Although CNN-based approaches have made great progress, they often require massive labeled training data. Medical image tasks are usually more difficult than natural image tasks because of little training data and high cost manual annotations, etc. In addition, most medical datasets are still constrained in limited size and application scenarios. Hence, it is a complex and expensive procedure to obtain large-scale medical labeled data.

© Springer Nature Switzerland AG 2019
Y. Zhao et al. (Eds.): ICIG 2019, LNCS 11902, pp. 459–470, 2019.
https://doi.org/10.1007/978-3-030-34110-7_38

In order to ease the effort of acquiring high-quality data, unsupervised learning is an alternative way to utilize massive unlabeled data. However, due to lacking the concept of classes, unsupervised learning methods have not attained convincing performance in segmentation. So semi/weakly-supervised methods have drawn much attention from many researchers in the community. These methods generally demand additional annotations or data, such as the image-level class label [18], box level [16,17], point level [19], or scribble level [1].

Recently, Generative Adversarial Networks (GANs) [22] have achieved a wide range of success due to their ability to generate high-quality realistic images [2,6,11,12]. It attracts extensive attention with successful applications in super-resolution [14], domain adaptation [8,15], zero-shot learning [13], etc. A classic GAN consists of two sub-networks (i.e., generator and discriminator) that play a min-max game in the training procedure where generator produces a sample of the target data distribution, while discriminator aims to differentiate between real and fake data repeatedly. The generator is then optimized to generate more realistic samples that are more close to target data distribution. Recently, several works have applied the GANs framework in semantic segmentation. Luc *et al.* [23] propose to apply a classifier discriminator to assist the training process for semantic segmentation in a fully-supervised way. But this method has not achieved distinguished results over the baseline scheme and fails to tackle unlabeled data for semi-supervised setting. Frid-Adar *et al.* [9] employ GANs to generate synthetic medical images to train segmentation network. Nie *et al.* [7] use sample attention mechanism to improve the network training. However, those jobs utilize the classification networks as their discriminators in fully-supervised ways, so those discriminators only can capture the global information of generated masks and ground truth masks without considering the local details, which is more important for the task of semantic segmentation.

In this paper, we propose a semi-supervised semantic segmentation algorithm (called ISDNet) based on GANs in order to alleviate the demand for large-scale medical labeled data. Inspired by [10] and [8], our network consists of three sub-networks: (1) segmentation network, (2) confidence network and (3) importance weight network. In this work, two semi-supervised loss are conducted to leverage the unlabeled data. First, Our FCN-based confidence network can generate confidence maps, which can guide our segmentation network in a self training strategy. The confidence maps provide us the trustworthy regions in the segmented label map, which can be selected to generate proxy label for unlabeled data. Second, we apply the adversarial loss on unlabeled data in the supervised setting, which encourages the model to predict segmentation outputs of unlabeled data close to the ground truth distributions. Then, our importance weight network can identify the importance score of unlabeled samples, which represents the probability of the sample come from the labeled data distribution. Finally, we integrate the importance score into semi-supervised loss and obtain our two weighted semi-supervised loss.

In sum, our main contributions include: (i) we develop an adversarial framework, which improves semantic segmentation performance without adding any

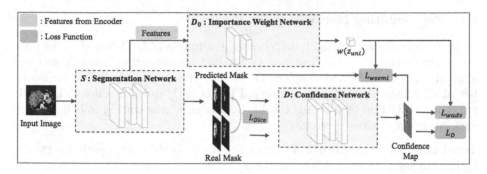

Fig. 1. Illustration of the architecture of our proposed ISDNet, which consists of a segmentation network, a confidence network and an importance weight network.

computational cost during inference; (ii) we propose a semi-supervised framework to improve the segmentation accuracy with unlabeled data; (iii) we combine a fully convolutional discriminator and a classifier discriminator to facilitate the semi-supervised learning, which can better use unlabeled data. To demonstrate the effectiveness of our proposed approach, ablation studies are conducted on the LASC 2013 dataset. Overall, our proposed approach brings 1.8% improvement on the LASC 2013 dataset and 11.4% improvement on the LiTS 2017 dataset.

2 Our Approach

The proposed ISDNet consists of three subnetworks, i.c., (1) segmentation network (denoted as S), (2) confidence network (denoted as D) and (3) importance weight network (denoted as D_0). The architecture of our proposed framework is presented in Fig. 1.

In order to facilitate elaboration, we first give the definitions of terminologies used throughout the paper. Given an input medical image X_n of dimension $H \times W \times 1$ and its one-hot encoded ground truth label Y_n, we denote the segmentation network as $S(\cdot)$, the features as $Z(X_n)$ extracted from the encoder of our segmentation network and the predicted probability map as $\hat{Y}_n = S(X_n)$ of size $H \times W \times C$, where C is the category number. We denote our fully convolutional discriminator as $D(\cdot)$ which takes class probability maps as the input (the output from segmentation network $S(X_n)$ or ground truth label maps Y_n) and then outputs a confidence map of size $H \times W \times 1$. Confidence map generated by D scores each pixel p, which represents whether that pixel is sampled from the ground truth label ($p = 1$) or the segmentation network ($p = 0$). The importance weight network denoted as $D_0(\cdot)$, takes $Z(X_n)$ (the features of labeled sample or unlabeled sample) as the input and outputs an importance weight. The importance weight represents whether that sample is sampled from the labeled data ($X_n = 1$) or the unlabeled data ($X_n = 0$).

2.1 Segmentation Network

In ISDNet as shown in Fig. 1, we employ a simplified 2D U-Net (SU-Net) as our segmentation network, but any end-to-end segmentation network can be applied, such as FCN and deeplabv3+, etc. In this paper, we halve the number of all convolutional layers in original U-Net [21], and use leaky ReLU and group normalization [3] instead of ReLU and batch normalization to balance the performance and memory cost.

Total Loss for Segmentation Network. We train the segmentation network by minimizing a multi-task loss function

$$L_{seg} = L_{Dice} + \lambda_{adv} L_{wadv} + \lambda_{semi} L_{wsemi}, \tag{1}$$

where L_{Dice}, L_{wadv} and L_{wsemi} denote the multi-class dice loss, adversarial loss and semi-supervised loss, respectively. In (1), λ_{adv} and λ_{semi} are two weights for minimizing the proposed multi-task loss function.

Multi-class Dice Loss. To overcome the class imbalance problem, we propose to use a weighted multi-class dice loss as the segmentation loss

$$L_{Dice} = 1 - 2 \sum_{c=1}^{C} \frac{w^c \hat{Y}_n^c Y_n^c}{w^c (\hat{Y}_n^c + Y_n^c)}, \tag{2}$$

where $\hat{Y}_n^c$ denotes the predicted probability belonging to class c (i.e. background, liver, or liver lesion), Y_n^c denotes the ground truth probability, and w^c denotes a class dependent weighting factor. Empirically, we set the weights to be 0.2 for background, 1.2 for liver, and 2.2 for liver lesion. But for left atrium (LA) segmentation, we use normal two-class dice loss.

2.2 Confidence Network

Different from using CNN-based discriminator, we propose to use a FCN-based discriminator called confidence network to generate more detailed adversarial information in local region. Hence, we combine adversarial learning in our work to further optimize the segmentation network.

Adversarial Loss of the Confidence Network. To train the confidence network, we minimize the binary cross-entropy loss L_D using

$$L_D = L_{bce}(D(Y_n)^{h,w}, 1) + L_{bce}(D(S(X_n))^{h,w}, 0), \tag{3}$$

where X_n and Y_n represent the input data and its corresponding ground truth label map (one-hot encoding scheme), respectively. In addition, $D(S(X_n))^{(h,w)}$ is the confidence map of X_n at location (h, w), and $D(Y_n)^{(h,w)}$ is defined similarly.

Adversarial Loss of the Segmentation Network. In the conventional GANs, generators and discriminators play a min-max game. Hence, there is another loss from D working as adversarial Loss to further improve segmentation network. It enforces higher-order consistency between ground truth label and predicted masks. We utilize the loss L_{adv} based on a fully convolutional discriminator network

$$L_{adv} = L_{bce}(D(S(X_n))^{h,w}, 1). \tag{4}$$

With this loss, we further improve the ability of segmentation network to fool the discriminator by maximizing the probability of the predicted results being more close to the ground truth distribution.

2.3 Importance Weight Network

Training with Unlabeled Data. In this work, we concern more about how to use unlabeled data to improve the performance of segmentation network. Since there is no corresponding ground truth label for unlabeled data, L_{Dice} no longer works. But the adversarial loss L_{adv} is still applicable as it only requires the discriminator network.

In addition, since our confidence network could provide local confidence information, we propose a self-taught learning framework with our trained discriminator D for unlabeled data. The main idea is that our confidence network can generate a confidence map $CM = D(S(X_n))^{h,w}$ to indicate us which regions of the predicted results are sufficiently close to the ground truth distribution. Then we process the confidence map with a threshold T_{semi} to obtain the confident regions. In this way, we can exploit these confident regions to filter the segmentation results of unlabeled data to improve the segmentation network. The semi-supervised loss is defined as

$$L_{semi} = 1 - 2 \sum_{c=1}^{C} \frac{w^c[CM > T_{semi}]\hat{Y}_n^c \bar{Y}_n^c}{w^c[CM > T_{semi}](\hat{Y}_n^c + \bar{Y}_n^c)}, \tag{5}$$

where $\bar{Y}_n$ is the one-hot encoding of $\arg\max(\hat{Y}_n)$. $[\cdot]$ is the indicator function.

Sample Weights Learning. Furthermore, we employ another discriminator named D_0. It can output the probability that an unlabeled sample belongs to labeled data distribution on the image level. Specifically, the importance weight network is similar to the original GANs with min-max loss

$$L_{adv} = L_{bce}(D_0(Z(X_l), 1) + L_{bce}(D_0(Z(X_{unl})), 0), \tag{6}$$

where $Z(\cdot)$ is the feature extractor (also is the encoder of our SU-Net) for labeled data X_l and unlabeled data X_{unl} respectively, and D_0 is a binary classifier with all the labeled data labeled as 1 and all the unlabeled data labeled as 0.

Assume that in the case of the optimal classifier D_0, the output value of D_0 is the probability that the sample comes from the labeled data distribution. If $D^*(z) \approx 1$, then the sample will highly likely originate from the labeled data distribution, since the features $Z(X_l)$ are quite different from the features $Z(X_{unl})$

and can be ideally separated from labeled data distribution by D_0. Then we should reduce the contribution of these samples because feature extractor has already been trained by some similar samples. On the other hand, if $D^*(z)$ is small, it means feature extractor has not been trained by those samples. A larger importance weight should be applied to these samples to improve segmentation network. Hence, the sample weights function should be inversely related to $D^*(z)$ and the importance weight function of the unlabeled samples is defined as

$$w(z) = 1 - D^*(z). \tag{7}$$

As can be seen that if $D^*(z)$ is small, $w(z)$ is large. Hence, the weights for unlabeled samples that are similar to the labeled data will be smaller than those are not similar to the labeled data. Our aim is to obtain the relative importance of unlabeled samples. The weight function can also be expressed as a function of density ratio between labeled and unlabeled features. If we apply the weights to D_0, then the Jensen-Shannon divergence between two densities can not be reduced from the theoretical results of the minimax game [8]. Hence, we utilize the weights to D to solve this issue. In this way, D_0 is only used for obtaining the importance weights for unlabeled samples. Thus, we will not update the encoder with the gradient of D_0. So we can integrate the importance weight into our semi-supervised loss.

$$L_{wsemi} = w(z)L_{semi}. \tag{8}$$

And adversarial loss for unlabeled data can be modified as

$$L_{wadv} = w(z)L_{adv}. \tag{9}$$

But for labeled data, $w(z)$ should be set to 1. By summing the above losses, the total loss to train the segmentation network can be defined as (1).

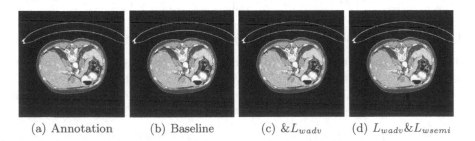

(a) Annotation   (b) Baseline   (c) $\&L_{wadv}$ (d) $L_{wadv}\&L_{wsemi}$

Fig. 2. Comparisons on the LiTS 2017 dataset using 1/2 labeled data. Green area and red area represent liver and lesion, respectively. It can be seen that our confidence network assists segmentation network discover parts of lesions while our baseline does not. Furthermore, our semi-supervised algorithm refines the segmentation results.

3   Experiments

Evaluation Datasets and Metrics. Experiments are conducted on two publicly available datasets to report the state-of-the-art performance of ISDNet. Ablation studies are conducted on LASC 2013 dataset [4]. We also conduct experiments on LiTS 2017 dataset to verify the validity of our method. For LASC 2013, we employ data augmentation and obtain $3\,K$ 2D images with size 320×320 in total. Dice index for left atrium (LA) and running time are selected to compare with other state-of-the-art method. For LiTS 2017, we use two metrics to evaluate the segmented liver lesions, including dice per case and global dice.

Implementation Details. All experiments are built with Pytorch framework on a single NVIDIA 1080ti GPU. We use the Adam optimizer for both our segmentation network and two discriminators with the learning rate 10^{-4}. For the hyper-parameters in the proposed method, λ_{adv} is set as 0.001 when trained with labeled and unlabeled data. We set λ_{semi} as 1 and T_{semi} as 0.1. For semi-supervised training, we randomly divide all dataset into labeled and unlabeled data. We initiate the semi-supervised learning after 5 epochs training with labeled data. In each epoch, we train both the segmentation network and two discriminator networks, only labeled data are used for training of the discriminator D while D_0 demands the part of unlabeled data.

Table 1. Results on the LASC test set. We utilize 1/2 images as labeled data, the rest as unlabeled data for semi-supervised learning. *Running time* indicates mean inference time on CPU.

Methods	Data amount		
	1/2	Full	Running time (sec)
LTSI_VRG [24]	N/A	91.0	3100
UCL_1C [25]	N/A	93.8	1200
UCL_4C [25]	N/A	85.9	1200
OBS_2 [4]	N/A	90.8	N/A
Hung et al. [10]	91.0	N/A	1.1
Luc et al. [23]	90.0	93.6	1.1
Liu et al. [26]	N/A	94.0	23.7
AF-CNN-SP [27]	N/A	**95.1**	450
U-Net [21]	87.4	90.8	1.4
Baseline (SU-Net)	89.5	93.2	1.1
Baseline+L_{wadv}	90.5	**94.0**	1.1
Baseline+L_{wadv}+L_{wsemi}	**91.3**	N/A	**1.1**

3.1   LASC 2013

Results and Analysis. Table 1 shows the evaluation results on the LASC 2013 test dataset. We randomly sample 1/2 images as labeled data, the rest as unlabeled data. We compare the proposed algorithm against LTSI-VRG [24], UCL-1C [25], UCL-4C [25], U-Net [21], [26] and [27] to demonstrate that our baseline model (SU-Net) performs comparably with the state-of-the-art schemes. LTSI-VRG, UCL-1C, UCL-4C are the top three methods in Dice index, which are all based on multi-atlas. OBS-2 [4] is the result from human observer. [26] combines CNN and recurrent neural network (RNN) to achieve a Dice index of 0.94, but it will greatly increase the inference time (22 times slower than our SU-Net). [27] is based on a multi-view CNN with an adaptive fusion strategy and a new loss function, which is 400 times slower than ours and use 20 times more data than us. Table 1 shows that the adversarial loss brings consistent performance improvement (from 0.8% to 1.0%) over different amounts of training data. Incorporating the proposed semi-supervised learning scheme brings overall 1.8% improvement. For [10] and [23], we use our SU-Net to replace its original segmentation network for equal comparisons. Specially, our importance weight network brings 0.3% improvement compared to [10]. It means our network makes better use of unlabeled data to improve network performance. Apart from this, our confidence network brings improvement (from 0.4% to 0.5%) compared to a typical classifier discriminator [23].

Table 2. Hyper parameter analysis.

Data amount	λ_{adv}	λ_{semi}	T_{semi}	Dice
1/2	0.0001	0	N/A	89.3
1/2	0.001	0	N/A	90.5
1/2	0.005	0	N/A	88.7
1/2	0.001	5	0.1	89.2
1/2	0.001	1	0.1	91.3
1/2	0.001	0.5	0.1	90.6
1/2	0.001	1	0	90.1
1/2	0.001	1	0.1	91.3
1/2	0.001	1	0.5	90.9
1/2	0.001	1	1	90.3

Hyper-parameter Analysis. The proposed algorithm is governed by three hyper parameters: λ_{adv} and λ_{semi} for balancing the multi-task learning in (1), and T_{semi} used to control the sensitivity in the semi-supervised learning described in (5). Table 2 shows sensitivity analysis of hyper parameters on the LASC 2013 dataset under semi-supervised setting. Different from [10], we find that smaller λ_{adv} must be used for medical image tasks, this is because the content of natural images is richer and requires larger loss to guide network learning.

Then, we conduct the experiments with different values of T_{semi}. With higher T_{semi}, our algorithm will select regions, which are more close to the ground truth distribution. When $T_{semi} = 0$, all the pixel predictions in unlabeled images will be applied for semi-supervised training, which leads to performance degradation. Overall, the proposed model achieves the best results when $T_{semi} = 0.1$.

Ablation Study. We present ablation study of our proposed system in Table 3 on LASC test dataset. Our confidence network gains 0.5% and 0.4% improvement compared to a classifier discriminator with half and full data, respectively. Then, we apply the semi-supervised learning method without the adversarial loss. The results show that the adversarial procedure on the labeled data is necessary to our semi-supervised scheme. If the segmentation network does not participate in adversarial training, the confidence maps generated by the discriminator would be pointless. As shown in Table 3, our semi-supervised methods in ISDNet help to improve segmentation performance.

Table 3. Ablation study of the proposed method on the LASC dataset. $\sqrt{}$ denotes the setting of corresponding column is employed. CN denotes confidence map.

L_{wadv}	L_{wsemi}	L_{adv}&L_{semi}	CN	Data amount	
				1/2	Full
				89.5	93.2
$\sqrt{}$			$\sqrt{}$	90.5	94.0
$\sqrt{}$				90.0	93.6
	$\sqrt{}$		$\sqrt{}$	89.1	N/A
$\sqrt{}$	$\sqrt{}$		$\sqrt{}$	91.3	N/A
		$\sqrt{}$	$\sqrt{}$	91.0	N/A

3.2 LiTS 2017

Results and Visualization. Furthermore, we extend the experiment on LiTS 2017 dataset. Figure 2 shows visual comparisons of the segmentation results on the LiTS 2017 validation dataset generated by our proposed method. It can be seen that no lesion is found in our baseline (Fig. 2(b)), but with the assistance of adversarial loss, segmentation network can detect parts of lesions (Fig. 2(c)). Further more, with our semi-supervised adversarial learning algorithm, segmentation network could segment a majority of lesions (Fig. 2(d)). Table 4 shows the liver lesion evaluation results on the LiTS 2017 test dataset with random sampled 1/2 images as labeled data. It can be seen that our methods have made the best dice per case of 50.6% with 10.5% gain and the best global dice of 72.5% with 11.4% gain.

Table 4. Results on the LiTS test set. *DPC* indicates dice per case. *GD* denotes global dice.

Methods	Data Amount	DPC	GD
Our baseline	Full	54.0	76.6
Baseline+L_{wadv}	Full	56.8	76.9
Our baseline	1/2	40.1	61.1
Baseline+L_{wadv}	1/2	45.9	64.0
Baseline+L_{wadv}+L_{wsemi}	1/2	50.6	72.5

4   Conclusion

In this work, we have presented a novel importance guided semi-supervised adversarial learning scheme (ISDNet) for medical image segmentation. Specifically, we train two discriminators to enhance the segmentation network with both labeled and unlabeled data to effectively address the insufficient labeled data problem. We combine FCN-based discriminator with CNN-based discriminator for our semi-supervised learning strategy. It can be seen that by integrating these components into our framework, the ISDNet has achieved significant improvement in terms of both accuracy and robustness.

Acknowledgement. This work is supported by: National Natural Science Foundation of China (61673269, 61273285).

References

1. Lin, D., Dai, J., Jia, J., et al.: ScribbleSup: scribble-supervised convolutional networks for semantic segmentation. In: Proceedings of the IEEE Conference on Computer Vision and Pattern Recognition, pp. 3159–3167 (2016)
2. Brock, A., Donahue, J., Simonyan, K.: Large scale GAN training for high fidelity natural image synthesis. arXiv preprint arXiv:1809.11096 (2018)
3. Wu, Y., He, K.: Group normalization. In: Ferrari, V., Hebert, M., Sminchisescu, C., Weiss, Y. (eds.) ECCV 2018. LNCS, vol. 11217, pp. 3–19. Springer, Cham (2018). https://doi.org/10.1007/978-3-030-01261-8_1
4. Tobon-Gomez, C., Geers, A.J., Peters, J., et al.: Benchmark for algorithms segmenting the left atrium from 3D CT and MRI datasets. IEEE Trans. Med. Imaging **34**(7), 1460–1473 (2015)
5. Chen, L.-C., Zhu, Y., Papandreou, G., Schroff, F., Adam, H.: Encoder-decoder with atrous separable convolution for semantic image segmentation. In: Ferrari, V., Hebert, M., Sminchisescu, C., Weiss, Y. (eds.) ECCV 2018. LNCS, vol. 11211, pp. 833–851. Springer, Cham (2018). https://doi.org/10.1007/978-3-030-01234-2_49
6. Radford, A., Metz, L., Chintala, S.: Unsupervised representation learning with deep convolutional generative adversarial networks. arXiv preprint arXiv:1511.06434 (2015)

7. Nie, D., Gao, Y., Wang, L., Shen, D.: ASDNet: attention based semi-supervised deep networks for medical image segmentation. In: Frangi, A.F., Schnabel, J.A., Davatzikos, C., Alberola-López, C., Fichtinger, G. (eds.) MICCAI 2018. LNCS, vol. 11073, pp. 370–378. Springer, Cham (2018). https://doi.org/10.1007/978-3-030-00937-3_43

8. Zhang, J., Ding, Z., Li, W., et al.: Importance weighted adversarial nets for partial domain adaptation. In: Proceedings of the IEEE Conference on Computer Vision and Pattern Recognition, pp. 8156–8164 (2018)

9. Frid-Adar, M., Diamant, I., Klang, E., et al.: GAN-based synthetic medical image augmentation for increased CNN performance in liver lesion classification. Neurocomputing **321**, 321–331 (2018)

10. Hung, W.C., Tsai, Y.H., Liou, Y.T., et al.: Adversarial learning for semi-supervised semantic segmentation. arXiv preprint arXiv:1802.07934 (2018)

11. Arjovsky, M., Chintala, S., Bottou, L.: Wasserstein GAN. arXiv preprint arXiv:1701.07875 (2017)

12. Gulrajani, I., Ahmed, F., Arjovsky, M., et al.: Improved training of Wasserstein GANS. In: Advances in Neural Information Processing Systems, pp. 5767–5777 (2017)

13. Zhu, Y., Elhoseiny, M., Liu, B., et al.: A generative adversarial approach for zero-shot learning from noisy texts. In: Proceedings of the IEEE Conference on Computer Vision and Pattern Recognition, pp. 1004–1013 (2018)

14. Lai, W.S., Huang, J.B., Ahuja, N., et al.: Deep Laplacian pyramid networks for fast and accurate super-resolution. In: Proceedings of the IEEE Conference on Computer Vision and Pattern Recognition, pp. 624–632 (2017)

15. Hu, L., Kan, M., Shan, S., et al.: Duplex generative adversarial network for unsupervised domain adaptation. In: Proceedings of the IEEE Conference on Computer Vision and Pattern Recognition, pp. 1498–1507 (2018)

16. Dai, J., He, K., Sun, J.: BoxSup: exploiting bounding boxes to supervise convolutional networks for semantic segmentation. In: Proceedings of the IEEE International Conference on Computer Vision, pp. 1635–1643 (2015)

17. Oh, S.J., Benenson, R., Khoreva, A., et al.: Exploiting saliency for object segmentation from image level labels. In: 2017 IEEE Conference on Computer Vision and Pattern Recognition (CVPR), pp. 5038–5047. IEEE (2017)

18. Pathak, D., Krahenbuhl, P., Darrell, T.: Constrained convolutional neural networks for weakly supervised segmentation. In: Proceedings of the IEEE International Conference on Computer Vision, pp. 1796–1804 (2015)

19. Bearman, A., Russakovsky, O., Ferrari, V., Fei-Fei, L.: What's the point: semantic segmentation with point supervision. In: Leibe, B., Matas, J., Sebe, N., Welling, M. (eds.) ECCV 2016. LNCS, vol. 9911, pp. 549–565. Springer, Cham (2016). https://doi.org/10.1007/978-3-319-46478-7_34

20. Long, J., Shelhamer, E., Darrell, T.: Fully convolutional networks for semantic segmentation. In: Proceedings of the IEEE Conference on Computer Vision and Pattern Recognition, pp. 3431–3440 (2015)

21. Ronneberger, O., Fischer, P., Brox, T.: U-Net: convolutional networks for biomedical image segmentation. In: Navab, N., Hornegger, J., Wells, W.M., Frangi, A.F. (eds.) MICCAI 2015. LNCS, vol. 9351, pp. 234–241. Springer, Cham (2015). https://doi.org/10.1007/978-3-319-24574-4_28

22. Goodfellow, I., Pouget-Abadie, J., Mirza, M., et al.: Generative adversarial nets. In: Advances in Neural Information Processing Systems, pp. 2672–2680 (2014)

23. Luc, P., Couprie, C., Chintala, S., et al.: Semantic segmentation using adversarial networks. arXiv preprint arXiv:1611.08408 (2016)

24. Sandoval, Z., Betancur, J., Dillenseger, J.-L.: Multi-atlas-based segmentation of the left atrium and pulmonary veins. In: Camara, O., Mansi, T., Pop, M., Rhode, K., Sermesant, M., Young, A. (eds.) STACOM 2013. LNCS, vol. 8330, pp. 24–30. Springer, Heidelberg (2014). https://doi.org/10.1007/978-3-642-54268-8_3

25. Zuluaga, M.A., Cardoso, M.J., Modat, M., Ourselin, S.: Multi-atlas propagation whole heart segmentation from MRI and CTA using a local normalised correlation coefficient criterion. In: Ourselin, S., Rueckert, D., Smith, N. (eds.) FIMH 2013. LNCS, vol. 7945, pp. 174–181. Springer, Heidelberg (2013). https://doi.org/10.1007/978-3-642-38899-6_21

26. Liu, X., Shen, Y., Zhang, S., et al.: Segmentation of left atrium through combination of deep convolutional and recurrent neural networks. J. Med. Imaging Health Inform. **8**(8), 1578–1584 (2018)

27. Mortazi, A., Karim, R., Rhode, K., Burt, J., Bagci, U.: *CardiacNET*: segmentation of left atrium and proximal pulmonary veins from MRI using multi-view CNN. In: Descoteaux, M., Maier-Hein, L., Franz, A., Jannin, P., Collins, D.L., Duchesne, S. (eds.) MICCAI 2017. LNCS, vol. 10434, pp. 377–385. Springer, Cham (2017). https://doi.org/10.1007/978-3-319-66185-8_43

Development and Application of Silkworm Disease Recognition System Based on Mobile App

Dingyuan Xia[1]([✉]), Zhen Yu[1], Anjun Cheng[1], Liang Tang[2], and Meining Shi[2]

[1] School of Information Engineering, Wuhan University of Technology, Wuhan 430070, China
labxiady@263.net
[2] Sericulture Technology Promotion Master Station of Guangxi, Nanning 530007, China

Abstract. Facing the characteristic agriculture of silkworm breeding in China, aiming at the technical requirements of silkworm farmers for accurate recognition and effective prevention and control of silkworm diseases, referring to the "flower companion" App for flower and grass recognition and the Taobao online commodity purchasing system, a silkworm disease image detection and recognition system based on mobile App is developed to fill the gaps in the industry. The system adopts the C/S network architecture mode, and users can collect silkworm disease images in real-time by mobile App and upload them to cloud server platform automatically. The cloud server platform uses efficient image segmentation, feature extraction, SVM-based classification, and feature matching and fast retrieval algorithm, automatically pushes the case analysis report to the mobile phone, displays the case image, and makes brief text descriptions. After online testing by Android mobile phone, the system runs smoothly and has no stagnation. The system response time is less than 0.5 s, and the average retrieval accuracy rate is about 75%. Compared with domestic similar systems, it has unique characteristics and achieves the expected goal of system design, which has certain theoretical significance and application value.

Keywords: Silkworm Disease Recognition · Mobile App · Android · SVM

1 Introduction

Silkworm industry is an important economic source in some areas of southern China and silkworm disease has an important impact on silkworm breeding. The recognition of silkworm disease is the primary task to prevent and control silkworm disease, and it is mainly based on the subjective judgment of silkworm experts in the past, which the efficiency is low and the intensity is high. Therefore, the requirements of online experts system of silkworm diseases recognition based on mobile application come into being. At present, machine learning has been widely used in the fields of bio-metrics (such as face recognition) and license plate recognition. The use of image processing to solve specific problems has become more and more widespread in various industries. With the advancement of machine learning technology and the popularity of mobile Internet

© Springer Nature Switzerland AG 2019
Y. Zhao et al. (Eds.): ICIG 2019, LNCS 11902, pp. 471–482, 2019.
https://doi.org/10.1007/978-3-030-34110-7_39

applications, many mobile applications based on intelligent recognition systems have emerged, such as the "flower companion" App for flower and grass recognition and the Taobao online commodity purchasing system. However, there is currently no nationwide coverage of silkworm disease automatic recognition mobile phone App that can directly serve for silkworm farmers.

At the same time, for the scattered breeding of silkworm farmers, mainly rely on the reading of silkworm disease prevention manual, using text-based silkworm disease retrieval diagnostic rules as the basis for reasoning. Because most of the symptoms of silkworm disease in manual are terminology, for some silkworm farmers who do not have professional knowledge background, it is difficult to grasp the way of silkworm disease by text description. In addition, in the past, most systems for the recognition of silkworm diseases were based on a single machine or a Web system, and the recognition process required computer terminal, which was not very convenient. The applications of artificial intelligence, system engineering and other multidisciplinary for the judgment and prevention of silkworm disease is of great significance to ensure the normal production of silkworm farmers. Flexible mobile devices have better portability and popularity, and can provide silkworm disease recognition and diagnosis services to silkworm farmers anytime and anywhere. However, this work is full of challenges. First, the structure, shape and details of the silkworm itself are complex. In the natural environment, it is highly susceptible to some background factors, such as the occlusion of mulberry leaves and changes in lighting conditions, which makes the recognition of silkworm diseases very different. Second, the existing silkworm disease data is scarce and messy, and the data set standards are not uniform. The third is the lack of application and system design for the recognition of silkworm disease.

In this paper, aiming at the technical requirements of silkworm farmers for accurate recognition and effective prevention of silkworm disease, we have developed a set of silkworm disease automatic detection and recognition system based mobile App, improving methods, achieving accurate recognition and prevention, filling the gaps in the industry. It is foreseeable that the App has broad prospects, great economic and social values.

2 Related Work

With the development and popularization of smart phones, the realization of silkworm disease recognition system based on mobile application is feasible and convenient. The design and development of silkworm recognition systems are relatively few at home and abroad.

However, there have been good progress and research on retrieval system in other fields. Dai et al. [1] developed an Android system for searching cotton pests and diseases, which realized the automatic diagnosis of cotton pests and diseases. Kumar et al. [2] developed the iOS software Leafsnap, which can identify trees. Zhao et al. [3] developed an Android application that can identify plant species. Qi et al. [4] developed an Android software for face detection. Wu et al. [5] developed an Android software for locating images. Li et al. [6] used different kernel function training support vector machines to realize the classification and recognition of cucumber, and the final result confirmed that SVM has good generalization ability in disease detection. Yang et al. [7] used color moments and lab operators as features to conduct SVM learning and training, and successfully identified various diseases of barley. Carmargo and Smith [8] used SVM to identify plant diseases in color images, extracted features such as gray scales on plant leaves, and used SVM to identify them, achieving a high recognition rate. Patil et al. [9] used SVM to classify cotton lesions, which had two processing: firstly, using pre-processing to extract image boundary and texture features, then using SVM to classify and recognize the features, the experiment results show that it may obtain a good precision. Sannakki et al. [10] used SVM to detect pomegranate disease. Chang [11] used SVM to study wheat pathological diseases.

Based on the research and reference of exiting image retrieval systems in different fields at home and abroad, by selecting and testing many classic classifiers under the factors of comprehensive retrieval efficiency and accuracy, we have developed a silkworm disease recognition system based on mobile App.

3   System Design

3.1   Overall System Design

To realize the recognition of silkworm disease based on the Android platform, the system is divided into a server module and a mobile client module. The system architecture is shown in Fig. 1.

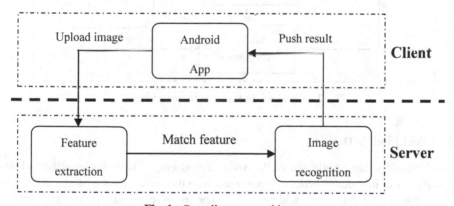

Fig. 1. Overall system architecture.

In the Fig. 1, the mobile clients and servers use wireless networks for data transmission. The mobile phone client is mainly responsible for real-time collection and automatic upload of local silkworm disease images, that is, taking photos by viewfinder frame or selecting photos from local album, and transferring the designated images to the server. The server processes the image according to the received image, extracts the image features, classifies them by the trained classifier, and returns the retrieval results to the mobile phone client. The process of silkworm disease recognition is shown in Fig. 2.

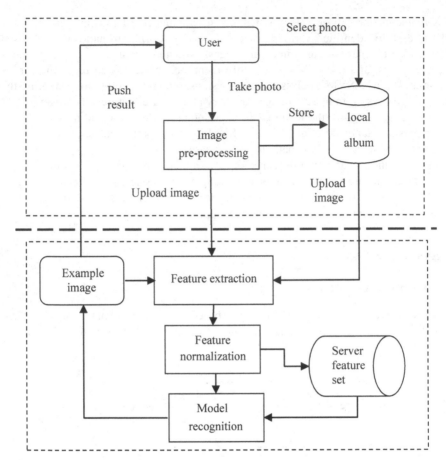

Fig. 2. Silkworm disease recognition process.

3.2 Client Module Design

Using Java to develop mobile App on the Android platform, we have designed the mobile client interface. In order to better communicate with the server, the registered users log in according to the user name and password. The image example can be collected at mobile phone by taking photos or selecting photos, while the retrieval results can be pushed to the mobile phone by the server.

3.3 Server Module Design

The important function of the server is to search and classify the images example sent by the mobile client. The main parts of the server module are the image pre-processing, the image feature extraction and the generation of the classification model, which the basic process includes below.

Image Pre-processing. In this paper, silkworm image samples are collected from the natural state, including 542 sick silkworm image samples and 610 normal silkworm image samples. Since the number of silkworm image samples is scarce, it is easy to produce an over-fitting in training, so image enhancement is performed. The basic enhanced method is to mirror, rotate and pan the existing silkworm image samples. After the silkworm image samples are expanded, 2,604 silkworm disease samples and 2,928 silkworm disease-free samples are obtained. Since the image is easily affected by lighting, environment and other conditions during the shooting process, there will be some noise and other interference in the image. Therefore, some simple pre-processing of the image is required, and then the image is derived from the characteristics of the silkworm disease itself. In this paper, the algorithm of marker and watershed is used to segment the image. The extracted marker is used as the minimum value of the gradient image, the gradient image is modified, and then the watershed algorithm is used to reconstruct the image to complete the image segmentation [12]. Finally, the image is subjected to adaptive threshold segmentation and morphological transformation to complete image pre-processing. The image pre-processing process is shown in Fig. 3.

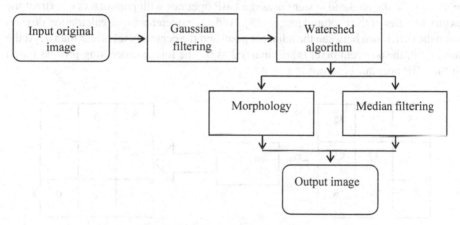

Fig. 3. Image pre-processing process.

Image Feature Extraction. This paper uses color moments to describe image color features because useful color information is concentrated in the first, second and third moments. Compared to other traditional color features, the use of the color moment method does not require more processing of color features, which is a very big advantage. A color feature is formed by taking 3 low-order moments for each component on the 3 components of the image and a total of 9 components are required. In practical applications, color moments are often rarely used alone because it is global in color description. The first, second and third moments of the two systems RGB and HSV are evaluated to identify the image color information.

The formula for calculating the first moment of R, G and B, or H, S and V is:

$$\mu = \frac{1}{p} \sum_{j=1}^{P} f_j p(f_i) \qquad (1)$$

The second-order moments of R, G and B, or H, S and V are calculated as:

$$\sigma^2 = \frac{1}{P} \sum_{j=1}^{P} (f_i - \mu)^2 p(f_i) \qquad (2)$$

The third-order moments for R, G and B, or H, S and V are calculated as:

$$\varepsilon^3 = \frac{1}{P} \sum_{j=1}^{P} (f_j - \mu)^3 p(f_i) \qquad (3)$$

Equations (1) to (3) constitutes the characteristics of the image color moment.

This paper uses the LBP operator to extract image texture features, while the traditional LBP operator is sensitive to subtle texture features. Because the images retrieved by the system come from the mobile phone client, they are easily affected by light, plant leaf occlusion and other factors, which the noise interference is a serious problem to be solved. So the backend system uses the LBP operator with parameters to extract the texture features of the captured image [13]. Add a parameter α to the calculation process when the difference between the adjacent pixel and the central pixel is less than α. At the same time, the adjacent pixel is still marked as 0. The image processing process based on the LBP operator is shown in Fig. 4.

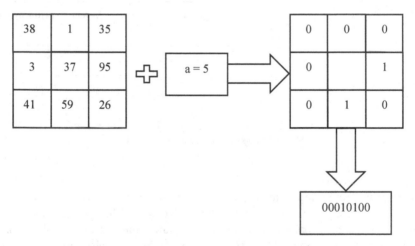

Fig. 4. Image processing process based on the LBP operator.

After obtaining the LBP encoding of the pixel, the LBP encoded value of all the pixels of entire image is counted.

The formula for calculating the LBP encoded value after adding parameters is as follows:

$$LBP_{P,R} = \sum_{0}^{P-1} s(g_p - g_c) 2^P \qquad (4)$$

$$s(x) = \begin{cases} 0, & x < 0 \\ 1, & x \geq 0 \end{cases} \tag{5}$$

Classification by Classifier. The SVM classifier and the KNN classifier are used in the experiment, while the color moment and the LBP feature vector are as input to the classifier. Use the cross-validation method to select the optimal model. The positive sample of silkworm disease is 2,604 and the normal silkworm sample is 2,928, while 108 of them are taken out as test sets. Since the "s" takes a value of 10, the training set is divided into 10 parts, 9 parts as a training set and 1 part as verification set. Then calculate the accuracy of each verification set, which the results are shown in Table 1. The model is with the highest accuracy as the final test model. The test model is tested with the test set and the final test error is as the standard deviation for the model. The classifier work flow is shown in Fig. 5.

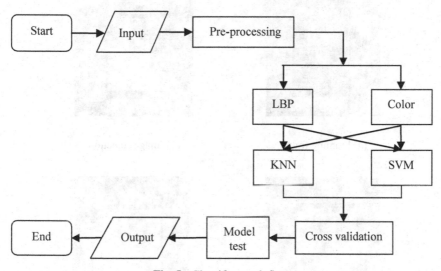

Fig. 5. Classifier work flow.

4   System Testing and Analysis of Experimental Results

4.1   System Testing

The system development environment is as follows:

*Development language: Java, Python
*Android platform: Android system 4.0 or above
*Operating system platform: CentOS 7.3

The mobile client user interface is shown in Fig. 6. There are two modes for user to collect the image example by mobile phone, taking photos by viewfinder frame or selecting photos from local album. When collecting the image example by taking photos, the user only needs to click the camera button, as shown in Fig. 6(a), or by selecting photos from the mobile phone album, as shown in Fig. 6(b). After the photo is collected and sent, the backend retrieval system returns the retrieval result at once, as shown in Fig. 6(c) and (d), which the Fig. 6(c) and (d) show the retrieval results of two different silkworm diseases. With the increasing of test data, the system can achieve higher recognition rate. Many of test results show that the system runs stably, and the retrieval accuracy and respond time are satisfactory.

(a) Framing frame

(b) Image selection

(c) Search result 1

(d) Search result 2

Fig. 6. Mobile client image retrieval interface.

4.2   Analysis of Experimental Results

Accuracy Test. This paper mainly uses the KNN and SVM classifiers to train the extracted image features. As mentioned above, the accuracy results obtained by the s-fold cross-validation are shown in Table 1.

Table 1. Image feature extraction training results.

Classifier	1set	2set	3set	4set	5set	6set	7set	8set	9 set	10set
KNN accuracy (%)	66.5	69.5	70.2	70.7	66.4	65.9	63.0	68.7	71.2	69.2
SVM accuracy (%)	77.0	70.1	78.5	77.5	74.3	72.1	69.1	73.1	71.1	73.2

From the data analysis in Table 1, it can be shown that SVM has strong generalization ability and small computational cost compared to KNN. The KNN algorithm is more suitable for classification with larger sample sizes, but it is more likely to cause misclassification for smaller sample sizes, while the SVM can solve the problem in small sample cases. The test results show that SVM is better than KNN algorithm, which proves that SVM has strong generalization ability for classification of insufficient data.

(a) Framing frame   (b) Search results

Fig. 7. "Flower Companion" App mobile client image retrieval interface.

Further experimental analysis shows that the mean of the cross-validation method under the KNN classifier is 0.681 and the standard deviation is 0.0246, while the mean obtained under the SVM classifier is 0.736 and the standard deviation is 0.0304. The best model is selected from different models and the average retrieval result is used to test the recognition effect, which the system response time is less than 0.5 s, the retrieval accuracy rate is 73.8% and the recall rate is 75.6%.

This system has certain characteristics compared with the domestic similar system, the "Flower Companion". The image retrieval interface of the "Flower Companion" at the mobile client is shown in Fig. 7. After testing, the "Flower Companion" App has a recognition rate of less than 60% for most kinds of flowers and plants.

Real-Time Test. The real-time test results for the silkworm disease recognition system based on mobile App are shown in Table 2.

Table 2. Real-time test results.

Device	RAM	CPU	Main screen resolution	Search time
Huawei Glory 7	3G	Hisilicon Kirin 935	1920 × 1080	0.29 s
Huawei p7	2G	Hisilicon Kirin 960	1920 × 1080	0.25 s

According to the data analysis in Table 2, the different models of Huawei mobile phones are selected to test for silkworm disease recognition system. The results show that the retrieval time can be completed within 0.5 s, and the system has good fluency and user experience.

Application Scenario Test. In order to test the recognition effect of the system in various scenarios, the experiment uses the control variable method to compare the recognition results under different conditions. We conducted experimental design based on the knowledge provided by the sericulture experts, and divided the test evaluation criteria into three levels: good recognition, qualified recognition, bad recognition. The experiment performs 240 tests on each group of scenes, while the result is judged as good recognition when the recognition ratio is greater than 80%, qualified recognition when it is between 50% and 80%, and bad recognition when it is smaller than 50%. The recognition results are shown in Table 3.

Table 3. Application scenario test results.

Test items	Scene description	Recognition result
Outdoor test	Blades blocked on sunny days	Qualified ($\geq$50%)
	Sunny without blade	Good ($\geq$80%)
	Blade blocking on cloudy days	Bad ($<$50%)
	Cloudless occlusion	Qualified ($\geq$50%)
Indoor test	Daytime, indoor lighting	Good ($\geq$80%)
	day	Qualified ($\geq$50%)
	Night, indoor lighting	Bad ($<$50%)

From the data analysis in Table 3, we can see whether the silkworm body is occluded by the leaves, and whether the light intensity will affect the retrieval results. However, after a large number of experimental results analysis, the system has better recognition effect in the case of good illumination, while qualified recognition effect under the condition of blurred background, which can satisfy the basic application needs.

5 Conclusions

In this paper, a silkworm disease recognition system based on mobile App is designed for several typical silkworm diseases, which the client platform is developed based on the Android platform and the App can get the silkworm disease recognition results by taking photo in real-time or selecting photo from local album. Firstly, the captured image example of silkworm body is pre-processed. Then, the silkworm disease features are extracted by the color moment and the LBP features, and the optimal classification model is gotten by the SVM training. Finally, the best retrieval result is achieved by matching features between the image example at client and the image database at the server. The experimental results show that the system can effectually achieve the retrieval of several typical silkworm diseases with higher retrieval accuracy and shorter respond time, which can meet the basic application needs. Due to the captured samples of different silkworm diseases are not enough, some comparative tests between a few kinds of typical silkworm diseases and normal silkworm are complied in the paper, which can only make high accuracy of classification between the white muscardine silkworm and normal silkworm, but the extraction of more silkworm disease features can not achieve better results. Thus, it provides a large margin for further improving the recognition rate and more tests will be done in the future to reach higher application levels.

Acknowledgments. This work was supported by the Key Research and Development Project in Guangxi Zhuang Autonomous Region, Nanning, China: the Research and Application of General Survey, Evaluation, Forecast and Prevention & Control Technology of Major Diseases and Pests of Silkworm in Guangxi under Grant No. AB16380102, while a part of this work was supported by the Key Lab. of Broadband Wireless Communications and Sensor Networks, Hubei Province, Wuhan University of Technology, Wuhan, China.

References

1. Dai, J., Lai, J.: Cotton pest and disease diagnosis system based on image rules and Android mobile phone. Trans. Chin. Soc. Agric. Mach. **46**(1), 35–43 (2015)
2. Kumar, N., Belhumeur, P.N., Biswas, A., et al.: Leafsnap: a computer vision system for automatic plant species identification. In: 12th European Conference on Computer Vision, pp. 502–516 (2012)
3. Zhao, Z.Q., Ma, L.H., Cheung, Y.M., et al.: Ap leaf: an efficient android-based plant leaf identification system. Neuro-Computing **151**, 1112–1119 (2015)
4. Yan, Z., Wang, J.: Image content detection based on android system. Software **33**(6), 35–37 (2012)
5. Wu, Y., Luo, T., Wang, M.: Research on image acquisition and retrieval methods of positionable images. Comput. Eng. **40**(7), 207–211 (2012)
6. Li, W., Tang, S., Chen, R.: Identification of cucumber leaf disease based on color feature and support vector machine. Agric. Mech. Res. **1**, 73–75 (2014)
7. Yang, Q., Gao, X.: Research on identification of main diseases of barley based on color and texture features. J. Chin. Agric. Univ. **5**, 129–135 (2013)
8. Carmargo, A., Smith, J.: Image pattern classification for the identification of disease causing agents in plants. Comput. Electron. Agric. **66**(2), 121–125 (2009)

9. Patil, S.P., Zambre, M.R.S.: Classification of cotton leaf spot disease using support vector, machine. Int. J. Eng. Res. Appl. **4**(5), 92–97 (2014)
10. Sannakki, S.S., Rajpurohit, V.S., Nargund, V.B.: SVM-DSD: SVM based diagnostic system for the detection of pomegranate leaf diseases. In: Kumar, M.A., Kumar, T. (eds.) Proceedings of International Conference on Advances in Computing, vol. 174, pp. 715–720 (2013). https://doi.org/10.1007/978-81-322-0740-5_85
11. Chang, T.: Research on wheat disease identification based on support vector machine. Shandong Agricultural University, Taian (2015)
12. Diao, Z.: Research and application of intelligent diagnosis system for wheat leaf disease in Datian. University of Science and Technology of China, Hefei (2010)
13. Wang, A.: Research on classification algorithm of floorboard texture based on mixed Gaussian model. Northeast Forestry University, Harbin (2013)

A Structural Oriented Training Method for GAN Based Fast Compressed Sensing MRI

Haotian An$^{(\boxtimes)}$ and Yu-Jin Zhang

Department of Electronic Engineering, Tsinghua University, Beijing 100084, China
aht15@mails.tsinghua.edu.cn

Abstract. Traditional strategies for reconstructing Compressed Sensing Magnetic Resonance Imaging (CS-MRI) may introduce computational redundancy, and deep learning-based methods can significantly reduce reconstruction time and improve restoration quality. However, many recent deep learning-based algorithms lay insufficient attention to spatial frequency information. In this paper, a Structural Oriented Generative Adversarial Network (SOGAN) is proposed aiming at restoring image domain information as well as refining frequency domain during the reconstruction of CS-MRI. Numerical Experiments showed our model's efficiency and capability for diagnostic purpose.

Keywords: Image restoration · Magnetic Resonance Imaging (MRI) · Compressed sensing · Deep learning · Generative Adversarial Networks (GAN) · Structural oriented

1 Introduction

In the past two decades, Magnetic resonance imaging (MRI) has revolutionized diagnostic and therapeutic imaging due to its non-radiation and non-ionizing nature. It can reveal the structure and the function of internal tissues and organs in a high-quality and safe manner. However, the main barrier in contemporary MRI technology is the slow process of data acquisition, resulting in long scan time and potentially more severe motion artefacts, hence accelerating MR acquisition is in high demand. Different efforts have been made to reduce scan time, which can be categorized into two complementary directions: physics and hardware-based methods as well as signal processing based methods. The former mainly lay emphasis on designing fast imaging sequences, as well as exploiting information from multiple receiving coils. For example, generalized autocalibrating partial parallel acquisition (GRAPPA) [1] aims to exploit the diverse information in coil sensitivity maps. The latter relies on the prior knowledge of the sparsity in k-space. Compressed Sensing MRI (CS-MRI) [2] is an important representative in signal processing based methods. k-space is the frequency domain, and randomly undersampled data (usually less than 50%) is often acquired in

© Springer Nature Switzerland AG 2019
Y. Zhao et al. (Eds.): ICIG 2019, LNCS 11902, pp. 483–494, 2019.
https://doi.org/10.1007/978-3-030-34110-7_40

such applications. In the theory of Compressed Sensing MRI, artefacts brought by random undersampling can be treated as noise-like interference and thus be recovered by the sparse representation [2]. Although this assumption based on the sparsity in the transformation domain succeeds in many applications [3–7], one problem still exists is the computational complexity.

Recent progress in artificial neural networks opens new opportunities to solve classification [8], recognition [9], and ill-posed inverse problems [10] more efficiently than conventional signal processing methods. When dealing with ill-posed inverse problems, Convolutional Neural Networks (CNNs) outperforms a great number of traditional model-based methods in different tasks, such as image super-resolution [11], segmentation [12], de-noising [13], and pose estimation [14] etc.

In order to address the problems regarding complexity resulted from the above assumption, there are preliminary researches focusing on deep learning based MRI reconstruction have made great progress. Wang et al. [15] first proposed using end to end CNN to learn the mapping between zero-filled and fully-sampled data. Schlemper et al. [16] incorporated data consistency as a layer when cascading CNNs for MRI reconstruction, also demonstrated that using different Cartesian masks to train is beneficial for generic applications. Yang et al. [17] took advantage of the algorithm in Alternating Direction Method of Multipliers (ADMM) and achieved results that reconstruction time was significantly reduced while producing the same quality as traditional model-based methods. Sun et al. [18] used a Recursive Dilated architecture aiming to reduce the network parameters while introducing dilated convolutions. However, training traditional end to end CNN with pixel-wise oriented loss function may result in overly smooth structure detail and lack perceptual coherent details for diagnostic purpose. Goodfellow et al. [19] proposed Generative Adversarial Networks (GANs) in which utilizing the generator network as a nonlinear transformation solves perceptually generating problems at a high level. Wang et al. [20] proposed a state of the art single image super-resolution (SISR) model called Enhanced SRGAN, taking advantage of a residual dense block with a GAN architecture. Such analogous computer vision tasks (e.g. super-resolution, de-noising, and reconstruction) with perceptual quality driven goal gradually make use of GAN architecture and showed promising results [20,21].

Mardani et al. [22] first incorporated GAN into Compressed Sensing MRI, Quan et al. [23] used a cyclic loss function while learned residual content of undersampled scans. Yang et al. [24] incorporated perceptual and frequency domain loss, Li et al. [25] introduced a structure regularization called Patch Correlation Regularization (PCR) which aims to restore structure information within both local and global scale. Chen et al. [26] trained a GAN to provide two MRI contrast during one single scan.

The motivation of this study mainly comes from two observations. In recent years, image restoration and de-noising tasks lay great emphasis on perceptual quality [27] based on the human visual system (HVS). Also, it is straightforward to formulate one single reconstruction based on a single observation instead of repeatedly refinement of the generated sample, which is beneficial for clinical hardware implementation.

Taken the above observations into consideration, in this study, we adopted and improved Generative Adversarial Network (GAN) to first time aimed at preserving global structure using an MS-SSIM oriented training purpose, while realizing data correction after single reconstruction. Specifically, our contributions are as follows:

- We proposed to incorporate MS-SSIM oriented loss function in an unbalanced U-Net based generator architecture, further balanced between NMSE loss and frequency domain loss.
- We proposed to add a single data consistency correction after one-time reconstruction using GAN, which can be further synthesized into the model.
- We presented a theoretical analysis of the proposed differentiable loss function, conducted numerous comparison experiments to examine our model and proved the efficiency of the proposed method.

The rest of this paper is organized as: In Sect. 2 the problem is stated, and Structure Oriented Generative Adversarial Networks (SOGAN) is proposed after the evaluation of conventional methods and deep learning methods. Section 3 reports the method as well as our contributions. In Sect. 4, training details and data evaluation are presented. Discussion and conclusion are in Sect. 5.

2   Problem Formulation

Compressed Sensing MRI can be treated as an ill-posed linear system $y = \boldsymbol{\Phi} x + \epsilon$ with $\boldsymbol{\Phi} \in \mathbb{C}^{M \times N}$. ϵ denotes the noise and other unmodeled dynamics. The observation and desired reconstruction are respectively denoted as y and x, where $y \in \mathbb{C}^M$ and $x \in \mathbb{C}^N$, note that $M \ll N$. The image acquisition process can be described by matrix $\mathbb{C}^{M \times N}$. Thus the desired goal is estimating the inverse matrix $\mathbb{C}^{N \times M}$ which is underdetermined. Another unstable factor is the unmodeled dynamics ϵ. The reconstructed image is often estimated by

$$\hat{x} = \arg \min_x \{ \frac{1}{2} \| \boldsymbol{\Phi} x - y \|_2^2 + \sum_{l=1}^L \lambda_l g(x) \} \tag{1}$$

in which $\boldsymbol{\Phi} = \boldsymbol{PF} \in \mathbb{C}^{M \times N}$ is the measurement matrix with $\boldsymbol{P}$ denoting undersample operation and $\boldsymbol{F}$ denoting Fourier transformation. $g(\cdot)$ is the regularization term, making use of prior information and l_q-regularizer ($q \in [0, 1]$) is usually adopted for compressed sensing problems.

For learning based problem formulation, no further information is obtained besides the training samples and the corresponding noisy observations. The goal is to estimate x' with newly acquired data y'. We denote the fully-sampled training data as set $\boldsymbol{X} = \{x_1, x_2, \ldots, x_t\}$, and the corresponding observations as set $\boldsymbol{Y} = \{y_1, y_2, \ldots, y_t\}$, thus the training process can be written as $\boldsymbol{S} = \{(x_1, y_1), (x_2, y_2), \ldots, (x_t, y_t)\}$.

2.1 Conventional Model-Based MRI

Magnetic Resonance Imaging takes advantage of the radio frequency pulse sequence. Model-based theories can be categorized into two parts: transform-based methods and dictionary learning-based methods. For conventional Compressed Sensing (CS) theory, utilizing the sparsity characteristic of acquired signal is important, and transforms such as Fourier transform, Wavelets [4] and discrete cosine transform [2] are used. However, solving the minimization problem may introduce computational complexity and also result in block artefacts [28]. The highlights for dictionary learning-based methods [29] is that it can specifically design a dictionary for the desired dataset.

2.2 Generative Adversarial Networks

General image processing aimed Generative Adversarial Networks derives from a zero-sum game between two CNN based neural networks, called the generator G and the discriminator D. The generator aims to learn the mapping from the manifold latent space z and the corresponding ground truth input x. The discriminator learns to classify whether the input sample lies within real data distribution P_{data} or in generated data distribution P_g. Together the training function L can be formulated by

$$\max_D \min_G L(D,G) = E_{x \sim P_{data}(x)}[logD(x)] + E_{z \sim P_{z(z)}}[log(1 - D(G(z)))] \quad (2)$$

GAN can be estimated by the simultaneous optimization of G and D, based on a stochastic gradient descent algorithm. However, at the initial stage, the over-confident discriminator may result in gradient vanishing problem, thus the gradient step for generator often takes

$$\Delta_G = \nabla_G E_{z \sim P_{z(z)}}[-log(D(G(z)))] \quad (3)$$

The optimized balance between generator and discriminator should finally reach at

$$D'_G(x) = \frac{P_{data}(x)}{P_{data}(x) + P_g(x)} \quad (4)$$

in which the discrimination process approximates random guess and the training process is then stopped. In the final stage, the generated sample distribution P_g approximates real data distribution P_{data}.

3 Method

In the proposed SOGAN architecture, U-Net based generator is adopted for several reasons. Skip connections between the down-sampling encoder and up-sampling decoder can preserve structure information within different scales, which have proven effective among medical image processing tasks [30]. Unlike the upscaling characteristic of super-resolution, the input and output of our task

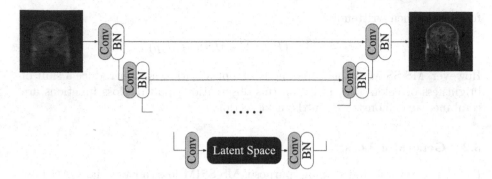

Fig. 1. U-Net structure of generator used in this study

should maintain the same size. Moreover, the residual connection can effectively propagate gradients and avoid gradient vanishing problem.

The generator used in this study is shown in Fig. 1 which utilizes skip connections, and each down-sampling decreases the feature map size by a factor of 2 and each up-sampling increase the feature map size by a factor of 2. Empirically doubling the feature maps in the decoder which results in an unbalanced U-Net helps to reconstruct more detail, and gain better results. Each down-sampling and up-sampling stage consists of three parts: convolutional layer (deconvolutional layer), batch normalization layer, Leaky ReLU layer.

3.1 Multi-scale SSIM Loss

In order to evaluate the content quality of a reconstructed image, PSNR and SSIM are the two important factors involved. More importantly, the perceptual quality of the image is often assessed by SSIM [31], thus the perceptually motivated error function is adopted in this study. To evaluate SSIM at pixel p,

$$SSIM(p) = \frac{2\mu_x\mu_y + C_1}{\mu_x^2 + \mu_y^2 + C_1} \cdot \frac{2\sigma_{xy} + C_2}{\sigma_x^2 + \sigma_y^2 + C_2} = l(p) \cdot cs(p) \tag{5}$$

SSIM driven loss function should be written as

$$L^{SSIM}(p) = \frac{1}{N}\sum_{p \in P}(1 - SSIM(p)) \tag{6}$$

In order to deal with boundary regions, we need to replace pixel patch p with center pixel $\tilde{p}$ to calculate SSIM and its derivatives. For back propagation need, the derivatives of SSIM function should be calculated as

$$\frac{\partial L^{SSIM}(p)}{\partial x(p)} = -\frac{\partial}{\partial x(q)}SSIM(\tilde{p}) = -(\frac{\partial l(\tilde{p})}{\partial x(q)} \cdot (\tilde{p}) + l(\tilde{p}) \cdot \frac{\partial cs(\tilde{p})}{\partial x(q)}) \tag{7}$$

where q is any other pixel in patch P, and $l(\tilde{p})$ and $cs(\tilde{p})$ denote two different terms in computing $SSIM(\tilde{p})$. For Multi-scale SSIM computation, the loss function is then written as

$$L^{MS-SSIM}(P) = 1 - MSSSIM(\tilde{p}) \qquad (8)$$

However, MS-SSIM as the goal of network optimization may introduce a shift of brightness or colors [31], based on this observation, multiple loss functions are combined as demonstrated in the next section.

3.2   Generator Loss

For structural oriented training purpose, MS-SSIM loss, adversarial GAN loss, pixel-wise l2 loss, and frequency domain l2 loss are combined as the total optimization goal. We use the loss function in Eq. (8) for MS-SSIM loss, which is the main training guidance. For fast convergence and robustness, pixel-wise NMSE loss dominates the training procedure at the starting point, which helps to guide the overall gradient descent procedure. For pixel NMSE the loss function can be written as

$$\min_{G} L_{NMSE}(G) = \frac{\|x_t - \hat{x}_g\|_2^2}{\|x_t\|_2^2} \qquad (9)$$

Recall that x_t denotes the ground truth and $\hat{x}_g$ is the generated sample. Different from single image super-resolution (SISR) tasks in which images do not have a clear frequency domain pattern, MRI data are naturally acquired from k-space. Thus at the same time, a frequency domain NMSE loss is added into the training loss

$$\min_{G} L_{k-space}(G) = \frac{\|f_t - \hat{f}_g\|_2^2}{\|f_t\|_2^2} \qquad (10)$$

where f_t and $\hat{f}_g$ are the corresponding k-space data of x_t and $\hat{x}_g$. At last, the adversarial loss based on the discriminator is written as

$$\min_{G} L_{GAN}(G) = -log(D(G(\hat{x}_g))) \qquad (11)$$

The total loss function for SOGAN generator is then as follows

$$L_{SOGAN}(G) = \alpha L_{MSSSIM} + \beta L_{NMSE} + \gamma L_{kspace} + \eta L_{GAN} \qquad (12)$$

3.3   Single Data Consistency Correction

The task of MRI reconstruction is analogous to super-resolution, de-noising but also different. The intrinsic down-sampling is operated in k-space, which result in global aliasing and blurring artefacts.

After training the network, a mapping from the observation sample x_t to the reconstructed samples $\hat{x}_g = f_{recon}(x_t)$ is obtained. In order to fully correct the original k-space data, we apply a data consistency layer after a single time reconstruction. As $\mathcal{F}(x_t)$ contains the original data from the fully-sampled data and the padded zeroes, the generator only tries to fill the zeroes in k-space as far as possible. During this nonlinear interpolation, $f_{recon}(x_t)$ also changed the original data inevitably because the reconstruction is performed in the image domain. Hence the correction is formulated in function $f_{DC}(\cdot)$ which is conducted in k-space, the output of the final network is

$$\hat{x}_g(t)' = \mathcal{F}^{-1}(f_{DC}(\mathcal{F}(\hat{x}_g))) \tag{13}$$

where we transform to frequency domain and replace corresponding data points. Finally, the undersampling and reconstruction process is illustrated in Fig. 2.

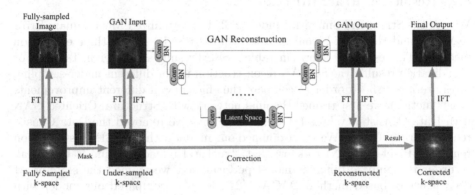

Fig. 2. Overall reconstruction process of SOGAN

4   Experiment Settings and Results

In the following, experiments are performed on testing the capability of SOGAN, and results are compared with other state-of-art methods.

4.1   Experiment Settings

Dataset. We tested SOGAN on MICCAI 2013 Grand Challenge on Multi-Atlas Labeling [32], and used deep brain structures data for training, testing and validating. For training purpose, 12729 T2 weighted brain scans were included, 3879 for validation and 7082 for testing purpose. All the images of T2 weighted brain scans are 256×256 and we normalize them into $[-1, 1]$. During the under-sampling process, all the networks are tested under different masks: 10%, 20%, and 30%, correspondingly yields 10, 5 and 3.3 times acceleration. For robustness of the training process, a time-decreasing data augmentation is added onto the training set. All the random added white Gaussian noise (AWGN) and random interpolation of the image starts at a ratio of 1, and decrease as the training epochs increase. In order to test the model, 50 images from the test set was randomly chosen.

Network Settings and Training Details. After empirically experiments, we set the loss function as $L_{SOGAN}(G) = \alpha L_{MSSSIM} + \beta L_{NMSE} + \gamma L_{kspace} + \eta L_{GAN}$, where $\alpha = 10, \beta = 15, \gamma = 0.5$, and $\eta = 1$. In the early stage, NMSE and frequency domain loss decreases dramatically as the main motivation, later on, SSIM and adversarial loss modify the details of the output. The architecture of SOGAN was inspired by [19] and we implemented on Tensorlayer API. The training was conducted on NVIDIA Tesla K80 of 12 GB memory. The initial learning rate was set to 1E-3, the batch size was set to 25.

4.2 Results on Real MRI Data

We use the Structural Similarity Index (SSIM), Normalized Mean Square Error (NMSE), and the Peak Signal to Noise Ratio (PSNR) as the three evaluation methods. The results are shown in Table 1, SSIM results are shown in Table 2. For visualization results, the SOGAN reconstruction under different under-sampling rates are in Fig. 3. In order to compare the efficiency of different improvements of our method, we first trained the final network with Structural Oriented GAN with Data Consistency Loss (SOGAN-DC), then we removed the Data Consistency layer (SOGAN). We also examined our model with the SSIM loss function removed (Pixel-SOGAN) to show that structural aimed training is beneficial. In order to compare different model performance, we trained the state-of-art deep learning based method DAGAN [24], we also compared our model with ADMM-Net [17].

Table 1. Evaluations for PSNR and NMSE

Method	10%		20%		30%	
	PSNR	NMSE	PSNR	NMSE	PSNR	NMSE
Zero-Filling	27.94 ± 3.75	0.33 ± 0.06	33.47 ± 4.23	0.18 ± 0.03	34.99 ± 4.47	0.15 ± 0.03
ADMM-Net	30.70 ± 3.94	0.24 ± 0.08	37.31 ± 4.14	0.16 ± 0.08	37.36 ± 3.84	0.15 ± 0.05
DAGAN	33.76 ± 4.20	0.17 ± 0.02	39.28 ± 3.41	0.09 ± 0.02	39.76 ± 3.62	0.08 ± 0.01
Pixel-SOGAN	34.02 ± 3.97	0.16 ± 0.03	40.02 ± 4.02	0.08 ± 0.02	40.87 ± 3.78	0.07 ± 0.02
SOGAN	34.22 ± 3.93	0.16 ± 0.03	40.10 ± 4.26	0.08 ± 0.02	41.07 ± 3.84	0.07 ± 0.02
SOGAN-DC	$\mathbf{35.08 \pm 4.47}$	$\mathbf{0.15 \pm 0.03}$	$\mathbf{41.87 \pm 4.56}$	$\mathbf{0.07 \pm 0.02}$	$\mathbf{42.70 \pm 4.48}$	$\mathbf{0.06 \pm 0.01}$

4.3 Comparison

Comparison of Different Training Variables. It can be observed that Data Consistency layer plays an important role in reconstruction quality, and the improvement becomes more efficient as the sampling rate increases, this is due to the correction involves more data as the sampling rate increases. Also, SSIM oriented loss function helps to improve the performance of the network not only in SSIM but also in PSNR. Note that, there is a significant help in Data Consistency layer but the correction does not introduce computational redundancy as the reconstruction time does not increase a lot.

Table 2. Evaluations for SSIM

Method	10%	20%	30%
Zero-Filling	0.77 ± 0.08	0.84 ± 0.06	0.88 ± 0.05
ADMM-Net	0.80 ± 0.04	0.89 ± 0.04	0.91 ± 0.02
DAGAN	0.88 ± 0.04	0.95 ± 0.01	0.96 ± 0.01
Pixel-SOGAN	0.93 ± 0.01	0.97 ± 0.01	0.97 ± 0.01
SOGAN	0.93 ± 0.01	$\mathbf{0.98 \pm 0.01}$	$\mathbf{0.99 \pm 0.01}$
SOGAN-DC	$\mathbf{0.95 \pm 0.03}$	$\mathbf{0.98 \pm 0.01}$	0.98 ± 0.01

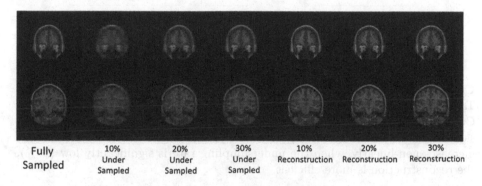

Fig. 3. SOGAN reconstruction results under different under-sampling rates

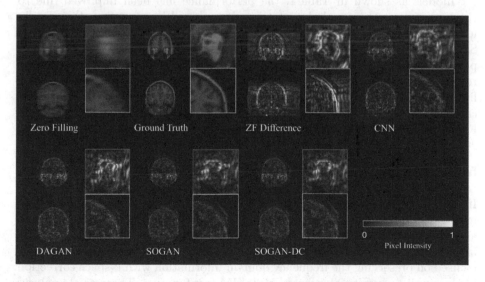

Fig. 4. The comparison of reconstructed samples' differences from fully sampled data under 10% under-sampling

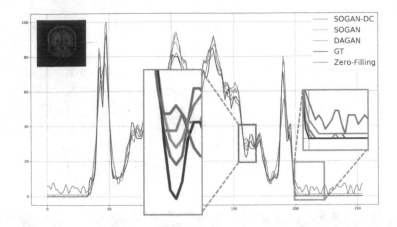

Fig. 5. Pixel values drawn from a horizontal line from reconstructed samples

Comparison with Different Sampling Rate. As can be observed from Table 1, different sampling rate did influence the reconstruction result a lot. Current reconstruction results for 10% undersampling is approximately at the same level of 30% undersampling with zero-filling images. Also, the performance increases non-linearly, when the undersampling rate is significantly low (10%), the reconstruction is more efficient.

Comparison with Other Models. We tested SOGAN with other state-of-art models as shown in Table 1, the performance has been improved due to the k-space correction and the introduced combined loss function. Specifically for structure evaluation methods, SOGAN-DC outperforms the other models in SSIM evaluation as shown in Table 2. As for visual comparison, we plotted the pixel values in a horizontal line from a reconstructed sample. The differences of reconstructed samples from fully sampled data between different methods are listed in Fig. 4, SOGAN-DC also has perceptually satisfying result. Moreover, it can be observed from the details of pixel values drawn from a horizontal line in Fig. 5 that SOGAN-DC preserved structure contrast most successful.

5   Discussion and Conclusion

In this paper, we propose to incorporate the structural training technique in image restoration into the reconstruction of compressed sensing MRI, formed and presented our novel SOGAN model. For compressed sensing MRI, preserving structural information is critical for clinical diagnostic purpose. This study focused on preserving the frequency domain information with k-space correction layer as well as structural oriented MS-SSIM loss function. Theoretical analyses of the structural loss function are given and the combined training strategies are illustrated.

Numerical experiments showed our architecture is efficient to learn the mapping from zero-filling acquisitions to the perceptually convincing reconstructions. For future exploration, it is interesting to form an architecture with fewer parameters and pruning strategy for hardware implementation.

Acknowledgement. This work was supported by National Nature Science Foundation of P.R. China under grand 61673234 and U1636124.

References

1. Griswold, M.A., et al.: Generalized autocalibrating partially parallel acquisitions (GRAPPA). Magn. Reson. Med. Official J. Int. Soc. Magn. Reson. Med. **47**(6), 1202–1210 (2002)
2. Lustig, M., Donoho, D., Pauly, J.M.: Sparse MRI: the application of compressed sensing for rapid MR imaging. Magn. Reson. Med. Official J. Int. Soc. Magn. Reson. Med. **58**(6), 1182–1195 (2007)
3. Candes, E.J., Wakin, M.B.: An introduction to compressive sampling (a sensing/sampling paradigm that goes against the common knowledge in data acquisition). IEEE Sig. Process. Mag. **25**(2), 21–30 (2008)
4. Lustig, M., Donoho, D.L., Santos, J.M., Pauly, J.M.: Compressed sensing MRI. IEEE Sig. Process. Mag. **25**(2), 72 (2008)
5. Usman, M., Prieto, C., Schaeffter, T., Batchelor, P.: k-t Group sparse: a method for accelerating dynamic MRI. Magnetic Reson. Med. **66**(4), 1163–1176 (2011)
6. Hollingsworth, K.G.: Reducing acquisition time in clinical MRI by data undersampling and compressed sensing reconstruction. Phys. Med. Biol. **60**(21), R297 (2015)
7. Gamper, U., Boesiger, P., Kozerke, S.: Compressed sensing in dynamic MRI. Magn. Reson. Med. Official J. Int. Soc. Magn. Reson. Med. **59**(2), 365–373 (2008)
8. Chen, Y., Lin, Z., Zhao, X., Wang, G., Gu, Y.: Deep learning-based classification of hyperspectral data. IEEE J. Sel. Top. Appl. Earth Obs. Remote Sens. **7**(6), 2094–2107 (2014)
9. He, K., Zhang, X., Ren, S., Sun, J.: Deep residual learning for image recognition. In: Proceedings of the IEEE Conference on Computer Vision and Pattern Recognition, pp. 770–778 (2016)
10. Li, H.: Deep learning for image denoising. Int. J. Sig. Process. Image Process. Pattern Recogn. **7**(3), 171–180 (2014)
11. Ledig, C., et al.: Photo-realistic single image super-resolution using a generative adversarial network. In: Proceedings of the IEEE Conference on Computer Vision and Pattern Recognition, pp. 4681–4690 (2017)
12. Noh, H., Hong, S., Han, B.: Learning deconvolution network for semantic segmentation. In: Proceedings of the IEEE international Conference on Computer Vision, pp. 1520–1528 (2015)
13. Zhang, K., Zuo, W., Chen, Y., Meng, D., Zhang, L.: Beyond a Gaussian denoiser: residual learning of deep CNN for image denoising. IEEE Trans. Image Process. **26**, 3142–3155 (2017)
14. Toshev, A., Szegedy, C.: DeepPose: human pose estimation via deep neural networks. In: Proceedings of the IEEE Conference on Computer Vision and Pattern Recognition, pp. 1653–1660 (2014)

15. Wang, S., et al.: Accelerating magnetic resonance imaging via deep learning. In: 2016 IEEE 13th International Symposium on Biomedical Imaging (ISBI), pp. 514–517. IEEE (2016)
16. Schlemper, J., Caballero, J., Hajnal, J.V., Price, A.N., Rueckert, D.: A deep cascade of convolutional neural networks for dynamic MR image reconstruction. IEEE Trans. Med. Imaging **37**(2), 491–503 (2017)
17. Yang, Y., Sun, J., Li, H., Xu, Z.: ADMM-Net: a deep learning approach for compressive sensing MRI. arXiv preprint arXiv: 1705.06869 (2017)
18. Sun, L., Fan, Z., Huang, Y., Ding, X., Paisley, J.: Compressed sensing MRI using a recursive dilated network. In: Thirty-Second AAAI Conference on Artificial Intelligence (2018)
19. Goodfellow, I., et al.: Generative adversarial nets. In: Advances in Neural Information Processing Systems, pp. 2672–2680 (2014)
20. Wang, X., et al.: ESRGAN: enhanced super-resolution generative adversarial networks. In: Leal-Taixé, Laura, Roth, Stefan (eds.) ECCV 2018. LNCS, vol. 11133, pp. 63–79. Springer, Cham (2019). https://doi.org/10.1007/978-3-030-11021-5_5
21. Li, W., Seitz, A.R.: Deep neural networks for modeling visual perceptual learning. J. Neurosci. **38**(27), 6028–6044 (2018)
22. Mardani, M., et al.: Deep generative adversarial neural networks for compressive sensing MRI. IEEE Trans. Med. Imag. **38**(1), 167–179 (2018)
23. Quan, T.M., Nguyen-Duc, T., Jeong, W.K.: Compressed sensing MRI reconstruction using a generative adversarial network with a cyclic loss. IEEE Trans. Med. Imaging **37**(6), 1488–1497 (2018)
24. Yang, G., et al.: DAGAN: deep de-aliasing generative adversarial networks for fast compressed sensing MRI reconstruction. IEEE Trans. Med. Imaging. **37**, 1310–1321 (2018)
25. Li, Z., Zhang, T., Zhang, D.: SEGAN: structure-enhanced generative adversarial network for compressed sensing MRI reconstruction. arXiv preprint arXiv: 1902.06455 (2019)
26. Chen, T., Song, X., Wang, C.: Preserving-texture generative adversarial networks for fast multi-weighted MRI. IEEE Access **6**, 71048–71059 (2018)
27. Zhang, L., Zhang, L., Mou, X., Zhang, D.: A comprehensive evaluation of full reference image quality assessment algorithms. In: 2012 19th IEEE International Conference on Image Processing, pp. 1477–1480. IEEE (2012)
28. Gho, S.M., Nam, Y., Zho, S.Y., Kim, E.Y., Kim, D.H.: Three dimension double inversion recovery gray matter imaging using compressed sensing. Magn. Reson. Imaging **28**(10), 1395–1402 (2010)
29. Caballero, J., Price, A.N., Rueckert, D., Hajnal, J.V.: Dictionary learning and time sparsity for dynamic MR data reconstruction. IEEE Trans. Med. Imaging **33**(4), 979–994 (2014)
30. Zhou, Z., Rahman Siddiquee, M.M., Tajbakhsh, N., Liang, J.: UNet++: a nested U-Net architecture for medical image segmentation. In: Stoyanov, D., et al. (eds.) DLMIA/ML-CDS -2018. LNCS, vol. 11045, pp. 3–11. Springer, Cham (2018). https://doi.org/10.1007/978-3-030-00889-5_1
31. Zhao, H., Gallo, O., Frosio, I., Kautz, J.: Loss functions for image restoration with neural networks. IEEE Trans. Comput. Imaging **3**(1), 47–57 (2016)
32. MICCAI Challenge Workshop on Segmentation: Algorithms, Theory and Applications ("SATA"). https://my.vanderbilt.edu/masi/workshops/. Accessed 9 May 2019

A Hybrid Model for Liver Shape Segmentation with Customized Fast Marching and Improved GMM-EM

Weizhuo Huang[1], Yinwei Zhan[1(✉)], and Rongqian Yang[2]

[1] School of Computer, Guangdong University of Technology, Guangzhou, China
ywzhan@gdut.edu.cn
[2] School of Materials Science and Engineering, South China University of Technology, Guangzhou, China

Abstract. This paper describes an approach to segment liver shape from abdominal CT sequences, required by the analysis of liver diseases. A rough segmentation is first conducted via a customized Fast Marching method to obtain an approximate 3D liver region for subsequent procedure. Then, an improvement of GMM-EM algorithm is made to extract the accurate liver region. Experimental results, evaluated on non-tumor series and tumor series of 10 cases, show that the proposed method performs better than several other typical segmentation models in running time and precision.

Keywords: Liver segmentation · Fast Marching · GMM-EM · K-means++

1 Introduction

Among the most common malignant diseases, liver diseases have the highest incidence rate in the world. Usually, liver diseases can be diagnosed in computed tomography (CT) images and the liver boundary delineation is a key step in the liver sequence analysis. While manual delineation being time-consuming and inefficient, automatic delineation is still facing with difficulties in that the liver is packed with organs of similar-looking tissues with fuzzy boundaries in grayscale.

In order to be more efficient and accurate in segmentation, various methods have been developed to improve the performance of the image processing approaches in liver extraction, including adaptive intensity thresholding [1], region growing, convolutional neural network [2] and so on.

Normally, there are three main stages in liver shape extraction, i.e., noise suppression, ROI initialization and final extraction. Many approaches concentrate on the initialization for the ROI [3], yet they fall short of accuracy because of the variability of liver shapes. Moreover, being highly dependent on initialization, some critical problems such as over-segmentation remain unsolved. In order not to count on initialization and iteration, a single-block linear detection model is presented [4]. But it is suffered from blurred edges between liver and abdominal wall. A customized level set method [5] is then proposed to segment liver shapes with an automatic seed point identification method

© Springer Nature Switzerland AG 2019
Y. Zhao et al. (Eds.): ICIG 2019, LNCS 11902, pp. 495–508, 2019.
https://doi.org/10.1007/978-3-030-34110-7_41

and achieves good performance. However, the seed points selection is performed under the threshold of empirical value, which means the method is not robust enough.

In order to enhance the performance of liver segmentation, we introduce a hybrid segmentation model. For a given abdominal CT sequence, a few seed points are manually selected after image pre-processing. Then a rough segmentation is conducted with a customized Fast Marching Method (FMM). We further make an improvement of GMM-EM [6] for a finer segmentation.

The remainder of this paper is organized as follows. The proposed hybrid method is introduced in Sect. 2 followed by the corresponding experiment in Sect. 3. We conclude the paper in Sect. 4.

2 Method

Let $I = \{I_n : D \rightarrow \mathbb{R}, n = 1, \ldots, L\}$ be an liver CT sequence of L consecutive slices, where each slice I_n is an image defined on a rectangular grid $D = \{1, \ldots, r\} \times \{1, \ldots, c\}$ of r rows and c columns. Here we are concerned with the 3D characteristics of the CT sequence and prefer to denote $\boldsymbol{D} = D \times \{1, \ldots, L\}$ and $D_n = D \times \{n\}$. Therefore the CT sequence has the volumetric representation as $I : \boldsymbol{D} \rightarrow \mathbb{R}$. Our objective is then to extract the liver region $\boldsymbol{\Omega}$ from $\boldsymbol{D}$, which is called the region of interest (ROI), $\boldsymbol{\Omega} \subset \boldsymbol{D}$. Correspondingly, the ROI on slice n is $\Omega_n = D_n \cap \boldsymbol{D}$.

To invoke FMM [7–9], let $\zeta(t) : [0, \infty) \rightarrow \mathbb{R}$ be a marching closed contour in I_n and F be the speed of propagation. Then we have $\partial \zeta / \partial t = |\nabla \zeta| F$ as the basic formulation of the level set equation. The essential idea of level set is to embed the marching contour as the zero set $\tau(s, t) = 0$ of $\tau(s, t) = \pm d$, where $s \in \mathbb{R}$ and d is the distance from s to $\zeta(t)$. The $\zeta(t)$ changes the topology of $\tau(s, t)$ when the $\zeta(t)$ is propagating [10]. The $\zeta(t)$ is the red one and $\tau(s, t)$ is the blue one in Fig. 1.

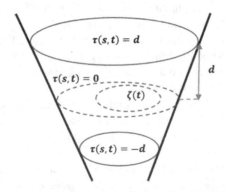

Fig. 1. The contour embeds in the level set distance function. (Color figure online)

In FMM, the F is restricted into a one-way speed term at time t, i.e.

$$F = \frac{1}{1 + e^{-\left(\frac{|\nabla I_n| - \beta}{\alpha}\right)}} \tag{1}$$

where $|\nabla I_n|$ is the magnitude of the gradient [11] and $\alpha < 0$ and $\beta > 0$ are constants that define the region of the image we are interested in. Our works on image preprocessing, consisting of the noise suppression, the edges enhancement and the calculation of F, follow the method in reference [12] implemented in the segmentation toolkit ITK [13].

Our segmentation model consists of two main ingredients, a customized FMM and an improved GMM-EM; the complete flowchart is shown in Fig. 2.

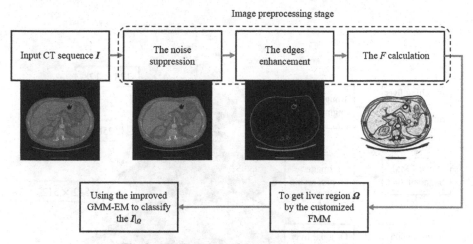

Fig. 2. The flowchart of the proposed approach.

Afterwards, several slices I_n are chosen from I such that $\Omega_n \neq \emptyset$ in an interval of $L/4$ to $L/3$ slices. Then multiple points on these slices are manually selected as seed points, the number of which on each slice is according to the area of its ROI. For instance, we select 5 to 9 points for a large ROI and 1 to 3 points for a small ROI; see Fig. 3. The experiment in [14] shows that the multiple seed points strategy does greatly help upon liver segmentation when using FMM.

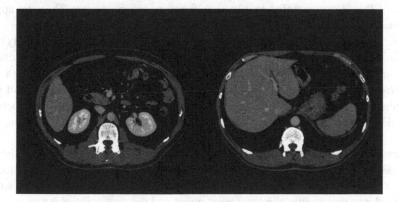

Fig. 3. The selection of seed points.

2.1 Customized FMM

In this part, a customized FMM is described to extract Ω from I. Moreover, a Gaussian image pyramid conducted by a series of down-sampling operation is employed in this pipeline. The Gaussian image pyramid approach is widely used in feature extraction, and it is proved to be facilitated in saving the pivotal feature in sampling operation [15]; the whole flow chart is presented in Fig. 4.

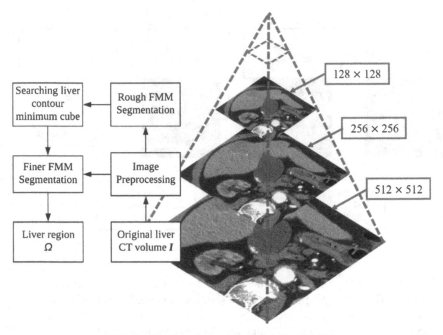

Fig. 4. The flowchart of the customized FMM.

In practice, the size of D is usually 512×512. In order to shorten the processing time, here D is down sampled to 128×128 before preprocessing. Then we applied FMM *twice* to extract Ω from I.

In the 1st FMM, the seed points we set before will start to propagate and finally result in obtaining a coarse Ω. Then a minimum bounding box algorithm [16] is to enclose the Ω_n in I_n by a square gird and form a minimum cuboid to contains the rough Ω as far as possible. It is not accurate enough because of the similar gray intensity of other organ edges. Especially in the similar gray intensity area such as adjacent edges between organs (Fig. 5), the propagation of the liver contour will not stop until the propagating time we set is arrived [17].

Then comes the 2nd FMM to get a finer Ω_n. Here we take every 3 points on the liver surface as a set, 2 of them considered as alive points which will not be readjusted and the 1 left as trait point that needs to be readjusted [18]. Then the points on the surface are divided into two groups, the alive point group and the trait point group.

Now, we set another arrival time smaller than that in the 1st FMM and the trait points are readjusted when the time is arrival. In addition, in order to smoothen sharp burr

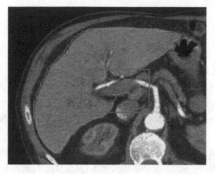

Fig. 5. The problem of leaking into adjacent organs.

edges, mathematical morphology methods, such as erosion and dilate, are used. The comparison between the rough ROI and its finer version is shown in Fig. 6. The region enclosed in blue represents the ROI. It can be seen that the FMM in the second round indeed provides better contours.

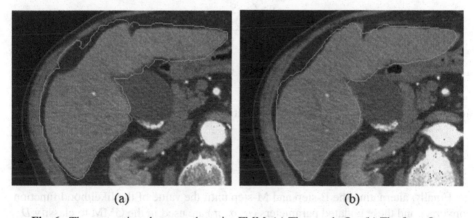

(a)   (b)

Fig. 6. The comparison between the twice FMM. (a) The rough Ω_n, (b) The finer Ω_n.

The FMM is still a low robustness algorithm in segmentation and has the problem of leaking into adjacent structures. In recent years, many researchers have done a lot in improving the FMM, such as adaptive arrival time [19], fuzzy generalized FMM [20, 21] and Fast Marching Spinning Tree [22]. These methods actually perform better than the traditional FMM, but the main problem, leaking to adjacent structures, is still unsolved. In the next part, we propose a new way to solve it by using improved GMM-EM which classifies the $I|_\Omega$ into two clusters, the false liver cluster and the true liver cluster.

2.2 Improved GMM-EM

For a slice $I_n: D \to R$, the GMM of I_n means that, for a pixel $p = (x, y) \in D$, its probability density function f is assumed to be a weighted sum of K Gaussian distributions $G_i-N_i(\mu_i, \sigma_i)$ of mean μ_i and covariance σ_i with weight π_i, $i\in\{1, ..., K\}$, i.e.

$$f(p) = \sum_{i=1}^{K} \pi_i G_i(p; \mu_i, \sigma_i) \tag{2}$$

where π_i sum up to 1. Let $C_i \subset D$ be the cluster i such that $\bigcup_{i=1}^{K} C_i = D$. Then the objective of GMM is to classify D into $C_1, ..., C_K$.

The EM algorithm is one of the general solutions to acquire parameters (μ, σ, π) for GMM and it can be divided into two step: E-step and M-step. More details are shown in Ref. [23].

In E-step, the main task is to calculate the posterior probability of the k-th Gaussian distribution N_k by randomly setting parameters (μ_k, σ_k, π_k), $k \in \{1, ..., K\}$. After that, to each pixel p, the generative probability from N_k can be described as

$$P_k(p) = \frac{\pi_k N_k(p|\mu_k, \sigma_k)}{\sum_{k=1}^{K} \pi_k N_k(p|\mu_k, \sigma_k)} \tag{3}$$

In the M-step, denoting rc as the number of p in D, we can re-estimate the parameters (μ_k, σ_k) with the results P_k and p:

$$\mu_k = \frac{1}{rc} \sum_{x=1}^{r} \sum_{y=1}^{c} P_k(p) \cdot p \tag{4}$$

$$\sigma_k = \frac{1}{rc} \sum_{x=1}^{r} \sum_{y=1}^{c} P_k(p) \cdot ||p - \mu_k||^2 \tag{5}$$

and update the weight π_k of the k-th distribution as

$$\pi_k = \frac{1}{rc} \sum_{x=1}^{r} \sum_{y=1}^{c} P_k(p) \tag{6}$$

Finally, alternating the E-step and M-step until the value of the likelihood function converges and these updated parameters (μ, σ, π) are used in the GMM to classify D.

The random mean, covariance and weight will increase the computational cost. Our improvement is to apply K-means++ to approximate the parameters (μ, σ, π) to restrain the impact of randomness [24]; a description of the algorithm is described in Table 1.

Table 1. Initializing the parameters for GMM-EM by K-means++

Algorithm 1. Using K-Means++ to initialize the parameters for GMM-EM

Input: The $I|_\Omega$, number of cluster k, maximum iteration θ and minimum error η.

Output: Classified clusters $C_1, ..., C_k$

Initialization: Randomly select a point from the input data and set as the first cluster center (x_0, y_0, z_0). Initialize iteration λ by 0 and error ε by infinity.

Classification:

Loop: for $n = 1 : L$ **do**

(1) For each slice $I_n|_{\Omega_n}$, calculate its total distance to the first cluster center:

$$D_0 = \sum_n^L \sum_c \sum_r \sqrt[2]{(x - x_0)^2 + (y - y_0)^2 + (n - z_0)^2}$$

where (x, y, n) is the pixel of $I|_\Omega$ and $(x, y) \in \Omega_n$.

(2) Randomly select value from 0 to D_0 which set as D_1, and calculate the distance D_2. When $D_2 \geq D_1$, this pixel is the new cluster center.

(3) Repeat 1 and 2 until k cluster centers are selected.

(4) Use the k initial cluster centers to run the standard K-means algorithm to form k clusters.

(5) Calculate mean μ, covariance σ and proportion π of each cluster.

End for

Do:

(1) Calculate probability P_k in E-step by parameters (μ, σ, π) in k cluster.

(2) Update parameters (μ, σ, π) and ε by the formulations in M-step .

(3) Assign points to their categories by updated parameters (μ, σ, π) in GMM to form $C_1, ..., C_k$.

While $\lambda < \theta$ **or** $\varepsilon > \eta$.

Exportation: Classified clusters $C_1, ..., C_k$

After applying the improved GMM-EM, the $I|_\Omega$ is divided into two categories which are the true liver area and the false liver area. Then we reserve the true liver area and draw its rim. Therefore, we not only gain an accurate Ω but also solve the leakage problem. The final result is shown in Fig. 7.

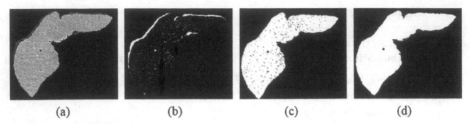

(a)   (b)   (c)   (d)

Fig. 7. The final result of improved GMM-EM. (a) A slice of the $I|_\Omega$, (b) the category of false liver area, (c) the category of true liver area, (d) the true liver area after a fill-hole operation.

3   Experimental Results

In order to evaluate our proposed method, we sampled liver CT dataset from Sun Yat-Sen Univ. Affiliated Tumor Hospital anonymously. The dataset was comprised of tumor or non-tumor cases from 10 patients, including 6 non-tumor cases (01–06), 2 close tumors (07, 08), and 2 open tumors (09, 10), each of consisting of an average of 300 CT slices. Each abdominal CT series was in a resolution of 512×512 in scale with a thickness of 3 mm.

Besides, we had the contour results of liver drawn manually from clinicians so that we could apply the Dice Similarity Coefficient (DSC) to evaluate the accuracy of our method. For ground truth image A and the predicted image B, their DSC defined as $DSC(A, B) = 2|A \cap B|/(|A| + |B|)$. The DSC of value 0 meant there was no overlap between the segmented region and ground truth while the value 1 meant perfect segmentation. We also used classification criteria evaluation method, such as Intersection-over-Union (IoU) and Accuracy, to do more objective analysis, which defined as: $IoU = TP/(FP + TP + FN)$, $Accuracy = (TP + TN)/(TP + TN + FN + FP)$, where TP denoted the number of true positive pixels, TN denoted the number of true negative pixels, FP denoted the number of false positive pixels and FN denoted the number of false negative pixels.

Firstly, we compared the GMM-EM and the improved GMM-EM under the same $I|_{\Omega}$ in run time. Apparently, our improvement was effective on reducing computing time according to the statistics (Fig. 8). The improvement achieved 83 s in average while unimproved method cost 169.6 s in average.

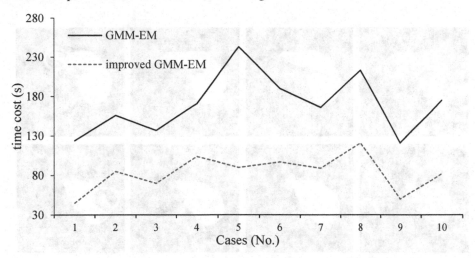

Fig. 8. The run time of the improved GMM-EM and the GMM-EM.

Also, we developed a comparative experiment upon the classification results from GMM-EM and improved GMM-EM, and the reference results were drawn by clinicians. We could infer that the improved GMM-EM performed better than the GMM-EM in accuracy from Table 2.

Table 2. Evaluation of improved GMM-EM and the GMM-EM.

Case No.	Improved GMM-EM		GMM-EM	
	IoU	Accuracy(%)	IoU	Accuracy(%)
1	0.94	99.32	0.93	99.04
2	0.94	99.58	0.90	98.80
3	0.90	99.47	0.89	98.77
4	0.93	99.61	0.93	99.04
5	0.92	99.52	0.92	99.00
6	0.91	99.44	0.90	99.13
7	0.82	86.71	0.80	86.03
8	0.81	87.16	0.80	87.01
9	0.80	86.17	0.79	85.97
10	0.79	85.40	0.78	85.28

Especially in dealing with redundant areas in the $I|_\Omega$, the improved GMM-EM reserved more features than the GMM-EM, which could gain liver contour accurately. The red circle denoted to the redundant area and the blue one was the failure. Both of the results had done the fill-hole operation.

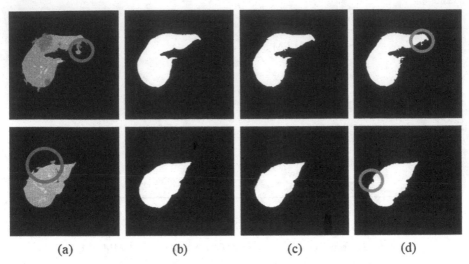

(a)   (b)   (c)   (d)

Fig. 9. The classification results of the improved GMM-EM and the GMM-EM. (a) A slice of the $I|_\Omega$, (b) a slice of the reference results, (c) the classification result of the improved GMM-EM, (d) the classification result of the GMM-EM.

We noticed that Ina [25] developed a method comprised of level set and K-mean on the liver shape segmentation. The essential idea of this method is to classify liver CT into 4 clusters and to draw the liver contour from those clusters. Also, Pankaj *et al.* [26] proposed a similar hybrid method to do hemorrhage segmentation, which consists of fuzzy c-mean (FCM) and a modified version of distance regularize level set evolution (MDRLSE). It applies FCM to do classification on brain CT and selects relative cluster as an initialization for MDRLSE to process hemorrhage area, which reduces the number of iterations in level set.

In order to figure out the performance of our method, we conduct a comparative experiment with the above mentioned methods. All of them are conducted on the same dataset and circumstances. See Table 3 for the evaluation. The performance of ours in segmenting the non-tumor liver sequence is better than the others. However, due to the large difference of the gradient between the tumor and the liver parenchyma, the accuracy drops suddenly when processing liver tumor series (Fig. 9).

The representative results are presented in Fig. 10. In the third horizontal group, being affected by the tumor area, the contour shrinks into the liver area, which lowers the accuracy of segmentation.

On the edge of the liver, the Ina's method is susceptible to the region of the similar gradient mutation and therefore fails to accurately segment the entire liver contour.

Table 3. Segmentation performances of different method.

No.	Our method			Ina's method [25]			Pankaj's method [26]		
	IoU	Acc(%)	DSC	IoU	Acc(%)	DSC	IoU	Acc(%)	DSC
1	0.94	99.32	0.977	0.83	97.22	0.974	0.91	98.99	0.974
2	0.94	99.58	0.985	0.89	99.27	0.938	0.90	99.39	0.955
3	0.90	99.47	0.975	0.84	97.90	0.951	0.89	99.04	0.964
4	0.93	99.61	0.967	0.90	99.32	0.955	0.91	99.48	0.964
5	0.92	99.52	0.988	0.88	98.60	0.947	0.92	99.50	0.973
6	0.91	99.44	0.977	0.87	98.86	0.939	0.88	99.11	0.950
7	0.82	86.71	0.922	0.76	80.43	0.902	0.79	85.90	0.916
8	0.81	87.16	0.932	0.72	78.96	0.895	0.77	86.24	0.909
9	0.80	86.17	0.943	0.77	80.97	0.911	0.77	84.55	0.932
10	0.79	85.40	0.917	0.70	74.28	0.860	0.74	80.71	0.894

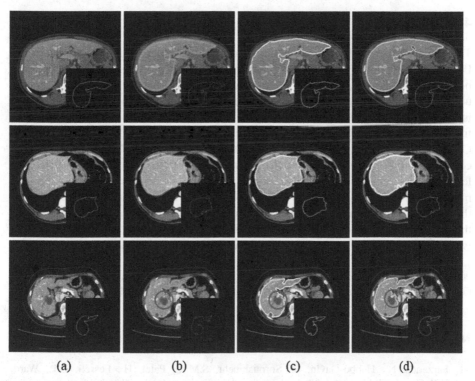

(a)   (b)   (c)   (d)

Fig. 10. The experimental results. (a) Original image and ground truth contour, (b) result of the Ina's method, (c) result of the Pankaj's method, (d) result of our method.

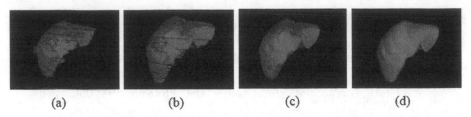

(a)   (b)   (c)   (d)

Fig. 11. The results in view of 3D. (a) The result of Ina's method, (b) the result of Pankaj's method, (c) our method result, (d) the ground truth result.

Although the Pankaj's method performs better than the Ina's method, it still cannot segment liver completely. Our method allows the contour front to propagate into abdominal wall and tumor area while detecting the entire liver shape, and then the improved GMM-EM algorithm is applied to intercept and remove the redundant contour, so as to solve the problem of leaking to adjacent structures.

In Fig. 11, we rebuild results above in 3D for objective comparison. Compared to the other methods, the result of ours is more reductive to the ground truth. The coarse boundary which leaks to other structures slightly in 2D, can cause a large error in 3D by the other methods.

4   Conclusion

This paper proposes a model combining level set method and classification algorithm. Firstly, the first time FMM is used for rough segmentation. The minimum bounding box algorithm is used to search the three-dimensional liver region so as to remove uninterested region and shorten the processing time. And then the second time FMM is further applied on the result of the first time FMM. Thirdly, we extract the finer liver region by using the binary form to search a corresponding region in the original CT sequence. Finally, the GMM-EM algorithm initialized by K-Means++ divides the corresponding region into two classes, the true liver region and the false liver region. The leaking edge problem is solved by our method. The experimental results show that, our method averagely achieves 0.923 in IoU and 0.978 in DSC evaluation on segmenting the tumor-free liver sequence, which performances better than the other methods. But the performance is poor when segmenting the tumor liver sequence. Next, in the future work, we will develop tumor segmentation algorithm to make up this shortcoming.

Acknowledgement. This work is supported by the Science and Technology Planning Project of Guangdong Province with grant numbers 2017B010110007 and 2017B010110015.

References

1. Farzaneh, N., Habbo-Gavin, S., Soroushmehr, S.M.R., Patel, H., Fessell, D.P., Ward, K.R., et al.: Atlas based 3D liver segmentation using adaptive thresholding and super-pixel approaches. In: 2017 IEEE International Conference on Acoustics, Speech and Signal Processing (ICASSP), pp. 1093–1097. IEEE, New Orleans (2017)

2. Lu, F., Wu, F., Hu, P., Peng, Z., Kong, D.: Automatic 3d liver location and segmentation via convolutional neural network and graph cut. Int. J. Comput. Assist. Radiol. Surg. **12**(2), 171–182 (2017)
3. Chen, Y., Wang, Z., Hu, J., Zhao, W.: The domain knowledge based graph-cut model for liver CT segmentation. Biomed. Signal Process. Control **7**, 591–598 (2012)
4. Huang, L., Weng, M., Shuai, H., Huang, Y., Sun, J., Gao, F.: Automatic liver segmentation from CT images using single-block linear detection. Biomed. Res. Int. **2016**, 1–11 (2016). Hindawi
5. Yang, X., et al.: Segmentation of liver and vessels from CT images and classification of liver segments for preoperative liver surgical planning in living donor liver transplantation. Comput. Meth. Programs Biomed. **158**, 41–52 (2018)
6. Xia, Y., Ji, Z., Zhang, Y.: Brain MRI image segmentation based on learning local variational Gaussian mixture models. Neurocomputing **204**, 189–197 (2016)
7. Osher, S., Sethian, J.A.: Fronts propagating with curvature-dependent speed: algorithms based on Hamilton Jacobi formulations. J. Comput. Phys. **79**, 12–49 (1988)
8. Sethian, J.A.: A fast marching level set method for monotonically advancing fronts. Proc. Natl. Acad. Sci. **93**(4), 1591–1595 (1996)
9. Ho, H., Bier, P., Sands, G., Hunter, P.: Cerebral artery segmentation with level set methods. In: Proceedings of Image and Vision Computing New Zealand, pp. 300–304. Hamilton, New Zealand, December 2007
10. Yan, J., Zhuang, T.: Applying improved fast marching method to endocardial boundary detection in echocardiographic images. Pattern Recogn. Lett. **24**(15), 2777–2784 (2003)
11. Campadelli, P., Casiraghi, E., Pratissoli, S.: Fully automatic segmentation of abdominal organs from CT images using fast marching methods. In: 21st IEEE International Symposium on Computer-Based Medical Systems, pp. 1–5. IEEE, Jyvaskyla, Finland (2008)
12. Lee, J., et al.: Efficient liver segmentation using a level-set method with optimal detection of the initial liver boundary from level-set speed images. Comput. Methods Programs Biomed. **88**, 26–38 (2007)
13. Ibáñez, L., et al.: The ITK Software Guide. 2nd ed., Kitware, Inc., Clifton Park (2005)
14. Yang, X., Yu, H.C., Choi, Y., Lee, W., Wang, B., Yang, J., et al.: A hybrid semi-automatic method for liver segmentation based on levelset methods using multiple seed points. Comput. Methods Programs Biomed. **113**, 69–79 (2014)
15. Ali, H., Elmogy, M., El-Daydamony, E., Atwan, A.: Multi-resolution MRI brain image segmentation based on morphological pyramid and fuzzy c-mean clustering. Arabian J. Sci. Eng. **40**(11), 3173–3185 (2015)
16. Campadelli, P., Casiraghi, E., Esposito, A.: Liver segmentation from computed tomography scans: a survey and a new algorithm. Artif. Intell. Med. **45**(2–3), 185–196 (2009)
17. Gómez, J.V., Álvarez, D., Garrido, S., Moreno, L.: Fast Methods for Eikonal equations: an experimental survey. IEEE Access **7**, 39005–39029 (2019)
18. Capozzoli, A., Curcio, C., Liseno, A., Savarese, S.: A comparison of Fast Marching, Fast Sweeping and Fast Iterative Methods for the solution of the eikonal equation. In: 21st Telecommunications Forum Telfor (TELFOR), pp. 685–688. IEEE, Belgrade (2013)
19. Breuß, M., Cristiani, E., Gwosdek, P., Vogel, O.: An adaptive domain-decomposition technique for parallelization of the fast marching method. Appl. Math. Comput. **218**(1), 32–44 (2011)
20. Forcadel, N., Guyader, C.L., Gout, C.: Generalized fast marching method: applications to image segmentation. Numer. Algorithms **48**, 189–211 (2008)
21. Baghdadi, M., Benamrane, N., Sais, L.: Fuzzy generalized fast marching method for 3d segmentation of brain structures. Int. J. Imaging Syst. Technol. **27**(3), 281–306 (2017)

22. Ascoli, Giorgio A., Hawrylycz, M., Ali, H., Khazanchi, D., Shi, Y. (eds.): BIH 2016. LNCS (LNAI), vol. 9919, pp. 52–60. Springer, Cham (2016). https://doi.org/10.1007/978-3-319-47103-7
23. Portela, N.M., Cavalcanti, G.D.C., Ren, T.I.: Semi-supervised clustering for MR brain image segmentation. Expert Syst. Appl. **41**(4), 1492–1497 (2014)
24. Kapoor, A., Singhal, A.: A comparative study of K-Means, K-Means++ and Fuzzy C-Means clustering algorithms. In: 3rd International Conference on Computational Intelligence & Communication Technology (CICT), pp. 1–6. IEEE, Palo Alto (2017)
25. Singh, I.: Segmentation of liver using hybrid K-means clustering and level set. Int. J. Adv. Res. Comput. Sci. Software Eng. **5**(8), 742–746 (2015)
26. Singh, P., Khanna, V., Kamal, M.: Hemorrhage segmentation by fuzzy c-mean with Modified Level Set on CT imaging. In: 5th International Conference on Signal Processing and Integrated Networks (SPIN), pp. 550–555. IEEE, Noida (2018)

Spatial Probabilistic Distribution Map Based 3D FCN for Visual Pathway Segmentation

Zhiqi Zhao[1], Danni Ai[1(✉)], Wenjie Li[1], Jingfan Fan[1], Hong Song[2], Yongtian Wang[1,3], and Jian Yang[1]

[1] School of Optics and Photonics, Beijing Engineering Research Center of Mixed Reality and Advanced Display, Beijing Institute of Technology, Beijing 100081, China
danni@bit.edu.cn
[2] School of Computer Science and Technology, Beijing Institute of Technology, Beijing 100081, China
[3] AICFVE of Beijing Film Academy, 4, Xitucheng Road, Haidian, Beijing 100088, China

Abstract. Image-guided surgery has become an important aid in sinus and skull base surgery. In the preoperative planning stage, vital structures, such as the visual pathway, must be segmented to guide the surgeon during surgery. However, owing to the elongated structure and low contrast in medical images, automatic segmentation of the visual pathway is challenging. This study proposed a novel method based on 3D fully convolutional network (FCN) combined with a spatial probabilistic distribution map (SPDM) for visual pathway segmentation in magnetic resonance imaging. Experimental results indicated that compared with the FCN that relied only on image intensity information, the introduction of an SPDM effectively overcame the problem of low contrast and blurry boundary and achieved better segmentation performance.

Keywords: Visual pathway segmentation · Optic nerve · 3D fully convolutional network · Spatial probabilistic distribution map

1 Introduction

At present, image-guided surgery (IGS) is important in sinus and skull base surgery. The anatomy of the sinus, skull base, and adjacent orbital area is complex and contains important neurological and vascular structures (e.g., visual pathway, internal carotid artery, etc.), and surgeons may inadvertently penetrate these critical structures during surgery and even cause severe complications. Therefore, the successful implementation of IGS requires the accurate delineation of vital structures in preoperative planning. The segmentation of these vital structures is often conducted by manual delineation, which is time-consuming and tedious for the operators. High inter-operator and intra-operator variability may also affect the reproducibility of the treatment plans. Hence, the automatic and precise segmentation of vital structures is highly desired.

The visual pathway is responsible for transmitting visual signals from the retina to the brain. It consists of (1) a paired optic nerve, also known as the cranial nerve II; (2)

© Springer Nature Switzerland AG 2019
Y. Zhao et al. (Eds.): ICIG 2019, LNCS 11902, pp. 509–518, 2019.
https://doi.org/10.1007/978-3-030-34110-7_42

the optic chiasm, which is the part of the visual pathway where nearly half the fibers from each optic nerve pair cross to the contralateral side; and (3) an optic tract pair. The optic tract is a continuation of the optic nerve that relays the information from the optic chiasm to the ipsilateral lateral geniculate body. Automatic segmentation of the visual pathway is challenging because of the elongated structure and low contrast in medical images. Some methods have been proposed in this area. These segmentation methods are mainly divided into three categories [1].

1. Atlas-based methods: For atlas-based methods, a transformation is computed between a reference image volume (i.e., atlas), where the structures of interest have been previously delineated, and the target image. Image registration is often used to compute such a transformation. This transformation is then used to project labels in the atlas onto the image volume to be segmented, thus identifying the structures of interest [2]. Multi-atlas-based methods use a database of atlas images and then fuse the projected labels with a specific label fusion strategy to produce the final segmentation result [3]. Atlas-based methods can segment the optic nerve and chiasm [4–6], with Dice similarity coefficients (DSCs) that range from 0.39 to 0.78, which proves that the methods are not robust.
2. Model-based methods: Based on either statistical shape or statistical appearance models, these methods typically produce closed surfaces that can effectively preserve anatomical topologies because the final segmentation results are constrained by the statistical models. Bekes et al. [7] proposed a semi-automated approach using a geometrical model for eyeballs, lenses, and optic nerve segmentation. However, the reproducibility of their approach was found to be less than 50%. Nobel et al. [8] proposed an atlas-navigated optimal medial axis and deformable model algorithm in which a statistical model and image registration are used to incorporate a priori local intensity and tubular shape information. Yang et al. [9] proposed a weighted partitioned active shape model (ASM) for visual pathway segmentation in magnetic resonance imaging (MRI) to improve the shape flexibility and robustness of ASMs to capture the visual pathway's local shape variability. Mansoor et al. [10] proposed a deep learning guided partitioned shape model for anterior visual pathway segmentation. Initially, this method exploited a marginal space deep learning concept-based stacked autoencoder to locate the anterior visual pathway. Then it combined a novel partitioned shape model with an appearance model to guide the anterior visual pathway segmentation.
3. Classification-based methods: Classification-based methods usually train the classifiers by using the features extracted from the neighborhood of each individual voxel. The trained classifiers are then used for voxel-wise tissue classification. The distinctive features and superior performance of the classifiers are integral to these methods. In 2015, Dolz et al. [2] proposed an approach based on support vector machine. The approach extracted features in 2D slices, including image intensity of the voxel and its neighborhood, gradient pixel value, voxel probability, and spatial information. In 2017, Dolz et al. [11] proposed a deep learning classification scheme based on augmented enhanced features to segment organs at risk on the optic region in patients with brain cancer. This method composed novel augmented enhanced

feature vectors that incorporate additional information about a voxel and its environment, such as contextual features, first-order statistics, and spectral measures. It also used stacked denoised auto-encoders as classifiers.

With the development of deep learning, convolutional neural networks (CNNs) in particular have been widely used in medical image segmentation and have achieved superior performance compared with previous methods. Moreover, the fully convolutional networks (FCNs) proposed by Long et al. [12] designed a dense training strategy to train a network on multiple or all voxels of a single volume per optimization step. Compared with classical machine learning algorithms, CNN does not require hand-crafted features for classification. Instead, the network is capable of learning the best features during the training process [1].

However, low tissue contrast or some artifacts in medical images may corrupt the true boundaries of the target tissues and adversely influence the precision of segmentation. Under these circumstances, CNNs cannot effectively extract discriminative features, leading to poor segmentation results. Unfortunately, this problem also exists in the visual pathway segmentation in MRI. Given the location and shape similarity of the target tissue between individuals, image intensity information can be combined with shape and position prior information to learn the neural network. On the basis of this hypothesis, we proposed a novel method based on 3D FCN combined with spatial probabilistic distribution map (SPDM) for visual pathway segmentation in MRI. SPDM reflects the probability that a voxel belongs to a given tissue, and it is obtained by summing all the manual labels contained in the training data set. The experimental results show that compared with the FCN relying only on image intensity information, the introduction of SPDM effectively overcomes the problem of low contrast and blurry boundary and achieves better segmentation performance. To the best of our knowledge, this deep learning method is the first to incorporate an SPDM into an FCN for visual pathway segmentation.

2   Method

Given the size of visual pathway accounts for a small proportion of the entire brain MRI, the task was divided into two stages, location of the region of interest (ROI) and target segmentation, to save computing resources and speed up the calculation. Figure 1 illustrates the entire scheme of the proposed method.

2.1   The Creation of SPDM and Extraction of ROI

SPDM was obtained by summing all the manual labels contained in the training data set. Specifically, each image in the training set was first registered to a selected reference image. Registration was implemented using the well-known and publicly available tool elastix [13]. Then, the transformation obtained by registration was used to project the attached label to the reference space. Finally, the registered binary labels were summed up to create an SPDM (Fig. 2). SPDM reflected the probability that a voxel belonged to a visual pathway, which was used to integrate shape and locality information into the

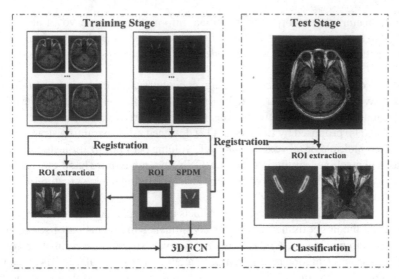

Fig. 1. The entire scheme of the proposed method

3D FCN training process, as described in the next section. SPDM also played another important role, which was to achieve the extraction of ROI. The starting and ending slice positions in the axial, coronal, and sagittal planes were calculated and expanded outward to form a bounding box $90 \times 54 \times 90$ in size. The morphological dilation operation was performed on the registered label to fill up the holes caused by registration. To eliminate the influence of very different images, we experimentally observed that the value of SPDM less than $2/n$ was set to 0, where n is the number of images in the training set.

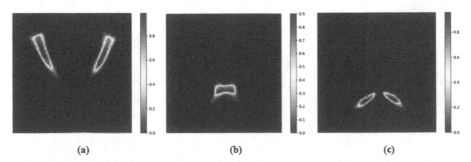

Fig. 2. The 2D representation of SPDM, which reflected the probability that a voxel belonged to a visual pathway. (a) optic nerves; (b) optic chiasm; (c) optic tracts.

2.2 3D FCN Architecture

The 3D FCN architecture used in this study was derived from Kamnitsas et al. [14] and Dolz et al. [15]. The baseline network architecture is shown in Fig. 3.

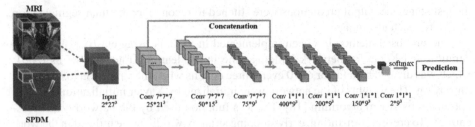

Fig. 3. The baseline 3D FCN architecture

The baseline network was composed of three convolutional layers with kernels of size $7 \times 7 \times 7$. Many studies have shown the benefits of using deeper network architectures. Following Simonyan et al. [16], the final network used three consecutive $3 \times 3 \times 3$ convolution kernels instead of the $7 \times 7 \times 7$ convolution kernel. Both cases have the same receptive field sizes. By using these smaller kernels, we obtained a deeper architecture that could learn a more discriminative hierarchy of features, with a reduced risk of overfitting. In addition, there were fewer parameters when smaller convolution kernels were used. Compared with CNN, FCN replaced the fully connected layer with $1 \times 1 \times 1$ convolution kernels, which allowed networks to be applied to images of arbitrary size. The dense training strategy enabled FCN to obtain predictions for multiple or all voxels in an image per step, thus avoiding redundant convolution and making the network more efficient. Each convolutional layer was followed by a PRelu nonlinear activation layer, and the final convolutional layer was followed by the Softmax function.

Furthermore, to use different levels of information, the network concatenated the feature maps of convolution layers at different stages (Fig. 3).

2.3 Experimental Details

After the SPDM was obtained, it was respectively registered to each image so that the SPDM and the image had one-to-one correspondence. At the same time, we obtained the ROI, including visual pathway, which removed most of the irrelevant information. Following the network of Dolz et al. [15], we obtained a network with the input size of $27 \times 27 \times 27$ and the network's output was the prediction of the input's central $9 \times 9 \times 9$ size patch. Thus, the volume data were cropped into $27 \times 27 \times 27$ size patches that corresponded to the central $9 \times 9 \times 9$ size labels. Image intensity information and SPDM were simultaneously fed into the neural network as two channels.

During the training stage, to alleviate the problem of class imbalance, we chose the target patches (patches that contain target voxels) and added the same number of background patches (all voxels belong to the background). However, owing to the intensity similarity between a few background patches and target patches, some voxels in the background patches may have been be misclassified as targets during the testing stage because not all background patches were sent to the network for training. The introduction of SPDM effectively solved this problem. For background patches, the value of SPDM was 0, meaning that the target did not appear in this spatial location. During the test stage, the output predictions were stitched to reconstruct the final segmentation results for each test image.

The proposed method has been implemented in Python, using elastix [13] for registration and Keras for network building. The initial learning rate was set as 0.001, which was divided by a factor of 10 every three epochs when the validation loss stopped improving. The weights of the network were initialized by Xavier initialization [17] and optimized by Adam algorithm [18]. The loss function used by the network was cross-entropy. To prevent over-fitting, early stopping strategy was likewise utilized in the work if no improvement arose in the validation loss after 10 epochs.

3   Results

MR 3T T1 brain images with voxel sizes of $1.0 \times 1.0 \times 1.0$ mm^3 were used in this experiment. A total of 93 images were provided by Beijing Tongren Hospital, 23 of which were used for testing. For each item of data, the ground truth for the visual pathway was manually delineated by radiologists. Intensity normalization was performed on the original image.

DSC was used as the quantitative evaluation metric, which reflects the overlap rate between the segmentation result and the ground truth. DSC is defined as follows:

$$DSC(A, B) = \frac{2|A \cap B|}{|A| + |B|} \tag{1}$$

where A and B represent the automatic segmentation result and the ground truth, respectively.

For the spatial distance-based metric, average symmetric surface distance (ASD) was used as another metric. ASD is defined as follows:

$$ASD(A, B) = \frac{\sum_{a \in S_A} d(a, S_B) + \sum_{b \in S_B} d(b, S_A)}{|S_A| + |S_B|} \tag{2}$$

$$d(a, S_B) = \min_{b \in S_B} (a - b) \tag{3}$$

where S_A and S_B represent the surface of the automatic segmentation result and the ground truth, respectively; $d(a, S_B)$ represents the shortest distance of an arbitrary point a on S_A to S_B; and $\|\cdot\|$ denotes the Euclidean distance.

Table 1 shows the quantitative analysis of the segmentation results under different methods, expressed as mean $\pm$ standard deviation. The text in bold indicates the best metrics. "FCN(MRI)" indicates that the network only learns image intensity information, and "FCN(SPDM)" indicates that only spatial probabilistic distribution information is learned. "Cascaded FCN" is a cascaded training strategy. On the basis of the previous FCN that relied only on MRI, the training set is sent to the network for prediction, in which the misclassified patches continue to be trained to fine-tune the network. Thus, the network can learn patches that are not easily discernible. "Our method" represents a combination of image intensity information and spatial probabilistic distribution information, which is the method proposed in this work.

Table 1. Quantitative analysis results of different methods

Methods	FCN(MRI)	Cascaded FCN	FCN(SPDM)	Our method
DSC(%)	82.92 ± 2.87	83.47 ± 3.62	68.58 ± 5.20	**84.89 ± 1.40**
ASD(mm)	0.94 ± 0.35	0.42 ± 0.08	0.68 ± 0.10	**0.37 ± 0.04**

Figure 4 shows the box plot of the DSC comparison results. The results of quantitative analysis indicate that FCN combined with SPDM achieves better performance and is more robust. Compared with the FCN that relied only on image intensity information, the introduction of spatial probability information in this paper has increased the DSC from (82.92 ± 2.87) % to (84.89 ± 1.40) %.

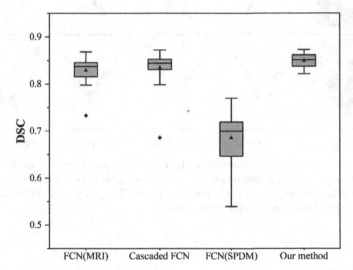

Fig. 4. The box plot of DSC comparison results

Figure 5 demonstrates the visual comparison of segmentation results for several cases of data. Each row represents the segmentation results of an example of MRI under different methods, in which the ground truth is represented by green and the automatic segmentation result is represented by red. The green curves in MRI outline the blurring boundary of the target. The segmentation results obtained by FCN that relied only on image intensity information have noise and breakage. Although the cascaded training strategy can suppress noise, it cannot identify the blurring boundary of the target; worse outcomes are possible as well. SPDM provides a complete shape of the visual pathway but deviates from the ground truth because of a few variations between individuals. To a certain extent, learning only with SPDM can be a type of multi-atlas-based segmentation, in which a network is used to determine the label fusion strategy. The obtained DSC also confirmed that it is similar to multi-atlas-based methods. Owing to the integration of shape and locality information, FCN combined with SPDM effectively solved the problem of background misclassification and discontinuity of segmentation results caused by low contrast.

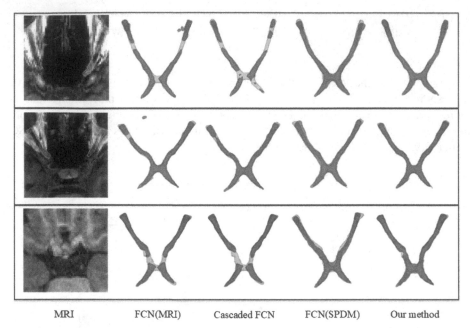

MRI   FCN(MRI)   Cascaded FCN   FCN(SPDM)   Our method

Fig. 5. Visual comparison of segmentation results. Each row represents the segmentation results of an example of MRI under different methods, in which the ground truth is represented by green and the automatic segmentation result is represented by red. The green curves in MRI outline the blurring boundary of the target. (Color figure online)

4 Conclusion

This study proposed a novel method based on 3D FCN combined with SPDM for visual pathway segmentation in MRI. SPDM reflects the probability that a voxel belongs to a given tissue and preserves the shape and locality information of the target. Experimental results show that compared with the FCN relying only on image intensity information, the introduction of SPDM effectively overcame the problem of background misclassification and discontinuity of segmentation results caused by low contrast. FCN combined with SPDM achieves improved segmentation performance, in which DSC is improved from $(82.92 \pm 2.87)\%$ to $(84.89 \pm 1.40)\%$.

Considering the similarity in the anatomy and location of tissues in medical images, useful shape and locality priori information may be provided for tissue segmentation. CNNs can automatically extract features from an image but may fail if the image is blurred. The experimental results in this work demonstrated that the combination of traditional shape and location information and FCN is promising. In the future, we will try to apply the approach to other tissue segmentation tasks that encounter similar problems.

Acknowledgments. This work was supported by the National Key Research and Development Program of China (2017YFC0112000), National Science and Technology Major Project of China (2018ZX10723-204-008), and the National Science Foundation Program of China (61672099, 61527827, 61771056).

References

1. Ren, X., et al.: Interleaved 3D-CNNs for joint segmentation of small-volume structures in head and neck CT images. Med. Phys. **45**(5), 2063–2075 (2018)
2. Dolz, J., Leroy, H.A., Reyns, N., Massoptier, L., Vermandel, M.: A fast and fully automated approach to segment optic nerves on MRI and its application to radiosurgery. In: IEEE International Symposium on Biomedical Imaging, pp. 1102–1105. IEEE, New York (2015)
3. Iglesias, J.E., Sabuncu, M.R.: Multi-atlas segmentation of biomedical images: a survey. Med. Image Anal. **24**(1), 205–219 (2015)
4. Gensheimer, M., Cmelak, A., Niermann, K., Dawant, B.M.: Automatic delineation of the optic nerves and chiasm on CT images. Medical Imaging, p. 10. SPIE, San Diego (2007)
5. Asman, A.J., DeLisi, M.P., Mawn, L.A., Galloway, R.L., Landman, B.A.: Robust non-local multi-atlas segmentation of the optic nerve. Medical Imaging 2013: Image Processing, pp. 86691L. International Society for Optics and Photonics (2013)
6. Harrigan, R.L., et al.: Robust optic nerve segmentation on clinically acquired computed tomography. J. Med. Imaging **1**(3), 034006 (2014)
7. Bekes, G., Mate, E., Nyul, L.G., Kuba, A., Fidrich, M.: Geometrical model-based segmentation of the organs of sight on CT images. Med. Phys. **35**(2), 735–743 (2008)
8. Noble, J.H., Dawant, B.M.: An atlas-navigated optimal medial axis and deformable model algorithm (NOMAD) for the segmentation of the optic nerves and chiasm in MR and CT images. Med. Image Anal. **15**(6), 877–884 (2011)
9. Yang, X., et al.: Weighted partitioned active shape model for optic pathway segmentation in MRI. In: Linguraru, M.G., et al. (eds.) CLIP 2014. LNCS, vol. 8680, pp. 109–117. Springer, Cham (2014). https://doi.org/10.1007/978-3-319-13909-8_14
10. Mansoor, A., et al.: Deep learning guided partitioned shape model for anterior visual pathway segmentation. IEEE Trans. Med. Imaging **35**(8), 1856–1865 (2016)
11. Dolz, J., et al.: A deep learning classification scheme based on augmented-enhanced features to segment organs at risk on the optic region in brain cancer patients (2017)
12. Long, J., Shelhamer, E., Darrell, T.: Fully convolutional networks for semantic segmentation. In: Proceedings of the IEEE Conference on Computer Vision and Pattern Recognition, pp. 3431–3440. IEEE, Boston (2015)
13. Klein, S., Staring, M., Murphy, K., Viergever, M.A., Pluim, J.P.: elastix: a toolbox for intensity-based medical image registration. IEEE Trans. Med. Imaging **29**(1), 196–205 (2010)
14. Kamnitsas, K., et al.: Efficient multi-scale 3D CNN with fully connected CRF for accurate brain lesion segmentation. Med. Image Anal. **36**, 61–78 (2017)
15. Dolz, J., Desrosiers, C., Ben Ayed, I.: 3D fully convolutional networks for subcortical segmentation in MRI: a large-scale study. Neuroimage **170**, 456–470 (2018)
16. Simonyan, K., Zisserman, A.: Very deep convolutional networks for large-scale image recognition. Comput. Sci. (2014)

17. Glorot, X., Bengio, Y.: Understanding the difficulty of training deep feedforward neural networks. In: Proceedings of the Thirteenth International Conference on Artificial Intelligence and Statistics, pp. 249–256 (2010)
18. Kingma, D.P., Ba, J.: Adam: a method for stochastic optimization. arXiv preprint arXiv:1412. 6980 (2014)

Automatic Image Annotation and Deep Learning for Tooth CT Image Segmentation

Miao Gou[1], Yunbo Rao[1(✉)], Minglu Zhang[1], Jianxun Sun[2], and Keyang Cheng[3]

[1] School of Information and Software Engineering, University of Electronic Science and Technology of China, Chengdu 610054, Sichuan, People's Republic of China
1003632332@qq.com, raoyb@uestc.edu.cn,
2016220302032@std.uestc.edu.cn
[2] West China School of Stomatology, Sichuan University, Chengdu 610041, Sichuan, People's Republic of China
jxsun@scu.edu.cn
[3] School of Computer Science and Telecommunications Engineering, Jiangsu University, Zhenjiang 212013, People's Republic of China
kycheng@ujs.edu.cn

Abstract. Recently, convolutional networks show great ability dealing with the problem of biomedical imaging, such as tooth image segmentation. In this paper, we propose a novel tooth-based computer tomography (CT) image segmentation approach that integrates U-Net with a level set model. Compared with a single U-Net, our method uses the level set method to build the mask for CT images. This allows automatic annotation in our model, improving the efficiency on image segmentation. Furthermore, we make some changes to the origin U-Net structure for the feasibility to images of any sizes. Using the combination of these two models, our integrated method shows its superiority dealing with problems on tooth image segmentation, outperforming the U-Net or the level set model alone.

Keywords: Image segmentation · Automation image annotation · Level set · U-Net · Convolutional networks

1 Introduction

Image segmentation has been one of the most essential tasks in biomedical imaging research. Biomedical image segmentation can be used to support medical diagnosis, displaying the real condition on patients. Here have two limitations of the traditional method. (1) due to the complexity of physical structure for human body, especially for tooth's image segmentation, building the mask for every image manually is time-consuming and tedious. (2) the number of labelled for image segmentation is also much smaller than other types on the internet. In this paper, our main aim is using the unlabeled data as the training set for tooth's image segmentation.

Some work has been done for achieving unlabeled data in image segmentation. Lin et al. [1] proposed a method using scribbles to annotate images, and train convolutional networks for semantic segmentation supervised by scribbles. That enables researchers

© Springer Nature Switzerland AG 2019
Y. Zhao et al. (Eds.): ICIG 2019, LNCS 11902, pp. 519–528, 2019.
https://doi.org/10.1007/978-3-030-34110-7_43

annotate training set in more efficient way. Pathak et al. [2] presented an approach to learn a dense pixel-wise labeling from image-level tags. So, image-level tags can be effectively used by Convolutional Neural Network (CNN) classifier to transfer them into predicted labels. Papandreou et al. [3] develop expectation-maximization methods for semantic image segmentation under these weakly supervised or semi-supervised settings. This deep convolutional network performs successfully even with significantly less annotation effort. However, these networks still need researchers to label every image more or less.

The level set method is popular in image segmentation. The traditional method represented the interface as the level-set of a higher dimensional function [4, 5]. The advantage of implicit representation of a moving front in level set method is its ability to naturally handle changes in topology. Li et al. [6] proposed distance regularized level set evolution as an edge-based active contour model. Though it can be implemented by a simpler and more efficient numerical scheme than conventional level set methods, it relies on good contour initialization. Recently, Allaire et al. [7] proposed a framework to handle geometric constraints related to local thickness. Since the initial guesses and the specific treatment of the constraints are crucial for some topological changes, the resulting shapes are strongly dependent on these. Yang et al. [8] embedded a Markov random field energy function to the conventional level set energy function. This method is robust against various kinds of noised. Morar et al. [9] proposed active contour model without edges. It has better noise immunity, and widely been spread widely now. The level set method has been widely used for tooth segmentation in biomedical imaging research due to its superiority dealing with topological changes and contour propagation, such as [10, 11]. However, all these methods need to iterate hundreds of times only for a single image segmentation.

To solve these problems, we adopt level set method for the automatic segmentation of tooth structure from CT image data, which use the curve evolution, the initial curve converges to the image boundary and the output is used as image annotation. In our work, we adopt some manual annotations as part of our training dataset to ensure the accuracy. And then, we combine these datasets and our new U-Net model to extract the feature map of the CT images, constructing the neural network, updating the weight of the model through iteration to obtain the optimal model. The final result of our method shows proved efficiency and accurate segmentation.

2 Methods

An overview of the proposed U-Net and Level-set framework is shown in Fig. 1. Automatic image annotation is pre-trained with a small dataset with labels. Then, we use the data enhancement strategy to better utilize the data and expand the dataset. A new level set method is inputted into our model for processing the dataset. Last, a new U-Net constitutes the next part of our method is proposed as training the model.

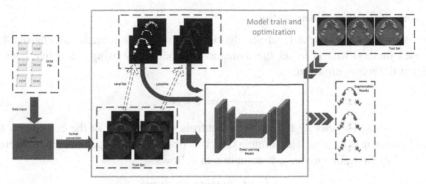

Fig. 1. The framework of our proposed method. The blue dotted box represents the input and output files, it is the pre-processing of DICOM images (Left). After conversion, the model is trained by our deep learning model, the automatic annotation using level set and manual annotation are also included in this part (Middle). The final result (Lower right) is tested by the test set (Upper right) (Color figure online)

2.1 Dataset

In this paper, we use the dataset from West China School of Stomatology. This dataset contains 5 group of complete scan results, 401 original CT images of tooth in total. Since the original DICOM image contains many other useless information for tooth segmentation, we filter out header data for communication and then transfer it into PNG images and converting the 16-bit int data to the 8-bit unit data. Besides, the Hounsfield unit (HU) of the annotated image in the dataset is [0, 1], and that range of value in our model is not obvious to identify. So, we modified the total range of the HU value in PNG image into [0, 255], contrasting the CT scanned tooth image and its mask. The transferred images and their masks are shown in Fig. 2.

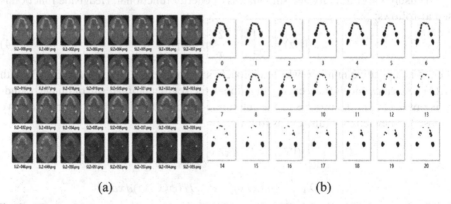

(a)   (b)

Fig. 2. The tooth images and image masks. (a) the sample of tooth images, (b) the sample of tooth masks

2.2 Automatic Image Annotation

In our work, we propose a level set algorithm to realize automatic annotation. The proposed method first is to set the dynamic parameters by using the active contour model of the following form:

$$\frac{\partial C(s, t)}{\partial t} = F * N \tag{1}$$

where F means the velocity function that controls the evolution of the curve, N is the normal vector in the curve. The formula C (s, t) is rewritten into a zero level set function φ (x, y, t), the initialization of φ is definition as follows:

$$\phi = \begin{cases} -d, & \text{outside the curve} \\ 0, & \text{on the curve} \\ +d, & \text{inside the curve} \end{cases} \tag{2}$$

where d defines the shortest distance from the point to the curve. The level set model has the energy function:

$$E = \mu \int_{\Omega} (|\nabla \phi| - 1)^2 dx dy + \lambda_1 \int_{inside(c)} |\mu_0(x, y) - c_1|^2 dx dy$$
$$+ \lambda_2 \int_{outside(c)} |\mu_0(x, y) - c_2|^2 dx dy \tag{3}$$

Ω is the whole image domain, c_1 denotes the gray mean inside the evolution curve, c_2 denotes the gray mean outside the evolution curve, μ, λ_1, λ_2 are constants. Where the $\mu \int_{\Omega} (|\nabla \phi| - 1)^2 dx dy$ is the distance constraint term, it keeps the level set function consistent with the sign distance function in the evolution process. The $\lambda_1 \int_{inside(c)} |\mu_0(x, y) - c_1|^2 dx dy$ and $\lambda_2 \int_{outside(c)} |\mu_0(x, y) - c_2|^2 dx dy$ defines the external energy term, they represent the difference of gray mean value of each region inside and outside evolutionary curve respectively.

To ensure the continuity and smoothness of energy functional, Heaviside function is used as follows:

$$H(z) = \frac{1}{2} \left[1 + \frac{2}{\pi} \arctan \left(\frac{z}{\varepsilon} \right) \right] \tag{4}$$

where ε is a positive number, which approaches 0. Joint energy functional Eq. (3) with Eq. (4), and calculate the new energy functional, the segmentation result of image boundary is obtained. On the process of the automatic annotation of the level set method, we propose the new energy function as follows:

$$E = \mu \int_{\Omega} (|\nabla \phi| - 1)^2 dx dy$$
$$+ \lambda_1 \int_{\Omega} |\mu_0(x, y) - c_1|^2 H(\phi(x, y)) dx dy$$
$$+ \lambda_2 \int_{\Omega} |\mu_0(x, y) - c_2|^2 H(\phi(x, y)) dx dy \tag{5}$$

These paramaters $\lambda 1$, $\lambda 2$, $c1$, $c2$ are consistent with formula (3). The final results of automatic image annotation prove our superiority and are shown in Fig. 3.

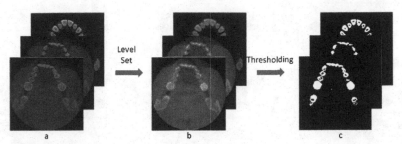

Fig. 3. The result of image boundary and image segmentation of level set method. (a) The original tooth CT images, (b) After 500 curve evolution results using level set, (c) automatic image annotation result.

2.3 Model Training and Optimization

Referring to the classical deep convolution network model U-Net [12–14], we build a new U-Net architecture for tooth segmentation in our work. The architecture consists of a contracting path for classification and an expanding path for precise localization. In this paper, the network is composed of 5 groups of nodes in the down-sampling stage, each follows two 3*3 convolutional layers and one 2*2 max pooling layer. In the up-sampling stage, each node contains two 3*3 convolutional layers and one 2*2 convolutional layer. The proposed method is shown Algorithm 1:

Algorithm 1   Model train stage method
Input : tooth images and annotation tooth CT images;
Ouput :
Step 1: Model weight initialization;
Step 2: Forward propagation and weighting operations using image data;
Step 3: Using loss function to compare image and mask weights;
Step 4: update weight and loss for back propagation: if the loss is small enough: save the model weight, if not: go to step 2;
Step 5: Optimal model obtained by iteration.

In this paper, our proposed new U-Net has 30 layers in total for model training. The network architecture is shown in Fig. 4.

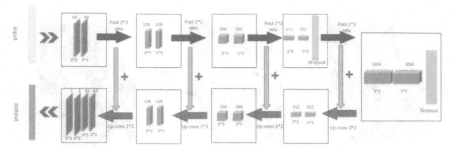

Fig. 4. The architecture of our proposed new U-Net (30 layers). The blue cuboid represents a 3*3 convolution layer, the cyan rectangle is one dropout layer, the blue arrow represents a 2*2 max pooling layer, the brown arrow represents a 2*2 deconvolution layer, pink arrows represent the clipping supplement of high-level information. (Color figure online)

3   Experiments and Analysis

Our method was evaluated with the dataset from West China School of Stomatology. After screening and pre-processing, we get 400 valid images. In this paper, these images are divided to training set and validation set according to the ratio of 3:1, training the deep network and test the prediction results, respectively. The final evolution curve is binarized, where the internal gray value of the curve is set to 255, the external gray value of the curve is set to 0. The marked pictures are obtained. The related constant parameters of the deep network are shown as follows Table 1:

Table 1. Deep network parameters (ES = evolutionary step)

Parameter	λ_1	λ_2	μ	ES	Iterations
Value (1)	1	1	0.02	0.5	500
Value (2)	0.5	2	0.02	1	500
Value (3)	1	1	0.02	0.5	800

Here, our experiment has been using three group parameters, $\lambda 1$ controls the influence of the internal energy term in the control curve for evolution results. $\lambda 2$ controls the influence of the external energy term in the control curve for evolution results. μ weakens the deviation between φ function and sign distance function while not affecting the evolutionary process. Evolutionary step determines the minimum step of curve evolution. Experiments show the inconformity between $\lambda 1$ and $\lambda 2$ can result in big error for curve convergence. And the target value of tooth size should not be too large. In our experiment, 500 iterations can complete the convergence, and 800 times of iterations can't improve the result. Ultimately, we choose Value (1) for the parameters.

We train the network under the keras framework for its wide and applicability for fast experimentation. Our experiment platform chooses NVIDIA GeForce GTX 1070 for its good performance in image processing and model train. About artificial image annotations, LabelMe software is used to annotate tooth images for its batch convert support. In order to enough dataset training, in our work also selects several methods for data enhancement, e.g. mirroring, rotating, moving, and flip.

During training, the batch size is set 300, and the maximum number of epochs is set 1. To ensure the accuracy of the gradient descent, and diminish the effect of noise, we introduce adaptive moment estimation (Adam) [15] into our method instead of stochastic gradient descent (SGD), and the learning rate is adjusted to 0.01. The best model on the validation set was stored and used for evaluations. To determine the proximity between the actual output and the expected output, the cross-entropy loss function is used in our experiment as follows:

$$loss = - \sum\nolimits_{i=1}^{n} \hat{y}_i \, log y_i + \left(1 - \hat{y}_i\right) \log\left(1 - \hat{y}_i\right) \qquad (6)$$

$$\frac{\partial loss}{\partial y} = - \sum\nolimits_{i=1}^{n} \frac{\hat{y}_i}{y_i} - \frac{1 - \hat{y}_i}{1 - y_i} \qquad (7)$$

Every model training takes about 60 s in our hardware platform, predicted results of the model are shown in Fig. 5.

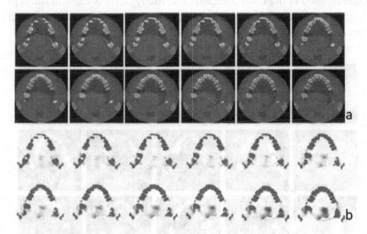

Fig. 5. The experimental results using our method. (a) the test original CT tooth image, (b) predicted results of our model.

To illustrate the precision of this method, we check the model results against real segmentation, and define the one which has more than 90% of the overlap to be success-fully segmented, the result is shown in Fig. 6. On the left of the black line is the result of successful segmentation. On the right side of the black line is an example of failure. In the right image, there are redundant parts in the segmentation result, e.g. excess teeth, noise shadow.

All experiences are performed on 2D slices. To show the superiority of our integrated U-Net and level-set method, we also compare the traditional method (watershed method [13], chan-vese model [16], and graph cut method [17]) with our method, it can be shown

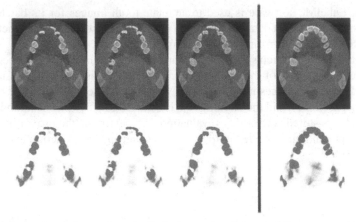

Fig. 6. Analysis of experimental results. Left: the results of successfully segmented tooth image, Right: the results of unsuccessfully segmented tooth image

in Fig. 7. From Fig. 7, we can find the graph cut method is least affected by noise and the watershed method is the most affected. Too many defects exist in the segmentation result of chan-vese model. Our method has clear segmentation result, no defect and little noise effect.

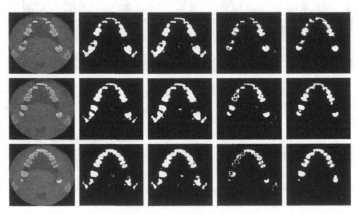

Fig. 7. Segmentation results with our method. (a) the original image, (b) our method, (c) watershed method [13], (d) chan-vese model [16], (e) graph cut method [17].

In order to performance automatic annotation and deep network well for tooth image segmentation, we also compare the traditional method and our method from Accuracy, artificial participation of image annotation, time-consuming. Table 2 illustrates that the graph cut method has the highest accuracy. Graph cut only processes one image at a time, and each processing requires a lot of manual delimitation of the segmentation area, it is difficult to automate, accurate segmentation of each graph requires artificial drawing of 3–4 lines, or even more. The accuracy of chan-vese model is close to our method, but it takes nearly 118 s to calculate an image, our method only takes about 10 s. The numerical calculation of chan-vese model is too large and it needs many iterations, so its time-consuming problem is very serious.

Table 2. Result analysis of the traditional methods and our method (MP = manual participation, TC = time-consuming)

Comparisons method	Accuracy	MP	TC (unit: second)
Watershed [13]	50.2%	Yes	23
Chan-Vese [16]	65.3%	No	118
Graph cut [17]	70.1%	Yes	27
Our method	66.7%	No	10

4 Conclusion

In this paper, a novel technique for integrating level set with a new U-Net is presented. This technique has two significant advantages which are shown in our work. First, the proposed method has better performance than the U-Net or level set alone. Second, introducing the level set method into this network enables unlabeled data to be used in our experiment and reaches semi-supervised learning. Although mask making and model training may take some time, our method can segment the tooth in very little time after the training of the model. In future work, as the medical environment always need digital 3D modeling, we will work on the issues dealing with 3D binary segmentation.

Acknowledgments. This work was supported in part by the Science and Technology Service Industry project of Sichuan under 2019GFW126, Key R&D project of Sichuan under 2019ZDYF2790.

References

1. Lin, D., Dai, J.F., Jia, J.Y.: ScribbleSup: scribble-supervised convolutional networks for semantic segmentation. In: the IEEE Conference on Computer Vision and Pattern Recognition (CVPR), Las Vegas, pp. 3159–3167 (2016)
2. Pathak, D., Krahenbuhl, P., Darrell, T.: Constrained convolutional neural networks for weakly supervised segmentation. In: The IEEE International Conference on Computer Vision (ICCV), Centro Parque Convention Center in Santiago, Chile, pp. 1796–1804 (2015)
3. Papandreou, G., Chen, L.C., Murphy, K.P., Yuille, A.L.: Weakly-and semi-supervised learning of a deep convolutional network for semantic image segmentation. In: The IEEE International Conference on Computer Vision (ICCV), Centro Parque Convention Center in Santiago, Chile, pp. 1742–1750 (2015)

4. Haslhofer, R.: Singularities of mean convex level set flow in general ambient manifolds. Adv. Math. **329**, 1137–1155 (2018)
5. Gibouab, F., Fedkiwc, R., Osher, S.: A review of level-set methods and some recent applications. J. Comput. Phys. **353**, 82–109 (2018)
6. Li, C.M., Xu, C.Y.: Distance regularized level set evolution and its application to image segmentation. IEEE Trans. Image Process. **19**(12), 3243–3254 (2010)
7. Allaire, G., Jouve, F., Michailidis, G.: Thickness control in structural optimization via a level set method. Struct. Multidisc. Optim. **53**, 1349–1382 (2016)
8. Yang, X., Gao, X.B., Tao, D.C., Li, X.L., Li, J.: An efficient MRF embedded level set method for image segmentation. IEEE Trans. Image Process. **24**, 9–21 (2014)
9. Morar, A., Moldoveanu, F., Gröller, E.: Image segmentation based on active contours without edges. In: IEEE 8th International Conference on Intelligent Computer Communication and Processing, Cluj-Napoca, pp. 213–220 (2012)
10. Gan, Y., Xia, Z., Xiong, J., Zhao, Q., Hu, Y., Zhang, J.: Toward accurate tooth segmentation from computed tomography images using a hybrid level set model. Med. Phys. **42**(1), 14–27 (2015)
11. Wang, L., Li, S., Chen, R., Liu, S.Y., Chen, J.C.: A segmentation and classification scheme for single tooth in micro CT images based on 3D level set and K-means++. Comput. Med. Imaging Graph. **57**, 19–28 (2017)
12. Ronneberger, O., Fischer, P., Brox, T.: U-net: convolutional networks for biomedical image segmentation. In: Navab, N., Hornegger, J., Wells, W.M., Frangi, A.F. (eds.) MICCAI 2015. LNCS, vol. 9351, pp. 234–241. Springer, Cham (2015). https://doi.org/10.1007/978-3-319-24574-4_28
13. Lu, S., Wang, S., Zhang, Y.: A note on the marker-based watershed method for X-ray image segmentation. Comput. Methods Program. Biomed. **141**, 1–2 (2017)
14. Li, H.W., Andrii, Z.G., Bjoern, M.: Automatic brain structures segmentation using deep residual dilated U-net. arXiv preprint arXiv:1811.04312 (2018)
15. Kingma, D.P., Ba, J.: Adam: a method for stochastic optimization. arXiv preprint arXiv:1412.6980 (2014)
16. Jung, M.Y., Chan, T.F., Vese, L.A.: Nonlocal Mumford-Shah regularizes for color image restoration. IEEE Trans. Image Process. **20**, 1583–1598 (2011)
17. Ju, W., Xiang, D., Zhang, B.: Random walk and graph cut for co-segmentation of lung tumor on PET-CT Images. IEEE Trans. Image Process. **24**, 5854–5867 (2015)

FU-Net: Multi-class Image Segmentation Using Feedback Weighted U-Net

Mina Jafari[1]([✉]), Ruizhe Li[1], Yue Xing[2], Dorothee Auer[2], Susan Francis[3], Jonathan Garibaldi[1], and Xin Chen[1]

[1] School of Computer Science, University of Nottingham, Nottingham, UK
Mina.jafari@nottingham.ac.uk
[2] School of Medicine, University of Nottingham, Nottingham, UK
[3] Sir Peter Mansfield Imaging Centre, University of Nottingham, Nottingham, UK

Abstract. In this paper, we present a generic deep convolutional neural network (DCNN) for multi-class image segmentation. It is based on a well-established supervised end-to-end DCNN model, known as U-net. U-net is firstly modified by adding widely used batch normalization and residual block (named as BRU-net) to improve the efficiency of model training. Based on BRU-net, we further introduce a dynamically weighted cross-entropy loss function. The weighting scheme is calculated based on the pixel-wise prediction accuracy during the training process. Assigning higher weights to pixels with lower segmentation accuracies enables the network to learn more from poorly predicted image regions. Our method is named as feedback weighted U-net (FU-net). We have evaluated our method based on T1-weighted brain MRI for the segmentation of midbrain and substantia nigra, where the number of pixels in each class is extremely unbalanced to each other. Based on the dice coefficient measurement, our proposed FU-net has outperformed BRU-net and U-net with statistical significance, especially when only a small number of training examples are available. The code is publicly available in GitHub (GitHub link: https://github.com/MinaJf/FU-net).

Keywords: Convolutional neural network · Medical image segmentation · U-net · Weighted cross entropy

1 Introduction

Image segmentation is a fundamental and crucial step in many image analysis tasks. In this paper, we focus on medical applications. From classical image segmentation methods (e.g. region growing) to more robust methods (e.g. level-set [1] and graph-cut [2]), various techniques have been proposed to achieve automatic image segmentation in a wide range of clinical problems. More recently, machine learning based methods have achieved superior performance against other traditional methods. It typically requires a training process, where a human-designed feature descriptor (e.g. SIFT [3] etc.) is applied to represent local image characteristics. Subsequently, the extracted features

© Springer Nature Switzerland AG 2019
Y. Zhao et al. (Eds.): ICIG 2019, LNCS 11902, pp. 529–537, 2019.
https://doi.org/10.1007/978-3-030-34110-7_44

are used to train a classification model for pixel-level classification to achieve image segmentation.

Since 2012, based on the idea of convolutional neural network (CNN) proposed by LeCun et al. [4] and followed by a technological breakthrough that allows deeper neural networks to be trained [5], deep CNNs have demonstrated remarkable capabilities in performing classification, segmentation, object detection, and other image processing tasks [6, 7]. Briefly, the CNN-based methods recognize objects based on a multi-scale feature representation obtained by applying many convolutional filters and non-linear activation functions at different image scales. The parameters of the convolutional filters are automatically learned during the training process through iterative back propagation of the errors between the predicted outputs and the ground truth images. This enables an automatic feature learning and representation, which is the key advantage against classical machine learning methods that are based on manually designed features.

Many deep CNN based methods have been proposed to address image segmentation tasks. In earlier approaches, image segmentation is treated as a pixel-wise classification problem [8]. Deep CNN classification models are trained in a patch-based manner. These methods require millions of image patches for training and suffer from low computational efficiency in both training and testing stages. One of the latest state-of-the art methods (known as U-net [9]) is based on an end-to-end deep CNN architecture. It is trained more efficiently and requires fewer training samples than the patch-based models. Following on this pioneer work, several improvements and modifications have been proposed. For instance, Drozdzal et al. [10] added short skip connections in addition to the long skip connections in the U-net to improve training efficiency and segmentation accuracy. RU-net and R2U-net, proposed by Alom et al. [11], are based on U-net plus recurrent neural network and U-net plus the combination of recurrent neural network and residual network respectively. A nested U-net architecture called U-net++ is introduced in [12] that is proposed to replace the direct skip connections from encoder to decoder part by dense skip connections. A chain of multiple U-nets are utilized in LadderNet [13] to improve the flow of information.

For most multi-class image segmentation problems, the number of pixels in each class is different from each other which potentially leads to less accurate predictions for some classes than others. Additionally, some of the image regions are easier to be classified (i.e. higher segmentation accuracy) than others due to more distinct local image characteristics. It would be more efficient if the network can be dynamically adapted to learn from pixel locations with lower predicted accuracies during the training process. There are a few methods have been proposed to address these issues. Focal loss [14] is proposed to modify the cross entropy loss function for addressing the class imbalance problem. Similarly, online hard example mining method proposed by Shrivastava et al. [15] balances class samples by mining hard examples based on the loss values. Both methods focus on the problem of object classification, while the application to image segmentation has not been thoroughly investigated.

As the main contribution of this paper, we improve the U-net method by introducing a dynamically weighted cross-entropy loss function. The weight for each pixel is calculated based on the predicted accuracy in each iteration. The pixel locations with higher prediction accuracies are assigned with lower weights, and vice versa. This enables the network to learn more from poorly predicted image regions. We name our proposed method as feedback weighted U-net (FU-net). We demonstrate the effectiveness of the FU-net using a challenging brain magnetic resonance image (MRI) dataset with extremely unbalanced classes as well as different numbers of training samples.

2 Methodology

2.1 Network Architecture

The U-net proposed by Ronnebergeret et al. [9] is based on convolutional neural network, and consists of a contracting path and an expansive path. In the contracting path, each layer consists of two 3×3 convolutions (Conv), and each convolution is followed by a rectified linear unit (ReLU) as illustrated in Fig. 1(a). The feature map in the next successive layer is a down-sampled version of the output from the previous layer by using a max pooling of stride 2. Due to the down-sampling process, only very abstracted information remained at the end of the contracting path. To capture and rebuild the spatial context, a decoding path is required. In the expansive (decoding) path, the output feature map in each layer is up-sampled using 2×2 up-convolution with halved number of feature channels in the previous layer. Each layer also has two 3×3 convolutions, and each followed by a ReLU. Additionally, there are some concatenation operations to combine feature maps from the contracting layers to the corresponding expansive layers. 1×1 convolution is used in the final layer to convert the dimension of feature maps to the number of classes. Subsequently, softmax function [16] is applied to map the output value of each pixel to the range of [0, 1]. In the U-net paper [9], the authors proposed a weighted cross entropy loss function E for parameter optimization that is expressed in Eq. (1).

$$E = \sum_{x \in \Omega} w(x) \, log(p_{l(x)}(x)) \tag{1}$$

where $p_{l(x)}(x)$ is the predicated probability value for the corresponding true class $l(x)$ of pixel x, and $x \in \Omega$ such that Ω indicating the domain of all image pixels. $w(x)$ is the weight for pixel x. In paper [9], the weights are pre-calculated by assigning higher values to challenging boundary pixels based on a distance map. The weights are pre-determined and application dependent.

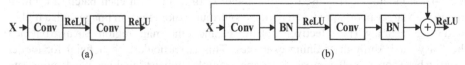

(a)   (b)

Fig. 1. (a) Layer of the original U-net. (b) Layer by adding batch normalization (BN) and residual block (RB).

In our proposed method, we firstly improve the U-net by adding batch normalization (BN) [17] and residual block (RB) [18] to the network layers, as illustrated in Fig. 1(b).

BN and RB are well-known techniques to achieve faster convergence and train deeper networks [19]. More importantly, we assign automatically calculated weight to $w(x)$ in Eq. (1). The weights are pixel-wise values which are iteratively updated in each training iteration for each training image. Calculation of the weight is introduced in Sect. 2.2.

2.2 Weighted Cross-Entropy Cost Function

In this section, we describe the method for automatically calculating the weight $w(x)$ in Eq. (1).

Object class with a larger number of pixels contributes more to the cross-entropy loss calculation and has larger influence on the gradient values for parameter optimization. Abraham and Khan [20] and Wang et al. [21] have applied dice coefficient loss to address the class imbalance issue. Weight calculated based on the number of pixels per class has also been proposed [6]. Different from these methods that use fixed weight calculations, we propose to calculate the weights dynamically according to the predication performance in each iteration. Our motivation is to increase the contribution from pixels that have larger prediction errors to the loss function calculation. This not only enables the balance of different classes implicitly, but also allows difficult local image regions to be emphasized for model training.

A pixel-wise weight map is generated based on the pixel-wise probability values that are produced in each training iteration. The pixel locations with lower prediction accuracies are assigned to higher weights and vice versa. Hence, the network is able to focus on learning from poorly predicted image regions. The feedback weight is a continuous function that maps the input values to the range of [0.01 1], which is expressed as:

$$w(x) = e^{-log\,100 \times p_{l(x)}^{\beta}} \tag{2}$$

In Eq. (2), larger values of $p_{l(x)}$ indicate higher predicated probability values of the true class, which are assigned to lower weights for calculating the loss function for network backpropagation. Figure 2 shows the behaviors of the weighting functions by varying the hyperparameter β in Eq. (2). β is experimentally determined in Sect. 3. Note that $log100$ is used to constrain the minimum weight to be 0.01 instead of 0, which prevents the pixels with high prediction accuracies being completely neglected from training.

Note that the same mapping function in Eq. (2) is applied to all training images, and mini-batch method [22] is used for parameter optimization. In each batch, a training image with larger poorly predicted regions contributes more than an image with a higher prediction accuracy. This effectively not only balances the image regions but also balance the 'easy' and 'difficult' training examples. This is particularly beneficial for model training based on a small number of training examples with certain bias. We demonstrate this advantage by varying the size of the training data in the evaluation section.

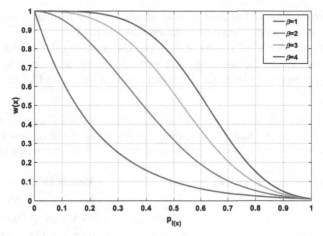

Fig. 2. Plot of the mapping function of Eq. (2) with different values of β.

3 Experiments and Results

In this section, we evaluate the proposed method based on T1-weighted brain MRI for segmentation of Midbrain (MB) and Substantia Nigra (SN). Certain quantitative measurements (e.g. volume) of SN has been found to associate with Parkinson disease [23]. However, it is extremely time consuming to annotate it manually and it is challenging to train a machine learning model for automatic segmentation due to the small size of SN. The T1-weighted brain MRI data were acquired in Nottingham University Hospital and was approved by the local ethics committee for this research. The dataset contains a total of 102 subjects with 30 axial image slices each. Experienced radiologist manually selected 3 or 4 slices that contain both the MB and SN, and annotated the contours of MB and SN. This resulted in a total of 310 2D slices for the segmentation evaluation in this paper.

Original U-net, U-net with batch normalization and residual block (BRU-net), BRU-net with feedback weight (FU-net) were compared with each other. The dice coefficient (DC) was used as the evaluation criterion. Note that the separate effects of adding batch normalization and residual block were not tested, as they were normally used simultaneously to achieve better performance. We performed three experiments for each method: randomly selected 200/100/50 images for training, 10 images for validation and the remaining 100/200/250 images for testing.

The parameters for model training are listed as follows. The batch size was 5. The optimizer was Adam [24] with learning rate of 0.001. The number of feature channels in the first layer was 16 and doubled in each of the down-sampled layers. The dropout rate was 0.25, and the number of epochs was 400. The number of iterations within each epoch for the three experiments were 40, 20 and 10 respectively (corresponding to experiments with 200, 100 and 50 training images). We evaluated the performances by varying the hyperparameter β (Eq. (2)) from 1 to 4 for the 100 training/200 testing experiment. When $\beta = 3$, it achieved the best performance. Hence, $\beta = 3$ was used for all the remaining experiments. The main aim of the evaluation is to compare the performances of the proposed improvements rather than achieve an ultimate performance for a particular medical application. Hence, data augmentation was not used.

Table 1 lists the numerical results of the mean DC ± standard deviation (Std) of the three methods by varying the number of training samples. We also report the P values of paired t-test by comparing U-net with BRU-net and BRU-net with FU-net respectively.

Table 1. Comparison of different methods using different number of training samples. The mean dice coefficient (DC) ± standard deviation (Std) and P values of paired t-tests are reported. Numbers in bold indicate the best method that statistically ($P < 0.01$) better than other methods.

Number of training/testing examples	Method	Mean of DC ± Std	
		MB	SN
200/100	U-net	0.9000 ± 0.03	0.7095 ± 0.17
	BRU-net	0.8775 ± 0.14	0.7164 ± 0.18
	FU-net	0.8929 ± 0.05	$\mathbf{0.7563 \pm 0.15}$
100/200	U-net	0.8584 ± 0.18	0.7022 ± 0.18
	BRU-net	0.8550 ± 0.16	0.7005 ± 0.15
	FU-net	0.8710 ± 0.15	$\mathbf{0.7575 \pm 0.16}$
50/250	U-net	0.8135 ± 0.19	0.4831 ± 0.26
	BRU-net	0.8088 ± 0.15	0.6387 ± 0.17
	FU-net	0.8182 ± 0.20	$\mathbf{0.7087 \pm 0.24}$
		P values of paired t-test	
200/100	U-net/BRU-net	0.0589	0.6086
	BRU-net/FU-net	0.1260	0.0026
100/200	U-net/BRU-net	0.6050	0.8706
	BRU-net/FU-net	0.6062	<0.0001
50/250	U-net/BRU-net	0.5725	<0.0001
	BRU-net/FU-net	0.3138	<0.0001

It is seen from the results in Table 1 that all three methods achieved similar segmentation performance (no statistical significance) for the MB segmentation regardless of the number of training samples. However, for the SN class where the number of pixels is much smaller than the MB class and more difficult to be segmented, the proposed FU-net consistently outperformed the U-net and BRU-net methods for all the experiments with statistical significance. When training using only 50 images, the performance of FU-net remained high (DC = 0.7087) which is much higher than the BRU-net (DC = 0.6387) and U-net (DC = 0.4831).

We also provide some visual examples to demonstrate the advantages of our proposed method. In Fig. 3, we present the segmentation results of an example image based on 50, 100 and 200 training images. Figure 3(a) and (b) are the original image and ground truth annotation respectively. In Fig. 3(b), the darker region is the MB and lighter region is the SN. Figure 3(c), (d) and (e) are the segmentation results for U-net, BRU-net and

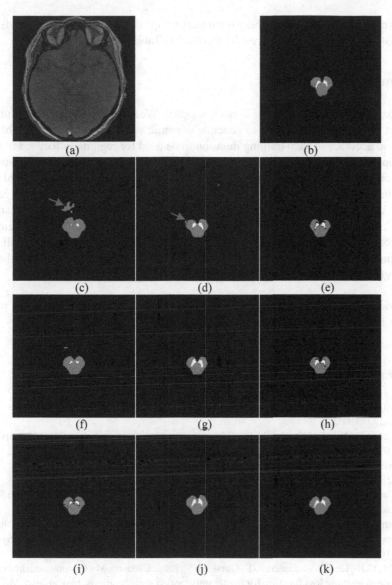

Fig. 3. (a) The original image. (b) The ground truth. (c) (d) (e) Segmentation results by U-net/BRU-net/FU-net respectively using 50 training samples. (f) (g) (h) Segmentation results by U-net/BRU-net/FU-net respectively using 100 training samples. (i) (j) (k) Segmentation results by U-net/BRU-net/FU-net respectively using 200 training samples.

FU-net respectively using 50 training examples. Some false positives and false negatives can be easily identified for the U-net and BRU-net methods, as indicated by red arrows. Figure 3(f), (g) and (h) and Fig. 3(i), (j) and (k) are the results for the three methods using 100 and 200 training examples respectively. Similarly, the FU-net results visually provide more similar outputs to the ground truth image than the other two methods. This is consistent with the numerical results reported in Table 1.

4 Conclusion

In this paper, the basic structure of U-net is adopted. We have improved the cost function of U-net by proposing a method to generate dynamic weight. This method enables the prediction accuracy at each training iteration to be used for regionally focused training. The proposed method has been evaluated on a challenging multi-class brain tissue segmentation task. Based on the results, FU-net significantly outperforms the original U-net and an improved version of U-net (BRU-net). We have shown that FU-net is a generic and useful technique for model training with unbalanced class labels and with smaller number of training examples. It can be easily applied to any DCNN based segmentation framework as long as cross entropy is used as the loss function. Future work will focus on method evaluation of different 2D/3D datasets and improvement of the method for tasks with a small number of training samples.

Acknowledgement. The authors acknowledge Nvidia for donating a graphic card for this research.

References

1. Chan, T.F., Vese, L.A.: Active contours without edges. IEEE Trans. Image Process. **10**(2), 266–277 (2001)
2. Boykov, Y., Veksler, O., Zabih, R.: Fast approximate energy minimization via graph cuts. IEEE Trans. Pattern Anal. Mach. Intell. **23**(11), 1222–1239 (2001)
3. Lowe, D.G.: Distinctive image features from scale-invariant keypoints. Int. J. Comput. Vision **60**(2), 91–110 (2004)
4. LeCun, Y., et al.: Gradient-based learning applied to document recognition. Proc. IEEE **86**(11), 2278–2324 (1998)
5. Krizhevsky, A., Sutskever, I., Hinton, G.E.: ImageNet classification with deep convolutional neural networks. In: International Conference on Neural Information Processing Systems, pp. 1097–1105 (2012)
6. Sudre, C.H., Li, W., Vercauteren, T., Ourselin, S., Jorge Cardoso, M.: Generalised dice overlap as a deep learning loss function for highly unbalanced segmentations. In: Cardoso, M.J., et al. (eds.) DLMIA/ML-CDS -2017. LNCS, vol. 10553, pp. 240–248. Springer, Cham (2017). https://doi.org/10.1007/978-3-319-67558-9_28
7. Simonyan, K., Zisserman, A.: Very deep convolutional networks for large-scale image recognition. arXiv preprint arXiv:1409.1556 (2014)
8. Farabet, C., et al.: Learning hierarchical features for scene labeling. IEEE Trans. Pattern Anal. Mach. Intell. **35**(8), 1915–1929 (2013)
9. Ronneberger, O., Fischer, P., Brox, T.: U-net: convolutional networks for biomedical image segmentation. In: Navab, N., Hornegger, J., Wells, W.M., Frangi, A.F. (eds.) MICCAI 2015. LNCS, vol. 9351, pp. 234–241. Springer, Cham (2015). https://doi.org/10.1007/978-3-319-24574-4_28

10. Drozdzal, M., Vorontsov, E., Chartrand, G., Kadoury, S., Pal, C.: The importance of skip connections in biomedical image segmentation. In: Carneiro, G., et al. (eds.) LABELS/DLMIA -2016. LNCS, vol. 10008, pp. 179–187. Springer, Cham (2016). https://doi.org/10.1007/978-3-319-46976-8_19

11. Alom, M.Z., et al.: Recurrent residual convolutional neural network based on u-net (R2U-net) for medical image segmentation. arXiv preprint arXiv:1802.06955 (2018)

12. Zhou, Z., Rahman Siddiquee, M.M., Tajbakhsh, N., Liang, J.: UNet++: a nested U-net architecture for medical image segmentation. In: Stoyanov, D., et al. (eds.) DLMIA/ML-CDS -2018. LNCS, vol. 11045, pp. 3–11. Springer, Cham (2018). https://doi.org/10.1007/978-3-030-00889-5_1

13. Zhuang, J.J.: LadderNet: multi-path networks based on U-Net for medical image segmentation (2018)

14. Lin, T.-Y., et al.: Focal loss for dense object detection. In: Proceedings of the IEEE International Conference on Computer Vision (2017)

15. Shrivastava, A., Gupta, A., Girshick, R.: Training region-based object detectors with online hard example mining. In: Proceedings of the IEEE Conference on Computer Vision and Pattern Recognition (2016)

16. Goodfellow, I., Bengio, Y., Courville, A.: Deep Learning. MIT Press, Cambridge (2016)

17. Ioffe, S., Szegedy, C.: Batch normalization: accelerating deep network training by reducing internal covariate shift. arXiv preprint arXiv:1502.03167 (2015)

18. He, K., et al.: Deep residual learning for image recognition. In: Proceedings of the IEEE Conference on Computer Vision and Pattern Recognition (2016)

19. Milletari, F., Navab, N., Ahmadi, S.-A.: V-net: fully convolutional neural networks for volumetric medical image segmentation. In: 2016 Fourth International Conference on 3D Vision (3DV). IEEE (2016)

20. Abraham, N., Khan, N.M.J.: A novel focal Tversky loss function with improved attention U-net for lesion segmentation (2018)

21. Wang, C., et al.: A two-stage 3D Unet framework for multi-class segmentation on full resolution image (2018)

22. Ruder, S.J.: An overview of gradient descent optimization algorithms (2016)

23. Schwarz, S.T., et al.: In vivo assessment of brainstem depigmentation in Parkinson disease: potential as a severity marker for multicenter studies. Radiology **283**(3), 789–798 (2016)

24. Kingma, D.P., Ba, J.: Adam: a method for stochastic optimization. arXiv preprint arXiv:1412.6980 (2014)

Scale Normalization Cascaded Dense-Unet for Prostate Segmentation in MR Images

Yuxuan Chen, Suiyi Li, Su Yang$^{(\boxtimes)}$, and Wuyang Luo

Shanghai Key Laboratory of Intelligent Information Processing, School of Computer Science,
Fudan University, Shanghai 201203, China
suyang@fudan.edu.cn

Abstract. Automated and accurate prostate segmentation technique from magnetic resonance images plays an important role in diagnostic and radiological planning. However, this task faces the challenge of extreme scale variation of prostate glands presented in the slices at different locations of MRI volumes. To alleviate problems arising from scale variation. We propose a cascaded prostate segmentation model that includes three stages: Coarse segmentation, segmentation result refinement, and scale normalization segmentation. Segmentation result refinement can remove the coarse segmentation results that do not contain prostates. More importantly, it normalizes the scale of the prostate region on different slice images of the same nuclear magnetic resonance volume according to the result of the coarse segmentation, thereby making the scale normalization segmentation network obtain scale-invariant magnetic resonance images as input. The experimental results demonstrate that this design can significantly reduce the degradation of segmentation performance arising from large scale variation.

Keywords: Prostate segmentation · Scale normalization · Cascaded model · MRI

1 Introduction

The prostate is an important reproductive organ for men. A young man's prostate is about the size of a walnut. It slowly grows larger with age. If it gets too large, this can cause problems, which is very common after age 50. The elder aging is more likely to prone prostate troubles. There are three major prostate diseases, including prostatitis, non-cancerous enlargement of the prostate (BPH), and prostate cancer. In particular, prostate cancer is the second leading cause of cancer death in American men. A sooner detection of prostate cancer can lead to higher probability of cure, such that it is important to utilize reliable computer-aided diagnosis solutions for prostate diseases. Prostate segmentation from MRI is an essential prerequisite for detecting prostate diseases, especially prostate cancer [1]. Prostate segmentation can be used to make radiotherapy plans to protect surrounding tissues and estimate volume of prostate [2]. There are some limitations to the traditional manual segmentation method: First, it relies on professional radiologists. In addition, the manual segmentation method is inefficient.

Although much progress has been made, there are still some challenges that have not yet been fully addressed, including the variation of scale and shape of prostates,

© Springer Nature Switzerland AG 2019
Y. Zhao et al. (Eds.): ICIG 2019, LNCS 11902, pp. 538–547, 2019.
https://doi.org/10.1007/978-3-030-34110-7_45

boundary blur caused by lesions, which has led to a gap between clinical needs and automatic segmentation performance. In particular, the scale of prostate gland varies greatly in the same patient's MRI volume, so the scale of the prostate gland presented in the slices at different locations of the MRI volume are very different, as shown in Fig. 1. This scale variation largely limits the accuracy of prostate segmentation. In this paper, we propose a cascaded scale normalization network to reduce the damage of scale variation to segmentation accuracy. The details of the model will be given in the third section.

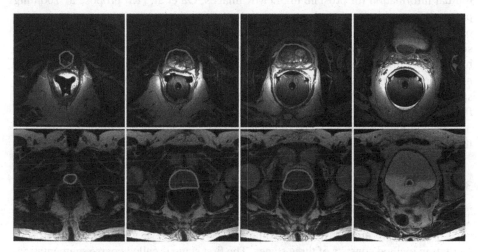

Fig. 1. Example of prostate MR images exhibiting large variations

2   Related Works

Automatic segmentation of different type medical images can provide important information for diagnosis and treatment of diseases. With the rapid development of deep learning in recent years, medical image segmentation technology has also made breakthroughs. Convolutional neural networks have been shown to provide robust feature representation for tasks such as classification and segmentation. Many medical image segmentation algorithms based on deep neural networks have emerged [3–7]. Ronneberger et al. [3] proposed u-net for biomedical image segmentation, which introduces skip connections between down-sampling paths and up-sampling paths to increase the transmission of features based on fully convolutional networks (FCN). Li et al. [5] proposed a hybrid model for liver and tumor segmentation from CT volumes, which consists of a 2D DenseUNet for efficiently extracting intra-slice features and a 3D counterpart for hierarchically aggregating volumetric contexts.

Many automatic prostate segmentation methods have been proposed for MR images. Because the trend of neural networks has been rekindled in recent years, many computer vision research fields, including image segmentation, have shown dramatic performance improvement by using deep neural networks. We divide the automatic prostate segmentation method into non-deep learning methods and deep learning-based methods. Non-deep learning methods can be further divided into deformable model based methods [8–10], atlas based methods [11–14], and graph based methods [15–17]. Pasquier et al. [9] present a method using SSM in a Bayesian classification framework, obtaining contextual information and priori knowledge by using Markov fields. To eliminate the restriction of landmarks, Toth et al. [10] proposed a novel landmark-free AAM model to capture shape information by a level set. This method can ease the difficulty of setting landmarks in ASMs. Klein et al. [11] employed multi-atlas matching and localized mutual information for prostate in 3D MR images. Ou et al. [13] propose a "zooming process" for multi-atlas-based prostate segmentation which overcome many limitations of the datasets. Zouqi et al. [15] proposed a method for prostate segmentation from ultrasound images, which contains the advantages of both graph cuts and domain knowledge based Fuzzy Inference Systems. Ever since entering the era of deep learning, many deep neural network models have been proposed [18–22]. Guo et al. [18] proposed a stacked sparse auto-encoder model. Milletari et al. [19] utilized 3D convolutional neural network for prostate segmentation. Yu et al. [20] introduced the mixed residual connections into 3D convolutional neural network. Jia et al. [21] employed the ensemble technique for fine prostate segmentation.

3   Method

The goal of the prostate segmentation task is to obtain the segmentation result for each slice image of the input MR image volume $V = \{v_1, v_2, ..., v_n\}$. The proposed segmentation method consists of three stages. The first stage is called coarse segmentation. The MRI volume is divided into single slice images, and all slice images are fed into the first dense-unet segmentation network to obtain the preliminary segmentation results of each slice image. The second stage is called morphological-based segmentation result refinement, which recombines the slice images obtained by the first stage segmentation into volumes. It employs the prior knowledge and morphology methods to obtain refined segmentation results from each MRI volume. The third stage is called scale normalization segmentation. Based on to the refined coarse segmentation result, the part of the slice images containing prostate is resized for normalizing the scale of the prostate regions. The resized slice images are fed into the second dense-unet segmentation network, and the final scale normalization segmentation results are obtained. An overview of proposed method is shown in Fig. 2.

3.1   Coarse Segmentation Network

The coarse segmentation stage and the scale normalization segmentation stage utilize the same dense-unet architecture proposed by Li et al. [23]. In order to more accurately segment prostates, this paper employs a dense-unet network model, as illustrated in Fig. 3. It can be seen as an extended version of densenet [24] architecture on u-net for semantic segmentation. The architecture follows the encoder-decoder fashion, which is composed of a down-sampling path and an up-sampling path. The down-sampling path extracts the semantic features of the input images, layer by layer through continuous

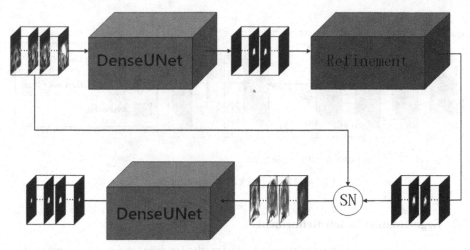

Fig. 2. An overview of the proposed model

convolution and down-sampling operations, from low-level to high-level. Up-sampling path expands the resolution of feature maps by deconvolution operation until the resolution of input images is completely restored. Both up-sampling path and down-sampling are composed of dense block and transition layer, which connects adjacent dense blocks. Their structure is shown in Fig. 4.

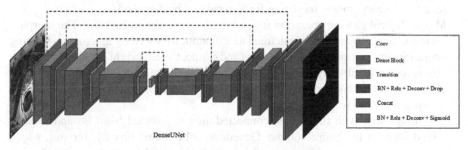

Fig. 3. Dense block and transition layer

Both up-sampling path and down-sampling path are composed of 4 dense blocks and 4 transition layers. A dense block consists of n consecutive convolution layers of the same resolution, each followed by a batch normalization (BN) rectified linear units (ReLU) and dropout layer. The Lth convolution layer takes the feature maps of all the previous layers as input.

The MRI volume $V = \{v_1, v_2, ..., v_n\}$ is split into individual slice images vi, all slice images are fed into the first dense-unet segmentation network to obtain the preliminary segmentation results $Sc = \{sc_1, sc_2, ..., sc_n\}$.

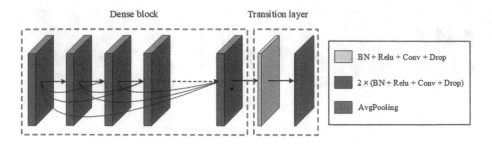

Dense block and Trasition layer

Fig. 4. Dense block and transition layer

3.2 Segmentation Result Refinement

The goal of this stage is to use the morphological method to refine the coarse segmentation results obtained in the previous stage based on prior knowledge. Human anatomy reveals that prostate is chestnut-shaped. Thus, in the MRI volume, a larger prostate area is present in the middle slice image, and the slice image near the sides of the MRI volume presents a smaller prostate area. Inspired by the above characteristics, we design the following refinement process:

1. First, the first stage coarse segmentation results are recombined into a volume $Sc = \{sc_1, sc_2, ..., sc_n\}$ according to the original arrangement order. Each segmentation result is a binary image, including foreground and background
2. Morphological closing operation is conducted separately on each sci. The morphological closing on an image is defined as a dilation followed by an erosion. Closing operations can remove small dark spots and connect small bright cracks. Then, each segmentation result only retain its largest connected area, and the remaining pixel values are set to background. After this step, the segmentation result volume is referred as $So = \{so_1, so_2, ..., so_n\}$.
3. The image som with the largest connected area is selected from So and used as a seed slice for the entire volume. Generating a bounding box B_m for so_m, which contains the entire largest connected area of the so_m with a small margin. Starting from the slice so_m, forward refinement ($m \rightarrow m + 1$) and backward refinement ($m \rightarrow m - 1$) are performed by sliding. Taking forward refinement as an example, in order to refine so_{m-1}, the region of so_{m-1} is selected, which corresponds to the region of the bounding box B_m of so_m. Only this region in the so_{m-1} is retained, and the rest region of so_{m-1} is set as background. Then the bounding box B_{m-1} of so_{m-1} is generated. Next, the segmentation result so_{m-2} can be refined using B_{m-1}. The backward refinement is the same as its forward counterpart. Through the above refining process, the refined segmentation results are obtained $Sr = \{sr_1, sr_2, ..., sr_n\}$. The above process is illustrated in Fig. 5
4. Finally, the segmentation results which only contain background are eliminated from the volume, and the final segmentation refinement results $R = \{r_s, r_{s+1}, ..., r_{e-1}, r_e\}$ ($e-s +1 <= n$) are obtained as the input of the third stage.

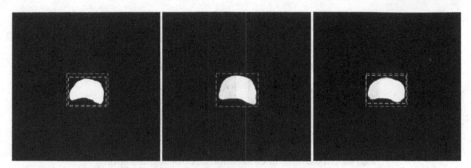

Fig. 5. Forward and backward refinement

3.3 Scale Normalization Segmentation

After the coarse segmentation and refinement process, we can get the refined segmentation results $R = \{r_s, r_{s+1}, ..., r_{e-1}, r_e\}$. Guided by the bounding box of each R_i, the foreground regions of the corresponding MRI slices are cropped and resized to the same scale (256×256, in experiments of this paper) to get the scale normalized input. Then, these scale normalized MR slices image are fed into the scale normalization segmentation network as proposed above to get final segmentation results.

3.4 Training

The coarse segmentation network and the scale normalization segmentation network are trained separately in the same way. Both networks were trained using Adam solver with a mini-batch size of 8 due to the limited capacity of GPU memory. Both models were trained for 500 epochs. The learning rate was set as 0.001 initially and is divided by 10 when training 50% of the total training epoch number.

4 Experiments

4.1 Dataset and Pre-processing

We validate our method on the MICCAI Prostate MR Image Segmentation (PROMISE12) challenge dataset [25]. This open dataset contains 50 training cases which include a transversal T2-weighted MR images of prostate and the corresponding expert-annotated segmentation results. We use 5-flod cross validation, which randomly divided the data set into 5 folds, each with 10 volumes, using a fold for testing, and the rest for training.

The data of PROMISE12 dataset is multi-center, multi-vendor and collected from clinical setting, causing large differences in slice thickness, with/without endorectal coil, dynamic range, voxel size, field of view, and position, all of which have directly effecting to the performance of the model.

In data processing, the first step is to sort the pixel values of each slice in order to remove noise. Then, set an pixel interval [min, max] to clip pixels, min is lower boundary

Fig. 6. An example of elimination of error segmentation

of smallest 2% of the pixels in the slice, while max is upper boundary of biggest 2% of the pixels. Pixel values outside the interval are clipped to the interval boundaries. Finally, all the slices are resized to 256*256, and their pixel values are mapped to 0–255.

4.2 Implementation

The proposed model was implemented based on Tensorflow. All the experiments were performed on server equipped with CPU, memory, and NVIDIA TITAN XP GPU.

4.3 Quantitative Analysis

In order to evaluate the performance of our model, we used dice score as the metrics to measure the overall region similarity of the segmentation results, and it is the same as the other prostate segmentation methods. The dice score is calculated via Eq. 1, where X denotes the volumetric ground truth, and Y the volumetric predicted value.

$$\text{dice} = \frac{2|X \cap Y|}{|X| + |Y|} \tag{1}$$

Table 1. Quantitative results

Model	Dice score
Only stage 1	0.849
Full model	0.878

Some quantitative results of the proposed method are shown in Table 1 through cross validation. Some segmentation results of our model are shown in Fig. 5. It is observed that the full model has achieved more accurate segmentation results than a single segmentation network. This is because we introduce the refinement process that can eliminate error segmentation. As shown in Fig. 6, Unreasonable foreground region is eliminated via our segmentation result refinement. On the other hand, the refinement process also provides scale normalized input for the second segmentation network. This makes the second network do not need to consider how to solve the extreme scale variation between slice images. Some segmentation results of our model are shown in Fig. 7.

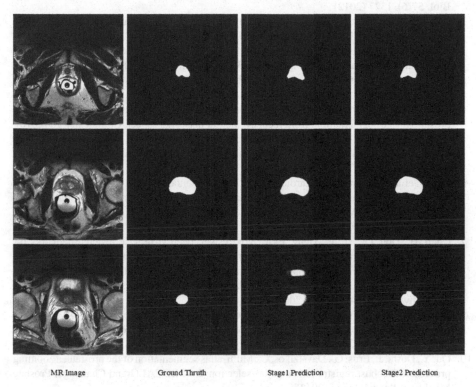

MR Image   Ground Thruth   Stage1 Prediction   Stage2 Prediction

Fig. 7. The results of the experiments

5 Conclusion

In this paper, we propose a cascaded prostate segmentation model to solve scale variation for automatic prostate segmentation from MR images. Through refining coarse segmentation results, the proposed method greatly alleviates the problem of scale variation in prostate segmentation task. Future investigations to be conducted include to integrating the framework into an end-to-end model for further improvement of performance.

Acknowledgement. This work is supported by Shanghai Science and Technology Commission (grant No. 17511104203) and NSFC (grant NO. 61472087).

References

1. Vos, P., Barentsz, J., Karssemeijer, N., Huisman, H.: Automatic computer-aided detection of prostate cancer based on multiparametric magnetic resonance image analysis. Phys. Med. Biol. **57**(6), 1527 (2012)
2. Toth, R., et al.: Accurate prostate volume estimation using multifeature active shape models on T2-weighted MRI. Acad. Radiol. **18**(6), 745–754 (2011)
3. Ronneberger, O., Fischer, P., Brox, T.: U-Net: convolutional networks for biomedical image segmentation. In: Navab, N., Hornegger, J., Wells, W.M., Frangi, A.F. (eds.) MICCAI 2015. LNCS, vol. 9351, pp. 234–241. Springer, Cham (2015). https://doi.org/10.1007/978-3-319-24574-4_28
4. Zhu, Q., Du, B., Turkbey, B., Choyke, P., Yan, P.: Exploiting interslice correlation for MRI prostate image segmentation, from recursive neural networks aspect. Complexity 10 (2018)
5. Li, X., Chen, H., Qi, X., Dou, Q., Fu, C., Heng, P.: H-DenseUNet: hybrid densely connected UNet for liver and liver tumor segmentation from CT volumes. IEEE Trans. Med. Imaging **37**(12), 2663–2674 (2018)
6. Yu, L., et al.: Automatic 3D cardiovascular MR segmentation with densely-connected volumetric convnets. In: Descoteaux, M., Maier-Hein, L., Franz, A., Jannin, P., Collins, D.L., Duchesne, S. (eds.) MICCAI 2017. LNCS, vol. 10434, pp. 287–295. Springer, Cham (2017). https://doi.org/10.1007/978-3-319-66185-8_33
7. Chen, H., Dou, Q., Yu, L., Heng, P.-A.: VoxResNet: deep voxelwise residual networks for volumetric brain segmentation. arXiv preprint arXiv:1608.05895 (2016)
8. Klein, S., van der Heide, U., Lipps, I., Vulpen, M., Staring, M., Pluim, J.: Automatic segmentation of the prostate in 3-D MR images by atlas matching using localized mutual information. Med. Phys. **35**(4), 1407–1417 (2008)
9. Martin, S., Daanen, V., Troccaz, J.: Automated segmentation of the prostate 3-D MR images using a probabilistic atlas and a spatially constrained deformable model. Med. Phys. **37**(4), 1579–1590 (2010)
10. Ou, Y., Doshi, J., Erus, G., Davatzikos, C.: Multi-atlas segmentation of the prostate: a zooming process with robust registration and atlas selection. In: MICCAI Grand Challenge: Prostate MR Image Segmentation (2012)
11. Yan, P., Cao, Y., Yuan, Y., Turkbey, B., Choyke, P.L.: Label image constrained multi-atlas selection. IEEE Trans. Cybernet. **45**(6), 1158–1168 (2015)
12. Pasquier, D., Lacornerie, T., Vermandel, M., Rousseau, J., Lartigau, E., Betrouni, N.: Automatic segmentation of pelvic structures from magnetic resonance images for prostate cancer radiotherapy. Int. J. Radiat. Oncol. Biol. Phys. **68**(2), 592–600 (2007)
13. Makni, N., Puech, P., Lopes, R., Dewalle, A.: Combining a deformable model and a probabilistic framework for an automatic 3-D segmentation of prostate on MRI. Int. J. Comput. Assisted. Radiol. Surg. **4**(2), 181–188 (2009)
14. Toth, R., Madabhushi, A.: Multifeature landmark-free active appearance models: application to prostate MRI segmentation. IEEE Trans. Med. Imag **31**(8), 1638–1650 (2012)
15. Moschidis E., Graham, J.: Automatic differential segmentation of the prostate in 3-D MRI using random forest classification and graph cuts optimization. In: Proceedings of IEEE International Symposium on Biomedical Imaging, pp. 1727–1730 (2012)
16. Zouqi M., Samarabandu, J.: Prostate segmentation from 2-D ultrasound images using graph cuts and domain knowledge. In: Proceedings of Computer and Robot Vision Conference, pp. 359–362 (2008)
17. Tian, Z., Liu, L., Zhang, Z., Fei, B.: Superpixelbased segmentation for 3D prostate mr images. IEEE Trans. Med. Imaging **35**(3), 791–801 (2016)

18. Guo, Y., Gao, Y., Shen, D.: Deformable MR prostate segmentation via deep feature learning and sparse patch matching. IEEE Trans. Med. Imag. **35**(4), 1077–1089 (2016)
19. Jia, H., Xia, Y., Song, Y., Cai, W., Fulham, M., Feng, D.D.: Atlas registration and en- semble deep convolutional neural network-based prostate segmentation using magnetic resonance imaging. Neurocomputing **275**, 1358–1369 (2017)
20. Milletari, F., Navab, N., Ahmadi, S.-A.: V-net: fully convolutional neural networks for volumetric medical image segmentation. In: 2016 Fourth International Conference on 3D Vision (3DV), pp. 565–571. IEEE (2016)
21. Yu, L., Yang, X., Chen, H., Qin, J., Heng, P.-A.: Volumetric ConvNets with mixed residual connections for automated prostate segmentation from 3D MR images. In: AAAI, pp. 66–72 (2017)
22. Yan, K., Wang, X., Kim, J., et al.: A propagation-DNN: deep combination learning of multi- level features for MR prostate segmentation. Comput. Methods Programs Biomed. **170**, 11–21 (2019)
23. Li, S., et al.: Cascade dense-Unet for prostate segmentation in MR images. In: ICIC (2019, accepted)
24. Huang, G., Liu, Z., Weinberger, K.Q., van der Maaten, L.: Densely connected convolutional networks. CoRR, abs/1608.06993 (2016)
25. Litjens, G., et al.: Evaluation of prostate segmentation algorithms for MRI: the PROMISE12 challenge. Med. Image Anal. **18**(2), 359–373 (2014)

Pulmonary Artery Segmentation Based on Three-Dimensional Region Growth Approach

Qing Guo[1], Chang Gao[1], Min Liu[2], Huaqing Wang[3(✉)], and Hongfang Yuan[1]

[1] College of Information Science and Technology,
Beijing University of Chemical Technology, Beijing 100029, China
[2] Department of Radiology, China-Japan Friendship Hospital, Beijing 100029, China
[3] College of Mechanical and Electrical Engineering,
Beijing University of Chemical Technology, Beijing 100029, China
hqwang@mail.buct.edu.cn

Abstract. Segmentation of pulmonary artery (PA) and its branches is the primary work to detect pulmonary embolism (PE). In order to achieve precise segmentation of the pulmonary artery, we propose an improved three-dimensional region growth (3D RG) method based on the anatomical features and spatial connectivity of the pulmonary artery. The three-dimensional vector is extracted from pulmonary trunk according to the mathematical theorem, and the isolation plane is introduced to prevent segmentation leakage. By adding an iteration parameter, the branches are segmented exactly. In this paper, three-dimensional segmentation and reconstruction of the pulmonary artery and its branches are carried out with pulmonary CTPA images provided by the China-Japan Friendship Hospital. The improved algorithm can effectively segment the pulmonary artery and its branches to the lung subsegments. High accuracy and three-dimensional connectivity are guaranteed and the research achieves a desired effect. According to the evaluation of radiologist, the segmentation result is accurate.

Keywords: Pulmonary artery segmentation · Three-dimensional region growth algorithm · Lung subsegment · CTPA images

1 Introduction

Pulmonary embolism (PE) is a blockage in the lungs that pulmonary artery (PA) is obstructed by emboli, leading to pulmonary circulatory disturbance with low diagnosis rate and high mortality. The emboli include thrombosis, fat, amniotic fluid, air and tumor, among which thrombosis is the most common. PE usually results from a blood clot in the leg where the thromboses fall off and move with blood circulation into PA. Therefore, the pulmonary embolism only occurs in the pulmonary artery and its branches. Symptoms of a PE include dyspnea, chest pain and hemoptysis. PE can be divided into

This work is supported by the Fundamental Research Funds for the Central Universities and Research Projects on Biomedical Transformation of China-Japan Friendship Hospital (No. PYBZ1804, No. PYBZ1807).

© Springer Nature Switzerland AG 2019
Y. Zhao et al. (Eds.): ICIG 2019, LNCS 11902, pp. 548–557, 2019.
https://doi.org/10.1007/978-3-030-34110-7_46

acute pulmonary embolism (APE) and chronic pulmonary embolism (CPE) according to the size and location of emboli. APE is the most common type of PE. According to the American Heart Association (AHA) 2015 data, PE is the third leading cause of cardiovascular death. It is difficult to diagnose PE definitively from other causes of symptoms for lack of clinical specific manifestation. The risk assessment is classified according to the pulmonary artery severity index, including the percentage of emboli volume to PA volume, the location of the emboli in the pulmonary artery branches, the spatial relationship between the emboli and the PA, and the type of emboli. They are all deemed as standard risk assessment indicators. We need computers to assist people to predict the risk of individual illness or death in diagnosing PE [1]. Since the PE only occurs in the pulmonary artery and its branches, accurate segmentation of the PA is the primary task.

Spiral CT pulmonary angiography (CTPA) is the golden standard for the PE diagnosis. CTPA images can clearly show the location, shape, size of the thromboses in the PA subsegment branches or above [2]. The sensitivity and specificity of the diagnosis are accurate, and it has many merits including non-invasive nature, fast scanning speed and powerful image processing ability. These advantages are instructive for clinical diagnosis and treatment plan, especially suitable for APE patients in emergency.

Medical image segmentation refers to extracting regions of interest according to the certain features or similarity of feature sets in medical images, and the images are divided into several non-overlapping regions with certain consistency. Traditional methods comprise threshold-based methods (Otsu method, etc.), region-based methods (Region Growth method, RG, etc.), boundary-based methods (Canny operator method, etc.). Kanas et al. proposed a random walk algorithm based on local intensity differences to segment the explicit boundaries of brain tumor [3]. Lesage D. et al. proposed a Bayesian random tracking algorithm based on particle filter for segmentation of coronary artery trees from cardiac CTA data. Using kernel density estimation to learn the entire Bayesian model, the results turned out to be a high robustness [4]. Zhang et al. proposed a piece-wise linear transformation for enhancing brain vessel boundaries and then segmenting blood vessels. The blood vessel was fused with weighted method to gain the entire vessels [5]. Zhou et al. presented a three-dimensional voxel clustering with multi-stage adaption method to segment pulmonary vessels based on expectation-maximization (EM) analysis. After analyzing connectivity of region on the segmentation results, blood vessels were tracked and reconstructed [6]. Some new methods, such as fuzzy mathematics-based methods (Fuzzy C-means algorithm, FCM) and neural network-based methods (Convolutional Neural Network, CNN), are put forward in later studies. Qin et al. proposed a convolutional-deconvolution depth network model with residual connections for segmenting the lesions of prostate in MR images. Combination of the U-Net and the ResNet network achieved a better result [7]. Xu et al. presented a new stage-wise convolution network for segmenting pulmonary vessels. The network was characterized by the automatic learning of pulmonary vessels in stages [8]. Pulmonary vascular segmentation is often used to detect pulmonary nodules [9], so the researchers did not separate the pulmonary artery and pulmonary veins.

The region growth (RG) method based on region segmentation has been widely applied to blood vessel segmentation, including two-dimensional RG and three-dimensional RG. The method fully considers the connectivity of blood vessels in space. In the study of Region Growth algorithm for pulmonary artery segmentation, scholars have proposed some improved methods. Zhang segmented the pulmonary trunk using a method based on RG and slice marching. The branches were tracked from the pulmonary trunk to branches, however, there existed fracture in branches and roughness in vascular wall after reconstruction [10]. Ebrahimdoost et al. took the pulmonary trunk extracted by the RG as the initial contour of the level set segmentation. They removed adhesions from other tissues and finally the pulmonary artery could be classified to the lung segment level [11]. Flores et al. proposed a 3D region growth plus progressive method on PA segmentation. They introduced boundary-based termination conditions, which could segment the PA to the segment level [12].

This paper proposes an improved three-dimensional region growth approach to segment pulmonary artery in the following three parts. Firstly, to separate vena cava, on the basis of mathematical principle and anatomical features, the vector of the pulmonary trunk in three-dimensional space is obtained. An isolation plane is introduced to remove vena cava. Secondly, in order to reduce error in different doctor's experience, the seed point is automatically obtained. Thirdly, to solve the precise segmentation to subsegmental branches, an adaptive parameter is introduced. The CT threshold will iterate according to the direction in which the CT value decreases. The approach for PA segmentation is presented in Sect. 2, and the results and conclusion are shown in Sect. 3 and 4, respectively.

2   The Proposed Method

In this paper, we fully take into account the connectivity nature of three-dimensional region growing algorithm. The false positives detected by the existing pulmonary embolism system mainly occur in the pulmonary vein and there is adhesion between the branches of pulmonary artery and pulmonary vein. So, the idea of connected domains is applied to address the problem. And in this part, the proposed 3D RG algorithm is illustrated in detail.

2.1   Remove Vena Cava

The blood from the vena cava flows through the heart into the pulmonary artery and there is little difference in CT value between the coterminous tissues. If the three-dimensional region growth is carried out directly, two regions will be segmented together. That is, the phenomenon of leakage occurs. In order to avoid leakage, we find the junction of pulmonary trunk and vena cava, then remove vena cava. We obtain normal vector of the pulmonary trunk in cross-section plane and add an isolation plane at the junction. Since obtaining the three-dimensional vector is difficult, we start from the two-dimensional vector. In CTPA images, the outline of the pulmonary trunk looks like a Chinese character- '人'. The main pulmonary artery (MPA) connected to the vena cava extends upward, the left pulmonary artery (LPA) and the right pulmonary artery

(RPA) extend downward. First, find the pulmonary trunk. Then, extract the skeleton of pulmonary trunk to gain the vector. Lastly, calculate the three-dimensional vector at the junction according to the vector projection theorem in mathematics. The detailed algorithm is as follows:

The first step, find the pulmonary trunk in the slice. We select a CTPA slice containing PA region (Fig. 1(a)). The major highlighted region on the image segmented with threshold method is the pulmonary trunk (Fig. 1(b)).

The second step, extract the skeleton of pulmonary trunk in the slice. The process of extracting the skeleton is performed in the region of '人'. Extraction Skeleton of the region uses a thinning algorithm in morphological principle called Medial Axis Transform (MAT) [13]. In the region R, the set of all elements is A. For any point p in set A, find the closest point on the boundary b. If there exist more than one closest point, it is considered that p is on the medial axis of the region R. So, the set of p is the skeleton of the region. The region R is eroded by the structuring element B, and the skeleton expressions are shown in the Eqs. (1) and (2):

$$S(A) = \bigcup_{k=0}^{K} S_k(A) \tag{1}$$

And

$$S_k(A) = (A \ominus kB) - (A \ominus kB) \circ B \tag{2}$$

Where: $A \ominus kB$ represents eroding k times to A, and k is the last time before being eroded into an empty set.

After pulmonary trunk is eroded k times according to Eqs. (1) and (2), the skeleton is obtained as shown in Fig. 1(c). So, we get the skeleton center point O and the endpoint P in MPA. And then, a vector $\overrightarrow{OP}$ or $\overrightarrow{n_0}$ (Fig. 1(d)) is obtained from point O and P, which is the vector in the slice of the MPA. The process of skeleton extraction is shown in Fig. 1. The original image is shown in Fig. 1(a). The pulmonary trunk in the slice is shown in Fig. 1(b). And the skeleton is shown in Fig. 1(c). The geometric diagram of skeleton is shown in Fig. 1(d).

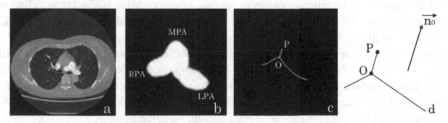

Fig. 1. (a) The original image. (b) The pulmonary trunk in the slice. (c) The skeleton. (d) Geometric diagram of skeleton.

The third step, get the spatial normal vector of MPA. According to the vector projection theorem, $\vec{n}$ is the vector of the three-dimensional space, and $\vec{n_0}$, the projection of $\vec{n}$ onto the XOY plane, is the vector of two-dimensional plane. $\left|\vec{n_0}\right|$ is the length of $\vec{n_0}$, and $\left|\vec{n}\right|$ is the length of $\vec{n}$. θ is the angle between $\vec{n_0}$ and $\vec{n}$ in the space. The theorem expression is shown in the Eq. (3):

$$\left|\vec{n_0}\right| = \left|\vec{n}\right| * \cos\theta \tag{3}$$

The pulmonary trunk is a spatial region at a certain angle from the XOY plane in the three-dimensional space (Fig. 2(a)). Figure 2(b) is the right view of Fig. 2(a). The pulmonary trunk, a short and wide vessel, ascends obliquely, being divided into LPA and RPA [14]. In our study, $\vec{n}$ is spatial normal vector of three-dimensional MPA in cross-section plane, XOY plane is horizontal plane, and $\vec{n_0}$ is the vector of the MPA in the XOY plane which has been obtained in second step. θ, between three-dimensional MPA and the XOY plane, is known according to anatomical features. And then vector $\overrightarrow{OQ}$ ($\vec{n}$), the actual MPA vector, is acquired (Fig. 2(c)). The 3D reconstruction result of pulmonary trunk is shown in Fig. 2(a), the right view of pulmonary trunk is shown in Fig. 2(b), and geometric diagram is shown in Fig. 2(c).

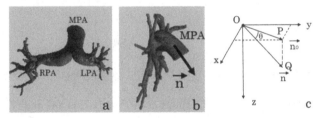

Fig. 2. (a) The 3D pulmonary trunk result. (b) The right view of pulmonary trunk. (c) Geometric diagram of MPA vector.

The fourth step, add the isolation plane at the junction. The MPA is approximately 5 cm in length and 3 cm in diameter [14]. The MPA endpoint W can be obtained from the point Q and vector $\vec{n}$ (Fig. 3(a)). $\left|\overrightarrow{OW}\right|$ is the length of MPA. It is confirmed that the point W must be in the pulmonary artery region. In space, MPA is similar as cylinder. With the endpoint W being the center and $\vec{n}$ being the normal vector, create a small circular plane that is the isolation plane for the three-dimensional region growth. The diameter of the circle is slightly larger than the MPA. This algorithm is suitable for angle between 0°–90°, except 0° and 90°. Figure 3(a) is the geometric diagram of the spatial position of the isolation plane. Figure 3(b) is a slice after adding isolation plane. Figure 3(c) is the detailed picture. Figure 3(d) is the traditional three-dimensional RG method result. Figure 3(e) is the result after adding isolation plane.

2.2 Confirm the Seed Point

The shape and location of the main pulmonary artery are relatively stable. Therefore, we choose the seed point in the main area of the PA because the area is large and the

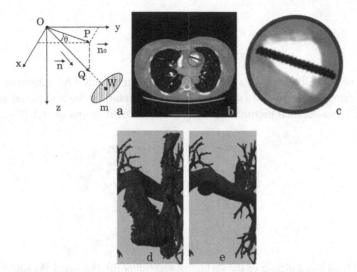

Fig. 3. (a) Geometric diagram of the spatial position of the isolation plane. (b) A slice after adding isolation plane. (c) The detailed picture. (d) The result of traditional method. (c) The result after adding isolation plane.

position is easy to judge. In the region, we select four different seed points, O, P, Q, W (Fig. 3(a)). In order to ensure the reliability of the segmentation, the average of four points is used as the initial value to avoid the inaccuracy of segmentation caused by the contingency of a single point. The method for determining four seed points is detailed in Sect. 2.1.

2.3 Adaptive Three-Dimensional Region Growth

Our improved 3D RG method selects the seeds automatically, and grows according to the criterion after adding an isolation plane. Until there are no pixel points meeting the threshold condition, growth is terminated. Clinically, doctors need to detect subsegmental branches of the PA for PE diagnosis and they hope the branches are conjoint and precise. In order to segment the branches to subsegments, an adaptive parameter is introduced to segment the PA and its branches accurately.

From pulmonary trunk to branches, CT value descends drastically. It is hoped that the finer we segment, the better effect we will get. That is, the seed iterates automatically on the direction in which the CT value is getting lower. Assume that the CT value of initial seed point in pulmonary trunk is s_0, and the ending point in the branch is s_n. After iterating its 26 neighborhoods in the first loop, the CT value along the direction decreases a bit. For this characteristic, a weight is assigned to the minimum value of 26 points, which makes seed value cuts down gradually. The weight, an adaptive iteration parameter, is called β. Through each loop, the CT value of 26 neighborhoods decreases by d, and the entire three-dimensional growth process needs to visit 26 neighborhoods n times. At the end of the first iteration, seed is alternative to s_1 that is used for the next round of growth. Similarly, we obtain s_2 to s_n. Variables, $s_0, s_1, s_2, \ldots s_n$ and d are known, and calculate β. The iteration Eq. (4) is shown below:

$$s_n = s_0 - \frac{n * d * \beta}{1 + \beta} \tag{4}$$

Experimental result turns out to be an accurate segmentation by adding an adaptive iteration parameter. The Fig. 4(a) below is a detailed picture of the traditional algorithm. The Fig. 4(b) is a detailed picture of adding adaptive iteration parameter β.

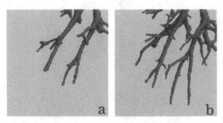

Fig. 4. (a) The detailed picture of the traditional algorithm. (b) The detailed picture of adding adaptive iteration parameter β.

By means of mathematical calculations and experimental verification, the best effect is acquired when $\beta = 0.0015$. It is proved that the descent direction of the seed iterated along the desired direction. As a result, the branches of the PA can be segmented to the subsegmental level. The improved method meets the doctor's requirements because of the accurate branches and vivid reconstruction model. The three-dimensional reconstruction result is in Fig. 5. Figure 5(a) shows the result when $\beta = 0.00015$. Figure 5(b) shows the result when $\beta = 0.0015$. Figure 5(c) shows the result when $\beta = 0.015$. It can be seen that the branch of Fig. 5(b) is finer and more detailed than Fig. 5(a). Figure 5(c) shows that all regions have been grown because the weight to the minimum point is too large. Therefore, when $\beta = 0.0015$ (Fig. 5(b)), the result is optimal.

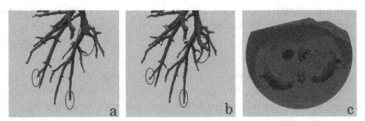

Fig. 5. (a) The result when $\beta = 0.00015$. (b) The result when $\beta = 0.0015$. (c) The result when $\beta = 0.015$.

3   Results and Discussion

In the experiment, eight groups of data with similar anatomic characteristics from China-Japan Friendship Hospital are tested. The lung CTPA images are grayscale images. The

MPA length of the patients is known, and at the junction of the pulmonary trunk and the heart, the angle between the pulmonary trunk and the XOY plane is about 20°–60°. The CTPA images of the experimental data come from the two devices of the China-Japan Friendship Hospital. The models include GE Healthcare SYSTEMS REVOLUTION CT of General Electric Company and TOSHIBA Aquilion ONE of Toshiba Medical Company. The experiments are carried out using MATLAB2014a on the PC with Inter Core i7-8700 K, CPU 3.70 GHz, and 32 GB RAM. Two results using our method to segment PA of two patients are shown in Fig. 6(a), (b):

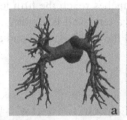

Fig. 6. (a) (b) The result using our method of with two patients.

Compared with other scholars' researches, the proposed three-dimensional region growth algorithm has improved in the number of PA branches, branches level, three-dimensional connectivity, and smoothness of pulmonary artery wall. The anatomical characteristic can be simulated veritably to analyze the degree of risk. The paper adopts volume rendering method to draw three-dimensional model. Medically, the level of pulmonary arteries and their branches is defined as follows. For example, the pulmonary trunk is the first level, the LPA is the second level, the left superior lobar artery is the third level, the segment is the fourth level, and the subsegment is the fifth level. Figure 7 shows the results of three other researchers in References [6, 11, 12]. Figure 7(a) shows the lobar arteries and segments and some branches reach the fourth level. But the branches are fractured, and the number of branches is incomplete. The pulmonary veins are mixed with PA, and the artery wall is rough. Figure 7(b) shows the lobar arteries and segments and some branches reach the fourth level. The number of branches is incomplete and the pulmonary artery wall is rough, too. Figure 7(c) shows that the pulmonary vessels are extracted completely, but the PA and pulmonary vein could not be separated.

Fig. 7. (a) (b) (c) Three results of other researchers in References [6, 11, 12].

The results of the traditional and improved approach are shown in Fig. 8. Figure 8(a) is the result of traditional method. Figure 8(a) shows the lobar arteries, segments and subsegments. The branches reach the fourth level and the number of branches is relatively complete. The artery wall is slightly rough and the vena cava is mis-segmented. Figure 8(b) is the result of the improved 3D RG approach with adaptive parameter. Figure 8(b) shows the lobar arteries, segments and subsegments. The branches reach the fifth level and the number of branches is complete and accurate. The artery wall is slightly rough and the vena cava is mis-segmented. Figure 8(c) is the result of the improved 3D RG approach adding the isolation plane. Figure 8(c) shows the lobar arteries, segments, and subsegments and the branches reach the fifth level. The number of branches is complete and accurate, and the artery wall is slightly rough. The segmentation effect is confirmed by radiologist that the result is good and achieves the desired goal.

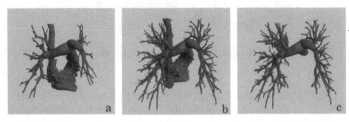

Fig. 8. (a) The result of traditional method. (b) The result of the improved 3D RG approach with adaptive parameter. (c) The result of the improved 3D RG approach adding the isolation plane.

4   Conclusions

In this paper, an adaptive three-dimensional region growth method is used to segment pulmonary artery and its branches. On the basis of vector projection theorem and anatomical characteristics, the skeleton and the normal vector are obtained. An isolation plane is introduced to remove the adhesion of the vena cava. The 3D RG algorithm is improved in choosing four seed points automatically and adding an adaptive parameter. Several sets of CTPA data are tested and it is proved that our approach can segment PA and its branches to subsegment level accurately. This method solves the following problems, including the fractured branches, incomplete branches and segmentation leakage. The results meet the requirements of radiologists, moreover, our method lays a solid foundation for the subsequent detection of pulmonary embolism and risk assessment.

References

1. Ozkan, H., Osman, O., Sahin, S., Boz, A.F.: A novel method for pulmonary embolism detection in CTA images. Comput. Methods Programs Biomed. **113**(3), 757–766 (2014)
2. Guo, D.J., et al.: Clinical analysis on the diagnosis and treatment of acute pulmonary embolism. Chin. J. Cardiol. **31**(1), 49–51 (2003)

3. Kanas, V.G., Zacharaki, E.I., Davatzikos, C., Sgarbas, K.N., Megalooikonomou, V.: A low cost approach for brain tumor segmentation based on intensity modeling and 3D random walker. Biomed. Signal Process. Control **22**, 19–30 (2015)
4. Lesage, D., Angelini, E.D., Funka-Lea, G., Bloch, I.: Adaptive particle filtering for coronary artery segmentation from 3D CT angiograms. Comput. Vis. Image Underst. **151**(C), 29–46 (2016)
5. Zhang, Y., Jiang, H.Q., Ma, L.: Blood vessel segmentation based on digital subtraction angiography sequence. In: 11th IEEE International Conference on Systems, Man, and Cybernetics, pp. 2049–2054. Institute of Electrical and Electronics Engineers Inc., Miyazaki (2018)
6. Zhou, C., et al.: Preliminary investigation of computer-aided detection of pulmonary embolism in three-dimensional computed tomography pulmonary angiography Images1. Acad. Radiol. **12**(6), 782–792 (2005)
7. Qin, X.X., Zhu, X., Zheng, B.B.: U-net model with residual connections fir automated prostate MR images segmentation. In: 11th International Congress on Image and Signal Processing, BioMedical Engineering and Informatics. IEEE, Beijing (2018)
8. Xu, Y.L., Mao, Z.D., Liu, C.X., Wang, B.: Pulmonary vessel segmentation via stage-wise convolutional networks with orientation-based region growing optimization. IEEE Access **6**, 71296–71305 (2018)
9. Setio, A.A.A., et al.: Pulmonary nodule detection in CT images: false positive reduction using multi-view convolutional networks. IEEE Trans. Med. Imaging **35**(5), 1160–1169 (2016)
10. Zhang, J.H., He, Z.S., Dehmeshki, J., Qanadli, S.D.: Segmentation of pulmonary artery based on CT angiography image. In: 4th Pattern Recognition. IEEE, Chongqing (2010)
11. Ebrahimdoost, Y., Qanadli, S. D., Nikravanshalmani, A., Ellis, T. J., Shoiaee, Z.F., Dehmeshki J.: Automatic segmentation of pulmonary artery (PA) in 3D pulmonary CTA images. In: 17th Digital Signal Processing. IEEE, Greece (2011)
12. Flores, J.M., Schmitt, F.: Segmentation, reconstruction and visualization of the pulmonary artery and the pulmonary vein from anatomical images of the visible human project. In: 6th Mexican International Conference on Computer Science. IEEE, Mexico (2006)
13. Rafael, C.G., Richard, E.W., Steven, L.E.: Digital Images Processing Using MATLAB, 2nd edn. Publishing House of Electronics Industry, Beijing (2005)
14. Mosby, Inc.: Mosby's medical dictionary. 9th edn. Elsevier (2009). https://medical-dictionary. thefreedictionary.com/pulmonary+trunk

A Comparative Study of CNN and FCN for Histopathology Whole Slide Image Analysis

Shujiao Sun[1,2], Bonan Jiang[3], Yushan Zheng[1,2(✉)], and Fengying Xie[1,2]

[1] Image Processing Center, School of Astronautics, Beihang University,
Beijing 100191, China
sunshujiao@buaa.edu.cn
[2] Beijing Advanced Innovation Center for Biomedical Engineering,
Beihang University, Beijing 100191, China
yszheng@buaa.edu.cn
[3] Beijing-Doblin International College, Beijing University of Technology,
Beijing 100124, China

Abstract. Automatic analysis of histopathological whole slide images
(WSIs) is a challenging task. In this paper, we designed two deep learning
structures based on a fully convolutional network (FCN) and a convolutional neural network (CNN), to achieve the segmentation of carcinoma
regions from WSIs. FCN is developed for segmentation problems and
CNN focuses on classification. We designed experiments to compare the
performances of the two methods. The results demonstrated that CNN
performs as well as FCN when applied to WSIs in high resolution. Furthermore, to leverage the advantages of CNN and FCN, we integrate the
two methods to obtain a complete framework for lung cancer segmentation. The proposed methods were evaluated on the ACDC-LungHP
dataset. The final dice coefficient for cancerous region segmentation is
0.770.

Keywords: Image segmentation · Computational pathology · CNN ·
FCN · Lung cancer

1 Introduction

Digital pathology has been gradually introduced in clinical practice. However,
the manual analysis of whole-slide images (WSIs) is a time-consuming task for
pathologists and prone to errors or intra-observer variability. The limited knowledge of pathologists also influences the veracity of diagnosis. As such, automatic
analysis of WSIs seems to be particular importance at the background of high
incidence of cancer. To relieve the dilemma we are facing [1], a large number of
researchers all around the world focus on studying algorithms for the automatic
analysis of WSIs.

© Springer Nature Switzerland AG 2019
Y. Zhao et al. (Eds.): ICIG 2019, LNCS 11902, pp. 558–567, 2019.
https://doi.org/10.1007/978-3-030-34110-7_47

In recent years, an increasing number of automatic analysis methods for WSIs have been developed based on machine learning algorithms. Cancerous region segmentation is a popular application among the existing methods based on deep learning networks. However, it's difficult to process a WSI directly using recent deep learning methods because of its high pixel resolution. Therefore, the first step is to divide the WSI into small patches and segment the cancerous regions patch by patch. Some segmentation methods for nature images are usually applied to WSIs analysis. For segmentation, one of the classic networks is Fully convolutional network (FCN) [8]. FCN is to segment images based on pixel-level, the input and output are both 2-D images with the same size. The segmentation results of the region of interest can be directly obtained. There are also many segmentation methods: SegNet [12], CRFs [14], DeepLab [4] and some aimed at WSIs, for instance, U-Net proposed in [9] adopt overlap-tile strategy for seamless segmentation of arbitrary large images and Yang et al. [13] combined U-Net and multi-task cascade network to segment WSIs and achieved better accuracy.

Besides FCN, convolutional neural networks (CNNs) including DenseNet [3], ResNet [2], GooLeNet [11] and graph CNN for survival analysis [5] arc also widely applied to the segmentation of WSIs. But the WSI should be firstly divided into small patches based on sliding window strategy because of the high resolution. Then, the patches are fed to the network and the labels of the patches are predicted. The segmentation results will be generated from the up-sampled probability maps similar to the result of FCN. This method is not sensitive to boundaries, while, for practical application, the segmentation result is sufficient to analyze WSI for pathologists. In addition, the small blank regions among the tissue would not be excessively segmented and pathologists can get a more integrated results.

In this paper, we conducted a series of experiments to segment cancerous regions from WSIs utilizing FCN and CNN frameworks and verified the feasibility and effectiveness of the two methods (FCN and CNN). Then, we compared the results from the two methods and found that they equally performed. All of our experiments are completed on a public lung histopathology dataset of ACDC-LungHP challenge [6].

Our work addresses the segmentation of lung carcinoma from WSIs. The main contributions of this paper can be summarized as:

(1) We designed two complete strategies for lung carcinoma segmentation based on CNN and FCN, respectively.
(2) We evaluated the accuracy and running time of CNN-based and FCN-based strategies and compared the segmentation performance of the two strategies.
(3) To leverage the advantages of both CNN and FCN, we proposed an integrated flowchart for lung carcinoma segmentation. Our method was evaluated on the ACDC-LungHP challenge and achieved the 4th rank with a dice coefficient 0.770.

The details of our methods and their results comparison are introduced in the following sections.

2   Method

The flowchart of our methods is illustrated in Fig. 1. To analyze histopathology images, pixel-wise segmentation based on FCN will be designed to segment lung carcinoma. Because histopathology WSIs are in high resolution, CNN for patch-level classification can accomplish the segmentation task when the patches are small enough relative to the whole slide. The ensemble of two networks is to leverage both advantages and further improve the segmentation performance.

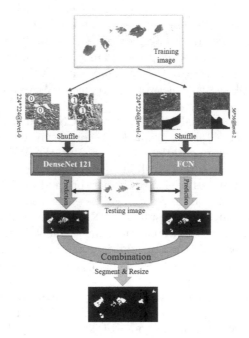

Fig. 1. The flowchart of our methods. It contains 3 sections: CNN, FCN and ensemble.

2.1   Segmentation Based on FCN

FCN is a conventional method for image segmentation. FCN framework can be used to process WSIs the same as nature images by dividing the whole WSI into smaller patches with size of 224×224. The FCN structure was designed based on DenseNet-1 structure [3], as shown in Fig. 2. To limit the computation, the last dense block of DenseNet structure was removed and two transposed convolution layers were connected instead, up-sampling the feature map to 56×56. Namely, the side length of output is $1/4$ to that of the input. Then, dice loss [10] and focal loss [7] were applied to train the networks with label masks. when predicting, the testing WSI was processed by the trained FCN with a sliding window of $1280 \times$

1280 pixels. To relieve the effect of the window border, the window region was padded to 1536 × 1536 pixels before feeding into the FCN. In corresponding, the output was cropped to remove the padded regions. After prediction, a probability map in high resolution was generated. Then, the segmentation was completed by the threshold on the probability maps.

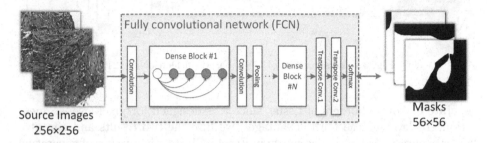

Fig. 2. The structure of FCN based on DenseNet.

2.2 Segmentation Based on CNN

CNNs have been proven effective in image classification and have been successfully introduced into histopathological image analysis because of the high resolution of WSIs. Specifically, to increase comparability, we also employed DenseNet-121 structure [3] with 2 output neurons (as shown in Fig. 3) as the classifier of cancer patches. The network was trained from randomly initial parameters. To relieve overfitting, color noise was randomly added to the patches. As for prediction, the testing WSIs were divided into patches (the same size with the CNN input) following the sliding window paradigm with sliding step set 112 (half of the patch side length) and fed into DenseNet structure. For each window, the output of the positive neural node was recorded and regarded as the probability of cancer. Thereby, a probability mat that indicates the location of cancerous patches was obtained after the sliding window paradigm. Then the mat was up-sampled to fit the original size of WSI. Finally, a threshold was selected to generate the mask for the WSI.

2.3 Ensemble

Finally, we have tried to assemble the probability maps obtained by the two frameworks. Specifically, the maps were averaged and then segmented by a threshold. The CNN can classify a patch into one single category according to the threshold. The small blank regions among the tissue would not be excessively segmented. Thereby, the cancerous regions segmented by CNN are more integrated than those obtained by FCN structure. On the contrary, the FCN can

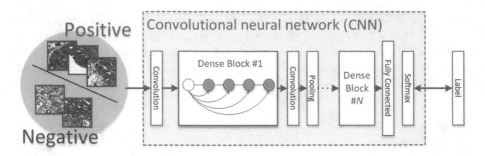

Fig. 3. The structure of CNN based on DenseNet-121.

generate elaborate borders of tissue, since it is designed for pixel-level segmentation. To leverage the both advantages, we fuse the two results and aim at a better accuracy. A diagram as shown in Fig. 4 indicates the process of generating segmentation results.

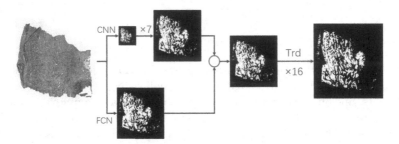

Fig. 4. The flowchart of generating masks from probability maps. The probability matrix obtained from CNN is up-sampled 7 times, to the same size with FCN and averaged with the probability matrix of FCN. A threshold ("Trd" in the figure) is applied to segment the averaged probability matrix. Finally, the segmentation result is resized 16 times to generate the pixel-wise segmentation result of the WSI.

3   Experiments

3.1   Experimental Setting

The proposed method was implemented in python. The experiments that involves CNNs were conducted based on the mxnet framework and the experiments for FCNs were on the tensorflow platform. The training patches along with the labels were transformed to the formats the platforms required.

All the experiments were conducted on a computer with an Intel Core i7-7700k CPU of 4.2 GHz and a GPU of Nvidia GTX 1080Ti.

3.2   Data Preparation

The data used in the experiments are ACDC-LungHP dataset. It concludes a mass of lung cancer biopsy samples stained with hematoxylin and eosin (H&E). To train the neural networks, we designed a flowchart (as shown in Fig. 5) to generate training samples from the WSIs. 150 WSIs with annotations are used to train our networks, among them, 80% are used as training set and the remaining are validation set.

At first, a bounding box was manually annotated to locate the tissue regions for each WSI. To reduce the computation, a threshold was applied to coarsely filter the blank areas (pure white and black pixels). Then, square patches in size of 224×224 pixels for CNN and 256×256 pixels for FCN were randomly sampled from the tissue regions to establish the training datasets. To balance the samples from each WSI, the patches from WSIs with small tissue regions were augmented through randomly flipping & rotating. Correspondingly, the patches from large WSIs were randomly reduced. Overall, about 2000 positive (contain more than 50% cancerous pixels referring to the annotation) and 2000 negative (less than 10% cancerous pixels) patches were generated from each WSI. For the training of FCNs, the mask of cancerous pixels for each patch was simultaneously cropped and used as the ground truth. All the patches and the corresponding labels and masks were shuffled to ensure each batch could contain the general allocation of the WSI data.

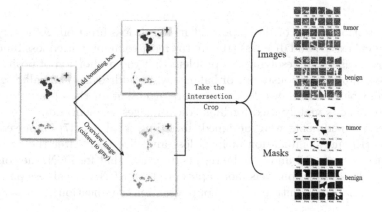

Fig. 5. The process of generating datasets for CNN and FCN.

3.3   Training

The CNN structure used in our experiment is the DenseNet-121 suggested in [3]. The training patches are sampled from WSIs under the resolution of level 0 (defined in ASAP, the resolution is 40× lens) and randomly flipped, rotated and scaled for augmentation. The cross-entropy with softmax output is used as the loss function. The SGD with momentum is applied as the optimizer.

The FCN consists of three dense blocks where the first block has 5 convolutional layers and the other two have 8 convolutional layers. Before the first dense block, two convolutional layers with 3×3 kernels are applied on the input images and each side of the input tensors is zero-padded by one pixel to keep the feature-map size fixed. Following the dense blocks, two transposed convolutional layers are used to upsample the feature maps to the same size of labels. Focal loss and dice loss were considered in the training stage. We conducted the experiment on WSIs under the resolution of level 2 (the pixel resolution is $1\times$ lens) and tried three kinds of loss combinations: focal loss only, dice loss only and both. Then, the loss type that achieves the best result is chosen for subsequent experiments.

3.4   Results and Discussions

Hyper-Parameter Setting. A number of experiments were conducted on the training and validation sets to determine the settings of our proposed approach. The CNN and FCN frameworks were conducted on resolution of level 0, level 1 and level 2 respectively. The results indicated that, as for CNN, the performance of level 0 was the best and level 2 for FCN achieved best accuracy. Besides, learning rate, batch size and growth rate were determined according to the performance of the validation set.

Loss Functions. One of the important factors is loss function. As for segmentation, focal loss [7] and dice loss [10] are the most commonly used loss functions. Focal loss is aimed at resolving the problem that the proportion of positive and negative samples is seriously out of balance when addressing two-value segmentation and bipartition. Dice loss pays more attention on the object needed be segmented and is mainly used for biomedical images segmentation.

Several experiments were designed, including focal loss [7] employed, only dice loss [10] and combination of focal loss and dice loss. After the prediction mentioned in Sects. 2.1 and 2.2, the results indicated that for FCN, the combination of both loss functions was more appropriate, for CNN, focal loss performed not better than cross-entropy (commonly used for classification).

Segmentation Accuracy. The dice coefficient and running time for different settings of FCN and CNN are presented in Table 1. The FCN achieved a dice score of 0.7525 and the CNN achieved a comparative score of 0.7528. It indicates both the two strategies are adequate for histopathological whole slide image analysis. Actually, the patch-based CNNs can generate a probability map of hundreds by hundreds pixels from high-resolution WSI (Level 0), which is sufficient to help pathologists recognize diagnostically relevant regions from the WSI. The running time of FCN structure is much shorter than CNN. The main reason is that the FCN structure uses a resolution that is much lower than that of CNN structure. Another reason is that the CNN structure utilizes overlapping patches in the analysis, which has further increased the computation. Furthermore, to exploit the advantages of the two frameworks, we assembled the CNN and FCN structures that achieved the best results separately (using the approach provided in Sect. 2.3). Consequently, the dice coefficient reached to 0.770. But, at the same time, it needs more time including the CNN's and FCN's. The result ranked No.4 in the ACDC-LungHP challenge. The leaderboard is listed in Table 2.

By analysis of each WSI result, several challenging WSIs for our method are displayed in Fig. 6, which are needed to be further improved. For visualization, the segmentation results obtained by our framework can be converted to free curves, which is able to be reloaded in ASAP tools. An instance of the visualization is presented in Fig. 7.

Table 1. The dice coefficients for different setting of the our methods.

Method	Image levels	Loss type	Dice coefficient	Time
CNN	Level-0	Cross entropy loss	**0.7528**	328.8 s
FCN	Level-2	Focal loss	0.7184	7.2 s
		Dice loss	0.7213	
		Focal+Dice loss	**0.7525**	
Combination	Level-0	Cross entropy loss	0.7700	336.0 s
	Level-2	Focal+Dice loss		

Table 2. The leaderboard of ACDC-LungHP challenge 2019.

Rank	Group name	Score (Dice mean)
1	PINGAN Technology	0.8373
2	Lunit Inc	0.8297
3	Turbolag	0.7968
4	**Ours**	**0.7700**
5	BUAA	0.7659
6	Arontier	0.7638
7	Frederick National Laboratory for Cancer Research	0.7552
-	**Ours(CNN)**	**0.7528**
-	**Ours(FCN)**	**0.7525**
8	National Taiwan University of Science and Technology	0.7510
9	Skychain	0.7456
10	University of Maryland	0.7394

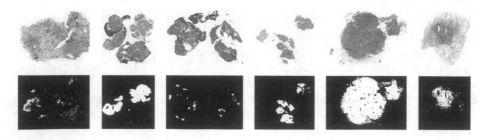

Fig. 6. The challenging WSIs and corresponding segmentation masks.

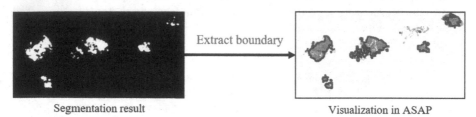

Segmentation result   Visualization in ASAP

Fig. 7. The flowchart of generating masks from probability maps.

4   Conclusion

According to the results, CNN and FCN both achieved satisfactory performance for histopathological whole slide image analysis. Furthermore, the frameworks based on CNN and FCN achieved comparable segmentation performance. It indicates that the segmentation via patch-wise classification on a high resolution could be equivalent to the segmentation by an FCN under lower resolutions. After a combination of the CNN and FCN results, the metric was further improved. It demonstrates that the information from high and low magnification of WSIs are complementary.

Acknowledgment. This work was supported by the National Natural Science Foundation of China (No. 61771031, 61371134, 61471016, and 61501009), China Postdoctoral Science Foundation (No. 2019M650446) and Motic-BUAA Image Technology Research Center.

References

1. Bejnordi, B.E., et al.: Diagnostic assessment of deep learning algorithms for detection of lymph node metastases in women with breast cancer. JAMA **318**(22), 2199–2210 (2017)
2. He, K., Zhang, X., Ren, S., Sun, J.: Deep residual learning for image recognition. In: The IEEE Conference on Computer Vision and Pattern Recognition (CVPR), June 2016

3. Huang, G., Liu, Z., van der Maaten, L., Weinberger, K.Q.: Densely connected convolutional networks. In: 2017 IEEE Conference on Computer Vision and Pattern Recognition (CVPR), pp. 2261–2269 (2017)
4. Chen, L., Papandreou, G., Kokkinos, I., Murphy, K., Yuille, A.L.: DeepLab: semantic image segmentation with deep convolutional nets, atrous convolution, and fully connected CRFs. IEEE Trans. Pattern Anal. Mach. Intell. **40**(4), 834–848 (2018). https://doi.org/10.1109/TPAMI.2017.2699184
5. Li, R., Yao, J., Zhu, X., Li, Y., Huang, J.: Graph CNN for survival analysis on whole slide pathological images. In: Frangi, A.F., Schnabel, J.A., Davatzikos, C., Alberola-López, C., Fichtinger, G. (eds.) MICCAI 2018. LNCS, vol. 11071, pp. 174–182. Springer, Cham (2018). https://doi.org/10.1007/978-3-030-00934-2_20
6. Li, Z., et al.: Computer-aided diagnosis of lung carcinoma using deep learning - a pilot study. CoRR abs/1803.05471 (2018)
7. Lin, T.Y., Goyal, P., Girshick, R., He, K., Dollar, P.: Focal loss for dense object detection. In: The IEEE International Conference on Computer Vision (ICCV), October 2017
8. Long, J., Shelhamer, E., Darrell, T.: Fully convolutional networks for semantic segmentation. In: The IEEE Conference on Computer Vision and Pattern Recognition (CVPR), June 2015
9. Ronneberger, O., Fischer, P., Brox, T.: U-Net: convolutional networks for biomedical image segmentation. In: Navab, N., Hornegger, J., Wells, W.M., Frangi, A.F. (eds.) MICCAI 2015. LNCS, vol. 9351, pp. 234–241. Springer, Cham (2015). https://doi.org/10.1007/978-3-319-24574-4_28
10. Sorensen, T.A.: A method of establishing groups of equal amplitude in plant sociology based on similarity of species content and its application to analyses of the vegetation on Danish commons. Biol. Skar. **5**, 1–34 (1948). https://ci.nii.ac.jp/naid/10008878962/en/
11. Szegedy, C., et al.: Going deeper with convolutions. In: The IEEE Conference on Computer Vision and Pattern Recognition (CVPR), June 2015
12. Badrinarayanan, V., Kendall, A., Cipolla, R.: SegNet: a deep convolutional encoder-decoder architecture for image segmentation. IEEE Trans. Pattern Anal. Mach. Intell. **39**(12), 2481–2495 (2017)
13. Yang, Q., et al.: Cervical nuclei segmentation in whole slide histopathology images using convolution neural network. In: Yap, B.W., Mohamed, A.H., Berry, M.W. (eds.) SCDS 2018. CCIS, vol. 937, pp. 99–109. Springer, Singapore (2019). https://doi.org/10.1007/978-981-13-3441-2_8
14. Zheng, S., et al.: Conditional random fields as recurrent neural networks. In: The IEEE International Conference on Computer Vision (ICCV), December 2015

Hybrid Simplified Spherical Harmonics with Diffusion Equation for X-Ray Luminescence Computed Tomography

Hengna Zhao[1,2], Jingxiao Fan[1,2], Hongbo Guo[1,2], Yuqing Hou[1,2],
and Xiaowei He[1,2(✉)]

[1] School of Information and Technology, Northwest University, Xi'an 710127, Shaanxi, China
hexw@nwu.edu.cn
[2] Xi'an Key Laboratory of Radiomics and Intelligent Perception,
No. 1 Xuefu Avenue, Xi'an 710127, Shaanxi, China

Abstract. X-ray luminescence computed tomography (XLCT) combines the high sensitivity of optical imaging with the high spatial resolution of X-ray imaging, and has a more extensive application prospect. An efficient and accurate optical transmission model is very important for XLCT. In optical molecular imaging, the light transmission models we often use are diffusion equation (DE) and simplified spherical harmonic (SP_N). DE has high efficiency but relatively low accuracy, while SP_N has high accuracy but low efficiency. Therefore, the hybrid simplified spherical harmonics with diffusion equation (HSDE) model is proposed. By coupling the DE and SP_N with boundary conditions, the HSDE obtained has both high accuracy and high efficiency. First, each tissue is simulated to determine the best model for it. Then the accuracy and the efficiency of HSDE are verified by forward simulation and inverse simulation for the whole digital mouse model. The results show that the accuracy of HSDE is better than SP_N and the efficiency is higher than DE.

Keywords: Hybrid optical transmission model · Diffusion equation · Simplified spherical harmonic · X-ray luminescence computed tomography

1 Introduction

Optical Imaging (OI) uses light to continuously observe the physiological activities of organisms at the molecular and cellular level, which is of great significance in the early detection of diseases, drug development, targeted therapy and other fields [1]. Fluorescence Molecular Tomography (FMT) has become a common optical imaging method due to its high sensitivity, non-ionizing radiation, etc. However, since FMT irradiates specific fluorescent molecular probes in biological tissues with near-infrared light, and it is stimulated to emit light, which leads to the absorption of nir light in the process of tissue transmission and the short penetration distance. In 2010, Carpenter et al. proposed the idea of combining hybrid X-ray and optical imaging, which come true X-ray molecular imaging [2]. Compared with FMT, X-ray luminescence computed

© Springer Nature Switzerland AG 2019
Y. Zhao et al. (Eds.): ICIG 2019, LNCS 11902, pp. 568–580, 2019.
https://doi.org/10.1007/978-3-030-34110-7_48

tomography (XLCT) uses X-ray to excitated specific fluorescent probes in biological tissues, so that X-ray can not be absorbed by tissues and has a longer detection range. Carpenter et al. has proved that the molecular imaging performance of finite Angle XLCT on deep targets is better than FMT through numerical simulation and simulation experiment [3]. XLCT combining high sensitivity of the optical imaging with high spatial resolution of the X-ray imaging, which can overcome defects of the optical molecular imaging, and achieve arbitrary Angle data acquisition. Meanwhile it will not be interfered by external signals, so it has a broad prospect of development.

At present, optical transmission model and reconstruction algorithm are still two important factors affecting XLCT reconstruction results. Radiative transport equation (RTE) can accurately describe the energy change of photons in turbid organisms. However, RTE is a complicated integral-differential process, and its solution is very difficult. In this regard, researchers have proposed various simplified approximate models. First, the diffusion equation (DE) is proposed, which is a first-order approximate model of RTE. However, when this model is used, it needs to meet certain conditions, that is, the scattering effect of biological tissue on light is much greater than the absorption effect. In addition, DE only achieves acceptable accuracy at a small computational cost, and its accuracy is relatively low [4]. In view of the shortcomings of the DE model, researchers further proposed a high-order approximate model of RTE, the simplified spherical harmonic approximation (SP_N), which is a more accurate RTE approximation model than DE. However, SP_N has a large demand for memory space, which makes it difficult for SP_N to be used on the fine mesh and limits its application in practice. Meanwhile, SP_N requires a relatively long running time. To sum up, the current optical transmission models are compromised between accuracy and computational efficiency, and there is no model that can guarantee both accuracy and efficiency.

According to the prior information of anatomical structure, we can decompose small animals such as mouse into the following major organs: adipose, muscle, liver, heart, kidney, stomach and lung. Since each tissue has different absorption and scattering characteristics of light, they will show different characteristics such as high scattering and non-high scattering. At the same time, the optical transmission model also has its own scope of application. For example, DE is suitable for describing the transmission of light in high-scattering tissue, while SP_N is suitable for describing the transmission of light in non-high-scattering tissue. In such a complex organism, a single model is inevitably insufficient to accurately describe transmission process of light in the organism. Hence, a hybrid model based on simplified spherical harmonic and diffusion equation is proposed, which can have the accuracy of SP_N and the high efficiency of DE at the same time, so as to achieve the balance between accuracy and efficiency.

In this paper, the hybrid simplified spherical harmonics with diffusion equation (HSDE) is proposed as the optical transmission model of XLCT. In HSDE, we divide tissues into two categories: high-scattering tissues and non-high-scattering tissues. Currently, the commonly used classification standard is defined according to the ratio of absorption coefficient and scattering coefficient [5–7]. When this ratio is greater than a value, DE is adopted, or else SP_N is adopted. This value is referred to as the threshold. It should be noted that there is no clear value for the threshold setting in this classification method, and researchers set it manually according to their own experiences or experimental requirements. For example, in some literatures, the threshold is set to 3, while in others it is set to 40 [6]. In order to classify the tissues accurately, we firstly set up a set of experiments to simulate each tissue of digital mouse by using DE and SP_N respectively. Then, we use the DE for high-scattering tissues and the SP_N for non-high-scattering tissues. Finally, DE and SP_N are connected through the boundary coupled equation, so that the high running time of DE is combined successfully with the high precision of SP_N to achieve the high efficiency and accuracy of HSDE.

In addition to the optical transmission model, reconstruction algorithm is another important factor affecting the quality of XLCT imaging. Due to the insufficient measurements and highly diffusive nature of the photon propagation within biological tissues, XLCT reconstruction is still a very challenging illposed inverse problem. Hence, the ill-posedness is the crucial issue that reconstruction algorithms have to address. The incomplete variables truncated conjugate gradient (IVTCG) algorithm proposed by He et al. has been proved to be able to accurately locate and quantify the light source distribution in the entire region under the condition of noise measurement and inaccurate optical parameters [8]. Therefore, we chose IVTCG as the reconstruction algorithm for our experimental reconstruction process.

The rest of the paper is arranged as follows. The optical transmission models, XLCT imaging principle, and reconstruction algorithm are introduced in Sect. 2 and the experiments and results are showed in Sect. 3. Finally, the conclusions are given in Sect. 4.

2 Methods

2.1 XLCT

In XLCT, X-rays generated by X-ray sources are high-energy electron streams. When the X-ray penetrates object, these electron streams will produce photoelectric effect, compton effect and coherent scattering effect in biological tissues. These effects will cause some of X photons to be completely absorbed or scattered, and eventually intensity of X-rays will decline to some extent. According to the Lambert-Beers law, energy attenuation of X-ray when passing through biological tissue can be expressed as [9]:

$$X(r) = X_0 e^{-(\tau + \sigma + \sigma_r) \cdot \Delta x} \tag{1}$$

where $X(r)$ is X-ray intensity at r in biological tissue, X_0 is initial intensity of the X-ray source, τ, σ, σ_r represent photoelectric effect, compton effect and attenuation coefficient of coherent scattering in biological tissue respectively. When absorption energy spectrum based on X-ray is reconstructed by back projection, Eq. (1) can be expressed as:

$$X(r) = X_0 e^{-\int_{r_0}^{r} \mu_x(\tau) d\tau} \tag{2}$$

where μ_x is X-ray attenuation coefficient.

In the excitation process of XLCT, Eq. (3) were used to obtain the boundary point information when X-ray passed through biological surface,

$$
\begin{cases}
\frac{X-X_s}{X_0-X_s} = \frac{Y-Y_s}{Y_0-Y_s} = \frac{Z-Z_s}{Z_0-Z_s} \\
\frac{X_1-X_s}{X_d-X_s} = \frac{Y_1-Y_s}{Y_d-Y_s} = \frac{Z_1-Z_s}{Z_d-Z_s}
\end{cases}
\tag{3}
$$

where (X_s, Y_s, Z_s), (X_0, Y_0, Z_0) and (X_1, Y_1, Z_1) are location of X-ray source, center position of source point, and known surface point respectively, (X, Y, Z) is location of the intersection of X-ray source and light source at imaginary plan, (X_d, Y_d, Z_d) is location of the intersection of point (X_s, Y_s, Z_s) and point (X_1, Y_1, Z_1) at imaginary plan. The schematic diagram is shown in Fig. 1:

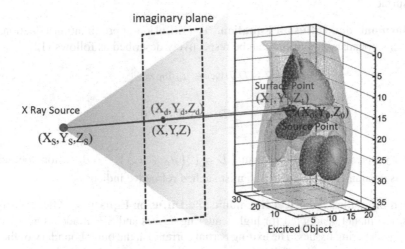

Fig. 1. XLCT image principle

2.2 Coupled Simplified Spherical Harmonic and Diffusion Model

According to the prior information of the dissection structure, a living animal, such as a mouse, can be divided into several major tissues, including heart, kidney, liver, lung, stomach and adipose. HSDE was used to describe the propagation process of light in high-scattering and non-high-scattering regions respectively after judging the light transmission model to be adopted by each tissue.

The Simplified Spherical Harmonic Equation. Liu et al. have confirmed that the third order SP$_N$ (SP3) can achieve relatively small calculation on the premise of ensuring accuracy, therefore we chose SP3 as an example of SP$_N$ in this work [10]. The optical transmission under the Sp3 can be expressed as follows [11]:

$$
\begin{cases}
-\nabla \cdot \frac{1}{3\mu_{a1}} \nabla \Phi_1 + \mu_a \Phi_1 - \frac{2}{3}\mu_a \Phi_2 = S \\
-\nabla \cdot \frac{1}{7\mu_{a3}} \nabla \Phi_2 - \frac{2}{3}\mu_a \Phi_1 + \left(\frac{4}{9}\mu_a + \frac{5}{9}\mu_{a2}\right)\Phi_2 = -\frac{2}{3}S
\end{cases}
\tag{4}
$$

where $\mu_{ai} = \mu_a + \mu_s(1 - g)$ is reduced scattering coefficient of biological tissue, g is Anisotropic factor, Φ_i represents spherical harmonic approximation of the light flux related to node flux density, S is light source. The solution of (2) must rely on a certain boundary prior condition, and commonly used Robin boundary condition, which has the following form under the SP$_3$ model [11]:

$$
\begin{cases}
\frac{1+B_1}{3\mu_{a1}}v \cdot \nabla\Phi_1 - \frac{D_1}{\mu_{a3}}v \cdot \nabla\Phi_2 = -\left(\frac{1}{2} + A_1\right)\Phi_1 + \left(\frac{1}{8} + C_1\right)\Phi_2 \\
-\frac{D_1}{\mu_{a1}}v \cdot \nabla\Phi_1 + \frac{1+B_2}{7\mu_{a3}}v \cdot \nabla\Phi_2 = \left(\frac{1}{8} + C_2\right)\Phi_1 - \left(\frac{7}{24} + A_2\right)\Phi_2
\end{cases}
\tag{5}
$$

where $A_n = \frac{1+R_n}{1-R_n}$, and $R_n = -1.4399n^{-2} + 0.7099n^{-1} + 0.0636n$, A_k, B_k, C_k, D_k (k = 1, 2) are boundary related parameters, and v is the unit direction vector toward the body surface.

The Harmonic and Diffusion Equation. The diffusion approximation equation and the robin's boundary conditions can be respectively described as follows [12]:

$$
-\nabla \cdot (D\nabla\Phi_0) + \mu_a\Phi_0 = S
\tag{6}
$$

$$
\Phi_0 + \frac{1}{\beta_0}D(v \cdot \nabla\Phi_0) = 0
\tag{7}
$$

where Φ_0 represents node flux density, $D = \left(3\left(\mu_a + \mu_s'\right)\right)^{-1}$ is diffusion coefficient, and β_0 is a parameter relevant to the mismatched refractive indices.

Coupled Simplified Spherical Harmonic and Diffusion Equation. After classifying tissues, DE model is adopted for high-scattering tissues and SP$_3$ model is adopted for non-high-scattering tissues. The exiting partial current J at the outer boundary of the SP$_3$ and DE can be expressed as follows:

$$
J_{SP3} = \beta_1\Phi_1 + \beta_2\Phi_2
\tag{8}
$$

$$
J_{DE} = \beta_0\Phi_0
$$

By combining the two models under boundary coupling conditions, that is to say that J_{SP3} is equal to J_{DE}. the following relationship can be addressed:

$$
\Phi_0 = \frac{\beta_1}{\beta_0}\Phi_1 + \frac{\beta_2}{\beta_0}\Phi_2
\tag{9}
$$

Then, the transmission equation of the coupled model can be obtained as follows:

$$
\begin{cases}
(1 - \sigma(r))\left(-\nabla\frac{1}{3\mu_{a1}(r)}\nabla\Phi_1(r) + \mu_a(r)\Phi_1(r) - \frac{2}{3}\mu_a(r)\Phi_2(r)\right) + \\
\sigma(r)\begin{pmatrix}-\nabla\left(D(r)\nabla\left(\frac{\beta_1(r)}{\beta_0(r)}\Phi_1(r) + \frac{\beta_2(r)}{\beta_0(r)}\Phi_2(r)\right)\right) + \\ \mu_a(r)\left(\frac{\beta_1(r)}{\beta_0(r)}\Phi_1(r) + \frac{\beta_2(r)}{\beta_0(r)}\Phi_2(r)\right)\end{pmatrix} = S(r) \\
(1 - \sigma(r))\begin{pmatrix}-\nabla\frac{1}{7\mu_{a3}(r)}\nabla\Phi_2(r) - \frac{2}{3}\mu_a(r)\Phi_1(r) + \\ \left(\frac{4}{9}\mu_a(r) + \frac{5}{9}\mu_{a2}(r)\right)\Phi_2(r)\end{pmatrix} = -\frac{2}{3}(1 - \sigma(r))S(r)
\end{cases}
\quad r \in \Omega
\tag{10}
$$

where $\sigma(r)$ is the introduced indicator factor and is defined as:

$$\sigma(r) = \begin{cases} 1 & r \in \Omega_l \ or \ \partial\Omega \subset \partial\Omega_l \\ 0 & r \in \Omega_h \ or \ \partial\Omega \subset \partial\Omega_h \end{cases} \tag{11}$$

where the Ω_l and Ω_h are regions containing high-scattering tissues and non-high-scattering tissues determined by experiments.

2.3 XLCT Inverse Model

We can get the linear relationship between the interior source density and the boundary photon flux rate are derived by solving boundary conditions with the finite element method for optical transmission model, and the matrix equation that connects the discretized fluence rate Φ and the discretized source distribution S can be expressed as [13, 14]:

$$M\Phi = FS \tag{12}$$

where M is a positive definite matrix and F is the source weight matrix. Thus, the photon fluence rate Φ is derived by

$$\Phi = M^{-1}F\,S = \overline{A}\,S \tag{13}$$

Since only partial photons on the boundary are captured by CCD in BLT experiments by retaining those rows associated with the boundary measurements Φ^m in the coefficient matrix $\overline{A}$, $\overline{A}$ becomes A, and then we obtain the inverse model of BLT:

$$AS = \Phi^m \tag{14}$$

where $A \in R^{M*N}$ ($M < N$).

2.4 Incomplete Variables Truncated Conjugate Gradient Algorithm

IVTCG transforms the XLCT inverse model into the following l_1 regularization minimization problem,

$$\min_s \frac{1}{2}\left\| AS - \Phi^m \right\|_2^2 + \tau \left\| S \right\| \tag{15}$$

where $S \in R^N$, $\Phi^m \in R^M$, $A \in R^{M*N}$ ($M < N$), $\tau > 0$ is a regularization parameter.

Since the objective function in Eq. (15) is convex but not differentiable, we reformulate it as a convex quadratic program with nonnegative constrained conditions by a similar method used in gradient projection for sparse reconstruction (GPSR), an efficient algorithm for large scale sparse problems in compressed sensing and other inverse problems in signal processing and statistics [8]. Hence, Eq. (15) can be rewritten as the following program:

$$\min_s c^T z + \frac{1}{2}z^T B z \equiv F(z), s.t.z \geq 0 \tag{16}$$

where $z = [u\ v]^T$, $c = \tau 1_{2N} + [-b\ b]^T$, $1_{2N} = [1, 1, \cdots, 1]^T$, $b = A^T\Phi^m$, and $B = \begin{bmatrix} A^T A & -A^T A \\ -A^T A & A^T A \end{bmatrix} = [A, -A\,]^T[A, -A]$.

3 Experiments and Results

3.1 Classification of Tissue

Before the hybrid model experiment, we need to select the best light transmission model for each tissue. The monte carlo method (MC), known as the 'gold standard', is believed to be the most accurate way to simulate propagation of light in biological tissues. The Molecular Optical Simulation Environment (MOSE) can realize MC simulation of complex biological organization and photon transmission in free space. Therefore, in this experiment, we take the results of MOSE as the standard, compared results of each tissue under DE and SP3, and selected a more appropriate model as model to be used in the hybrid model of this tissue.

The parameters involved in this experiment are as follows. XLCT often uses Eu^{3+} as luminescent material, and optimal divergence wavelength of Eu^{3+} is 612 nm [11], so wavelength used in this experiment is 610 nm. The absorption coefficients (μ_a), scattering coefficients (μ_s) and anisotropy coefficient (g) of involved tissues are shown in Table 1. For each tissue, we set a sphere of radius 1 mm as the internal light source. In the case of the heart, we set a small ball with a radius of 1 mm at (19, 6, 18) mm as the light source for heart.

Table 1. Optical properties at 610 nm.

Tissue	$\mu_a\left(mm^{-1}\right)$	$\mu_s\left(mm^{-1}\right)$	g
Heart	0.199872	1.102260	0.9
Liver	1.198672	0.748263	0.9
Lung	0.663226	2.284711	0.9
Muscle	0.294651	0.559023	0.9
Stomach	0.380180	1.573821	0.9
Kidney	0.223914	2.595900	0.9

First, it is crucial for HSDE to select the appropriate light transport model for each tissue. DE and SP3 are used for experiments in each tissue, and MOSE results were used as the standard for comparison. Figure 2 shows individual tissues and their experimental results. One to six lines are heart, kidney, liver, lung, muscle and stomach respectively. Vertical view, the first column is every tissue and its internal source, the second to the fourth column are simulated photon distribution on the surface of MOSE, DE and SP3 respectively. The fifth column is drawn energy surface of MOSE, DE and SP3, which the red crosses, blue asterisks and green circles represents the MOSE, DE and SP3 respectively.

The sixth column shows the difference of surface energy between DE, SP3 with MOSE, the red crosses is the difference between MOSE and DE, while the blue asterisks is the MOSE and SP3. Table 2 quantitatively describes the difference between DE, SP3

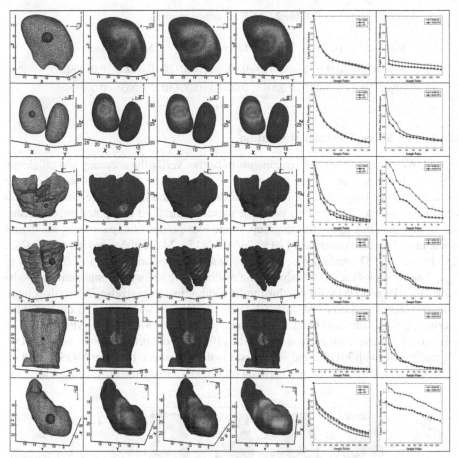

Fig. 2. Result of classification tissues. One to six lines are heart, kidney, liver, lung, muscle and stomach respectively. The first column is simulation model, the second to the fourth column are simulated photon distribution on the surface of MOSE, DE and SP3 respectively, the fifth column and sixth column are Surface photon diagram. (Color figure online)

and MOSE by calculating the average relative error (ARE) of the numerical models and MOSE. ARE is calculated as follows:

$$ARE = \frac{\sum_{i=1}^{N}(abs(Simulation_i - Mose_i)/max(Mose_i))}{N} \quad (17)$$

where $Simulation_i$ is the surface energy value obtained by MATLAB simulation and $Mose_i$ is the surface energy value obtained by MOSE, N is the total number of sample points. In Table 2, DE-MOSE is the ARE of DE relative to MOSE, while SP3-MOSE is the SP3 relative to MOSE. Both the Fig. 2 and Table 2 indicate that the heart, kidneys, liver and stomach are more suitable for SP3 than for DE, and lungs and muscles are more suitable for DE.

Table 2. ARE of surface energy

Method	Heart	Kidney	Liver	Lung	Muscle	Stomach
DE-MOSE	0.00074	0.00110	0.00260	0.00120	0.00033	0.01390
SP$_3$-MOSE	0.00037	0.00093	0.00180	0.00130	0.00036	0.000980

3.2 Digital Mouse Forward Simulation

Second, We set up four sets of experiments to further verify the accuracy and efficiency of HSDE. In the first group and the second group, the light source was placed in liver and heart, respectively. In the third and fourth groups, the light source was located in the muscle, but the distance between light source in the third group and subcutaneous was shorter than that in the fourth group. In the four groups of experiments, the digital mouse model are discretized into 19036, 24642, 24453, 24474 nodes and 99890, 130743, 129819 and 129587 tetrahedrons, and are shown in the first column of Fig. 3. Similar to Figs. 2 and 3 shows the MOSE simulation results in the second column and the results using DE, SP$_3$ and HSDE in the third to fifth columns respectively. The sixth column is drawn energy surface of MOSE, DE, SP$_3$ and HSDE, which the red crosses, blue asterisks, green circles and black dotted line represents the MOSE, DE, SP$_3$ and HSDE respectively. The seventh column shows the difference of surface energy between DE, SP$_3$ and HSDE with MOSE, the red crosses is the difference between MOSE and DE, the blue asterisks is the difference between MOSE and SP$_3$, while the green circles is the

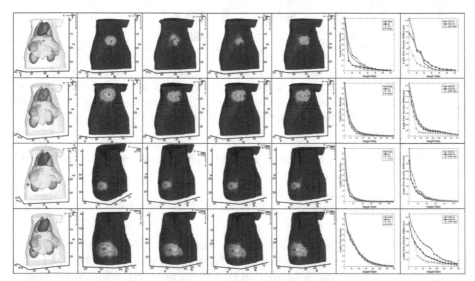

Fig. 3. Result of forward simulation. The first column is simulation model, the second to the fifth column are simulated photon distribution on the surface of MOSE, DE, SP3 and HSDE respectively, the sixth column and seventh column are Surface photon diagram. (Color figure online)

MOSE and HSDE. It can be seen from Fig. 3 that in the first two groups of experiments, HSDE always had the best effect. But it is worth noting that in the third and fourth groups of experiments, when the light source is close to subcutaneous area in the muscle, the effect of DE is better than that of SP3 and HSDE, while when the light source is far away from the subcutaneous area, HSDE is still the best. We can see this phenomenon in the last two rows of the last two columns in Fig. 3. This is because the muscle belongs to the highly scattered tissue, which is more suitable for the use of DE compared with SP3, which is consistent with the conclusion in Sect. 3.1, but the effect of HSDE in deep muscle is already better than that of DE. We can conclude that HSDE can be applied to tissues of all properties, compared with DE for tissues with high scattering and SP3 for tissues without high scattering.

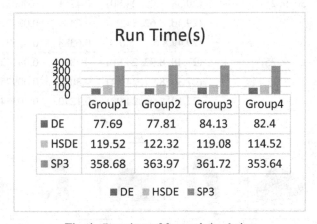

Fig. 4. Run time of forward simulation

We can see from Fig. 4, in the four groups of experiments, the running time of DE, HSDE and SP3 are around 80 s, 120 s and 360 s, respectively. Although the efficiency of HSDE is not as high as that of DE, it is more than three times higher than that of SP3, which is enough to explain the high efficiency of HSDE. Up to now, the accuracy and efficiency of HSDE have been proved.

3.3 Digital Mouse Inverse Simulation

Third, we further demonstrated the accuracy of HSDE through inverse simulation. We used IVTCG as the reconstruction algorithm, it can obtains fast and stable source reconstruction, even without a priori information of the permissible source region and multispectral measurements [8]. In this part of the experiment, the four groups of digital mouse models used in 3.2 are still adopted, and the results are shown in Fig. 5. Similar to Fig. 3, each row represents a group of experiments. Vertically, column 1, column 3, and column 5 are the 3D results of DE, SP3, and HSDE respectively. In the 3D image, the red part is real light source and the blue part is reconstructed light source. Column 2, 4, and 6 are the corresponding 2D effects, and the black circle is real light source and the fluorescent color is reconstructed light source. In order to quantitatively evaluate

Table 3. Reconstruction results

Group	Model	True light source location (mm)	Recon. light source location (mm)	LE (mm)	Fluorescence yield (nW/mm^3)
1	DE	(19, 7.5, 15)	(17.90, 7.36, 16.32)	1.7248	0.000249
	SP$_3$		(19.72, 6.43, 14.42)	1.4111	0.000476
	HSDE		(18.76, 7.78, 15.39)	0.5374	0.001185
2	DE	(19, 8, 7.5)	(19.30, 6.50, 6.83)	1.6638	0.000395
	SP$_3$		(18.76, 7.80, 7.55)	0.3069	0.017932
	HSDE		(18.62, 7.85, 7.50)	0.3978	0.001524
3	DE	(30, 9, 25)	(30.38, 8.79, 24.80)	0.4771	0.000317
	SP$_3$		(29.46, 8.62, 24.98)	0.6486	0.021291
	HSDE		(29.49, 8.61, 25.02)	0.6383	0.025272
4	DE	(27, 9, 25)	(27.48, 8.92, 24.96)	0.4893	0.001428
	SP$_3$		(27.30, 8.97, 24.94)	0.3072	0.009750
	HSDE		(27.10, 8.96, 24.92)	0.1270	0.003543

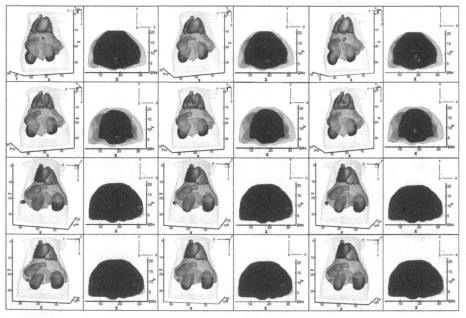

Fig. 5. Result of inverse simulation. The odd numbers are classified as 3D reconstruction results, while even numbers are classified as corresponding 2D reconstruction results. (Color figure online)

the reconstruction quality, the light source position error (LE) and fluorescence yield were used to illustrate the reconstruction effect, and the results are shown in Table 3.

According to the quantitative comparison, the reconstruction quality of HSDE is not much different from that of SP$_3$, or even better than that of SP$_3$. Moreover, the effect of DE is not always the worst. As can be seen from the third group of experiments, when the light source is located in the muscle and close to the skin surface, the effect of DE is better than that of SP$_3$ and HSDE, which is also consistent with the conclusion in Sect. 3.2.

4 Conclusion

In this paper, a hybrid light propagation model based on simplified spherical harmonic approximation and diffusion equation is proposed to describe the propagation of X-ray luminescence computed tomography in biological tissues. HSDE perfectly combines the calculation accuracy of SP$_N$ and the high efficiency of DE, so that HSDE can accurately and quickly describe the propagation process of light and achieve a perfect balance between accuracy and efficiency. First, each tissue was simulated separately to determine its optimal transmission model, and then the accuracy and efficiency of HSDE were demonstrated by comparing the simulation with DE and SP$_3$. Experiments show that HSDE can achieve a balance between accuracy and efficiency.

Acknowledgments. This work was supported by the National Natural Science Foundation of China under Grant Nos. 2016JM6025, 11571012, the Postdoctoral Innovative Talents Support Program under Grant No. BX20180254, the Project funded by China Post-doctoral Science Foundation under Grant No. 2018M643719, the education department served local special projects under Grant No. 17JF027.

References

1. Massoud, T.F., Gambhir, S.S.: Molecular imaging in living subjects: seeing fundamental biological processes in a new light. Genes Dev. **17**(5), 545–580 (2003)
2. Carpenter, C.M., Sun, C., Pratx, G., et al.: Hybrid x-ray/optical luminescence imaging: characterization of experimental conditions. Med. Phys. **37**(8), 4011–4018 (2010)
3. Carpenter, C.M., Pratx, G., Sun, C., et al.: Limited-angle x-ray luminescence tomography: methodology and feasibility study. Phys. Med. Biol. **56**(12), 3487 (2011)
4. Gao, H., Lin, Y., Gulsen, G., et al.: Fully linear reconstruction method for fluorescence yield and lifetime through inverse complex-source formulation: simulation studies. Opt. Lett. **35**(11), 1899–1901 (2010)
5. Chen, X., Yang, D., Qu, X., et al.: Comparisons of hybrid radiosity-diffusion model and diffusion equation for bioluminescence tomography in cavity cancer detection. J. Biomed. Opt. **17**(6), 066015 (2012)
6. Dehghani, H., Delpy, D.T., Arridge, S.R.: Photon migration in non-scattering tissue and the effects on image reconstruction. Phys. Med. Biol. **44**(12), 2897 (1999)
7. Tarvainen, T., Vauhkonen, M., Kolehmainen, V., et al.: Coupled radiative transfer equation and diffusion approximation model for photon migration in turbid medium with low-scattering and non-scattering regions. Phys. Med. Biol. **50**(20), 4913 (2005)
8. He, X., Liang, J., Wang, X., et al.: Sparse reconstruction for quantitative bioluminescence tomography based on the incomplete variables truncated conjugate gradient method. Opt. Express **18**(24), 24825–24841 (2010)

9. Chen, D., Zhu, S., Yi, H., et al.: Cone beam x-ray luminescence computed tomography: a feasibility study. Med. Phys. **40**(3), 031111 (2013)

10. Liu, K., Lu, Y., Tian, J., et al.: Evaluation of the simplified spherical harmonics approximation in bioluminescence tomography through heterogeneous mouse models. Opt. Express **18**(20), 20988–21002 (2010)

11. Han, D., Tian, J., Liu, K., et al.: Sparsity-promoting tomographic fluorescence imaging with simplified spherical harmonics approximation. IEEE Trans. Biomed. Eng. **57**(10), 2564–2567 (2010)

12. Arridge, S.R.: Optical tomography in medical imaging. Inverse Probl. **15**(2), R41 (1999)

13. Cong, W., Wang, G., Kumar, D., et al.: Practical reconstruction method for bioluminescence tomography. Opt. Express **13**(18), 6756–6771 (2005)

14. Singh, D., Tanwar, V., Bhagwan, S., et al.: Synthesis and optical characterization of europium doped MY_2O_4 (M = Mg, Ca, and Sr) nanophosphors for solid state lightening applications. Indian J. Mater. Sci. **2015**, 8 (2015)

Gradient Projection for Sparse Reconstruction Method for Dynamic Fluorescence Molecular Tomography

Jingxiao Fan[1,2], Hengna Zhao[1,2], Hongbo Guo[1,2], Yuqing Hou[1,2], and Xiaowei He[1,2(✉)]

[1] School of Information and Technology, Northwest University, Xi'an 710127, Shaanxi, China
hexw@nwu.edu.cn
[2] Xi'an Key Laboratory of Radiomics and Intelligent Perception,
No.1 Xuefu Avenue, Xi'an 710127, Shaanxi, China

Abstract. Dynamic fluorescence molecular tomography (FMT) is a promising optical imaging technique for three-dimensionally demonstrating the metabolic process of fluorophore in small animals. Conventional FMT methods focus on reconstructing static distribution of fluorescent yield, and the reconstruction results may perform poorly if the boundary measurement data, acquired from time-varying fluorophore, were directly used in these methods. In this study, we apply joint ℓ_1 and Laplacian manifold regularization model to dynamic FMT. The ℓ_1-norm regularization method is used to deal with the ill-posedness of FMT, and the Laplacian manifold regularization is introduced to obtain spatial structure information of boundary measurements. Then, we use gradient projection for sparse reconstruction (GPSR) method to solve the joint regularization model. Since the boundary measurements are obtained from different time points, the input data is converted from a vector to a matrix, and each column of the matrix corresponds to a time point. Thus, a sequence of fluorophore concentration images, corresponding to different time points, can be reconstructed in one step. Numerical simulation experiments are performed and the results indicate that the proposed method can recover the dynamic fluorophore well.

Keywords: Dynamic fluorescence molecular tomography · Regularization method · Gradient projection for sparse reconstruction method

1 Introduction

Dynamic fluorescence molecular tomography (FMT), as a promising optical tomographic imaging technique, provides richer information than conventional static imaging, and has the ability to capture the absorption, distribution, and elimination of fluorescent bio-markers within small animals [1–3]. It is helpful in better studying drug delivery and disease progression.

© Springer Nature Switzerland AG 2019
Y. Zhao et al. (Eds.): ICIG 2019, LNCS 11902, pp. 581–592, 2019.
https://doi.org/10.1007/978-3-030-34110-7_49

In static FMT, the traditional methods [4–6] assumed the concentration of fluorescent probe is constant, so these methods only reconstruct static distribution of fluorescent yield from data sets acquired within several minutes, but fail to capture the temporal information of the time-varying fluorophore. Besides, the reconstructed results perform poorly if the measurements, corresponding to the non-stationary fluorophore concentration, are directly used in the static FMT reconstruction, especially when the fluorophore concentrations vary rapidly.

To address the problem, some theoretical and experimental solutions have been proposed [7–10], and the fluorophore is assumed as a discrete time stochastic process. These methods allows the fluorophore concentration change over time, and they are capable to solve the dynamic FMT reconstruction problem. Since the fluorephore concentrations, viewed as a random variable at each time point, are temporally correlated, the acquired measurement data are highly correlated with one another along the time axis. These methods, however, obtain measurement data from different time first, and then reconstruct a series of static distributions of fluorescent yield respectively, fail to make full use of the temporal correlations of boundary measurements.

To overcome these limitations, in this paper, we propose a joint regularization model to reconstruct a sequence of FMT images of different time points in one step. Both accurate transportation model and sophisticated inverse algorithm are indispensable in FMT. To deal with the high ill-posedness of FMT, many regularization methods have been introduced to solve the inverse problem. ℓ_2-norm regularization, such as Tikhonov regularization [11, 12], was widely used in FMT. However, ℓ_2-norm regularization tends to incur over-smoothness in reconstructed image. To improve the imaging quality, ℓ_1-norm regularization, as an alternative solution, was used to promote the sparsity of the solution [13–15]. For dynamic FMT, spatial structure is significant information for reconstructing the distribution of fluorophore. To utilize both sparsity and spatial structure information, manifold-based learning method [16–19] is needed. Thus, we introduce Laplacian manifold regularization and combine it with ℓ_1-norm regularization to improve dynamic FMT reconstruction. Then, we use gradient projection for sparse reconstruction (GPSR) method [20, 21] to solve the joint regularization model.

The outline of this paper is as follows. In Sect. 2, the methods are detailed. Section 3 presents the experimental materials, and the reconstruction results are shown. In Sect. 4, we draw conclusions based on the simulation results.

2 Methods

2.1 Dynamic FMT Forward Model

For dynamic FMT, the photon propagation in biological tissues can be modeled using the diffusion equation (DE). In a continuous-wave domain with point excitation sources, the propagation of excitation and emission lights can be presented as follows:

$$
\begin{cases}
\nabla \cdot [D_x(r)\nabla\Phi(r,t)] - \mu_{ax}(r)\Phi_x(r,t) = -\Theta\delta(r - r_s, t) & (r \in \Omega) \\
\nabla \cdot [D_m(r)\nabla\Phi_m(r,t)] - \mu_{am}(r)\Phi_m(r,t) = -\Phi_x\eta\mu_{\alpha f}(r,t) & (r \in \Omega)
\end{cases}
\tag{1}
$$

where Ω is the domain of the imaged object, r is the position vector. $\mu_{ax,m}(r)$ represents the absorption coefficient, t denotes time. The subscript x and m represent the excitation process and emission progress respectively. $\Phi_{x,m}(r,t)$ denotes photon intensity and $D_{x,m}(r)$ is the diffusion coefficient of the tissue at position r. $\delta(r - r_s, t)$ is the point excitation source and Θ is the amplitude. r_s is the position vector of different excitation sources. η denotes the fluorescent yield efficiency, $\mu_{af}(r,t)$ is the absorption coefficient of fluorescent to the excitation light.

In this paper, finite element method (FEM) is chosen to solve the diffusion equations that the imaged domain is discretized into a mesh with N nodes. Equation (1) is converted into the following linear equations:

$$\begin{cases} K_x \Phi_x = S_x \\ K_m \Phi_m = FX \end{cases} \tag{2}$$

where K_x and K_m represent the system matrix in excitation process and emission process, respectively. S_x denotes the excitation source distribution, F is an $N \times N$ symmetric matrix. Based on Eq. (2), the final equation can be formulated as:

$$AX = \Phi \tag{3}$$

Equation (3) shows the linear relationship between the unknown fluorescent yield X and the boundary measurements Φ. A is an $M \times N$ weight matrix depending on the geometry and optical parameters.

For static FMT, the fluorophore is assumed to be stationary that it does not change during FMT imaging processes. Thus, X is a $N \times 1$ vector represents the fluorescent yield at a given time t, and Φ, also a $N \times 1$ vector, is the corresponding boundary measurements. However, in dynamic FMT, a time series of boundary measurements are acquired at intervals of minutes over time and the fluorescent yield can be denoted as $X = \{X_1, X_2, \cdots, X_t, \cdots, X_k\}$, where k is the number of time points. As a consequence, both of X and Φ are $N \times k$ matrices.

2.2 Dynamic FMT Inverse Model

The static reconstruction algorithms fail to solve the time-varying measurements, in this paper, we proposed a joint ℓ_1 and Laplacian manifold regularization model to improve the reconstruction performance.

To cope with the high ill-posed nature of Eq. (3) and the existence of noise, some form of regularization method is indispensable in the inversion. Compared with ℓ_2-norm regularization method, ℓ_1-norm regularization is used in this paper due to its sparsity. The inverse problem can be formulated as:

$$\arg \min_X \frac{1}{2} \|AX - \Phi_m\|_2^2 + \tau \|X\|_1 \tag{4}$$

In order to improve the quality of reconstruction, both structural priors and temporal correlations of boundary measurements should be fully utilized. Thus, we introduce the Laplacian manifold regularization into the inverse process:

$$\arg\min_{X} \frac{1}{2}||AX - \Phi_m||_2^2 + \tau||X||_1 + \frac{\lambda}{2}X^T LX \tag{5}$$

where $X^T LX$ is the Laplacian manifold regularization term and L is the regularization.

Let $p_i (i = 1, 2, \ldots, N)$ denotes the space nodes, $e_{i,j}(i, j = 1, 2, \ldots, N)$ denotes the edges of FEM mesh. $e_{i,j} = 1$ represents there is an edge between p_i and p_j, otherwise, $e_{i,j} = 0$.

The Laplacian manifold regularizer is defined as:

$$\sum_{i=1}^{N} \sum_{j=1}^{N} w_{i,j}(x_i - x_j)^2 \tag{6}$$

where $w_{i,j}$ is the weight of the edge between node p_i and p_j, defined as:

$$w_{i,j} = \begin{cases} \exp(-\frac{||p_i - p_j||_2^2}{\sigma^2}) & \text{if } e_{i,j} = 1 \\ 0 & \text{if } i = j \text{ or } e_{i,j} = 0 \end{cases} \tag{7}$$

where $\sigma > 0$ is the parameter to adjust the weight matrix. It is apparent that $w_{i,j} \in [0, 1]$, and the closer p_i from p_j, the closer $w_{i,j}$ to 1. By simple mathematical derivation, we can obtain the formula:

$$\sum_{i=1}^{N} \sum_{j=1}^{N} w_{i,j}(x_i - x_j)^2 = 2X^T (D - W)X \tag{8}$$

where W is a symmetrical weight matrix, which equals to $(w_{ij})_{N \times N}$. D is a diagonal matrix, which equals to $diag(d_1, d_2, \ldots, d_N)$. Let $L = D - W$, then we obtain the Laplacian manifold regularization item of Eq. (5).

2.3 Gradient Projection for Sparse Reconstruction Method

To resolve the dynamic optical imaging problem, the conventional approach estimates each image independently, and then assembles these results into a time sequence. The reconstruction results show good quality at each time point, but it fails to make full use of the measurements $\Phi = \{\Phi_1, \Phi_2, \ldots, \Phi_k\}$ that every column is temporarily correlated with one another. In this paper, GPSR is utilized to solve Eq. (5).

Through GPSR approach, the variable X is split into positive and negative parts. Equation (5) can be rewritten as the following quadratic program:

$$\arg\min \frac{1}{2}Z^T BZ + C^T Z \ s.t. Z \geq 0 \tag{9}$$

where $Z = \begin{bmatrix} Z_p \\ Z_n \end{bmatrix}$, $C = \begin{bmatrix} \tau 1_N - A^T \Phi \\ \tau 1_N + A^T \Phi \end{bmatrix}$, and $B = \begin{bmatrix} A^T A + \lambda L & -(A^T A + \lambda L) \\ -(A^T A + \lambda L) & A^T A + \lambda L \end{bmatrix}$.

These relationships are satisfied by $Z_p = (x_i)_+$ and $Z_n = (-x_i)_+$ for all $i = 1, 2, \ldots, N$, where $(\cdot)_+$ denotes the positive-part operator. Then gradient projection algorithm is used to solve the problem in Eq. (9).

Let $F(Z) = 1/2 Z^T B Z + C^T Z$, we search from each iterate $Z^{(v)}$ along the negative gradient $-\nabla F(Z^{(v)})$, and iterate $Z^{(v)}$ evolves to iterate $Z^{(v+1)}$ as follows:

$$Z^{(v+1)} = (Z^{(v)} - \alpha^{(v)} \nabla F(Z^{(v)}))_+ \tag{10}$$

where $\alpha^{(v)} > 0$ is the scalar parameter. We define the vector $g^{(v)}$ as:

$$g_i^{(v)} = \begin{cases} [\nabla F(Z^{(k)})]_i & if \ z_i^{(v)} > 0 \ or \ [\nabla F(z^{(v)})]_i < 0 \\ 0 & otherwise \end{cases} \tag{11}$$

The initial value of $\alpha^{(v)}$ can be computed as:

$$\alpha_0 = \frac{(g^{(v)})^T g^{(v)}}{(g^{(v)})^T B g^{(v)}} \tag{12}$$

Compared with other methods, the proposed method has several features: First, the joint ℓ_1 and Laplacian manifold regularization model makes full use of the temporal correlations of boundary measurements. Second, the input data Φ is a $N \times 4$ matrix, each column corresponds to a set of boundary measurements that obtained from different time points. The proposed algorithm could output the reconstructed results X, a $N \times 4$ matrix, in one step.

2.4 Evaluation Index

To quantify the reconstruction performance, position error (PE) was calculated to measure the distance variation between the reconstructed region and real region. The definition of PE is:

$$PE = ||P_r - P_0||_2 \tag{13}$$

where P_r and P_0 are the center coordinates of reconstructed and actual fluorescent sources respectively. We also calculated the volume of the reconstructed fluorophore, to compare with the volume of real target. The results is shown in Sect. 3.

3 Experiments

3.1 Experimental Setup

Numerical simulation is implemented to validate the performance of the joint regularization model and the proposed algorithms. A virtual mouse atlas was employed to provide the 3-D information, the mouse torso from the neck to the base of the kidneys was selected as the investigated region. As shown in Fig. 1(a), the simulation model includes five organs: muscle, heart, lungs, liver and kidneys. To simplify the simulation of the metabolic processes of drug, we focus on imaging kinetic behavior in liver.

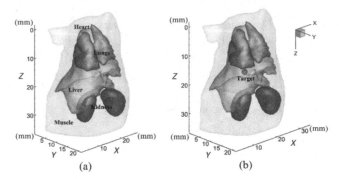

Fig. 1. (a) The mouse 3-D geometry model used in simulation studies. (b) Shows the position of the spherical target.

The spherical target is set in the liver and the center of it is at (16.4, 11, 16.4) mm, as shown in Fig. 1(b). The positions of four excitation point sources is located at $Z = 16$ mm. For each excitation location, the fluorescence is measured from the opposite side within 120 deg field of view.

The absorption and the scattering coefficients are essential in the photon propagation simulation. The following Table 1 gives the optical parameters of the mouse organs. The optical properties outside these organs were regarded as homogeneous.

Table 1. Optical parameters of the mouse organs.

Organ	$\mu_{ax}\,(\mathrm{mm}^{-1})$	$\mu'_{sx}\,(\mathrm{mm}^{-1})$	g
Muscle	0.0052	1.08	0.9
Heart	0.0083	1.01	0.85
Lungs	0.0133	1.97	0.9
Liver	0.0329	0.70	0.9
Kidneys	0.0066	2.25	0.86

To simulate the metabolic process, a series of spherical targets with different concentrations and sizes should be set as different fluorescents. We planned to set three simulation experiments: (a) Spherical targets with same concentration and different radii. (b) Spherical targets with different concentrations and same radius. (c) Spherical targets with different concentrations and different radii.

In this paper, we mainly focus on testing the proposed model and the algorithm, only the first experiment is illustrated, the other experiments would be done in the future work. According to the ICG concentration curves in [22], which mimic the metabolic processes of ICG in different organs and tissues, we set four spherical targets with four different radii: 1.0, 1.5, 2.0, 2.5 (mm) to simulate the diffusion progress of fluorescent at the four time points: 10, 15, 30, 60 (min). The variation of target concentration within each time point is neglected for simplification.

3.2 Forward Simulation

The photo propagation model of dynamic FMT reconstruction is illustrated in this section. Four spherical targets with different radii: 1.0, 1.5, 2.0, 2.5 (mm) and same concentration was set in the liver, as shown in Fig. 2.

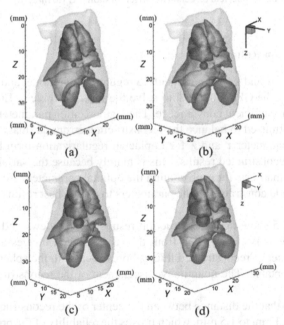

Fig. 2. Four mouse models with different spherical targets. The radius are 1.0, 1.5, 2.0 and 2.5 mm, corresponding to (a) to (d), to simulate the diffusion progress of fluorescent.

The photon density on the mouse surface was simulated using the FEM approach. In order to obtain the measurements, the four models was discretized into 10689, 10793, 10869, 10750 nodes, respectively. Figure 3 shows the forward results. 3-D reconstructions were performed on a tetrahedral mesh discretizing the mouse model with 7712 nodes.

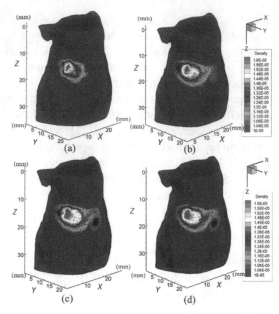

Fig. 3. Forward results of spherical targets with different radii: (a) 1.0 mm, (b) 1.5 mm, (c) 2.0 mm, and (d) 2.5 mm.

3.3 Reconstruction Results

Based on the joint ℓ_1 and Laplacian manifold regularization model and the experiment settings, we utilize the GPSR method to solve the inverse problem. Enough iterations were used to ensure sufficient convergence. The regularization parameters of the method were manually optimized to balance the reconstruction error and image contrast.

Specifically, parameter τ and λ for Laplacian regularization term have significant influence on the reconstructed results. This is mainly because the variable X and input data Φ are $N \times 4$ matrices, for each column the optimal parameters are different. Thus, it is necessary to add constraints to the parameters to get the best results of each column at once.

Figures 4 and 5 show the reconstruction results in 3-D views and cross-sectional views respectively. It is clearly seen from the reconstructed images at different time points that the center of reconstructed fluorophores is close to the spherical targets and the quality is acceptable. The quantitative assessment of the reconstruction results are shown in Table 2.

Table 2 shows that the distance between the center of the reconstructed fluorophore and real target is 1.1 mm to 1.5 mm, which proves the reliability of the proposed method. Besides, in consideration of the radius of target varies from 1.0 mm to 2.5 mm, the proposed algorithms shows stability in reconstructing small target and big target.

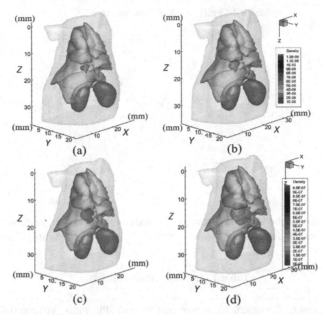

Fig. 4. Reconstruction results. (a), (b), (c) and (d) shows the reconstruction results of spherical targets with radius equals to 1.0, 1.5, 2.0, 2.5 mm, respectively.

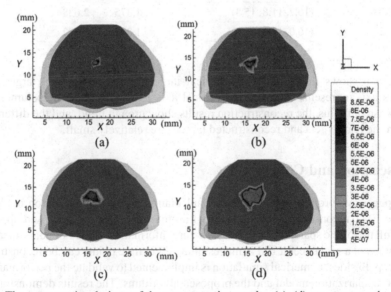

Fig. 5. The cross-sectional views of the reconstruction results. (a)–(d) are correspond to Fig. 4. (a)–(d). The black circle is the real position of target.

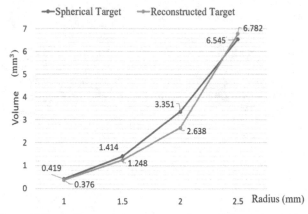

Fig. 6. The volume of spherical target and reconstructed target. The curves are depicted to different colors (spherical target: dark yellow; reconstructed target: grey) (color figure online).

Table 2. Quantitative assessment

Radius (mm)	Reconstructed source center (mm)	PE (mm)	Volume (mm^3)
1.0	(17.1, 11.8, 16.1)	1.139	0.376
1.5	(15.7, 11.7, 15.2)	1.503	1.248
2.0	(16.7, 11.8, 15.3)	1.375	2.638
2.5	(16.0, 12.3, 16.0)	1.382	6.782

Figure 6 shows the volume of spherical targets and reconstructed targets. The transvers axis represents time and the vertical axis represents value of volume. With the increase of radius, the reconstruction results show growth trend, and the differences between the real targets and reconstructed targets are relatively small.

4   Discussion and Conclusion

In this paper, we propose a joint ℓ_1 and Laplacian manifold regularization model for dynamic FMT reconstruction. Compared with other methods, the proposed approach makes full use of the sparsity and spatial structure information of the boundary measurement data, and a sequence of FMT images of different time points can be reconstructed in one step. Besides, numerical simulation is implemented to validate the performance of the joint regularization model and the proposed algorithms. The results demonstrate the reliability and stability of the proposed approach. In general, this approach for dynamic FMT can provide satisfactory reconstructed images.

In the simulation section, we mainly focus on testing the proposed model and the algorithm, only the first experiment, assuming that all the fluorescent targets have the same concentration, was illustrated. The other comprehensive experiments will be carried out in future works.

Acknowledgements. This work is supported by the National Natural Science Foundation of China under Grant Nos. 2016JM6025, 11571012; the Project funded by China Post-doctoral Science Foundation under Grant No. 2018M643719; the Postdoctoral Innovative Talents Support Program under Grant No. BX20180254; the education department served local special projects under Grant No. 17JF027.

References

1. Patwardhan, S., Bloch, S., Achilefu, S., Culver, J.: Time-dependent whole-body fluorescence tomography of probe bio-distributions in mice. Opt. Express **13**(7), 2564–2577 (2005)
2. Zhang, X., Liu, F., Zuo, S., Zhang, J., Bai, J., Luo, J.: Fast reconstruction of fluorophore concentration variation based on the derivation of the diffusion equation. J. Opt. Soc. Am. A **32**(11), 1993–2001 (2015)
3. Zhang, G., Pu, H., He, W.: A direct method with structural priors for imaging pharmacokinetic parameters in dynamic fluorescence molecular tomography. IEEE Trans. Biomed. Eng. **61**, 986–990 (2014)
4. Vasquez, K.O., Casavant, C., Peterson, J.D.: Quantitative whole body biodistribution of fluorescent-labeled agents by non-invasive tomographic imaging. PLoS ONE **6**(6), e20594 (2011)
5. Gao, X., Cui, Y., Levenson, R.M., Nie, S.: In vivo cancer targeting and imaging with semiconductor quantum dots. Nat. Biotechnol. **22**(8), 969–976 (2004)
6. Pierce, M.C., Javier, D.J., Richards-Kortum, R.: Optical contrast agents and imaging systems for detection and diagnosis of cancer. Int. J. Cancer **123**(9), 1979–1990 (2008)
7. Hiltunen, P., Sarkka, S., Nissila, I., Lajunen, A., Lampinen, J.: State space regularization in the nonstationary inverse problem for diffuse optical tomography. Inverse Probl. **27**(2), 025009 (2011)
8. Prince, S., Kolehmainen, V., Kaipio, J.P., Franceschini, M.A., Boas, D., Arridge, S.R.: Time-series estimation of biological factors in optical diffusion tomography. Phys. Med. Biol. **48**(11), 1491–1504 (2003)
9. Kolehmainen, V., Prince, S., Arridge, S.R., Kaipio, J.P.: State-estimation approach to the nonstationary optical tomography problem. J. Opt. Soc. Am. A **20**(5), 876–889 (2003)
10. Liu, X., Zhang, B., Luo, J., Bai, J.: 4-D reconstruction for dynamic fluorescence diffuse optical tomography. IEEE Trans. Med. Imag. **31**(11), 2120–2132 (2012)
11. Tikhonov, A., Goncharsky, A., Stepanov, V., Yagola, A.: Numerical Methods for the Solution of ill-Posed Problem. Kluwer Academic Publishers, Dordrecht (2013)
12. Bangerth, W., Joshi, A.: Adaptive finite element methods for the solution of inverse problems in optical tomography. Inverse Probl. **24**, 034011 (2008)
13. Shi, J., et al.: Enhanced spatial resolution in fluorescence molecular tomography using restarted l1-regularized nonlinear conjugate gradient algorithm. J. Biomed. Opt. **19**, 046018 (2014)
14. Yi, H., et al.: Reconstruction algorithms based on l1-norm and l2-norm for two imaging models of fluorescence molecular tomography: a comparative study. J. Biomed. Opt. **18**, 056013 (2013)
15. Ye, J., et al.: Fast and robust reconstruction for fluorescence molecular tomography via a sparsity adaptive subspace pursuit method. Biomed. Opt. Express **5**, 387–406 (2014)
16. Babaeian, A., et al.: Angle constrained path for clustering of multiple manifolds. In: IEEE International Conference Image Processing, pp. 4446–4450 (2015)
17. Tenenbaum, J., Silva, V., Langford, J.: A global geometric framework for nonlinear dimensionality reduction. Science **290**, 2319–2323 (2000)

18. Wang, Z., Nasrabadi, N., Huang, T.: Semisupervised hyperspectral classification using task-driven dictionary learning with Laplacian regularization. IEEE Trans. Geosci. Remote Sens. **53**, 1161–1173 (2015)
19. Roweis, S., Sau, L.: Nonlinear dimensionality reduction by locally linear embedding. Science **290**, 2323–2326 (2000)
20. Figueiredo, M., Nowak, R., Wright, S.: Gradient projection for sparse reconstruction: application to compressed sensing and other inverse problems. IEEE J. Sel. Top. Signal Process. **1**, 586–597 (2007)
21. He, X., Wang, X., Yi, H.: Laplacian manifold regularization method for fluorescence molecular tomography. Biomed. Optics **22**(4), 045009 (2017)
22. Shinohara, H., Tanaka, A., Kitai, T., Yanabu, N., Inomoto, T., Satoh, S.: Direct measurement of hepatic indocyanine green clearance with near-infrared spectroscopy: separate evaluation of uptake and removal. Hepatology **23**(1), 137–144 (1996)

Artificial Intelligence

Accelerating Deep Convnets via Sparse Subspace Clustering

Dong Wang$^{(\boxtimes)}$, Shengge Shi, Xiao Bai, and Xueni Zhang

School of Computer Science and Engineering,
Beijing Advanced Innovation Center for Big Data and Brain Computing,
Qingdao Research Institute, Beihang University, Beijing 100191, China
dongwang@buaa.edu.cn

Abstract. While the research on convolutional neural networks (CNNs) is progressing quickly, the real-world deployment of these models is often limited by computing resources and memory constraints. In this paper, we address this issue by proposing a novel filter pruning method to compress and accelerate CNNs. Our method reduces the redundancy in one convolutional layer by applying sparse subspace clustering to its output feature maps. In this way, most of the representative information in the network can be retained in each cluster. Therefore, our method provides an effective solution to filter pruning for which most existing methods directly remove filters based on simple heuristics. The proposed method is independent of the network structure, and thus it can be adopted by any off-the-shelf deep learning libraries. Evaluated on VGG-16 and ResNet-50 using ImageNet, our method outperforms existing techniques before fine-tuning, and achieves state-of-the-art results after fine-tuning.

Keywords: Convolutional neural networks · Network acceleration · Filter pruning · Clustering

1 Introduction

With the collection of huge volume of labeled data, tremendous power of graphical processing units (GPUs) and parallel computation, convolutional neural networks (CNNs) have achieved the state-of-the-art performance in a wide variety of computer vision tasks, such as image classification [4], and object detection [13]. As flexible function approximators by scaling to millions of parameters, CNNs can extract high-level and more discriminative features compared with the traditional elaborative hand-crafted ones.

However, modern CNNs heavily rely on the intensive computing and memory resources despite their overwhelming success. For instance, the ResNet-50 [4] has more than 50 convolutional layers, requiring over 95 MB storage memory and over 3.8 billion floating number multiplications when processing an image. The

---

S. Shi—This work was done when Shengge Shi was a visiting scholar at Beihang University while he works in the fifth military representative office of the navy in Beijing.

© Springer Nature Switzerland AG 2019
Y. Zhao et al. (Eds.): ICIG 2019, LNCS 11902, pp. 595–606, 2019.
https://doi.org/10.1007/978-3-030-34110-7_50

VGG-16 model [15] has 138.34 million parameters, taking up more than 500 MB storage space, and needs 30.94 billion float point operations (FLOPs) to classify a single image. It is very difficult to deploy these complex CNN models in some specific scenarios where computing resource is constrained, i.e., a task must be completed with limited resources such as computing time, storage space, and battery power.

Both academia and industry have developed methods to reduce the amount of parameters in CNNs. Ba *et al.* [1] used class probabilities produced by a pre-trained model as "soft targets" to feed a tiny network, successfully transferring the cumbersome model to a compact one while maintaining the generalization capability of the model. The student-teacher paradigm in [1] has shown its effectiveness in accelerating CNNs. However, to devise a new tiny network is not a trivial task. Moreover, it remains an open problem on how to define the inherent "knowledge" in the teacher model. Tensor factorization based methods [16] factorize an over-parameterized convolutional layer into several light ones. However, decomposing 1×1 convolution favoured by modern CNNs is still an intractable problem.

Filter pruning [5,11] has been proposed to address this issue. Since the network architecture is constant after the filter pruning, the obtained model is compatible with any off-the-shelf deep learning frameworks. In addition, since volumes of both convolutional kernels and intermediate activations are shrunken, the required memory is reduced remarkably. This strategy also allows complementary acceleration methods to be employed to gain a more compact model. The advantages of filter pruning lead to increasing attention to research in this direction. He *et al.* [5] learned a sparse weight vector to measure the importance of filters by applying the LASSO regression. Luo *et al.* [11] used statistical information computed from the next layer to guide the filter pruning for the current layer in a greedy way. Both methods directly prune some filters. It is obvious that the information contained in pruned filters can no longer be utilized once the filters have been pruned.

In this paper, we propose a novel filter pruning method to accelerate CNNs through sparse subspace clustering [3]. What motivates us is that feature maps would highly correlate if much redundancy exists in one convolutional layer, which is also shown in prior literature [2,5], and we can alleviate the serious correlation through clustering. As shown in Fig. 1, since different feature maps from one convolutional layer derive from the same input with different convolutional filters by a linear operation, the outputs will highly correlate when the redundancy is heavy. Thus, instead of measuring the importance of filters [10] or feature maps [5,11] and subsequently removing the trivial kernels, we attempt to seek the most representative information by casting the filter selection problem into a clustering problem on intermediate activations. Furthermore, since the convolution is a linear operation and the subspace clustering can work as a powerful tool to exploit the linear representation, we employ the subspace clustering to cluster feature maps. Concretely, we select the sparse subspace clustering (SSC) [3,18,19] as the representative. We firstly cluster feature maps with SSC.

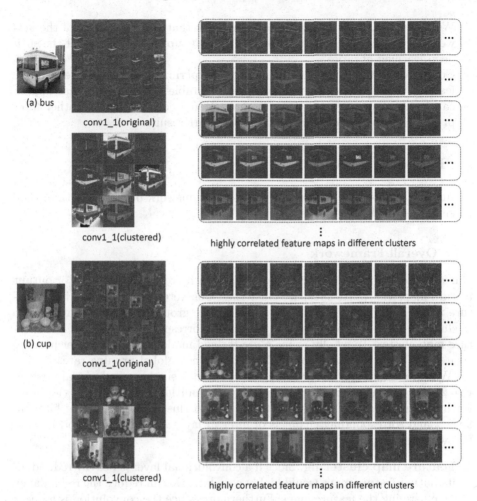

Fig. 1. Visualization of the output feature maps produced by the first convolutional layer of VGG-16 [15]. The example images are randomly chosen from ILSCVR-12 [14]. We show the highly correlated feature maps in different clusters and the feature maps produced by 8 clustered convolutional filters. It is obvious that redundant feature maps can be reduced through clustering.

This allows the clustering of the corresponding filters in the next layer which take these feature maps as input. Also, filters in the upper layer that produce these feature maps can be clustered. Then, we iterate this process to prune the whole network layer by layer.

In summary, this paper makes the following contributions:

- We propose a novel filter pruning method to accelerate CNNs through feature map clustering. We can reduce the redundant information in feature maps and simultaneously retain the most representative information.

- We devise a flexible filter pruning framework that is independent of the network structure. Thus our method can be well supported by any off-the-shelf deep learning libraries.
- Compared to the original heavy network, experiments demonstrate that the learned portable network achieves a comparable accuracy, but has significantly lower memory usage and computational cost. We exceed other filter pruning works, and obtain the state-of-the-art results.

2   Proposed Method

In this section, we first introduce the overall framework of our algorithm, then present the details of each step.

2.1   Overall Framework

Our method prunes a single convolutional layer by reducing its input or output feature maps via sparse subspace clustering. Concretely, to prune the input feature maps from c to desired c' $(0 < c' < c)$, we group the c feature maps into c' clusters. Then we calculate the average of corresponding filters of each feature map cluster. To wholly prune a pre-trained model, our single layer pruning strategy is applied layer by layer with a predefined global pruning rate.

We summarize our filter pruning method on a single convolutional layer in Fig. 2. We aim to prune the filters in layer i and layer $i + 1$. Once the input feature maps of layer $i + 1$ are clustered, we can cluster corresponding filters in layer i and corresponding channels of filter in layer $i + 1$. The method has the following key steps:

1. **Feature map clustering.** Since if a convolutional layer is heavily redundant its output feature maps would highly correlate, we can reduce the redundancy by clustering the feature maps. Furthermore, since the convolution is a linear operation and the subspace clustering can work as a powerful tool to exploit the linear representation, we employ the subspace clustering, concretely the sparse subspace clustering, to cluster feature maps.
2. **Filter clustering and reconstruction.** After clustering feature maps, we can cluster corresponding input channels of filter in the next layer which take these feature maps as input. Filters in the upper layer that produce these feature maps can also be clustered. Then we reconstruct the following feature maps using the pruned filters.
3. **Fine-tuning.** Fine-tuning is a necessary step to recover the generalization ability influenced by filter pruning, which is time consuming on large datasets and complex models. For efficiency considerations, we fine-tune part of epochs after all pruned feature maps have been reconstructed.
4. **Iterate to step 1 to prune the next layer.**

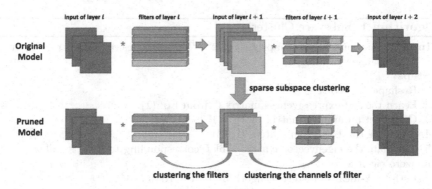

Fig. 2. Illustration of our filters pruning method. First, we cluster the input feature maps of layer $i+1$ by the sparse subspace clustering. Then the filters in layer i and the channels of filters in layer $i+1$ can be pruned by respectively calculating the average of corresponding filters and channels of each feature map cluster.

2.2 Filter Pruning

Formally, we use $(X^{(i)}, W^{(i)}, *)$ to denote the convolution process in layer i, where $X^{(i)} \in \mathbb{R}^{c_i \times H \times W}$ is the input tensor which has c_i feature maps of $H \times W$ in size. $W^{(i)} \in \mathbb{R}^{c_{i+1} \times c_i \times k_h \times k_w}$ is a set of filters with kernels of $k_h \times k_w$ in dimension, which generates a new tensor $X^{(i+1)}$ with c_{i+1} feature maps.

Sparse Subspace Clustering. To prune the channels of feature maps from c_i to desired c'_i $(0 < c'_i < c_i)$, we cluster the c_i feature maps into c'_i clusters. To achieve it, we leverage the sparse subspace clustering [3] to cluster the feature maps. Mathematically, this idea is formalized as an optimization problem

$$\min_C \|C\|_1 \; s.t. \; X = XC, \; (diag(C) = 0) \tag{1}$$

where $X \in \mathbb{R}^{HW \times c_i}$ is reshaped by $X^{(i)}$, and C is a self-expressiveness matrix. Since X is various with different training samples, to ensure the stability of clustering we solve C by iteratively optimizing Eq. (1) through Adam [9]. In addition, feature maps clustering should be employed before non-linear activation in our scenario since it would superficially mitigate the redundancy. The subspace clustering algorithm is summarized in Algorithm 1.

Filter Clustering. After clustering c_i feature maps into c'_i clusters, we represent the indices of each cluster as $I_1, I_2, \ldots, I_{c'_i}$. Then, we can prune the channels of filter in layer i by calculating the average channel of each cluster. For the m-th filter $W_m^{(i)}$, the average channel can be calculated through the clustering index

$$V_j^{(i)} = \frac{1}{|I_j|} \sum_{p \in I_j} W_{m,p}^{(i)}, \; j = 1, 2, \ldots, c'_i \tag{2}$$

Algorithm 1. Subspace Clustering.

Input: The input feature maps $X^{(i)} \in \mathbb{R}^{c_i \times H \times W}$, the desired number of input channels of filter, c_i'.

Steps:

1. Reshape $X^{(i)}$ to $X \in \mathbb{R}^{HW \times c_i}$.
2. Learn the self-expressiveness matrix C from Eq. (1).
3. Construct an affinity matrix by $W = |C| + |C^T|$.
4. Calculate the Laplacian matrix L of W.
5. Calculate the eigenvector matrix V of L corresponding to its c_i' smallest nonzero eigenvalues.
6. Perform k-means clustering algorithm on the rows of V.

Output: The clustering result of $X^{(i)}$ with c_i' clusters.

---

where $W_{m,p}^{(i)}$ is the p-th channel of filter $W_m^{(i)}$, $|I_j|$ is the number of elements in I_j. Then the pruned m-th filter $W_m'^{(i)}$ is the concatenation of $V_j^{(i)}$, $j = 1, 2, \ldots, c_i'$. For $m = 1, 2, \ldots, c_{i+1}$, we can obtain their pruned filters using Eq. (2). Then the pruned filters for layers i are $W'^{(i)} = [W_1'^{(i)} \ W_2'^{(i)} \ \ldots \ W_{c_{i+1}}'^{(i)}] \in \mathbb{R}^{c_{i+1} \times c_i' \times k_h \times k_w}$.

Naturally, the filters of upper layer $i - 1$ that produce feature maps $X^{(i)}$ can also be clustered

$$W_j'^{(i-1)} = \frac{1}{|I_j|} \sum_{p \in I_j} W_p^{(i-1)}, \ j = 1, 2, \ldots, c_i' \tag{3}$$

where $W_p^{(i-1)}$ is the p-th filters of $W^{(i-1)}$, $|I_j|$ is the number of elements in I_j. The result is $W'^{(i-1)} = [W_1'^{(i-1)} \ W_2'^{(i-1)} \ \ldots \ W_{c_i'}'^{(i-1)}] \in \mathbb{R}^{c_i' \times c_{i-1} \times k_h \times k_w}$, where c_{i-1} is the number of filters in layer $i - 1$.

Reconstruction Error Minimization. We reconstruct the output feature maps $X^{(i+1)}$ with pruned filters $W'^{(i)}$ by linear least squares. This problem can be formulated as:

$$\min_{W'^{(i)}} \|X^{(i+1)} - X'^{(i)} * W'^{(i)}\|_F^2, \tag{4}$$

where $\| \cdot \|_F$ is the Frobenius norm, $*$ is the convolution operation. $X'^{(i)} = X^{(i-1)} * W'^{(i-1)} \in \mathbb{R}^{c_i' \times H \times W}$ are the feature maps produced by the pruned layer $i - 1$. The complete filter pruning process is summarized in Algorithm 2.

2.3 Pruning Strategy

The network architectures can be divided into two types, i.e., the traditional single path and multi-path convolutional architectures. VGGNet [15] is the representative for the former, while the latter mainly includes some recent networks equipped with some novel structures like residual blocks in ResNet [4].

We use different strategies to prune these two types of networks. For VGG-16, we apply the single layer pruning strategy to the convolutional layer step by

---

Algorithm 2. Filter Pruning.

Input: The original convolutional filters $W^{(i-1)}$ and $W^{(i)}$, the indices of
    clustering result $I_1, I_2, \ldots, I_{c'_i}$.
Steps:
1. For layer i, calculate the aggregated channel for each filter through the
clustering indices, $W'^{(i)} \in \mathbb{R}^{c_{i+1} \times c'_i \times k_h \times k_w}$.
2. For layer $i - 1$, calculate the aggregated filter for each cluster through the
clustering indices, $W'^{(i-1)} \in \mathbb{R}^{c'_i \times c_{i-1} \times k_h \times k_w}$.
3. Minimize the reconstruction error between the original output and the
pruned output of layer i by Eq. (4).
Output: The pruned convolutional filters $W'^{(i-1)}$ and $W'^{(i)}$.

---

step. For ResNet, some restrictions are incurred due to its special structure. For
example, the channel numbers of the residual learning branch and the identity
mapping branch in the same block need to be consistent in order to finish the
sum operation. Thus it is hard to directly prune the last convolutional layer
in the residual learning branch. Since most parameters appear in the first two
layers, pruning the first two layers is a feasible option which is illustrated in
Fig. 3.

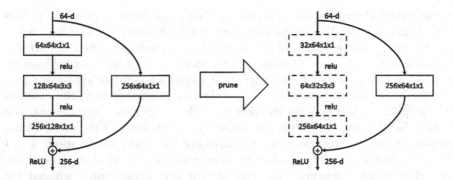

Fig. 3. Illustration of the ResNet pruning strategy. For each residual block, we only
prune the first two convolutional layers, keeping the block output dimension unchanged.

3   Experiment

Our method is tested for VGG-16 [15] and ResNet-50 [4] on ILSCVR-12 [14].
Firstly, we compare several filter selection strategies including ours by pruning
single layer for VGG-16 [15] on ILSCVR-12 to exhibit efficiency of our algorithm.
Then, whole model pruning for VGG-16 [15] is shown. Secondly, we show the
performance of pruning the ResNet-50 [4]. All the experiments were implemented
within Caffe [8]. The performance of ConvNets acceleration is evaluated with the
number of float-point operations (FLOPs).

3.1   Experiments on VGG-16

VGG-16 [15] is a classic single path CNN with 13 convolutional layers, which has been widely used in vision tasks as a powerful feature extractor. We use single layer pruning and whole model pruning to evaluate the efficiency of our method. The effectiveness is measured by the decrease of top-5 accuracy on validation dataset. The top-5 accuracy of VGG-16 [15] on ILSCVR-12 [14] validation dataset is 89.9%.

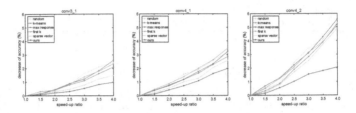

Fig. 4. Single layer performance analysis under different speed-up ratios (without fine-tuning), measured by decrease of top-5 accuracy on ILSCVR-12 validation dataset.

Single Layer Pruning. We first evaluate the single layer acceleration performance of our method. We compare our approach with several existing filter selection strategies. *sparse vector* [5] preserves filters according to their importance scores learned by a sparsity regularization method. *max response* [10] selects channels based on corresponding filters that have high absolute sum of weights. To differentiate our approach based on subspace clustering from the counterpart equipped with common clustering algorithms, we also select *kmeans* as a baseline. In addition, to validate the necessity of elaborative hand-crafted filter selection algorithm, we also take two naive criteria into consideration. *first k* selects the first k channels. *random* randomly selects a fixed amount of filters. After filter pruning, feature maps reconstruction is implemented without the fine-tuning step. The effectiveness of the methods is measured by reduction of top-5 accuracy on the validation dataset after the reconstruction procedure is accomplished.

Similar to [5], we extracted 10 samples per class, i.e. a total of 10000 images, to prune channels and minimize reconstruction errors. Images were resized such that the shorter dimension is 256. Then 224 × 224 random cropping was applied and the resulting image patches were fed into the network. The testing was made on a crop of 224 × 224 pixels at the center of the image. The self-expressiveness matrices for convolutional layers were learned with mini-batch size of 128 and the learning rate varied from $1e^{-3}$ to $1e^{-5}$ in 15 epochs. After pruning filters, we used a batch size of 64 and varied the learning rate from $1e^{-3}$ to $1e^{-5}$ to minimize the reconstruct error until the loss did not drop continuously. All parameters were optimized with Adam [9]. We pruned three convolutional layers, i.e., conv3_1, conv4_1 and conv4_2, with aforementioned methods including ours under several speed-up ratios. The results are shown in Fig. 4.

As expected, the loss on accuracy is proportional to the speed-up ratio, i.e., error increases as speed-up ratio increases. With the same speed-up ratio, our approach consistently outperforms other methods in different convolutional layers under different speed-up ratios. This shows that our subspace clustering based pruning method can retain more representative information. This enables the feature maps to be reconstructed more effectively. Although the key idea of the *kmeans* option is also clustering, it works poorly for feature maps which are generated by the linear operation and can not well exploit the correlation between feature maps, obtaining a coarse clustering result. Thus, subspace clustering is vital in our method and we will aggressively improve our approach with more efficient subspace clustering counterparts in our future work. Nevertheless, the performance of *kmeans* is consistently better than the two naive approaches, indicating clustering based pruning strategy is feasible in practice. *max response* performs with high loss of accuracy, sometimes even worse than *first k*. This is probably because *max response* ignores correlations between different filters. The *random* selection option shows good performance, even better than the heuristic methods in some cases. However, this method is not robust in feature maps reconstruction, making it not applicable in practice. In summary, the naive pruning strategies have shown some weakness, which implies that proper filter selection is vital for filter pruning.

It is also noticeable that pruning gradually becomes more difficult from shallow to deep layers. It indicates that whereas shallow layers have much more redundancy, deeper layers make more contribution to the final performance, which is consistent with the observation in [17] and [5]. This means it is preferable to prune more parameters in shallow layers rather than deep layers to accelerate the model. Moreover, Fig. 4 shows that our filter pruning method leads to smaller increase of error compared with other strategies when the deeper layers are compressed.

Table 1. Accelerating the VGG-16 model using a speedup ratio of 2×, 4×, and 5× respectively. The results show decreases of top-5 validation accuracy (1-view, baseline 89.9%).

Method	2×	4×	5×
Jaderberg et al. [7]	–	9.7	29.7
Asym. [17]	0.28	3.84	–
Filter pruning [10] (fine-tuned)	0.8	8.6	14.6
He et al. [5] (without fine-tune)	2.7	7.9	22.0
Ours (without fine-tune)	**2.6**	**3.7**	**8.7**
He et al. [5] (fine-tuned)	0	1.0	1.7
Ours (fine-tuned)	**0**	**0.5**	**1.1**

Whole Model Pruning. The whole model acceleration results under 2×, 4×, 5× are demonstrated in Table 1. Firstly, we applied our approach layer by layer sequentially. Then, our pruned model was fine-tuned for 10 epoches with a fixed learning rate $1e^{-5}$ to gain a higher accuracy. We augmented the data by random cropping of 224 × 224 pixels and mirror the cropped patch. Other parameters were the same as in our single layer pruning experiment. Since the last group of convolutional layers (i.e., conv5_x) affects the classification more significantly, these layers were not pruned. After the filter pruning and reconstruction, our approach outperforms the *sparse vector* method [5] by a large margin, which is consistent with the results of single layer analysis. After fine-tuning, our method achieves 2× speed-up without decrease of accuracy. Under 4× and 5×, the accuracy of our method only drops by 0.5% and 1.1% respectively. Our approach outperforms the state-of-the-art filter level pruning approaches ([10] and [5]). This is because our method retains as much representative information as possible by exploiting correlation between feature maps via subspace clustering, thus, recovering better approximation to the original data in the subsequent output volume.

3.2   Experiments on ResNet-50

We also tested our method on the popular multi-path network ResNet-50 [4]. During the implementation, we merged batch normalization [6] into convolutional weights. This does not affect the outputs of the networks, so that each convolutional layer is followed by ReLU [12]. Since ResNet-50 consists of residual blocks, we pruned each block step by step, i.e., we pruned ResNet-50 from block 2a to 5c sequentially. In this experiment, for each block, we only pruned the convolutional layers that learned the residual mapping. Therefore, we only pruned the first two layers of each block in ResNet-50 for simplicity, leaving the block output and projection shortcuts unchanged. Pruning these parts may lead to further acceleration, but can be quite difficult if not entirely impossible. We leave this exploration as a future work. After each block had been pruned, we used Adam [9] with mini-batch size of 64 and varied the learning rate from $1e^{-3}$ to $1e^{-5}$ to minimize reconstruction error until the loss did not drop continuously. The model was fine-tuned in 20 epochs with fixed learning rate $1e^{-5}$ to gain a higher accuracy.

The results of 2× acceleration on ResNet-50 are presented in Table 2. Our approach outperforms the state-of-the-art method [5] both before or after the fine-tuning. In addition, while pruning ResNet-50, He *et al.* [5] kept 70% and 30% channels for sensitive residual blocks and other blocks respectively. Our approach, without these constraints, is simpler and more efficient. Our pruning strategy can obtain more representative filters by eliminating redundancy in feature map subspace, enabling the reconstruct error to be better minimized.

Table 2. 2× acceleration for ResNet-50 on ILSCVR-12. The results show decrease from the baseline networks top-5 accuracy of 92.2% (one view).

Method	Increased err.
He *et al.* [5]	8.0
Ours (without fine-tune)	**5.2**
He *et al.* [5] (enhanced)	4.0
He *et al.* [5] (enhanced, fine-tuned)	1.4
Ours (fine-tune)	**1.0**

4   Conclusion

Current deep CNNs are accurate with high inference costs. In this paper, we have presented a novel filter pruning method for deep neural networks. Different from existing filter pruning methods which directly remove filters based on their importance, our approach better retrieves the representative information by applying subspace clustering to feature maps, so most important information can be retained by the mean of each cluster. The reduced CNNs are inference efficient networks while maintaining accuracy. Compelling speed-up and accuracy are demonstrated on both VGG-Net and ResNet with ILSCVR-12.

Acknowledgments. This work was supported by the National Natural Science Foundation of China project no. 61772057 and the support funding from State Key Lab. of Software Development Environment and Qingdao Research Institute.

References

1. Ba, J., Caruana, R.: Do deep nets really need to be deep? In: NIPS, pp. 2654–2662 (2014)
2. Denton, E.L., Zaremba, W., Bruna, J., LeCun, Y., Fergus, R.: Exploiting linear structure within convolutional networks for efficient evaluation. In: NIPS, pp. 1269–1277 (2014)
3. Elhamifar, E., Vidal, R.: Sparse subspace clustering: algorithm, theory, and applications. TPAMI **35**(11), 2765–2781 (2012)
4. He, K., Zhang, X., Ren, S., Sun, J.: Deep residual learning for image recognition. In: CVPR, pp. 770–778 (2016)
5. He, Y., Zhang, X., Sun, J.: Channel pruning for accelerating very deep neural networks. In: ICCV, pp. 1–9 (2017)
6. Ioffe, S., Szegedy, C.: Batch normalization: accelerating deep network training by reducing internal covariate shift. In: ICML, pp. 448–456 (2015)
7. Jaderberg, M., Vedaldi, A., Zisserman, A.: Speeding up convolutional neural networks with low rank expansions. In: BMVC, pp. 1–12 (2014)
8. Jia, Y., et al.: Caffe: convolutional architecture for fast feature embedding. In: ACM MM, pp. 675–678 (2014)
9. Kingma, D.P., Ba, J.: Adam: a method for stochastic optimization. In: ICLR, pp. 1–14 (2015)

10. Li, H., Kadav, A., Durdanovic, I., Samet, H., Graf, H.P.: Pruning filters for efficient convnets. In: ICLR, pp. 1–13 (2017)
11. Luo, J.H., Wu, J., Lin, W.: ThiNet: a filter level pruning method for deep neural network compression. In: ICCV, pp. 1–9 (2017)
12. Nair, V., Hinton, G.E.: Rectified linear units improve restricted Boltzmann machines. In: ICML, pp. 807–814 (2010)
13. Ren, S., He, K., Girshick, R., Sun, J.: Faster R-CNN: towards real-time object detection with region proposal networks. In: NIPS, pp. 91–99 (2015)
14. Russakovsky, O., et al.: ImageNet large scale visual recognition challenge. IJCV 115(3), 211–252 (2015)
15. Simonyan, K., Zisserman, A.: Very deep convolutional networks for large-scale image recognition. In: ICLR, pp. 1–13 (2015)
16. Wang, P., Cheng, J.: Accelerating convolutional neural networks for mobile applications. In: ACM MM, pp. 541–545 (2016)
17. Zhang, X., Zou, J., He, K., Sun, J.: Accelerating very deep convolutional networks for classification and detection. TPAMI 38(10), 1943–1955 (2016)
18. Zhou, L., Bai, X., Liu, X., Zhou, J.: Binary coding by matrix classifier for efficient subspace retrieval. In: ICMR, pp. 82–90. ACM (2018)
19. Zhou, L., Bai, X., Wang, D., Liu, X., Zhou, J., Edwin, H.: Deep subspace clustering via latent distribution preserving. In: IJCAI, pp. 1–10 (2019)

Personalized Micro-video Recommendation Based on Multi-modal Features and User Interest Evolution

Yingying Jin[1], Juan Xu[1,2](✉), and Xin He[1]

[1] College of Computer Science and Technology,
Nanjing University of Aeronautics and Astronautics, Nanjing, China
{yingyingjin2017,hexin}@nuaa.edu.cn
[2] Collaborative Innovation Center of Novel Software Technology
and Industrialization, Nanjing 210023, China
juanxu@nuaa.edu.cn

Abstract. Personalized recommendation plays a critical role in maintaining active users for most micro video applications. Previous methods up to now are not always feasible, such as the problems of cold-start and mismatch meta-data. In this paper, we propose a novel method, named Multi-Modal Interest Evolution (MMIE), to deal with these problems. MMIE consists of three parts: feature extraction, user interest modeling and personalized recommendation. We extract multi-modal features rather than unreliable meta-data to represent videos' content, which alleviates the problem of video cold-start. Furthermore, considering the diversity and evolution of user interests, we design a new evolving layer to capture the interest evolving process related to the target video. The combination of Gated Recurrent Unit and attention mechanism in this layer strengthens the effect of relevant interests and improves the accuracy of recommendation. Experiments on real-world dataset show that the MMIE performs better than other state-of-the-art methods. Moreover, the MMIE achieves 7.37% improvement on NDCG@10 by introducing multi-modal features.

Keywords: Multi-modal features · Attentive interest evolution · Micro-video recommendation

1 Introduction

With the popularity of smart mobile devices and the development of multimedia technology, the video has gradually become a carrier of information transmission. More and more people choose to record life stories with micro-videos and then share them in social media applications such as Snapchat[1], Tik Tok[2], and

---

[1] Snapchat: https://www.snapchat.com.
[2] Tik Tok: https://www.douyin.com.

© Springer Nature Switzerland AG 2019
Y. Zhao et al. (Eds.): ICIG 2019, LNCS 11902, pp. 607–618, 2019.
https://doi.org/10.1007/978-3-030-34110-7_51

Kuaishou[3]. Kuaishou, for example, has 110 million active users and 10 million videos uploaded daily at the end of June 2017[4], while Snapchat users watch 7 billion videos every day in 2016 [1]. The sheer volume of micro-videos available in applications often undermines users' capability to choose the micro-videos that best fit their interests.

Video recommendation is gradually becoming a key solution to this problem. Many state-of-the-art methods have been proposed and have achieved great practical success in long video recommendation [2,3]. Collaborative filtering (CF) and contend-based filtering are most widely used, which are the basis of most recommendation approaches.

CF-based recommendation suggests videos based on other users with similar taste generally, which often works well when enough users' interactive behaviors are available. However, it suffers from the cold-start problem seriously. The cold-start problem means when a new video joins the system, as the video has never been viewed by any user, the system is unable to recommend it to suitable users. The cold-start problem causes most videos neglected or less interested compared with popular ones. The situation becomes worse when videos are uploaded at a fast pace.

Content-based recommendation has been proposed to overcome the limitation of CF-based approaches. In general, videos with similar contents that users viewed or liked before are recommended. However, most researches up to now are not always feasible, as they rely on meta-data rather than raw video contents. However, meta-data of micro-videos is uploaded by users, which may not be available or precise for videos.

In this paper, we proposed a novel method, named Multi-Modal Interest Evolution (MMIE), relying on native video and audio content. Figure 1 depicts the structure of the proposed method. MMIE is combined with three parts. Firstly, we extract video and audio features by pre-trained Convolution Natural Networks (CNNs) [4,5] to represent videos' content comprehensively. Secondly, the user's interest evolving process is learned adaptively by Gated Recurrent Unit (GRU) and attention mechanism. Finally, a Multi-Layer Perceptron (MLP) is applied to generate a reasonable recommendation list.

The main contributions of this paper can be summarized as follows:

- We extract video and audio features rather than meta-data to represent videos' content, which alleviates the problem of video cold-start. These multi-modal features are fused in a novel way which represent latent interests more precisely.
- We design an novel evolving layer, where the combination of GRU and attention mechanism strengthens the effect from relevant interests to the target video and improves the accuracy of recommendation.

The rest of the paper is organized as follows. Section 2 reviews related works. Then, Sect. 3 illustrates the method proposed. In Sect. 4, we show experiment details and discuss the results. Finally, conclusions are drawn in Sect. 5, along with the future work.

---

[3] Kuaishou: https://www.kuaishou.com.
[4] Kuaishou report: https://www.kuaishou.com/about/.

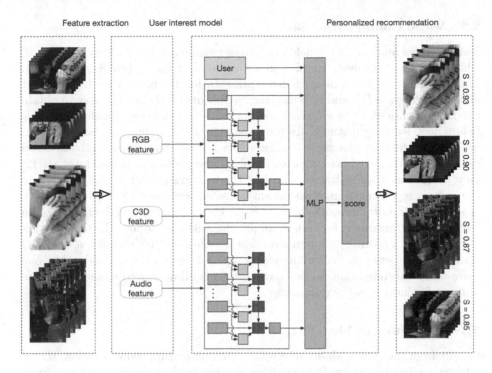

Fig. 1. The overall structure of MMIE.

2   Related Work

Compared to long videos or movies, micro-videos have more diverse themes, and uneven quality, which make it more difficult to analyze. We divide the recommendation task into two parts: video content analysis and user interest modeling, and view some literatures about them.

2.1   Micro-video Recommendation Methods

More recent researches have focused on video content-based methods [1, 6–9]. Redi et al. [6] achieve creative micro-video automatic detection by quality evaluation of similar images. McParlane et al. [7] combine video features and video popular patterns to predict the popularity of video. Ma et al. [1] propose a novel model, which uses the text information and the RGB feature to learn a latent genre of the video and optimize recommendation scores. Huang et al. [8] propose a hierarchical user interests recommendation model based on multi-modal features.

2.2   Video Content Analysis

Video content analysis in the field of computer vision has been widely researched, which can be extensively applied in many fields, such as intelligent security. Many of these works are about video representation learning [5,10–13]. Wang et al. [10,11] propose DT and iDT methods, which utilize the optical flow to obtain the motion trajectory in videos. These methods are the best classical methods before deep learning methods are proposed. The shortcomings of these methods are the high feature dimension and slow speed. Therefore, more methods based on deep learning have been proposed to solve these problems. Karpathy et al. [12] view a video as a set of frames, and fuse the features of each frame to generate the video's representation. Two-stream ConvNet architecture [13] incorporates spatial and temporal networks to learn static image features and dynamic motion features simultaneously. In Tran et al. [5], the authors propose the Convolution 3D feature, a generic spatiotemporal feature obtained by training a deep 3D convolutional network. In summarize, compared with image, a video has one more temporal dimension, so the above methods all devote to making good use of it, and achieve good performance.

2.3   User Interest Modeling

Benefit from the strong ability of deep learning on feature representation, recent interest models transform from tradition models to deep models, and pay more attention on the interaction of features, such as PNN [14], DeepFM [15]. However, in these models, user history behaviors are embedded into low-dimension vectors and pooled into a fixed vector in final, which ignores the relationship between behaviors and the target video. DIN [16] introduces the attention mechanism to activate the related behaviors locally, and captures the diversity of user interests successfully. However, DIN [16] is weak in learning the dependencies in sequential behaviors. Some recently work show that the temporal information of videos can help to build richer user interest model. TDSSM [17] optimizes long-term and short-term user interests to improve the recommendation quality. DREAM [18] uses Recurrent Neural Network for next basket recommendation. Inspired from the above methods, we combine the GRU and the attention mechanism to capture interest evolving process.

3   Multi-Modal Interest Evolution

In this section, we describe MMIE in detail. Started by describing how to extract video and audio features, using GPU to accelerate the process. Then, we introduce the multi-modal user interest evolution model in detail.

3.1   Feature Extraction

Inspired by the previous work in micro-video recommendation [1,8,9], we extract multi-modal features for micro-videos, including RGB feature, C3D feature and audio feature. RGB feature is widely used to recognize objects or scenes in video analysis tasks. C3D feature has achieved state-of-the-art performance in action recognition, which can extract motion information between consecutive frames. So this paper introduces this feature to evaluate its utility on recommendation task. Moreover, audio feature can provide a wealth of background information about emotions and scenes, which is helpful for analyzing video content. Therefore, the objects, activities and background information in videos can be represented directly by these features replacing meta-data.

RGB Feature Extraction. In this paper, ResNet152 [4] is applied, which can extract higher-level features. The ImageNet is used to pre-train ResNet152 which is beneficial for identifying objects and extracting RGB features. Concretely, we decode each video at dynamic frame-per-second firstly to ensure every second sampled at least one frame. Then, each frame is extracted into a 1000-dimension vector by the pre-trained ResNet152. Finally, these frame-level feature vectors are fused into a video-level feature by average pooling for simplicity.

C3D Feature Extraction. Similar with the process of RGB feature extraction, C3D model [5] is used as the spatiotemporal feature extractor. The sport-1M dataset is used to pre-train the model. We sample 16 consecutive frames from each video. Then, a 4096-dimension vector is extracted by the pre-trained model as video's C3D feature.

Audio Feature Extraction. The most representative audio feature is the Mel Frequency Cepstrum Coefficient (MFCC). In addition to MFCC, we utilize the other 21 dimension features as well, such as the zero crossing rate. Firstly, we use FFmpeg to separate the audio file from the video. Then pyAudioAnalysis [19] is applied as the audio feature extractor. Finally, the audio features are represented as a combination of the mean and variance of these 34 features (including 13-dimension MFCC).

3.2 User Interest Evolution Model

It is necessary to capture user interests behind user behaviors effectively for the recommendation task. Users' feature representations are usually learnt from user behaviors [1,8,20–23]. However, in past work, user interests features are used to be represented in fixed vectors, which makes it difficult to represent the user interests precisely, as user interests vary over different videos [16]. Inspired from the past work [14,16,18], this paper focuses on capturing user evolving interests by combining attention mechanism and GRU. As shown in Fig. 2, MMIE is composed in several parts. First, all modal features are transformed into the same semantic space through an embedding layer. Next, MMIE takes interest evolution layer to capture users' interest based on each modal feature, the specific implementation process is shown in Fig. 3. Finally, all modal interest representation vectors, target video's embedding vector and user profiles' embedding

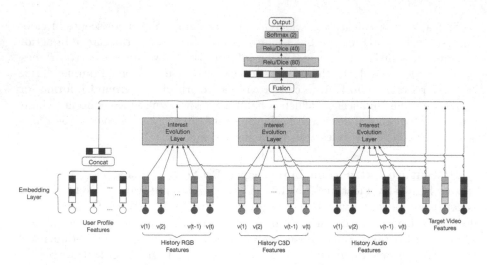

Fig. 2. The structure of the multi-modal interest evolution model.

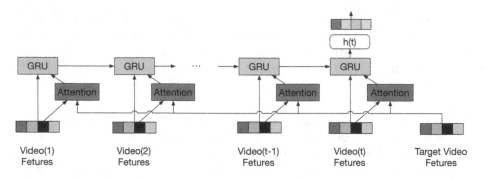

Fig. 3. The structure of the interest evolution layer.

vector are concatenated into one vector and fed into MLP to predict the user interests of the target video. In the rest of this section, we detail the core module of MMIE.

Interest Evolution Layer. As user interests evolve over time, we take Gated Recurrent Unit (GRU) [24] to model the dependency between behaviors, and the input of GRU is ordered behaviors. The formulations of GRU are as follows:

$$u_t = \sigma(W_u \cdot [h_{t-1}, x_t] + b_u) \tag{1}$$

$$r_t = \sigma(W_r \cdot [h_{t-1}, x_t] + b_r) \tag{2}$$

$$\tilde{h}_t = tanh(W_h \cdot [r_t \odot h_{t-1}, x_t] + b_h) \tag{3}$$

$$h_t = (1 - u_t) \odot h_{h-1} + u_t \odot \tilde{h}_t \tag{4}$$

where σ is the sigmoid activation function, $\odot$ is element-wise product, $W_u, W_r, W_h \in R^{n_H \times n_I}$, n_H is the hidden size, and n_I is the input size. x_t is the input of GRU, representing the t-th video that user liked. h_t is the t-th hidden state, representing user interest at t-th moment which can be seen as user's current interest.

In addition, each of diverse interests only relates to parts of behavior sequences [16], so attention mechanism is combined with GRU. The attention mechanism is used to activate related behaviors locally, then GRU is used to learn the evolving process of these related behaviors. Different from traditional attention-based GRU, attention score controls the update gated directly during each step of GRU, which can intensify relative behaviors' effort and is helpful for capturing the interest related to the target video. The formulations of the combination are as follows:

$$u_t' = a_t * u_t \tag{5}$$

$$h_t' = (1 - u_t') \odot h_{h-1} + u_t' \odot \tilde{h}_t \tag{6}$$

$$a_t = \frac{exp(h_t W e_a)}{\sum_{j=1}^{T} exp(h_j W e_a)} \tag{7}$$

where e_a is the multi-modal feature vectors of video, $W \in R^{n_H \times n_A}$, n_H is the dimension of hidden state and n_A is the target video's output size. Attention score means the relationship between video e_a and hidden state h_t, the attention score is larger when relationship is stronger.

Multi-modal Fusion. There are several ways to fuse multi-modal features, including pre-fusion, mid-fusion, and post-fusion. Experiments show that fusing all modal interest features gets the best result. What's more, product operation [14] is introduced to capture high-order feature interactions.

Loss Function. The objective function used is the negative log-likelihood function, which is defined as:

$$L = -\frac{1}{N} \sum_{x,y \in S} (y * log(p(x)) + (1 - y) * log(1 - p(x))) \tag{8}$$

where S is the training set of size N. $y \in \{0, 1\}$ represents whether the user likes target video. $p(x)$ is the output of the network.

4 Experiments

4.1 Dataset and Parameters Setting

Since there is no public dataset of micro-videos, we build a real-world dataset for our experiments. The dataset is collected from a well-known micro-video platform, Tik Tok, via web crawlers including 6293 users, 23343 micro-videos and 129423 user behavior logs. To avoid data sparseness, we remove users with less than ten records.

The behavior sequence of a user is set as $(b_1, b_2, ..., b_k, ..., b_n)$. We split the dataset into training dataset which is generated with $k = 1, 2, ..., n - 2$ for each user, while test dataset, which we use to predict the last one contains the first $n - 1$ behaviors. SGD is used to optimize all models, and learning rate starts at 1 and gradually decay to 0.1. The mini-batch is 32. The activation function is Dice [16].

4.2   Evaluation Metric

We evaluate recommendation performance in two widely-used ranking metrics: Hit Ratio (HR@k) and Normalized Discounted Cumulative Gain (NDCG@k).

HR@k is the measure of test samples that contain at least one of the ground truth in the top-k predictions.

NDCG@k considers the order of recommendation items in the top-k list.

4.3   Results and Discussion

Comparison of Multi-modal Feature Combinations' Performances.
Table 1 shows the performance of the combination of different modalities on the same dataset. Obviously, models that using video or audio feature performs better than using only audio feature. For example, the HR@10 result of RGB feature increases from 44.55% to 49.18%. Among the results of the single-modal feature, RGB achieves the best results (HR@10: 49.18%, NDCG@10: 26.25%), which is slightly better than C3D feature.

Table 1. Comparison of multi-modal feature combinations.

Model	HR@1	HR@10	NDCG@1	NDCG@10
Baseline	7.43%	44.11%	7.43%	22.75%
Audio	8.15%	44.55%	8.15%	23.69%
RGB	9.16%	49.18%	9.16%	26.25%
C3D	10.10%	46.16%	10.10%	26.13%
Audio+RGB	12.21%	**51.61%**	12.21%	30.11%
Audio+C3D	10.80%	46.43%	10.80%	26.66%
Audio+RGB+C3D	**12.75%**	50.77%	**12.75%**	**30.12%**

In the results of the multi-modal combination, it can be seen that the combined feature results are better than corresponding single feature results on HR@1. Although the audio feature achieves the lowest results in the comparison of a single-modal feature, when combined with RGB feature, accuracy improves further as audio feature can provide more different information. As C3D and RGB contain too much repetitive information, we don't experiment with this combination. Moreover, the results of the model incorporating all features are not excellent as the dataset we collected is not large enough to train the optimal parameters of model.

Comparisons of Different Models' Performances

- PNN [14]. Product-based Neural Networks introduces a product layer after embedding layer to capture high-order feature interactions, which is referred to in the modal fusion module and is as a baseline in this paper.
- DIN [16]. In this model, the attention mechanism is used to weight the hidden interest feature at all moments.
- DeepFM [15]. DeepFM combines low-order features and high-order ones to improve the power of expression.
- MMIE. The model is proposed in this paper, which focuses on learning the user evolving interests by combining attention mechanism and GRU.

Table 2. Comparison of different model on RGB feature.

Model	HR@1	HR@10	NDCG@1	NDCG@10
PNN [14]	3.17%	25.33%	3.17%	12.41%
DIN [16]	6.19%	32.81%	6.19%	17.84%
DeepFM [15]	8.17%	37.99%	8.17%	20.76%
MMIE	**9.16%**	**49.18%**	**9.16%**	**26.25%**

Table 2 indicates the results of different models on the same dataset. Obviously, the model we proposed achieves best performance (HR@10:49.18%, NDCG@10: 26.25%), which is 13.83% better than PNN [14] on NDCG@10. Contrasted to DIN [16], HR@10 of MMIE increases from 32.81% to 49.18%. Compared DIN [16] with DeepFM [15], the result of DeepFM has improved 2.92% than DIN on NDCG@1, which indicates the importance of low-order features.

Comparisons of Different Components' Performances

- GRU+Att. In this model, the attention mechanism is used to weight the hidden interest feature at all moments. The model is used to evaluate the effect of the combination of GRU and attention mechanism.
- MMIE-GRU, i.e. DIN [16]. Its structure is equivalent to removing the GRU from MMIE. The model is used to evaluate the utility of GRU.
- MMIE-Att. Its structure is equivalent to removing the attention from MMIE. The model is used to evaluate the utility of attention.

- MMIE-Product. Its structure is equivalent to removing the product operation in the fusion module from MMIE. The model is used to measure the effect of product operation.
- MMIE. The model is proposed in this paper, which focuses on learning the user evolving interests with all components.

Table 3 indicates the effect of different components on the same dataset. Compared MMIE-Att with MMIE, only 1.01% decreases on HR@1. Besides, MMIE-Product achieves 42.52% on HR@10, which is a little better than MMIE-GRU. These results indicate that compared with attention mechanism and product operation, GRU plays a more important role in interest evolution modeling. Moreover, the result of GRU+Att is worse MMIE, which shows that a reasonable combination of GRU and attention mechanism leading to better performance. Hence, we can devoted to improving GRU to get better results.

Table 3. Comparison of different components on RGB feature.

Model	HR@1	HR@10	NDCG@1	NDCG@10
GRU+Att	6.91%	37.94%	6.91%	20.46%
MMIE-GRU	6.19%	32.81%	6.19%	17.84%
MMIE-Product	6.96%	42.52%	6.96%	21.82%
MMIE-Att	8.77%	48.17%	8.77%	25.62%
MMIE	**9.16%**	**49.18%**	**9.16%**	**26.25%**

Comparison of Different Parameters' Performances. Figure 4 indicates the results of model with different values of parameters based on RGB feature.

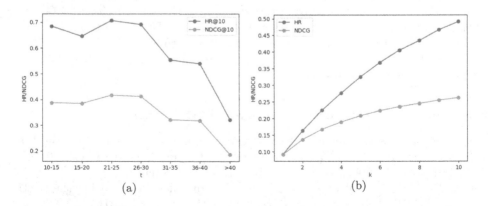

(a)   (b)

Fig. 4. (a) HR@10 and NDCG@10 of different behavior lengths t on RGB feature. (b) HR and NDCG of different top k on RGB feature.

Figure 4(a) shows the performance of HR@10 and NDCG@10 at different behavior lengths t. We can see that as t increases, HR@10 and NDCG@10 improve firstly but fall later. As the larger t is, the more information model can learn and the better result is. However, limited by the optimization algorithm of RNN, when t is too large, the information will loss in the process of back propagation, so the result falls finally. How to model longer sequence effectively will be our future research direction. Figure 4(b) show the performance of HR@k and NDCG@k. Obviously, the larger k is, the better result is.

5   Conclusion

In conclusion, this paper focuses on the task of personalized recommendation in the scenario of a sheer volume of micro-videos available. The extraction of user interest is the key to personalized recommend successfully. In this paper, we propose a micro-video recommendation method, named MMIE. In order to model user interests effectively, we directly rely on raw video and audio content rather than utilizing unreliable text information. We designed attention-based GRU to obtain an adaptive representation vector for user interests, which varies over different videos. Experiments on real-world micro-video dataset demonstrate the state-of-the-art performance of our proposed method.

In the future, we will focus on a better way to model user interests, since GRU is weak in capturing long-term behavioral dependencies and is difficult to parallel computing.

References

1. Ma, J., Li, G., Zhong, M., Zhao, X., Zhu, L., Li, X.: LGA: latent genre aware micro-video recommendation on social media. Multimed. Tools Appl. **77**(3), 2991–3008 (2018)
2. Davidson, J., et al.: The youtube video recommendation system. In: Proceedings of the Fourth ACM Conference on Recommender Systems, RecSys 2010, New York, NY, USA, pp. 293–296. ACM (2010)
3. Deng, Z., Yan, M., Sang, J., Xu, C.: Twitter is faster: personalized time-aware video recommendation from twitter to youtube. ACM Trans. Multimed. Comput. Commun. Appl. **11**(2), 31:1–31:23 (2015)
4. He, K., Zhang, X., Ren, S., Sun, J.: Deep residual learning for image recognition. In: The IEEE Conference on Computer Vision and Pattern Recognition (CVPR), June 2016
5. Tran, D., Bourdev, L.D., Fergus, R., Torresani, L., Paluri, M.: C3D: generic features for video analysis (2014). CoRR, abs/1412.0767
6. Redi, M., O'Hare, N., Schifanella, R., Trevisiol, M., Jaimes, A.: 6 seconds of sound and vision: creativity in micro-videos. In: The IEEE Conference on Computer Vision and Pattern Recognition (CVPR), June 2014
7. McParlane, P.J., Moshfeghi, Y., Jose, J.M.: "Nobody comes here anymore, it's too crowded"; predicting image popularity on flickr. In: Proceedings of International Conference on Multimedia Retrieval, ICMR 2014, New York, NY, USA, pp. 385:385–385:391. ACM (2014)

8. Huang, L., Luo, B.: Personalized micro-video recommendation via hierarchical user interest modeling. In: Zeng, B., Huang, Q., El Saddik, A., Li, H., Jiang, S., Fan, X. (eds.) PCM 2017. LNCS, vol. 10735, pp. 564–574. Springer, Cham (2018). https://doi.org/10.1007/978-3-319-77380-3_54

9. Chen, J., Song, X., Nie, L., Wang, X., Zhang, H., Chua, T.-S.: Micro tells macro: predicting the popularity of micro-videos via a transductive model. In: Proceedings of the 24th ACM International Conference on Multimedia, MM 2016, New York, NY, USA, pp. 898–907. ACM (2016)

10. Wang, H., Kläser, A., Schmid, C., Liu, C.-L.: Dense trajectories and motion boundary descriptors for action recognition. Int. J. Comput. Vis. **103**(1), 60–79 (2013)

11. Wang, H., Schmid, C.: Action recognition with improved trajectories. In: IEEE International Conference on Computer Vision, ICCV, December 2013

12. Karpathy, A., Toderici, G., Shetty, S., Leung, T., Sukthankar, R., Fei-Fei, L.: Large-scale video classification with convolutional neural networks. In: The IEEE Conference on Computer Vision and Pattern Recognition (CVPR), June 2014

13. Simonyan, K., Zisserman, A.: Two-stream convolutional networks for action recognition in videos. In: Ghahramani, Z., Welling, M., Cortes, C., Lawrence, N.D., Weinberger, K.Q. (eds.) Advances in Neural Information Processing Systems 27, pp. 568–576. Curran Associates Inc. (2014)

14. Qu, Y., et al.: Product-based neural networks for user response prediction. In: 2016 IEEE 16th International Conference on Data Mining (ICDM), pp. 1149–1154. IEEE (2016)

15. Guo, H., Tang, R., Ye, Y., Li, Z., He, X.: DeepFM: a factorization-machine based neural network for CTR prediction. arXiv preprint arXiv:1703.04247 (2017)

16. Zhou, G., et al.: Deep interest network for click-through rate prediction. In: Proceedings of the 24th ACM SIGKDD International Conference on Knowledge Discovery and Data Mining, pp. 1059–1068. ACM (2018)

17. Song, Y., Elkahky, A.M., He, X.: Multi-rate deep learning for temporal recommendation. In: Proceedings of the 39th International ACM SIGIR Conference on Research and Development in Information Retrieval, pp. 909–912. ACM (2016)

18. Yu, F., Liu, Q., Wu, S., Wang, L., Tan, T.: A dynamic recurrent model for next basket recommendation. In: Proceedings of the 39th International ACM SIGIR Conference on Research and Development in Information Retrieval, pp. 729–732. ACM (2016)

19. Giannakopoulos, T.: pyAudioAnalysis: an open-source Python library for audio signal analysis. PLoS ONE **10**(12), e0144610 (2015)

20. Lee, J., Abu-El-Haija, S.: Large-scale content-only video recommendation. In: IEEE International Conference on Computer Vision, ICCV Workshops, October 2017

21. Donkers, T., Loepp, B., Ziegler, J.: Sequential user-based recurrent neural network recommendations. In: Proceedings of the Eleventh ACM Conference on Recommender Systems, pp. 152–160. ACM (2017)

22. Du, N., Wang, Y., He, N., Sun, J., Song, L.: Time-sensitive recommendation from recurrent user activities. In: Cortes, C., Lawrence, N.D., Lee, D.D., Sugiyama, M., Garnett, R. (eds.) Advances in Neural Information Processing Systems 28, pp. 3492–3500. Curran Associates Inc. (2015)

23. Loyola, P., Liu, C., Hirate, Y.: Modeling user session and intent with an attention-based encoder-decoder architecture. In: Proceedings of the Eleventh ACM Conference on Recommender Systems, pp. 147–151. ACM (2017)

24. Cho, K., et al.: Learning phrase representations using RNN encoder-decoder for statistical machine translation. arXiv preprint arXiv:1406.1078 (2014)

Multi-dimensional Feature Fusion Modulation Classification System Based on Self-training Network

Jingpeng Gao[1], Yi Lu[1(✉)], Lu Gao[2], and Liangxi Shen[1]

[1] College of Information and Communication Engineering, Harbin Engineering University, Harbin, China
louis@hrbeu.edu.cn

[2] National Key Laboratory of Science and Technology on Test Physics and Numerical Mathematics, Beijing Institute of Space Long March Vehicle, Beijing, China

Abstract. To solve the problem that the single feature extraction method cannot fully express the radar signal at low SNR and the large-scale deep learning network cannot deal with small sample size of radar signal, this paper proposes a multi-dimensional feature fusion modulation classification system, which can classify radar signals including CW, BPSK, LFM, COSTAS, FRANK, T1, T2, T3 and T4. The machine could extract time-frequency feature of radar signal automatically through small self-training network. Combined with the idea of multi-dimensional feature fusion, the time-frequency entropy feature, the higher-order statistics feature and network self-extraction feature are normalized and fused by non-negative matrix factorization (NMF), which improves the classification performance of the proposed system at low SNR. The simulation results show that the recognition rate of the proposed system is 78% at −3 dB. Compared with the traditional method, the recognition rate of proposed system has a significant improvement.

Keywords: Feature fusion · Self-training network · Dimension reduction · Modulation classification

1 Introduction

Electronic warfare has become an indispensable part of modern warfare, which is the key to contend for the information superiority of the whole battlefield. With the increasing complex electromagnetic environment, the classification of radar emitter signal modulation becomes an urgent problem to be solved [1].

With the application of the new radar system, the modulation mode of radar emitter signal becomes more and more complex and the feature of signal changes and develops ceaselessly. Hence the traditional classification methods of modulation cannot meet the requirements of present electronic reconnaissance [2]. Traditional feature analysis methods mostly focus on the feature in a certain domain, while ignoring other domains. So it cannot effectively extract modulation feature of signal, thus affecting the electronic reconnaissance [3]. In [4], the deep belief network was used to realize the automatic

© Springer Nature Switzerland AG 2019
Y. Zhao et al. (Eds.): ICIG 2019, LNCS 11902, pp. 619–629, 2019.
https://doi.org/10.1007/978-3-030-34110-7_52

extraction of feature parameters of large-sample data. The extracted feature is of a large order of magnitude, which makes the computational complexity of system high. And deep layer of network will easily cause gradient dispersion and gradient explosion. Literature [5] used LeNet-5 network to recognize document, which achieved good results. LeNet-5 is a small network that can adaptively train network parameters to make the network more suitable for current data processing. What's more, higher-order statistics (HOS) feature can improve the anti-noise performance [6], Renyi entropy feature can reflect the energy concentration level of the signal [7], and the fusion of them is helpful to improve recognition rate at low SNR.

Based on the self-training network, a multi-dimensional feature fusion modulation classification system is proposed in this paper. The system uses self-training network to extract time-frequency feature of radar signal, then fuses the network extracted feature with HOS feature and Renyi entropy feature, finally sends them into extreme learning machine (ELM) to realize the accurate classification.

The rest of this paper is organized as follows. In Sect. 2, model of system and signal is established. Section 3 introduces the radar signal process. Section 4 shows methods of feature extraction. Section 5 describes the classifier. Simulation results and analysis are given in Sect. 6. At last, conclusions are drawn in Sect. 7.

2   Model of System and Signal

In order to realize the multi-dimensional feature fusion modulation classification based on self-training network, time-frequency transform, image preprocessing, feature extraction, feature fusion and feature classification needed to be introduced. Firstly, the pseudo Wigner-Vile distribution (PWVD) is used to transform radar signals into time-frequency images. Secondly, time-frequency images need to be preprocessed before feature extraction. Thirdly, LeNet-5, a small self-training network, is used to extract features. Fourthly, to express information of radar signals more comprehensively, network feature, Renyi entropy feature and HOS feature are fused together based on non-negative matrix factorization (NMF). Finally ELM can realize the classification. The structure of the proposed system is showed in Fig. 1.

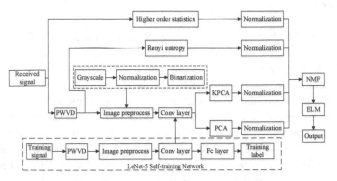

Fig. 1. The structure of the proposed system.

To implement the proposed algorithm, it is necessary to generate radar signal to train the network parameters. The unified model of radar signal is as follow.

$$s(t) = A(t) \exp[j(2\pi f_0 t + c(t) + \varphi_0)] \qquad (1)$$

where $A(t)$ represents the amplitude function, f_0 is the carrier frequency, $c(t)$ means phase function and φ_0 is the original phase.

The classical nine types of radar signal include CW, BPSK, LFM, COSTAS, FRANK, T1, T2, T3 and T4, detailed models are showed in Table 1.

Table 1. Models of nine types of radar signal.

Type	Formula
CW	$s(t) = Arect(\frac{t}{T}) \exp(j2\pi f_0 t + \varphi_0) \qquad 0 < t \le T$
BPSK	$s(t) = A \sum_{i=1}^{N} \exp\{j(2\pi f_0 t + \varphi_i)\} u_{T_p}(t - iT_p)$
LFM	$s(t) = Arect(\frac{t}{T}) \exp\left\{ j \left[2\pi(f_0 t + \frac{kt^2}{2}) + \varphi_0 \right] \right\}$
COSTAS	$s(t) = \frac{1}{\sqrt{N_1}} \sum_{n=1}^{N_1} u(t - (n-1)T_r) \exp(j2\pi f_n t)$ $u(t) = \frac{1}{\sqrt{T}} rect(\frac{t - T/2}{T})$
FRANK	$\varphi_{i,j} = \frac{2\pi}{M}(i-1)(j-1)$
T1	$\phi_{T1} = \mathrm{mod}\left\{ \frac{2\pi}{n} INT\left[(kt - jT)\frac{jn}{T} \right], 2\pi \right\}$
T2	$\phi_{T2} = \mathrm{mod}\left\{ \frac{2\pi}{n} INT\left[(kt - jT)\left(\frac{2j-k+1}{T}\right)\frac{n}{2} \right], 2\pi \right\}$
T3	$\phi_{T3} = \mathrm{mod}\left\{ \frac{2\pi}{n} INT\left[\frac{n\Delta Ft^2}{2t_m} \right], 2\pi \right\}$
T4	$\phi_{T4} = \mathrm{mod}\left\{ \frac{2\pi}{n} INT\left[\frac{n\Delta Ft^2}{2t_m} - \frac{n\Delta Ft}{2} \right], 2\pi \right\}$

3 Signal Processing

Because radar signal is a non-stationary signal, the traditional methods would cause signal aliasing, which leads to in low recognition rate. Therefore, time-frequency transform is adopted.

3.1 Time-Frequency Transform

Wavelet transform and short-time Fourier transform (STFT) are two common methods of time-frequency transform, but wavelet transform is sensitive to noise, STFT can only deal with stationary signal [8, 9]. Wigner-vile distribution (WVD) has good time-frequency aggregation, and PWVD could further enhance the aggregation of distribution, which is helpful to classification [10].

$$P_x(t, f) = \int_{-\infty}^{+\infty} h(\tau)x(t + \tau/2)x(t - \tau/2)e^{-jf\tau}d\tau \tag{2}$$

where $h(\tau)$ is window function. Figure 2 shows different time-frequency images without noise obtained by PWVD.

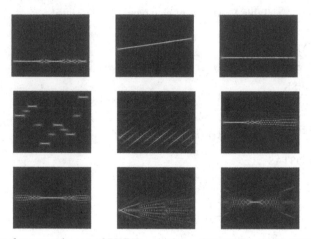

Fig. 2. The time-frequency image of PWVD, which are CW, BPSK, LFM, COSTAS, FRANK, T1, T2, T3 and T4.

3.2 Image Preprocessing

With the development of artificial intelligence, the application of neural network1 is more and more extensive. To apply LeNet-5 to radar signal, the images need to be preprocessed before being sent into network. The image preprocessing could eliminate noise and reduce the computational complexity of the LeNet-5 network. Most image preprocessing algorithms are defined by grayscale or binary image. In grayscale preprocessing, the original image information brightness is expressed by grayscale, thus changing the color image into grayscale format.

The time-frequency image could be represented by a $M \times N$ matrix, and the brightness of image pixel points can be calculated by grayscale formula.

$$I_{fg} = 0.3B_{fg} + 0.59G_{fg} + 0.11R_{fg} \tag{3}$$

where f, g represent the pixel point of image, $0 < f \le M, 0 < g \le N$.

Because the dynamic range of gray value of time-frequency images is different to their corresponding signals, the range of gray value would affect the classification.

In order to reduce the data imbalance on classification, the gray value needs to be normalized.

$$\hat{I}_{fg} = (I_{fg} - \bar{I}) \bigg/ \sqrt{\frac{1}{MN-1} \sum_{f=1}^{M} \sum_{g=1}^{N} (I_{fg} - \bar{I})^2} \tag{4}$$

where $\bar{I}$ is the average of gray value.

In order to further enhance signal, reduce the influence of noise and the amount of data, binary process could be carried out.

$$P_{fg} = \begin{cases} 1 & I_{fg} \geq \partial \\ 0 & I_{fg} < \partial \end{cases} \tag{5}$$

where the ∂ is the binary threshold, in this paper it equals to 0.4.

4 Feature Extraction

In the classification of radar signal, feature extraction is an essential part, this paper proposes a method of multi-dimensional feature extraction, which enables the extracted feature to represent information of signal more comprehensively.

4.1 LeNet-5

LeNet-5 was proposed in 1998, which is the most representative among the early neural networks. It was initially used in document recognition. The network structure is simple so that it is suitable for small sample size training. The application of LeNet-5 on feature extraction can make information of radar signal more comprehensive, which can improve the reliability of the system at low SNR. The structure of LeNet-5 network is showed in Fig. 3.

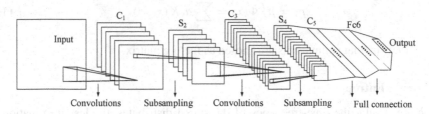

Fig. 3. The structure of LeNet-5 network.

After the training of LeNet-5, it can be used to extract feature. This paper chooses principal component analysis (PCA) and kernel principal component analysis (KPCA) to deal with network extracted feature. To be specific, PCA treats the extracted feature as a data matrix F, the covariance matrix could be represented as $R = FF^T$.

$$R = UAU^T \tag{6}$$

where A is the eigenvalue diagonal matrix of covariance matrix, U is the correspond feature matrix.

$$P = U^T F = [p_1, p_2, \cdots p_K]^T \tag{7}$$

where p is the principal component of extracted feature matrix. The first K principal components are chosen as feature matrix.

The difference between PCA and KPCA is that KPCA would map the feature matrix to high-dimensional feature space by nonlinear mapping. To feature matrix F, it would be mapped to high-dimensional space Φ to get $\Phi(f)$, the covariance matrix is $R = \frac{1}{M} \sum_{c=1}^{M} \Phi(f_c)\Phi(f_c)^T$. Eigen value λ_c and eigenvector μ_c can be get from following equation.

$$R\mu_c = \lambda_c \mu_c \tag{8}$$

Eigenvector μ_c can be represented by the linear combination of c.

$$\mu_c = \sum_{c=1}^{M} a_c \Phi(x_c) \tag{9}$$

$$\lambda_c a = \frac{1}{M} \Phi(x_c)\Phi(x_c)^T \cdot a \tag{10}$$

where a is the linear combination coefficient $a = (a_1, a_2, \ldots a_n)^T$. A kernel function can be defined as follow.

$$K_{cs} = K(f_c, f_s) = \Phi(f_c)^T \Phi(f_c) \tag{11}$$

$$N\lambda_c a = Ka \tag{12}$$

The k th kernel principal component through KPCA mapping is

$$p_k = \mu_t^T \Phi(x) = \sum_{s=1}^{M} a_s K(x_s, x) \tag{13}$$

The first k principal components are chosen as feature matrix.

4.2 Renyi Entropy

The more regular the time-frequency of the signal distributes, the less information it contains, and the smaller the entropy value. When the components of signal are cluttered, it means that it contains more information and the entropy will increase. The Renyi entropy of time-frequency image can be represented as

$$R^\alpha = \frac{1}{1-\alpha} \log_2 \iint P_x^\alpha(t, f) dt df \tag{14}$$

Order can reflect feature well, and this paper chooses the order α of Renyi entropy in 3, 5, 7, 9 and 11 as signal feature.

4.3 Higher-Order Statistic

HOS can express the essential feature of signal well, which can improve the robustness of system. Kurtosis and margin of signal are extracted in time domain. The average of time domain signal $x(t)$ is

$$\bar{X} = \frac{1}{N} \sum_{i=1}^{N} x_i(t) \tag{15}$$

where N is the number of $x(t)$. The mean-square value can be represented as

$$X_{rms}^2 = \frac{1}{N} \sum_{i=1}^{N} x_i^2(t) \tag{16}$$

Thus, the margin of signal is

$$C_e = \frac{X_{rms}}{\bar{X}} \tag{17}$$

The kurtosis of signal is

$$C_q = \frac{\frac{1}{N} \sum_{i=1}^{N} (|x_i| - \bar{x})}{X_{rms}^4} \tag{18}$$

The time domain signal could be transformed into frequency domain signal $X(f)$ by Fourier Transform. We extract the kurtosis and margin feature of frequency as the spectral kurtosis and spectral margin feature.

4.4 Feature Fusion

This paper applies self-training network LeNet-5 to extract features, and the extracted feature is reduced by PCA and KPCA. What's more, the Renyi entropy feature and HOS feature would be extracted as supplement to make feature extraction more accurate. But the ranges of feature value of different extraction methods are different, which may affect the accuracy of subsequent classifier greatly. So it is necessary to normalize the extracted features respectively.

$$T = \left[T_{PCA}, T_{KPCA}, T_{HOS}, T_{Renyi} \right] \tag{19}$$

where T_{PCA} is the normalized feature reduced by PCA, T_{KPCA} is the normalized feature reduced by KPCA, T_{HOS} is the normalized feature extracted by HOS, T_{Renyi} is the normalized feature extracted by Renyi entropy. When different features are normalized, NMF is used to fuse them together, which can reduce the redundant information of features. The NMF can be expressed as

$$\min_{W,H} f(W, H) = \frac{1}{2} \sum_{i=1}^{m} \sum_{j=1}^{n} \left(T_{ij} - (WH)_{ij} \right)^2 \tag{20}$$

where $m \times n$ is the size of T, W and H are two matrixes. W is the feature matrix after being fused. Then the fused feature is sent into classifier to realize classification.

5 Feature Classification

ELM overcomes the shortcomings of traditional neural network such as low training rate, easy to fall into local optimum and sensitive to learning rate [11]. During the process of training, ELM could randomly generate the connection weights between input layer and hidden layer and threshold of hidden layer. There is no need to adjust them in the training, the global optimal can be obtained by setting the number of hidden layer neuron.

The mathematical expression of ELM is

$$v_k = \omega^T g(W_{in}u_k + b), k = 1, 2, \cdots, N \tag{21}$$

where v_k is the output vector, ω is the output weight, g is the activation function, W_{in} is the input weight, u_k is the input vector, b is the bias value of hidden layer, N is the sum of sample.

During the training process, the W_{in} and b are randomly initialized and unchanged, the only parameter need to be trained is ω. The detailed calculation method is as followed.

$$\omega = H^+ I \tag{22}$$

where H^+ is the Moore-Penrose generalized inverse matrix of hidden layer input matrix H. We can expand the H as

$$H = \begin{bmatrix} g(W_{in}u_1 + b_1) & \cdots & g(W_{in}u_1 + b_n) \\ \vdots & \ddots & \vdots \\ g(W_{in}u_N + b_1) & \cdots & g(W_{in}u_N + b_n) \end{bmatrix}_{N \times n} \tag{23}$$

The expected output matrix I is

$$I = (I_1, I_2, \cdots, I_N)^T \tag{24}$$

Thus, the training process of ELM is a simple linear regression process. When the ω is found, the training is finished.

6 Simulation Results and Analysis

To test and verity the feasibility of the proposed algorithm, we set the parameters of radar signal as follow. The sampling frequency is $f_s = 32$ MHz, the sampling point is $N = 512$ and the noise is white Gaussian noise, the pulse width of signal is 10us, the carrier frequency is 10 MHz. According to the signal models in Table 1, we generate nine types of radar signal in random under -3–6 dB respectively, and do time-frequency transform on them. For each SNR, we randomly choose 100 signals from each type of signals. In addition, we generate nine types of radar signal without noise to train LeNet-5 network, each signal is chosen 300 randomly to do time-frequency transformation and image preprocessing.

Figure 4 shows the proportion of each component of total component under 0 dB. From Fig. 4, we can see that both in PCA and KPCA, as the increase of subcomponent, the proportion of subcomponent decreases, while the proportion of sum component increases. In PCA, first 20 subcomponents can account for 90% of the total components, which is enough to represent most feature information. The proportion of the component after 20th component is smaller and smaller, which is easily disturbed by noise, so it is ignored. We can get 20 features after PCA. Similar to PCA, first twelve subcomponents can account for 90% of the total components in KPCA. We choose first 12 subcomponents of KPCA as feature matrix. If we output the features from C5 convolutional layer, 4096 features will be obtained. But the number of features after dimension reduction is only 32, which greatly reduces the computational complexity.

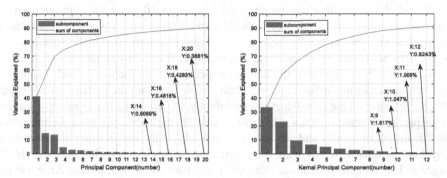

Fig. 4. The proportion of each component in PCA and KPCA.

Figure 5 shows the recognition rate curves of training set and test set of the proposed algorithm under −3–6 dB, in which the number of PCA components is 20, the number of KPCA components is 12, each type of signal is randomly divided into training set and test set according to 7:3, and the experiment results take the mean by 500 times repeat.

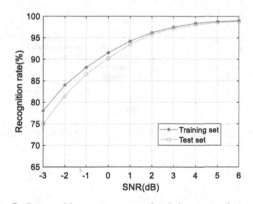

Fig. 5. Recognition rate curves of training set and test set.

Figure 5 shows that the recognition rate of the training set and test set of proposed algorithm would increase as the SNR increases. The recognition rate of training set reaches 91% under 0 dB, which indicates that the proposed algorithm has a good recognition rate. What's more, the recognition rate trend of the test set is similar to that of the training set, and the difference between them is not obvious, which indicates that there is no over-fitting or over-fitting in classifier. The Fig. 5 proves that the proposed algorithm can be well applied to radar signal modulation classification.

Figure 6 shows that the recognition rates of the test set based on four method all increase as the SNR increases. What' more, the recognition rate of algorithm based on LeNet-5 + HOS + Renyi entropy is higher than that of LeNet-5, which proves that feature fusion in proposed algorithm can improve the recognition rate. The recognition rate of proposed algorithm tends to stable after 4 dB, the recognition rate under 4 dB is 96% and the recognition rate under low SNR of −3 dB up to 78%. In addition, it is obvious that the performance of LeNet-5 extracted feature is worse that of Renyi entropy feature. This is mainly because the signal is chaotic under the influence of noise in low SNR, Renyi entropy feature can explain the energy concentration level of the signal, which can improve the anti-noise performance effectively, and fusing the HOS feature can further enhance the reliability. However, with the increase of SNR, the influence of noise on the signal decreases gradually, the ability of Renyi entropy feature to interpret modulation regulation becomes weak. On the contrary, LeNet-5 can extract signal features completely and accurately, which makes the recognition rate better than Renyi entropy after 3 dB. All in all, after fusing the LeNet-5 extracted feature with HOS feature and Renyi entropy feature, although a small amount of cumulative error will be included, the fused feature expresses modulation information more comprehensive and the performance is further improved.

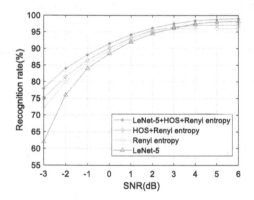

Fig. 6. Recognition rate of test set based on four algorithms.

7   Conclusion

A multi-dimensional feature fusion modulation classification algorithm based on self-training network is proposed in this paper. The algorithm applies LeNet-5 network to extract the modulation regulation feature automatically, which can solve the problem that traditional algorithms extract feature incompletely and deep learning neural network is not suitable for small sample training. Renyi entropy feature and HOS feature are fused by NMF to increase the recognition rate of proposed algorithm. The simulation results show that the recognition rate of modulation classification based on fused feature is better than other classification algorithms, and it performs well under low SNR.

Acknowledgements. This paper is funded by the International Exchange Program of Harbin Engineering University for Innovation-oriented Talents Cultivation, the National Natural Science Foundation of China (61701134), China Shipbuilding Industry Corporation 722 Research Institute Fund Project (KY10800170051), Equipment Pre-research Fund (61404150101), SAST2017-068 and the Fundamental Research Funds for the Central Universities (HEUCFG201832).

References

1. Dudczyk, J., Kawalec, A.: Specific emitter identification based on graphical representation of the distribution of radar signal parameters. Bull. Polish Acad. Sci. Tech. Sci. **63**(2), 391–396 (2015)
2. Guo, Q., Nan, P., Zhang, X., et al.: Recognition of radar emitter signals based on SVD and AF main ridge slice. J. Commun. Netw. **17**(5), 491–498 (2015)
3. Ma, J., Huang, G., Zuo, W., et al.: Robust radar waveform recognition algorithm based on random projections and sparse classification. IET Radar Sonar Navig. **8**(4), 290–296 (2014)
4. Wang, X., Zhou, Y., Zhou, D., et al.: Research on low probability of intercept radar signal recognition using deep belief network and bispectra diagonal slice. J. Electron. Inf. Technol. **38**(11), 2972–2976 (2016)
5. Lecun, Y.L., Bottou, L., Bengio, Y., et al.: Gradient-based learning applied to document recognition. Proc. IEEE **86**(11), 2278–2324 (1998)
6. Wei, S.: Feature space analysis of modulation classification using very high-order statistics. IEEE Commun. Lett. **17**(9), 1688–1691 (2013)
7. Aguiar, V., Guedes, I., Pedrosa, I.A.: Tsallis, Rényi, and Shannon entropies for time-dependent mesoscopic RLC circuits. Prog. Theor. Exp. Phys. **2015**(11), 113A01 (2015)
8. Samiee, K., Kovacs, P., Gabbouj, M.: Epileptic seizure classification of EEG time-series using rational discrete short-time Fourier transform. IEEE Trans. Biomed. Eng. **62**(2), 541–552 (2015)
9. Huynh, Q.Q., Cooper, L.N., Intrator, N., et al.: Classification of underwater mammals using feature extraction based on time-frequency analysis and BCM theory. IEEE Trans. Signal Process. **46**(5), 1202–1207 (2016)
10. Wang, Y., Wu, X., Li, W., et al.: Analysis of micro-Doppler signatures of vibration targets using EMD and SPWVD. Neurocomputing **171**(C), 48–56 (2016)
11. Ding, S., Xu, X., Nie, R.: Extreme learning machine and its applications. Neural Comput. Appl. **25**(3–4), 549–556 (2014)

Soft Actor-Critic-Based Continuous Control Optimization for Moving Target Tracking

Tao Chen, Xingxing Ma, Shixun You[(✉)], and Xiaoli Zhang

College of Information and Communication Engineering, Harbin Engineering University,
Heilongjiang 150001, China
youshixun@hrbeu.edu.cn

Abstract. In the field of cognitive electronic warfare (CEW), unmanned combat aerial vehicle (UCAV) realize moving targets tracking is a prerequisite for effective attack on the enemy. However, most of the traditional target tracking use intelligent algorithms combined with filtering algorithms leads to the UCAV flight motion discontinuous and have limited application in the field of CEW. This paper proposes a continuous control optimization for moving target tracking based on soft actor-critic (SAC) algorithm. Adopting the SAC algorithm, the deep reinforcement learning technology is introduced into moving target tracking train. The simulation analysis is carried out in our environment named Explorer, when the UCAV operation cycle of is 0.4 s, after about 2000 steps of iteration, the success rate of UCAV target tracking is above 92.92%, and the tracking effect is improved compared with the benchmark.

Keywords: Cognitive electronic warfare · Target tracking · SAC

1 Introduction

Deep reinforcement learning (DRL) has achieved great success in many domains, such as automatic driving, robot control, path planning and so on. Deep learning has strong perception ability, but lacks certain decision-making ability; while reinforcement learning has decision-making ability, and has no way to deal with perception problems. Therefore, combining the advantages of the two and complementing each other provides a solution to the perceptual decision-making problem of complex systems [1]. Applying this method to UCAV, DRL can make decision for UCAV flight without knowing or limited understanding of the environment, and plan the best flight route.

In recent years, many methods are used to solve the problem of target tracking. For example, intelligent algorithms [2] and Kalman filter [3]. However, most of the methods are computationally intensive and have limited applications in complex problems. Zhao hui presented a fusion tracking algorithm of fire solution for MMW/Tv combined guidance UCAV based on IMM-PF [4]. However, the tracking trajectory is discrete and the trajectories need to be synthesized. Wu proposed a square root orthogonal Kalman

© Springer Nature Switzerland AG 2019
Y. Zhao et al. (Eds.): ICIG 2019, LNCS 11902, pp. 630–641, 2019.
https://doi.org/10.1007/978-3-030-34110-7_53

filter (SRQKF) algorithm to realize target tracking [5], but it increased the computational complexity and took a long time. Therefore, to relieve the abovementioned drawback, Sun proposes a time method for autonomous vehicle tracking moving target based on regularized extreme learning machine (relm). Typical Q-learning algorithm was used to generate strategies suitable for autonomous navigation [6], but its force constraints were not considered.

With the development of deep reinforcement learning methods, more methods are used to solve UCAV target tracking or navigation problems. However, most of the papers do not consider UCAV's flight action and constraints in three-dimensional (3D) space or discretize UCAV flight action, so it is difficult to apply UCAV to the actual scene.

In this paper, we propose a continuous control optimization for moving target tracking based on soft actor-critic (SAC) algorithm. Takes full account of UCAV flight environment and 3D space action characteristics, and carefully designs reward conditions. The SAC algorithm in deep reinforcement learning is used to train UCAV and complete the moving target tracking. Finally, the effectiveness of the method is demonstrated by experimental simulation. The simulation experiments verify the effectiveness of the proposed method.

The rest of the paper is organized as follows. Section 2 describe the problem of moving target tracking. In Sect. 3, the DRL and SAC algorithm are introduced. Results and related discussion are provided in the following section. The conclusion will be discussed in the last section.

2   Moving Target Tracking Research

Aiming at the traditional target tracking model is two-dimensional (2D) and UCAV motion is discontinuous. In this paper, SAC algorithm of deep reinforcement learning algorithm is used to train UCAV to track moving targets in 3D continuous model. This work mainly refers the CEW in [7].

2.1   Map

In order to view the flight trajectory of UCAV and moving target conveniently, we define a flight map (15 km × 15 km) named Explorer, Because it is difficult to visualize continuous motion in three-dimensional (3D) space on the dimension of altitude, so projected it into a (2D) plane in the negative direction of the Z-axis, and the flight altitude information is expressed numerically in the attribute box on the right side (Fig. 1).

Fig. 1. The map of the moving target tracking and the size of the map is 15×15 (km). The left side displays the map from the global perspective, and the right sides display the attributes of the UCAV and target, contains location, speed, etc. information.

2.2 Tracking Structure

A modular moving target track system is proposed for the target action continuous. Different parts of tracking system are shown in Fig. 2, and will be elaborated in detail in the following sections.

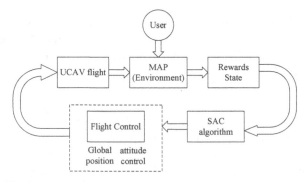

Fig. 2. Modular tracking system functional structural diagram.

2.3 Confrontation Model and Training Constraints

In order to simulate the actual battlefield environment more realistically, we take full account of UCAV's flight state and action constraints in 3D space and design the reward conditions of UCAV.

States

At any time t, the state of the UCAV can be expressed as:

$$S_t = CON(p_{u,t}, p_{a,t} - p_{u,t}, v_{a,t} - v_{u,t})$$
$$= CON([x_{u,t}, y_{u,t}, h_{u,t}], [dx_t, dy_t, dh_t],$$
$$[dv_{x,t}, dv_{y,t}, dv_{z,t}]) \tag{1}$$

where CON represents a function used to concatenate vectors.

$$[dx_t, dy_t, dh_t] = [x_{a,t} - x_{u,t}, y_{a,t} - y_{u,t}, h_{a,t} - h_{u,t}] \tag{2}$$

$$[dv_{x,t}, dv_{y,t}, dv_{z,t}] = [v_{ax,t} - v_{ux,t}, v_{ay,t} - v_{uy,t}, v_{az,t} - v_{uz,t}] \tag{3}$$

The $[dx_t, dy_t, dh_t]$ is relative displacement of UCAV and moving target, $[dv_{x,t}, dv_{y,t}, dv_{z,t}]$ is relative velocity of UCAV and moving target. The transformation formula between Z-axis coordinates of any point in space and ground height:

$$h = \sqrt{x^2 + y^2 + z^2} - R \tag{4}$$

where R is the radius of the earth and h is the height from UCAV to the surface of the earth.

In our environment Explorer, we only consider the case of 1v1, that is, a UCAV tracks only one moving target. The trajectory of the UCAV tracking moving target is shown as Fig. 3.

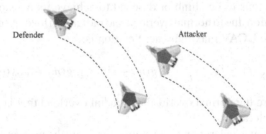

Defender   Attacker

Fig. 3. The trajectory of UCAV tracking moving target, the red and blue represent attacker and defender respectively. (Color figure online)

Action

In the actual battlefield, UCAV cannot change the flight speed, direction, position and other information arbitrary and quickly because of its physical constraints. The constraints must be well considered in order to design UCAV flight action (Fig. 4).

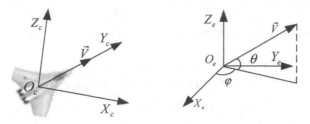

Fig. 4. Description of the constraint reference frame.

According to [8], define the UCAV's constraint reference frame and the local geographic Cartesian reference frame is $(O_cX_cY_cZ_c)$ and $(O_eX_eY_eZ_e)$ respectively. θ is the pitching angle of UCAV, φ represents the angle between UAV velocity and velocity projection. Then, the transformation matrix from $(O_eX_eY_eZ_e)$ to $(O_cX_cY_cZ_c)$ is:

$$C_e^c = \begin{bmatrix} \sin\varphi & -\cos\varphi\cos\theta & -\cos\varphi\sin\theta \\ \cos\varphi & \sin\varphi\cos\theta & \sin\varphi\sin\theta \\ 0 & -\sin\theta & \cos\theta \end{bmatrix} \tag{5}$$

The arbitrary position P_c of UCAV in the constrained reference frame is expressed by formula:

$$P_c = \begin{bmatrix} x_c \\ y_c \\ z_c \end{bmatrix} = C_e^c \begin{bmatrix} x_e - x_u \\ y_e - y_u \\ z_e - z_u \end{bmatrix} \tag{6}$$

When the UCAV needs to be climb or descend to achieve its mission, there will be a maximum acceleration due to normal overload and radial overload. According to formula in [13] and [10], the UCAV maximum acceleration is:

$$a_{\max}(t) = (g\sqrt{n_f^2 - 1}, g(n_g - \sin(\theta_t)), g(n_f - \cos(\theta_t)) \tag{7}$$

where n_f and n_g are the normal overload and radial overload that UAV can withstand. g gravitational acceleration.

Adopting constant acceleration (CA) control strategy, the motion state of UCAV can be expressed as:

$$U_{t+1} = \Phi_{CA}U = \Phi_{CA} \begin{bmatrix} p_{u,t} \\ v_{u,t} \\ a_{u,t} \end{bmatrix} \tag{8}$$

where $p_{u,t}, v_{u,t}, a_{u,t}$ represents the position, velocity, and acceleration of the UCAV. Additionally, Φ_{CA} is:

$$\Phi_{CA} = \begin{bmatrix} I & \tau I & \tau^2 I/2 \\ 0 & I & \tau I \\ 0 & 0 & I \end{bmatrix} \tag{9}$$

where τ is the sampling cycle, $\mathbf{I}$ is the third-order unit matrix, and $\mathbf{0}$ is the third-order zero matrix.

The maximum flight speed is a key factor in the UCAV flight process. In the acceleration process, in order to ensure the safety of UCAV during flight, UCAV cannot exceed its maximum sustainable speed, assuming that the maximum speed of UCAV is v_{max}, the flight speed must satisfy the constraint:

$$||v|| < v_{max} \tag{10}$$

Rewards

In the process of UCAV tracking target, we use the distance between UCAV and enemy target as the size of reward. When the distance between the two is less than the threshold we set, the reward will gradually increase, otherwise, will be given a negative reward.

$$R_t = \begin{cases} 1 - \|p_{a,t} - p_{u,t}\| & if \ \|p_{a,t} - p_{u,t}\| < \rho_{max} \\ -\|p_{a,t} - p_{u,t}\| & else \end{cases} \tag{11}$$

where $p_{a,t}$ and $p_{u,t}$ represents UCAV and target location respectively.

3 Deep Reinforcement Learning

Reinforcement learning is a kind of method in machine learning and artificial intelligence. It studies how to achieve a specific goal through a series of sequential decisions. The process of reinforcement learning is realized through Markov Decision Making (MDP), it can be defined by the tuple (S, A, p, r), where the state space S and the action space A, and the state transition probability $p(s'|s, a)$ represents the probability density of the next state $s_{t+1} \in S$ given the current state $s \in S$ and action $a_t \in A$. The environment emits a bounded reward $r : S \times A \rightarrow [r_{min}, r_{max}]$ on each transition. The state transition process can be represented in Fig. 5.

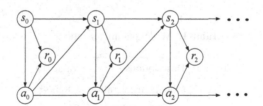

Fig. 5. The process of state transition

When the agent's actions are continuous or high dimensional, traditional reinforcement learning is difficult to deal with. DRL combines high-dimensional input of deep learning with reinforcement learning.

Standard RL maximizes the expected sum of rewards $\sum_t E_{(s_t,a_t)\sim\rho_\pi}[r(s_t, a_t)]$, soft actor-critic (SAC) requires actors to maximize the entropy of expectation and strategy distribution at the same time.

$$J(\pi) = \sum_{t=0}^{T} E_{(s_t,a_t)\sim\rho_\pi}[r(s_t, a_t) + \alpha H(\pi(\cdot|s_t))] \tag{12}$$

The temperature parameter α determines the relative importance of the entropy term against the reward.

SAC incorporates three key factors:

(1) An actor-critic structure consists of a separated policy and a value function network, in which the policy network is random;
(2) An off-policy updating method, which updates parameters based on historical experience samples more efficiency;
(3) Entropy maximization to ensure stability and exploratory ability.

Because SAC algorithm adopts above three points, it achieves state-of-the-art results on a series of continuous control benchmarks.

4   Simulated Experiment and Results

As mentioned before, we propose a continuous control optimization for moving target tracking based on soft actor-critic. In this section, we will discuss simulation results of the moving target tracking model. A total of 10000 iterations training were performed using a computer with a NVIDIA GeForce GTX 970M GPU card and 8G RAM in Explorer. Table 1 summarizes the parameter in the numerical simulations. For DRL, parameter setting has a greater impact on the results, and the super parameters need to be adjusted carefully. The SAC parameters used in the simulation experiments are listed in Table 2.

Table 1. Model parameter setting

Notation	Descriptions	Value
g	Gravity acceleration	9.8 m/s^2
n_f	Normal overload	8
n_q	Radial overload	8
ρ_{max}	Reward threshold	3 km
v_{max}	Maximum speed	300 m/s

Table 2. SAC algorithm parameter setting

Parameter	Value
Actor learning rate	2×10^{-5}
Critic learning rate	10^{-4}
Replay buffer size	3×10^5
Discount	0.99
Number of hidden layers	2
Optimizer	Adam
Number of hidden units per layer	300
Target smoothing coefficient	0.995
Nonlinearity	ReLu

In this paper, to evaluate the performance of SAC algorithm in moving target tracking mission in Explorer. We set up four different difficulties missions, each difficult task is executed with 10000 episodes, and each episode has a tracking time of 400 s. Obviously, as the operation cycle decreases, the task becomes more difficult. At the beginning of each episode, UCAV and the location of the target are randomly reset. The maximum steps and operating cycles of UCAV with different difficulty are shown in Table 3.

Table 3. UCAV operational steps and operating cycles

Level	Operational steps	Operating cycle
0	400	1
1	500	0.8
2	800	0.5
3	1000	0.4

4.1 Reward Analysis

To test the performance of missions on Explore at different difficulty levels, the mission completion is measured according to the mean accumulated reward (MAR), and the calculation formula is:

$$\overline{MAR} = \frac{1}{ep} \sum_{e=1}^{ep} R_e \tag{13}$$

where ep represents the size of dividing the total steps of UCAV training. In order to more intuitively observe the performance of the algorithm, In the simulation, we set it to 40, R_e means the reward of UCAV in each step.

The simulation results of our system for different difficult missions are shown in Fig. 6.

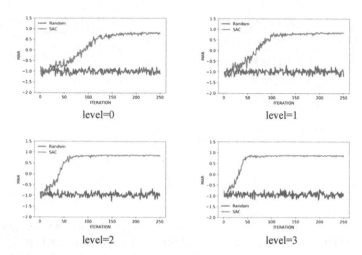

level=0   level=1

level=2   level=3

Fig. 6. Evaluating the performance of the SAC algorithm in Explorer, the red line and the blue line represent the MAR of UCAV using SAC algorithm and random strategy, respectively. (Color figure online)

By comparing the simulation diagrams of different difficult missions, we observed that UCAV performs poorly at the beginning of the missions and get the same rewards as adopting random policy. But when it learning a certain number of steps, the UCAV can get a reward close to 1, and the success rate of target tracking increases gradually.

4.2 Behavior Analysis

Although we can obtain from *MAR* that UCAV can track moving targets after a certain amount of training. In order to explain the flight situation of UCAV from different perspectives, we define the behavior angle (BHA) to describe the flight direction of UCAV:

$$\theta = \langle \vec{a}_t, \vec{n}_t \rangle \tag{14}$$

where $\vec{a}_t, \vec{n}_t$ represents the target and UCAV flight direction respectively. For analysis convenience, θ can be normalized into: $\bar{\theta} = \theta / \pi$, where $\bar{\theta} \in [0, 1]$, when $\bar{\theta} < 0.5$ can be considered that UCAV has a tendency to toward the target. In different difficult missions, UCAV's behaviors are shown in Fig. 7.

As shown in Fig. 7, the BHA of UCAV after training is smaller than that using random strategy. which indicates that UCAV has a tendency towards the target after a certain number of steps of training. By comparing the game environments with different difficulty, the performance of UCAV gradually improves with the increase of the difficulty of the mission from the perspective of reward and behavior angle, which shows that the convergence of SAC algorithm is better in the more complex environment.

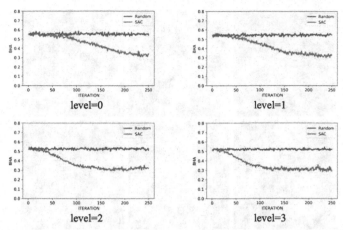

level=0   level=1

level=2   level=3

Fig. 7. The simulation results of BHA for different mission, the red line and the blue line represent the BHA of UCAV using SAC algorithm and random strategy, respectively. (Color figure online)

4.3 Trajectory Analysis

In order to see the UCAV and the target flight trajectory clearly, we chose an episode with an operating cycle of 0.4 s. UCAV and target flight trajectory as shown in Fig. 8.

As shown in Fig. 8, the UCAV's maneuvers at different time have different purposes. During the early operating cycles of UCAV, it began to fly towards moving targets. With the increase of UCAV operating steps, UCAV plans to track moving target.

5   Conclusion

In this paper, we build a three-dimension UCAV flight model named Explorer and combining with the deep reinforcement learning theory, design the flight motion and reward of UCAV. Using SAC algorithm realizes the UCAV tracking moving targets. The experimental results also show that UCAV can successfully track the moving target of the enemy after the number of iterations reaches a certain number of steps. It has strong application value in the field of cognitive electronic warfare.

Acknowledgment. This paper is funded by the International Exchange Program of Harbin Engineering University for Innovation-oriented Talents Cultivation.

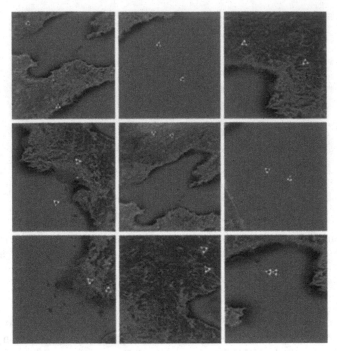

Fig. 8. UCAV and target flight trajectory, the red and blue represent attracter and defender respectively. The number of UCAV operational steps between each image are 100. (Color figure online)

References

1. Sutton, R.S., Barto, A.G.: Reinforcement Learning: An Introduction. MIT Press, Cambridge (1998)
2. Niu, C.F., Liu, Y.S.: Hierarchic particle swarm optimization based target tracking. In: International Conference on Advanced Computer Theory and Engineering, Cairo, Egypt, pp. 517–524 (2009)
3. Mu, C., Yuan, Z., Song, J., et al.: A new approach to track moving target with improved mean shift algorithm and Kalman filter. In: International Conference on Intelligent Human-machine Systems and Cybernetics (2012)
4. Hui, Z., Weng, X., Fu, Y., et al.: Study on fusion tracking algorithm of fire calculation for MMW/Tv combined guidance UCAV based on IMM-PF. In: Chinese Control and Decision Conference. IEEE (2011)
5. Wu, C., Han, C., Sun, Z.: A new nonlinear filtering method for ballistic target tracking. In: 2009 12th International Conference on Information Fusion. IEEE (2009)
6. Sun, T., He, B., Nian, R., et al.: Target following for an autonomous underwater vehicle using regularized ELM-based reinforcement learning. In: OCEANS 2015 - MTS/IEEE Washington. IEEE (2015)
7. You, S., Diao, M., Gao, L.: Deep reinforcement learning for target searching in cognitive electronic warfare. IEEE Access **7**, 37432–37447 (2019)
8. Zhu, L., Cheng, X., Yuan, F.G.: A 3D collision avoidance strategy for UAV with physical constraints. Measurement **77**, 40–49 (2016)

9. Haarnoja, T., Zhou, A., Abbeel, P., et al.: Soft actor-critic: off-policy maximum entropy deep reinforcement learning with a stochastic actor (2018)
10. Imanberdiyev, N., Fu, C., Kayacan, E., et al.: Autonomous navigation of UAV by using real-time model-based reinforcement learning. In: International Conference on Control. IEEE (2017)
11. You, S., Gao, L., Diao, M.: Real-time path planning based on the situation space of UCAVs in a dynamic environment. Microgravity Sci. Technol. **30**, 899–910 (2018)
12. Ma, X., Xia, L., Zhao, Q.: Air-combat strategy using deep Q-learning 3952–3957 (2018). https://doi.org/10.1109/cac.2018.8623434
13. Dionisio-Ortega, S., Rojas-Perez, L.O., Martinez-Carranza, J., et al.: A deep learning approach towards autonomous flight in forest environments. In: 2018 International Conference on Electronics, Communications and Computers (CONIELECOMP). IEEE (2018)
14. Yun, S., Choi, J., Yoo, Y., et al.: Action-driven visual object tracking with deep reinforcement learning. IEEE Trans. Neural Netw. Learn. Syst. **29**, 2239–2252 (2018)

A Pruning Method Based on Feature Abstraction Capability of Filters

Yi Tang, Xiang Zhang$^{(\boxtimes)}$, and Ce Zhu

University of Electronic Science and Technology of China, Chengdu 611731, China
uestchero@uestc.edu.cn

Abstract. With the wide application of convolutional neural network, the optimization of CNN has received ever-increasing research focus. This paper proposes a new pruning strategy, which aims to accelerate and compress off-the-shelf CNN models. Firstly, we propose the pruning criteria for the feature abstraction capability of the filter, which is evaluated by combining the kernel sparsity of the filter with the dispersion of the feature maps activated by the filter. Then, the filter with weak Feature Abstraction Capability (FAC) is pruned to obtain a compact CNN model. Finally, fine-tuning is used to restore the generalization ability. And Compared with other pruning methods which use filters of the same layer for contrast, Our method normalizes each layer, the proposed criterion can be applied to the filters between cross-layer of CNN. Experiments on CAFAR-10 and CUB-200-2011 datasets verify the effectiveness of our method. The FAC-based method achieves better performance than previous filter importance evaluation criteria.

Keywords: Accelerate · Kernel sparsity · Dispersion · Feature Abstraction Capability

1 Introduction

In recent years, It is well known that convolutional neural networks have achieved great success in various computer vision tasks [1], including object detection [2–4], object classification [5,6] and semantic segmentation [7,8] and many others. CNNs have achieved state-of-the-art performance in these fields compared with traditional methods based on manually designed visual features [9]. However, with the deepening and widening of CNN convolution layer, higher computational overhead and larger memory are required, so it is difficult to deploy CNN model to resource-limited devices, such as mobile phones and embedded devices. As a result, the application of convolutional neural network in practical scenarios will be limited by various hardware equipment resources, such as storage space, computing power and battery power. For instance, AlexNet [10] network contains about 6×10^6 parameters, while some better networks like VGG [11] contain about 1.38×10^8 parameters. For less complex tasks, such as simple image recognition, the VGG network will require more than 500 MB memory

© Springer Nature Switzerland AG 2019
Y. Zhao et al. (Eds.): ICIG 2019, LNCS 11902, pp. 642–654, 2019.
https://doi.org/10.1007/978-3-030-34110-7_54

and 1.56×10^{10} Float Point Operations (FLOPs). The over-parameterized [12] of deep learning is a major obstacle to deployment on mobile devices.

Thus, network compression has drawn a significant amount of interests from both academia and industry. In recent years, numerous efficient compression methods have been proposed, including low-rank approximation [12,13], parameter quantization [14,15], and binarization [16]. Among them, network pruning [17–20] has excellent performance in reducing redundancy of CNNs, and it has better model deployment ability compared with parameter quantization. simultaneous pruning can be applied to different elements of CNNs, such as weights, filters, and layers. Early works in network pruning mainly resort to removing several unimportant weight connections from a well-trained network with negligible impact on network performance.

In this paper, a pruning strategy based on Feature Abstraction Capability (FAC) of filters is proposed. Zhou et al. [21] have shown that the features extracted by convolution kernels across layers or even the same layer have significant differences in the contribution of the final prediction results. The more information the feature map represents, the more important it is to the network. Therefore, we believe that the Feature Abstraction Capabilities of different filters are different, and use this criterion to guide the pruning of network elements.

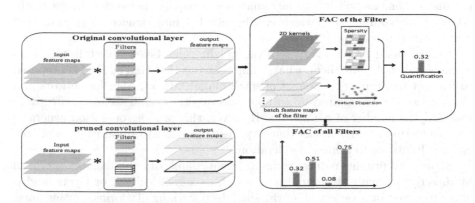

Fig. 1. The framework of our method, in the original convolution layer, the input feature graph is convoluted with the 3D filter to obtain the output feature map. In our FAC method, we first obtain the sparsity of the 3D filter and the dispersion of the batch feature maps by the L1-norm [24] and the data-driven method [18]. Finally, the quantized value of the FAC is obtained as the pruning index in combination with the sparsity and dispersion, and the filter with the lower FAC value in the volume layer is pruned to generate a more Compact network.

As shown in Fig. 1, the Feature Abstraction Capability (FAC) of the filter is obtained by evaluating the sparsity of the convolution kernel of the filter and the information richness contained in the feature map activated by the filter. Our main insight is that the feature map activated by the filter with lower Feature Abstraction Capability (FAC) is redundant. Pruning unimportant filters and fine-tuning the network to restore its generalization capabilities. Finally, the CNN model accelerates and compresses during the training and testing phases, transforming the cumbersome network into a smaller model with a slight performance degradation. At the same time, we propose to normalize the quantized value of each filter's FAC, the proposed pruning strategy can be extended to all layers of the deep CNN, eliminating the need for threshold sensitivity analysis for each layer.

We evaluated our pruning framework by using two commonly used CNN models: VGG-16 [22] and Resnet-110 [23]. These two models are pruned on two benchmark datasets CIFAR10 and CUB_200_2011. These two data sets are representative. In the CIFAR10 dataset, our method still achieves 4.9× compression and 1.77× acceleration on VGG-16, with about 0.3% top-1 accuracy drop. Similarly, in the CUB_200_2011 dataset with 200 kinds of complex tasks of fine-grained classification, our method still had 4.2× acceleration on VGG-16 with roughly 0.6% top-1 accuracy drop, which was better than most similar pruning algorithms.

2   Related Work

In this section, we will briefly introduce some popular network pruning methods in CNN compression, which can be divided into structured pruning and unstructured pruning.

Unstructured pruning is to zero the weight value below a certain threshold in the weights. Among them, what is impressive is that Han et al. [17] proposed to connect by pruning the weight of small magnitudes on AlexNet network and VGG network, and then retrain without affecting the overall accuracy, effectively reducing the number of parameters. However, this pruning operation generates an unstructured sparse model that requires sparse BLAS libraries or even specialized hardware to achieve acceleration.

Structured pruning reduces computational complexity and memory overhead by directly removing structured parts, such as kernels, filters, or layers, and is well supported by a variety of off-the-shelf deep learning platforms. For instance, One pruning criterion is sparsity activated by non-linear ReLu mappings. Hu et al. [18] proposed a data-driven neuron pruning approach to remove unimportant neurons. They argue that if most of these activated feature maps are zero, it is not important for neurons to have a high probability. The criterion measures the importance of neurons by calculating the average percentage of zeros (APoZ) in the activated feature map. However, the APoZ pruning criterion requires the introduction of different threshold parameters for each convolutional layer, which are difficult to accurately determine. Li et al. [24] proposed to remove unimportant filters based on the L1-norm. Molchanov et al. [19] calculated the influence of filters on network loss function based on Taylor expansion. According to the criterion, if the filter has little influence on the loss function, the filter can be safely removed. So they use Taylor expansion to approximate the change in loss. He et al. [23] proposes a channel selection method based on LASSO regression, which uses least squares reconstruction to eliminate redundant filters. Similar to our study, Luo et al. [20] proposed a method to calculate entropy of filters to measure the information richness of the convolution kernel. However, only the information richness of the filter is considered in the method, and the strategy can only compare the entropy value of the same convolutional layer. Most of these methods need to accurately obtain the pruning threshold of each convolutional layer, but this is difficult to achieve. If fixed compression rate is used for pruning, it may lead to irreparable accuracy reduction.

In addition to the network pruning method, some other CNN compression methods are introduced, such as designing a more compact architecture. For example, it is known that most parameters of the CNN model exist in fully-connected layers, so the global average pooling is proposed to replace the full connection layer in the Network-In-Network [26]. Son et al. [27] reconstructed the network by unified representation of similar convolutions, so as to achieve effective compression of the network. However, this method has some limitations. It is only effective for 3×3 convolution kernels. Sandler et al. [28] proposed the use of depthwise separable convolution to build a lightweight network, which has also been widely used in mobile devices. It's important to note that our approach can be combined with these strategies to achieve a more compact and optimized network. As for ResNet-50, there exists less redundancy compared with classic CNN models. We can still bring $1.63\times$ acceleration and achieves $2.48\times$ reduction in FLOPs and parameters with 0.007 decrease in accuracy.

3   Pruning Method

In this section, we will describe in detail our pruning method based on the Feature Abstraction Capability of the filter. First, the general framework is given. Our main idea is to quantify the FAC of all convolutional layer filters, discard those filters with poor performance in each pruning, and restore their performance by fine-tuning. These implementation details will be released later. Finally, the training and pruning planning strategy we used in the experiment is introduced, which has less impact on the final prediction accuracy compared with other previous strategies.

3.1   Framework

Figure 1 illustrates the overall framework of our proposed FAC pruning method. We first obtain the weight values of all 2D kernels in the 3D filter, obtain the sparsity of the 3D filter from the sum of the L1-norm [24] of the 2D kernels, at the same time obtain the batch feature maps of the filter by the data-driven method [18], and then calculate the discreteness of batch feature maps. We use the discreteness of the filter batch feature maps to evaluate the richness of the information contained in the activated feature map, because if the difference in the feature map of the filter is small each time, we have enough reason to believe that the filter Feature Abstraction Capability is weak. Finally, we combine the sparsity of the convolution kernel with the information dispersion of the activated feature map to make the estimated filter feature abstraction more accurate and robust.

Then, all weak filters are pruned from the original model to achieve a more optimized network architecture. Note that the corresponding input channels of filters in the next layer should be removed. Finally, the network is fine-tuned to restore its generalization performance.

3.2 Filter Sparsity

In the convolution layer i, the input tensor $I_i \in \mathbb{R}^{C \times H_{in} \times W_{in}}$ is convolved with a set of filter weights $W_i \in \mathbb{R}^{N \times C \times K_h \times K_w}$ to get the output tensor $Y_i \in \mathbb{R}^{N \times H_{out} \times W_{out}}$. Here, C is the number of the input feature maps, H_{in} and W_{in} are the height and width of the input feature maps, N is the number of the filters, H_{out} and W_{out} are the height and width of the output feature maps, K_h and K_w are the height and width of a filter. The convolution operation can be expressed by the following formula:

$$Y_n = I_i * W_n \tag{1}$$

Where denote the convolution operation, W_n is the weight of the nth filter in the convolutional layer I, $W_n \in \mathbb{R}^{C \times K_h \times K_w}$. Y_n is the feature map of nth filter, $Y_n \in \mathbb{R}^{H_{out} \times W_{out}}$.

We evaluate the sparsity of the filter by calculating the L1-norm of W_n, because it is known from Eq. (1) that if the absolute value of the weights value in W_n is mostly close to zero, the L1-norm will be small and the value in the output feature map of the filter will also be closer to zero. We think that such a feature map is approximately sparse, indicating that the filter's Feature Abstraction Capability is also weaker. Therefore, for the n-th input feature map, we define its sparsity as:

$$S_n = \sum_{c=0}^{C} \sum_{i=0}^{K_h} \sum_{j=0}^{K_w} |W_{n,c,i,j}|, \quad n = 0, 1, 2, \ldots, N \tag{2}$$

3.3 Discreteness of Feature Maps

In this paper, we propose a criterion based on the FAC of the filter to evaluate the importance of each filter. We believe that if the difference between the feature maps of each output of the filter is greater, the filter's Feature Abstraction Capability will be stronger.

As shown in Fig. 2, we use global average pooling [26] for the activated feature maps output of layer i, in this way, a $N \times H_{out} \times W_{out}$ output tensor will be converted into a $1 \times N$ vector. At the same time, a corresponding score is obtained for each feature map output of the filter. In order to calculate the dispersion of each filter's output feature map score, more output results are needed, so we calculate a score for each batch of the data set, and finally we will get a matrix

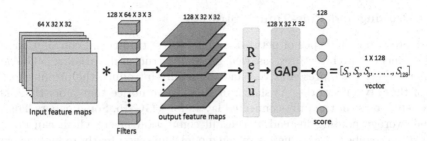

Fig. 2. How to use Global Average Pooling (GAP) to calculate the score of output feature map in convolutional layer i, it should be noted that feature maps are activated by ReLu function before GAP, because we think that the negative values in feature maps are filtered out in the network.

$M \in \mathbb{R}^{B \times N}$, where B refers to the number of batches in the training data set, and N is the output channel number.

Then, for $M_{:,j}$ in the matrix M represents the output scores vector of the j-th filter, let μ_j be the average of the scores of the j-th filter, the formula is as follows:

$$S_n = \sum_{i=0}^{B} M_{i,j}, \quad j = 0, 1, 2, \ldots, N \tag{3}$$

Then, the feature maps dispersion of the j-th filter is:

$$D_j = \begin{cases} 0, & \mu_j = 0 \\ \sqrt{\frac{\sum_{i=0}^{B}(M_{i,j}-\mu_j)^2}{B}}, & otherwise \end{cases} \tag{4}$$

3.4 Definition of the FAC

From the above discussion, we know that the importance of the filter depends on two parts, the sparsity of the convolution kernel and the discreteness of the feature maps. Therefore, we combine the two parts to propose the Feature Abstraction Capability (FAC) to measure the importance of the filter by:

$$FAC = S_n * D_j \tag{5}$$

3.5 Normalization

In many papers, the pruning criterion is only applicable to the convolution kernel comparison between the same layers, and the scale inconsistency will occur when applied to the cross-layer. Therefore, in our method, we uses layer-wise L2-normalization to achieve reasonable rescaling:

$$\Theta^{(i)} = \frac{\Theta^{(i)}}{\sqrt{\sum_{j=0}^{N}(\Theta^{(i)})^2}} \tag{6}$$

Where, $\Theta^{(i)}$ refers to the set of all FAC filters in the layer i, which can be understood as a vector. $\Theta^{(i)}$ refers to the FAC of the j-th filter in the layer i.

3.6   Pruning and Fine-Tuning Strategy

There are two main types of network architectures: traditional convolution and fully-connected architectures, as well as some structural variants. VGG and Resnet are typical representatives, and we mainly introduce the pruning methods of these two networks. As shown in Table 1, we notice that more than 39% parameters exist in the fully-connected layers for VGG-16. Some papers [20] use global average pooling instead of the full connection layer, which can greatly reduce the number of parameters of the model, but also greatly reduce the convergence speed of the model, which may make it difficult to train the model back to the original accuracy. Therefore, we reduce the parameters of the full connection layer by pruning the filter of the last convolution layer to reduce the input channel of FC1 layer.

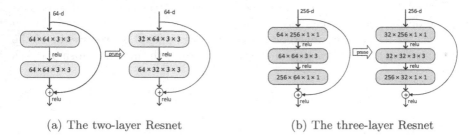

(a) The two-layer Resnet   (b) The three-layer Resnet

Fig. 3. Our pruning strategy for ResNet. For each residual block, the final convolutional layer filter cannot be pruned, reducing its input channel by pruning of the previous layer.

For ResNet, there are some restrictions in the pruning process due to the introduction of so-called "identity shortcut connection". For example, the summation operation requires that the number of output channels per block in the same group needs to be consistent (see Fig. 3). In the ResNet network structure, two kinds of residual modules are mainly used, one is that two 3×3 convolution networks are connected in series as one residual module, and the other is 1×1, 3×3, 1×1 of 3 convolutional networks are concatenated together as a residual module.

The final question is how to fine tune the entire network during the pruning process. Our strategy is prune and retrain iteratively. We found that most of the pruning method is to pruning filter of each layer at a fixed rate of pruning, and then fine-tuning the model a few times, but if the pruning rate is too high, the filter structure of the layer may be damaged. This problem will become more apparent in more complex task networks because too many filters are pruned at once in this layer.

So our method is to preset a compression ratio α for the whole network. We need to pruning $N \times (1 - \alpha)$ filters, and then we only pruned β filters each time, finally whole network is fine-tuned with few epochs to recover its performance slightly. In this way, we only need to perform $N \times (1 - \alpha)/\beta$ pruning, and those β filters that are pruned each time are distributed across all convolutional layers of the network, not concentrated on one layer at a time. And the value of β in the experiment is 256. The fine-tuning method obtained better results in experiments than other methods.

Table 1. Overall performance of our approach to reduce FLOPs and parameters on the VGG-16 model. The experiment is based on the CIFAR10 dataset. Note that we will resize the 32×32 image size in CIFAR to 128×128.

Layer	Feature map size	FLOPs			Parameters		
		Original	Pruned	Percentage	Original	Pruned	Percentage
Conv1-1	128×128	29.36M	21.56M	73.4%	1.79K	1.32K	73.5%
Conv1-2	128×128	605.02M	305.65M	50.5%	36.92K	18.65K	46.7%
Conv2-1	64×64	302.51M	37.4M	12.4%	73.85K	9.13K	12.4%
Conv2-2	64×64	604.50M	18.74M	3.1%	147.58K	4.58K	3.1%
Conv3-1	32×32	302.25M	5.91M	2.0%	295.16K	5.77K	1.9%
Conv3-2	32×32	604.24M	9.39M	1.5%	590.08K	9.17K	1.6%
Conv3-3	32×32	604.24M	16.83M	2.8%	590.08K	16.43K	2.8%
Conv4-1	16×16	302.12M	10.69M	3.5%	1.18M	41.74K	3.5%
Conv4-2	16×16	604.11M	24.84M	4.1%	2.36M	97.04K	4.1%
Conv4-3	16×16	604.11M	32.37M	5.3%	2.36M	126.44K	5.4%
Conv5-1	8×8	151.02M	9.63M	6.4%	2.36M	150.48K	6.4%
Conv5-2	8×8	151.02M	16.68M	6.9%	2.36M	260.69K	11.1%
Conv5-3	8×8	151.02M	20.62M	13.6%	2.36M	322.18K	13.7%
FC1	1	8.39M	2.92M	34.8%	8.39M	2.92M	34.8%
FC2	1	1.05M	1.05M	100.0%	1.05M	1.05M	100.0%
FC3	1	10.24K	10.24K	100.0%	10.24K	10.24K	100.0%
Total	–	5.02B	534.29M	10.6%	24.17M	5.03M	20.9%

4   Experiments

We used our pruning method to pruning two typical CNN models: VGG-16 and ResNet-50. We have implemented our approach using the deep learning framework Pytorch. The validity of the algorithm is verified on two datasets, CIFAR-10 and CUB_200_2011. The CIFAR-10 dataset consists of 60000 images, whose size is 32×32, and the number of images in each category is 6000, with 10 categories. During training, images are converted to 128×128, because if the image is too small, the FLOPs of the network itself will be very small, and the deceleration effect after pruning is not obvious. The Cub_200_2011 is a birds data set for fine-grained classification tasks, which contains 11788 images of 200 different bird species. It presents a significant challenge for pruning algorithms to maximize model compression and acceleration without reducing accuracy too much. During training, all images of Cub_200_2011 are resize to 320×320, After each pruning, we fine-tune the whole network in 8 epochs with learning rate varying from 10^{-3} to 10^{-5}. During the last pruning, the network is fine-tuned in 20 epochs with learning rate varying from 10^{-3} to 10^{-8}. All experiments are run on a computer equipped with Nvidia GTX 1080Ti GPU.

4.1 VGG-16 Pruning

The detailed distribution of FLOPs and parameters in each layer of VGG-16 is shown in Table 1. As we have seen, the 2nd - 12th layer convolutional layer contains 90% FLOPs. And we can see that our pruning method is also mainly aimed at layer 3–12. For the first two layers of convolutional layer, there is no large-scale pruning. We think that the first two layers of filters contain rich feature information, so they have stronger Feature Abstraction Capability than other filters in the layer. The side proves that our method has a certain degree of interpretability. The pruning rate we set is 80%, that is, 80% of the filters in the model are pruned off. Finally, we compare our method with following baselines on the VGG-16 model:

Taylor Expansion [19]: The effect of the filter on the network loss function is calculated based on the Taylor expansion method. According to this criterion, if the filter has little effect on the loss function, the filter can be safely removed.

APoZ [18]: The criterion measures the importance of filters by calculating the average percentage of zeros (APoZ) in the activated feature map.

Entropy [20]: The method to calculate entropy of filters to measure the information richness of the convolution kernel.

Table 2. Comparison of different model compression methods for VGG-16 network on CIFAR10.

Method	Top-1 Acc	FLOPs (%)	Params (%)	Speed up	Compression
Original	0.916	5.02B	24.17M	1.0×	1.0×
APoZ-50%	0.912	1.27B (25.3%)	8.39M (34.7%)	1.61×	2.7×
APoZ-80%	0.803	0.19B (3.8%)	3.34M (13.8%)	1.92×	5.4×
Taylor-50%	0.922	1.42B (28.2%)	6.94M (28.71%)	1.48×	3.8×
Taylor-80%	0.908	0.56B (11.2%)	1.03M (4.3%)	1.72×	6.1×
Entropy_GAP	0.868	1.56B (31.1%)	4.22M (17.5%)	1.49×	4.8×
FAC-50%	0.925	1.26B (25.1%)	11.09M (45.9%)	1.54×	2.0×
FAC-80%	0.913	0.53B (10.6%)	5.03M (20.8%)	1.77×	4.9×

Table 3. Comparison of different model compression methods for VGG-16 network on CUB_200_2011.

Method	Top-1 Acc	Top-5 Acc	FLOPs (%)	Params (%)	Speed up
Original	0.764	0.939	31.64B	304.1M	1.0×
APoZ-80%	0.556	0.833	1.40B (4.4%)	80.6M (26.5%)	5.6×
Taylor-50%	0.772	0.948	13.96B (44.1%)	91.8M (30.2%)	2.7×
Entropy-50%	0.728	0.932	9.42B (29.8%)	64.6M (21.2%)	3.5×
FAC-50%	0.786	0.950	11.62B (36.7%)	122.6M (40.3%)	3.1×
FAC-80%	0.758	0.937	6.74B (21.3%)	66.6M (21.9%)	4.2×

As shown in Tables 2 and 3, we used different algorithms for pruning VGG-16 networks in CIFAR10 and CUB_200_2011 datasets, among which the APOZ method pruned the filter of each layer with a fixed prune rate. We can see that when the pruning rate reaches 80%, the accuracy of the model drops very seriously. In the Entropy method, Luo et al. used GAP instead of the fully-connected layer, which greatly reduced the parameters of the model, but had a greater impact on the prediction accuracy of the model (which greatly increased the difficulty of convergence of the model). The Taylor method uses a pruning strategy similar to ours. It can be seen that the Taylor criterion has better performance for model size compression, but at the same pruning rate, our method has less precision loss and more excellent acceleration performance. As can be seen from the two tables, the larger the size of the input image, the greater the clipping acceleration. In the CUB_200_2011 dataset, the size of the input image is 320 × 320. Our method can achieve about 4.7× reduction in FLOPs and parameters with 0.006 decrease in accuracy. When the pruning rate is 50%, the accuracy of the pruned model is even higher than the original model, and higher than other pruning methods.

By comparison, we can see that our FAC-based pruning method has better overall performance, and there is a better balance between model compression and model acceleration at the same pruning rate.

4.2 ResNet-110 Pruning

In the network structure of ResNet-110, it is divided into three hierarchies by the residual block, and the size of its corresponding feature maps are 32 × 32, 16 × 16, and 8 × 8, respectively. According to the process of pruning for ResNets in Sect. 3.5, the pruned model for ResNet-110 was obtained on CIFAR-10. During the training process, the images are randomly cropped to 32 × 32.

The overall performance of our method on pruning ResNet-110 is shown in Table 4, We prune this model with 2 different pruning rate (pruning 20%, 30% filters respectively). The best pruned model achieves 2.48× reduction in FLOPs and parameters with 0.007 decrease in accuracy. Unlike traditional CNN architectures, ResNet is more compact. There is less redundancy than the

Table 4. The pruned model for ResNet-110 on CIFAR-10 with different pruning rate.

Model	Top-1 Acc	Speed-up		Compression		Time
		#FLOPs	FLOPs%	#Para.	Para.%	
ResNet110	0.937	2.53×10^8	–	1.72×10^6	–	1.0×
FAC-20%	0.933	1.46×10^8	57.7%	1.02×10^6	59.3%	1.34×
FAC-30%	0.928	1.02×10^8	40.3%	0.72×10^6	41.9%	1.63×

VGG-16 model, so it seems more difficult to delete a large number of filters. However, when small pruning rate is adopted, our method can improve the performance of ResNet-110 to the maximum extent.

5   Conclusion

In this paper, we propose a pruning framework based on the Feature Abstraction Capabilities of filters to accelerate and compress the CNN model simultaneously in the training and inference phases. Compared with the previous pruning strategy, the pruning model has better performance. Our approach does not depend on any proprietary libraries, so it can be widely used in a variety of practical applications of current deep learning libraries.

In the future, we want to further explore the interpretability of model pruning, and then design pruning strategies that are more suitable for different visual tasks (such as semantic segmentation, target detection, image restoration, etc.). The pruned network will greatly accelerate these visual tasks.

References

1. Girshick R.: Fast R-CNN. In: The IEEE International Conference on Computer Vision (ICCV), pp. 1440–1448 (2015)
2. Redmon, J., Farhadi, A.: YOLO9000: better, faster, stronger. In: The IEEE Conference on Computer Vision and Pattern Recognition (CVPR), pp. 7263–7271 (2017)
3. Hu, H., Gu, J., Zhang, Z., et al.: Relation networks for object detection. In: The IEEE Conference on Computer Vision and Pattern Recognition (CVPR) (2018)
4. He, K., Gkioxari, G., Dollár, P., et al.: Mask R-CNN. In: The IEEE International Conference on Computer Vision (ICCV), pp. 2961–2969 (2017)
5. He, K., Zhang, X., Ren, S., et al.: Deep residual learning for image recognition. In: The IEEE Conference on Computer Vision and Pattern Recognition (CVPR) (2016)
6. Huang, G., Liu, Z., Van Der Maaten, L., et al.: Densely connected convolutional networks. In: The IEEE Conference on Computer Vision and Pattern Recognition (CVPR) (2017)
7. Long, J., Shelhamer, E., Darrell, T.: Fully convolutional networks for semantic segmentation. In: The IEEE Conference on Computer Vision and Pattern Recognition (CVPR) (2015)

8. Xu, Y.S., Fu, T.J., Yang, H.K., et al.: Dynamic video segmentation network. In: The IEEE Conference on Computer Vision and Pattern Recognition (CVPR), pp. 6556–6565 (2018)

9. Kuhn, M., Johnson, K.: An introduction to feature selection. In: Kuhn, M., Johnson, K. (eds.) Applied Predictive Modeling, pp. 487–519. Springer, New York (2013). https://doi.org/10.1007/978-1-4614-6849-3_19

10. Krizhevsky, A., Sutskever, I., Hinton, G.E.: ImageNet classification with deep convolutional neural networks. In: International Conference on Neural Information Processing Systems (NIPS), pp. 1097–1105 (2012)

11. Simonyan, K., Zisserman, A.: ImageNet classification with deep convolutional neural networks. In: International Conference on Learning Representations (ICLR) (2015)

12. Lin, S., Ji, R., Chen, C., et al.: Holistic CNN compression via low-rank decomposition with knowledge transfer. IEEE Trans. Pattern Anal. Mach. Intell. (TPAMI) (2018)

13. Krizhevsky, A., Sutskever, I., Hinton, G.E.: Coordinating filters for faster deep neural networks. In: The IEEE International Conference on Computer Vision (ICCV) (2017)

14. Wu, J., Leng, C., Wang, Y., et al.: Quantized convolutional neural networks for mobile devices. In: The IEEE Conference on Computer Vision and Pattern Recognition (CVPR), pp. 4820–4828 (2016)

15. Jacob, B., Kligys, S., Chen, B., et al.: Quantization and training of neural networks for efficient integer-arithmetic-only inference. In: The IEEE Conference on Computer Vision and Pattern Recognition (CVPR) (2017)

16. Lin, X., Zhao, C., Pan, W.: Towards accurate binary convolutional neural network. In: International Conference on Neural Information Processing Systems (NIPS), pp. 345–353 (2017)

17. Han, S., Mao, H., Dally, W.J.: Deep compression: compressing deep neural networks with pruning, trained quantization and Huffman coding. In: International Conference on Learning Representations (ICLR) (2016)

18. Hu, H., Peng, R., Tai, Y.W., Tang, C.K.: Network trimming: a data-driven neuron pruning approach towards efficient deep architectures. arXiv preprint arXiv:1607.03250 (2016)

19. Molchanov, P., Tyree, S., Karras, T., et al.: Pruning convolutional neural networks for resource efficient inference. In: International Conference on Learning Representations (ICLR) (2017)

20. Luo, J.H., Wu, J.: An entropy-based pruning method for CNN compression. arXiv preprint arXiv:1706.05791 (2017)

21. Zhou, B., Sun, Y., Bau, D., et al.: Revisiting the importance of individual units in CNNs via ablation. arXiv preprint arXiv: 1806.02891 (2018)

22. Simonyan, K., Zisserman, A.: Very deep convolutional networks for large-scale image recognition. In: International Conference on Learning Representations (ICLR) (2015)

23. He, K., Zhang, X., Ren, S., et al.: Deep residual learning for image recognition. In: The IEEE Conference on Computer Vision and Pattern Recognition (CVPR), pp. 770–778 (2016)

24. Li, H., Kadav, A., Durdanovic, I., et al.: Pruning filters for efficient convnets. In: International Conference on Learning Representations (ICLR) (2016)

25. He, Y., Zhang, X., Sun, J.: Channel pruning for accelerating very deep neural networks. In: International Conference on Computer Vision (ICCV) (2017)

26. Lin, M., Chen, Q., Yan, S.: Network in network. In arXiv preprint arXiv:1312.4400 (2013)
27. Son, S., Nah, S., Lee, K.M.: Clustering convolutional kernels to compress deep neural networks. In: Ferrari, V., Hebert, M., Sminchisescu, C., Weiss, Y. (eds.) ECCV 2018. LNCS, vol. 11212, pp. 225–240. Springer, Cham (2018). https://doi.org/10.1007/978-3-030-01237-3_14
28. Sandler, M., Howard, A., Zhu, M., et al.: MobileNetV2: inverted residuals and linear bottlenecks. In: Computer Vision and Pattern Recognition (CVPR) (2018)

DFQA: Deep Face Image Quality Assessment

Fei Yang[1,2(✉)], Xiaohu Shao[1,2], Lijun Zhang[1,2], Pingling Deng[1,2],
Xiangdong Zhou[1,2], and Yu Shi[1,2]

[1] Chongqing Institute of Green and Intelligent Technology, CAS,
Beijing 400714, China
yangfei@cigit.ac.cn
[2] University of Chinese Academy of Science, Beijing 100049, China

Abstract. A face image with high quality can be extracted dependable
features for further evaluation, however, the one with low quality can't.
Different from the quality assessment algorithms for general images, the
face image quality assessment need to consider more practical factors
that directly affect the accuracy of face recognition, face verifcation, etc.
In this paper, we present a two-stream convolutional neural network
(CNN) named Deep Face Quality Assessment (DFQA) specifically for
face image quality assessment. DFQA is able to predict the quality score
of an input face image quickly and accurately. Specifcally, we design a
network with two-stream for increasing the diversity and improving the
accuracy of evaluation. Compared with other CNN network architectures
and quality assessment methods for similar tasks, our model is smaller
in size and faster in speed. In addition, we build a new dataset containing 3000 face images manually marked with objective quality scores.
Experiments show that the performance of face recognition is improved
by introducing our face image quality assessment algorithm.

Keywords: Face image · Quality assessment · Deep learning · Face
recognition

1 Introduction

The image quality assessment algorithms [1–3] are widely used in medical, information technology, military and other fields. In the aspects of image content
understanding and video understanding analysis, image quality directly affects
the discrimination effect of subsequent modules. For example, in the process
of face recognition, the images of poor quality may directly lead to the face
recognition module can't accurately verify user's identity information.

The image quality assessment algorithms mainly include full reference (FR)
quality assessment, partial reference (PR) quality assessment and no reference
(NR) quality assessment. FR methods mainly use the ideal image and the distorted image, comparing the difference between the distorted image and the

© Springer Nature Switzerland AG 2019
Y. Zhao et al. (Eds.): ICIG 2019, LNCS 11902, pp. 655–667, 2019.
https://doi.org/10.1007/978-3-030-34110-7_55

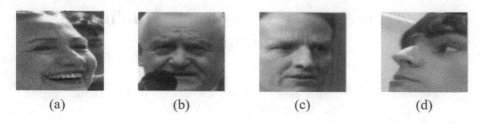

(a)   (b)   (c)   (d)

Fig. 1. Examples of face images. (a)–(d) show that the image quality is good, but the face image quality is poor.

ideal image, so as to evaluate the image quality scores. However, ideal images are difficult to obtain in practice. And the speed of this method is slow in actual evaluation, such as PSNR [4] and SSIM [5].

In contrast, the NR methods don't include ideal images and estimate quality scores from input images directly. The method proposed in this paper belongs to NR quality assessment algorithm. NR methods mainly include the algorithms which based on distortion types and machine learning. Zhou [6] proposed the fuzzy degree caused by the error when quantizing by DCT transform coefficient as the evaluation standard of image quality. Cohen, Erez and Yitzhaky [7] combined two factors of noise and fuzziness to evaluate the image quality scores. These methods use distortion types to calculate image quality scores have certain effect, but the calculation speed is slow.

With the rapid development of deep learning, more and more scholars begin to use deep learning technology to evaluate the quality of images. Gao and Wang [8] used pre-trained VGG model to extract image features and then used SVM to complete the prediction process. Ma, Liu [9] used RankNet to learn a blind image quality assessment (BIQA) model, which predicted the quality scores of images without a reference image. The CNN model can independently learn the content information of images and accomplish different tasks by learning various information based on the prior knowledge during training processing.

At present, although many scholars have begun to study CNN to predict image quality scores, they all studying on the datasets of some image quality assessment fields. However, the face image quality assessment problems are different from the traditional image quality assessment problems. It is more concerned with the change of face angle, blur, illumination and other factors in the actual scene. For example, in Fig. 1(a), the image quality is good. While the face image quality is poor due to poor face angle. In Fig. 1(b), the face is obscured. In Fig. 1(c), the face's illumination is uneven. In Fig. 1, the image quality is better from the perspective of traditional image quality assessment. However, the image quality is poor from the perspective of face image quality assessment. On the other hand, as shown in Fig. 2, in the process of face recognition training, some face images of extremely poor quality will affect the recognition effect and lead to the recognition error. Filtering out the worst quality images can help

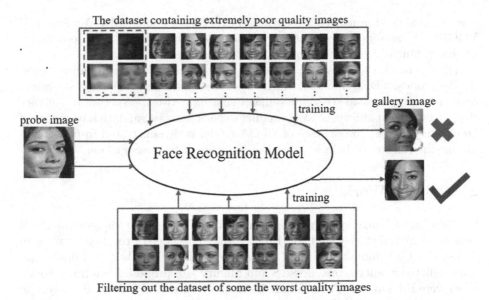

Fig. 2. In the process of face recognition training, some face images of extremely poor quality will affect the recognition effect. Filtering out the worst quality images can help face recognition systems improve their accuracy and effectiveness. Toward this end, we propose a two-stream CNN model to filter out the worst quality images.

face recognition systems improve their accuracy and effectiveness. Toward this end, we propose a two-stream CNN model to filter out the worst quality images.

This paper proposes a two-stream CNN model, named Deep Face Quality Assessment (DFQA) for the quality assessment of face images. Instead of the Euclidean loss used in other methods, we exploit the SVR loss [10] as the objective function, because SVR has been successfully applied to the regression function in many practices in the previous image quality assessment tasks [11,12]. Since the image quality assessment task is a small module in practice, the space size and time complexity occupied by it should not be too high from the practical point of view. The single branch of the proposed DFQA model chooses the Squeezenet [14], which is a lightweight CNN model, it has advantages in both size and speed. In this paper, the quality scores of 3000 images are marked firstly. And the comprehensive quality scores are given according to the face angle, sharpness, illumination and other factors from six volunteers. After that, the 3000 images are used to train the pre-trained squeezenet model using Imagenet dataset. Using the scores-trained squeezenet model to predict the image quality scores of the MS-Celeb-1M [14] dataset as label. Then, the MS-Celeb-1M dataset is used to train the DFQA network to obtain the final face image quality assessment model. The comparison experiment results show that our model is smaller in size and faster in speed, which is suitable for quality assessment tasks. The branch comparison experiments show the validity of the double branch network than single branch. Face recognition experiments on CASIA-WebFace and VGGFace2 datasets prove that our model can help improve face recognition accuracy. Our main contributions can be summarized as follows:

(1) We build a new dataset manually marked with objective quality scores. (2) We propose a DFQA model, which based on the face image quality assessment task and using the two-stream parameter sharing network structure to enhance the prediction capability. (3) We conduct experiments to validate advantages of DFQA model. The importance of DFQA model is demonstrated in face recognition experiments to help improve the accuracy of face recognition.

2   Related Work

In the task of image quality assessment using CNN, many classical methods emerge. Bare Bahetiyaer and Ke [15] used the knowledge of residual network to design the CNN model, and used FSIM to calculate the label, and finally got the predicted quality score. Bosse S and Maniry [16] proposed two frameworks. They were FR and NR. The 32 image blocks were extracted from each image, one network branch predicted image block weight, and one network branch predicted image quality score. Kim and Lee [17] got the weight of each image block and extracted features to predict the quality score. These methods all use CNN to predict the image quality score.

At present, there are few methods for face image quality assessment based on CNN. Nasrollahi and Moeslund [18] used four simple features to assess face quality in video sequence. Truong and Dang [19] used contrast, brightness, focus and illumination factors to assess face image quality score. Ranjan, Rajeev and Bansal [20] mentioned using the probability score of face detection as the quality score of face image. Chen and Yu [21] extracted Hog feature, Gabor feature, Gist feature, LBP feature and CNN feature. Then the weight value of each feature was obtained by sorting algorithm. Finally, the quality score was obtained by fusion. These methods use some image features or factors to predict the quality score of the face image, but don't start from the essence of the face image to consider a variety of factors in the face image, such as face angle, face sharpness, face illumination and other factors. The method proposed in this paper starts from the perspective of manual annotation, taking all kinds of factors of face image into consideration. This paper designs a lightweight two-stream CNN model, and uses SVRloss constraint to predict the quality score of face image.

3   Method

In order to predict the quality score of face image, we select 3000 face images for annotation in the IJB-A dataset from six volunteers. We propose a two-stream CNN model called Deep Face Quality Assessment (DFQA). In this section, we introduce the tagging process and DFQA's framework structure and parameter setting.

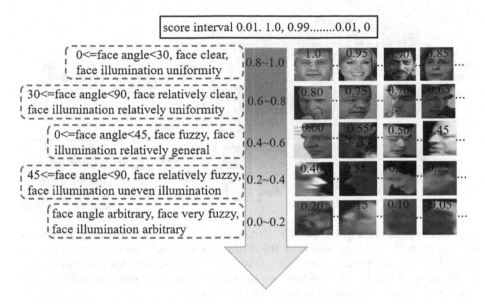

Fig. 3. Manually graded face image quality score results. The final score range is between [0, 1].

3.1 Annotation

We select 3000 face images for manual annotation. Based on the essence of face image, various factors are considered to score face images. We chose six volunteers that all image area researchers and ranging in age from 25 to 35 to score the quality scores of face images. For example, as shown in Fig. 3, we divide the scores into 5 segments from 0 to 1 and label the quality score according to the labeling criteria in Fig. 3. We mainly consider the face angle, face clear and face illumination. But in labeling proceesing, we also consider face visibility, facial expression and other factors, it's not a requirement. Six volunteers score the images according to the requirements, and then calculate an average value as the final quality score of the images based on their results.

As can be seen from Fig. 3, the marked quality scores are between [0, 1]. The score interval is 0.01. Currently, there is no public face image quality score datasets and no standard to mark face image quality score. We carry out a comprehensive assessment score from practical point of view which may affect face recognition of some factors. In the labeling process, we mainly consider several factors: face angle, face sharpness, face illumination and face expression and occlusion. These factors will affect the quality of face in practice and further affect accuracy of the face recognition system.

3.2 DFQA

The framework diagram of DFQA is shown in Fig. 4. The single channel network structure of DFQA uses squeezenet. Since the quality assessment module is a

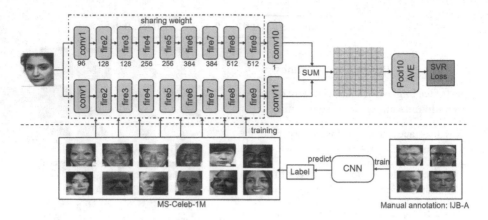

Fig. 4. The framework of DFQA. The DFQA model adopts the two-stream parameter sharing network structure, and fuses the features at the tenth layer, and then passing through the average pooling to get the quality score. We first annotate 3000 face images to pre-train a CNN model, and then use the CNN model to predict the quality scores label of MS-Celeb-1M dataset to train the DFQA model.

relatively small module in practical application, it has high requirements on size and speed. So, with a size of only 3M, squeezenet has strong prediction ability and fast calculation speed. Although the structure of single branch network also has good prediction ability, the feature learning of single branch is not sufficient and can't represent the quality score due to the numerous factors that need to be considered in face image. The choice of double branch network structure can enhance the expression of features, and more comprehensively consider various factors to better characterize the image quality.

DFQA is a two-stream parameter sharing network structure. And each branch consists of two convolutional layers and eight fire layers (conv10 and conv11 layer parameters are not shared). The input is a 128×128 face image. The conv10 convolutional layer consists of a 1×1 convolution kernel, and the final output is a 9×9 matrix X_1. The output of another branch conv11 layer is X_2. Sum fusion method is used to fuse X_1 and X_2, as shown in formula 1.

$$X_{fusion} = \lambda X_1 + (1 - \lambda)X_2 \tag{1}$$

Among, λ represents the weight of X_1. As the first nine layers share parameters, the parameters are not shared at conv10 layer. So the X_1 and X_2 matrix data are not the same. X_1 and X_2 represent the distribution of the quality scores. Because of the structure setting of the two-stream parameter sharing network, the parameters of the previous layers are shared in the process of forward and reverse propagation. The parameters are not shared at the conv10 layer to increase diversity of the fraction distribution, but the weight distribution of X_1 and X_2 shouldn't be too different to maintain the uniformity of the data. Considering the above problems, the parameter λ is set to 0.5 to achieve the effect of balance and further improve the accuracy.

X_{fusion} is a 9×9 matrix where the values are the quality scores in each block of the map. Then, the X_{fusion} through a pooling layer. The pooling layer calculates the mean of the X_{fusion}, as shown in formula 2.

$$score = \frac{1}{81} \sum_{i=1}^{9} \sum_{j=1}^{9} X_{fusion}(i,j) \tag{2}$$

Among, $score$ is the predicted quality score. The overall framework is constrained by the objective function, as shown in formula 3.

$$W^* = argmin \frac{1}{N} \sum_{i=1}^{N} \|f(w, x_i) - y_i\| + \beta \|W\| \tag{3}$$

Among, W is the learning parameters of DFQA. N is the predicted quality score dimension, in this case, $N=1$. y represents label. β is a constant that controls the norm of parameters in DFQA.

Through minimization formula 3, DFQA model can well predict the quality score of face image and comprehensively analyze the content information of face image to get the most appropriate score value by integrating multiple factors. To train the DFQA model, we select the Caffe platform and use a batch size of 100. We adopt the step training method, and set the initial learning rate at 10^{-3}. The learning rate drops once for every 20 rounds of iteration, and drops three times in total. Moreover, the momentum is set to 0.96. The weight decay is set to 0.0005. DFQA model fully analyzes the content information of face image by considering various factors in practice and applies the characteristics of CNN independent learning, and finally predicts the quality score of face image.

We use the 3000 face annotation images mentioned in Sect. 3.1 to finetune the squeezenet model using the ImageNet dataset for pre-training. The model is then used to predict the label of the MS-Celeb-1M dataset. In this way, we get the label information of the MS-Celeb-1M dataset, and train the DFQA model with the MS-Celeb-1M dataset to get the most appropriate training parameters. At this point, DFQA model complete training, inputing face image can get the quality score.

4   Experiment

In order to verify the effectiveness of DFQA model, we design a series of experiments, including:

(1) Loss function test: Comparing the performance impact of Euclidean loss and SVRloss on DFQA model, and proves the effectiveness and necessity of selecting SVRloss.
(2) Classical method contrast test: Making comparison between resnet10 [22], squeezenet [14], NRIQA [10], RankIQA [23] and DFQA for face image quality assessment, and verifies the accuracy and efficiency of DFQA.

Table 1. Loss function results

Loss function	0.2	0.1	0.05
DFQA+Euclidean loss	1	0.9898	0.8429
DFQA+SVR loss	**1**	**0.9999**	**0.9784**

(3) Face recognition test: DFQA model is used to filter out face images with poor quality in the training process of face recognition model to improve the accuracy of face recognition.

(4) Branch selection test: Different branches were selected for quality evaluation experiment. Single branch, three branches and four branches (referred to as Model-1, Model-3 and Model-4) were compared with DFQA to verify the effectiveness and necessity of selecting the structure of double branch network.

During the training and testing phase of DFQA model, we select the MS-Celeb-1M dataset. The MS-Celeb-1M dataset consists of 2,000 person ids with a total of 165155 images. We use the pre-trained CNN model of 3,000 manually labeled face images to predict the labels of the 165155 images. These images are assigned to a quality score level with an interval of [0,1] and a scale of 0.01. We select 400 face images as the training set and 100 images as the testing set in each quality score level. In the end, the training set contains 37409 face images. The testing set contains 9100 face images.

4.1 Loss Function Test

In the loss function test, we compare Euclidean loss with SVRloss. Euclidean loss is a common objective function for regression problems. In order to verify the advantages and effectiveness of SVRloss, we replace the SVRloss of DFQA model with Euclidean loss, remaining the network structure unchanged. And MS-Celeb-1M dataset is used for training with consistent parameters. The experiment results are shown in Table 1.

In the testing stage, because the predicted quality score is a high precision value, some images with very close scores can be regarded as correct within a certain acceptable range. Three thresholds of score difference between predicted score and groundtruth are selected in the experiment, which are 0.2, 0.1 and 0.05 respectively, as shown in formula 4. The values in Table 1 represent the prediction accuracy. The predicted result should be true when the difference of predicted score and groundtruth is less than the threshold value. And the predicted result should be wrong when it is greater than the threshold value. The ratio of the final true numbers and the total number represents the prediction accuracy, as shown in formula 5.

$$|S_{pre} - S_{gnd}| < threshold \tag{4}$$

$$Acc = Num(|S_{pre} - S_{gnd}| < threshold)/N \tag{5}$$

As can be seen from Table 1, SVRloss has obvious advantages and can be used for better regression of quality scores. In the case that the threshold of score difference is very small, the results can be predicted with high accuracy.

4.2 Classical Method Contrast Test

In the classical model test, we use resnet10, NRIQA and RankIQA to predict the quality scores of face images, compared with DFQA. Since the quality assessment is a small module, the model selected in the comparison experiment should not be too large considering the size and speed of the model. Otherwise, it doesn't meet the size and speed requirements in the actual module. And the model size, speed and accuracy of DFQA have reflected high performance from Table 1. We use MS-Celeb-1M dataset to train the resnet10, NRIQA and RankIQA. The experiment results are shown in Table 2. All the speed values of experiment results were obtained on the 64-bit Windows 10 system, Intel i5 processor, and Caffe platform.

As can be seen from Table 2, DFQA has the highest accuracy under various thresholds. Although NRIQA's model is smaller, its accuracy is lower than the DFQA model. The resnet10 and RankIQA model not only has more parameters, but also performs worse in face image quality assessment. The predicted accuracy of resnet10 and RankIQA is good under the condition of loose threshold. However, with the decrease of the threshold value, the predicted precision significantly reduced. This means it is a certain gap between the predicted quality score and groundtruth. But the DFQA model still maintains a higher prediction precision under the conditions of extremely low threshold. The comparison experiment illustrates the prediction ability is strong of DFQA. The DFQA model is faster and applicable to practical applications. The two-stream parameter sharing structure can further analyze the image content information and improve the accuracy of the estimated quality score.

Table 2. Classical method contrast results

Model	0.2	0.1	0.05	Size	Speed
Resnet10 [22]	0.9920	0.8816	0.6066	21.7M	70 ms
NRIQA [14]	0.4	0.2	0.1	3M	11 ms
RankIQA [23]	0.9870	0.8284	0.5512	260M	85 ms
DFQA	1	**0.9999**	**0.9784**	5.9M	18 ms

4.3   Face Recognition Test

In face recognition test, we select DFQA model to screen out the poor quality face images in training stage. We select CASIA-WebFace [24] and VGGFace2 [25] as the training dataset and use the LFW [26] as the testing dataset.

We select 6000 person ids from CASIA-WebFace and VGGFace2. Each person id includes about 60 images. Finally, a total of 338307 face images are selected as the training set in the CASIA-WebFace dataset, and 360000 face images as the training set in the VGGFace2 dataset. For the face recognition model, we choose FaceNet [27]. During the training, we use CASIA-WebFace and VGGFace2 to train the FaceNet model, and use LFW as the test dataset to obtain baseline. Then, we use DFQA model to predict the quality scores of face images in CASIA-WebFace and VGGFace2 dataset, and filter the quality scores of face images less than 0.1 to obtain a new training set, and then retrain the FaceNet model. The experiment results are shown in Table 3.

Table 3. Face recognition results

	Testing	CASIA-WebFace	CASIA-WebFace+DFQA	VGGFace2	VGGFace2+DFQA
Acc	LFW	0.9541	**0.9632**	0.9625	**0.9735**

Table 4. Branch selection results

Model	0.2	0.1	0.05	Size	Speed
Model-1	1	0.9993	0.9473	3M	11 ms
Model-3	1	0.9999	0.9771	8.9M	29 ms
Model-4	1	0.9999	0.9792	11.8M	40 ms
DFQA	1	0.9999	0.9784	5.9M	18 ms

As can be seen from Table 3, DFQA can help face recognition to improve the recognition accuracy. There are many particularly poor quality face images in the CASIA-WebFace and VGGFace2 dataset. Some of them are vague, and some couldn't see faces in the dark. These face images with poor quality will affect the adjustment direction of training parameters in the training process. Because there are some very fuzzy and dark face images under different person ids at the same time, during the training process, it is difficult for the model to distinguish differences between face images of different characters with poor quality. In the process of training, filtering some poor quality images can enhance the robustness of the face recognition model and improve the anti-interference ability.

4.4   Branch Selection Test

In branch selection test, we select single branch, three branches and four branches (referred to as Model-1, Model-3 and Model-4) to conduct face image assessment experiment to validate necessity of selecting double branches. The experiment results are shown in Table 4.

As can be seen from Table 4, the prediction accuracy will not change much after three branches or four branches. The model size will be larger. And the speed will be slower. As can be seen from Table 2, with the decrease of threshold value, the accuracy of many models will be greatly reduced. This phenomenon shows that it is very difficult to improve the prediction accuracy when the threshold value is very low. For example, when the threshold value is 0.05, the difference between the predicted quality score and groundtruth can only be maintained at the tiny difference of 0.05. It can also be seen from Fig. 3 that in the process of labeling, 0.2 is a threshold with a relatively high degree of discrimination, while the threshold of 0.05 is already a threshold with a very low degree of discrimination in manual labeling, making it difficult to distinguish the quality score of face images. Therefore, under the strict threshold constraint of 0.05, it is extremely difficult for DFQA to improve 3 points compared with Model-1, which also indicates that DFQA model has a strong ability of prediction and characterization. Although the performance of Model-1 is also good, considering the difficulty in improving the prediction accuracy in the case of model size and speed already good, we choose DFQA model with stronger prediction ability to predict the quality score of face image.

5   Conclusion

In this paper, we propose a two-stream network structure called DFQA to predict quality score of face image. Considering a variety of practical factors, we make a comprehensive score of 3000 face images by manual annotation. The single branch of DFQA uses the lightweight model squeezenet to realize parameter sharing and co-learning in the ninth layers to further analyze the quality information of face images. SUM fusion method is used to fuse the quality information. And SVRloss is used to further constrain the overall framework. Finally, a quality assessment model with fewer parameters and high accuracy is obtained. The experiment results prove the validity and necessity of the overall architecture selection. The proposed model can help improve the accuracy of face recognition.

In our future work, we will apply this idea to more practical scenarios, such as pedestrian detection, video analysis, image search to help them more quickly and accurately remove some unnecessary interference information and improve the accuracy rate.

Acknowledgments. This work was supported by National Key Research and Development Program of China (2018YFC0808300), CAS Light of West China Program (2017), National Natural Science Foundation of China (6180021609, 6180070559, 61602433).

References

1. Kim, J., Zeng, H., Ghadiyaram, D., et al.: Deep convolutional neural models for picture-quality prediction: challenges and solutions to data-driven image quality assessment. IEEE Signal Process. Mag. **34**(6), 130–141 (2017)
2. Simone, B., Luigi, C., Paolo, N., Raimondo, S.: On the use of deep learning for blind image quality assessment. Signal Image Video Process. (3), 1–8 (2016)
3. Pittayapat, P., Oliveira, S., Thevissen, P., Michielsen, K., Bergans, N., Willems, G., et al.: Image quality assessment and medical physics evaluation of different portable dental X-ray units. Forensic Sci. Int. **201**(1–3), 112–117 (2010)
4. Tanchenko, A.: Visual-PSNR measure of image quality. J. Vis. Commun. Image Represent. **25**(5), 874–878 (2014)
5. Wang, Z., Bovik, A.C., Sheikh, H.R., Eero, P.S.: Image quality assessment: from error visibility to structural similarity. IEEE Trans. Image Process. **13**(4), 600–612 (2004)
6. Zhou, W., Hamid, R.S., Alan, C.B.: No-reference perceptual quality assessment of JPEG compressed images. In: International Conference on Image Processing (2002)
7. Erez, C., Yitzhak, Y.: No-reference assessment of blur and noise impacts on image quality. Signal Image Video Process. **4**(3), 289–302 (2010)
8. Gao, F., Wang, Y., Pan, P.L., Tan, M., Jun, Y., Yan, Z.: DeepSim: deep similarity for image quality assessment. Neurocomputing **257**, S0925231217301480 (2017)
9. Ma, K., Liu, W., Liu, T., Wang, Z., Tao, D.: dipIQ: blind image quality assessment by learning-to-rank discriminable image pairs. IEEE Trans. Image Process. **26**(8), 1–1 (2017)
10. Kang, L., Ye, P., Li, Y., et al.: Convolutional neural networks for no-reference image quality assessment. In: IEEE Conference on Computer Vision and Pattern Recognition (CVPR). IEEE Computer Society (2014)
11. Mittal, A., Moorthy, A.K., Bovik, A.C.: No-reference image quality assessment in the spatial domain. IEEE Trans. Image Process. **21**(12), 4695 (2012)
12. Kang, L., Ye, P., Li, Y., David, D.: Convolutional neural networks for no-reference image quality assessment. In: IEEE Conference on Computer Vision Pattern Recognition (2014)
13. Forrest, N.I., Song, H., Matthew, W.M., Khalid, A., William, J.D., Kurt, K.: SqueezeNet: AlexNet-level Accuracy with 50x Fewer Parameters and ¡0.5 MB Model Size (2016)
14. Guo, Y., Zhang, L., Hu, Y., He, X., Gao, J.: MS-Celeb-1M: a dataset and benchmark for large-scale face recognition. In: Leibe, B., Matas, J., Sebe, N., Welling, M. (eds.) ECCV 2016. LNCS, vol. 9907, pp. 87–102. Springer, Cham (2016). https://doi.org/10.1007/978-3-319-46487-9_6
15. Bahetiyaer, B., Li, K., Yan, B.: An accurate deep convolutional neural networks model for no-reference image quality assessment. In: IEEE International Conference on Multimedia Expo (2017)
16. Bosse, S., Maniry, D., Muller, K.R., Wiegand, T., Samek, W.: Deep neural networks for no-reference and full-reference image quality assessment. IEEE Trans. Image Process. **27**(1), 206–219 (2017)
17. Kim, J., Lee, S.: Fully deep blind image quality predictor. IEEE J. Sel. Top. Signal Process. **11**(1), 206–220 (2017)

18. Nasrollahi, K., Moeslund, T.B.: Face quality assessment system in video sequences. In: Schouten, B., Juul, N.C., Drygajlo, A., Tistarelli, M. (eds.) BioID 2008. LNCS, vol. 5372, pp. 10–18. Springer, Heidelberg (2008). https://doi.org/10.1007/978-3-540-89991-4_2

19. Truong, Q.C., Dang, T.K., Ha, T.: Face quality measure for face authentication. In: Dang, T.K., Wagner, R., Küng, J., Thoai, N., Takizawa, M., Neuhold, E. (eds.) FDSE 2016. LNCS, vol. 10018, pp. 189–198. Springer, Cham (2016). https://doi.org/10.1007/978-3-319-48057-2_13

20. Rajeev, R., Ankan, B., Xu, H.Y., Swami, S., Rama, C.: Crystal loss and quality pooling for unconstrained face verification and recognition (2018)

21. Chen, J.S., Deng, Y., Bai, G.C., Su, G.D.: Face image quality assessment based on learning to rank. IEEE Signal Process. Lett. **22**(1), 90–94 (2014)

22. Marcel, S., Erik, R., Joachim, D.: ImageNet pre-trained models with batch normalization. arXiv preprint arXiv:1612.01452 (2016)

23. Liu, X., Joost, V.D.W., Bagdanov, A.D.: RankIQA: learning from rankings for no-reference image quality assessment (2017)

24. Yi, D., Lei, Z., Liao, S.C., Stan, Z.L: Learning face representation from scratch. In: Computer Science (2014)

25. Qiong, C., Shen, L., Xie, W.D., Omkar, M.P., Andrew, Z.: VGGFace2: a dataset for recognising faces across pose and age (2017)

26. Gary, B.H., Manu, R., Tamara, B., Erik, L.M.: Labeled faces in the wild: a database for studying face recognition in unconstrained environments (2007)

27. Florian, S., Dmitry, K., James, P.: FaceNet: a unified embedding for face recognition and clustering (2015)

U-Net with Attention Mechanism for Retinal Vessel Segmentation

Ze Si, Dongmei Fu$^{(\boxtimes)}$, and Jiahao Li

School of Automation and Electrical Engineering,
University of Science and Technology Beijing, No.30 Xueyuan Road,
Haidian District, Beijing, China
fdm2003@163.com

Abstract. Retinal vessel is the only vessel which can be observed directly, retinal vessel analysis is a crucial method for the screening and diagnosis of related diseases. In this paper, we propose a retinal vessel segmentation method based on U-Net and attention mechanism. Fully convolutional network (FCN) like U-Net have excellent performance on segmentation tasks, but there are problems for it to build long-range dependencies amoung different part of images because convolution layers extract features in local area, local feature based methods can lead to mistake in some segmentation scenes. In this paper, attention mechanism is used to solve this problem, and a new attention module is proposed, with two different attention module, long-range dependencies in different part of the image can be built efficiently. The proposed method was evaluated on DRIVE dataset, experiment result demonstrate that proposed method have better performance than the state-of-art methods.

Keywords: Segmentation · Deep learning · U-Net · Retinal vessel · Attention mechanism

1 Introduction

Retinal vessels are branches of the cerebral blood vessels, main function of retinal vessels is to provide nutrition to the retina. Retinal vessels at bottom of the eye are the only non-invasive parts of the vascular system, features of retinal vessels like width, angle and branch morphology can be used as a basis for diagnosis of vascular-related diseases. Ophthalmological blindness diseases such as glaucoma and diabetic retinopathy, etc. can be directly observed from retinal vasculopathy. So, retinal vessels segmentation is indispensable in clinical diagnosis. Figure 1 shows a retinal image and retinal vessel segmented by expert. Manual segmentation of retinal vessels is time consuming, due to the growing

Supported by Beijing Engineering Research Center of Industrial Spectrum Imaging, School of Automation and Electrical Engineering, University of Science and Technology Beijing (No.BG0150).

number of patients with retinal vasculopathy and lacking of trained specialists, an effective and precise method for retinal vessel segmentation is meaningful in clinical.

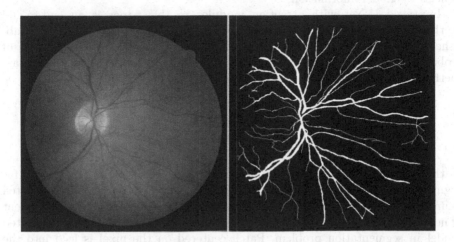

Fig. 1. Retinal images and vessel area's pixel level label in DRIVE database.

Reasearch of retinal vessel segmentation method has attract researchers in cv field. Deep learning method showed great performance in semantic segmentation task these years, some researches have tried related method on retinal vessle segmentation, for example, Hu et al. [1] proposed a method based on FCN for retinal vessel segmentation which perform state-of-the-art. Although deep learning method like FCN have great performance on related tasks, there are still some limitations for normal FCN model on retinal vessel segmentation task. Convolution operator has a local receptive field, and long-range dependencies in different regions of the image can be processed only after passing through many convolutional layers. Therefore, small scale neural network will not be able to learn and represent long-range dependencies across different image regions. Even for deep model, there's still some problems prevent the model from learning long-range dependencies. For example, optimization algorithms may have trouble discovering parameter values that carefully coordinate multiple layers to capture these dependencies, and these parameterizations may be statistically brittle and prone to failure when applied to previously unseen inputs [2].

There's less semantic information in retinal images compared with images in other complex tasks, in some cases, it is difficult to distinguish pixels belong to the vessels and some retinal tissues by local features solely. Therefore, it is necessary to make use of global information and establish long-range dependencies in different regions of the image.

U-Net is one of the most common segmentation model for medical image segmentation. U-Net is an encoder-decoder model with skip connection structure, encoder extract features, decoder maps the low-resolution features to the high-resolution space, skip connection structure fuse multi-features to enhance the details of the segmentation. Based on the improved U-Net, in this paper, attention modules are added to encoders and decoders to build long-range dependencies by global information.

Improved U-Net with attention modules in this paper is an end-to-end method. Different from previous deep learning method, proposed method established position-wise and channel-wise long-range dependencies. By the use of global information, proposed method performed better than the state-of-the-art methods.

2   Related Work

2.1   Segmentation Model

In the early years, fully connected neural networks was the first ANN used for segmentation task, features around each pixel are extracted and fully connected neural network work as a classifier to classify all the pixels. With the development of neural networks, convolutional neural network (CNN) replaced fully connected model in segmentation problem. Patch centered on the pixel is feed into the model to extract features, and a fully connected layer is trained as a classifier. Application of CNN avoids feature extraction process, but repeated storage and redundant convolution computation caused by overlapping image patches makes it time consuming and inefficiency [3]. Long et al. [4] proposed fully convolutional network (FCN), which is more precise and efficient, from then on, almost all semantic segmentation studies have adopted this basic structure. Deeplab series model [5–7] showed impressive results in the semantic segmentation tasks by the use of dilated convolution, conditional random field, ASPP and other techniques. U-net [8] is widely used in medical image segmentation, with dense encoder-decoder and skip-connection structure, it have great advantage in clinical image segmentation.

2.2   Attention Mechanism

Attention mechanism was proposed by Benigio et al. [9]. Similar to human attention, attention mechanism intended to screen the high value information that is most useful for current task in the overall information received. Vaswani et al. [10] proposed a method for establishing global dependencies of input information using self-attention mechanism and applied this in machine translation. Attention mechanism was widely used in the field of NLP in the early years. In recent years, attention mechanism has attracted researchers in CV field. Wang et al. used attention module to establish the temporal and spatial dependencies of video sequences. This method had greatly improved the video classification performance [11]. Zhang et al. introduced self-attention mechanism in GAN to generate consistent scenes using complementary features of images [2].

Retinal vessel segmentation methods based on FCN in the published works improve the segmentation performance by feature fusion, but during the feature extraction process and mapping process, global features are not used and relationship between different features is not considered. So in this paper, a retinal vessel segmentation method with attention mechanism is proposed.

3   Method

3.1   Model Structure

The basic segmentation network in this paper is an improved U-net. For an input image, the model outputs a probability map which indicate the probability of all the pixels belong to the vessel area. A module called channel attention module is proposed, and it is added after each skip-connection structure, in second basic block we introduced a position attention module based similar to the non-local model proposed by Wang et al. [11]. Figure 2 shows the structure of proposed model.

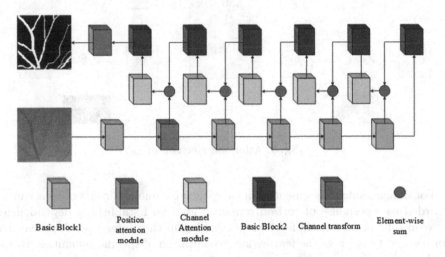

Fig. 2. Structure of proposed model.

Basic block1 in Fig. 2 consists of three residual blocks [12] and a convolutional layer with 3*3 kernel and 2 strides, basic block2 consists of three residual blocks and a deconvolutional layer. Compared with U-net in previous work, max-pooling is replaced by convolutional layer with 2 strides to reduce loss of information. Batch normalization layers [10] are used to reduce the risk of overfitting and simplify the training process. To reduce computing cost, concats in feature fusion stages are replaced by summation.There are two kinds of attention moudles in proposed model, position attention moudle and channel attention moudle, position attention moudle same as non-local moudle proposed by Wang [11] is used to build long-range dependencies of different regions of the feature map, channel attention moudle is used to build long-range dependencies of different channels of the feature map.

3.2 Channel Attention Mechanism

Figure 3 shows the basic idea of attention mechanism, each point of the feature map can be treated as a Query, points around the Query point are treated as Key, each S is calculated as the similarity of corresponding Key and Query, weights A is normalization of S weighted sum of Value is the attention value. In general, Key and Value is the same, A is Query element's encode vector, which contains Query's relationship with both local and global features. So attention module can capture both local and long-range dependencies.

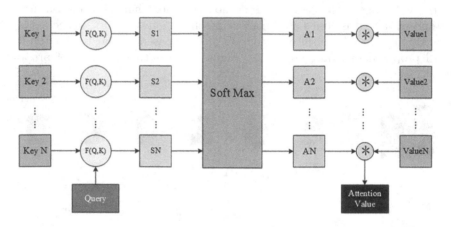

Fig. 3. Attention mechanism

For image semantic segmentation task, each channel of layer's output can be regarded as a response of certain semantic feature. Establishing dependencies between different semantic features is meaningful that interdependent features can be used to improve the feature's representation of specific semantics. Based on this motivation, channel attention mechanism is proposed in this paper.

Analogy the position attention module like non-local module, each channel of channel attention module's output is a weighted sum of all the input feature map's channels as shown in Fig. 4.

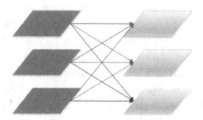

Fig. 4. Channel attention mechanism schematic diagram.

Channel attention mechanism proposed in this paper indicated as (5)

$$y_i = \frac{1}{C(x)} \sum_{\forall j} f(x_i, x_j) x_j \tag{1}$$

x_i is the ith channel of input feature map, y_i is the corresponding output channel. x_i and y_i are transformed into column vectors, $\{x_i, y_i\} \in R^N$, N is the size of each channel, f is the correlation measurement (6)

$$f(x_i, x_j) = e^{E((x_i - E(x_i))(x_j - E(x_j)))} \tag{2}$$

$E((x_i - E(x_i))(x_j - E(x_j)))$ is covariance of x_i and x_j, $E(x_i)$ is replaced by the mean value of x_i, f is expressed as (7) in this way.

$$f(x_i, x_j) = e^{\frac{(x_i - \bar{x}_i)'(x_j - \bar{x}_j)}{N}} \tag{3}$$

C is normalization coefficient like it in non-local module [11].

$$C(x) = \sum_{\forall j} f(x_i, x_j) \tag{4}$$

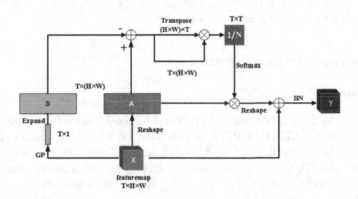

Fig. 5. Channel attention module.

The implementation process of channel attention module is shown in Fig. 5. Input feature map $X \in R^{T \times H \times W}$ is reshaped to $A \in R^{T \times N}$. The ith row of A corresponds to the vector expansion from the ith channel of original feature map. Expected value of the ith channel is approximated by the mean value of it. A global pooling layer is used to calculate the mean value of each channel of original feature map X, the output of global pooling layer is expanded to $B \in R^{T \times N}$. The result of element-wise subtraction between A and B preform matrix multiplication with the transpose of itself and then each element is multiplied by the factor $1/N$ to get the covariance matrix for all the channels of input feature map. Finally, a SoftMax layer is applied to get the channel attention map $CM \in R^{T \times T}$, each element in CM can be expressed as (9)

$$CM_{ij} = \frac{e^{\frac{\sum_{k=1}^{N}(A-B)_{ik}(A-B)'_{kj}}{N}}}{\sum_{w=1}^{T} e^{\frac{\sum_{k=1}^{N}(A-B)_{ik}(A-B)'_{kw}}{N}}} \tag{5}$$

Here CM_{ij} represents the correlation of the jth channel and the ith channel of input feature map. Result of a matrix multiplication between CM and A is reshaped and add back the input feature map to obtain Y.

3.3   Data Processing Method

During the training of deep model, a large number of training samples with labels are required. For retinal vessel segmentation task, training samples with labels is limited, data augmentation is necessary.

Medical images generally have large size, it is a common method to cut image into patches. In this way, all the patch can be treated as training samples. In this paper, attention mechanism is used to build position-wise and channel-wise long-range dependencies, we need sufficient information in a single patch, therefore, patches with 256 * 256 size are used, in this paper, all the images and labels are flip and rotated (30° each time), then sliding window with 256 * 256 size and 128 strides is used to cut the images into patches.

4   Experiments and Results

4.1   Materials

To demonstrate the performance of proposed method, we evaluated our method on public dataset DRIVE. DRIVE is consisted of 40 retinal images, in which 20 images in both training set and testing set, All the images have the same size of 565 * 584. To get more and larger patches, in the training stage, all the images are resized to 1695 * 1752, in testing stage, the segmentation result will be resized back to 565 * 584.

4.2   Result Comparison

Commonly used evaluation metrics for retinal vessel segmentation task are accuracy (ACC), sensitivity (SE), specificity (SP), and AUC. Figure 6 shows several segmentation results generated by proposed method, from which we can see proposed method have a good performance on both thick vessels and tiny vessels. To prove the validity of proposed method, comparison of proposed method with other methods in this years on DRIVE is shown in Table 1.

As shown in Table 1 proposed method performs better than other methods on most of the evaluate index. Among these evaluate metrics, Se, Sp and Acc are

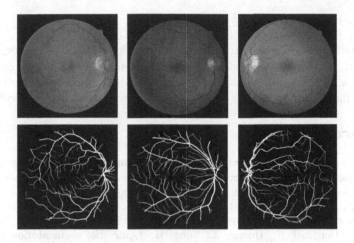

Fig. 6. Segmentation result

associated with select of threshold, Se and Sp can not measure the performance of model solely, Acc in class imbalance task is not an appropriate metric for model evaluation. Compared with other metrics, AUC not rely on the threshold, and it's a suitable metric to evaluate models for class imbalance tasks. As shown in Table 1, we got highest AUC which demonstrate the effectiveness of our proposed method.

Table 1. Performance comparision of proposed method on DRIVE

Method	Year	Se	Sp	Acc	AUC
Marin [13]	2011	0.7067	0.9801	0.9452	0.9588
Cheng [14]	2014	0.7252	0.9798	0.9474	0.9648
Roychowdhury [15]	2014	0.7250	0.9830	0.9520	0.9620
Wang [16]	2015	0.8173	0.9733	0.9533	0.9475
Azzopardi [17]	2015	0.7655	0.9704	0.9442	0.9614
Liskowski [18]	2016	0.7569	0.9816	0.9527	0.9738
Li [19]	2016	0.7569	0.9816	0.9527	0.9738
Dasgupta [20]	2017	0.7691	0.9801	0.9533	0.9744
Alom [21]	2018	0.7798	0.9813	0.9556	0.9784
Hu [1]	2018	0.7772	0.9793	0.9533	0.9759
Proposed	**2019**	**0.8156**	**0.9837**	**0.9687**	**0.9807**

5   Conclusion

In this paper, a U-Net with attention mechanism for retinal vessel segmentation is proposed. For the data imbalanced problem, a novel loss function called dice entropy loss function is used, that allowed the model to focus more on the vessel area. Comparative experiments show the efficiency of proposed method.

References

1. Kai, H., et al.: Retinal vessel segmentation of color fundus images using multi-scale convolutional neural network with an improved cross-entropy loss function. Neurocomputing **309**, 179–191 (2018)
2. Zhang, H., Goodfellow, I., Metaxas, D., Odena, A.: Self-attention generative adversarial networks. arXiv preprint. arXiv:1805.08318 2018
3. Liu, Y., Dongmei, F., Huang, Z., Tong, H.: Optic disc segmentation in fundus images using adversarial training. IET Image Process. **13**(2), 375–381 (2018)
4. Long, J., Shelhamer, E., Darrell, T.: Fully convolutional networks for semantic segmentation. In: Proceedings of the IEEE Conference on Computer Vision and Pattern Recognition, pp. 3431–3440 (2015)
5. Chen, L.C., Papandreou, G., Kokkinos, I., Murphy, K., Yuille, A.L.: Semantic image segmentation with deep convolutional nets and fully connected crfs. arXiv preprint arXiv:1412.7062 (2014)
6. Chen, L.C., Papandreou, G., Schroff, F., Adam, H.: Rethinking atrous convolution for semantic image segmentation. arXiv preprint arXiv:1706.05587 (2017)
7. Chen, L.C., Papandreou, G., Kokkinos, I., Murphy, K., Yuille, A.L.: Deeplab: semantic image segmentation with deep convolutional nets, atrous convolution, and fully connected crfs. IEEE Trans. Pattern Anal. Mach. Intell. **40**(4), 834–848 (2018)
8. Ronneberger, O., Fischer, P., Brox, T.: U-Net: convolutional networks for biomedical image segmentation. In: Navab, N., Hornegger, J., Wells, W.M., Frangi, A.F. (eds.) MICCAI 2015. LNCS, vol. 9351, pp. 234–241. Springer, Cham (2015). https://doi.org/10.1007/978-3-319-24574-4_28
9. Bahdanau, D., Cho, K., Bengio, Y.: Neural machine translation by jointly learning to align and translate. arXiv preprint arXiv:1409.0473 (2014)
10. Ioffe, S., Szegedy, C.: Batch normalization: accelerating deep network training by reducing internal covariate shift. arXiv preprint arXiv:1502.03167 (2015)
11. Wang, X., Girshick, R., Gupta, A., He, K.: Non-local neural networks. In: Proceedings of the IEEE Conference on Computer Vision and Pattern Recognition, pp. 7794–7803 (2018)
12. He, K., Zhang, X., Ren, S., Sun, J. Deep residual learning for image recognition. In: Proceedings of the IEEE Conference on Computer Vision and Pattern Recognition, pp. 770–778 (2016)
13. Marín, D., Aquino, S., Gegúndez-Arias, M.E., Bravo, J.M.: A new supervised method for blood vessel segmentation in retinal images by using gray-level and moment invariants-based features. IEEE Trans. Med. Imaging **30**(1), 146–158 (2011)
14. Cheng, E., Du, L., Wu, Y., Zhu, Y.J., Megalooikonomou, V., Ling, H.: Discriminative vessel segmentation in retinal images by fusing context-aware hybrid features. Mach. Vis. Appl. **25**(7), 1779–1792 (2014). https://doi.org/10.1007/s00138-014-0638-x

15. Roychowdhury, S., Koozekanani, D.D., Parhi, K.K.: Blood vessel segmentation of fundus images by major vessel extraction and subimage classification. IEEE J. Biomed. Health Inf. **19**(3), 1118–1128 (2014)
16. Wang, S., Yin, Y., Cao, G., Wei, B., Zheng, Y., Yang, G.: Hierarchical retinal blood vessel segmentation based on feature and ensemble learning. Neurocomputing **149**, 708–717 (2015)
17. Azzopardi, G., Strisciuglio, N., Vento, M., Petkov, N.: Trainable cosfire filters for vessel delineation with application to retinal images. Med. Image Anal. **19**(1), 46–57 (2015)
18. Liskowski, P., Krawiec, K.: Segmenting retinal blood vessels with deep neural networks. IEEE Trans. Med. Imaging **35**(11), 2369–2380 (2016)
19. Li, Q., Feng, B., Xie, L.P., Liang, P., Zhang, H., Wang, T.: A cross-modality learning approach for vessel segmentation in retinal images. IEEE Trans. Med. Imaging **35**(1), 109–118 (2016)
20. Dasgupta, A., Singh, S.: A fully convolutional neural network based structured prediction approach towards the retinal vessel segmentation. In: 2017 IEEE 14th International Symposium on Biomedical Imaging (ISBI 2017), pp. 248–251. IEEE (2017)
21. Alom, M.Z., Hasan, M., Yakopcic, C., Taha, T.M., Asari, V.K.: Recurrent residual convolutional neural network based on u-net (r2u-net) for medical image segmentation. arXiv preprint arXiv:1802.06955 (2018)

Learning to Detect License Plates Using Synthesized Data

Yanhui Pang, Wenzhong Wang, Aihua Zheng, and Jin Tang[✉]

Anhui University, Hefei, China
yanhuipang@foxmail.com, ahzheng214@foxmail.com,
{wenzhong,tj}@ahu.edu.cn

Abstract. Due to the lack of large-scale license plate dataset, existing license plate detection methods are usually conducted on small and unrepresentative datasets. Therefore, the training of these models maybe insufficient and only sub-optimal results can be achieved. In this paper, we propose a simple but effective method to handle this issue by automatically synthesizing license plate images. Specifically, we utilize Blender as a modeling and rendering engine to simulate various environmental factors and create scenes with diverse vehicle models. With these created models, we can obtain massive training data by synthesizing unique license plate. The benefits of our proposed method are: (1) we cannot only automatically provide pixel-level bounding box annotation of license plate, but also avoid errors caused by manual labeling. (2) the introduced algorithm is more efficient than manual labelling and thus we can generate a large-scale dataset in a rather short term. Based on these synthesized data, we propose a dilated convolutional attention augmentation module in conventional deep license plate detection algorithm to further boost the final detection performance. Extensive experiments on two benchmarks validate the effectiveness of our proposed algorithm.

Keywords: Data rendering · License plate detection · Attention mechanism · Dilated convolution

1 Introduction

With the development of modern traffic, license plate detection (LPD) and recognition technology have attracted more and more attention. It is commonly used in traffic monitoring, highway toll station, parking lot entrance, exit management and other actual monitoring systems. Although it has achieved great success in recent years, LPD is still a difficult task under the unconstrained scenarios, such as rotation, distortion, uneven illumination and vagueness. Most previous works [1,14,18,26] usually achieve good performance on extremely limited datasets. In some extremely complex real scenes, the performance may not satisfying due to the manual collected LP data is insufficient in both quantity and diversity. One intuitive idea is to collect and annotate a massive LP data

Y. Zhao et al. (Eds.): ICIG 2019, LNCS 11902, pp. 678–689, 2019.
https://doi.org/10.1007/978-3-030-34110-7_57

to obtain better detection results. However, this procedure is rather time and energy consuming. In addition, the human labelling may also introduce bias or errors.

Recently, some works [6, 7] have applied synthetic training dataset to the field of object detection. Inspired by the work of Peter Slosar et al. [24] which uses synthetic data for vehicle detection. In this paper, we propose a novel synthetic data generation approach for license plate detection. Specifically, we use Matlab (version R2016b) and Blender[1] (version 2.79) with bundled Python (version 3.6) scripting for the rendering. We simulate various factors affecting license plate acquisition in natural scenes, and render different types of license plate images containing different regions. We extract the depth map of each rendered image for pixel-wise segmentation of the license plate in a given view, then compute an axis-aligned 2D bounding box, and realize automatic labelling of the license plate bounding box. The image of our synthesized dataset contains the LP images with various tilt angles, light intensities, and degrees of blur, which can cover a large diversity of the vehicles in the real scene.

The current state-of-the-art detection methods can be divided into two categories: the two-stage approach [5,8,9,23] and the one-stage approach [17,21]. However, these methods are not specifically designed for license plate detection, so the accuracy and efficiency of these methods for license plate detection maybe not optimal. In recent years, some works [6,16,25] have introduced dilated convolutional operation and attention mechanism into the field of object detection. Dilated convolution can help the network to expand the receptive field of convolutional kernels and obtain higher resolution features without increasing the parameter amount. Attention mechanisms can help the network better focus on the object area. Based on these observations, we propose to jointly integrate the dilated convolutional operations and attention model into a unified model, which can help the network to detect the small object license plate and improve the final detection performance. We first propose a dilated convolutional attention enhancement block for license plate detection. It introduces dilated convolutional operation into the Faster R-CNN [23] framework to increase the receptive field of convolution kernels and obtain higher resolution feature maps. Then the attention mechanism is introduced to weight the feature maps and help the neural network to achieve better classification performance.

In summary, this paper makes the following contributions:

- We propose a method to synthesize the license plate images, which can not only generate license plates of different provinces, cities and different types, but also realize the accurate labelling of the bounding box of the license plate area.
- We propose an novel license plate detection method based on Faster R-CNN. Specifically, we introduce the dilated convolutional operation and attention mechanism into the conventional convolutional network to generate more discriminative feature representations to achieve better performance of license plate detection.

---

[1] https://www.blender.org.

- Evaluations of the proposed LPD model on generated LP dataset demonstrate the validity of the synthetic license plate method and the proposed license plate detection model.

2   Related Work

2.1   Dateset of Synthetic LP

Most license plate datasets [3] tend to collect images from traffic monitoring systems, highway toll stations or parking lots. The collected license plate images usually have some shortcomings, such as small tilt angle, small number, uneven distribution of license plate types, manual annotation and so on. Therefore, these datasets can not evaluate LP detection algorithm very well. At present, the largest public license plate dataset is CCPD [27], but the CCPD dataset comes from the same city with limited types of license plate. On this basis, we propose to use the synthetic license plate dataset to simulate the real license plate data to train the detector. Our method can not only change the angle of license plate and various environmental factors, but also generate various license plate data from different provinces and cities with annotation.

2.2   LP Detection Algorithms

With the rapid development of region-based convolutional neural network [8], the currently popular object detection models have been widely applied in LP detection [10,14,15]. Faster R-CNN [23] utilizes a region proposal network which can generate high-quality region proposals for detection, so as to detect objects more accurately and quickly. YOLO [21] and YOLO9000 [22] frame object detection as a regression problem to spatially separated bounding boxes and associated class probabilities. SSD [17] combines the regression idea in YOLO and Anchor mechanism in Faster R-CNN, completely eliminate proposal generation and subsequent pixel or feature resampling stage, and encapsulate all calculations in a network.

2.3   Attention Mechanism

Attention mechanism in deep learning is essentially similar to human selective visual attention mechanism, whose goal is to select more critical information from a large number of information for the current task. At present, attention model has been widely used in various types of deep learning tasks, such as image recognition [6], speech recognition [2] and sequence learning [19], location and understanding of images [4,13]. Recently, the representative Squeeze-and-Excitation [11] reweights feature channels using signals aggregated from entire feature maps, while BAM [20] and CBAM [25] refine convolutional features independently in the channel and spatial dimensions.

Algorithm 1. License plate synthesizing algorithm

Input: M(total,savedir,camx,camy,sunx,suny,suni,brightness,contrast,licenseplate
map,backgroundmap)
Output: License plate image(Image) and bounding box coordinates(label)
1: **function** RENDER(M)
2:    **while** $i < total$ **do**
3:       **if** M *is* True **then**
4:          **camera**$_{horizontal}$ = **random**($camx$)
5:          **camera**$_{vertical}$ = **random**($camy$)
6:          **sun**$_{azimuth}$ = **random**($sunx$)
7:          **sun**$_{height}$ = **random**($suny$)
8:          **sun**$_{intensity}$ = **random**($suni$)
9:          **brightness** = **random**($brightness$)
10:          **contrast** = **random**($contrast$)
11:          **licenseplatemap** = **random**($licenseplatemap$)
12:          **backgroundmap** = **random**($backgroundmap$)
13:       **end if**
14:       [**Image**^{i}, **label**^{i}] = **render**(M)
15:    **end while**
16: **end function**

3 Overview of the Synthetic Dataset

3.1 LP Rendering Methodology

The main idea of our license plate rendering system is illustrated in Fig. 1.
First, we generate different types of license plate maps (Fig. 1(a)) of different
provinces, and load these license plate maps into the defined vehicle object model
(Fig. 1(b)). The object is instantiated with a given set of parameters of material properties (vehicle color, windows material properties, etc.). For this image,
depth map of LP is also rendered (Fig. 1(d)) which is used to determine the
bounding box of the license plate in the image. Algorithm 1 summarizes the
license plate synthesizing algorithm.

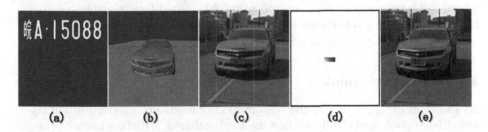

(a)   (b)   (c)   (d)   (e)

Fig. 1. The procedure of our license plate rendering framework. First we use MATLAB
to generate a license plate map (a) and load it into a defined set of vehicles (b). Then
we create a synthetic image of the vehicle and license plate from the defined collection
(c) and render a depth map of the license plate (d). The depth map is used to obtain
the precise segmentation of pixels in the license plate bounding box (e).

3.2   Viewpoint and Sunlight of LP

In order to obtain realistic and useful dataset, it is very important to control the camera angle and the illumination. As shown in Algorithm 1, we simulate the camera angle, solar direction and illumination intensity in natural scenes by specifying function parameters. We use variables **cmax** and **cmay** to control the horizontal and vertical view of the camera, **sunx** and **suny** to control the azimuth and height of the sun, **suni** to control the intensity of the sun. At the same time, we use **brightness** and **contrast** variables to adjust the brightness and contrast of the image.

4   Detection Approach

4.1   Model

The network architecture is shown in Fig. 2. We employ the Faster R-CNN [23] as the base network.

We propose a dilated convolutional attention block based on RFNet [16] and the attention model proposed by Woo *et al.* [25] called DCA Block. The feature map **FM** of the base network is fed into the dilated convolution layer and the attention module respectively. Then the merged feature map is used as the input feature map of the RPN network and the detection network. Compared with the whole image, the license plate is small. Therefore features from the convolution layer of the original model can not accurately describe the license plate, so the dilated convolution layer is added to obtain higher resolution features. Additionally, we apply channel attention and spatial attention to the feature map to enhance the features of the object area. The whole process is summarized as follows:

$$
\begin{aligned}
FM^{'} &= M_{dc}(FM) \\
FM^{''} &= [M_{sp}(M_{ch}(FM) \otimes FM)] \otimes [M_{ch}(FM) \otimes FM] \\
FM^{'''} &= FM^{'} + FM^{''}
\end{aligned}
\tag{1}
$$

where $\otimes$ denotes element-wise multiplication. $\mathbf{M_{dc}}$ is a dilated convolution attention map, $\mathbf{M_{ch}}$ is a one-dimensional channel attention map and $\mathbf{M_{sp}}$ is a two-dimensional spatial attention map. $\mathbf{FM^{'''}}$ is the final refined output.

4.2   Dilated Convolution

As shown in Fig. 2, we utilize the combination of multi-branch convolution layer and dilated pool. Specifically, we first use the bottleneck structure in each branch, consisting of a 1×1 convolution layer plus an n × n convolution layer, followed by a pooling or convolution layer with a corresponding dilation. The detailed process is as follows:

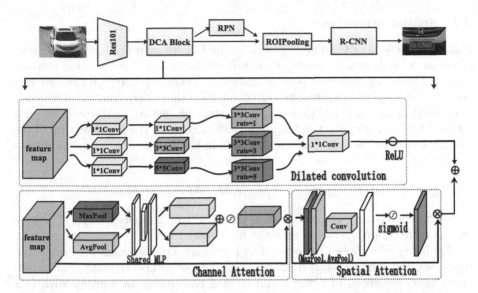

Fig. 2. The overall structure of our network. In the Faster R-CNN base network output feature map, we introduce the dilated convolution layer to obtain higher resolution features while maintaining the parameters and the same receptive field. In addition, we use the feature map channel and spatial attention to enhance the object features. Finally, we fuse the two output results and feed them to RPN and subsequent detection network.

$$
\begin{aligned}
M_{dc}(FM) =& \varphi[f^{1\times1}(concat(f^{3\times3}_{r=1}(f^{1\times1}(f^{1\times1}(FM))), \\
& f^{3\times3}_{r=3}(f^{3\times3}(f^{1\times1}(FM))), f^{3\times3}_{r=5}(f^{5\times5}(f^{1\times1}(FM)))))] \quad (2) \\
=& \varphi[f^{1\times1}(concat(FM_{r=1}, FM_{r=3}, FM_{r=5}))]
\end{aligned}
$$

where φ denotes the Relu activation function and $f^{n\times n}$ represents a convolution operation with the filter size of n × n, $f^{3\times3}_r$ denotes an dilated convolution operation with a convolution kernel of size 3 and an dilation rate of r.

4.3 Channel Attention

As in Fig. 2, we utilize average pooling and maximum pooling operations to aggregate the spatial information of the feature map, and generate two different spatial average pool features and maximum pool features. Then both are fed to the shared network to generate our channel attention map. The shared network consists of a multilayer perceptron (MLP) and a hidden layer. After sharing the network layer, we use element summation to merge the output eigenvectors.

$$
M_{ch}(FM) = \sigma(MLP(AvgPool(FM)) + MLP(MaxPool(FM))) \quad (3)
$$

4.4 Spatial Attention

Following the idea of CBAM [25] module, the feature map produced by channel attention module is used as the input feature map of spatial attention module. First, we make a global max pooling and global average pooling on channel, and then concatenate the two results. After a convolution operation, the dimension is reduced to one channel, then a spatial attention feature can be acquired via sigmoid function. Finally, the feature is multiplied with the input feature of the module to obtain the final feature, as shown in Fig. 2. The specific calculation is as follows:

$$M_{sp}(FM) = \sigma(f^{7\times7}([AvgPool(M_{ch}(FM)), MaxPool(M_{ch}(FM))])) \qquad (4)$$

where σ denotes the sigmoid function, the MLP weight shared and $f^{7\times7}$ represents a convolution operation with the filter size of 7×7.

Training. We choose Resnet-101 as backbone. Our model is pre-trained on ImageNet and then fine-tuned on synthetic dataset of license plate. The experiment is implemented in pytorch and trained end-to-end on a group with four Tesla P100 GPUs, with Stochastic Gradient Descent (SGD) and a weight decay of 0.0001 and momentum of 0.9. At the beginning of the training process, the learning rate is set to 0.001. After 20 epochs, the learning rate decreases by 0.1 times for every 5 epochs.

5 Experiments

In this section, we give a detailed description of our synthetic dataset, further more, we evaluate the the performance of different detectors on our synthetic dataset and CCPD dataset. We show that the detectors trained with the synthetic dataset are comparable with those trained with the real license plate dataset. Finally, we synthesize a dataset of 20,000 yellow, blue and new energy license plates, and compare the performance of the prevalent detection algorithm with our algorithm. We show that the proposed method improves the accuracy of license plate detection compared with the original method.

5.1 Data Preparation

As aforementioned in Sect. 3, we render and synthesize a large license plate dataset (SLPD100) containing only **blue plates**, which contains about 100 K images with resolution of 800 (Width) × 1160 (Height) × 3 (Channels). For each image, the bounding box label contains (x, y) coordinates of the top left and bottom right corner of the bounding box are used to locate the minimum bounding rectangle of LP. The CCPD dataset is the largest license plate dataset in public, which contains about 250 k images. We divide CCPD into two parts, the default training set containing about 100 k images, and the default evaluation set containing about 20,000 images. The training set and test set of our experiment are shown in Table 1.

Table 1. The division of training set and test set and the numbers in brackets represent the size of dataset.

Training set	Test set	License plate type
SLPD100 (100 k)	CCPD [27] (20 k)	Blue license plate
CCPD [27] (100 k)	CCPD [27] (20 k)	Blue license plate
SLPD20 (20 k)	LPD3000 (3 k)	Blue, yellow and new energy license plate

In order to verify the validity of our proposed license plate detection method, we also synthesize another dataset of about 20 k (SLPD20), including **yellow license plate, blue license plate and new energy license plate**. Our test dataset for evaluating detector performance is about 3,000 license plate images (LPD3000) taken by surveillance cameras and hand-held cameras.

5.2 Experiment Analysis

Evaluation Criterion. We follow the standard protocol (Intersection-over-Union (IoU)) [12] of object detection. The bounding box is considered to be correct if and only if its IoU with the ground-truth bounding box is more than 70% (IoU > 0.7).

Experimental Results on Different Datasets. We synthesize a dataset similar to the CCPD dataset and conduct experiments by the current prevalent YOLO9000, SSD, Faster R-CNN detection algorithm. Table 2 shows the experimental results. In the experiment, we set the same parameters for the same dataset. As shown in Table 2, we use the synthetic license plate datasets (SLPD100) and CCPD datasets to train SSD, Faster R-CNN and YOLO9000 detectors and use CCPD (20k) as the test set. The test accuracy on SSD and Faster R-CNN are about 2% to 3% lower than the real dataset CCPD, and the performance on YOLO9000 is only 0.2% higher. The main reason may be that the data distribution of the synthetic datasets is not comprehensive enough. Because we do not consider these factors such as license plate occlusion, rain, snow and fog, which may be a gap between our synthetic datasets and the license plate image collected by the natural scene. In future work, we will consider further increasing the data diversity in the synthetic datasets. Generally speaking, the detector trained with the synthetic license plate dataset is comparable to the detector trained with the real license plate dataset, which shows the effectiveness the synthetic license plate datasets.

Experimental Results on Different Detectors. We evaluate different detectors on the synthetic dataset. The experimental results are shown in Table 3. We evaluate the current prevalent detectors, SSD [17], YOLO9000 [22], R-FCN [5] and Faster R-CNN [23]. The results show that the performance of our detector based on Faster R-CNN improves about 2.2% compared with other detectors. In Sect. 5.3, we will analyse the effectiveness of our proposed method in detail.

Table 2. Comparison of license plate testing accuracy between different datasets of the same detector.

Dataset	Model	blue_licenceplate(%)
CCPD [27] (100 k)	SSD300+VGG16	99.1
	YOLO9000+Darknet19	98.8
	Faster R-CNN+Resnet-101	98.1
OurDataset (100 k)	SSD300+VGG16	**97.4**
	YOLO9000+Darknet19	**99.0**
	Faster R-CNN+Resnet-101	**96.2**

Table 3. Test accuracy of different detectors.

NAME	mAP(%)	yellowlp(%)	bluelp(%)	nelp(%)
R-FCN [5]	87.9	86.1	89.3	88.4
SSD300 [17]	86.0	86.5	88.1	83.4
YOLO9000 [22]	84.3	83.4	89.0	80.6
Faster R-CNN [23](**baseline**)	88.9	87.9	88.8	90.1
Faster R-CNN+Channel Attention	89.5	89.3	89.3	89.8
Faster R-CNN+Dual Attention	90.0	90.4	89.5	90.3
Faster R-CNN+Dilated convolution	89.8	90.0	89.3	90.2
Faster R-CNN+DCABlock(our)	**91.1**	**90.9**	**91.3**	**91.2**

5.3   Ablation Studies

For ablation study, we use the SLPD20 and LPD3000 as training and test dataset. In the experiment, we progressively introduce the channel attention on Faster R-CNN, the spatial attention, and then the dilation convolution module, and report the results on Table 3.

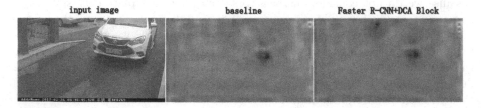

Fig. 3. Feature visualization. We compare the visualization results of our method (Faster R-CNN + DCA Block) with baseline (Faster R-CNN).

Dilated Convolution. As shown in Table 3, after the introducing the dilated convolution module, the detection accuracy on the test set increases by 0.9% (from 88.9% to 89.8%) compared to the baseline.

Channel Attention. We choose Faster R-CNN as our baseline, and we introduce the channel attention module between the base network Resnet-101 and the RPN network. As shown in Table 3, introducing channel attention, the mAP increases after by about 0.6% (from 88.9% to 89.5%), which demonstrates the effectiveness of the channel attention model.

Dual Attention. As shown in the experiment in Table 3, the introduction of the channel and spatial dual attention model improves the license plate detection accuracy by 1.1% (from 88.9% to 90.0%), which demonstrates the effectiveness of the dual attention model.

DCA Block. Based on the above analysis, we consider combining the dilated convolution and the dual attention module. The feature maps generated by the dilated convolution module and the dual attention module are fused. The experimental results show that the accuracy of our method is about 2.2% (from 88.9% to 91.1%) higher. For qualitative analysis, we compare the visualization results of our method (Faster R-CNN + DCA Block) with baseline (Faster R-CNN) in Fig. 3. We can see that our method pays more attention to the object area than baseline. Meanwhile, as in Fig. 4, our method can detect almost all the objects in the image. The result shows the effectiveness of the method.

Fig. 4. Comparison of results. The first line is the baseline method test result picture, in which the blue rectangle represents the undetected object, the second line is our method test result picture.

6   Conclusions

In this paper, we present a method to synthesize license plate datasets and a dilated convolutional attention augmentation module in conventional deep license plate detection. The proposed license plate synthesis method can not only simulate the real scene by controlling the illumination intensity and other environmental factors of the synthetic images, but also can automatically label the license plate area as ground truth. It is very useful to solve the problems of limited license plates in training dataset and high cost manual labeling under some specific conditions. The proposed dilated convolutional attention augmentation module uses the dilated convolutional operation with different dilation rates to increase the receptive field of convolution kernels and obtain the higher resolution feature maps. In addition, the attention mechanism is added to learn the weight map for better classification. Extensive evaluations on two benchmarks demonstrate that our method improves the performance of license plate detection over the baseline methods.

Acknowledgements. This work is supported by the National Natural Science Foundation of China (No. 61472002) and the Open Project Program of the National Laboratory of Pattern Recognition (NLPR)(No. 201900046).

References

1. Al-Shemarry, M.S., Li, Y., Abdulla, S.: Ensemble of adaboost cascades of 3l-lbps classifiers for license plates detection with low quality images. Exp. Syst. Appl. **92**, 216–235 (2018)
2. Bluche, T.: Joint line segmentation and transcription for end-to-end handwritten paragraph recognition. In: Advances in Neural Information Processing Systems (2016)
3. Caltech: Caltech licese plate dataset. http://www.vision.caltech.edu/html-files/archive.html
4. Cao, C., et al.: Look and think twice: capturing top-down visual attention with feedback convolutional neural networks. In: Proceedings of the IEEE International Conference on Computer Vision (2015)
5. Dai, J., Li, Y., He, K., Sun, J.: R-fcn: Object detection via region-based fully convolutional networks. In: Advances in Neural Information Processing Systems (2016)
6. Duan, S., Hu, W., Li, R., Li, W., Sun, S.: Attention enhanced convnet-RNN for Chinese vehicle license plate recognition. In: Lai, J.H., et al. (eds.) PRCV 2018. LNCS, vol. 11257, pp. 417–428. Springer, Cham (2018). https://doi.org/10.1007/978-3-030-03335-4_36
7. Georgakis, G., Mousavian, A., Berg, A.C., Kosecka, J.: Synthesizing training data for object detection in indoor scenes (2017)
8. Girshick, R.: Fast R-CNN. In: The IEEE International Conference on Computer Vision (ICCV) (2015)
9. Girshick, R., Donahue, J., Darrell, T., Malik, J.: Rich feature hierarchies for accurate object detection and semantic segmentation. In: Proceedings of the IEEE Conference on Computer Vision and Pattern Recognition (2014)

10. Hsu, G.S., Ambikapathi, A., Chung, S.L., Su, C.P.: Robust license plate detection in the wild. In: 2017 14th IEEE International Conference on Advanced Video and Signal Based Surveillance (AVSS) (2017)

11. Hu, J., Shen, L., Sun, G.: Squeeze-and-excitation networks. In: Proceedings of the IEEE Conference on Computer Vision and Pattern Recognition (2018)

12. Hui, L., Peng, W., Shen, C., Hui, L., Peng, W., Shen, C.: Towards end-to-end car license plates detection and recognition with deep neural networks. IEEE Trans. Intell. Transp. Syst. (2017)

13. Jaderberg, M., Simonyan, K., Zisserman, A., et al.: Spatial transformer networks. In: Advances in Neural Information Processing Systems (2015)

14. Laroca, R., et al.: A robust real-time automatic license plate recognition based on the yolo detector. In: 2018 International Joint Conference on Neural Networks (IJCNN) (2018)

15. Li, H., Wang, P., Shen, C.: Towards end-to-end car license plates detection and recognition with deep neural networks. corr abs/1709.08828 (2017)

16. Liu, S., Huang, D., et al.: Receptive field block net for accurate and fast object detection. In: Proceedings of the European Conference on Computer Vision (ECCV) (2018)

17. Liu, W., et al.: SSD: single shot multibox detector. In: Leibe, B., Matas, J., Sebe, N., Welling, M. (eds.) ECCV 2016. LNCS, vol. 9905, pp. 21–37. Springer, Cham (2016). https://doi.org/10.1007/978-3-319-46448-0_2

18. Masood, S.Z., Shu, G., Dehghan, A., Ortiz, E.G.: License plate detection and recognition using deeply learned convolutional neural networks (2017)

19. Miech, A., Laptev, I., Sivic, J.: Learnable pooling with context gating for video classification. arXiv preprint arXiv:1706.06905 (2017)

20. Park, J., Woo, S., Lee, J.Y., Kweon, I.S.: Bam: bottleneck attention module (2018)

21. Redmon, J., Divvala, S., Girshick, R., Farhadi, A.: You only look once: unified, real-time object detection. In: Proceedings of the IEEE conference on computer vision and pattern recognition (2016)

22. Redmon, J., Farhadi, A.: Yolo9000: better, faster, stronger. In: Proceedings of the IEEE Conference on Computer Vision and Pattern Recognition (2017)

23. Ren, S., He, K., Girshick, R., Sun, J.: Faster R-CNN: towards real-time object detection with region proposal networks. In: Advances in Neural Information Processing Systems (2015)

24. Šlosár, P., Juránek, R., Herout, A.: Cheap rendering vs. costly annotation: rendered omnidirectional dataset of vehicles. In: Proceedings of the 30th Spring Conference on Computer Graphics. ACM (2014)

25. Woo, S., Park, J., Lee, J.Y., So Kweon, I.: Cbam: convolutional block attention module. In: Proceedings of the European Conference on Computer Vision (ECCV) (2018)

26. Xie, L., Ahmad, T., Jin, L., Liu, Y., Sheng, Z.: A new CNN-based method for multi-directional car license plate detection. IEEE Trans. Intell. Transp. Syst. **19**, 507–517 (2018)

27. Xu, Z., et al.: Towards end-to-end license plate detection and recognition: a large dataset and baseline. In: Proceedings of the European Conference on Computer Vision (ECCV) (2018)

Large-Scale Street Space Quality Evaluation Based on Deep Learning Over Street View Image

Mei Liu[1], Longmei Han[2], Shanshan Xiong[1], Linbo Qing[1,3(✉)], Haohao Ji[1], and Yonghong Peng[4]

[1] College of Electronics and Information Engineering,
Sichuan University, Chengdu 610065, China
qing_lb@scu.edu.cn
[2] Chengdu Institute of Urban Planning and Design,
No. 399 Fucheng Avenue, Chengdu 610065, China
[3] Key Laboratory of Wireless Power Transmission of Ministry of Education,
Chengdu 610065, China
[4] Faculty of Computer Science, University of Sunderland,
St. Peters Campus, Sunderland SR6 0DD, UK

Abstract. In the quantitative study of cities, the extraction and appropriate evaluation of the space quality information of urban streets can provide great insight and guidance to urban planners to build more livable urban public space, which is also of great significance for urban management. However, the traditional methods, which mostly use the manual statistical investigation to carry on, are difficult to carry out large-scale objective quantification. To tackle this challenge, this paper presents a complete quantitative analysis method for street space quality score based on street view image analysis. Three quantitative indices (i.e. cleanliness, comfort and traffic) for the evaluation of street space qualities are employed in this study as suggested in literature on urban planning. A new deep learning approach, named as Cross-connected CNN + SVR, is proposed to estimate the street space quality score. A new dataset is constructed based on Baidu Street View image for the training and validation of the proposed framework. Experimental results suggested that the three indices used in this paper is able to reflect the street's objective visual attributes effectively and the proposed CNN + SVR approach has produced insightful results. The proposed approach has been applied to evaluate the street space quality score of the 2nd ring road district of Chengdu, to demonstrate the value and effectiveness of the proposed work for providing data support and analytics support to urban planners.

Keywords: Space quality · Computer vision · Street view image · Quantitative evaluation · Urban planning

1 Introduction

The 2015 Central Urbanization Work Conference emphasized the importance to "implement innovation, coordination, green, open, and shared development concepts", urban

© Springer Nature Switzerland AG 2019
Y. Zhao et al. (Eds.): ICIG 2019, LNCS 11902, pp. 690–701, 2019.
https://doi.org/10.1007/978-3-030-34110-7_58

design and the improvement of urban public space quality have become an important factor for the improvement of living environment. As a microscopic component of living environment, the street's traffic value, communication value and aesthetic value contribute a lot to livability, good street space can form a friendly neighborhood and a vibrant public life, promote social integration. Besides, a comfortable street environment can enhance the frequency of walking and improve the health of individuals.

Different schools have formed diverse theories and methods on the basis of urban landscape research, including visual impact evaluation method, landscape quality evaluation model, landscape comparative evaluation method and environmental evaluation model [24, 25]. However, until now, research on road landscape and aesthetics are still subject to technical deficiencies and shortages of data sources, which make it difficult to obtain complex information and assess space quality.

Computer vision techniques on the other hand, has been developed fast in the last decade, which has been boosted by deep learning. In most cases, computer vision involves image processing techniques. With the rapid development of image processing, it also brings many new opportunities in the field of urban planning. Based on remote sensing image processing, Zhang [1] studied urban green space to provide more reliable data resources for urban detection and construction. Gu [2] used the change detection technology in remote sensing image processing to detect the change of two remote sensing images in the same area at different times, which can timely monitor the change and development of the city. Xing [3] analyzed the lawn scene image based on the image processing technology to improve the working ability of the intelligent lawn mowing robot. Emerging street view images can effectively depict urban public space scenes and make up for the deficiency of non-visual data, which have indispensable advantages in urban street spatial attribute extracting [21]. Using computer vision technology to analyze street view images can enrich the number and the coverage of research samples and provide data support for urban planners.

Our goal in this paper is to establish a complete quantitative analysis method to assess the space quality of streets based on street view images. We choose three physical qualities to quantify space quality, which are cleanliness, comfort and traffic. A Cross-connected CNN + SVR scheme is proposed to predict scores of street space quality, the numerical results indicate that the computer vision model we have proposed can reach a mean squared error (MSE) of 0.0306 in the regression classification task.

The remaining structure of the paper is arranged as follows: Sect. 2 reviews existing relevant researches on street space environment evaluation; Sect. 3 illustrates the definitions and impacts of the three indices we use to evaluate space quality; The street space quality dataset and methodology are given in Sect. 4; Sect. 5 presents the numerical evaluation results of the proposed work and a case study is also given for demonstrating the application value of the proposed work; Sect. 6 concludes the paper and makes extended discussion for limitations and future work.

2 Related Works

2.1 Subjective and Objective Evaluation Towards Urban Environment

Evaluation of urban environment has an important impact on promoting urban development and improving the quality of public life. At present, there are many indicators used in urban environmental evaluation, including green view rate, street enclosure and street accessibility et al. Generally speaking, there are two methods for the evaluation of urban environment: subjective and objective.

The research method of urban environment based on subjective feelings is mainly image evaluation method. This method of artificial evaluation is limited by the number and scale of survey objects, and cannot objectively and comprehensively reflect the comprehensive spatial feelings of people in real scenes. Shao et al. [11] conducted a questionnaire survey to evaluate the spatial quality of the square in the main city of Harbin. Ewing et al. [10] constructed the urban design quality evaluation system, and carried on the comprehensive evaluation analysis to the urban street.

There are also many objective studies on the physical space of the street. Tang et al. [13] applied street view picture data to measure the openness, enclosure and motorization of Beijing and Shanghai streets by combining the pedestrian subjective evaluation method [10] with the street element objective composition analysis method. Wang et al. [12] used semantic differential method to conduct a research towards 8 streets in Shanghai, specifically analyzing the correlation between street space characteristics and objective indices.

2.2 Applying Machine Learning Algorithms to Street View Images

With the unceasingly mature of artificial intelligence, big data and visual analysis technologies, new opportunities are provided for the space quality evaluation of urban public space. Computer vision techniques have been successfully applied for urban environments evaluation by researchers.

Hazelhoff et al. [4] used the method of combining direction gradient histogram (HOG) and scale invariant feature transformation (SIFT) to extract the feature set of traffic signs in street view images, and then used SVM for classification to realize large-scale detection of traffic signs in street image. Abhimanyu et al. [5] utilized street view images to understand the city, and used machine learning method to understand the relationship between the urban appearance and the social economy by quantifying the six indexes of the city: safety, vitality, boredom, wealth, depression and beauty. Nikhil et al. [6] used Place Pulse 1.0 data to calculate streetscape safety indices using regression models based on two image local features (GIST and texture map). Porzi et al. [7] proved that the Convolutional Neural Network (CNN) feature is superior to the traditional description feature (such as SIFT, HOG, and LBP) in predicting human perception. Liu et al. [8] combined machine-learning with street view images to evaluate the urban environment in terms of the quality level of the building facade and the continuity of the walls. Ye et al. [9] used machine learning algorithms to extract street space elements based on street view image data, and then used neural network algorithms to train evaluation models to build large-scale and high-quality street place quality measures.

3 Three Quantitative Indices Selected for This Research

The Street View image is a more realistic representation of the urban public space scene with rich realism and strong information. It is convenient and free from weather, time and place. Besides, it has been proved to be an effective means of quantitative research on the street [14]. In this work, we select cleanliness, comfort and traffic for the research. We are not saying that these three chosen quantitative indices are the most appropriate or most important for this study. They are just as the beginning of this series of studies.

Cleanliness refers to the cleanliness level of public streets. If there no rubbish on the streets, the vehicles are neatly arranged, and there is no obviously dilapidated building,then the streets are considered to be well-kept. The comfort characterizes street's human scale and the rationality of the design structure. If the street have beautifully designed structures and humanized infrastructure, such street can bring people great comfort. Traffic emphasizes the traffic function of the street, if the street has convenient transportation and the lanes are clearly divided. It is easy to generate a higher street vitality index.

4 Data and Methodology

In this work, we try to apply machine learning to evaluate the street space quality. The work flow of the proposed work is shown in Fig. 1. Firstly, we used Baidu dynamic web pages to crawl street view images as the dataset,among all the images captured by Baidu street view, some images are not facing the street but the buildings on both sides of the street. Such images cannot be used for the evaluation of street space quality, so they need to be removed. To tackle this issue, a computer vision algorithm named Inception_v3 [17] was applied. Then, based on existing literature and experts' opinions, the scoring criteria was established, we recruited volunteers to manually score the dataset as the label of the dataset according to the scoring criteria. After that, a Cross-connected CNN + SVR scheme was used to train the model. In the end, 2nd ring road district of Chengdu was chosen as the case study area, we applied the proposed method to evaluate the street space quality score of the case study area and obtained map of space quality in 2nd ring road district of Chengdu.

Fig. 1. Working flow

4.1 Dataset and Data Augment

Our dataset is used to train the CNN + SVR model, which is composed of a small number of public data sets Cityscapes [22] and BDD [23] as well as street view images crawled in China using Baidu dynamic web pages.

For the pictures crawled by Baidu dynamic web pages using keyword "street", the space environment is mostly at the medium level, and the streets with good environment and bad environment only account for a small part, so the data distribution obtained by crawling is not balanced, which is go against training our machine learning model. To solve this problem, we process the data set as follows:

Firstly, In order to crawl pictures with high spatial environment, use keywords like "beautiful street" and "scenic street". For streets with poor spatial environment, keywords such as "ruined street" is used for crawling. Then, expand the category images with insufficient samples by mirroring, rotating or adding noise. At last, we got 4307 street view images as the street spatial quality dataset.

4.2 Dataset Scoring

In order to label the dataset, we need to firstly design the criteria of each aspect according to existing literature and experts' opinions. We selected 10 volunteers [8] (including 5 males and 5 females) with relevant majors to rate the dataset. In order to ensure the objectivity of the manual grading scoring, we took the following measures. Firstly, we held a seminar for the volunteers to understand the scoring rules (Tables 1, 2 and 3, Fig. 2) of street space quality.

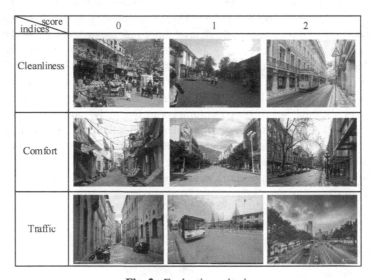

Fig. 2. Evaluation criteria

Then, we randomly selected 50 images and asked all the volunteers to score them until their scores were consistent in most cases.

$$s = s_1 + s_2 + s_3 \tag{1}$$

$$s \xrightarrow{\text{Normalized}} s^* \tag{2}$$

Table 1. Scoring standard for the cleanliness

Scorings	Scoring standard
2	The street is clean and tidy, without messy vehicles, there are no stains or messy attachments on both sides of the street, such as rusty iron railings, hanging or loose wires, etc.
1	There is a little rubbish in the street or a little messy vehicle, or may have a little dirt and stains on the sides of the street, etc.
0	The street is littered with garbage or parked cars, people are not willing to stay or be active here

Table 2. Scoring standard for the comfort

Scorings	Scoring standard
2	Attractive street design, exquisite materials, beautiful environment, greening, building without damage and aging, no walls or fences that obstruct the sight, reasonable street openness, etc.
1	The street design has a certain attraction, the environment is acceptable, the greening is insufficient, the building is a little damaged and aging, and further improvement is needed
0	The street design is unattractive, built with low-quality materials, poor environment, no greening, building with damage and aging, unreasonable street opening, etc.

Table 3. Scoring standard for the traffic

Scorings	Scoring standard
2	Reasonable road design (e.g. sidewalk, bicycle lane division), convenient transportation, good accessibility, unified road indication system, etc.
1	Convenient transportation, moderate accessibility, unified road indication system, but no obvious road division, etc.
0	Inconvenient transportation, poor accessibility, no unified road indication system, etc.

Where s is the total score of space quality, s_1, s_2, s_3 denote score of cleanliness, comfort and traffic respectively.

4.3 Score Estimation Based Deep Learning

On the basis of manual scoring, we try to apply deep learning to evaluate space quality of streets. Since SVR is skilled in solving complex nonlinear problems with small and medium-sized datasets, this paper selects SVR to predict space quality. In the traditional SVM model, local features such as SIFT, HOG and LBP are mainly used, but these features cannot describe the subtle differences of images in the same scene. Deep convolutional neural networks have the characteristics of flexible structure and the extracted feature is abundant. Drawing on the idea of DeepID [15] network, we modified the AlexNet [16] network structure and proposed a Cross-connected CNN + SVR (Support Vector Regression) network model (Fig. 3).

The advantage of applying Cross-connected convolutional neural network to feature extraction is that, integrating high-level features with low-level features, it is possible to obtain more abundant features than traditional convolutional neural network. Given input feature vector x and their corresponding label y, we can understand the principle of SVR as find a function $f(x)$ that approximates y. $f(x)$ can be expressed as

$$f(x) = (w \cdot x) + b, \qquad w, x \in R^N, b \in R \tag{3}$$

SVR problems can be formalized as

$$\min_{w,b} \frac{1}{2}\|w\|^2 + C \sum_{i=1}^{m} l_e(f(x_i) - y_i) \tag{4}$$

Where C is the regularization constant, l_e is the e-insensitive loss. By introducing slack variables ξ_i and $\hat{\xi}$, Eq. (4) can be rewritten as

$$\min_{w,b,\xi_i,\hat{\xi}_i} \frac{1}{2}\|w\|^2 + C \sum_{i=1}^{m} \left(\xi_i + \hat{\xi}_i\right) \tag{5}$$

Subject to

$$f(x_i) - y_i \le \varepsilon + \xi_i \tag{6}$$

$$y_i - f(x_i) \le \varepsilon + \hat{\xi}_i$$

$$\xi_i \ge 0, \ \hat{\xi}_i \ge 0, \ i = 1, 2, \ldots, m.$$

We used the output of FC8 layer to train a SVR classifier. Here, the feature vector where FC8 outputs is equal to x, and the score that model estimates can be thought as $f(x)$. What we try to do is make $f(x)$ approximates y. Since the regression task does not need to calculate the accuracy, the accuracy layer in the AlexNet network is removed.

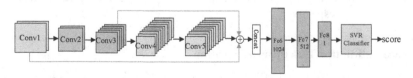

Fig. 3. Cross-connected CNN + SVR model structure

5   Results

In order to verify the validity of the proposed model, numerical experiments have been firstly conducted based on proposed dataset given in Sect. 4. Then, taking ratio of 8:1:1, the dataset were divided into 3445 training set pictures, 431 test set pictures, and 431 validation set pictures randomly.

To evaluate the performance of the regression model, we used Mean Square Error (MSE) as a metric, which was calculated as follows:

$$MSE = \frac{1}{n} \sum (y_i - t_i)^2 \tag{7}$$

Where n denotes the total number of samples, y_i and t_i denote machine scoring and volunteer scoring for each image respectively.

Then the proposed model is applied to analyze the street space quality of the case study area, i.e. the 2nd ring road district of Chengdu.

5.1   Overall Model Evaluation

We train the SVR using Caffe [26] and choose RBF kernel with following parameters: $C = 1e3$ and gamma $= 0.01$. Table 4 shows the performance of the image gray value, HOG feature, LBP feature, AlexNet feature and improved AlexNet feature on test set of the regression task.

Table 4. Performance of the regression model

Model	MSE
Image + SVR	0.0736
HOG + SVR	0.0737
LBP + SVR	0.0511
AlexNet + SVR	0.0348
Cross-connected AlexNet + SVR	0.0306

It can be seen from Table 4 that CNN features performed better than the traditional image description features, image gray value, HOG and LBP features. This is consistent with Porzi's [7] experimental results, which fully demonstrates that CNN features are more suitable for image prediction and classification tasks. In addition, our proposed Cross-connected AlexNet + SVR scheme showed the best performance with the lowest MSE 0.0306. It is proved that the accuracy of the street space quality assessment is greatly improved by the Cross-connected AlexNet + SVR network proposed in this paper.

In order to more intuitively show the accuracy of our proposed method for space quality assessment, we randomly chose several pictures from the test set and applied the trained network model to score the space quality of the streets. Figure 4 shows the quantitative results. In the lower right corner of the picture, the right side is the manual scoring and the left side is the value that network estimated.

Fig. 4. Quantitative examples of space quality

5.2   Case Study for Space Quality Evaluation—Chengdu 2nd Ring Road District

We took 2nd ring road district of Chengdu as the case study area to show the application value of our proposed work. Specifically, we used Baidu Street View map considering that Baidu Street View is convenient and has a wide coverage. The street view samples were obtained by using ArcGIS to carry out random sampling operation along the road network at intervals of 100–200 m, resulting in 9842 street sample points. Each sampling point includes street view images in four directions: east, south, west and north. A total of 39368 images were obtained using the BaiDu panoramic static picture API. The crawling technique is illustrated in detail in reference [19, 20]. Scoring map of street space quality (Fig. 5) was made by calculating the average score of each street view sample. It needs to be noted that the result we have displayed is definitely not an exact match with the actual situation, and there is a certain error. However, we can know the space quality distribution of Chengdu 2nd ring road in general, so as to provide certain reference for researchers to do further research and planners to make decisions and judgments.

We grouped the street space quality in five levels, with values ranging from [0–0.4], (0.4–0.5], (0.5–0.6], (0.6–0.7] and (0.7–1.0]. Level 5 indicates the highest space quality while level 1 indicates the lowest. The main proportion of street space quality are grade 3 and grade 4, 30% and 30% respectively (Fig. 5), indicating that the overall space quality of the case study area is of medium level. The top five streets with the highest space quality were Linjiangxi road, Gaoshengqiao road, Jinlidong road, Hongxingqiao and Yuzhangnan road. The bottom five were Shirenzheng street, Guojielou street, Chengke road, Xiangheli, Dongli road.

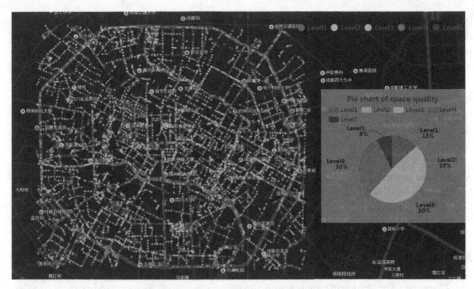

Fig. 5. Street space quality distribution

6   Conclusion and Prospect

6.1   Summarizing the Work

In this paper, we proposed a complete quantitative analysis method for street space quality evaluation based on street view image analysis. We hope that the score of street space quality can be assessed accurately using the scheme. To achieve this goal, we have made the following efforts. Firstly, three key indices were selected as the starting points in this field: cleanliness, comfort and traffic. Secondly, we utilized BaiDu panoramic static picture API to download street view images as the database. Thirdly, by applying Cross-connected CNN + SVR scheme, we could achieve satisfactory computer vision performance on the datasets. The MSE for the regression task was 0.0306 on test set. The score of space quality of each sample point was calculated by aggregating the images at the sample point. Finally, we have demonstrated a case study by analyzing the space quality distribution of Chengdu 2nd ring road.

6.2   Potential Applications and Future Work

This study provides a new way and data analytics support to urban planners and researchers to understand the space quality distribution of selected area of the city. The space quality can be used by urban planners as a reference indicator when they consider socio-economic variables such as real estate pricing, education quality and street safety [18]. This can facilitate urban design better. For regions with poor space quality, planners can consider improving urban appearance from aspects of architectural structure, greenness and enclosure. For researchers, the computer vision model proposed in this paper can be applied to more similar studies. Most of the traditional researches use questionnaire survey, field research and other methods to evaluate the urban physical environment, which will undoubtedly consume a lot of manpower and material resources. The method proposed in this paper can improve this situation to some extent.

Future research will include the combination of other urban quantitative index to verify the rationality of space quality, and provide a predicative analytics on the impact of a new change to be implemented in the urban plan. This is our first attempt to apply deep learning to space quality evaluation, future work will compare our proposed method with more major methods.

Acknowledgments. The authors would like to thank the anonymous reviewers for their comments. This work was supported by the National Natural Science Foundation of China (No. 61871278) and the Sichuan Science and Technology Program (No. 2018HH0143).

References

1. Zhang, X.: Application of remote sensing image processing in city greenland extraction. Xi'an University of Architecture and Technology (2018)
2. Gu, W.: Application of change detection method in urban planning. Graduate School of Chinese Academy of Sciences (Research Institute of Remote Sensing Applications) (2003)
3. Xing, M.: Research on the analysis algorithm of lawn scenes based on digital image processing. Zhejiang Sci-Tech University (2016)
4. Hazelhoff, L., Creusen, I.M.: Exploiting street-level panoramic images for large-scale automated surveying of traffic signs. Mach. Vis. Appl. **25**(7), 1893–1911 (2014)
5. Dubey, A., Naik, N., Parikh, D., Raskar, R., Hidalgo, César A.: Deep learning the city: quantifying urban perception at a global scale. In: Leibe, B., Matas, J., Sebe, N., Welling, M. (eds.) ECCV 2016. LNCS, vol. 9905, pp. 196–212. Springer, Cham (2016). https://doi.org/10.1007/978-3-319-46448-0_12
6. Naik, N., Kominers, S., Raskar, R., et al.: Computer vision uncovers predictors of physical urban change. Proc. Natl. Acad. Sci. **114**(29), 7571–7576 (2017)
7. Porzi, L., Rota, B., Lepri, B., et al.: Predicting and understanding urban perception with convolutional neural networks. In: Proceedings of the 23rd ACM International Conference on Multimedia, pp. 139–148. ACM, Brisbane (2015)
8. Liu, L., Wang, H., Wu, C.: A machine learning method for the large-scale evaluation of urban visual environment. Comput. Environ. Urban Syst. **65**, 113–125 (2017)
9. Ye, Y., Zhang, Z., Zhang, X., et al.: Human-scale quality on streets: a large-scale and efficient analytical approach based on street view images and new urban analytical tools. Urban Plan. Int. **34**(01), 18–27 (2019)
10. Ewing, R., Clemente, O.: Measuring Urban Design: Metrics for Livable Places. Island Press, Washington (2013)
11. Shao, J., Zhang, H., Liu, J.: Quality evaluation of square space based on the aging - friendly city: central city plaza in Harbin. Build. Energ. Effi. **46**(03), 78–83 (2018)
12. Wang, D., Zhang, Y.: Study of street space perception in Shanghai based on semantic differential method. J. TongJi Univ. (Nat. Sci.). **39**(07), 1000–1006 (2011)
13. Tang, J., Long, Y.: Metropolitan street space quality evaluation: second and third ring Of Beijing, inner ring of Shanghai. Planners **33**(2), 68–73 (2017)
14. Gebru, T., Krause, J., Wang, Y., et al.: Using deep learning and Google street view to estimate the demographic makeup of the US. arXiv preprint arXiv:1702.06683, pp. 1–41 (2017)

15. Sun, Y., Wang, X., Tang, X., et al.: Deep learning face representation from predicting 10 000 classes. In: IEEE Conference on Computer Vision and Pattern Recognition 2014, pp. 1891–1898. IEEE, Columbus (2014)
16. Krizhevsky, A., Sutskever, I., Hinton, G.: ImageNet classification with deep convolutional neural networks. Adv. Neural. Inf. Process. Syst. **25**(2), 1097–1105 (2012)
17. Szegedy, C., Vanhoucke, V., Ioffe, S., et al.: Rethinking the inception architecture for computer vision. In: IEEE Conference on Computer Vision and Pattern Recognition, pp. 2818–2826. IEEE, Las Vegas (2016)
18. Naik, N., Philipoom, J., Raskar, R., et al.: Streetscore - predicting the perceived safety of one million streetscapes. In: IEEE Conference on Computer Vision and Pattern Recognition, pp. 793–799. IEEE, Columbia (2014)
19. Li, X., Zhang, C., Li, W., et al.: Assessing street-level urban greenery using google street view and a modified green view index. Urban For. Urban Greening **14**(3), 675–685 (2015)
20. Li, X., Zhang, C., Li, W., et al.: Environmental inequities in terms of different types of urban greenery in Hartford. Connecticut. Urban For. Urban Greening **18**, 163–172 (2016)
21. Chen, Y.: Streetscape renewal: designing livable urban space. Chin. Garden **34**(11), 69–74 (2018)
22. Cordts, M., Omran, M., Ramos, S., et al.: The cityscapes dataset for semantic urban scene understanding. In: IEEE Conference on Computer Vision and Pattern Recognition, pp. 3213–3223. IEEE, Las Vegas (2016)
23. Yu, F., Xian, W., Chen, Y., et al.: BDD100K: a diverse driving video database with scalable annotation tooling. arXiv preprint arXiv:1805.04687 (2018)
24. Antrop, M.: Background concepts for integrated landscape analysis. Agric. Ecosyst. Environ. **77**(1), 17–28 (2000)
25. Daniel, T.C.: Whither scenic beauty? visual landscape quality assessment in the 21st century. Landsc. Urban Plan. **54**(1), 267–281 (2001)
26. Jia, Y., Shelhamer, E., Donahue, J., et al.: Caffe: convolutional architecture for fast feature embedding. In: ACM Multimedia, pp. 675–678. Orlando (2014)

UCAV Path Planning Algorithm Based on Deep Reinforcement Learning

Kaiyuan Zheng, Jingpeng Gao[✉], and Liangxi Shen

College of Information and Communication Engineering, Harbin Engineering University,
Heilongjiang 150001, China
gaojingpeng@hrbeu.edu.cn

Abstract. In the field of the Unmanned Combat Aerial Vehicle (UCAV) confrontation, traditional path planning algorithms have slow operation speed and poor adaptability. This paper proposes a UCAV path planning algorithm based on deep reinforcement learning. The algorithm combines the non-cooperative game idea to build the UCAV and radar confrontation model. In the model, the UCAV must reach the target area. At the same time, in order to complete the identification of the radar communication signal based on ResNet-50 migration learning, we use the theory of Cyclic Spectrum(CS) to process the signal. With the kinematics mechanism of the UCAV, the radar detection probability and the distance between the UCAV and center of the target area are proposed as part of the reward criteria. And we make the signal recognition rate as another part of the reward criteria. The algorithm trains the Deep Q-Network(DQN) parameters to realize the autonomous planning of the UCAV path. The simulation results show that compared with the traditional reinforcement learning algorithm, the algorithm can improve the system operation speed. The accuracy reaches 90% after 300 episodes and the signal recognition rate reaches 92.59% under 0 dB condition. The proposed algorithm can be applied to a variety of electronic warfare environment. It can improve the maneuver response time of the UCAV.

Keywords: UCAV · Signal recognition · Path planning · Cyclic spectrum · Reward criteria · Deep Q-Network

1 Introduction

The appearance of new system radar brings new requirements to the UCAV on electronic warfare, thus the UCAV path planning has become an urgent problem. Good path planning can improve the safety performance of the UCAV and help UCAV accomplish their tasks well.

Currently, the main methods of UCAV path planning include intelligent algorithms, and neural networks [1]. Sun proposes quantum genetic algorithm for mobile robot path planning [2]. He guides and realizes path optimization by introducing genetic operators including quantum crossover operator and quantum gate mutation operator with the essential characteristics of quantum. However, the algorithm is easy to fall into local extreme points and the convergence speed is slow. To achieve a fast search of the path,

© Springer Nature Switzerland AG 2019
Y. Zhao et al. (Eds.): ICIG 2019, LNCS 11902, pp. 702–714, 2019.
https://doi.org/10.1007/978-3-030-34110-7_59

Wang uses the fuzzy neural network to plan the path of the mobile robot [3]. But in electronic warfare, there is a lack of training samples, resulting in poor applicability. In order to overcome the shortcomings of small samples, Peng proposes the 3-D path planning with Multi-constrains [4]. He takes multi-constrains into account in the planning scheme. A path is generated by searching in the azimuth space using genetic algorithm and geometry computation. It causes the algorithm to converge slowly.

With the development of artificial intelligence, more path planning algorithms have been proposed [5–8]. In [9], Q-learning-based path planning algorithm is presented to find a target in the maps which are obtained by mobile robots. Q-learning is a kind of reinforcement learning algorithm that detects its environment. It shows a system which makes decisions itself that how it can learn to make true decisions about reaching its target. However, because the limitations of the Q table of the algorithm [10], its calculation accuracy is poor. Although he uses the reward criteria, the reward values is too single, which makes it less accurate.

Under the UCAV and radar confrontation model, this paper proposes a UCAV path planning algorithm based on deep reinforcement learning to solve the UCAV signal recognition and path planning problem. In order to enable the UCAV to complete the task of identifying the radar signal while reaching the target area, the proposed method combines the neural network of deep learning with the reward criteria of reinforcement learning. We set the reasonable reward values, state values and action values of the UCAV. Then, we use ResNet migration learning to improve the recognition rate of radar signals. The Deep Q-Network is trained to realize adaptive generation of UCAV path. Finally, simulation experiments verify the effectiveness of the proposed method.

The structure of this paper is organized as follows: The model of deep reinforcement learning is described in the Sect. 2. The Sect. 3 introduces the system structure of the path planning. It includes confrontation model and training constraints. The Sect. 4 shows the simulation results. The conclusion will be discussed in Sect. 5.

2 Deep Reinforcement Learning

On one hand, the traditional reinforcement learning algorithms rely on human-involved feature design [11], on the other hand they rely on approximations of values functions and strategy functions. Deep learning, especially Convolutional Neural Networks (CNN), can extract high-dimensional features of images [12]. The Google technical team combines the CNN in deep learning with the Q-learning algorithm in reinforcement learning. They propose the Deep Q-Network (DQN) algorithm [13]. As a pioneering work of deep reinforcement learning, the DQN can finish end-to-end learning from perception to action.

Figure 1 shows the structure of the DQN algorithm. DQN effectively removes the instability and divergence caused by neural network nonlinear action values approximator. It greatly improves the applicability of reinforcement learning. First, the experience replay in the figure randomizes the data. Thereby, it can remove the correlation between the observed data, smooth the data distribution and increase the utilization of historical data. Secondly, the CNN is used to replace the traditional reinforcement learning table mechanism. By using two networks to iteratively update, the algorithm uses the DQN loss function to adjust the direction of the current network values toward the target values network. It is also periodically updated to reduce the correlation with the target network. In addition, through truncating the rewards and regularizing the network parameters, the gradient is limited to the appropriate range, resulting in a more robust training process.

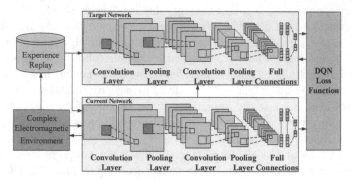

Fig. 1. The structure of DQN model.

3 UCAV Path Planning Research Program

Aiming at the problem that the UCAV avoids the ground radar detection to effectively break through the defense area and accurately identify radar signals, the deep reinforcement learning algorithm is used to train the model to realize the automatic generation of the UCAV path. This paper considers how to plan a reasonable path for a UCAV to arrive at the target area, which makes the UCAV not detected by the two radar.

3.1 Path Planning System Structure

The structure of the path planning system of the UCAV is shown in Fig. 2. Under the background of complex electromagnetic environment, we build a model of the UCAV and radar confrontation. On the one hand, we use the radar signal-to-noise ratio to calculate the radar detection probability. On the other hand, we analyze the UCAV kinematic constraints to study the state values and action values of the UCAV in intelligent decision. These two factors are combined as the reward criteria of the UCAV path planning, which is used to train the intelligent decision network parameters of the UCAV. Finally, a real and reliable path of the UCAV is obtained according to the result.

3.2 Confrontation Model and Training Constraints

In order to simulate the real confrontation environment, it is assumed that there are two random search radars. The distance between the radars satisfies:

$$0.5R_{\max} \leq d < 3R_{\max} \tag{1}$$

where $R_{\max}$ is the maximum working distance of the radar.

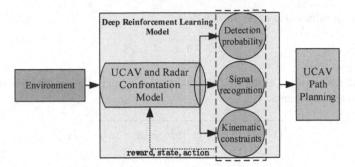

Fig. 2. The structure of path planning system.

The initial position of UCAV is fixed, and the target area is the ground hemisphere with a radius of d_0. After establishing the battlefield environment, the training constraints for the path planning include the reward values, the state values, and the action values constraints. These three types of constraints are the basis for training the parameters of the UCAV intelligent decision network.

Kinematic constraints of the UCAV
Set the random speed vector of the UCAV to:

$$A = [v_x, v_y, v_z] \tag{2}$$

where: v_x is the velocity component of the north direction of the UCAV; v_y is the velocity component of the east direction of the UCAV; v_z is the velocity component of the UCAV facing upward.
The UCAV uses uniform motion:

$$\sqrt{v_x^2 + v_y^2 + v_z^2} = C_0 \tag{3}$$

where C_0 is the UCAV speed values.
The coordinate position $[x, y, z]$ of the UCAV is taken as the state values S, where x represents the coordinates of the north of the UCAV, y represents the coordinates of the east, and z represents the height of the UCAV, and satisfies $0 \leq z \leq 2.5$ km.
After moving for Δt time, according to the action constraints and the current state values, the next state values of the UCAV is:

$$S' = [x + v_x \Delta t, y + v_y \Delta t, z + v_z \Delta t] \tag{4}$$

The action values of UCAV after Δt time is:

$$A' = [v_x', v_y', v_z'] \tag{5}$$

The action values also needs to satisfy (6):

$$\sqrt{v_x'^2 + v_y'^2 + v_z'^2} = C_0 \tag{6}$$

When the state values of the UCAV satisfies (7), it can be determined that the UCAV has reached the target area:

$$\sqrt{(x - x_0)^2 + (y - y_0)^2 + (z - z_0)^2} \leq d_0 \tag{7}$$

where:

[x_0, y_0, z_0] is the target point coordinate;
d_0 is the target area radius.

Signal recognition

The traditional signal recognition based on radar characteristic parameters can not meet the recognition requirements in complex electromagnetic environment in modern electronic countermeasures. In recent years, the development of deep learning, especially the widespread use of neural networks, has provided new ideas and methods for signal processing and recognition. The recognition based on neural network image features can be well applied in the field of radar signal recognition. However, the reasonable conversion of radar signals into images is the key to reliable identification.

First, generating a reliable signal is the basis for signal processing:

$$x(t) = ae^{j\varphi(t)} + n(t) \tag{8}$$

where a is the amplitude, we suppose $a = 1$ in this paper; $\varphi(t)$ is the instantaneous phase of the radar signal; $n(t)$ is the white Gaussian noise. The radar communication signal are BPSK, QPSK, 8PSK, ASK, OQPSK, QAM16, QAM32, QAM64, QAM256.

The theory of Cyclic Spectrum(CS) is established based on the cyclic and stationary characteristics. The signal processing of the communication signal by the cyclic spectrum can obtain good results. Therefore, after receiving the communication modulation signal, the signal processing of the cyclic spectrum analysis is performed:

$$S_x^\alpha(f) = \int_{-\infty}^{\infty} R_x^\alpha(\tau) e^{-j2\pi f\tau} d\tau \tag{9}$$

where α is the cyclic frequency and $R_x^\alpha(\tau)$ is the cyclic autocorrelation of the signal $x(t)$:

$$R_x^\alpha(\tau) = \lim_{T \to \infty} \frac{1}{T} \int_{-\frac{T}{2}}^{\frac{T}{2}} x(t + \frac{\tau}{2}) x^*(t - \frac{\tau}{2}) e^{-j2\pi\alpha t} dt \tag{10}$$

Figure 3 shows nine types of radar communication signals according formula (10).

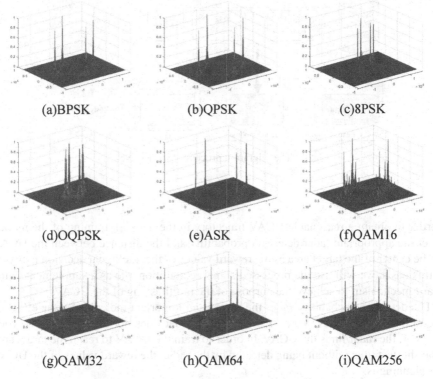

(a)BPSK   (b)QPSK   (c)8PSK

(d)OQPSK   (e)ASK   (f)QAM16

(g)QAM32   (h)QAM64   (i)QAM256

Fig. 3. Nine types of radar communication signals

Compared with the common convolutional neural network, the ResNet network mainly adds a shortcut connection between the input and the output, so that the network can make the subsequent layer can directly learn the residual. When the traditional convolutional layer or fully connected layer is used for information transmission, there will be problems of information loss due to inconvenient connection between input and output. ResNet solves this problem to some extent, and the ResNet network passes the input information. Therefore, we use the ResNet network to extract features from the three-dimensional spectrum of the cyclic spectrum of the communication signal. Migration learning is a new machine learning method. It has good adaptability and can improve the quality of feature extraction. Therefore, the above network application migration learning is adapted to the communication field. Figure 4 shows the migration process of the ResNet. We use pre-training model ResNet to process the signal. Finally, the system uses the Support Vector Machine(SVM) to reach the purpose of classification and identification and get the communication signal recognition rate η.

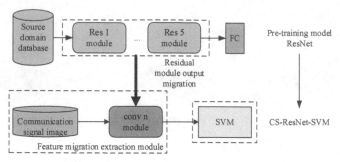

Fig. 4. The migration process of the ResNet.

3.3 Reward Criteria

In order to obtain a reasonable UCAV trajectory in the network training of the model, we set the appropriate radar detection probability and the distance between the UCAV and the center of the target area as the reward values of the intelligent decision network. On this basis, we will use the processed signal recognition rate as a supplement to the reward mechanism to achieve the purpose of the multitasking of the UCAV.

The detection probability P_d of the radar is an important indicator for the effective penetration of the UCAV. When $P_d \leq 0.1$, the radar does not find the UCAV; when $P_d > 0.1$, the radar finds the UCAV. In order to train the UCAV to reach the target area in the shortest time without being detected by the radar, the reward values of the UCAV path planning is:

$$R(\omega) = P_d(\omega_1) + D(\omega_2) \tag{11}$$

where: D is the distance between the UCAV and the center of the target area; $\omega = [\omega_1, \omega_2]$ are the weights of the detection probability and the flight time of the UCAV respectively. Different weights can get different reward trends. In this paper, we set the reward as:

$$R = \frac{\omega_1}{\log_2 P_d^{-1}} - \omega_2(D - 250)^3 + 2 \tag{12}$$

where: $\omega_1 = 1$, $\omega_2 = 0.001$.

However, in order to enable the UCAV to better identify the radar communication signal. We improve the reward with communication signal recognition rate η:

$$R = \eta(\frac{\omega_1}{\log_2 P_d^{-1}} - \omega_2(D - 250)^3 + 2) \tag{13}$$

3.4 Path Planning Algorithm

Intelligent decision making is the core of the UCAV path planning algorithm. In the traditional reinforcement learning algorithm, the state and action space are discrete and the dimension is low. Q table can be used to store the Q values of each state action. In solving the problem of UCAV path planning, the state and action of the UCAV are highly dimensionally continuous, and the data is also very large. Due to the limitations of the Q table, it is very difficult to store data, which makes the traditional reinforcement learning algorithm cannot solve the problem of path planning. The DQN algorithm replaces the Q table by fitting a loss function so that similar states get similar action outputs. We propose that the path planning algorithm based on deep reinforcement learning, which can effectively solve the problem that the data is too large to be trained. Besides, it can break the correlation between data and improve the training efficiency. We have discussed the three elements of the DQN algorithm: state, action, and reward. Figure 4 shows the DQN algorithm flow.

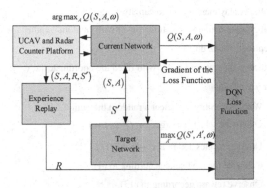

Fig. 5. DQN algorithm flow.

In Fig. 5, the experience replay is used to learn the previous experience. We send (S, A, R, S') to the experience replay for learning. At the same time, we send the output reward values R to the DQN loss function. The current state action pair is sent to the current values network, and the next state S' is sent to the target values network. The DQN loss function can be expressed by (14):

$$L(\omega) = E[(r + \gamma \max_{A'} Q(S', A', \omega) - Q(S, A, \omega))^2] \tag{14}$$

where: γ is attenuation coefficient of the reward values; ω is the weight of the loss function; $r + \gamma \max_{A'} Q(S', A', \omega)$ is the values of the target values network; $Q(S, A, \omega)$ is the Q values of the current values network.

It can be seen that the loss function is calculated by the mean square error of the difference between the target values and the current values. After the loss function is derived, we can calculate the gradient of the loss function:

$$\frac{\partial L(\omega)}{\partial \omega} = E[(r + \gamma \max_{A'} Q(S', A', \omega) - Q(S, A, \omega)) \frac{\partial Q(S, A, \omega)}{\partial \omega}] \tag{15}$$

Therefore, we use stochastic gradient descent to update parameters to obtain an optimal values $Q(S, A, \omega)$. The current values network in DQN uses the latest parameters, which can be used to evaluate the values function of the current state action pair. But the target values network parameters are a long time ago. After the current values network is iterated, the UCAV takes action on the environment to update the target values network parameters according to (15). In this way, a learning process is completed. The optimal Q values is stored in the network to realize the practical application of the optimal track (Table 1).

Table 1. The process described by algorithm 1

Algorithm1 DQN for path planning
Input: (S, A, R, S')
Output: $Q(S, A, \omega)$
1: Initialize replay memory D to capcity N ;
2: Initialize state-action values function Q with random weights ω ;
3: for episode $= 1, M$ do:
4:     Initialize the state of UCAV with fixed the coordinate $[x, y, z]$.
5:     for $t = 1, T$ do:
6:         With probability ε select a random the action A .
7:         Otherwise select $A = \arg\max_a Q(S, A, \omega)$.
8:         UCAV executes action according to (2).
9:         Calculate the next state according to (4).
10:        Observe reward according to (13).
11:        Store transition (S, A, R, S') in D .
12:        Sample random the minibatch from D .
13:        Update the Q-network with the sample according to (15).
14:     end for.
15: end for.

4 Simulation Experiment and Results

After analyzing the UCAV motion constraints and the path planning algorithm, UCAV and radar confrontation model parameters are set in Table 2. The simulation experiment parameters are shown in Table 3.

Table 2. UCAV and Radar Confrontation Platform parameters

Flight Altitude Of UCAV	0–2.5 (km)
Speed Of UCAV	120–180 (km/h)
Flight Area	500 * 500 (km)
Radar Position	Random

Combined with the UCAV and radar confrontation model parameters in Table 3 and the simulation experiment parameters in Table 3, we use the DQN algorithm to achieve simulation training. Then we normalize the data of the reward values. The normalization function is:

$$f(x) = 1/(1 + e^{-x}) \tag{16}$$

Table 3. Simulation experiment parameters

Network Update Times	200
Episodes Of Training	300
Time Interval	$\Delta t = 0.5\,\text{s}$

On this basis, in order to observe the relation between the reward values and the episodes, we take the reward values of 10 times to do an average. Finally, we can obtain the following simulation results by combining the above parameters and conditions.

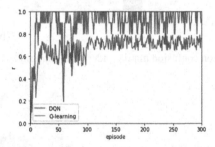

Fig. 6. The reward values of 300 episodes conversion curve.

Figure 6 shows the variation of the overall reward values for each episode of the UCAV. The abscissa represents the number of episode and the ordinate is the reward values after normalization. The reward values 0 and 1 represent the minimum and maximum values after normalization respectively. Figure 6 shows that compared with Q-learning, the DQN overall reward values gradually increases, and eventually stabilizes after the episodes reaches 80, and the average reward values is close to 0.9. This is because the DQN network uses the gradient descent method to correct the loss function, so that the Q values of the intelligent decision network is optimized. When the episode is 60, the reward values is abrupt. This is because after a certain number of trainings, the algorithm will re-randomly search for the optimal solution to avoid falling into local optimum.

When the episodes are 190 and 240, due to the random sampling of the experience replay in the DQN algorithm, the correlation between data is cut off. The simulation shows that the accuracy of the algorithm reaches 90%.

In each modulation category, 100 tests are implemented. It is clear from Fig. 7(a) that the classification accuracy of BPSK, QAM16, QAM64, QPSK and 8PSK is 100%.

The classification accuracy of OQPSK, ASK, QAM256 and QAM64 becomes worse, especially for QAM32 and QAM256. Figure 7(b) shows the recognition rate curve based on the CS method signal recognition and the recognition rate curve based on the traditional signal recognition. This indicates that the residual neural network signal recognition based on cyclic spectrum has a good recognition rate. The proposed method is lower than the traditional method at -6 dB, but the proposed method is superior to the traditional method with the improvement of signal-to-noise ratio. This is because by transmitting the input information directly to the output, the ResNet network only needs to learn the difference between input and output, which simplifies the learning goal and difficulty, protects the information integrity to a certain extent.

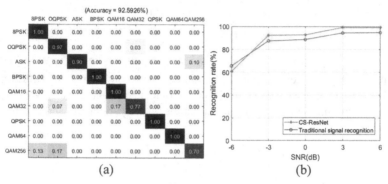

(a)   (b)

Fig. 7. (a) Signal recognition confusion matrix under 0 dB condition; (b) The recognition rate of proposed algorithm.

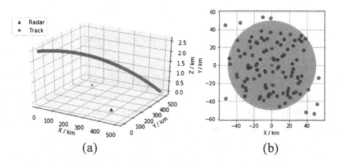

(a)   (b)

Fig. 8. (a) The 3D renderings of the UCAV single-shot to the target; (b) The 2D renderings of the UCAV multiple times to the target. (Color figure online)

Figure 8(a) shows the effect of the UCAV reaching the target area. The black point represents the radar and the red curve represents the path of the UCAV. This shows that the UCAV can independently plan a path to the target area without being detected by the radar.

In Fig. 8(b), a light blue circle represents the target area, a red star represents the center ground projection of the target area, and a red projected point represents a of the UCAV approaching the target area. Figure 8(b) shows that after 300 episodes, the success rate of the UCAV reaching the target reaches 90%. This is because the deep reinforcement learning algorithm has good self-learning and correction capabilities. The simulation results show that the UCAV path planning algorithm based on deep reinforcement learning can independently plan a reasonable path in the unknown space.

5 Conclusion

This paper proposes a UCAV path planning algorithm based on deep reinforcement learning, which solves the problem of poor adaptability and slow calculation speed in traditional track planning algorithm. Besides, it realizes the aircraft signal recognition. The simulation results show that the proposed algorithm achieves 90% accuracy under the conditions of compromise planning time and flight quality. Besides, the signal recognition rate reaches 92.59% under 0 dB condition. It has good convergence, which can be applied in the field of modern electronic warfare.

Acknowledgment. This paper is funded by the International Exchange Program of Harbin Engineering University for Innovation-oriented Talents Cultivation, the Fundamental Research Funds for the Central Universities (HEUCFG201832), the Key Laboratory Foundation Project of National Defense Science and Technology Bureau (KY10800180080) and the China Shipbuilding Industry Corporation 722 Research Institute Fund Project (KY10800170051).

References

1. Zou, A.M., Hou, Z.G., Fu, S.Y., Tan, M.: Neural networks for mobile robot navigation: a survey. In: Wang, J., Yi, Z., Zurada, J.M., Lu, B.L., Yin, H. (eds.) Advances in Neural Networks - ISNN 2006. Lecture Notes in Computer Science, vol. 3972, pp. 1218–1226. Springer, Berlin (2006). https://doi.org/10.1007/11760023_177
2. Sun, Y., Ding, M.: Quantum genetic algorithm for mobile robot path planning. In: Fourth International Conference on Genetic and Evolutionary Computing, pp. 206–209 (2010)
3. Wang, H., Duan, J., Wang, M., Zhao, J., Dong, Z.: Research on robot path planning based on fuzzy neural network algorithm. In: IEEE 3rd Advanced Information Technology, Electronic and Automation Control Conference (IAEAC), pp. 1800–1803 (2018)
4. Peng, J., Sun, X., Zun, F., Zhang, J.: 3-D path planning with multi-constrains. In: IEEE. Chinese Control and Decision Conference, pp. 3301–3305 (2008)
5. Challita, U., Saad, W., Bettstetter, C.: Interference management for cellular-connected UAVs: a deep reinforcement learning approach. IEEE Trans. Wireless Commun. 1–32 (2019)
6. Beomjoon, K., Pineau, J.: Socially adaptive path planning in human environments using inverse reinforcement learning. Int. J. Soc. Robot. **8**(1), 51–66 (2016)
7. Wang, C., Wang, J., Shen, Y.: Autonomous navigation of UAVs in large-scale complex environments: a deep reinforcement learning approach. IEEE Trans. Vehicular Technol. **68**(3), 2124–2136 (2019)
8. Wu, J., Shin, S., Kim, C.: Effective lazy training method for deep q-network in obstacle avoidance and path planning. In: IEEE International Conference on Systems, Man, and Cybernetics (SMC), pp. 1799–1804 (2017)

9. Çetin, H., Durdu, A.: Path planning of mobile robots with Q-learning. In: 22nd Signal Processing and Communications Applications Conference (SIU), pp. 2162–2165 (2014)
10. Richard, S., Andrew, G.: Reinforcement Learning: An Introduction. MIT press, Cambridge (2018)
11. Lei, T., Ming, L.: A robot exploration strategy based on q-learning network. In: IEEE International Conference on Real-time Computing and Robotics, pp. 57–62 (2016)
12. Mnih, V., et al.: Human-level control through deep reinforcement learning. Nature **518**(7540), 529–533 (2015)
13. Mnih, V., Kavukcuoglu, K., Silver, D., et al: Playing atari with deep reinforcement learning. arXiv preprint arXiv:1312.5602, pp. 1–9 (2013)

Efficient and Accurate Iris Detection and Segmentation Based on Multi-scale Optimized Mask R-CNN

Zhi Li[1,2]([✉]), Di Miao[3], Huanwei Liang[3], Hui Zhang[3], Jing Liu[3],
and Zhaofeng He[3]

[1] Criminal Investigation Department of Public Security Bureau of Xinjiang Uygur
Autonomous Region, Xinjiang Uygur, China
708832309@qq.com
[2] School of Economics and Management,
University of Chinese Academy of Sciences, Beijing, China
[3] Beijing IrisKing Tech Co., Ltd., Beijing, China
{miaodi,lianghw,zhanghui,liujing,hezhf}@irisking.com

Abstract. Iris segmentation plays an important role in iris recognition.
However, traditional iris segmentation performance decreases dramatically on non-constrained conditions, which stops iris recognition system
from being widely deployed. In this paper, an efficient and accurate iris
detection and segmentation method based on multi-scale optimized Mask
R-CNN method is proposed. The proposed method introduces the attention module and multi-scale fusion module to the iris segmentation task.
The attention module accelerate the procedure by detecting a smaller
iris region for segmentation, while the multi-scale fusion module faithfully preserves the explicit spatial position of iris region. Experimental
results on UBIRIS.v2 and CASIA.v4-Distance demonstrate the superior
performance of the proposed method.

Keywords: Iris segmentation · Attention · Multi-scale fusion

1 Introduction

Iris recognition [1–4] is one of accurate and widely adopted approaches to the
automated personal identification and has become increasingly integrated into
our daily life. Performance of iris recognition systems highly relies on effectiveness of iris segmentation. Iris detection and segmentation [1–8] aims at locating
and isolating valid iris texture regions from eye images. The accuracy of iris
segmentation greatly impacts the performance of subsequent procedures such as
image normalization, feature extraction, and pattern matching in iris recognition. However, traditional iris segmentation methods require the subjects to be
captured under strictly constrained condition, and their performance decreases
dramatically in non-cooperative environments such as remote iris recognition

© Springer Nature Switzerland AG 2019
Y. Zhao et al. (Eds.): ICIG 2019, LNCS 11902, pp. 715–726, 2019.
https://doi.org/10.1007/978-3-030-34110-7_60

systems and on-the-move systems. The degradation is mainly caused by occlusions, specular reflections, blur and off-axis. That is one of the major difficulties restricting iris recognition systems from being deployed in civilian and surveillance applications more widely.

For friendly user experience, various iris segmentation methods have been proposed to improve the performance especially in non-cooperative environments and achieve remarkable performance. The existing methods can be divided into two categories, boundary based methods [2–7,9,10] and pixel based methods [11–13]. Boundary based methods segment iris texture regions by locating pupillary, limbic and eyelid boundaries, while pixel based methods directly distinguish iris pixels from non-iris pixels according to the appearance features around. However, boundary based methods are easy to be severely influenced by noise data around iris boundaries in especially low quality images, and pre-knowledge such as shapes of boundaries is usually required as the constraint. Though pixel based methods do not require any assumption of boundary shapes, handcrafted appearance features are still not able to distinguish the differences between iris region and non-iris region. Due to those shortcomings, the existing methods fail to facilitate a more robust and accurate iris recognition system in a further step.

To address the problems mentioned above, inspired by the procedure that human being recognize an iris, an efficient and accurate iris detection and segmentation network based on multi-scale optimized Mask R-CNN (IDSN-MS) is introduced. It is an efficient and flexible model which detects iris in a captured image while simultaneously generating a high-quality segmentation result for the iris. To reduce the influence of noisy data on boundaries and extract more distinct features, the proposed method utilized deep neural networks which segment the iris texture region directly according to its learnt features. Moreover, to reduce the time consumption of deep neural networks, it detects an iris region at first, and then segment the iris in the detected region. As the detection procedure is much faster than segmentation, segmentation on the small detected region is a wise choice in the consideration of time cost. That also makes the network concentrate on iris region rather than the whole image. Thus more parameters of the network are utilized to learn detailed features from the Regions of Interest (RoI), instead of rough boundaries. It benefits both accuracy and efficiency as the segmentation branch could pay much attention on the actual iris region. What's more, the multi-scale fusion branch is introduce to fully utilized boundary information of feature maps in various scale levels. It facilitates faithfully preserve the information derived from local texture and global structure simultaneously.

The rest of the paper is organized as follows. Section 2 review the related work on iris segmentation. The proposed method is introduced in Sect. 3, and experimental results are shown in Sect. 4. Finally, the conclusion is drawn in Sect. 5.

2 Related Work

2.1 Boundary Based Methods

The boundary based iris segmentation methods are proposed as early as the primary research on iris recognition. The integrodifferential operator [5] proposed by Daugmand is one of the classic iris segmentation methods. The integrodifferential operator is an edge detector that searches the best fitted circle boundary over the whole image. Hough transform [9] is another iris segmentation method with the assumption of circle boundaries. After deriving a binary edge map, it finds the best set of boundary parameters that most of edge pixels in the map vote for. Similar methods [2–4] are also proposed. An elastic model called pulling and pushing method [7] which is inspired by Hookes law, treats boundaries of iris as circles as well. However, further researches indicate that circles are not always able to fit iris boundaries precisely due to non-circular iris boundaries in captured images, and the bad fitted boundary is one of the reasons for false reject matching. To address this problem, active contour model is introduced to iris segmentation [6] in Daugmans follow up work. Shah and Ross [10] further improve this kind of method by utilizing geodesic active contour and achieve accurate iris segmentation results. All these methods all achieve remarkable iris segmentation performance, but the shapes of segmented iris region by these methods will be severely influenced by noise data especially in the images with low quality or in non-cooperated environment, and result in failure of iris recognition.

Some iris detection methods [14,15] are also performed based on the iris boundary. These methods determine whether an candidate pre-detected region is an iris region or not. Similar to boundary-based iris segmentation methods, the boundary based iris detection methods are also easy to be influenced by noise data.

2.2 Pixel Based Methods

Different from the boundary based methods utilizing gradient and geometry information, pixel based methods mainly focus on how to distinguish the pixel of iris region from that of non-iris region according to the appearance features such as texture around the pixel. Various of handcrafted features such as Gabor filters [11], Zernike moments [12], location and color features [13] are employed as appearance features, and classic classifiers such as support vector machines (SVMs), graph cut methods and Gaussian mixture models (GMMs) are trained to distinguish iris region features from non-iris region features. In this way, noise boundaries can be removed. These methods segment and isolate iris texture region from well captured images exactly, without any assumption of boundary shapes. However, handcrafted appearance features are still not able to distinguish the differences between iris region and non-iris region.

2.3   Deep Neural Network Based Methods

Nowadays, deep neural networks are paid more attention, as they achieve remarkable results in object instance segmentation tasks. A variety of iris segmentation work based on convolution neural networks (CNNs) are proposed recently. Fully convolution deep neural network (FCDNN) [16], multi-scale fully convolutional networks (MFCNs) [8] and Seg-Edge bilateral constraint network (SEN) [17] are proposed specifically for the iris segmentation task. MFCN [8], an end-to-end iris segment model, is a extension of FCNs. MFCN fuse multi layers from shallow-and-fine layers to deep-and-coarse layers, which balances the information from local texture and global structure. Their superior performance illustrates outstanding effectiveness of Deep Neural Networks (DNNs) on iris segmentation. However, the above remarkable performance highly relies on a large number of parameters of the model, which are time consuming. That stops the above methods to be deployed in real time iris recognition systems.

3   Proposed Method

In this section, the proposed iris detection and segmentation method is illustrated in detail. At first, it detects actual iris location, and crop an RoI based on the detection result. Then iris segmentation is performed on the RoI, which is much faster than the segmentation on the whole image. The proposed model is an extension of the Mask R-CNN, and achieves more accurate iris segmentation results with the attendance of the multi-scale fusion. Superior performance suggests the proposed method is not only an accurate but also efficient iris detection and segmentation method, which makes more accurate iris segmentation available in real time iris recognition systems.

The Mask R-CNN [18] approach is an extension of Faster R-CNN [19]. The approach is able to accomplish object detection, classification and object instance segmentation simultaneously in its network architecture. On the part of object instance segmentation, it predicts a segmentation mask on each RoI in a pixel-to-pixel manner, by adding a mask branch. The mask branch is in parallel with the branch for classification. That prevents it from being influenced by the classification task and makes it fully focus on the segmentation task to faithfully preserve the explicit instance spatial position. In addition, the mask branch is a small FCN which does not consume much time. That allows the approach available in real time segmentation systems.

3.1   Backbone Structure

ResNet-50 [20] is used as the basic network here, due to its efficiency and expressive feature extractors benefitted from its deep but less complex architecture. Then feature pyramid network (FPN)[21] is adopted to enhance the expression ability of features.

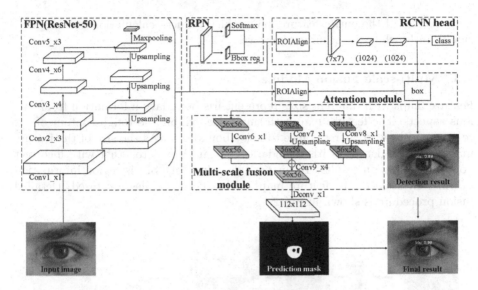

Fig. 1. Network architecture of the proposed method. The iris image is fed into the ResNet-FPN backbone for feature extraction. The RPN and RCNN head are standard components of Mask R-CNN. Attention module obtains the feature map to be segmented, and multi-scale fusion module fuses feature maps with different scales.

The overall architecture of the proposed method is shown in Fig. 1. Features of input images are extracted by the ResNet-50, from which rough candidate feature maps are obtained through the Region Proposal Network (RPN). The generated feature maps are used for iris detection and iris segmentation. After the attention module [22], iris bounding box is generated, along with the extracted feature map. Then the multi-scale fusion module expends feature map into various scales to fully investigate iris boundary information. The final iris segmentation mask are gained afterward.

3.2 Attention Module

In terms of iris segmentation, most of the incorrect segmentation appears in the eyelids or glasses frames. It will be more effective in reducing the incorrect segmentation, if iris regions are paid more attention. More accurate areas to be segmented will be more conducive to network learning, due to the limited representation ability of the network.

Therefore, the detection network is used to obtain the bounding box of the iris, and the correct bounding boxes are reserved as the pre-selection box of masks. On the corresponding feature map, ROIAlign is used to extract feature maps of 14×14, 28×28 and 56×56 pixels according to the pre-selected boxes. In this way, the mask network obtains different scale features and is able to focus on segmentation much better. Meanwhile, the iris mask is extracted on the feature map instead of the entire feature map, which reduces calculation consumption significantly while the accuracy improves.

3.3   Multi-scale Fusion Module

Feature maps with different sizes represent iris boundary information from various aspects. The feature map with small size exhibit the rough contour of iris region, and have great resistance to noisy boundaries. As the size of the feature map increases, details of iris boundaries appear clearly, together with incorrect noisy segmentation results. To further take advantage of iris region information in different scale levels, feature maps with different scales are fused. Detailed fusion procedure is shown in Fig. 2.

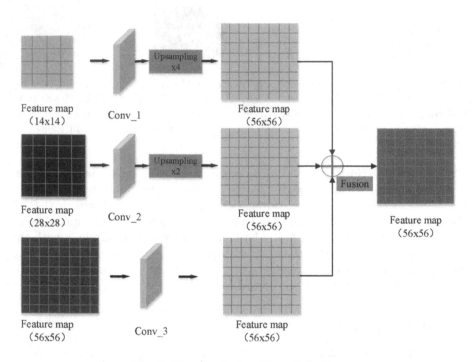

Fig. 2. Flowchart of multi-scale fusion.

Specifically, feature maps which are resized into 14×14, 28×28 and 56×56 pixels, are derived from attention module. Convolution operations are performed on the three feature maps to obtain segmentation features of different scales. After the upsampling operation by bilinear interpolation, feature maps of different scales are all interpolated to 56×56 pixels. To balance the robustness and precision of different scales, feature maps are fused into a single feature map based on the weighted sum rule. Then the fused feature map gets through four convolution operations and one deconvolution operation. At last, the fused feature map is resized into 112×112 pixels for iris segmentation. The fusion operation can be expressed as:

$$F(x,y) = \delta_1 * V_1(x,y) + \delta_2 * V_2(x,y) + \delta_3 * V_3(x,y) \qquad (x,y) \in M \qquad (1)$$

where $F(x,y)$ represents the fusion features in position (x,y). $V_1(x,y)$, $V_2(x,y)$ and $V_3(x,y)$ represent features of three different scales after sampling on different scale feature maps in position (x,y). δ_1, δ_2 and δ_3 represent the weights of the feature maps. M represents the set of points in the feature map.

The output probability is obtained with the help of sigmod function. Cross entropy function is adopted as the loss function. The cross entropy loss function is formulated as follows:

$$L = \sum_{i=0}^{N} y_i log\hat{y}^i + (1 - y^i)log(1 - \hat{y}^i) \qquad (2)$$

$$\hat{y}^i = g(F(x,y)) = g(\delta_1 * V_1(x,y) + \delta_2 * V_2(x,y) + \delta_3 * V_3(x,y))$$

where $\hat{y}^i$ represents the probability of each pixel. $g(*)$ is the predicted probability. Each predicted pixels is obtained by the fusion of corresponding features at different scales. N represents the total number of pixels to be split.

4 Experiment

4.1 Datasets

Two public datasets UBIRIS.v2 [23] and CASIA.v4-Distance [24] are utilized to evaluate segmentation accuracy and efficiency of the proposed methods. UBIRIS.v2 contains 945 visible wavelength images captured on non-constrained conditions with various capture distance and illumination. There are 500 images and 445 images used for training and test respectively. Image in CASIA.v4-Distance are captured by the near-infrared device, and the dataset is separate into two parts, 300 images for training and 100 images for test. Iris regions in the images above are all well labeled with masks and bounding boxes.

4.2 Datasets Augmentation

To enhance robustness and generalization ability of the proposed method, training datasets are augmented by adding additional illumination, shadows and blur to images. Furthermore, images are also resized by 1 to 2 times randomly, to simulate various captured iris images on non-constrained conditions. All the images are cropped with the size of 480×360 pixels as the standard input. The total number of training images in UBIRIS.v2 and CASIA.v4-Distance is 5000 and 15000 respectively.

4.3 Training Pipeline

Mask R-CNN is employed as the backbone in the iris segmentation task. On the concern of time consumption, ResNet-50 is used to learn qualified feature extractor, due to its superior efficiency and feature discrimination. Then multi-scale fusion module is adopted to facilitate precise spatial locations of iris regions.

Training: Parameters of ImageNet are used to initialize the backbone network. The training schedule is extended to 160k iterations in which the learning rate is reduced from 0.0025 by 10 at 60k iterations. In the Region Proposal Network (RPN) module, the number of output bounding boxes is fixed to 2,000. The bounding boxes whose Intersection over Union (IoU) is larger than 0.7 are treated as positive samples. The mask prediction threshold is 0.5.

Testing: The number of output bounding boxes in RPN is set to 1,000, while the detection threshold is set to 0.7.

4.4 Experimental Results

Average segmentation error (ASE), a widely used indicator, is adopted to evaluate accuracy of the proposed method. It is computed as follow:

$$ASE = \frac{1}{N \times H \times W} \sum_{i,j \in (H,W)} G(i,j) \oplus M(i,j) \tag{3}$$

where N is total number of test images. H and W denote the height and width of image, G(i,j) and M(i,j) are the ground truth mask and predicted iris segmentation mask. $\oplus$ represents the XOR operation.

Baseline. Mask R-CNN, which is utilized as the backbone of the proposed method, is used as the baseline of iris segmentation. The size of the convolution kernel is 3×3 pixels, and the padding is 1. The size of mask feature map is 14×14 pixels (i.e. the size of RoI is 14×14 pixels) after 4 convolutions layers. Then the feature map is upsampled to 28×28 pixels. The ASEs of the baseline on the UBIRIS.v2 and CASIA.v4-Distance are 1.01% and 0.739%, respectively.

Table 1. Performance of feature maps with various scales. Results of RoI with the sizes 14×14, 28×28 and 56×56 before upsampling are demonstrated.

Method	UBIRIS.v2		CASIA.v4-Distance	
	ASE(%)	Time(ms)	ASE(%)	Time(ms)
Mask R-CNN(14×14)	1.010	57.58	0.739	57.58
Mask R-CNN(28×28)	0.890	59.06	0.452	59.06
Mask R-CNN(56×56)	0.883	60.66	0.444	60.66

To investigate the influence of different feature maps size on iris segmentation, performance of feature maps (i.e. RoI) with sizes of 14, 28 and 56 are evaluated. Then the feature maps are upsampled to 28, 56 and 112 respectively. Experimental results are shown in Table 1. It illustrates that performance of different feature map sizes vary a lot and the feature map with larger size provides significant improvement on iris segmentation.

Multi-scale Fusion. Information of feature maps with different scales result in various iris segmentation results. Feature map with small size can learn the rough outer contour of the segmented image and have great resistance to noise. As the size of the feature map increases, the details of segmentation get better, while incorrect segmentation results appear due to noise.

To further enhance the segmentation performance, feature maps with multi-scale are fused as described in Subsect. 3.3. The multi-scale fusion result of feature maps with the sizes of 14×14, 28×28 and 56×56 pixels is shown in Table 2. δ_1, δ_2 and δ_3 in formula (1) are fixed to 1, so that feature maps with different scales have the same right to exhibit their information for segmentation. For purpose of illustrating the positive impact of smaller feature maps, the feature map with the size 14×14 is removed and then the model is fine-tuned. That result can also be found in Table 2. Segmentation results of fusing feature maps with different scales differ a lot. The fusion of the three scales has a lower ASE than the fusion of two. It can be inferred that the rough boundary indicated by smaller feature maps help to resist noisy boundaries while larger feature maps faithfully preserving detailed boundaries.

Table 2. Multi-scale fusion segmentation results. (28-56) and (14-28-56) indicate the scales of feature maps to be fused.

Method	UBIRIS.v2		CASIA.v4-Distance	
	ASE(%)	Time(ms)	ASE(%)	Time(ms)
Fusion(28-56)	0.879	65.51	0.443	65.51
Fusion(14-28-56)	**0.873**	69.42	**0.439**	69.42

Comparison with Other Iris Segment Algorithms. To illustrate the superior performance of the proposed method, it is compared with public state-of-the-art iris segmentation methods. Results are shown in Table 3.

The training sets of all the methods in the table are the same. It can be seen that the proposed method not only achieve the most accurate segmentation result, but also accelerate the iris detection and segmentation procedure by nearly 3 times. Some iris segmentation results of images in UBIRIS.v2 and CASIA.v4-Distance are shown in Fig. 3.

Table 3. Comparisons of the proposed methods and other iris segmentation method. '-' indicates the result is not reported in their work.

Method	UBIRIS.v2		CASIA.v4-Distance	
	ASE(%)	time(ms)	ASE(%)	time(ms)
Our method	**0.87**	69.42	**0.44**	69.42
SEN [17]	0.88	200.00	0.46	200.00
MFCN [8]	0.90	200.00	0.59	200.00
RTV-L1 [25]	1.21	–	0.68	–
Tan et al. [26]	1.31	–	–	–
Tan and Kumar [27]	1.72	750.00	0.81	1530.00
Proenca [13]	1.87	780.00	–	–
Tan and Kumar [28]	1.90	–	1.13	–

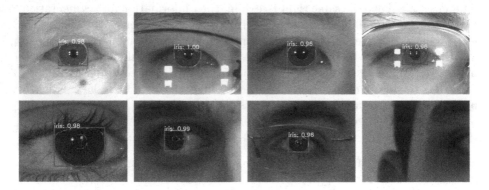

Fig. 3. Segmentation results of the proposed method on CASIA.v4-Distance (the first row) and UBIRIS.v2 (the second row). The red pixels indicate the iris regions which are incorrectly predicted as non-iris regions, and the green pixels indicate the non-iris regions which are incorrectly predicted as iris regions. 'iris' is the probability that there exists an iris in the bounding box.

5   Conclusions

In this paper, a novel iris detection and segmentation method named IDSN-MS is proposed. It utilizes the location information of the iris to provide a more accurate segmentation feature for iris segmentation. Fusion of multi-scale feature maps improves the segmentation performance by utilizing segmentation information in various scale levels. Finally, the state-of-the-art iris segmentation results on two challenging UBIRIS.v2 and CASIA.v4-distance datasets are shown to demonstrate the superiority of the proposed method.

Acknowledgement. This work was support by the National Key R & D Program of China [2018YFC0807303].

References

1. Daugman, J.: Statistical richness of visual phase information: update on recognizing persons by iris patterns. Int. J. Comput. Vision **45**(1), 25–38 (2001)
2. Ma, L., Wang, Y., Tan, T.: Iris recognition using circular symmetric filters. In: Object Recognition Supported by User Interaction for Service Robots, vol. 2, pp. 414–417. IEEE (2002)
3. Tisse, C.-L., Martin, L., Torres, L., Robert, M., et al.: Person identification technique using human iris recognition. Proc. Vision Interface **294**, 294–299 (2002)
4. Kong, W.K., Zhang, D.: Accurate iris segmentation based on novel reflection and eyelash detection model. In: Proceedings of 2001 International Symposium on Intelligent Multimedia, Video and Speech Processing. ISIMP 2001 (IEEE Cat. No. 01EX489), pp. 263–266. IEEE (2001)
5. Daugman, J.: How iris recognition works. In: The Essential Guide to Image Processing, pp. 715–739 (2009)
6. Daugman, J.: New methods in iris recognition. IEEE Trans. Syst. Man Cybern. Part B (Cybern.) **37**(5), 1167–1175 (2007)
7. He, Z., Tan, T., Sun, Z., Qiu, X.: Toward accurate and fast iris segmentation for iris biometrics. IEEE Trans. Pattern Anal. Mach. Intell. **31**(9), 1670–1684 (2009)
8. Liu, N., Li, H., Zhang, M., Liu, J., Sun, Z., Tan, T.: Accurate iris segmentation in non-cooperative environments using fully convolutional networks. In: 2016 International Conference on Biometrics (ICB), pp. 1–8. IEEE (2016)
9. Wildes, R.P.: Iris recognition: an emerging biometric technology. Proc. IEEE **85**(9), 1348–1363 (1997)
10. Shah, S., Ross, A.: Iris segmentation using geodesic active contours. IEEE Trans. Inf. Forensics Secur. **4**(4), 824–836 (2009)
11. Li, Y.-H., Savvides, M.: An automatic iris occlusion estimation method based on high-dimensional density estimation. IEEE Trans. Pattern Anal. Mach. Intell. **35**(4), 784–796 (2013)
12. Tan, C.-W., Kumar, A.: Unified framework for automated iris segmentation using distantly acquired face images. IEEE Trans. Image Process. **21**(9), 4068–4079 (2012)
13. Proenca, H.: Iris recognition: on the segmentation of degraded images acquired in the visible wavelength. IEEE Trans. Pattern Anal. Mach. Intell. **32**(8), 1502–1516 (2010)
14. Kawaguchi, T., Rizon, M.: Iris detection using intensity and edge information. Pattern Recogn. **36**(2), 549–562 (2003)
15. Mäenpää, T.: An iterative algorithm for fast iris detection. In: Li, S.Z., Sun, Z., Tan, T., Pankanti, S., Chollet, G., Zhang, D. (eds.) IWBRS 2005. LNCS, vol. 3781, pp. 127–134. Springer, Heidelberg (2005). https://doi.org/10.1007/11569947_16
16. Bazrafkan, S., Thavalengal, S., Corcoran, P.: An end to end deep neural network for iris segmentation in unconstrained scenarios. Neural Networks **106**, 79–95 (2018)
17. Hu, J., Zhang, H., Xiao, L., Liu, J., He, Z., Li, L.: Seg-edge bilateral constraint network for iris segmentation. In: 2019 International Conference on Biometrics (ICB), pp. 1–8. IEEE (2019)
18. He, K., Gkioxari, G., Dollár, P., Girshick, R.: Mask R-CNN. In: Proceedings of the IEEE International Conference on Computer Vision, pp. 2961–2969 (2017)
19. Ren, S., He, K., Girshick, R., Sun, J.: Faster r-cnn: towards real-time object detection with region proposal networks. In: Advances in Neural Information Processing Systems, pp. 91–99 (2015)

20. He, K., Zhang, X., Ren, S., Sun, J.: Deep residual learning for image recognition. In: The IEEE Conference on Computer Vision and Pattern Recognition (CVPR), pp. 770–778, June 2016
21. Lin, T.Y., Dollár, P., Girshick, R., He, K., Belongie, S.: Feature pyramid networks for object detection (2016)
22. Woo, S., Park, J., Lee, J.-Y., So Kweon, I.: Cbam: Convolutional block attention module. In: Proceedings of the European Conference on Computer Vision (ECCV), pp. 3–19 (2018)
23. Proenca, H., Filipe, S., Santos, R., Oliveira, J., Alexandre, L.A.: The UBIRIS.v2: a database of visible wavelength images captured on-the-move and at-a-distance. IEEE Trans. PAMI 32(8), 1529–1535 (2010)
24. Biometrics Ideal Test. CASIA.v4-database. http://www.idealtest.org
25. Zhao, Z., Ajay, K.: An accurate iris segmentation framework under relaxed imaging constraints using total variation model. In: The IEEE International Conference on Computer Vision (ICCV), December 2015
26. Tan, T., He, Z., Sun, Z.: Efficient and robust segmentation of noisy iris images for non-cooperative iris recognition. Image Vis. Comput. 28(2), 223–230 (2010). Segmentation of Visible Wavelength Iris Images Captured At-a-distance and On-the-move
27. Tan, C., Kumar, A.: Towards online iris and periocular recognition under relaxed imaging constraints. IEEE Trans. Image Process. 22(10), 3751–3765 (2013)
28. Tan, C., Kumar, A.: Unified framework for automated iris segmentation using distantly acquired face images. IEEE Trans. Image Process. 21(9), 4068–4079 (2012)

Attention to Head Locations
for Crowd Counting

Youmei Zhang[1(✉)], Chunluan Zhou[2], Faliang Chang[3], Alex C. Kot[2],
and Wei Zhang[3]

[1] School of Mathematics and Statistics, Qilu University of Technology
(Shandong Academy of Sciences), Jinan 250353, People's Republic of China
zym5289@gmail.com
[2] Nanyang Technological University, 50 Nanyang Avenue, Singapore, Singapore
[3] School of Control Science and Engineering, Shandong University, Jinan 250061,
People's Republic of China

Abstract. Occlusions, complex backgrounds, scale variations and non-uniform distributions present great challenges for crowd counting in practical applications. In this paper, we propose a novel method using an attention model to exploit head locations which are the most important cue for crowd counting. The attention model estimates a probability map in which high probabilities indicate locations where heads are likely to be present. The estimated probability map is used to suppress non-head regions in feature maps from several multi-scale feature extraction branches of a convolutional neural network for crowd density estimation, which makes our method robust to complex backgrounds, scale variations and non-uniform distributions. Experiments on ShanghaiTech dataset demonstrate the effectiveness of our method.

Keywords: Crowd counting · Convolutional Neural Network · Attention model

1 Introduction

With increasing demands for intelligent video surveillance, public safety and urban planning, improving scene analysis technologies becomes pressing [6]. As an important task of scene analysis, crowd counting has gained more and more attention in recent years for its applications such as crowd control, traffic monitoring and public safety. However, the crowd counting task comes with many challenges such as occlusions, complex backgrounds, non-uniform distributions and variations in scale and perspective [12], as Fig. 1 shows. Many algorithms have been proposed to address these challenges and increase the accuracy of crowd counting [11, 14, 17].

Recent methods based on convolutional neural networks (CNNs) have achieved a significant improvement in crowd counting [12]. A multi-column CNN (MCNN) is proposed in [17] to address the scale-variation problem by using

© Springer Nature Switzerland AG 2019
Y. Zhao et al. (Eds.): ICIG 2019, LNCS 11902, pp. 727–737, 2019.
https://doi.org/10.1007/978-3-030-34110-7_61

(a) Occlusion   (b) Complex background

(c) Scale variation   (d) Non-uniform distribution

Fig. 1. Challenges for crowd counting.

several CNN branches with different receptive fields to extract multi-scale features. A cascaded CNN [10] learns high-level prior which is incorporated into the crowd density estimation branch of the CNN to boost the performance. In [11], both global and local context are exploited to generate high-quality crowd density maps. Despite these methods have achieved promising performance, they neglect one important aspect which could be exploited to further improve the accuracy of crowd counting. These methods do not well exploited head locations in images which are the most important cue for crowd counting. Actually, head locations are usually used to generate ground-truth density maps in crowd counting datasets. Although the generated ground-truth density maps from head locations are used to learn a CNN for regression, these methods do not explicitly give more attention to head regions during training and testing.

In this paper, we propose a novel method to address the above-mentioned limitation. Figure 2 shows the network architecture used in the proposed method. We incorporate an attention model into the MCNN [17] to guide the network to focus on head locations during training and testing. Specifically, the attention model learns a probability map in which high probabilities indicate locations where heads are likely to be present.

The advantage of the proposed method can be summarized as follows:
• We introduce an attention model into the MCNN for crowd counting. By incorporating the attention model into the CNN, the proposed method can filter

most of background regions and body parts, therefore improving its robustness to complex backgrounds and non-uniform distributions.

• The proposed method is robust to variations in scale because of the use of multi-scale feature extraction branches and the capability of the attention model to locate heads of different sizes.

The remainder of the paper is organized as follows. Section 2 presents some related works about crowd counting. In Sect. 3, our proposed attention model convolutional neural network (AM-CNN) is introduced. Experimental results are given and discussed in Sect. 4. Finally, Sect. 5 concludes the paper.

2   Related Work

CNN-based counting approaches have become the main tend for its great success in various computer vision tasks, such as person re-identification [16], object recognition [13] and terrain perception [15]. Inspired by the successful applications of CNN, some researchers began to design CNN architecture fot crowd counting. Early CNN-based counting methods [3,5,18] predict the number of objects instead of density map. Hu et al. [3] exploit a density level classification task to enrich the features, therefore increasing the counting accuracy. Similarly, method in [18] classifies the appearance of the crowds while estimating the counts, which forms auxiliary CNN for crowd counting. Authors of [5] address the appearance change problem by multiplying appearance-weights output by a gating CNN to a mixture of expert CNNs. As aforementioned, estimating the crowd distribution while getting the counts is more applicable in some specific scenarios. Therefore, some researchers attempt to get the counts by density map prediction based on CNN architectures.

Zhang et al. make their first attempt to address the challenge of complex backgrounds by utilizing CNN to estimate the density map, which also denotes the counts by the sum of pixel values. To make use of both high-level semantic information and low-level features, Boominathan et al. [1] makes a combination of deep and shallow, fully convolutional network to estimate the density maps. Some algorithms [7–9,17] are proposed to cater to large variations in scale and perspective. The MCNN [17] presents several CNN branches with different receptive fields, which could extract multi-scale features and enhance the robustness to large variations in people/head size. The Hydra CNN in [7] provides a scale-aware solution to generate the density maps by training the regressor with a pyramid of image patches at multiple scales. To make full use of sharing computations and contextual information, local and global information are leveraged in [9] by learning the counts of both local regions and overall image. Authors of [8] propose a switching-CNN by adding a switch to the MCNN [17]. They utilize an improved version of VGG-16 as the switch classifier to choose a best CNN regressor for the original image. Sindagi et al. [11] aims at generating high quality density maps by using a Fusion CNN to concatenate features extracted by Global Context Estimator (GCE), Local Context Estimator (LCE) and Density Map Estimator (DME). In addition, their counting architecture is trained in a Generative Adversarial Network to get shaper density maps.

3   The Proposed Method

The proposed AM-CNN consists of 3 shallow CNN branches and an attention model. The CNN branches with different receptive fields are firstly exploited to extract multi-scale features. Then the attention model is incorporated to emphasize head locations regardless of the complexity of scenes, the non-uniformity of distributions and the variability of scale and perspective.

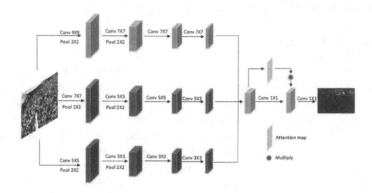

Fig. 2. Architecture of the AM-CNN. The image is firstly fed into three shallow CNN branches to extract multi-scale features. These branches are with different sizes of filters, which can be represented as large (9-7-7-7), medium (7-5-5-5) and small (5-3-3-3). Then the feature maps from different branches are concatenated to generate attention features by the attention model. Since containing 2 max pooling layers in each CNN branches, this architecture finally outputs a density map with 1/4 size of the original image.

3.1   Feature Extraction with Multi-receptive Fields

Some of previous works [7,8,11,17] exploited multi-column networks with different receptive fields to address the variations in scale since different sizes of receptive fields can cope with the diversity in object-size [19]. Inspired by successful use of the MCNN [8,11,17], we select part of it to extract multi-scale features. The multi-column architecture with larger filter sizes or more columns may cater to larger variations in scale, but it brings a time-consuming parameter adjustment task. Since the proposed method mainly focuses on the effect of the attention model for crowd counting, we use the same filter sizes and channels as [17] and [8]. But different from them, the multi-column network in this paper is used to generate high-dimensional feature maps rather than transforming the input into a density map directly.

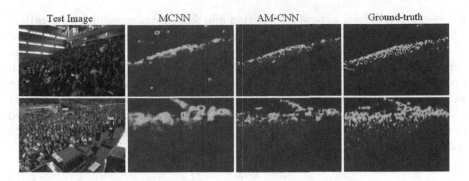

Fig. 3. Density maps generated by different methods. Best viewed in color.

Density maps generated by the MCNN [17] contain complex backgrounds, which impact the counting accuracy seriously. In addition, the distinction between large and small objects is not so obvious in density map, as Fig. 3 shows. The most important cue for crowd counting, head locations, is the key to address the above problems. Therefore, we need an operation to guide the network to give more attention to head locations and suppress non-head regions. In virtue of the strong object-focused capability, an attention model is incorporated into the MCNN and thus forming a new architecture which could generate more accurate density maps. We will describe the attention model in Sect. 3.2.

3.2 The Attention Model for Crowd Counting

Visual attention is an essential mechanism of the human brain for understanding scenes effectively [2]. Therefore, we aim to guide the network selectively focus on head regions when estimating the density maps for crowd counting, no matter how complex the background is and how various the distributions are.

The attention model has been widely used for different tasks with different focuses, e.g. focusing on different patches that relevant to task domain and specific objects for image classification and scene labeling, respectively; focusing on feature maps with different resolutions for image segmentation and focusing on different joints for action recognition. For crowd counting, the attention model could be an effective tool to guide the network focusing on head locations, which are the most important cue for crowd counting. Therefore, an attention model is introduced to identify how much attention to pay to features at different locations. Concretely, we use the attention model to concentrate more on head regions, meanwhile suppressing the background regions and body parts in images.

Herein, we briefly introduce the implementation of the attention model used in this work. Suppose convolutional features in layer i as f^i, the soft attention is generated as:

$$S = \varphi(W \textcircled{c} f^i + b) \tag{1}$$

where φ is a nonlinear activation function and © denotes convolution operation. The attention model aims to identify how much attention to pay to features at different locations, which could be achieved by generating the probability scores with a softmax operation applied to S spatially. Different from traditional AM, we use a Sigmoid function instead of Softmax since the AM is used to learn whether there is head in the location. Then we will get an probability map M from the attention model. Note that M is shared across all channels. The learned probability map is finally multiplied to feature maps in layer $i + 1$ to generate attention features, as Eq. 2 shows:

$$F^{att} = f^{i+1} \odot M \qquad (2)$$

Where $\odot$ denotes element-wise product. Before this operation, the channel of M is expanded as the same as f^{i+1}. F^{att} is the refined attention feature map, which is the feature re-weighted by the probability scores, and has the same size as f^{i+1}. Figure 4 illustrates the detailed implementation of the attention model.

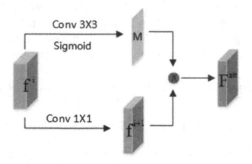

Fig. 4. The attention model

To this end, the trained attention model could adaptively select the relevant positions where the heads are located and assigned them higher weights. This makes the AM-CNN very suitable for crowd counting.

As most of previous methods use Euclidean distance as the loss function for counting task. As Eq. 3 shows:

$$L_{ED} = \frac{1}{N} \sum_{i=1}^{N} (F(X_i, \Theta) - D_i)^2 \qquad (3)$$

Where N is the number of the training samples, D is the ground-truth density map and F is the function that mapping the input X_i to the estimated density map with parameters Θ.

4   Experimental Results

This section presents the experimental results on the ShanghaiTech dataset. For fair comparison, we use 2 standard metrics for evaluation as other CNN-based counting methods did. The 2 metrics are defined as:

$$
MAE = \frac{1}{N} \sum_{i \in N} |y_i - y_i'|,
$$
$$
MSE = \sqrt{\frac{1}{N} \sum_{i \in N} (y_i - y_i')^2}
$$

(4)

Where MAE represents mean absolute error and MSE stands for mean squared error, respectively. y_i is the ground-truth count and y_i' is the estimated count of the AM-CNN for the i-th sample.

We shall first introduce the details of the datasets, and then discuss the counting results. The ShanghaiTech dataset was published in [4], it contains 2 subsets: Part-A mainly consists of dense crowd examples and Part-B mainly focuses on sparse crowd examples. There are 300 training images and 182 testing images in Part-A whereas Part-B contains 400 images for training and 316 for testing. The crowd density varies greatly in this dataset, making the counting task more challenging than other datasets. We compare our method with other 5 recent CNN-based methods in Table 1.

Zhang et al. [14] mainly focus on the cross-scene crowd counting by an operation of candidate scene retrieval. They retrieve images with similar scenes from training data to fine-tune the trained-CNN for target scene. In [10], high-level prior is learned by utilizing feature maps trained for density level classification and thus getting better results than former methods. On the basis of the MCNN [17], which concatenate feature maps with multi-scale receptive fields, Sam et al. [8] train a switch-CNN to select a specific CNN regressor for the images. In addition, they enforced a differential training regimen to tackle the large scale and perspective variations. Their method improves the performance obviously compared with the MCNN. Apart from increasing the counting accuracy by adding contextual information, Sindagi et al. [11] use Generative Adversarial Network to sharper the density maps. Based on the concatenation of multi-scale feature maps, the proposed method exploit an attention model to emphasize head regions when generating the density map. For Part-A which mainly contains dense crowds, the AM-CNN performs better than other methods expect for the CP-CNN [11]. It may result from that the proposed method only uses a density estimator while Sindagi et al. [11] add contextual information which is trained by other two complex structures to their counting architecture. But the addition of contextual information comes with spurt growth of parameters. Images in Part-B mainly focus on sparse crowds, and the proposed AM-CNN gets the state-of-the-art performance on this subset. Density maps illustrated in Figs. 5 and 6 show that the AM-CNN could focus on every specific head regions in sparse crowds, which may result in good performance for sparse crowds. Notably, by integrating an attention model, the proposed method performs much better than the MCNN [17]. The MAEs/MSEs of the AM-CNN for these 2 sub-sets are 20.6/37.0 and 10.2/11.5 lower than that of the MCNN, which demonstrate a significant performance improvement. Overall, the attention model guides the network ignore most of the complex backgrounds and give more attention to head regions.

Table 1. Results on ShanghaiTech dataset

Dataset	Part-A		Part-B	
Method	MAE	MSE	MAE	MSE
Cross-Scene [14]	181.8	277.7	32.0	49.8
MCNN [17]	110.2	173.2	26.4	41.3
Cascaded-MLT [10]	101.3	152.4	20.0	31.1
Switching-CNN [8]	90.4	135.0	21.6	33.4
CP-CNN [11]	73.6	106.4	20.1	30.1
AM-CNN	89.6	136.2	16.2	29.8

4.1   Probability Maps

This section displays the probability maps and density maps to explore the influence of the attention model. Figures 5 and 6 illustrate representative samples from ShanghaiTech dataset. To explore whether the probability maps present higher probability scores in head locations, we overlay them on the original images. As Fig. 6 shows, the AM-CNN could concentrate on specific head regions accurately for sparse crowds. However, for the dense crowds, it can only emphasize the general regions that crowds are located. It is well known that given an image which contains too many objects to concentrate on, humans usually focus on the regions where most of the objects are located. Similarly, it is hard for the attention model to focus on every specific head in a dense crowd, and it concentrates on the region where the crowd is located. The probability and density maps displayed in this section demonstrate that the attention model could roughly filtered complex background regions and body parts before the generation of density maps. As a result, the density maps become clear and head-focused under the effect of the attention model.

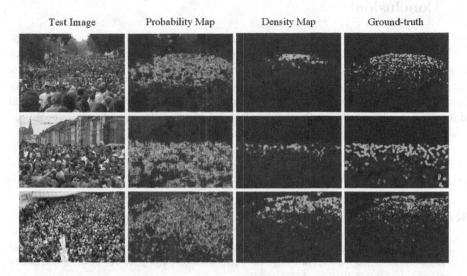

Fig. 5. Probability and density maps of ShanghaiTech-A dataset generated by the AM-CNN. To illustrate the effectiveness of the attention model concisely, we overlay the probability maps on the original images and set the transparency as 0.7, as the second column shows. Best viewed in color.

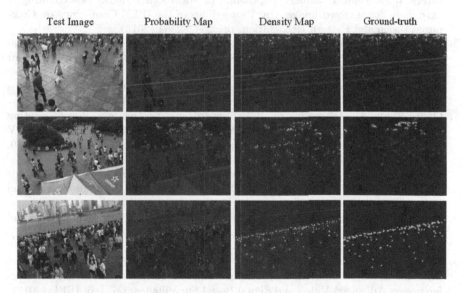

Fig. 6. Probability and density maps of ShanghaiTech-B dataset generated by the AM-CNN. To illustrate the effectiveness of the attention model concisely, we overlay the probability maps on the original images and set the transparency as 0.7, as the second column shows. Best viewed in color.

5   Conclusion

In this paper, we proposed an attention model convolutional neural network (AM-CNN) to well exploit head locations for crowd counting. The architecture explicitly gives more attention to head locations and suppresses non-head regions by exploiting an attention model to generate a probability map which presents higher probability scores in head regions. Experiments on the ShanghaiTech dataset demonstrate the robustness of the AM-CNN to complex backgrounds, scale variations and non-uniform distributions.

Acknowledgment. This work was supported in part by the National Natural Science Foundation of China under Grant61673244, Grant61273277 and Grant61703240.

References

1. Boominathan, L., Kruthiventi, S.S., Babu, R.V.: Crowdnet: a deep convolutional network for dense crowd counting. In: Proceedings of the 2016 ACM on Multimedia Conference, pp. 640–644. ACM (2016)
2. Chu, X., Yang, W., Ouyang, W., Ma, C., Yuille, A.L., Wang, X.: Multi-context attention for human pose estimation. arXiv preprint arXiv:1702.07432 (2017)
3. Hu, Y., Chang, H., Nian, F., Wang, Y., Li, T.: Dense crowd counting from still images with convolutional neural networks. J. Vis. Commun. Image Represent. **38**, 530–539 (2016)
4. Idrees, H., Saleemi, I., Seibert, C., Shah, M.: Multi-source multi-scale counting in extremely dense crowd images. In: Proceedings of the IEEE Conference on Computer Vision and Pattern Recognition, pp. 2547–2554 (2013)
5. Kumagai, S., Hotta, K., Kurita, T.: Mixture of counting CNNs: adaptive integration of cnns specialized to specific appearance for crowd counting. arXiv preprint arXiv:1703.09393 (2017)
6. Li, T., Chang, H., Wang, M., Ni, B., Hong, R., Yan, S.: Crowded scene analysis: a survey. IEEE Trans. Circuits Syst. Video Technol. **25**(3), 367–386 (2015)
7. Oñoro-Rubio, D., López-Sastre, R.J.: Towards perspective-free object counting with deep learning. In: Leibe, B., Matas, J., Sebe, N., Welling, M. (eds.) ECCV 2016. LNCS, vol. 9911, pp. 615–629. Springer, Cham (2016). https://doi.org/10.1007/978-3-319-46478-7_38
8. Sam, D.B., Surya, S., Babu, R.V.: Switching convolutional neural network for crowd counting. In: Proceedings of the IEEE Conference on Computer Vision and Pattern Recognition, vol. 1, p. 6 (2017)
9. Shang, C., Ai, H., Bai, B.: End-to-end crowd counting via joint learning local and global count. In: 2016 IEEE International Conference on Image Processing (ICIP), pp. 1215–1219. IEEE (2016)
10. Sindagi, V.A., Patel, V.M.: Cnn-based cascaded multi-task learning of high-level prior and density estimation for crowd counting. In: 14th IEEE International Conference on Advanced Video and Signal Based Surveillance, pp. 1–6. IEEE (2017)
11. Sindagi, V.A., Patel, V.M.: Generating high-quality crowd density maps using contextual pyramid CNNs. In: 2017 IEEE International Conference on Computer Vision (ICCV), pp. 1879–1888. IEEE (2017)
12. Sindagi, V.A., Patel, V.M.: A survey of recent advances in CNN-based single image crowd counting and density estimation. Pattern Recogn. Lett. **107**, 3–16 (2018)

13. Yu, T., Meng, J., Yuan, J.: Multi-view harmonized bilinear network for 3d object recognition. In: Proceedings of the IEEE Conference on Computer Vision and Pattern Recognition, pp. 186–194 (2018)
14. Zhang, C., Li, H., Wang, X., Yang, X.: Cross-scene crowd counting via deep convolutional neural networks. In: Proceedings of the IEEE Conference on Computer Vision and Pattern Recognition, pp. 833–841 (2015)
15. Zhang, W., Chen, Q., Zhang, W., He, X.: Long-range terrain perception using convolutional neural networks. Neurocomputing **275**, 781–787 (2018)
16. Zhang, W., Ma, B., Liu, K., Huang, R.: Video-based pedestrian re-identification by adaptive spatio-temporal appearance model. IEEE Trans. Image Process. **26**(4), 2042–2054 (2017)
17. Zhang, Y., Zhou, D., Chen, S., Gao, S., Ma, Y.: Single-image crowd counting via multi-column convolutional neural network. In: Proceedings of the IEEE Conference on Computer Vision and Pattern Recognition, pp. 589–597 (2016)
18. Zhang, Y., Chang, F., Wang, M., Zhang, F., Han, C.: Auxiliary learning for crowd counting via count-net. Neurocomputing **273**, 190–198 (2018)
19. Zhou, B., Khosla, A., Lapedriza, A., Oliva, A., Torralba, A.: Object detectors emerge in deep scene CNNs. arXiv preprint arXiv:1412.6856 (2014)

Optimization of Excess Bounding Boxes in Micro-part Detection and Segmentation

Yining Qian and Fei Chen[✉]

College of Mathematics and Computer Science, Fuzhou University,
Fuzhou 350116, Fujian, China
qian_yi_ning@foxmail.com, chenfei314@fzu.edu.cn

Abstract. As an important application field for object detection and instance segmentation, industrial inspection has attracted more and more attention from the manufacturing industry in recent years. Improving the performance of existing algorithms in the field of industrial inspection has many advantages such as reducing costs and increasing safety. In this paper, we select the four most representative types of watch parts and use them to build a micro-part dataset for training. Given a test image with small parts, the learned model can detect and segment all parts effectively. In addition, by optimization of excess bounding boxes, we modify the NMS and propose a novel loss function to solve the problem on the number of bounding boxes that arise during the procedure of detection and segmentation. Experimental results on the micro-part dataset demonstrate that our method can reduce the number of error bounding box and improve the performance on detection and segmentation in contrast to Mask R-CNN.

Keywords: Instance segmentation · Micro-part dataset · NMS · Mask R-CNN

1 Introduction

In the related field of the clock and watch manufacturing, mechanical parts with small size and large difference in shape often appear on the assembly line. These different types of parts are often mixed with each other and difficult to distinguish manually. Improving the performance of the existing instance segmentation algorithm on mechanical parts not only saves labor, reduces costs, but also has important significance for the convenience and accuracy of subsequent inventory of the pipeline. To achieve this goal, as Fig. 1, we collect and label a micro-part dataset which targeting four types of watch parts, and train an instance segmentation model with this dataset.

This work is supported by the National Natural Science Foundation of China (61771141), the Natural Science Foundation of Fujian Province (2017J01751), and the Seed Foundation of Tianjin University & Fuzhou University (TF-1902).

ⓒ Springer Nature Switzerland AG 2019
Y. Zhao et al. (Eds.): ICIG 2019, LNCS 11902, pp. 738–749, 2019.
https://doi.org/10.1007/978-3-030-34110-7_62

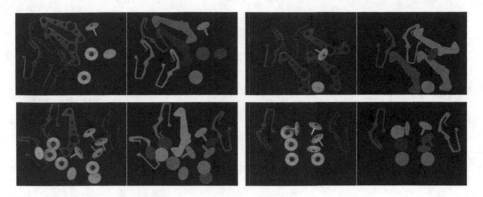

Fig. 1. Four samples in micro-parts dataset

Unlike object segmentation [2,19] and semantic segmentation, which only classifies each pixel of an image, the instance segmentation task must distinguish pixels belonging to the same category according to their corresponding targets. In view of the property that be able to distinguish different instances, instance segmentation contains the elements of the object detection. Therefore, it is similar to detecting the results of semantic segmentation, or the semantic segmentation of each object detection result. Mask R-CNN [8] involved in this article is one of the best algorithms based on the latter thought.

However, when Mask R-CNN is used to perform instance segmentation on the micro-part dataset, two kinds of abnormal detection appear in the result, as shown in the Fig. 2, where G_1 and G_2 are groundtruth detection boxes, and P_1 and P_2 are predicted boxes corresponding to G_1, P_3 and P_4 are predicted boxes corresponding to G_2. In the first case (Fig. 2a), for the same target, when the detection network produces a more accurate detection box P_1, it also incorrectly produces a false box P_2 that its area is smaller than P_1 and it is almost surrounded by P_1. In the second case (Fig. 2b), for the same target, the detection network incorrectly produces two false detection box P_3, P_4 whose area is smaller than the groundtruth box. They overlap less with each other, and they are similar to the split from the groundtruth box.

We will optimize these two situations by improving the structure and parameters of network. The main work of this paper is:

Firstly, we collect and label the micro-part dataset which targeting four types of watch parts for instance segmentation; Secondly, we solve the problem about the number of bounding box that arise during the process of Mask R-CNN by improving the network structure; Thirdly, according to the prior knowledge of mechanical parts in the dataset, such as size, shape [3,18] and distribution [4], we adjust the network parameters of Mask R-CNN to improve its performance on the micro-part dataset.

By comparing the results before and after the changes of the network, we can prove that the improved network has a significant optimization on the micro-part dataset.

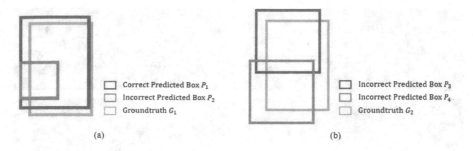

(a)   (b)

Fig. 2. Two kinds of abnormal detection

2 Related Work

2.1 Mask R-CNN

By merging the semantic segmentation framework FCN [13] (full convolutional network) into the object detection framework Faster R-CNN [14], Mask R-CNN achieves a fine combination of these two algorithms. As the fundamental structure, here are some brief introduction about Faster R-CNN and FCN.

The overall structure of the Faster R-CNN consists of two parts. The first part is the regional suggestion network RPN. After inputting image, classification and bounding box regression according to the IOU (Intersection over Union) are performed on a large number of anchors generated by each pixel of the image, and finally many candidate detection boxes which closer to the groundtruth boxes are extracted as outputs. The second part is Fast R-CNN [7], which includes the classification branch and the bounding box regression branch. After extracting the feature map of the input image, RoIPool layer of the network will extract the part, which corresponds a candidate detection box in the feature map, and the part will be further classified and bounding box regressed. According to the comparison from recent research [10], Faster R-CNN using the residual network model [9] as the feature extraction network has the highest accuracy in the object detection frameworks.

The FCN implements an end-to-end network structure by removing the fully connected layer in the classification model to classify each pixel in the image. Mask R-CNN applies the two-stage structure from Faster R-CNN. In order to implement the function of instance segmentation, Mask R-CNN adds the FCN to the second part of Faster R-CNN as a mask branch in parallel with the original classification and regression branches. This branch takes the candidate detection box and the feature map obtained by the RPN as input, extracts corresponding part of the detection box on the whole feature map via RoIAlign layer, then uses the groundtruth mask as a label to train the full convolution network. The loss function of Mask R-CNN is:

$$L = L_{cls} + L_{box} + L_{mask} \tag{1}$$

where L_{cls} is the classification loss, L_{box} is the bounding box regression loss, and L_{mask} is the mask loss, that is, the total loss function L is the sum of the respective loss functions of classification, bounding box regression and mask. Among them, L_{cls} and L_{box} are the same as in Faster R-CNN basically, but for L_{mask}, it is different from the cross entropy loss with multi-class (depending on the total number of classes) used in the FCN, Mask R-CNN uses the two-class cross entropy loss. The reason is that the rough classification has been performed in the RPN, and the mask branch only need to perform the two-class classification on the pixels of the candidate detection box according to the classification result. This structure can well shield the effect of the inter-class competition, and then the precision of instance segmentation is well improved.

2.2 NMS

In the object detection task, since the anchors layer inevitably generates a large number of detection bounding boxes with high overlap, it is necessary to perform non-maximum suppression [15]. The NMS calculates the IoU between the detection box with highest classification score and the remaining detection boxes of the same class, and removes the box whose IoU is higher than threshold to reduce the overlap. When the calculation of the box whose classification score is the highest is over, move that box to the output list. Repeat the above process until there are no remaining boxes.

In the related research of NMS, Soft-NMS [1] showed us that the network can improve performance without retraining existing models by modifying the suppression rules of NMS.

3   Proposed Method

3.1   Analysis on Failure Cases

Figures 3 and 4 show the typical situations of abnormal detection. In Fig. 3, when the network outputs a correct box P_1, it also generates a false box P_2 which is almost included in P_1. In Fig. 4, the network erroneously outputs two false boxes P_3 and P_4, which are small in area and less overlapped with each other.

For convenience of description, the first case is referred to as S_1 (Fig. 3), and the second case is S_2 (Fig. 4). For detection, the above cases will result in a situation that more targets being detected than the true value, which will affect the detection accuracy and cause serious interference to the application which counts number of parts through the object detection. For segmentation, the above cases have no effect on the normal generation of the masks of P_1 to P_4, and the overlaps between masks will complement each other, so the effect on the final mask accuracy is small.

For S_1, it may be caused by NMS failure. When S_1 occurs, it may be due to P_1 containing P_2, and the area of P_2 is too small, then the IoU between P_1 and P_2 is smaller than the IoU threshold in NMS. It causes that P_2 is not suppressed

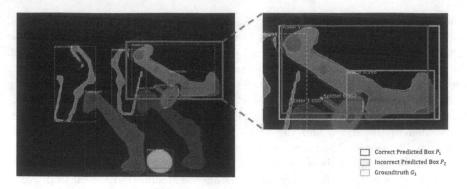

Fig. 3. S_1: when the network outputs a correct box P_1, it also outputs a false box P_2

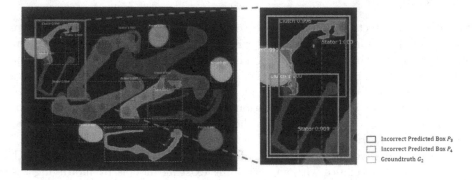

Fig. 4. S_2: the network erroneously outputs two false boxes P_3 and P_4

by NMS. If this argument is tenable, S_1 can be solved by decreasing the NMS threshold.

However, it found by experiment that adjusting the NMS threshold in the detection process can not completely solve S_1. When the threshold is greatly reduced, although the frequency of occurrence of S_1 can be reduced, if there is a neighboring target P_{ner} next to P_1, the IoU of P_1 and P_{ner} may be larger than the reduced threshold. It will cause P_1 to be erroneously suppressed. Therefore, more effective improvements are needed to solve S_1.

For S_2, it usually happens that when the target with fail detection is partially blocked by other target, it looks like the groundtruth bounding box is divided into P_3 and P_4 by other groundtruth box. The classification scores of P_3 and P_4 whose position is not accurate enough that calculated by network are too high, which cause them to become the standard for suppression. At the same time, because the overlap between P_3 and P_4 is usually small, NMS cannot suppress one of them according to their IoU and threshold, which result in the appearing of two incomplete wrong bounding box.

3.2   Optimization of Excess Bounding Boxes

For S_1, we improves the performance of detection by modifying the process of NMS (Algorithm 1). When the NMS filters the bounding box with the same class according to the IoU between the box with highest classification score and the remaining boxes, we calculate the intersection over min-area (IoMA) between them, that is,

$$IoMA = \frac{area(B_i \cap B_j)}{min(area(B_i), area(B_j))} \tag{2}$$

where B_i and B_j are any two detection boxes of the same class. The result of IoMA indicates the proportion of the overlapping area between the two boxes in the area of box whose area is smaller.

If the IoMA is larger than a threshold δ which is a relatively larger preset value (in this paper, $\delta \geq 0.8$), it can be considered that the smaller box is included in the larger box. According to the prior knowledge of this dataset, the sizes of the parts with same class is very close, the size of bounding boxes is also very close, and there is no possibility of a large degree of inclusion between two boxes. Therefore, the situation at this time can be considered as S_1, and the box with a lower classification score (usually a box with a smaller area) is an unnecessary false bounding box, and S_1 can be solved by eliminating that box.

For S_2, by adding a loss function $L_{distance}$, we reduces the distance and increase the overlap between the bounding boxes which corresponding to a same target. For a single image, we define $P_+ = \{P\}$ for all positive samples anchors (IoU > 0.5), $G_{all} = \{G\}$ for all groundtruth boxes. Then for an anchor $P \in P_+$, we can calculate the IoU between it and all the groundtruth boxes G_{all} by the following formula [17], and take a groundtruth box with the largest IoU as the target G^P corresponding to P:

$$G^P = argmax_{G \in G_{all}} IoU(G, P) \tag{3}$$

According to their corresponding G^P, P_+ can be divided into $|G_{all}|$ groups, that is, $P_+ = P_1 \cap P_2 \cap ... \cap P_{|G_{all}|}$. For two overlapping boxes $B_i^{P_a}$ and $B_j^{P_a}$ which are selected randomly from a same group corresponding to P_a, we hope that the IoU between them will increase as large as possible. Therefore, with reference to the repulsion loss L_{RepBox} [17], the loss function $L_{distance}$ is designed as follows:

$$L_{distance} = \frac{\sum_{P_a \in P_+, i \neq j} Smooth_{-ln}(IoU(B_i^{P_a}, B_j^{P_a}))}{\sum_{P_a \in P_+, i \neq j} \mathbf{1}[IoU(B_i^{P_a}, B_j^{P_a}) > 0] + \epsilon} \tag{4}$$

$$Smooth_{-ln}(x) = \begin{cases} -\ln x & x \geq \delta \\ -\frac{x-\delta}{\delta} - \ln x & x < \delta \end{cases} \tag{5}$$

Where P_a represents a any group of anchors corresponding to a same groundtruth box, and B^{P_a} is the set of predicted boxes corresponding to P_a. $B_i^{P_a}$ and $B_j^{P_a}$ represent any two predicted boxes in the B^{P_a}. $\mathbf{1}$ is an indication function. To prevent the denominator from being zero, a small constant ϵ is added.

Algorithm 1. IoMA-NMS

Input: B= $\{b_1,...,b_N\}$,S= $\{s_1,...,s_N\}$, N_t, δ
     B is the list of initial detection boxes
     S contains corresponding detection scores
     N_t is the NMS threshold
     δ is the IoMA-NMS threshold
Output: list of detection boxes D, list of corresponding detection scores S
1: initialize D={}
2: **while** $B \neq empty$ **do**
3:    $m \leftarrow argmaxS$
4:    $M \leftarrow b_m$
5:    $D \leftarrow D \cup M; B \leftarrow B - M$
6:    **for** b_i in B **do**
7:        **if** $iou(M,b_i) \geq N_t$ **or** $ioma(M,b_i) \geq \delta$ **then**
8:            $B \leftarrow B - b_i; S \leftarrow S - s_i$
9:        **end if**
10:   **end for**
11: **end while**

$Smooth_{-ln}(x)$ is obtained by $Smooth_{ln}(x)$ [17] fliped along straight line $x = 0.5$. $Smooth_{ln}(x)$ is monotonically increasing, then $Smooth_{-ln}(x)$ is monotonically decreasing. In L_{RepBox}, the purpose of applying $Smooth_{ln}(x)$ is to minimize the IoU of the two input boxes by reducing the IoU as the L_{RepBox} is minimized. In this paper, the purpose of $L_{distance}$ is to make the IoU increase as much as possible. Therefore, by applying $Smooth_{-ln}(x)$ which was monotonically decreasing, the IoU is increased with the minimization of $L_{distance}$, so as to maximize the IoU between the input boxes. Referring to $\delta = 0$ in L_{RepBox}, we take $\delta = 1$ in $L_{distance}$.

$$Smooth_{ln}(x) = \begin{cases} -\ln(1-x) & x \leq \delta \\ \frac{x-\delta}{1-\delta} - \ln(1-\delta) & x > \delta \end{cases} \tag{6}$$

As the above formula, minimizing $L_{distance}$ will increase the IoU between any two overlapping boxes generated for a same target, so that their degree of overlap is increased as much as possible, thereby increasing the sensitivity of NMS to them, and finally remove the predicted box whose classification score is smaller through NMS. The final total loss function is as follows:

$$L = L_{cls} + L_{box} + L_{mask} + \alpha \cdot L_{distance} \tag{7}$$

4 Experiment

4.1 Dataset

As the basis of the research, we collected 550 images of 3664×2748 pixels about the parts of watches and scaled them to 512×384 pixels to improve the speed of training. Among these, 339 images were taken on a black background, and the backgrounds of remaining 211 images were replaced with white. During the process of collection, the balance of four classes and the diversity of the state of the parts are guaranteed as much as possible, to reduce the interference caused by background color, state of the parts, distribution of classes and so on.

We randomly selected 478 images for training, 48 images for validation and the rest for testing. In order to avoid over-fitting and other problems caused by the number of training data, we performed a series of augmentation on the dataset before training and testing, including multi-directional flip, rotation, pixel multiplication and Gaussian blur.

4.2 Parameter Settings

The Number of Anchors and ROIs for each Training Image. As a general-purpose instance segmentation model, MS COCO dataset [12] is used as a standard training set of Mask R-CNN. Such dataset have a large number of images with a bright background, their targets are mostly pedestrians, animals, and vehicles, and some of images contain a large number of targets that should be detected. In order to ensure that targets are detected as many as possible, the original Mask R-CNN sets a lots of anchors and RoIs for a single image (256 and 200).

According to the Hard Negative Mining strategy [7,16] obtained from previous experience, the decrease of detection accuracy is well avoided when the ratio of positive and negative samples is close to 1:3. However, in the dataset used herein, the single image contains a constant range of targets, and the maximum value is usually less than 20 due to the size of the part. If the original training parameters is still used, the RPN cannot produce enough positive samples to maintain a 1:3 positive-negative sample ratio, resulting in a decrease in accuracy.

Therefore, in our experiments, according to the prior knowledge [2–4,18,19] that the range of targets is constant, we reduce the number of training anchors to 128 and the number of RoIs to 50 for a single image. The experimental results show that this modification can improve the overall performance (Tables 1 and 2).

Preference of FPN Feature Layer. Mask R-CNN uses a ResNet-based FPN network [11] as a feature extraction network. Similar to the effect of DENets which integrates the deep hierarchical context of image and the local optic disc region [6], the FPN fuses and outputs multi-scale feature layers by performing top-down side concatenation on the bottom-up convolution results. In Mask R-CNN, there are five levels of feature maps from P_2 to P_6. RoIs of different scales should use the FPN feature layer of its corresponding scale as the input of the RoIAlign layer, and the corresponding relationship is determined by the K value:

$$k = \lfloor k_0 + \log_2(\frac{\sqrt{wh}}{\rho}) \rfloor \qquad (8)$$

Table 1. The improvement of changing number of anchors

Number of anchors	Precision	Recall	AP_{50}	AP
256	77.6	52.2	75.0	38.2
128	77.7	53.2	76.1	35.4

Table 2. The improvement of changing number of RoIs

Number of RoIs	Precision	Recall	AP_{50}	AP
200	77.7	53.2	76.1	35.4
50	82.5	54.6	84.5	44.5

Where k_0 is the initial number of level, the default is 5, which is the P_5 layer, w and h are the width and height of the current RoIs region, and finally the Pk layer is selected as the input of the RoIAlign layer.

In the original formula, $\rho = 224$, which corresponding to the standard width and height of the images in ImageNet [5]. It is still different from the zoomed height and height of the dataset involved in this paper, which may cause the mismatch between RoIs and feature layer. So we changed this parameter to 384 during the experiment, corresponding to the smaller side length of this dataset. The experimental results show that this modification can better match the RoIs and FPN feature layers, and the evaluation results are improved (Table 3).

Table 3. The improvement of changing ρ

ρ	Precision	Recall	AP_{50}	AP
224	82.5	54.6	84.5	44.5
384	83.2	56.7	87.6	46.5

4.3   Results

As shown in Fig. 5(a) and (b), according to IoMA-NMS, when the overlap between two bounding boxes with a same class is too high, the box with a smaller classification score is removed. The problem that network outputs repeated predicted boxes (S_1) is well suppressed and the number of predicted boxes is no longer more than the number of groundtruth.

As shown in Fig. 5(c) and (d), by adding $L_{distance}$, the S_2 problem that originally appeared in the result is improved to a certain extent, and the distance between the two overlapping boxes is generally reduced. The IoU between them increases, making the NMS more sensitive to them, which make some redundant fail predicted boxes correctly removed. It also correct the number of predicted box in results, which improve the performance of segmentation.

Table 4. The improvement of changing network structure

Methods	Precision	Recall	AP_{50}	AP
Mask R-CNN	83.2	56.7	87.6	46.5
Ours	84.8	54.7	88.0	48.2

Table 5. Comparison of different methods

Methods	Precision	Recall	AP_{50}	AP
Mask R-CNN	77.6	52.2	75.0	38.2
Ours	84.8	54.7	88.0	48.2

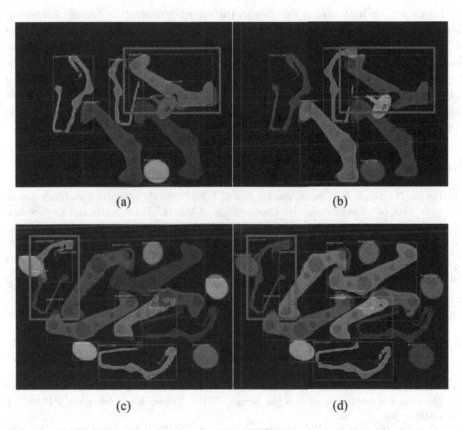

Fig. 5. The (a) and (b) show the improvement of S_1, and (c) and (d) show the improvement of S_2

As shown in Table 4, comparing the improved network structure with the Mask R-CNN adjusted with the above parameters, it can be found that the results are improved in most of the instance segmentation evaluation criteria. This shows that the improvement of the network structure is effective for improving the performance of segmentation.

As shown in Table 5, compared with original Mask R-CNN, our approach with optimization in parameter and structure has better accuracy, recall and accuracy on the micro-part dataset. And the problem that original network outputs too many predicted boxes is also well solved in this paper, which will help to improve the efficiency of the inventory management about workpieces.

5 Conclusion

In this paper, we have built a micro-part instance segmentation dataset targeting four types of watch parts, and used prior knowledge to optimize the performance of Mask R-CNN in this dataset by adjusting the anchors, RoIs number and FPN feature layer selection rule. Meanwhile, for two problems that caused the network to output too many predicted boxes in the process of segmentation, we propose the IoMA-NMS based on NMS and a new loss function to solve. From the above improvements, the performance of Mask R-CNN on the micro-part dataset is optimized, and the detection about the quantity of objects is more accurate.

References

1. Bodla, N., Singh, B., Chellappa, R., Davis, L.S.: Soft-NMS-improving object detection with one line of code. In: Proceedings of the IEEE International Conference on Computer Vision, pp. 5561–5569 (2017)
2. Chen, F., Yu, H., Hu, R.: Shape sparse representation for joint object classification and segmentation. IEEE Trans. Image Process. 22(3), 992–1004 (2012)
3. Chen, F., Yu, H., Hu, R., Zeng, X.: Deep learning shape priors for object segmentation. In: Proceedings of the IEEE Conference on Computer Vision and Pattern Recognition, pp. 1870–1877 (2013)
4. Chen, F., Yu, H., Yao, J., Hu, R.: Robust sparse kernel density estimation by inducing randomness. Pattern Anal. Appl. 18(2), 367–375 (2015)
5. Deng, J., Dong, W., Socher, R., Li, L.J., Li, K., Fei-Fei, L.: ImageNet: a large-scale hierarchical image database. In: 2009 IEEE Conference on Computer Vision and Pattern Recognition, pp. 248–255. IEEE (2009)
6. Fu, H., Cheng, J., Xu, Y., Zhang, C., Cao, X.: Disc-aware ensemble network for glaucoma screening from fundus image. IEEE Trans. Med. Imaging PP(99), 1 (2018)
7. Girshick, R.: Fast R-CNN. In: Proceedings of the IEEE International Conference on Computer Vision, pp. 1440–1448 (2015)
8. He, K., Gkioxari, G., Dollár, P., Girshick, R.: Mask R-CNN. In: Proceedings of the IEEE International Conference on Computer Vision, pp. 2961–2969 (2017)
9. He, K., Zhang, X., Ren, S., Sun, J.: Deep residual learning for image recognition. In: Proceedings of the IEEE Conference on Computer Vision and Pattern Recognition, pp. 770–778 (2016)

10. Huang, J., et al.: Speed/accuracy trade-offs for modern convolutional object detectors. In: Proceedings of the IEEE Conference on Computer Vision and Pattern Recognition, pp. 7310–7311 (2017)
11. Lin, T.Y., Dollár, P., Girshick, R., He, K., Hariharan, B., Belongie, S.: Feature pyramid networks for object detection. In: Proceedings of the IEEE Conference on Computer Vision and Pattern Recognition, pp. 2117–2125 (2017)
12. Lin, T.-Y., et al.: Microsoft COCO: common objects in context. In: Fleet, D., Pajdla, T., Schiele, B., Tuytelaars, T. (eds.) ECCV 2014. LNCS, vol. 8693, pp. 740–755. Springer, Cham (2014). https://doi.org/10.1007/978-3-319-10602-1_48
13. Long, J., Shelhamer, E., Darrell, T.: Fully convolutional networks for semantic segmentation. In: Proceedings of the IEEE Conference on Computer Vision and Pattern Recognition, pp. 3431–3440 (2015)
14. Ren, S., He, K., Girshick, R., Sun, J.: Faster R-CNN: towards real-time object detection with region proposal networks. In: Advances in Neural Information Processing Systems, pp. 91–99 (2015)
15. Rosenfeld, A., Thurston, M.: Edge and curve detection for visual scene analysis. IEEE Trans. Comput. 5, 562–569 (1971)
16. Shrivastava, A., Gupta, A., Girshick, R.: Training region-based object detectors with online hard example mining. In: Proceedings of the IEEE Conference on Computer Vision and Pattern Recognition, pp. 761–769 (2016)
17. Wang, X., Xiao, T., Jiang, Y., Shao, S., Sun, J., Shen, C.: Repulsion loss: detecting pedestrians in a crowd. In: Proceedings of the IEEE Conference on Computer Vision and Pattern Recognition, pp. 7774–7783 (2018)
18. Zeng, X., Chen, F., Wang, M.: Shape group Boltzmann machine for simultaneous object segmentation and action classification. Pattern Recogn. Lett. 111, 43–50 (2018)
19. Zeng, X., Chen, F., Wang, M., Lai, C.H.: Circulant dissimilarity-based shape registration for object segmentation. Int. J. Comput. Math. 96(4), 753–766 (2019)

Dual-Cross Patterns with RPCA of Key Frame for Facial Micro-expression Recognition

Xinhe Yu, Zhihua Xie$^{(\boxtimes)}$, and Wenjun Zong

Key Lab of Optic-Electronic and Communication, Jiangxi Sciences and Technology Normal
University, Nanchang, Jiangxi, China
xie_zhihua68@aliyun.com

Abstract. Fast and discriminative feature extraction has always been a critical issue for spontaneous micro-expression recognition applications. In this paper, a micro-expression analysis framework based on new facial representation is proposed. Firstly, to remove redundant information in the micro-expression video sequences, the key frame is adaptively selected on the criteria of structural similarity index (SSIM) between different face images. Then, robust principal component analysis (RPCA) obtains the sparse information of the Key frame, which not only retains the expression attributes of the micro-expression sequence, but also eliminates useless information. Furthermore, we use Dual-cross patterns (DCP) to extract features of sparse key frame. Repeated comparison experiments were performed on the SMIC database to evaluate the performance of the method. Experimental results demonstrate that our proposed method achieves promising performance for micro-expression recognition.

Keywords: Micro-expression recognition · Key frame · Robust principal component analysis · Dual-cross patterns · Feature extraction

1 Introduction

In recent years, micro-expressions have received more and more attention. In many cases, people hide, camouflage or suppress their true emotions [1], so they produce partial, fast facial expressions, which we call micro-expressions. Compared to ordinary expressions, the short duration of micro-expressions is a typical feature, usually they last 1/25 s to 1/3 s [2]. In addition, micro-expressions have potential uses in many areas, such as national security, interrogation, and medical care. It should be noted that only trained people can distinguish micro-expressions, but even after training, the recognition rate is only 47% [3]. Therefore, the research of micro-expression recognition is of great significance.

Previous research on facial expressions focused on facial micro-expressions [4] found in macroscopic expressions. In recent years, spontaneous facial expressions have attracted more and more researchers' attention. The recognition of micro-expressions requires a large amount of data for training and modeling, but it is difficult for non-professionals to collect data, which is also the difficulty of micro-expression recognition.

Y. Zhao et al. (Eds.): ICIG 2019, LNCS 11902, pp. 750–759, 2019.
https://doi.org/10.1007/978-3-030-34110-7_63

Commonly used spontaneous micro-expression data sets are: SMIC [5] of the University of Oulu and CASME [6], CASME2 [7] of the Chinese Academy of Sciences. The SMIC dataset consists of three subsets of HS, VIS, and NIR captured by a high-speed camera, a normal camera, and a near-infrared camera, respectively.

The object of micro-expression processing is a video clip, and a gray-scale video clip can be regarded as 3D, and many micro-expression algorithms focus on extracting 3D texture features. Local binary pattern from three orthogonal planes (LBP-TOP) [8] is an extension of LBP in three-dimensional space and is widely used in micro-expression analysis. Since then, LBP-TOP has proven to be effective in micro-expression recognition, and many researchers have proposed improvements based on LBP-TOP. For example, Huang et al. proposed a Completed Local Quantized Pattern (CLQP) [9] to reduce the dimensions of features. Subsequently, an integral projection method based on a difference image (STLBP-IP) [10] is also proposed. This method first obtains the difference image of the micro-expression sequence, and then uses the integral projection method to combine the LBP to obtain the feature vector. In 2017, Huang et al. [11] proposed an RPCA-based integral projection (STLBP-RIP) method for identifying spontaneous micro-expressions. This method has better performance than other methods.

In this paper, we present a new algorithm Dual-cross patterns with RPCA of Key frame (DCP-RKF) for feature extraction of micro-expressions. For each video sequence, starting frames and ending frames are used as standard frames, and structural similarity index (SSIM) [12] is used to find key frames in the video sequence. Sparse information is extracted from key frames using RPCA, and feature extraction is performed using DCP [13].

2 Key Frame Based on Structural Similarity (SSIM)

The spatial domain SSIM index is based on similarities of local luminance, contrast, and structure between reference and distorted image. In fact, because it is a symmetric measure, it can be thought of as a similarity measure for comparing any two signals [16]. Given two image x and y, SSIM index is defined as

$$SSIM(x, y) = \frac{(2\mu_x\mu_y + c_1)(2\delta_{xy} + c_2)}{(\mu_x^2 + \mu_y^2 + c_1)(\delta_x^2 + \delta_y^2 + c_2)} \tag{1}$$

Where μ_x, μ_y are the pixel average of the image x and y, σ_x^2 and σ_y^2 are the variance of x, y, σ_{xy} is the covariance of x, y. c_1 and c_2 are used to maintain stability when the pixel average are close to zero. By default, $c_1 = (0.01 * L)^2$, $c_2 = (0.03 * L)^2$, where L is the specified 'Dynamic Range' value. SSIM range from 0 to 1, when the two images are identical, the value of SSIM is equal to 1.

The pioneering work by Wang et al. [12] showed that SSIM-motivated optimization for video coding played a very important role in video processing, which is more relative to micro-expression recognition.

For micro-expression video sequence, the traditional feature extraction method is to consider the entire sequence or part of it for reproduction. There are always problems with alignment, lighting, etc. in the micro-expression database, so too much data is the bane of accurate identification [14]. A novel proposition is presented in this paper, whereby we utilize only one image per video, called key frame. The key frame of a video contains the highest intensity of expression changes among all frames, while the onset and offset frame is the perfect choice of a reference frame with neutral expression and SSIM is used to extract key frame.

Given a micro-expression video sequence $f_i|i = 1, \ldots, n$, R_1 and R_2 are the reference frames of this sequence which are the first and last frames, respectively, defined as $R_1 = f_1$, $R_2 = f_n$. For each frame in the video sequence, the total SSIM is represented as:

$$TSSIM_i = SSIM_{1i} + SSIM_{2i} = SSIM(f_i, R_1) + SSIM(f_i, R_2) \tag{2}$$

Combine the previously proposed SSIM index (Eq. (1)), Eq. (2) can be re-defined as:

$$TSSIM_i = \frac{(2\mu_{f_i}\mu_{R_1} + c_1)(2\delta_{f_i R_1} + c_2)}{(\mu_{f_i}^2 + \mu_{R_1}^2 + c_1)(\sigma_{f_i}^2 + \sigma_{R_1}^2 + c_1)} + \frac{(2\mu_{f_i}\mu_{R_2} + c_1)(2\delta_{f_i R_2} + c_2)}{(\mu_{f_i}^2 + \mu_{R_2}^2 + c_1)(\sigma_{f_i}^2 + \sigma_{R_2}^2 + c_1)} \tag{3}$$

Where $i = 2, 3, \cdots, (n-1)$. According to the definition of total SSIM, we can get TSSIM except for the first and last frames. Finally, by comparing the size of TSSIM, can get key frame. We think that TSSIM value is the smallest, that is, the frame with the largest difference compared with the reference frame is the key frame.

$$keyframe = f_i = \min\{TSSIM_i\} \tag{4}$$

3   Sparse Information Extracted from Key Frame Using RPCA

Although the key frame based on structural similarity preserves the main information of different micro-expression and discriminative ability, it also has a lot of facial information. Just as STLBP-IP [10] considers video clips from difference image method can well characterize the different micro-expression. Next, we exploit the nature of STLBP-IP to get the motion feature from the robust principal component analysis.

Based on Eq. 4, we can obtain the key frame of any video sequence. For convenience, we denote it as M. First we know that M is a large data matrix and the data are characterized by low-rank subspaces, so it may be decomposed as

$$M = L_0 + S_0 \tag{5}$$

Where L_0 is a low-rank matrix and S_0 is sparse matrix, aiming at recovering S_0. This problem can be solved by tractable convex optimization. Equation 5 is formulated as follows

$$\min \|L\|_* + \lambda \|S\|_1 \Leftrightarrow \textbf{subject to } L + S = M \tag{6}$$

Where $\|.\|_*$ denotes the nuclear norm, which is the sum of its singular values, λ is a positive weighting parameter. The iterative threshold technique minimizes the combination of the L_0 norm and the 'nuclear' norm, and the scheme converges very slowly.

Now discuss the Augmented Lagrangian Multiplier (ALM). The ALM method operates on the augmented Lagrangian

$$l(L, S, Y) = ||L||_* + \lambda ||S||_1 + \langle Y, M - L - S \rangle + \frac{\mu}{2}||M - L - S||_F^2 \qquad (7)$$

Where Y is a Lagrange multiplier and μ is a positive scalar. A genetic Lagrange multiplier algorithm would solve PCP (principle component pursuit) by repeatedly setting $(L_k, S_k) = \arg\min l(L, S, Y_k)$, and then updating the Lagrange multiplier matrix via $Y_{k+1} = Y_k + \mu(M - L_k - S_k)$. Equation 7 can resolved by ALM proposed by EJ et al. [15] Fig. 1 shows the key frame selected from a micro-expression video clip, in which it is labeled as negative. It is found from Fig. 2 that after using RPCA, the sparse part we extracted is used to extract the feature part, and the information is reduced more, which also reflects the simplicity of the proposed method. As seen from Fig. 1, the subtle motion image obtained by RPCA well characterizes the specific regions of facial movements.

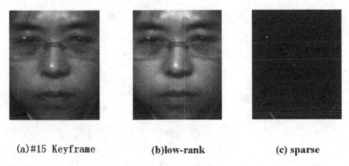

(a)#15 Keyframe   (b)low-rank   (c) sparse

Fig. 1. Sparse information extracted from key frame using RPCA

4 Dual-Cross Patterns (DCP)

DCP is a kind of local binary descriptors focus on local sampling and pattern encoding, which are the important part of a face image descriptor. DCP encodes the second-order statistical information in the most abundant direction of the face image. The research of Ding et al. [13] shows that DCP has strong recognition ability and strong robustness to posture, expression and illumination changes. Compared to LBP, the local sampling method of DCP is different, as shown in Fig. 2.

The purpose of DCP is to perform local sampling and mode encoding on the direction in which the amount of information contained in the face image is the largest. After the face image is normalized, some facial expressions such as eyes, nose, mouth, and eyebrows extend horizontally or outward, and converge toward the diagonal direction ($\pi/4$ and $3\pi/4$). As shown in Fig. 2(a), for each pixel in an image, sample in 8 directions, such as 0, $\pi/4$, $\pi/2$, $3\pi/4$, π, $5\pi/4$, $3\pi/2$ and $7\pi/4$. Two pixels are sampled in each direction. The final sampling points are $\{A_0, B_0; A_1, B_1; \ldots; A_7, B_7\}$, we define the radius of A is R_{in} and the radius of B is R_{ex}.

Define the encoding for each direction as follows

$$DCP_i = S(I_{A_i} - I_O) \times 2 + S(I_{B_i} - I_{A_i}), 0 \leq i \leq 7 \tag{8}$$

Where $S(t) = \begin{cases} 1, t \geq 0 \\ 0, t < 0 \end{cases}$, and I_o, I_A, I_B are the gray value of points O, A_i and B_i, respectively.

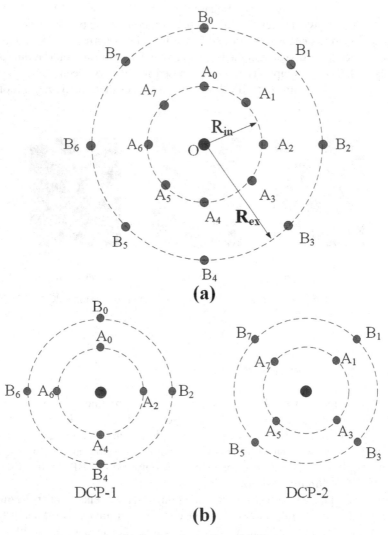

Fig. 2. Local sampling of DCP

In order to reflect the horizontal and diagonal information of the image, the DCP_i is further divided into two cross encoders. We define $\{DCP_0, DCP_2, DCP_4, DCP_6\}$ as the first subset and name is DCP-1; $\{DCP_1, DCP_3, DCP_5, DCP_7\}$ as the second subset and name is DCP $-$ 2 as shown in Fig. 2(b). The codes at each pixel are represented as

$$DCP-1 = \sum_{i=0}^{3} DCP_{2i} \times 4^i \qquad (9)$$

$$DCP-2 = \sum_{i=0}^{3} DCP_{2i+1} \times 4^i \qquad (10)$$

Thus, the DCP descriptor for each pixel in an image can be represented by the two codes generated by the cross encoders.

5 Results and Discussion

For evaluating DCP-RKF, the experiments are implemented on SMIC-HS databases for micro-expression recognition [10]. The SMIC-HS database consists of 16 subjects with 164 spontaneous micro-expressions recorded by a 100-fps camera and spatial resolution with 640×480 pixel size. There are 3 classes of the micro-expressions in this database: negative (70 samples), positive (51 samples) and surprise (43 samples)

For SMIC-HS databases, we firstly use active shape model (ASM) to extract the 68 facial landmarks for a micro-expression image and aligned to a standard frame. And then we crop facial images into 170×139. In the experiments, we use leave-one-sample out cross validation protocol, one of which was used for testing and the remaining samples were used for training. For the classification, we use the chi-square distance.

We introduce the Dual-cross patterns with RPCA of key frame (DCP-RKF). The block size N of sparse key frame, the inner and outer radius (R_{in}, R_{ex}) of DCP are two important parameters for DCP-RKF, which determine the complexity of the algorithm and the performance of the classification. In this subsection, our aim is to evaluate the effects of parameters N and (R_{in}, R_{ex}). This paper evaluates the performance of DCP-RKF caused by various N on SMIC-HS database. We know that the number of blocks of a sparse key frame is represented by the number of rows and the number of columns, defined as $N = (row, col)$. In order to avoid bias and compare the performance of features at a more general level, we extract features by changing the number of blocks without regard to the radius effect of DCP. The results of DCP-RKF on SMIC-HS databases are presented in Fig. 3, at this point we take (R_{in}, R_{ex}) as (5, 7).

It is known from Fig. 3 that when the radius of the DCP is (5, 7), the DCP-RKF recognition rate is up to 62.8% when the blocks are at (8, 9) and (10, 10). If the block is (1, 1), that is, without block, the overall recognition rate will be lower, which also indicates that the block is helpful for the recognition rate. Theoretically, we believe that blocking helps to improve the positional information of the micro-expressions. Overall, within a certain range, as the number of blocks increases, the recognition rate generally has an upward trend. However, exceeding a certain range, the increase in the number of blocks does not increase the recognition rate.

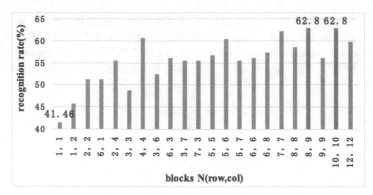

Fig. 3. Performance of DCP-RKF using different blocks of sparse Keyframe on SMIC-HS databases (%)

Based on the designed N(8, 9), we verify the influence of $(R_{in}, R_{ex})(R_{in}, R_{ex}|1, 2, 3, 4, 5, 6, 7, 8, 9$ and $R_{in} < R_{ex})$ on SMIC-HS database, of which results are shown in Table 1. From Table 1, we can see that when the sparse Keyframe is divided into 8×9 blocks, the micro-expression recognition rate of DCP-RKF is related to the radius of the DCP. For DCP-RKF, the greater the difference between R_{in} and R_{ex}, the better recognition we obtain. However, if the radii differ too much, the effect may be reduced. In the case of 8×9 blocks, the best recognition rate 63.41% we get is at radius (4, 9).

Table 1. Recognition rates with different radius of DCP under the 8×9 blocks (%)

R_{in}	R_{ex}								
	1	2	3	4	5	6	7	8	9
1	null	56.71	53.66	62.2	62.2	56.71	58.54	57.93	61.59
2	null	null	54.88	56.7	56.7	61.59	57.93	59.15	57.93
3	null	null	null	60.4	60.4	62.2	59.15	58.54	60.37
4	null	null	null	null	56.1	54.27	59.76	54.88	**63.41**
5	null	null	null	null	null	57.32	62.8	59.76	60.37
6	null	null	null	null	null	null	53.05	59.15	57.32
7	null	null	null	null	null	null	null	56.1	62.8
8	null	null	null	null	null	null	null	null	58.54

To verify the proposed method, we compare the recognition rate of DCP-RKF with the algorithm of LBP-TOP [7], STLBP-IP [10], STLBP-RIP [11] on SMIC-HS database. It should be noted here that DCP-1-RKF and DCP-2-RKF means that we only use DCP-1, DCP-2 for feature extraction of sparse Key frame.

Table 2. Micro-expression recognition rates of different methods (%)

Methods	Block number (BN)	Recognition rate (%)
LBP-TOP	8 × 9	55.49
STLBP-IP	8 × 9	50
STLBP-RIP	8 × 9	50
DCP-RKF	**8 × 9**	**63.41**

For DCP-RKF, we use 8 × 9 blocks on sparse key frame, and the radius of DCP is (4, 9). Leave-one-sample-out cross validation protocol is used to select the training and testing samples, the last chi-square distance is used for classification. For LBP-TOP, STLBP-IP, STLBP-RIP, in order to reflect the experimental contrast, we use the 8*9 block, and the other optimal parameters proposed in the respective articles, the same classification method, and repeatedly implement the related algorithm on the SMIC-HS database. Results on recognition rate are reported in Table 2. As seen from the table, LBP-TOP achieves the recognition rate of 55.49%, at the same time, STLBP-IP and STLBP-RIP only achieve a recognition rate of 50%. However, DCP-RKF reaches the best recognition rate of 63.41%, which is 7.92% higher than LBP-TOP. These results

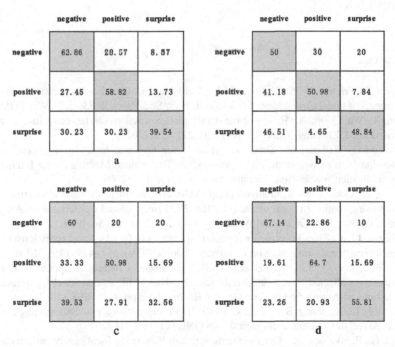

Fig. 4. The confusion matrix of (a) LBP-TOP, (b) STLBP-IP, (c) STLBP-RIP, (d) DCP-RKF for micro-expression recognition on SMIC-HS databases

show that DCP-RKF has good geometric and texture features, and can be well applied to micro-expression feature extraction.

The confusion matrix of LBP-TOP, STLBP-IP, STLBP-RIP and our methods are shown in Fig. 4. Compared to other methods, DCP-RKF performs better on all emoticons (negative, positive, surprise). On the negative micro-expression, DCP-RKF achieved a recognition rate of 67.14%, higher than 62.86% of LBP-TOP, 50% of STLBP-IP, and 60% of STLBP-RIP. Similarly, on positive and surprise micro-expression, DCP-RKF achieved 64.7% and 55.81%, which are also higher than the other three methods.

6 Conclusions

In this paper, we propose Dual-cross patterns with RPCA of key frame (DCP-RKF) for micro-expression recognition. Specifically, we first use SSIM to obtain the key frame of the micro-expression sequence, then apply RPCA to obtain the sparse information of the key frame, and finally use DCP to extract the features. Experimental results demonstrate that our proposed method gets higher recognition rates and achieves promising performance, compared with the state-of-the-art performance on the SMIC-HS micro-expression database.

Acknowledgments. This paper is supported by the National Nature Science Foundation of China (No. 61861020), the Natural Science Foundation of Jiangxi Province of China (No. 20171BAB202006).

References

1. Ekman, P., Friesen, W.V., O'sullivan, M., et al.: Universals and cultural differences in the judgments of facial expressions of emotion. J. Pers. Soc. Psychol. **53**(4), 712–717 (1987)
2. Shen, X., Wu, Q., Fu, X.: Effects of the duration of expressions on the recognition of micro-expressions. J. Zhejiang (Univ. Sci. B) **13**(3), 221–230 (2012)
3. Frank, M.G., Herbasz, M., Sinuk, K., et al.: I see how you feel: training laypeople and professionals to recognize fleeting emotions, In: The Annual Meeting of the International Communication Association, Sheraton New York, pp. 1–2 (2009)
4. Shreve, M., Godavarthy, S., Goldgof, D., et al.: Macro-and micro-expression spotting in long videos using spatio-temporal strain. In: 2011 IEEE International Conference on Automatic Face & Gesture Recognition and Workshops (FG 2011), pp. 51–56. IEEE (2011)
5. Pfister, T., Li, X., Zhao, G., et al.: Recognizing spontaneous facial micro-expressions. In: 2011 IEEE International Conference on Computer Vision (ICCV), pp. 1449–1456. IEEE (2011)
6. Yan, W.J., Wu, Q., Liu, Y.J., et al.: CASME database: a dataset of spontaneous micro-expressions collected from neutralized faces. In: 10th IEEE International Conference and Workshops on Automatic Face and Gesture Recognition, pp. 1–7, IEEE (2013)
7. Yan, W.J., Li, X., Wang, S.J., et al.: CASME II: an improved spontaneous micro-expression database and the baseline evaluation. PLoS ONE **9**(1), e86041 (2014)
8. Zhao, G., Pietikainen, M.: Dynamic texture recognition using local binary patterns with an application to facial expression. IEEE Trans. Pattern Anal. Mach. Intell. **29**(6), 915–928 (2007)

9. Huang, X., Zhao, G., Hong, X., Pietikäinen, M., Zheng, W.: Texture description with completed local quantized patterns. In: Kämäräinen, J.-K., Koskela, M. (eds.) SCIA 2013. LNCS, vol. 7944, pp. 1–10. Springer, Heidelberg (2013). https://doi.org/10.1007/978-3-642-38886-6_1

10. Huang, X., Wang, S.J., Zhao, G., et al.: Facial micro-expression recognition using spatiotemporal local binary pattern with integral projection. In: Proceedings of the IEEE International Conference on Computer Vision Workshops, pp. 1–9. IEEE (2015)

11. Huang, X., Wang, S.J., Liu, X., et al.: Discriminative spatiotemporal local binary pattern with revisited integral projection for spontaneous facial micro-expression recognition. IEEE Trans. Affect. Comput. 10(1), 32–47 (2019)

12. Wang, S., Rehman, A., Wang, Z., et al.: SSIM-motivated rate-distortion optimization for video coding. IEEE Trans. Circuits and Syst. Video Technol. 22(4), 516–529 (2012)

13. Ding, C., Choi, J., Tao, D., et al.: Multi-directional multi-level dual-cross patterns for robust face recognition. IEEE Trans. Pattern Anal. Mach. Intell. 38(3), 518–531 (2016)

14. Liong, S.T., See, J., Wong, K.S., et al.: Less is more: micro-expression recognition from video using apex frame. Signal Process.: Image Commun. 62(1), 82–92 (2018)

15. Candès, E.J., Li, X., Ma, Y., et al.: Robust principal component analysis? J. ACM (JACM) 58(3), 11–12 (2011)

Author Index